BILLY KIDD'S AMERICAN SKI GUIDE

ART DIRECTION	David C. Bilotti
EDITORS	Michael Nordine Les Plesko
COVER PHOTOGRAPHY	Michael Salas
ACTION PHOTOGRAPHY	Ron Dahlquist
SKI AREA MAPS	John Andrews

ISBN 0-899-23-015-6

BILLY KIDD'S AMERICAN SKI GUIDE is published by CITRUS HOUSE PUBLISHERS, INC., P.O. BOX 2061, Beverly Hills, California 90213. Telephone number (213) 463-4306.

INTRODUCTION

Over the past 33 years, I've had the opportunity to ski all over the world, from Europe to Australia to South America to Japan. Wherever I've gone, I've had a good time, because skiing is such a great sport. But I must say that I'm always glad to get back to the mountains of North America. This is not just because it's my home, but because I've found American skiing to be truly the best in the world. Let me tell you why.

As a group, Americans are seldom satisfied with the status quo—we're always looking for ways to make things better. This is especially true in skiing, where American innovations have set the pace all over the world. Americans invented the metal ski, the honeycomb ski, the plastic boot, and the aluminum ski pole, to name just a few. These were all key developments in the sport that made it easier to learn and provided much more performance on the slopes.

In resort management, Americans were responsible for the development of artificial snowmaking, slope grooming, and the most widely-used mode of uphill transport, the chair lift, which appeared for the first time in Sun Valley in the late '30s, the basic design having been adapted from a United Fruit Co. banana conveyor.

In ski area design and planning, Americans have also been in the forefront. Major resorts like Vail, Snowmass, and Snowbird were designed to make access to the slopes as easy as possible, with lodging, restaurants, and entertainment close by. At my home area, Steamboat, Colo., the trails are laid out in such a way that novice runs don't suddenly turn into expert slopes halfway down the mountain, so that there is a variety of terrain to choose from off each lift, allowing family members to ride up together, separate to ski the trail of their choice, and then meet again at the bottom of the same lift.

Finally, ski area managers in America make an effort to ensure that their employees—lift operators, ski instructors, ski patrollers, and food service people—are not only conscientious when it comes to your safety and comfort, but are also friendly and courteous. That's the kind of added bonus that can make a ski vacation in America truly enjoyable.

Where can you find all this good skiing? That's what this book will tell you. As you'll see, you don't have to go all that far from home. If you live in Washington D.C., for instance, you'll find skiing less than two hours away; if you're from Minneapolis, there are ski areas just 20 minutes distant; if Detroit is your hometown, you can be on the slopes in half an hour. Artificial snowmaking systems and lights for night skiing have given Americans skiing opportunities that just don't exist in other parts of the world.

Now let's take a look at what the various regions have to offer in the way of fine skiing:

THE EAST. I grew up in Stowe, Vermont, so I've done quite a lot of skiing in the East. I can tell you that Eastern skiing is definitely underrated. In addition to excellent novice and intermediate terrain, the East also has some of the most challenging slopes in the U.S. Trails like Goat, Starr, and National at Stowe, which are justly famed for their steepness, provide even top experts with an exhilerating ride. It's true that snow conditions in the East are generally not as predictable as in the West, but with the massive snowmaking systems now in place at most areas, the chances are excellent that you'll have good skiing. And there's a special atmosphere about Eastern skiing that really enhances the experience. The East was home to the first ski lifts in the country, the first ski clubs, and the original ski trains from Boston and New York, and that feeling of a long tradition is still alive. You can still find country ski lodges where the accomodations are cozy and the food and service make you feel like a member of the family, and there are still lots of picturesque New England villages to explore and enjoy. It's a great region for either a vacation or a weekend.

THE SOUTHEAST. Skiers who live near the big mountains of the West sometimes get a little blase about their sport. Not so the Southern skier. When the first blast of winter hits the South each year, skiers from Alabama, Georgia, Mississippi, North and South Carolina, and Virginia literally swarm to their local ski areas in the Smokies, the Blue Ridge mountains, the Poconos, and the Appalachians. On the enthusiasm scale, Southern skiers rate a "10," and that same feeling of fun can be found at the Southeast's ski areas as well, all of which have snowmaking systems to ensure good snow cover, modern facilities, a wide variety of terrain, and some pretty impressive verticals.

THE MIDWEST. Though the mountains here are little more than hills, the Midwest still produces excellent skiers, people like Cindy Nelson, who has been a mainstay of the U.S. Ski Team stand out. In addition, the ski clubs in the Midwest consistently field racing teams that dominate national recreational racing programs. The reason for this is not hard to discover. The verticals in the Midwest may not be great, but there are lots and lots of places to ski here, many of them easily accessible to major metropolitan areas. Snowfall along the Great Lakes is invariably consistent and deep, and there are many areas that offer night skiing. You don't need a big hill to learn and improve your skiing–or to learn to race. All you need is determination. And Midwesterners, many of whom have skiing in their blood from Scandinavian forebears, have plenty of that.

THE ROCKIES. Rocky Mountain skiing is famous all over the world–and with good reason. The special mixture of low humidity, high altitude, and wind-protected slopes produces snow that is light, long-lasting, fluffy, and dry–what the locals at Steamboat call "champagne powder." Surprisingly, there's also plenty of sunshine. This, coupled with the high altitude, gives you the kind of tan that you can be proud to wear home. Each resort in the Rockies has its own special flavor. There are restored mining towns like Aspen, Park

City, Breckenridge, and Telluride; planned modern villages like Vail, Snowmass, Big Sky, and Sun Valley; and cowboy towns like Steamboat and Jackson Hole. In short, the Rockies have it all—great snow, big mountains, beautiful scenery, fine weather, and amazing diversity.

THE FAR WEST. The same Pacific Coast mountain range extends from the Canadian border south to Mexico, but there is quite a difference between the skiing in California and the Pacific Northwest. Since California has the nation's largest population, it's understandable that it also has the nation's largest ski areas—Mammoth Mountain, Squaw Valley, and Heavenly Valley. The Sierra is a huge mountain range, with impressive verticals, so you get long runs here as well as great scenery. It's also located right next to the Nevada desert, so there's plenty of sunshine. Because of the deep snowfalls, the season is exceptionally long here. California skiers, as a rule, are fast, fearless, and fun-loving.

The Northwest has equally deep snow, equally impressive scenery, but not quite so much sunshine. It's also a bit further off the standard ski vacation route, which is a plus for those who discover it, because the natives tend to overwhelm you with hospitality. Another advantage of Northwest skiing is that it is very accessible. Skiers in Portland and Seattle think nothing of jumping in the car and heading to the slopes on a moment's notice. And there's quite a tradition of racing here, best exemplified these days by the World Cup champion, Phil Mahre, and his equally hot twin brother, Steve, who are from White Pass, Washington.

CANADA. Just as there is quite a different feeling between the skiing in the eastern and western parts of the U.S., so is there a different atmosphere between Canada East and Canada West. The mountains of eastern Canada are similar to those in the eastern U.S.—tree-covered and rolling. Here you'll find plenty of snow, challenging runs, and the kind of superb food that only a French heritage can provide. The West is wild, with spectacular mountains, consistent snowfall, and world-famous helicopter skiing operations that offer skiing's greatest adventures.

So there it is—North American skiing. Now you can see why I call it the best in the world. With the help of this book, I hope you'll take full advantage of it—and have a great time.

BILLY KIDD

Billy Kidd's American Ski Guide contains information about 1,302 ski areas. Each area includes up to date factual information regarding ski terrain, facilities, snow phone numbers, lodgings, restaurants, and area services. Maps of larger areas pinpoint lifts and runs, as well as travel information for the nearest major city.

TABLE OF CONTENTS

ALPINE

ADDENDA

CROSS-COUNTRY

CITIES

REGIONAL SKI CONDITIONS

UPDATED AT 8:30 A.M., 11:00 A.M., 3:00 P.M., 5:00 P.M. & 10:00 P.M. CODE 900 RATE + TAX.

DIAL 900 + NUMBER
(No coin or operator-handled calls)

EASTERN NEW ENGLAND
Maine, New Hampshire, E. Massachusetts, Rhode Island 976-3700

VERMONT/ADIRONDACKS
Vermont, Central & Northern New York . . . 976-3710

MID-ATLANTIC
Berkshires, Connecticut, Southern New York, New Jersey, Eastern Pennsylvania. 976-3720

ALLEGHENY/BLUE RIDGE
W. New York, W. Pennsylvania, West Virginia, Virginia, Maryland, North Carolina 976-3730

MID-WEST
Ohio, Indiana, Michigan 976-3740

NORTH CENTRAL
Illinois, Iowa, Wisconsin, Minnesota 976-3750

ROCKIES/NORTH
North Dakota, South Dakota, Wyoming, Idaho, Montana 976-3760

ROCKIES/SOUTH
Utah, Colorado, Arizona, New Mexico 976-3770

PACIFIC NORTHWEST
Washington, Oregon 976-3780

CALIFORNIA/NEVADA 976-3790

ALASKA

ALYESKA

P.O. BOX 578, GIRWOOD, AK 99587 (908) 783-6000

AREA INFORMATION

BASE ELEVATION
200 feet

HOURS
10:00 a.m. to 3:00 p.m., weekdays
9:00 a.m. to 3:00 p.m., weekends

LIFTS
4 chairs, 2 tows

LODGING
Hotel and condos
Central Reservations: 783-6000

LONGEST RUN
2 miles

NURSERY
Weekends only, call ski area

SEASON
Mid-November to end of April

SNOW PHONE
Call ski area

TRAILS
Open bowls and slopes
25% beginner, 25% intermediate, 50% difficult

TRAVEL
From Anchorage: International Airport Rd. to Old Seward Hwy. south to New Seward Hwy.
Bus and car rental from Anchorage Airport.

VERTICAL DROP
2,800 feet

CALIFORNIA/NEVADA

ALPINE MEADOWS

P.O. BOX AM, TAHOE CITY, CA 95730 (916) 583-4232

AREA INFORMATION

BASE ELEVATION
6,970 feet

HOURS
9:00 a.m. - 4:00 p.m., Winter
8:30 a.m. - 4:00 p.m., Spring

LIFTS
10 chairlifts, 3 bars, 14,000 capacity per hour

LONGEST RUN
5,420 feet

NURSERY
Ages 2 - 8, call Ski Area

SEASON
Thanksgiving to Memorial Day, snowmaking

SNOW PHONE 583-6914

TRAILS
25% beginner, 40% intermediate, 35% expert

TRAVEL
I-80 to Hwy. 89 for 10 miles, then
Alpine Meadows Rd. to Ski Area

VERTICAL DROP
1,700 feet

FOR LODGING, RESTAURANTS, SERVICES, STORES & SKI SHOPS, SEE N. LAKE TAHOE

DONNER

NORDEN, CA 95724 (916) 426-3578

AREA INFORMATION

BASE ELEVATION
7,135 feet

HOURS
9:00 a.m. - 4:00 p.m.

LIFTS
3 chairlifts, 2 bars, 3,500 capacity per hour

LONGEST RUN
¾ mile

SEASON
Mid-December to mid-April

TRAILS
21 trails

TRAVEL
3½ miles off I-80, Soda Springs, Norden exit

VERTICAL DROP
825 feet

FOR LODGING, RESTAURANTS, SERVICES, STORES & SKI SHOPS, SEE N. LAKE TAHOE

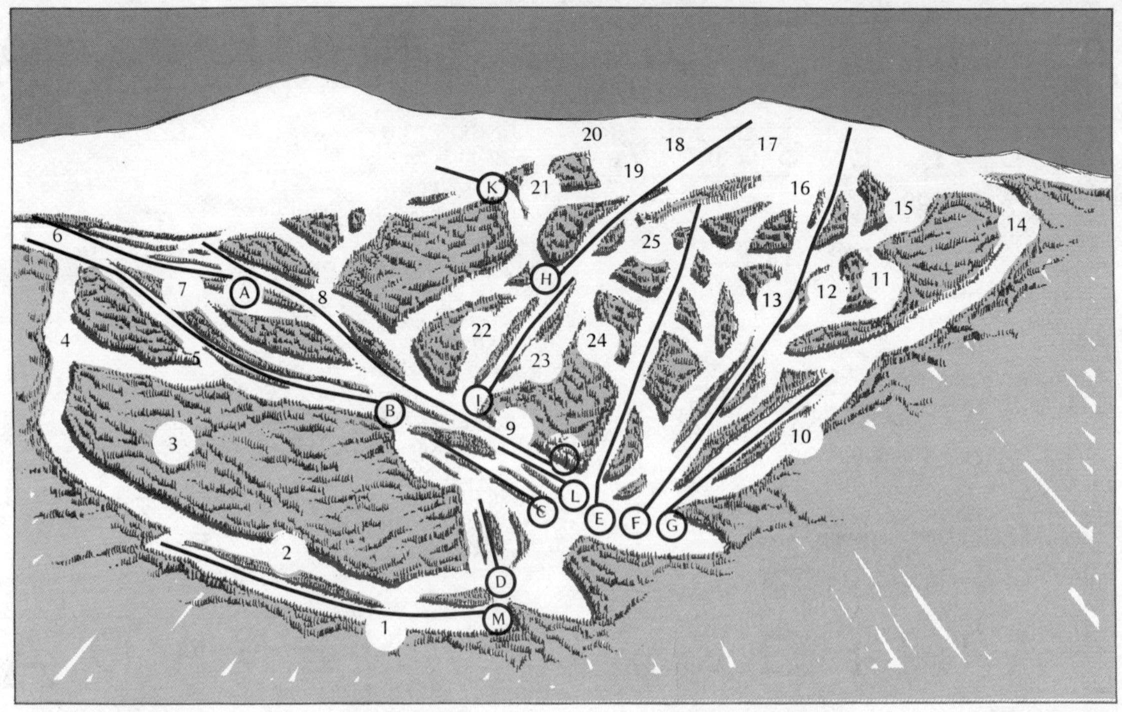

ALPINE MEADOW LIFTS

A SCOTT T-BAR
B SCOTT CHAIR
C MEADOW CHAIR
D SUBWAY CHAIR
E VICTORIA STATION CHAIR
F SUMMIT CHAIR
G KANGAROO CHAIR
H ALPINE BOWL CHAIR
I YELLOW CHAIR
J WEASEL CHAIR
K SHERWOOD CHAIR

ALPINE MEADOWS RUNS

1 LOWER FORTY POMA
2 LOWER FORTY
3 PROMISED LAND
4 GENTIAN GULLY
5 SCOTT CHUTE
6 SCOTT MEADOW
7 SCOTT RIDGE RUN
8 WEASEL RUN
9 MEADOW
10 NASTAR SLOPE
11 THREE SISTERS
12 WATERFALL
13 THE FACE
14 BEAVER BOWL
15 WOLVERINE BOWL
16 ALPINE BOWL
17 HIGH TRAVERSE
18 PALISADES
19 TERRY RETURN
20 LOWER SADDLE
21 HIGH YELLOW
22 YELLOW TRAIL
23 LADIES SLALOM
24 DANCE FLOOR
25 ART'S KNOLL
26 ROCK GARDEN

HEAVENLY VALLEY

BOX AT, S. LAKE TAHOE, CA 95705 (702) 588-4584

BASE ELEVATION
6,550 ft.
BUS
Shuttle to S. Lake Tahoe daily to 5:15
CENTRAL RESERVATIONS
(702) 588-4584
CHILD CARE
See S. Lake Tahoe
HELICOPTER SKIING
Full service, 541-1330
HOURS
9 a.m. to 4 p.m.
LODGING
See S. Lake Tahoe
LONGEST RUN
6.8 miles
LIFTS
1 triple chair, 14 chairs, 6 tows,
18 passenger train, 19,100 capacity per hr.
RESTAURANTS
See S. Lake Tahoe
SEASON
Nov. to May
SERVICES
See S. Lake Tahoe
SKI SHOPS, RENTALS
See S. Lake Tahoe
SNOWFALL
400 inches
SNOW PHONE
541-SKII
TRAILS
20 miles, 25% beginner,
50% intermediate, 25% advanced
TRAVEL
1 mi. from S. Lake Tahoe
VERTICAL DROP
4,000 feet

HOMEWOOD

P.O. BOX 165, HOMEWOOD, CA 95718 (916) 525-7256

AREA INFORMATION

BASE ELEVATION
6,230 feet
HOURS
Winter: 9:00 a.m. - 4:00 p.m.
8:30 a.m. - 4:00 p.m., weekends
Spring: 9:00 a.m. - 4:30 p.m.
8:00 a.m. - 4:30 p.m., weekends
LIFTS
3 chairs, 6 surface lifts, 5,350 capacity per hour
LONGEST RUN
2 miles
SEASON
Late November to mid-April
SNOW PHONE
Call Ski Area
TRAILS
20% novice, 50% intermediate, 30% advanced
TRAVEL
In the California Sierras on the west shore of Lake Tahoe, six miles south of Tahoe City on Hwy. 89. From San Francisco or Sacramento, I-80 E. to Lake Tahoe exit, Rt. 89 S., six miles to Ski Area. From Reno Int'l. or South Lake Tahoe Airports you can rent a car. By prior arrangement, connecting air service from Cal-Vada Aircraft Inc. to Sea Plane Base adjacent to lifts.
VERTICAL DROP
1,650 feet

FOR EMERGENCY LISTINGS, LODGINGS, RESTAURANTS, SERVICES, STORES & SKI SHOPS, SEE N. LAKE TAHOE

NORTHSTAR AT TAHOE

P.O. BOX 129, TRUCKEE, CA 95734 (916) 562-1212

AREA INFORMATION

ELEVATIONS
Village - 6,400 ft.
Day Lodge - 6,800 ft.
Lookout Mtn. - 8,100 ft.
Mt. Pluto - 8,600 ft.
LIFTS
6 double chairs, 2 triple chairs, 10,680 capacity per hr.
LOCATION
Placer County, btwn. Truckee & Lake Tahoe, Hwy 267
LOCKERS
In Village & Day Lodge areas
LONGEST RUN
2.84 miles
MESSAGES - EMERGENCY
If your name appears on one of the blackboards at the top of each lift, contact the ski patrol or the information booth near T lift or in Northstar Village.
SEASON
Late Nov. to mid-April
SNOW PHONE 562-1330
SNOWFALL
400 inches
TRAILS
41 runs, 19.5 miles, beginner 33%, intermediate 50%, advanced 17%
VERTICAL DROP
2,200 ft.

LODGING

CENTRAL RESERVATIONS
Northstar Village, Aspen Grove, Ski Trail, Gold Bend, Indian Hills
P.O. Box 2499, Truckee, CA 95734 562-1000

NEARBY LODGING, TRUCKEE, CA 95734

ALPINE VILLAGE MOTEL
P.O. Box 790 587-3801
ALTA MOTEL
P.O. Box 2118. 587-6668
BIG CHIEF LODGE
P.O. Box 2427. 587-9813
COTTAGE HOTEL
P.O. Box 878 587-3108
COZY MOTEL
P.O. Box 905 587-3093
DONNER LAKE VILLAGE
P.O. Box 2348. 587-6081
DONNER TRAIL CABINS
P.O. Box 937 587-3462
GATEWAY MOTEL
P.O. Box 175 587-3182
LA MARINA LODGE
P.O. Box 157 587-9968
HILLTOP LODGE
P.O. Box 1196. 587-2545
SAN SOUCI LODGINGS
P.O. Box 476 587-3730
TRUCKEE HOTEL
P.O. Box 565 587-4444

RECREATION

BOATING
Boca Reservoir 587-3558
Donner Lake. 587-3090
Prosser & Stampede Reservoir. 587-3558
Tahoe-Donner Marina 587-9820
CAMPING, HIKING
Donner Memorial Park 587-3789
Other parks 587-3558
CROSS COUNTRY SKIING
Golf Course Club House 562-1010
GOLF
Northstar at Tahoe 562-1333
Ponderosa Golf Club 587-3501
Tahoe-Downer Golf. 587-6046
HUNTING & FISHING
Fish & Game Dept. 583-3325

NORTHSTAR AT TAHOE CONT.

RAFTING
- High Wheeler 583-5606
- Truckee River Runner 583-9724

RIDING
- Boreal Stables 426-3769
- Coldstream Corral. 587-4121
- Innis Free Equestrian. 587-2216
- Tahoe Donner Center. 587-9807
- Tahoe Stables, Northstar. 562-1230
- Thousand Trails. 426-3191

RESTAURANTS

AT THE SLOPE

BIG SPRINGS DAY LODGE
- Cafeteria, bar, ice cream parlor

NORTHSTAR DELI (Sandwiches)
- At ski area

SCHAEFFER'S MILL (Seafood, bar, entertainment)
- Ski season only 562-1015

WINE & CHEESE HOUSE (beer & wine)
- At day lodge

INCLINE VILLAGE

BALLARD INN (Steak, prime rib) . . . . . (702) 831-2450
HUGO'S (Continental). . . . . (702) 831-1111
MARGARITA'S (Mexican). . . . . (702) 831-3500

KING'S BEACH

CANTINA LOS TRES HOMBRES (Mexican) 546-4052
LANZA'S (Italian) 546-2434

TAHOE CITY

BACCHI'S INN (Italian) 583-3324
CHART HOUSE (Steak, lobster, prime rib) 583-0233
PFEIFER HOUSE (German) 583-3102
SWISS LAKEWOOD LODGE (Continental). . . . 525-7814
TOMFOOLERY (Fondue). 583-5700
WATER WHEEL (Mandarin, Szechwuan) 583-4404

TAHOE VISTA

BON VIVANT (French) 546-5888
LA PETITE PIER (Gourmet French). 546-4464

TRUCKEE

GREY'S TOLL STATION (crepes, seafood, steak)587-2626
LA VIELLE MAISON (French). 587-2421
O.B.'S BOARD (ribs, steak,seafood) 587-4164
A WILD THYME (Continental). 587-3764

SERVICES

AIRPORTS
- Reno Int'l, Tahoe & Tahoe-Truckee

AUTO RENTAL
- Avis. (702) 831-1111
- Hertz . . . . (702) 831-2214
- Thrifty 587-2588
- National 587-6748

BABY SITTING
- Call rental office 562-1111

BUSES
- Greyhound from Truckee 587-3822

CHECK CASHING
- Up to $25.00 at front desk with I.D.

CONFERENCES
- Village Conference Room 562-1010

EMERGENCY
- C.H.P. 587-3518
- Fire. 562-0911
- Hospital 587-3541
- Security 562-1010
- Sheriff 583-4244

LOST & FOUND
- Ski Hill & Recreation Center 562-0320

PHARMACIES
- King's Beach. 546-4231
- Tahoe City. 583-3888
- Vail's 583-1300

PHOTOGRAPHY
- General Store 562-0140
- Tahoe City (N. Lake Photo). 583-1300

RENTAL SHOP
- At ski area 562-1010

TAXI
- Draney's 546-3324
- Incline 546-3181
- Yellow Cab 587-6336

TOWING, AUTO EMERGENCY
- AAA 587-6021
- National 587-2055

TRAINS
- Amtrak from Truckee 587-2515, (800) 648-3850

TRANSPORTATION
- Bus to Village Rec. Ctr., Golf Course/Nordic Center, Stables, Condos, etc., continuous daily

STORES & SKI SHOPS

KING'S BEACH

NORTH SHORE HARDWARE 546-3505
WILDERNESS SHOP. 546-4815

TAHOE CITY

ALPINE SPORTING GOODS 583-3266
BASECAMP 583-5306
CASA ANDINA (Hwy. 89) 583-4123
THE MOUNTAIN SHOP. 583-3120
PORTER'S. 583-2314

TRUCKEE

HIDESIDE/ALPINE GLOW 587-2025
MOUNTAIN HARDWARE 587-4844
WESTGATE SPORTS 587-4667

NORTHSTAR AT TAHOE RUNS

1 EAST RIDGE
2 CORRIDOR
3 WEST RIDGE
4 DELIGHT
5 SHARK'S CHUTE
6 TONINI'S
7 CUTOFF
8 POWDER BOWL
9 GROUSE ALLEY
10 PLUNGE
11 MOGUL RUN
12 LUGGI'S RUN
13 SKID TRAIL
14 MARTIS LANDING
15 RENDEZVOUS
16 SULLY'S
17 CASCADES
18 HALFWAY
19 LOOKOUT TRANSFER
20 GOOFY'S SLIDE
21 TURKEY CHUTE
22 THE FACE
23 LOGGER'S LOOP
24 THE STRAITS
25 SUNSHINE
26 AIRPORT
27 GULLY RUN
28 DEER SKIN
29 LOOK-UP
30 GOLD BEND
31 BOONDOCK'S
32 HORNET'S NEST
33 EASY OVER
34 SURPRISE
35 DROP OUT
36 BY WAY
37 GULCH
38 MOLE HILL
39 OVERPASS
40 BEAVER BEND
41 VILLAGE RUN

SIERRA SKI RANCH

TWIN BRIDGES P.O., CA 95735 (916) 659-7453

AREA INFORMATION

BASE ELEVATION

7,280 feet

EMERGENCY

California Highway Patrol 577-1001
Hospital 541-3420
Sheriff 544-3464
Other . . . . Zenith 1-2000

HOURS

9 a.m. to 4:30 p.m., no night skiing

LIFTS

8 chairs, approx. 7,000+ capacity per hr.

SIERRA SKI RANCH CONT.

LODGING
2 lodges at slope, call ski area for other lodging
See S. Lake Tahoe
RENTALS
Under the porch of the Main Lodge
RESTAURANTS
Cafeterias at ski area. For nearby restaurants, see S. Lake Tahoe
SEASON
Nov. to April
SERVICES
See S. Lake Tahoe
SNOW PHONE
Call ski area
SNOWFALL
470 inches, no snowmaking
TRAILS
21 runs, 25% beginner, 40% intermediate, 35% difficult
TRAVEL
12 miles from S. Lake Tahoe, off Hwy. 50
VERTICAL DROP
1,585 feet

RESTAURANTS

ALL CASINOS HAVE RESTAURANTS ON THE PREMISES—SEE S. LAKE TAHOE NIGHTLIFE AND NORTHSTAR AT TAHOE

SKI INCLINE

P.O. DRAWER AL INCLINE VILLAGE, NV 89450
TELEPHONE: (702) 831-1821

AREA INFORMATION

BASE ELEVATION
6,700 feet
HOURS
9:00 a.m. - 4:00 p.m.
LIFTS
6 chairs, 1 bar, 6,465 capacity per hour
LONGEST RUN
1 mile
NURSERY
Sierra Nursery in the Village. 831-2486
SEASON
Mid-November to mid-April, snow making
SNOW PHONE 831-3211
TRAILS
30% beginner, 50% intermediate, 20% advanced
TRAVEL
On Lake Tahoe's north shore, 28 miles from Reno. I-80 to U.S. Rt. 395 S. to Rt. 27 W. to Rt. 28 S. Or, from California, I-80 to Rt. 267 S., then east on Lake Shore Drive to Nevada's Rt. 28.
VERTICAL DROP
900 feet

LODGING

CAL-NEVA LODGE (hotel, casino)
P.O. Box 368
Crystal Bay, 89402 . . . . . . (800) 684-4577, 831-1511
CRYSTAL BAY MOTEL
P.O. Box 254, Crystal Bay, 89402 831-0287
GARNI MOTOR LODGE (walk to restaurants, clubs)
P.O. Box 295, Crystal Bay, 89402 831-4414
HOWELL LAKE TAHOE REALTY
Raley's Incline Center, Hwy. 28
Box 31771, Incline Village. 831-0334
INCLINE MOTOR LODGE
P.O. Box 4545, Incline Village 831-1052
INCLINE VILLAGE SALES COMPANY (rentals)
940 Hwy. 28, P.O. Box 3033, Incline Village . 831-3333
TYROLIAN VILLAGE REALTY
1036 Lucerne (Lower Tyrolia)
P.O. Drawer AB, Incline Village. 831-3600

RESTAURANTS

BRONZE BULL (steaks, prime rib, happy hour)
931 Tahoe Bl., across from Raley's. 831-6501
THE CHESSMEN (steaks, cocktails, Wed. - Sun.)
907 Tahoe Bl. 831-1377
GASTHAUS ZUM JAGERMEISTER
(German, cocktails, live entertainment, all day menus)
798 Southwood, Village Shopping Center . . . 831-2659
LAS MARGARITAS
Christmas Tree Village, Incline 831-3500
PANCHO'S (Mexican, steaks, cantina, lunch, dinner)
Raley's Incline Center 831-4048

STORES & SKI SHOPS

INCLINE SPORTS HAUS
Raley's Incline Center, behind Valley Bank . . 831-5050
SKI RENTS USA
869 Tahoe Bl. 831-4724
TIMBERLINE CRAFTS GALLERY
590 Lakeshore Bl.. 831-2460
T-SHIRTS BY CAVARICCI (large selection of ski prints)
Country Club Mall No. 7. 831-4248
VILLAGE SKI LOFT
800 Tahoe Bl. 831-3537

FOR OTHER LODGING, RESTAURANTS, STORES & SKI SHOPS, SEE N. LAKE TAHOE

SKI RENO

P.O. BOX 2406, RENO, NV 89505 (702) 849-0704

AREA INFORMATION

BASE ELEVATION
8,200 feet
HOURS
9:00 a.m. to 4:00 p.m., night skiing
LIFTS
2 chairs, bar and tow, 3,000 capacity per hour
LODGING
Call ski area

LONGEST RUN
1.5 miles
NURSERY
Call ski area
SEASON
Mid November to Mid May
SNOW PHONE
(702) 849-0706
TRAILS
14+ runs,
30% Beginner, 30% Intermediate, 40% Difficult
TRAVEL
40 minutes Southeast of Reno on Hwy. 27,
Airport in Reno
VERTICAL DROP
1,500 feet

SODA SPRINGS

P.O. BOX 67, SODA SPRINGS, CA 95728 (916) 426-3801

AREA INFORMATION

BASE ELEVATION
6,700 feet
HOURS
9:00 a.m. - 4:30 p.m.
LIFTS
3 chairlifts, 4,500 capacity per hour
ROAD CONDITIONS
California . . . . (916) 587-3806
Nevada . . . . (702) 793-1313
SEASON
Mid-November to end of April
No snowmaking, but has northern exposure
TRAILS
40% beginner, 50% intermediate, 10% expert
TRAVEL
2 miles off I-80, Soda Springs, Norden exit
4 miles west of Donner Summit, 87 miles from Sacramento, 45 miles from Reno/Sparks, Nevada
VERTICAL DROP
700 feet

FOR LODGING, RESTAURANTS, SERVICES, STORES & SKI SHOPS, SEE N. LAKE TAHOE

SQUAW VALLEY

OLYMPIC VALLEY, CA 95730 (916) 583-6985

AREA INFORMATION

BASE ELEVATION
6,200 feet
HOURS
Daily, 9:00 a.m. - 4:00 p.m.
8:00 a.m. - 4:00 p.m., weekends
Spring, thru April, 8:30 a.m. - 4:30 p.m.
LIFTS
21 chairlifts
1 tram, 1 gondola, 26,300 capacity per hour
LONGEST RUN
3 miles
NURSERY
Ages 2-6, call Ski Area
SEASON
November 15th to May 15th, no snowmaking
SNOW PHONE 583-0121
TRAILS
30% beginner, 40% intermediate, 30% advanced
TRAVEL
I-80 to Rt. 89, 10 miles
VERTICAL DROP
2,700 feet

FOR LODGING, RESTAURANTS, SERVICES, STORES & SKI SHOPS, SEE N. LAKE TAHOE

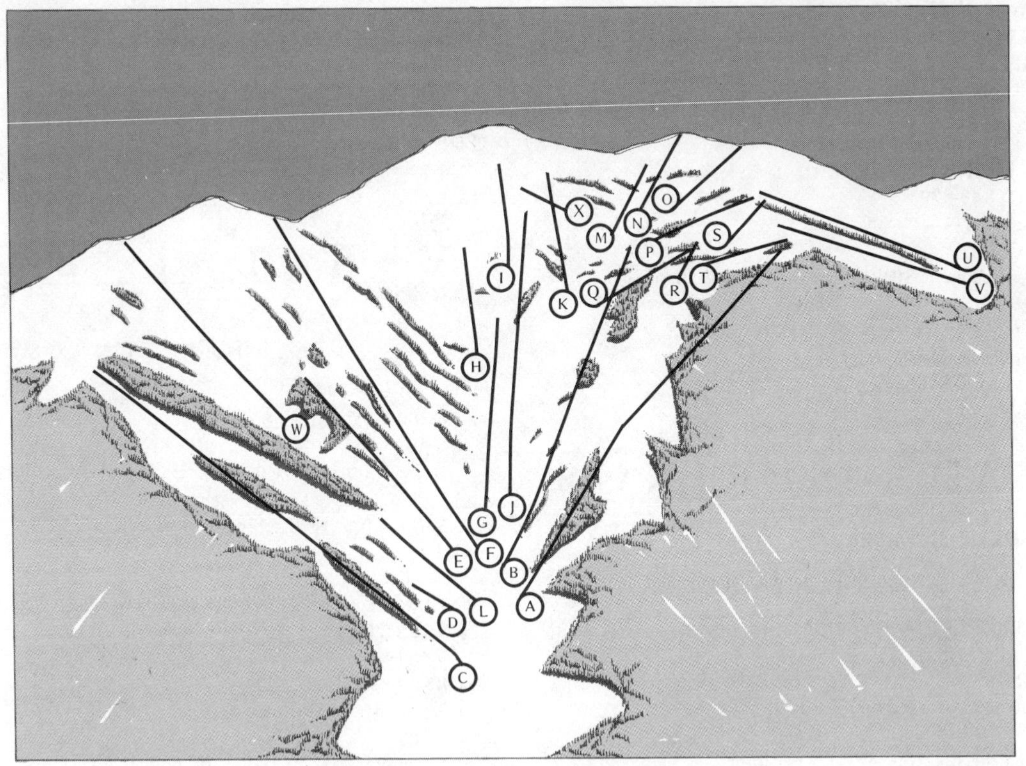

SQUAW VALLEY LIFTS

A RED DOG
B OLYMPIC LADY
C TORCHLIGHT
D PLATTERS
E EXHIBITION
F KT 22
G CORNICE I
H CORNICE II
I HEADWALL
J SUPER SQUAW
K SIBERIA
M MAINLINE
N GOLD COAST
O EMIGRANT
P EAST BROADWAY
Q RIVIERA
R BELMONT
S LINKS
T BAILEY'S BEACH
U SHIRLEY LAKE
V SULLUDE
W GONDOLA
X NEWPORT

SUGAR BOWL

P.O. BOX 5, NORDEN, CA 95724 (916) 426-3651

AREA INFORMATION

BASE ELEVATION
6,881 feet
HOURS
9:00 a.m. - 4:00 p.m., 7:30 - 10:00 p.m., Tues. & Sat.
LIFTS
8 chairs, 1 gondola, 7,000 capacity per hour
LONGEST RUN
3 miles
SEASON
November to May 15th, no snowmaking
SNOW PHONE 426-3651
TRAILS
20% beginner, 30% intermediate, 50% expert
TRAVEL
Just off I-80, 40 miles west of Reno, 90 miles east of Sacramento, 190 miles east of San Francisco.
VERTICAL DROP
1,500 feet

FOR LODGING, RESTAURANTS, SERVICES, STORES & SKI SHOPS, SEE N. LAKE TAHOE

TAHOE DONNER

DRAWER G, TRUCKEE, CA 95734 (916) 587-6046

AREA INFORMATION

BASE ELEVATION
6,750 feet
HOURS
9:00 a.m. to 4:00 p.m.
LIFTS
2 chairlifts, 1 tow, 2,000 capacity per hour
LONGEST RUN
1 mile
SEASON
Thanksgiving to Easter
TRAILS
50% beginner, 50% intermediate
TRAVEL
I-80, Donner Memorial State Park exit, west on old U.S. 40 to Ski Area
VERTICAL DROP
600 feet

FOR LODGING, RESTAURANTS, SERVICES, STORES & SKI SHOPS, SEE N. LAKE TAHOE

NORTH LAKE TAHOE

CONDOMINIUMS

CARNELIAN BAY, 95711

CARNELIAN BAY RENTALS
P.O. Box 62 546-5924

INCLINE VILLAGE, 89450

COEUR DU LAC
P.O. Box 7107. . . . . (702) 831-3318
INCLINE VILLAGE REALTY
P.O. Box 3549. . . . . (702) 831-1515

KINGS BEACH, 95719

KINGSWOOD VILLAGE
P.O. Box 1919. 546-2501
MC KINNEY'S LANDING
P.O. Box 206 546-4074

NORTHSTAR, 95734

NORTHSTAR AT TAHOE
P.O. Box 2499, Truckee 562-1111
SUGAR PINE LAKESIDE
P.O. Box 185, Homewood 525--7042

TAHOE CITY, 95730

CHINQUAPIN
P.O. Box RR. 583-6911
LAKE FOREST GLEN
Drawer U.U.. 583-0151
TAHOE MARINA LODGE
P.O. Box 82 583-2365

TAHOE DONNER, 95734

TAHOE DONNER RESORT
Drawer G, Truckee 587-2551

CASINOS - NEVADA

CAESAR'S TAHOE . . . . (702) 588-3515
CAL - NEVA LODGE . . . . (702) 831-1511
CRYSTAL BAY CLUB. . . . . (702) 831-0512
HARRAH'S . . . . (702) 588-6611
HYATT LAKE TAHOE . . . . (702) 831-1111
SAHARA TAHOE . . . . (702) 588-6211
TAHOE MARINER. . . . . (702) 831-3100

EMERGENCY

AMBULANCE, TAHOE CITY 583-6911
FIRE, TAHOE CITY. 583-6911
HIGHWAY PATROL, TRUCKEE 587-3518
SHERIFF, TAHOE CITY 583-4244

LODGING

HOTELS - MOTELS

ALPINE MEADOWS / SQUAW VALLEY

ALPINE MOTOR INN
P.O. Box 32, Tahoe City 583-4266
CAL NEVA LODGE
368 Crystal Bay 831-1511
SQUAW VALLEY INN
P.O. Box 2407, Olympic Valley. 583-4211
SQUAW VALLEY INN
P.O. Box 2407, Olympic Valley. 583-4211
SQUAW VALLEY LODGE
P.O. Box 23930, Olympic Valley 583-0121
TRUCKEE RIVER RANCH
P.O. Box 197, Tahoe City 583-4264

CARNELIAN BAY, 95711

ZELMAR LODGE
P.O. Box 125, Carnelian Bay 546-3133

INCLINE VILLAGE, 89450

INCLINE MOTOR LODGE
4545 Incline Village 831-1052

KINGS BEACH, 95719

BLUE VUE LODGE
P.O. Box 291 546-3871
CARAVELLE
P.O. Box 67 546-2842
EDGE LAKE RESORT
P.O. Box 366 546-5974
GOLDCREST RESORT
P.O. Box 579 546-3301
STEVENSON'S HOLIDAY INN
P.O. Box 235 546-3845
WOOD VISTA LODGE
P.O. Box 63 543-3839

SODA SPRINGS

DONNER SUMMIT LODGE
P.O. Box 115 426-3538

TAHOE CITY, 95730

LAKE OF THE SKY
P.O. Box 227 583-3305
TRAVELODGE
P.O. Box 84 583-3766

NORTH LAKE TAHOE CONT.

TAHOE VISTA, 95732

CHARMEY CHABET
P.O. BOX 316 546-2529
CEDAR GLEN LODGE
P.O. Box 188 546-4281
DUNES
P.O. Box 34 546-2196
HORSESHOE LODGE
P.O. Box 17 546-3386
RUSTIC COTTAGES
P.O. Box 138 546-3523
SILVER SANDS RESORT
P.O. Box 109 546-2592

TRUCKEE / DONNER LAKE, 95734

ALPINE VILLAGE MOTEL
P.O. Box 730, Truckee 587-3801
COTTAGE PINE
P.O. Box 905, Truckee 587-3634
DONNER LAKE VILLAGE
P.O. Box 2348, Truckee 587-6081

WEST SHORE / HOMEWOOD, 95733

HOMEWOOD MARINA LODGE
P.O. Box 526, Homewood 525-6728
SWISS LAKEWOOD LODGE
P.O. Box 205, Homewood 525-7814

RESTAURANTS

A CATERED AFFAIR (catering)
Tahoe Vista 546-3074
BENISSIMO'S (Italian)
By Brockway Theatre
King's Beach 546-7385
BLUE WATER SEA GARDEN
Back of Country Club Mall
Incline Village . . . . (702) 831-2086
BON VIVANT (French)
Hwy. 28, Tahoe Vista 546-5903
CANTINA LOS TRES HOMBRES
Foot of Brockway Hill, Kings Beach 546-4052
CARNELIAN HOUSE (Continental)
Hwy. 28, Carnelian Bay on the Lake 546-5954
CHINA CHEF
874 Tahoe Bl., Incline Village 831-0953
ERNIE'S BISTRO (European)
Commercial Row, Truckee. 587-4936
FIRESIGN CAFE (vegetarian, espresso)
Hwy. 89, Tahoe Park 583-0871
GREY'S TOLL STATION (American)
Downtown Truckee. 587-2626
JAKE'S ON THE LAKE (American, seafood)
780 N. Lake Bl., Tahoe City. 538-0188
THE LOFT (American, seafood)
8393 N. Lake Bl., Kings Beach 546-4778
NORTHWOODS CLUBHOUSE (steak, seafood, live music)
Northwoods Bl. at Tahoe Donner. 587-6131
OFF SHORE BAR & GRILL (American, seafood)
Atop Village Store, Truckee 583-4550
THE PASSAGE (American, Continental)
Truckee Hotel, Bridge St. & Commercial Row 587-7619
RIVER RANCH (ribs, steak, Italian)
Hwy. 89 & Alpine Meadows Rd. 583-4264
SCHAFFER'S MILL (American, seafood, entertainment)
Village Mall @ Northstar 562-1015
THE SIERRA CHILI CO. (also take-out)
930 Tahoe Bl., Incline Village 831-6466
STEREOSCOPE CAFE (bag lunches)
Next to the Bronze Bull, Incline Village 831-2043
SWISS LAKEWOOD (Swiss)
Hwy. 89, 6 mi. S. of Tahoe City 525-5211
TAHOE HOUSE (Swiss)
Hwy. 89, 1 mi. S. of the "Y" 583-1377
VAL D'ISERE (coffee house)
Village Shopping Center, Incline Village 831-7474
VALLEY FLOOR (steak, seafood, dancing)
2nd fl., Olympic House, Squaw Valley 583-0121 X 109
WATER WHEEL (Chinese)
115 W. Lake Bl. 583-4405
WOLFDALE'S (seafood)
Hwy. 89, Homedale. 525-7833

SERVICES

AIR

CAL-VADA AIRCRAFT (charter)
Between Reno & Homewood
Seaplane Base . . . . (916) 525-7143
RENO INTERNATIONAL AIRPORT (60 miles via I-80)
Air Cal, American, Braniff, Delta, Eastern, PSA,
Republic, TWA, United, and Western Airlines

AUTOMOTIVE

DOLLAR POINT SHELL
3205 N. Lake Bl., Tahoe City 583-5885
SIERRA TOW SERVICE (24 hours)
Truckee 587-6021

BABYSITTING

DIAL-A-SITTER . . . . (702) 323-8588

BOAT

THE TAHOE I (cruise boat)
Between South Lake Tahoe & Tahoe City. . . 541-4569

BUS

GREYHOUND
To Truckee
SHUTTLE BUS
Between Tahoe City and Homewood Ski Area
TAHOE AREA REGIONAL TRANSIT
North & west shore 583-1658

DRUG STORE

TAHOE CITY PHARMACY
Tahoe City 583-3888

LIMOS

C T S . . . . (702) 831-3967
DRANEY'S 546-3324

TAXI

INCLINE 546-3181
TRUCKEE YELLOW CAB 587-6336

THEATRES

CALL FOR INFORMATION 583-5403

STORES & SKI SHOPS

ALPINE MARINA SPORTS (rentals)
7360 N. Lake Bl., Tahoe Vista 546-7255
BIRKENSTOCKS OF TAHOE
Lighthouse Shopping Center 583-0951
LA BOUTIQUE GOURMANDE
8160 N. Lake Bl., Kings Beach 546-3252
BUTLERS OF TAHOE (skiwear)
531 N. Lake Bl., Tahoe City 583-5777
CASA ANDINA (ski shop, skiwear)
Hwy. 89 at Alpine Meadows Rd. 583-4123
EARTHSONGS (gifts)
Loading Dock, Commercial Row, Truckee. . . 587-2458
GRAPE OF THE LAKE (wine)
700 N. Lake Bl., Tahoe City 583-5456
GUNDY OF SCANDINAVIA (gifts)
Cobblestone Mall, Tahoe City 583-4533
HEAVENLY HIDES (sheepskin, leather)
Downstairs, Bratworks Mall, Tahoe City 583-1455
THE HIGH SIERRA (rentals)
1 blk. up Old Hwy. 40, Soda Springs 426-3567
INCLINE SPORTS HAUS (rentals)
910 Tahoe Bl. . . . . (702) 831-5050
THE INN AT SKI SLOPE (rentals)
Squaw Valley Inn 583-2195
OVERLAND SHEEPSKIN CO.
Old Ice House Mall, Truckee 587-2167
THE SKI RENTER
265 N. Lake Bl., Basecamp 583-2548
SKI RENTS USA
185 River Rd., Tahoe City 583-9724
8345 N. Lake Bl., Kings Beach 546-7191
VILLAGE SPORTS
Tahoe City 583-3722
THE WEARHOUSE (gifts, clothing)
No. 4 Country Club Mall, Incline Village. . . . 831-1003

SOUTH LAKE TAHOE

AREA CODE 916 - CA, 702 - NEVADA

EMERGENCY

AMBULANCE 541-3333
BARTON HOSPITAL 541-3420
FIRE 541-1226
COAST GUARD 583-4433
AAA 541-2430
LOCKSMITH 541-5545
TOW TRUCK 541-2720
FOREIGN LANGUAGE BANK. . . . . . . (702) 323-0500
RESCUE / FOREST FIRE. 541-5468
VETERINARIAN. 541-0150

CAMPGROUNDS

CITY

S. LAKE TAHOE - EL DORADO
Box 1212, 95705 (write first) 541-4611
D.L. BLISS STATE PARK
Hwy. 89, 11 miles N. of Hwy. 50 525-7277
EMERALD BAY STATE PARK
Hwy. 89, N. of "Y". 541-3030
SUGAR PINE POINT
Hwy 89, 20 miles N. of "Y" 525-7982

U.S. FOREST SERVICE

FALLEN LEAF
Fallen Leaf Rd. off Hwy. 89, call Ticketron. . 541-3366
MEEKS BAY CAMPGROUND
15 miles N. of the "Y" on Hwy. 89, call Ticketron
NEVADA BEACH
Elk Point Rd. off Hwy. 50, call Ticketron
WILLIAM KENT CAMP
20 miles N. of the "Y" 544-6420

PRIVATE CAMPGROUNDS

KOA OF S. LAKE TAHOE
Hwy. 50 & Upper Truckee Rd. 577-3693
MEEKS BAY RESORT
15 miles N. of the "Y" on Hwy. 89. 525-7242
TAHOE PINES
Hwy. 50, N. of Junction 89 577-1653
TAHOE VALLEY
Hwy. 50 at "C" St. 541-2222
ZEPHYR COVE CAMPGROUND
Hwy. 50, Zephyr Cove . . . . (702) 588-6644

LODGING

* TOLL FREE NUMBER FROM THE
7 WESTERN STATES . . . . (800) 648-5450

SOUTH LAKE TAHOE CONT.

† FROM CALIFORNIA
S. TAHOE TOURS . . . . (800) 822-5974
NATIONWIDE . . . . (916) 544-2244

ALDER INN *
1072 Ski Run Bl. 544-4485
AMERICANA INN †
3845 Pioneer Trail 541-8022
BEACHCOMBER INN *
999 Lakeview 544-2426
BIG 7 MOTEL †
3790 Hwy. 50 544-7696
BLACK JACK MOTEL
985 Park Ave. 544-3902
BLUE LAKE MOTEL *
1055 Ski Run Bl. 544-4853
BONANZA MOTEL
3800 Hwy. 50 544-8688
CAL VA RADO
988 Stateline 544-3393
CASINO TRAVELODGE
4003 Hwy. 50 . . . . 541-5000, (800) 255-3050
CONDOR LODGE †
3838 Hwy. 50 541-5400
ELM INN *
4082 Hwy. 50 . . . . . . .541-7900, CA (800) 822-5955
FLAMINGO LODGE*
3961 Hwy. 50 544-5288
HANSEN'S RESORT
1360 Ski Run Bl. 544-3361
HIGH COUNTRY LODGE
1227 Emerald Bay Rd. 541-0508
INN BY THE LAKE *
3300 Hwy. 50 542-0330
LAKELAND VILLAGE *
3535 Hwy. 50 . . . . . . .541-7711, CA (800) 822-5969
LAKE TAHOE INN
4110 Hwy. 50 . . . . 541-2010, (800) 528-1234
MARK TWAIN MOTEL
947 Park Ave. 544-5733
MONACO MOTEL *
4140 Pine Bl. 544-4300
OLYMPIC MOTEL †
3901 Pioneer Trail 541-2119
RED CARPET INN
4100 Hwy. 50 . . . . . . .544-2261, CA (800) 822-5972
SKI HAUS LODGE
977 Park Ave. 544-2544
ST. MORITZ LODGE
1261 Ski Run Bl. 544-4244
SIERRA HOUSE INN
968 Park Ave. 541-4800
SLALOM INN *
1195 Ski Run Bl. 544-5765
STARDUST LODGE
4061 Hwy. 50 . . . . . . .544-5211, CA (800) 822-5972
SUN 'N SKI LODGE
3530 Hwy. 50 544-3445

TAHOE MARINA INN
Bal Bijou 541-2180
TAHOE SHORES *†
3717 Hwy. 50 544-2244
TIMBER COVE LODGE
3411 Hwy. 50 . . . . 541-6722, (800) 528-1234
WATERFRONT MOTEL *
953 Ski Run Bl. 544-3457, (800) 238-5511

CABIN / CONDO RENTALS

ACCOMODATION STATION 541-2355
LAKESIDE COVE . . . . (702) 588-4455
LAKE TAHOE ACCOMODATIONS 544-3230
PARADISE RENTALS 542-1329
RESORT MANAGEMENT 544-5791
TAMARACK RENTALS 541-2595
TAHOE VILLAGE CONDOS . . . . (702) 588-3537

NIGHTLIFE

ALL CASINOS ARE ON THE STRIP

BARNEY'S . . . . (702) 588-2455
CAESAR'S TAHOE . . . . (702) 588-3515
HARRAH'S . . . . (800) 648-3773, (702) 588-6606
HARVEY'S . . . . (800) 648-3361, (702) 588-2411
MONTE VISTA, Round Hill Mall
2 miles N. of Stateline . . . . (702) 588-7200
ROJO'S
Hwy. 50 & San Francisco St. 541-9086
SAHARA TAHOE . . . . (800) 648-3322, (702) 588-6211
SOUTH TAHOE NUGGET . . . . (702) 588-6288

RECREATION

AVIATION
Tahoe Valley Airport 541-2110
BIKING
Map of Bike paths
1180 Rufus Allen Bl. 541-4611
BOATING - CRUISES
High Water Princess, S. Shore Marina 544-0503
Lake Tahoe Cruises, Ski Run Marina 541-4652
Miss Tahoe, Lakeside, Marina 541-3364
M.S. Dixie, Zephyr Cove . . . . (702) 588-3508
Tahoe I, Timber Cove Marina 541-4911
Woodwind Trimaran, Zephyr Cove 588-3000
BOATING - RENTALS
Beachcomber Marina
999 Lakeview Ave. & Hwy. 50 544-2426
Lakeside Marina, Park Ave. & Lakeshore Bl. 541-6626
Ski Run, Ski Run Bl. 544-0200
Tahoe Keys, Venice Dr. 541-0790
Timber Cove, opposite Safeway 544-2942
Zephyr Cove, Hwy. 50 . . . . (702) 588-6644
FISHING LICENSES
Dept. of Fish & Game 583-3325
U.S. Forest Service 544-6420
Tahoe Trout Farm (no license required)
1023 Blue Lake Ave. 544-0761
GOLF
Edgewood by Sahara Tahoe . . . . (702) 588-3566
Glenbrook . . . . (702) 749-5201

Bijou, Hwy. 50 & Johnson Bl. 544-0611
Lake Tahoe Country Club
Hwy. 50 @ Meyers 577-0788
Tahoe Paradise, Hwy. 50 @ Meyers. 577-0797

HIKING & RAFTING
U.S. Forest Service 544-6420
Sandpiper Whitewater Guides
Box 11752, Zephyr Cove . . . . (702) 588-4074

HOT TUBS
Nephele (cocktails)
1169 Ski Run Bl. 544-8130
Shingle Creek (cocktails)
1142 Ski Run Bl. 544-5400

RACQUET BALL
Sierra Tahoe Athletic Club (Open 24 hrs.). . . 544-6222

RIDING
Camp Richardson, Hwy. 89 541-3113
Cascade Stables 541-2055
Stateline Stables, end of Park Ave. 541-9909
Sunset Corral, ¼ mi. S. of airport, Hwy. 50 . . 541-9944
Zephyr Cove, Hwy. 50 . . . . (702) 588-6644

SKIING CROSS COUNTRY
Echo Nordic Center, 10 miles of trails 659-7221
Kirkwood . . . . (209) 258-8864
Sugar House West, Tahoe Paradise 577-6811
Zephyr Cove, 760 Hwy. 50 . . . . (702) 588-4490

SNOWMOBILING
Sunset Corral, ¼ mi. past airport, Hwy.50. . . 541-9944
Tahoe Paradise, 2 miles S. of airport, Hwy. 50, 577-0797

RESTAURANTS

BELLA UNION (American)
4090 Hwy. 50. 544-3565

BUDAPEST TAHOE (Hungarian)
Hwy. 50 & C St.. 541-3515

THE CHART HOUSE (Steakhouse, view)
Kingsbury Grade . . . . (702) 588-6276

CHEZ VILLARET (French)
636 Hwy. 89. 541-7860

DORY'S OAR (New England seafood)
1041 Fremont Ave.. 541-6603

EPPAMONIDAS (International)
3678 Hwy. 50. 542-1242

GREENHOUSE (American, bar)
4140 Cedar 544-6278

LOS AGUIRRES (Mexican)
Hwy. 50 near Tahoe Keyes Bl. 541-9849

MIDNITE MINE (American)
Round Hill Mall, N. of Stateline. 588-5395

MINE SHAFT (American)
Hwy. 89, 2 bl. N. of the "Y" 544-0456

GROFINOS (Eastern seafood)
2660 Hwy. 50. 542-0285

SQUIRES (Continental)
1142 Ski Run Bl. 542-0708

TAHOE STEAKERY (choose your own cut)
1 bl. W. of Stateline, Hwy. 50 541-5077

TEP'S VILLA ROMA (Italian)
2588 Hwy. 50 @ Reno Ave. 541-8227

THE WAY STATION (American)
½ bl. from Ski Run on Hwy. 50. 541-6220

WILDWOOD RESTAURANT
Elmwood Inn, Hwy. 50 & Wildwood 541-6030

SERVICES

CHILDCARE
A-1, 1931 D St. 541-4688
Heavenly Baby Care, 3624 Needle Peak Rd. 544-6323
Kindertown, 2249 Helen. 541-7310
Tiny Piny, Pioneer Trail 544-5444

CATERING (full service)
Pat's, 3733 Hwy. 50 541-5750

LAUNDROMATS
Al Tahoe, Hwy. 50 @ Tallac
Bijou Moonlight, Sandy Way
Crescent V, Crescent V Center
Town & Country, across from Community College

SECRETARIAL SERVICE (full service)
Dictating, copying 542-1411

TRAVEL SERVICE
3449 Hwy. 50 544-5205

WEDDINGS
Fond du Lac Chapel, Hwy. 50 & Ski Run Bl. 544-3409
Tahoe Chapel, call . . . . (702) 588-6112
Woodwind (on Trimaran) 588-3000
California information 541-5707
Nevada information. 588-2044

STORES & SKI SHOPS

HOUSE OF SKI (rentals, sales)
209 Kingsbury Grade, Stateline . . . . . (702) 588-5935

LITTLE SWITZERLAND (rentals, sales)
Hwy. 50 & Navahoe, Meyers. 577-5646

THE OUTDOORSMAN (rentals, sales, clothing)
Hwy. 50, Tahoe 541-1660

PYRAMID PEAK (rentals)
3729 Hwy. 50. 541-5550

SKI COUNTRY RENTALS
1140 Ski Run Bl. 541-6883
Hwy. 89, ¼ mi. N. of the "Y". 544-3111

THE SKI RENTER (short & demo skis)
S. Lake Tahoe 544-2100

THE SKI SHOP (rental, clothing)
Across from Harvey's. 541-7111

THE SUGAR HOUSE (rental, clothing)
4045 Hwy. 50. . . . . 541-SKIS

THE SUGAR HOUSE TOO!
2205 Hwy. 50. . . . . 544-SKIS

WINTER WONDERLAND (rental)
3672 Verdon Lane 544-7903

TRANSPORTATION

AIR

ASPEN AIR
From Burbank, L.A., Bakersfield, San Jose,
San Francisco 544-8193, (800) 525-0256

YOSEMITE AIRLINES
Weekends . . . . (209) 532-6946

AUTO RENTALS

ADEQUATE (24 hrs.) 544-4099
AVIS (till 9 p.m.). 541-7800
DOLLAR (from Caesar's) 588-4562
NATIONAL (till 9 p.m.). 541-2277
SIERRA EXECUTIVE. 541-8087

CHARTERS

GRAY LINE TOURS. . . . . (702) 588-6688
SAFARIS & TOURS . . . . (702) 831-4567
TRAVEL SYSTEMS . . . . (702) 588-5656

GROUND

CASINO LIMO (to Reno) . . . . (702) 588-4562
GREYHOUND BUS
1099 Park Ave. 544-2241
LAKE TAHOE LIMO
Casinos to Tahoe Airport . . . . (702) 588-6688

CHINA PEAK

P.O. BOX 236, LAKESHORE, CA 93634 (209) 893-3316

AREA INFORMATION

BASE ELEVATION
7,030 feet
HOURS
9:00 a.m. to 4:00 p.m., weekdays
Opens 8:30 a.m. weekends, holidays
Night skiing, call first
LIFTS
3 chairs, 2 bars, 2 tows, 4,900 capacity per hour
LODGING
Central reservations: 893-3316
LONGEST RUN
3 miles
SEASON:
Mid-November to mid-April
TRAILS
200 acres
15% beginner, 50% intermediate, 35% difficult
TRAVEL
1½ hours from Fresno on Hwy. 168
Airport and transportation at Fresno Airport
VERTICAL DROP
1,500 feet

K I R K W O O D

P.O. BOX 1, KIRKWOOD, CA 95646 (209) 258-6000

AREA INFORMATION

BASE ELEVATION
7,800 ft.
HOURS
9 a.m. to 4:30 p.m., no night skiing
LIFTS
8 chairs, 10,500 capacity per hr.
LOCATION
On Hwy. 88. From Tahoe S. on 89, off U.S. 50, W. on Hwy. 88 for 30 miles. From Reno, S. on 395, S.W. on Hwy. 88
LONGEST RUN
2½ miles
SEASON
Mid Nov. to late April
SNOW PHONE 258-6000
SNOWFALL
460 ins., no snowmaking
TRAILS
50 runs, 25% beginner, 50% intermediate, 25% advanced
TRAVEL
Limousine, auto rentals available from S. Lake Tahoe Airport
VERTICAL DROP
2,000 ft.

LODGING

CENTRAL RESERVATIONS. 258-7247

BASE CAMP
Base of chairs 5 & 6, condos, fireplaces
EDELWEISS
Next to chairs 7 & 9, bedroom units
KIRKWOOD TOWERS
Base of Snowkirk lift
THIMBLEWOOD
Bottom of lifts 7 & 9, townhouses

FOR OTHER LODGING, SEE SOUTH LAKE TAHOE

RESTAURANTS

THE DELI (picnic service)
8:30 a.m. - 5 p.m., Kirkwood Cafeteria
HAUS HAHNENKAMM (Continental)
Base of lifts 7 & 9. 258-7267
KIRKWOOD INN (bar, American)
At the ski area. 258-7218
THE SNOWFLAKE (Steakhouse)
Main Lodge 258-7262
ZACHARY'S BAR (live music)
Kirkwood Main Lodge 258-7223

FOR OTHER RESTAURANTS SEE SOUTH LAKE TAHOE

SERVICES

AIR TRAVEL
Aspen Airways to S. Lake Tahoe, major airlines to Reno
AUTO RENTAL
National from Reno or S. Lake Tahoe (800) 328-4567
BUS SHUTTLE
From Reno & Tahoe . . . . (702) 329-1425
CHILD CARE
3 to 7 yrs., 9 a.m. to 5 p.m., Main Lodge
GAS STATIONS
Union 76, 2 mi. E. on Hwy. 88 258-8888
Chevron, 5 mi. W. on Hwy. 88 258-8598
Kirkwood Center, at resort
MEDICAL CLINIC
9 a.m. to 5 p.m., MD on duty
POST OFFICE
9 a.m. to 1 p.m., Main Lodge
RENTALS
At Main Lodge & Hahnenkamm Lodge
STORES
General Store, open till 7 p.m. 258-7217
Kirkwood Mt. Outfitters, at base of Main Lodge, open till 5 p.m.

FOR OTHER NEARBY SERVICES SEE SOUTH LAKE TAHOE

M A M M O T H

BOX 24, MAMMOTH LAKES, CA 93546 (714) 934-2571

AREA INFORMATION

BASE ELEVATION
7,900 feet
HOURS
9:00 a.m. - 4:30 p.m.
8:30 a.m. - 4:30 p.m., weekends & holidays
LIFTS
19 chairlifts, 2 gondolas, 2 T-bars, 2 poma lifts, 25,000 capacity per hour
LONGEST RUN
2½ miles
SEASON
October or November to June, no snowmaking
SNOW PHONE 934-6166
TRAILS
30% beginner, 40% intermediate, 30% expert
VERTICAL DROP
3,100 feet

EMERGENCY

AMBULANCE. 934-3049
FIRE 934-2200
HOSPITAL
Mammoth Lakes Hospital 934-3311
PHARMACY (open 24 hrs., call first)
Medical Arts Pharmacy
Minaret Rd. towards Devil's postpile 934-2711
POLICE 934-2566
SKI PATROL
Call Ski Area. 834-2571

LODGING

A-LEE LODGE
471548 Mammoth Tavern Rd.
P.O. Box 1241. . . . . 934-6709, (213) 360-8851

ALPENHOF LODGE
Minaret Rd., Highway 203
P.O. Box 1157. 934-6330

ALPINE LODGE
Minaret Rd., Highway 203
P.O. Box 359 934-8526

AUSTRIA HOF
End of Canyon Bl., near Lifts 7, 8, 16 & 17
P.O. Box 8227. 934-2764

BEST WESTERN WILDWOOD INN
Main St. in the Village
P.O. Box 568 934-6855

CHATEAU RESERVATIONS
Box A-2, Mammoth Lakes 93546. 934-2600
Toll Free . . . . (800) 462-5585

DISCOVERY 4 (condos)
Lake Mary Road
P.O. Box 789 934-6410

EDELWEISS LODGE
2½ miles from Village on Old Mammoth Rd.
P.O. Box 658 934-2445

1849 CONDOMINIUMS
Next to Warming Hut 2
P.O. Box 835 934-6998

THE ENGELHOF
Millers Siding Rd., behind Whiskey Creek Restaurant
P.O. Box 349 934-2417

HOLIDAY HAUS
Main Street, Highway 203
P.O. Box 107 . . . . 934-2414, 934-2426

HORIZONS 4 (Condos)
Meridian Bl., 1 bl. off Old Mammoth Rd.
P.O. Box 175 . . . . 934-2460, 934-6779

INNSBRUCK LODGE
Forest Trail, 2 bl. E. of Minaret Rd.
P.O. Box 758 934-3035

INTERNATIONAL INN
Main Street, Highway 203
P.O. Box 1089. 934-2542

JAGERHOF LODGE
Old Mammoth Road
P.O. Box A-6 934-6162

KITZBUHEL DORM
Berner Rd., off Minaret Rd., across from Alpine Lodge
P.O. Box 1132. 934-2669

KRYSTAL VILLA EAST (condos)
Corner of Laurel Mtn. & Mammoth Tavern Roads
P.O. Box 1132. 934-2669

MAMMOTH LAKES RESERVATION BUREAU
Box 8, Mammoth Lakes 93546 934-2528
Toll Free . . . . (800) 462-5571

MAMMOTH RESERVATION SERVICE
Old Mammoth Rd. & Highway 203
Box 277MS, Mammoth Lakes 93546. 934-2522

THE RENTAL PLACE
Old Mammoth Road
P.O. Box 8841, Mammoth Lakes 93546 934-6181

SKI TIME
P.O. Box 911 . . . . 934-8144, 934-6885

RECREATION

BODIE GHOST TOWN
U.S. 395 N. past Lee Vining, follow signs, 75 mi. away

CROWLEY LAKE (fishing, boat rentals)
25 min. S. of Mammoth on U.S. 395

DEVIL'S POSTPILE NATIONAL MONUMENT
In Red's Meadow, 15 minute walk from parking lot

EARTHQUAKE FAULT (self-guided tour 55 ft. down)
2 mi. N. of Mammoth on Minaret Rd.

HOT CREEK (swimming, fishing, hot springs)
10 min. S. of Mammoth on U.S. 395

HOT CREEK FISH HATCHERY
10 min. S. of Mammoth on U.S. 395

INYO CRATERS (volcano pits, lakes)
5 mi. N. of Mammoth on U.S. 395

JUNE LAKE LOOP (fishing, boating, skiing)
20 mi. N. of Mammoth off U.S. 395

MAMMOTH VISITOR CENTER (various tours)
Hwy. 203 at entrance to Mammoth Lakes

MINARET VISTA
One mi. N. of Mammoth Mountain

MONO LAKE & TUFA TOWERS (saline lake)
25 mi. N. of Mammoth on U.S. 395

OBSIDIAN DOME (volcanic glass mountain)
20 mi. N. of Mammoth Mountain off U.S. 395

RAINBOW FALLS
15 min. from Rainbow Falls Parking lot

RED'S MEADOW (virgin forest, campgrounds)
4 mi. N.W. of Mammoth Mountain

RESTAURANTS

AUSTRIA HOF (German-American)
End of Canyon Bl. 934-2764

BUS STOP CAFE (open till midnight, home cooking)
Corner of Main St. & Lupin 934-3454

CAPTAIN'S TABLE (American, seafood, entertainment)
Main St. 934-3241

CARSON PEAK INN (American, seafood)
June Lake Loop Rd., call 1st 648-7575

CHEZ MICHEL (French)
Laurel Mtn. Road in Mini-Mall 934-2155

CLOCKTOWER (American, disco, cocktails)
Minaret Rd. at Alpenhof Lodge 934-6160

COMSTOCK LODE (American, bar, entertainment)
Main St. 934-2594

CONVICT LAKE (Continental, cocktails)
8 mi. S. of Mammoth, Airport turnoff 935-4213

FAT ALBERT'S (Continental, American, deli, catering)
Highway 203 934-6267

HOT TO GO (take out, American)
Center St., behind Pea Soup 934-8648

LA FONDUE (Swiss)
Viewpoint Rd., by Swiss Chalet. 934-2007

LAS MONTANAS (Mexican, live entertainment)
Highway 203 & Sierra B7 934-8014

MILL CITY (American, cocktails, disco)
Old Mammoth Rd. & Sierra Nevada Rd. 934-8539

MOGUL STEAKHOUSE (cook your own)
Mammoth Tavern Rd., behind Safeway 934-3039
MOUNTAIN OMELETTES (also Mexican, juices)
Sierra Manor Rd. @ the High School 934-4260
NICOLOSI'S (Italian)
Old Mammoth Rd., across from Safeway . . . 934-6400
THE NORMANDY INN (Continental)
Crowley Lake Dr., 2 mi. S. of Mammoth Airport
on Highway 395. 935-4406
PEA SOUP ENDERSEN'S (adjacent saloon)
Village Center, Main St. 934-2264
THE RAFTERS (American, seafood, cocktails)
Old Mammoth Rd. by Sierra Nevada Inn. . . . 934-2537
ROGET'S (American, seafood, bar)
Corner of Main St. & Minaret Rd.. 934-4466
THE STOVE (Country, home made)
Old Mammoth Rd. @ Chateau. 934-2821
SWENSEN'S (ice cream)
Main Street Center 934-3200
SWISS CAFE
Old Mammoth Road 934-6196
WHISKEY CREEK (American, entertainment, bar)
Corner of Hwy. 203 & Minaret Rd.. 934-2555

SERVICES

NURSERY

MAMMOTH DAY CARE NURSERY (2 - 7 years)
Mammoth Mountain Inn, Nov. to April
Forest Trail at Pinecrest
Box 805, Mammoth Lakes, 93546 934-2894

TRAVEL

AIR

Sierra Pacific has daily flights from Los Angeles. Connections are available from other cities.
Sierra Pacific Airlines. . . . . (800) 462-4487
Outside of 714, 213, 805 areas . . . . . (800) 854-5511

BUS

Shuttle service runs throughout the Main Lodge parking lot area, 7 a.m. to 5 p.m. weekdays and 7 a.m. to 6 p.m. weekends. The warming Hut 2 has shuttle service that makes a loop starting at the Lodge, goes down Lakeview Bl. to Forest Trail Rd., then back up Lakeview to the Lodge. Buses also run to Chair 15. Chair 15 has a shuttle that runs between the lift area and Old Mammoth Rd. via Meridian Bl.

Quicksilver Stagelines has daily scheduled service in the village to the airport and the Ski Area from 7a.m. to 5:30 p.m. with stops in town, the Main Lodge, Warming Hut 2 and Chair 15. Saturdays they run till midnight and they offer charter service. Call 934-3868.

Greyhound runs twice daily, north & south into Mammoth. Call your local Greyhound station.

CAR

From the South take Highway 395 N. and turn at the Mammoth Lakes junction.

From the North take Highway 395 out of Reno and follow it south to the Mammoth Lakes junction.

From the Bay Area Mammoth is reached via Hwy. 80 to Reno and Highway 395 to the Mammoth Lakes junction. This is the most snow free though longest route. The shortest winter route is Hwy. 50 to South Shore Lake Tahoe, at which point, depending on snow conditions, you can either go over Hwy. 19 (Kingsbury Grade) to U.S. 395 and then south to Mammoth, or Hwy. 89 (Luther Pass) to U.S. 395. Approximate driving time using this route is about 6 hours. In the spring when Tioga Pass is open the driving time is 5 hours by going through Yosemite Valley. Roads may close any time due to bad weather.

HIGHWAY REPORT NUMBERS
Bay Area . . . . (415) 864-6440
Mammoth Area 873-6366
Sacramento . . . . (916) 445-0120
Reno . . . . (702) 793-1313
24 Hour Snow Report 934-6166
Southern California. . . . . (213) 626-7231
Mammoth Chamber of Commerce 934-2712

TAXI
Quicksilver Taxi Service 934-3838

STORES & SKI SHOPS

CORNICE (sporting goods, sportswear)
Main St., across from Fat Albert's 934-2955
COUNTRY COMFORT (antiques)
Village Center West, Main St. 734-6442
FILSON'S TACKLE & SPORTS
Gateway Shopping Center 934-2290
THE GARMENT STORE (clothing)
Red Rooster Mall, Main St. 934-4219
GRAPHIC CONCLUSION (T-shirts)
Village Center West, Main St. 934-2187
HIGH COUNTRY WESTERN ART GALLERY
U.S. 395 N. of Bishop 873-5509
HIGH MOUNTAIN TRADING CO. (sportswear, gifts)
Sherwin Plaza IV, Old Mammoth Rd. 934-3885
THE HOLE IN THE WALL (art gallery)
Main St., across from Las Montanas 934-6228
INSIGHTS (gifts, jewelry)
Pine Tree Plaza 934-2745
MAMMOTH MOUNTAIN RENTAL SHOPS
In the Main Lodge & Warming Hut
MAMMOTH VILLAGE PHARMACY (necessities, etc.)
Gateway Shopping Center 934-8561
NOW & THEN (antiques, gifts)
Red Rooster Mall 934-4280
THE OUTFITTER (sportswear)
Pine Tree Plaza 934-2335
SKY KING PHOTO
Sherwin Plaza, Old Mammoth Rd. 934-8415
SPORTS & TRAILS (mountaineering, rentals)
Old Mammoth & Mammoth Tavern Roads. . . 934-3078
THE STORE (natural foods)
Sherwin Plaza by the Post Office 934-8122
TEX'S MOUNTAIN SHOP (sporting goods, rentals)
Center of June Lake Village 648-7370

MAMMOTH CONT.

20TH CENTURY FOX (women's fashions, sportswear)
Village Center West, Main St. 934-4482

UPHILL SPORTS
Village Center West, Main St. 934-6955

THE WINERY (wines, gourmet foods)
Next to Safeway 934-2700

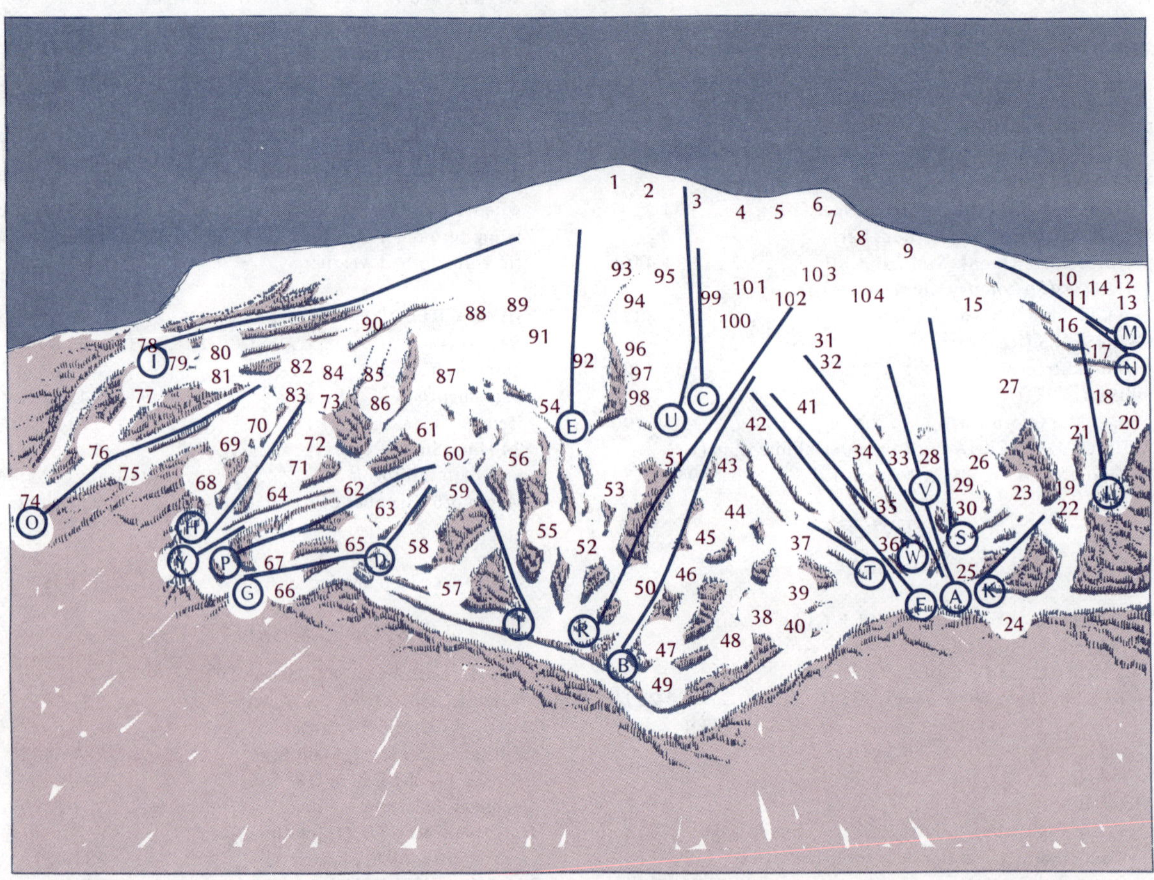

MAMMOTH RUNS

1 DAVE'S RUN
2 HUEVOS GRANDE
3 CLIMAX
4 HANGMAN'S HOLLOW
5 CORNICE BOWL
6 DROP OUT
7 WIPE OUT
8 SCOTTY'S RUN
9 RED'S LAKE RUN
10 ARRIBA
11 DOS PASOS
12 HEMLOCK RIDGE
13 HEMLOCK BOWL
14 SANTIAGO
15 ROAD RUNNER
16 SURPRISE
17 OOPS
18 WHITE BARK RIDGE
19 ROAD RUNNER
20 SECRET SPOT
21 LODGE POLE
22 CRITTERS
23 COMIN' THRU
24 SESAME ST. WEST
25 SESAME ST.
26 LOWER SAN ANTON
27 WHITE BARK BOWL
28 TERRY'S RUN
29 AGEE'S RUN
30 BLUE OX
31 UPPER BLUE OX
32 GRAVY CHUTE
33 POWDER BOWL
34 FASCINATION
35 BROADWAY
36 THUNDER MOUNTAIN
37 LOWER FOREST TRAIL
38 JILL'S RUN
39 ST MORITZ
40 GUS' PASTURE
41 WALL
42 BOWLING ALLEY
43 FOREST TRAIL
44 MAMBO
45 PATROLMEN
46 OVER EASY
47 LOWER PATROLMEN'S
48 PHAMTON'S ESCAPE
49 LOWER MAMBO
50 STUMP ALLEY
51 EGO BOWL
52 EASY RIDER
53 COME BACK TRAIL
54 LOWER DRY CREEK
55 WALL STREET
56 LOST IN THE WOODS
57 BIG BIRD
58 ROLLER COASTER
59 ROLLER COASTER WEST
60 AVALANCHE
61 DOWNHILL
62 ROUND ROBIN
63 SPRING CANYON
64 GINGER BREAD
65 ROUNDABOUT
66 GRETEL
67 HANSEL
68 BLUE JAY
69 CHICKA DEE
70 SWELL
71 CLOVERLEAF
72 GOFER TRAIL
73 HULLY GULLY
74 LUPIN
75 HANS GEORG
76 SLEEPY HOLLOW
77 PUMPKIN
78 RICOCHET
79 HOLIDAY
80 GOLD HILL
81 QUICKSILVER
82 SUNSHINE
83 MILK RUN
84 GRIZZLY
85 SHAFT
86 VIVA
87 ONE CHANCE
88 SPOOK
89 SOLITUDE
90 GOLD HILL
91 FACE OF FIVE
92 SANCTUARY
93 SLIVER
94 DRY CREEK
95 ROOSTER TAIL
96 CHINA BOWL
97 CHRISTMAS BOWL
98 EAST BOWL
99 CENTER BOWL
100 WEST BOWL
101 SADDLE BOWL
102 GREMLINS GULCH
103 ST. ANTON
104 PARANOID FLAT

MAMMOTH LIFTS

A CHAIR 1
B CHAIR 2
C CHAIR 3
D CHAIR 4
E CHAIR 5
F CHAIR 6
G CHAIR 7
H CHAIR 8
I CHAIR 9
J CHAIR 10
K CHAIR 11
L CHAIR 12
M CHAIR 13
N CHAIR 14
O CHAIR 15
P CHAIR 16
Q CHAIR 17
R CHAIR 18
S CHAIR 19
T GONDOLA 1
U GONDOLA 2
V T-BAR 1
W T-BAR 2
X POMA 1
Y POMA 2

EMERGENCY

BEAR VALLEY COMMUNITY HOSPITAL
41870 Garstin Bl., Big Bear Lake 866-7526
CALIFORNIA HIGHWAY PATROL
Ask Operator for . . . . Zenith 1-2000
Road Condition Information 887-7977
FIRE-RESCUE
Big Bear City 585-2555
Big Bear Lake, Fawnskin. 866-4666
U.S. Forest Service Fire Emergency 383-5651
SAN BERNARDINO COUNTY SHERIFF 866-7581
OTHER IMPORTANT NUMBERS
Animal Control . . . . (800) 472-5609
Contact The Help Line. 867-3500
County Library, 40940 Big Bear Bl. 866-4190
Humane Society. 866-5555
Time 866-8111

CAMPGROUNDS

ASPEN GLEN (picnic area, open all year)
2 miles west of Big Bear Lake
Post Office on Mill Creek Rd.
BARTON FLATS (open year round)
7½ mi. E. of Camp Angelus on Hwy. 38 794-1123
COLDBROOK (open all year)
1½ miles west of Big Bear Lake on Hwy. 18,
then ½ mile southwest on Tulip Lane 866-3437
COUNCIL GROUP CAMP (Open May 15th to Oct. 15th)
7½ miles east of Camp Angelus on Hwy. 38
FALLS (open year round)
2½ mi. E. of Forest Home via Mill Creek Rd. . 794-1123
GRAY'S PEAK GROUP CAMP
1½ mile N.W. on 2N13 from Fawnskin, then ½ mi. S.W.
on 2N68A, then 1 mi. S.W. on 2N68 866-3437
GREEN SPOT PICNIC AREA (open all year)
3 mi. S. of Big Bear City, & ½ W. of Hwy. 38
GROUT BAY (open April 1st to Nov. 30th)
½ mi. S. of Fawnskin on Hwy. 38. 866-3437
GROUT BAY PICNIC AREA (open all year)
½ mile south of Fawnskin on Hwy. 38
HANNA FLATS (open May 15th to Oct. 1st)
2½ mi. N.W. on Coxey Rd. (2N13) from Fawnskin,
then ½ mi. N.W. on 3N14 866-3437
HEART BAR HORSE CAMP
13 mi. E. of Camp Angelus off Hwy. 38 on
Coon Creek Rd., Mill Creek Station, Mentone
HOLCOMB VALLEY (open May 15th to Oct. 1st)
2 mi. E. on Hwy. 38 from Fawnskin, then 3 mi. N.
on Palique Canyon Rd. (2N09), then east on 3N08
LIGHTHOUSE TRAILER PARK (May 1st to Nov. 1st)
On North Shore Drive, 2 mi. E. of Fawnskin 866-7855
MILL CREEK (open all year)
7 mi. S.W. of Camp Angelus on Hwy. 38. . . . 794-1123
PINE KNOT (May 1st to Oct. 1st)
1½ mi. E. of Big Bear Lake Village,
then ½ mi. S. of Hwy. 18 866-3437
PIPES CANYON (June 15th to Sept. 15th)
9 mi. S.E. on Hwy. 38 from Big bear City,
then 7½ mi. S.E. on 1N01 866-3437
ROUND VALLEY GROUP CAMP (open all year)
8 mi. S.E. of Big Bear City on Hwy. 38,
then 6 mi. E. via 2N01 866-3437
SAN GORGONIO (open May 15th to Oct. 15th)
8 mi. E. of Camp Angelus 794-1123
SNOW VALLEY PICNIC AREA (open all year)
Between Running Springs & Big Bear Lake on Hwy. 18
SOUTH FORK
11 mi. E. of Camp Angelus on Hwy. 38 794-1123
TANGLEWOOD GROUP CAMP
E. of Holcomb Valley Area, N. of Big Bear Lake off
3N16. Big Bear Ranger Station, Big Bear City, 92314
THURMAN FLATS PICNIC AREA (open all year)
2½ mi. E. of Mill Creek Ranger Station on Hwy. 138

LODGING

ALL WAYS INN
40994 Pennsylvania Ave., P.O. Box 462 866-3576
AMBASSADOR LODGE
P.O. Box 1705. 866-2350
BIG BEAR RESERVATION SERVICE
Next to Bank of America
Mix Real Estate office 866-3671, 866-3676
BLACK FOREST LODGE
Between the Village & Snow Summit on Big Bear Bl.
P.O. Box 156 866-2166
BLUE SKIES RESERVATIONS SERVICE
24 hours 866-7415
CAL PINES CHALETS
Big Bear Blvd. across from The Alpine Restaurant
P.O. Box 3422. 866-2574
CONDOS. 866-2223
COOK'S 7 OAKS CABINS (Fawnskin)
P.O. Box 54, Fawnskin, 92333 866-2933
EMBERS LODGE
40229 Big Bear Bl., P.O. Box 335. 866-2371
ESCAPE FOR ALL SEASONS
Base of Snow Summit Ski Area
P.O. Box 1909B. 866-7504
FAWN VIEW CABINS
39117 No. Shore Dr., Fawnskin
P.O. Box 132, Fawnskin, 92333 866-2023
FIRESIDE LODGE
P.O. Box 635 866-2253
FRONTIER LODGE
Hwy. 18, ½ mi. W. of Big Bear Lake Village
P.O. Box 186 866-2232
FULLER'S GUEST LODGE
40687 Big Bear Blvd., P.O. Box 105 866-4684
GOLDEN BEAR COTTAGES, STOVALLS
2 mi. E. of the dam on Hwy. 18 in Boulder Bay
P.O. Box 5424. 866-2010
GOLDMINE LODGE (Moonridge)
Moonridge Rd. near Goldmine ski area
P.O. Box 198 866-8786

BIG BEAR AREA CONT.

GREY SQUIRREL CABINS
2 mi. E. of the dam on Hwy. 18
P.O. Box 5404. 866-4335

HENRY'S CABINS
Lagunita Point, P.O. Box 147 866-2526

HILLCREST LODGE
40241 Big Bear Blvd., P.O. Box G 13-8 866-2345

KRISKAY LODGE
3 mi. E. of the dam on Hwy. 18
P.O. Box 665 866-4646

LAGUNITA MOTOR LODGE
Hwy. 18, 3.7 mi. E. of the dam to Lakeview Dr.,
left ½ mi., P.O. Box 665 866-2190

LAKESHORE LODGE
Hwy. 18, 3.7 mi. E. of dam to Lakeview Dr., left
P.O. Box 1178. . . . . 866-7393, 866-7960

MARINA RIVIERA MOTEL
Hwy. 18 thru Village to the Post Office
P.O. Box 979 866-7545

PARAMOUNT LODGE
In the Village, P.O. Box1715 866-4672

PINE HAVEN COTTAGES
Big Bear Blvd., ½ mi. E. of Bank of America
P.O. Box 201 866-2637

PONDEROSA MOTEL
2 mi. E. of the dam on Hwy. 18, Boulder Bay
P.O. Box 5414. 866-2435

ROBINHOOD INN & LODGE
Lakeview Dr. & Hwy. 18, P.O. Box 2826 . . . 866-4643

SHANGRI-LA LODGE
¾ of a mile W. of the village, P.O. Box 2801. . 866-2415

SHORE ACRES
Lakeview Dr., P.O. Box GC 4-1 866-4386

SOUTH SHORE LODGE
Hwy. 18 to Lagunita, then right
P.O. Box 1316. 866-2368

SUMMIT INN
Snow Summit, at the slope 866-4601

TEOLA PINES
547 Main St., P.O. Box 1746 866-2720

THREE PINES LODGE
39268 Big Bear Bl, P.O. Box 186 866-4103

THUNDERCLOUD LODGE
1 block from the lake, W. of the Village
P.O. Box 1773. 866-4543

TIMBERLINE LODGE
39921 Big Bear Bl., P.O. Box 186. 866-3546

TOWN & COUNTRY LODGE
Hwy. 18, 2¾ mi. E. of the dam, P.O. Box 142 866-2723

TRAVEL INN
3 blocks E. of the traffic signal on Big Bear Bl.
P.O. Box 1565. 866-2133

WAWONA LODGE
Big Bear Bl., 2 blocks E. of the high school
P.O. Box 34 866-2644

WISHING WELL MOTEL
Hwy. 18 & Pineknot Bl.
P.O. Box 577 . . . . 866-3505, 866-5709

UNLESS OTHERWISE NOTED, ALL MAILING ADDRESSES ARE FOR BIG BEAR LAKE, CA 92315
AREA CODE IS 714

RECREATION

BIG BEAR AVIATION (flight charter & rental)
At the airport 585-2514

BIG BEAR HONDA (cycle, snowmobile rentals)
Near Moonridge Rd. 866-7554

BIG BEAR ROLLER RINK
40679 Lakeview Dr. 866-3535

BIG BEAR VALLEY RECREATION & PARK DISTRICT
Parks & various activities. 866-3652

PAN HOT SPRINGS
Hwy. 18, 4½ blocks east of Greenway
on N. Shore Drive. 585-2757

SUPER BEAR ARCADE
Big Bear Bl., by Jack-in-the-Box. 866-8620

WATERFALL MINIATURE GOLF & ARCADE
42123 Big Bear Bl., Moonridge 866-7877

RESTAURANTS

A LITTLE BIT OF QUEBEC (French-Canadian)
40037 Big Bear Blvd. 866-4263

BIG BEAR INTERNATIONAL DELI
41011 Big Bear Blvd. 866-4363

BIT AND SPUR (steak, seafood, beer & wine)
Hwy. 18, at Moonridge Rd., Moonridge 866-2411

BOSTON PROPER
(Steak, seafood, cocktails, entertainment)
40615 Big Bear Bl., ... 866-3155

CAPTAIN'S ANCHORAGE (steak, seafood, cocktails)
Big Bear Bl., to Moonridge cut-off 866-3997

CHAD'S PLACE (American, cocktails, entertainment)
Big Bear Village 866-2162

CROW'S NEST RESTAURANT & POOP DECK LOUNGE
(American, cocktails, entertainment)
One block E. of traffic signal on the lake . . . 866-5771

FAWN LODGE (American, cocktails, entertainment)
North Shore, Fawnskin. 866-2525

THE GALLERY INN (American, beer, wine, entertainment)
337 W. Big Bear Bl. 585-3232

THE HIGHLANDER RESTAURANT
(American, cocktails, dancing, entertainment)
1 block W. of the Post Office 866-3602

HOOGIES (American)
40211 Big Bear Bl. 866-2664

LOG CABIN RESTAURANT
(French, German, American, cocktails)
Hwy. 18 & Edgemoor 866-2639

SANDWICH HAUS (Gourmet sandwiches, omelets)
On Pineknot in the Village
Across from Ronardo's. 866-5413

SUGAR BEAR SMORGASBORD (beer & wine)
Big Bear Bl., 2 blocks E. of traffic signal 866-5611

SWISS CHALET (Swiss, Continental, cocktails)
646 Pineknot 866-2026

ALL RESTAURANTS ARE IN BIG BEAR LAKE UNLESS OTHERWISE NOTED. AREA CODE - 714.

SERVICES

AIR

BIG BEAR AVIATION
Big Bear City Airport. 585-2514
MOUNTAIN AIR SERVICE
Big Bear City Airport. 585-2511

AUTO RENTAL

MOUNTAIN TOP CAR RENTALS
Big Bear Lake 585-2514

AUTO REPAIR & SERVICE

ARCHIES - MOONJEAN TIRE & BATTERY SERVICE
40182 Big Bear Bl. 866-2333
ARROWBEAR GARAGE
33211 Hilltop Bl., Arrowbear 867-2361
BEAR CITY GARAGE
336 W. Big Bear Bl.. 585-2272
BILL'S AUTO & TRUCK REPAIR
Edgemoor & Big Bear Bl.. 866-3142
CENTRAL AUTOMOTIVE
Hwy. 18 & Paine Rd.. 866-3626
CITY EXXON
225 W. Big Bear Bl., Big Bear City 585-2630
D & D AUTO PARTS & REPAIR
41505 Big Bear Bl. 866-3488
MERCER TIRE & AUTO SERVICE
42181 Big Bear Bl. 866-7222
MOONRIDGE EXXON
Hwy. 18 & Garstin 866-4480
PRECISION MOTORS
685 Pine Knot Bl.. 866-7234
STOCK'S AUTO REPAIR
41390 Big Bear Bl. 866-5361
T & S AUTOMOTIVE REPAIR
42159 Big Bear Bl. 866-2400

BANKS

BANK OF AMERICA
40865 Big Bear Bl. 866-7575
SECURITY PACIFIC NATIONAL BANK
42142 Big Bear Bl. 866-3447
WELLS FARGO BANK
Big Bear Bl. & Pine Knot. 866-4661

BOATS, RENTAL & CHARTER

BIG BEAR MARINA
Paine & Spruce 866-3218
BOULDER BAY VILLAGE
39166 Big Bear Bl. 866-7557
COOKE MARINE
1 Pine Knot Boat Landing 866-7717
GRAY'S BOAT LANDING
Fawnskin. 866-2443
HOLLOWAY'S MARINA
Edgemoor Rd.. 866-5706
LEONARD'S NORTH SHORE LANDING
Just over a mile from dam, Fawnskin. 866-2018
PLEASURE POINT BOAT LANDING
Metcalf Bay 866-2455

CLOTHING

BENO'S FAMILY APPAREL
Interlaken Shopping Center 866-5435
CHILDREN'S CLOSET
40764 Big Bear Bl. 866-7474
LE ROY'S
598 Paine Rd.. 866-4887
MC NEAL'S TRADING POST
40712 Big Bear Bl. 866-2115
VILLAGE SPORTSWEAR
40760 Big Bear Bl. 866-3658
WR BRAND WESTERN APPAREL
40645 Big Bear Bl. 866-8733

DENTISTS

CHUKA, RONALD
41628 Big Bear Bl. 866-2646
CRANE, EARL R. (Orthodontist)
41628 Big Bear Bl. 866-2646
DAVIS, ROBERT C.
40712 Lakeview. 866-2233
PEARSON, WILLIAM
40643 Big Bear Bl. 866-4994
TURNEY, KENNETH
40798½ Lakeview Dr. 866-3935

DRY CLEANING

BIG BEAR CLEANERS 866-2418
KIMBRO'S LAUNDROMAT
41114 Big Bear Bl. 866-3132

FLORIST

THE LITTLE GREEN HOUSE
563 Pine Knot Bl.. 866-5352

GIFT SHOPS

ARNETT'S
40750 Big Bear Bl. 866-7321
BROWN BEAR GIFT SHOP
675 Pine Knot Bl.. 866-2514
CROW'S NEST BOUTIQUE
40835 Pennsylvania Ave.. 866-8773
DELANO'S UNIQUE GIFT BOUTIQUE
1117 W. Big Bear Bl., Big Bear City. 585-2929
ELIZABETH'S GIFT SHOP
600 Pine Knot Bl.. 866-8601
HARVEST MOON EMPORIUM
40754 Big Bear Bl. 866-7321
HIGH CHAPARRAL JEWELERS
596 Bonanza Terrace 866-5500
HIGH COUNTRY POTTERY & LEATHER
The Hutch 866-4882

LISA'S HOUSE OF IMPORTS
652 Pine Knot Bl. 866-8541
ROOM TO ROOM
40768 Big Bear Bl. 866-4464
THE SERVICE STATION
204 W. Big Bear Bl., Big Bear City 585-4263
TOTEM POLE
605 Pine Knot Blvd. 866-3838
TRAVEL INN
41066 Big Bear Bl. 866-2133
WOODLAND GIFT SHOP
133 W. Big Bear Bl., Big Bear City 585-2726

GROCERY STORES

BOULDER BAY MARKET 866-4927
CIRCLE K MARKET
Big Bear City 585-2626
COMMUNITY MARKET
100 E. Big Bear Bl., Big Bear City. 585-2641
DENNY'S MEAT & DELI
42180 Moonridge Rd., Moonridge 866-8771
EASY'S GENERAL STORE
Maple & Barton Lane, Sugarloaf 585-2134
EMINGER'S BEAR VALLEY MARKET 866-2366
FAWNSKIN MARKET
39187 N. Shore Dr., Fawnskin 866-2129
HOLIDAY MARKET
40133 Big Bear Bl. 866-3192
MOONRIDGE MARKET
Moonridge 585-3456
MURPHY'S MARKET
Maple & Barton Lane, Sugarloaf 585-2134
REEDY'S LIQUOR & GROCERIES
40517 Big Bear Bl. 866-2120
SAFEWAY STORES
42170 Big Bear Bl. 866-5331
Pennsylvania Ave.. 866-4403
TRIANGLE MARKET
Moonridge 866-7218

LIQUOR STORES

ALPINE LIQUORS
41532 E. Big Bear Bl.. 866-4400
HOLIDAY MARKET
40133 Big Bear Bl. 866-3912
L & H LIQUOR. 866-3528
VILLAGE WINE & SPIRITS
40568 Big Bear Bl. 866-2330

LOCKSMITHS

ART MURRAY LOCKSMITH
929 W. Big Bear Bl., Big Bear City 585-3527
ARROWBEAR LOCK & KEY
32875 Hilltop Bl., Arrowbear 867-7994

PHARMACIES

BIG BEAR PHARMACY
In the Village 866-2112
THRIFTY DRUG STORES CO.
42146 Big Bear Bl. 866-3901

SKI SHOPS

ALPINE SPORTS CENTER
41530 Big Bear Bl. 866-7542
BIG BEAR SPORTING GOODS
40544 Big Bear Bl. 866-3222
BLAUER SKI RENTALS
Knight & Big Bear Blvd. 866-5689
FRED'S SKI & SPORT
Pine Knot in Village 866-3500
LEROY'S
598 Paine Rd. 866-4887
RED WING SKI RENTAL
41207 W. Big Bear Bl. 866-7608
SKI-HAUS. 866-7411

THEATRE

VILLAGE THEATRE (movie)
Program information 866-5115

VETERINARIAN

STEPHENS, H. A. 866-2021

ALL SERVICES ARE IN BIG BEAR LAKE UNLESS NOTED OTHERWISE. AREA CODE - 714.

G O L D M I N E

BOX 68112, BIG BEAR LAKE, CA 92315 (714) 585-2517

AREA INFORMATION

BASE ELEVATION
7,100 feet
HOURS
8:00 a.m. - 4:00 p.m., weekdays
7:00 a.m. - 4:00 p.m., weekends
LIFTS
4 chairlifts, 3 rope tows, 5,000 capacity per hour
LONGEST RUN
2½ miles
NURSERY
Call Ski Area
SEASON
Thanksgiving thru April, snowmaking
SNOW PHONE 585-2517
TRAILS
30% beginner, 40% intermediate, 30% advanced
TRAVEL
Big Bear Lake, 2 miles; San Bernardino, 32 miles. Located in the San Bernardino Mountains via I-10 to San Bernardino, then Hwy. 330 through Running Springs, Hwy. 38 through Redlands, or Hwy. 18 through Lucerne Valley.

VERTICAL DROP
1,500 feet

FOR LODGINGS, RESTAURANTS, SERVICES, STORES & SKI SHOPS, SEE BIG BEAR

SNOW SUMMIT

BOX 77, BIG BEAR LAKE, CA 92315 (714) 866-5766

AREA INFORMATION

BASE ELEVATION
7,000 feet
HOURS
8:00 a.m. - 4:30 p.m., 4:30 - 10:00 p.m., nights
LIFTS
5 chairs, 3 tows, capacity per hour, 9,000
LONGEST RUN
1¼ miles
NURSERY
Ages 4 - 8, call Ski Area
SEASON
End of November thru end of March, snowmaking
SNOW PHONE 866-4621
Out of State 462-4071
TRAILS
25% beginners, 50% intermediate, 25% advanced
TRAVEL
Big Bear Lake, 1 mile, Los Angeles, 100 miles.
I-10 to San Bernardino, then Rt. 330 to Rt. 18
to Big Bear Lake.
VERTICAL DROP
1,200 feet

FOR LODGINGS, RESTAURANTS, SERVICES, STORES & SKI SHOPS, SEE BIG BEAR

CRESTLINE/LAKE ARROWHEAD

AREA CODE - 714

EMERGENCY

CALIFORNIA HIGHWAY PATROL
Ask Operator for . . . . Zenith 1-2000
Road Condition Information 887-7977
FIRE-RESCUE-PARAMEDICS
Blue Jay, Crestline, Twin Peaks 338-3310
Crest Forest Fire District. 337-1414
Lake Arrowhead Fire District 337-2525
U.S. Forest Service Fire Emergency 383-5651
MOUNTAINS COMMUNITY HOSPITAL 337-2495
SAN BERNARDINO COUNTY SHERIFF
Call 337-6131
Otherwise ask Operator for . . . . Zenith 7-1234

CAMPGROUNDS

BAYLIS PARK PICNIC AREA (open all year)
1 mi. E. of Arrowhead Highlands on Hwy. 18
BIG PINE FLATS (19 campsites)
½ mi. S.W. from Green Valley Lake on 2N13,
3½ mi. N. on 3N16 866-3437
CAMP SWITZERLAND
P.O. Box 967, Crestline, 92325 338-2731
CRAB FLATS (open May 15th to Oct. 15th)
1½ mi. S.W. from Green Valley Lake on 2N13,
then 3½ mi. N. on 3N16 337-2444
CREST PARK PICNIC AREA (open all year, no water)
2 mi. S. of Lake Arrowhead on Hwy. 18
CRESTLINE MOUNTAIN PARK RESORT
Hwy. 138 to V.O.E., then left fork on Waters Dr. ½ mi.
P.O. Box 663, Crestline, 92325 338-2388
DOGWOOD (open May 15th to Oct. 15th)
½ mi. N.E. of Rim Forest on Hwy. 18 337-2444
FISHERMAN'S (open May 1st to Oct. 15th)
1½ mi. E. of Lake Arrowhead on Hwy. 173,
then 4 mi. E. on 2N18 337-2444
GREEN VALLEY (open all year)
1 mi. N.E. of Green Valley Lake on 2N13. . . 337-2444
HORSE SPRINGS (open June 15th to Sept. 15th)
5 mi. N.W. of Big Pine Flats campground on 3N14,
then ½ mi. N.E. on 3N17 866-3437
IRONWOOD GROUP CAMP
½ mi. S.W. on 2N13 from Green Valley Lake, then
9 mi. N.E. on 3N16, then ½ mi. E. on 3N97. . 866-3437
NORTH SHORE (open all year)
3 mi. N. of Lake Arrowhead via
North Shore Hwy. 173. 337-2444
SIBERIA CREEK GROUP CAMP
Hwy. 18, 7 miles east of Running Springs,
then 2½ mi. by trail. 866-3437
TOLL ROAD
6½ mi. N.W. of Lake Arrowhead via
North Shore Rd., Hwy. 173 337-2444

LODGING

ANTLER'S INN & LODGE
P.O. Box B, Twin Peaks, 92391 337-3374
ARROWHEAD INN & COTTAGES
P.O. Box 280, Lake Arrowhead, 92352 337-2411
ARROWHEAD ROAD RESORT
P.O. Box 31, Twin Peaks, 92391 337-2341
CREST LODGE
23508 Lake Drive
P.O. Box 2269, Crestline, 92325 338-2418
CUSTER'S LODGE
Lake Dr. & Friendly Lane
P.O. Box 785, Crestline, 92325 338-3313
LAKESIDE REALTY (Twin Peaks & Lake Arrowhead)
Hwy. 189, Twin Peaks, P.O. Box 268,
Lake Arrowhead, 92352 . . . . . . .337-6105, 337-2403

CRESTLINE/LAKE ARROWHEAD CONT.

MILE HIGH RESORT
Hwy. 18 to Twin Peaks, then 2 mi. on Hwy. 189
to Twin Peaks 337-3115

SLEEPY HOLLOW
24033 Lake Dr.
P.O. Box 632, Crestline, 92325 338-2718

TANGLED PINES
23998 Straight Way Rd.
P.O. Box 37, Crestline, 92325 338-2339

WHITELY MOTEL
580 Forest Shade Rd.
P.O. Box 152, Crestline, 92325 338-2755

WOODY'S MOTEL & ANTIQUES
23854 Lake Dr.
P.O. Box 1667, Crestline, 92325 338-3439

RECREATION

DEEP CREEK LAKE
Hwy. 18, E. on Deep Creek Dr., N. Badger . . 867-7127

LAKE ARROWHEAD EQUESTRIAN CENTER
Grand View Rd., turn @ County Bldg. 337-6616

THE QUEEN ARROWHEAD (boat excursion)
Lake Arrowhead Village 337-1555

SANTA'S VILLAGE (Skyforest)
Hwy. 18, 2 mi. E. of Lake Arrowhead turn-off 337-2481

VILLAGE ARCADE & MINIATURE GOLF
Crestline Village 338-4592

RESTAURANTS

ANTLERS INN (family dining, entertainment, dancing)
Twin Peaks 337-3374

CLIFFHANGER RESTAURANT (Continental)
Arrowhead Highlands, Hwy. 18 between Crestline
& Lake Arrowhead 338-3806

COUNTRY STORE (American, Italian, beer & wine)
Hwy. 18 & Kuffel Cyn. Rd. 337-7100

DAS SCHNITZELHAUS (German, beer & wine)
Crestline 338-9016

ELKS RESTAURANT
(steaks, cocktails, entertainment Sat. night)
26584 Hwy. 18, Rim Forest. 337-4111

ENCHANTED LODGE
(steaks, seafood, Italian, piano bar Fri. & Sat.)
22730 Waters Dr., Valley of Enchantment. . . 338-1214

GOLDEN ELK RESTAURANT & COCKTAILS
(live entertainment Fri. & Sat., dancing)
Hwy. 18 in the middle of Arrowbear 867-3130

GREGORY INN (seafood, cocktails, music & dancing)
End of Lake Gregory
Lake Dr. & Dart Canyon Rd. 338-4401

THE LAKE INN
(home cooked meals, cocktails, entertainment Fri., Sat.)
Green Valley Lake, south side of lake 867-3832

THE LAKESIDE RESTAURANT (beer & wine)
23941 Lake Dr., Crestline 338-2112

MOUNTAIN MUNCH & CRAFT CO.
(deck dining, picnic packaging, beer &wine to go)
24048 Lake Dr., Crestline 338-5352

RICARDO'S (Mexican & American)
Agua Fria, 26824 Hwy. 189,
½ mi. S. of Blue Jay 337-1817

ROYAL OAK (European, cocktails, entertainment)
Next to the Ice Rink, Blue Jay 337-6018

SALA'S ITALIAN RESTAURANT
(gourmet dining, beer & wine)
Agua Fria Mall, Blue Jay 337-5054
23775 Lake Dr. 338-2035

THE SPORTMAN (steak, seafood, entertainment, cocktails)
28949 Hook Creek Rd., Cedar Glen 337-9036

SUZIE'S SWEET SHOP (ice cream)
23822 Lake Dr., Crestline 338-4518

TONY'S (Mexican, margaritas, disco)
29090 Hook Creek Rd., Cedar Glen 337-9037

SERVICES

AUTO REPAIR & SERVICE

ARROWBEAR GARAGE
33211 Hilltop Bl., Arrowbear 867-2361

ARROWHEAD AUTOMOTIVE
Hook Creek Rd. & Arrowhead Dr., Cedar Glen 337-8002

ART'S CORNER CHEVRON SERVICE
26816 Hwy. 189, Blue Jay. 337-3505, 337-5793

BEN'S AUTO REPAIR
27445 Hwy. 189, Lake Arrowhead 337-2633

SUBARU MOUNTAIN SERVICE CENTER
24051 Lake Dr., Crestline 338-4949

BANKS

BANK OF AMERICA
62 Lake Arrowhead Village 337-2465

SECURITY PACIFIC NATIONAL BANK
27235 Hwy. 189, Blue Jay. 337-2546

WELLS FARGO BANK
23860 Lake Dr., Crestline 338-1718

BOOKS

THE BOOK EXCHANGE
23875 Lake Dr., Lake Gregory Village 338-5550

MC CABE & COMPANY BOOKSEELERS
23898 Lake Dr., Lake Gregory Village 338-1088

CLOTHING

BABIANA
At Shanty Towne, Hwy. 18, Sky Forest 337-7741

CLIFF'S TRADING POST
23459 Crest Forest Dr., Crestline 338-2521

MARGUERITE'S
27244 Hwy. 189, Blue Jay. 337-1111

MAXINE'S
26139 Hwy. 189, Twin Peaks 337-2777

MILES FROM NOWHERE
Blue Jay Mall 337-4914

MOUNTAIN JEANERY
27211 Hwy. 189, Blue Jay. 337-9223

MOUNTAINEER SPORTSWEAR
23815 Lake Drive, Crestline. 338-2611

REDHEAD'S CLOTHESLINE
23758 Manzanita, Crestline 338-2324
SPORTS MODEN
Lake Dr. & Thousand Pines, Crestline 338-3215

DENTISTS

ANDERSON, RICHARD
251 N. Hwy. 173, Cedar Glen 337-6227, 337-2495
COX, VANCE J.
Crestline Dental Bldg.
23571 Lake Dr. at Fern, Crestline 338-1782
HAGGARD, FRANK R.
Hook Creek Rd., Cedar Glen 337-4222
MARKHAM FAMILY DENTAL
26108 Hwy. 189, Twin Peaks 337-2013
SALSBURY, RICHARD S. (Orthodontics)
Hook Creek Rd., Cedar Glen 337-1931
SMITH, GREGORY J.
Lake Arrowhead 337-6227, 337-7764
VAN, FAY C. (Orthodontist)
Lake Arrowhead Professional Ctr., Cedar Glen 337-3613

DRY CLEANING

MOUNTAIN WASH
29003 Oak Terrace, Cedar Glen. 337-4811
WASH HAUS
Blue Jay 337-3113

FLORIST

FLORIST IN THE FOREST
850 S. Hwy. 138, Crestline 338-1311
HILTON'S FLOWERS & GIFTS
Hwy. 18 at Kuffel Cyn., Sky Forest 337-5718

GIFTS

ARROW WAY INTERIORS
28966 Hook Creek Rd., Cedar Glen Village . . 337-2112
DEB'S PLACE
31960 Hilltop Bl., No. C, Running Springs . . 867-7800
MOUNTAIN GIFT SHOP
Hwy. 189, Blue Jay Mall. 337-4112
MOUNTAIN MUNCH & CRAFT CO.
24048 Lake Dr., Crestline 338-5352
PINE CONE BOUTIQUE
Alpine Mall, 23930 Lake Dr., Crestline. 338-2994
THE PLANT TREE
Blue Jay Mall 337-4208
THE RAINBOW TREE
Shanty Towne, Sky Forest. 337-4519
YANKEE PEDDLER
556 Springy Path, Crestline 338-4818

GROCERY STORES

ALPINE STORE
Twin Peaks. 337-1912
BURDEN'S MARKET
23484 Crest Forest Dr., Crestline 338-4647
CEDAR GLEN MARKET
Cedar Glen Village 337-1514
GOODWIN & SONS MARKET
23919 Lake Dr., Crestline 338-1757
JENSEN'S COMPLETE SHOPPING
Blue Jay 337-8484
JOHNNIE'S MARKET
23019 Waters Dr., V.O.E. 338-2817
RIM FOREST MARKET
Hwy. 18 337-1913

ICE RINK

BLUE JAY ICE CHALET
Blue Jay 337-1511

LOCKSMITHS

AAA "MOUNTAIN" LOCKSMITH
P.O. Box 1255, Blue Jay. 337-6479
ARROWBEAR LOCK & KEY
32875 Hilltop Bl., Arrowbear 867-7994

PHARMACIES

CEDAR GLEN PHARMACY
Hook Creek Rd., Cedar Glen 337-2611
CRESTLINE PHARMACY
854 S. Hwy. 138, Crestline 338-3516

SPORTING GOODS

HILLTOP SPORTING GOODS
Blue Jay Mall 337-1832
LAKE ARROWHEAD MARINAS' SPORTING GOODS
North Shore at the dam 337-2501
South Shore, Lake Arrowhead Village 337-1555

HOLIDAY HILL

DRAWER C, WRIGHTWOOD, CA 92397 (714) 249-3256

AREA INFORMATION

BASE ELEVATION
6,600 feet
HOURS
7:30 a.m. - 4:30 p.m.
4:30 - 10:00 p.m., Weds. thru Sat., night skiing
LIFTS
4 chairlifts, 3 T-bars, 3,000 capacity per hour
LONGEST RUN
1½ miles
SEASON
Mid-November to Mid-April, snowmaking
SNOW PHONE
Call Ski Area
TRAILS
25% beginner, 50% intermediate, 25% advanced
TRAVEL
I-15 to Wrightwood exit; Ski Area is 2
miles west of Wrightwood on Rt. 2.

HOLIDAY HILL CONT.

VERTICAL DROP
1,600 feet

FOR LODGING & RESTAURANTS, SEE MOUNTAIN HIGH

MOUNTAIN HIGH

P.O. BOX 993, WRIGHTWOOD, CA 92397 (714) 249-3226

AREA INFORMATION

BASE ELEVATION
6,900 feet
HOURS
8:00 a.m. - 4:30 p.m.
3:30 - 11:00 p.m., night skiing
LIFTS
5 chairs, 7,000 capacity per hour
SEASON
Thanksgiving to April, snowmaking
SNOW PHONE 249-6169
TRAILS
40% beginner, 30% intermediate, 30% advanced
TRAVEL
I-15 to Wrightwood exit, 3 miles west of Wrightwood.
VERTICAL DROP
1,200 feet

LODGING

BIG PINES LODGE - CABINS
Base of slopes, call Ski Area
EVERGREEN MOTEL
Box 97 249-3503
MOUNTAIN VIEW MOTEL
Box 458 249-3553
PINES MOTEL
6045 Pine 249-3931
SKYLODGE MOTEL
Box 516 249-3953

RESTAURANTS

BLUE RIDGE INN (cocktails)
6060 Park Drive. 249-3440
BULL WHEEL SALOON (Country-Western music)
Big Pines Lodge, call Ski Area
LYLES PINE MANOR
Park Drive 249-6393
MOUNTAIN HIGH BASE LODGE (soups/sandwiches)
At the slopes, 9 a.m. to 4:30 p.m.
MOUNTAIN INN RESTAURANT
Park Drive,. 249-6954
MOUNTAIN TOP CAFE (Italian sandwiches, beer, wine)
Wrightwood 249-3920
THE YODELER (steaks, sandwiches, dancing)
Park Dr. & Evergreen 249-6482

STORES & SKI SHOPS

RENTAL SHOP
At the slopes, call Ski Area
SKI SHOP (complete line of ski wear)
At the slopes. 249-6671

MT. BALDY

P.O. BOX 567, MT. BALDY, CA 91759 (714) 982-4208

AREA INFORMATION

BASE ELEVATION
6,500 feet
HOURS
8:00 a.m. - 4:30 p.m.
7:30 a.m. - 4:30 p.m., weekends
LIFTS
4 chairlifts, 3,500 capacity per hour
SEASON
Late November to late April, snowmaking
SNOW PHONE
Call Ski Area
TRAILS
15% beginner, 50% intermediate, 35% advanced
TRAVEL
I-10 to Upland, then 11 miles north on Mountain Ave. to Ski Area; from Los Angeles, 49 miles.
VERTICAL DROP
2,100 feet

LODGING, RESTAURANTS & LOUNGES AT SKI AREA

RUNNING SPRINGS

CAMPGROUNDS

CANYON PARK
1 mile east on Hwy. 18
P.O. Box 356, 92382. 867-2090
SHADY COVE GROUP CAMP
Hwy. 18, 7 mi. E. of Running Springs, then 2½ mi. by trail - no road - closed winters 337-2444

LODGING

CLOUD 9 LODGE
P.O. Box 54, 92382. 867-2400
GIANT OAKS MOTEL
Hwy. 18, 1 block from Union 76
P.O. Box 1145, 92382 867-2231

EMERGENCY

CALIFORNIA HIGHWAY PATROL
Ask Operator for . . . . Zenith 1-2000
FIRE/RESCUE/PARAMEDICS. 867-2626
MOUNTAINS COMMUNITY HOSPITAL 337-2495
U.S. FOREST SERVICE EMERGENCY. 383-5651
SAN BERNARDINO COUNTY SHERIFF
Ask Operator for . . . . Zenith 1-1234
OTHER IMPORTANT NUMBERS
Animal Control . . . . (800) 472-5609

Contact - The Help Line 867-3500
Humane Society. 867-7616
County Library, 31896 Hilltop Bl. 867-2554
Time 867-8111

RESTAURANTS

ALT HEIDELBERG
(German, American, German entertainment)
At the crossroads of Hwy. 330 & Hwy. 18. . . 867-4245
DON PEPE (Mexican, American, wine & beer)
31956 Hilltop Bl. 867-3050
CHATEAU PINES
(home cooking country style, full bar, entertainment Fri. & Sat., dancing)
1 mile west of Running Springs 867-7355
LLOYD'S OF RUNNING SPRINGS
(entertainment weekends, cocktails) 867-2731

SERVICES

BANK

BANK OF AMERICA
2625 Whispering Pines Dr. 867-2761

CLOTHING

GILBERT & STEWARD
31900 Hilltop Bl. 867-3585
SLEIGH BELLES
31945 Hilltop Bl. 867-2991

DENTISTS

CHRISTENSON, DONALD M., DDS
32194 Hilltop Bl. 867-2771

GROCERY STORES

ARROWBEAR LIQUOR & DELI
32861 Hilltop Bl., Arrowbear 867-2410
DUTCH'S MARKET & LIQUOR STORE
31941 Hilltop Bl. 867-2212
GREGORY'S MARKET
31987 Hilltop Bl. 867-2228

LAUNDROMATS

ANDY'S WASH & DRY
Post Office Bldg. 867-7610
SUDSY BELLE
31951 Hilltop Bl. 867-7610

SERVICE STATIONS

ARROWBEAR GARAGE
33211 Hilltop Bl., Arrowbear 867-2361
MAYO'S UNION 76
Hwy. 18 & Hunsaker 867-2324

SKI SHOPS

BLAUER SKI RENTALS & CLOTHING
32170 Hilltop Bl. 867-7201
LEROY'S
32759 Hwy. 18, Arrowbear 867-3110
SNOW VALLEY SKI AREA 867-2434

SKI SUNRISE

P.O. BOX 645, WRIGHTWOOD, CA 92397 (714) 249-6150

AREA INFORMATION

BASE ELEVATION
6,800 feet
HOURS
8:30 a.m. - 4:30 p.m.
8:00 a.m. - 4:30 p.m., weekends
LIFTS
1 quad chair, 3 tows, 2 bars, 8,000 capacity per hour
LONGEST RUN
1 mile
SEASON
December 1st to March 31st, no snowmaking
SNOW PHONE
Call Ski Area
TRAILS
35% beginner, 45% intermediate, 20% advanced
TRAVEL
I-15 to Wrightwood exit, 5 miles west of Wrightwood.
VERTICAL DROP
800 feet

FOR LODGING & RESTAURANTS
SEE MOUNTAIN HIGH

SNOW VALLEY

P.O. BOX 8 RUNNING SPRINGS, CA 92382
TELEPHONE: (714) 867-7182, 867-3677

AREA INFORMATION

BASE ELEVATION
6,800 feet
HOURS
7:00 a.m. - 4:30 p.m., 3:00 - 11:00 p.m., 7 nights
LIFTS
12 chairs, 3 tows
LONGEST RUN
1¼ miles
SEASON
Thanksgiving to mid-April, snowmaking
SNOW PHONE . . . . (714) 867-2434
Out of State . . . . (800) 462-4930
TRAILS
45% beginner, 30% intermediate, 25% advanced
TRAVEL
I-10 to San Bernardino, then Hwy. 330 to Rt. 18 to Ski Area. San Bernardino, 30 minutes, Los Angeles, 85 miles. Running Springs, 5 miles.
VERTICAL DROP
1,000 feet

FOR LODGING, RESTAURANTS & SERVICES
SEE RUNNING SPRINGS

COLORADO

ASPEN HIGHLANDS

ASPEN, COLORADO 81611 (303) 925-5300

AREA INFORMATION

BASE ELEVATION
8,000 feet
HOURS
9:00 a.m. to 4:00 p.m.
LIFTS
8 chairs, 4 bars, 10,000 capacity per hour
LONGEST RUN
2 miles
SEASON
Late November to early April
SNOW PHONE
Call ski area
TRAILS
56 miles
25% Beginner, 50% Intermediate, 25% Difficult
TRAVEL
1 mile from Aspen City, 5 hours from Denver via I-70 to Glenwood Springs, to Hwy. 82, Airport in Denver
VERTICAL DROP
3,800 feet

ASPEN MTN.

BOX 1248, ASPEN, CO 81611 (303) 925-1220

AREA INFORMATION

BASE ELEVATION
7,930 feet
HOURS
9 a.m. to 4 p.m.
LIFTS
7 chairs, 6,757 capacity per hr.
LONGEST RUN
3 miles
LOST & FOUND
Ski Patrol Headquarters near the Sundeck Restaurant or the Ski Area Headquarters at the bottom of Little Nell.
PARKING
Below the Bottom Terminal of Lift A
SEASON
Late Nov. to early April
SKI SCHOOL
Intermediate & advanced only, Gretl's Restaurant on upper slopes . . . . 925-1220 X 271
SNOW CONDITION PHONE . . . . 925-1220 X 290
TRAILS
620 acres, 75% advanced, 25% intermediate
TRAVEL
4½ hours from Denver, I-70 W. to Glenwood Springs, Hwy. 82 to Aspen. By plane: Aspen Airways & Rocky Mountain Airways.
VERTICAL DROP
3,300 feet

ASPEN RUNS

1 1 & 2 LEAF
2 SNOW BOW
3 BUCKHORN CUTOFF
4 BUCKHORN TRAIL
5 NORTH STAR
6 SILVER BELL
7 PUSSY FOOT
8 DIPSEY DOODLE
9 SUMMIT
10 MIDWAY ROAD
12 COPPER CUT-OFF
13 SILVER DIP
14 BLONDIES
15 SILVER BELL
16 SHOW-OFF ALLEY
17 MIDNIGHT CUT-OFF
18 GENTLEMAN'S RIDGE
19 COPPER CUTOFF
20 COPPER TRAIL
21 NO. 2 LEAF
22 PUMP HOUSE HILL
23 NORTH AMERICAN
24 MIDWAY ROAD
25 TOURTELOTTE PARK
26 GENTLEMAN'S RIDGE
27 SEIBERTS
28 CHRISTMAS TREE
29 SUNSET
30 DEER PARK
31 TOURTELOTTE PARK
32 LITTLE PERCY
33 CATWALK TO GRETL'S
34 MIDWAY
35 TO GENTS
36 BACK OF BELL NO. 1
37 RED'S RUN
38 LITTLE CORK SCREW
39 COPPER CONNECTOR
40 BACK NO. 2
41 BELL MOUNTAIN RIDGE
42 FACE OF BELL
43 FIS TRAIL
44 INTERNATIONAL
45 GLADE 1
46 GLADE 2
47 BACK 3
48 BELL MOUNTAIN RIDGE
50 BEAR PAW
51 ZIG-ZAUGG
52 GLADE 3
53 SHORT SNORT
54 ZAUGG DUMP
55 PERRY'S PROWL
56 LAST DOLLAR
57 SILVER QUEEN
58 KREUZECK
59 ROCH RUN
60 RUTHIE'S RUN
61 AZTEC
62 ZAUGG PARK
63 SNOW BOWL
64 ELEVATOR SHAFT
65 GRAND JUNCTION
66 JACKPOT
67 KLEENEX CORNER
68 BINGO SLOT
69 NIAGARA
70 UPPER MAG.
71 MAGNIFICO CUT-OFF
72 POINT OF NO RETURN
73 SPRING PITCH
74 DAGO CUT ROAD
75 SCHUSS GULLEY
76 FRANKLIN DUMP ROAD
77 F/S SLALOM SLOPE
78 LOWER MAGNIFICO
79 TOWER TEN ROADS
80 CORKSCREW
81 CORKSCREW GULLEY
82 STRAW PILE
83 THE ISLAND
84 CATWALK
85 WILLOUGHBY JUMPS
86 LITTLE NELL
87 NORWAY SLOPE

ASPEN LIFTS

A 1A
B 2
C 3
D LITTLE NELL
E BELL MTN.
F 6
G RUTHIE'S RUN

BUTTERMILK RUNS

1 TOM'S THUMB
2 WESTWARD HO
3 FRIEDL'S
4 UPPER SAVIO
5 TIEHACK PARKWAY
6 TIMBER DOODLE GLADE
7 STERNER
8 PTARMIGAN
9 CLINIC HILL
10 BUCKSKIN
11 NO PROBLEM
12 OVERPASS
13 RIDGE TRAIL
14 HOMESTEAD ROAD
15 BUCKSKIN
16 STERNER GULCH
17 TIEHACK TRAIL
18 JAVELIN
19 RACER'S EDGE
20 EGO HILL
21 SLALOM PRACTICE HILL
22 RABBIT RUN
23 MAGIC CARPET
24 TO EGO HILL
25 STERNER'S CATWALK
26 LOVER'S LANE
27 HOMESTEAD RD.
28 LOWER SAVIO
29 UPPER BYPASS
30 LOWER BYPASS
31 BEAR MIDWAY
32 COLUMBINE
33 BABY DOE
34 SPRUCE
35 JACOB'S LADDER
36 SPRUCE
37 GOVERNMENT (Nastar)
38 EASY WAY
40 WEST BUTTERMILK RD.
41 RED'S ROVER
42 LARKSPUR
43 HOMESTEAD RD.
44 HOMESTEAD TRAIL
45 BLUE GROUSE
46 CAMPBIRD
47 TEASER
48 CATWALK
49 LOWER LARKSPUR
50 LOWER HOMESTEAD TRAIL

BUTTERMILK LIFTS

A MAIN BUTTERMILK
B SAVIO
C BUTTERMILK WEST
D LOWER TIEHACK
E UPPER TIEHACK
F BABY T-BAR
G PONY

BUTTERMILK MTN.

P.O. BOX 1248, ASPEN, CO 81611 (303) 925-1220

AREA INFORMATION

BASE ELEVATION
7,860 feet

HOURS
9:00 a.m. - 4:00 p.m.

LIFTS
5 chairlifts, 1 T-bar, 1 pony lift, 6,600 capacity per hour

LONGEST RUN
2 miles

SEASON
Late November to Late March, snowmaking

SNOW PHONE
Call Ski Area

TRAILS
50% easier, 30% more difficult, 20% most difficult

TRAVEL
From Denver, 205 miles, Grand Junction, 140 miles, via I-70 and Rt. 82; Colorado Springs, 260 miles via I-25, I-70 and Rt. 82. By air: Aspen & Rocky Mtn. Airways.

VERTICAL DROP
2,000 feet

FOR LODGINGS, RESTAURANTS, SERVICES, STORES & SKI SHOPS, SEE ASPEN

ASPEN CITY

EMERGENCY

AMBULANCE. 925-1911
FIRE DEPT.. 925-1911
POLICE 925-1911
SHERIFF 925-1911
STATE PATROL .945-6198

LODGING

CENTRAL RESERVATIONS. 925-9000

ASPEN SKI LODGE
101 W. Main St. 925-3434
ALPENBLICK
747 S. Galena St., Box 1750
between the 2 Aspen Mtn. chairlifts 925-2260
APPLEJACK INN
311 W. Main St., 2nd & Main 925-7650
THE ASPEN ALPS (restaurant, health spa, tennis courts, pool and beauty shop)
700 Ute Ave., P.O. Box 1228 925-7820
ASPEN CHATEAUX / REID RENTALS (views of the Roaring Fork River and Independence Pass)
720 E. Hyman, Box 4949 925-1400
ASPEN INN (Gourmet Restaurant)
Box 680, downtown 925-6300
ASPEN MANAGEMENT COMPANY
606 E. Hyman, P.O. Box 9649,
Aspen, CO 81611 . . . . .925-2811, 925-5513
ASPEN MEADOWS (mountain views)
845 Meadows Rd., P.O. Box 220 925-3426
BAVARIAN INN (near the Institute and golf course)
801 W. Bleeker St. 925-7391
BEST WESTERN ASPENALT LODGE
Roaring Fork Valley, 16 miles from Aspen
Box 428, Basalt, CO . . . . (800) 528-1234
THE BRASS BED
926 E. Durant 925-3622
BLUE SPRUCE LODGE
Across from Wagner Park, Box 596 925-3991
BOOMERANG LODGE
500 W. Hopkins Ave 925-3416
CHALET KISL
100 E. Hyman Ave., Box 152 925-3520
CHRISTIANIA LODGE AND CHALETS
Walking distance to Music Festival and mall
501 W. Main St. 925-3014
CHRISTMAS INN
232 W. Main St. 925-3822
COACHLIGHT CHALET
3 blocks from center of town - faces Aspen Mtn.
232 W. Hyman 925-3809
CONTINENTAL INN (full-service hotel)
Box 388 925-1150
THE COPPER HORSE (shared bath)
328 W. Main, Box 4948 925-7525
CRESTAHAUS LODGE (eastern part of Aspen)
1301 E. Hwy. 82 925-7081
DEEP POWDER SKI LODGE APARTMENTS
Family-oriented, 2 blocks from the center of Aspen
410 S. Aspen 925-2290
DOLOMITE VILLAS OF ASPEN (foot of Aspen Mtn.)
650 S. Monarch 925-7624
EDELWEISS CHALET (central location)
201 E. Hopkins Ave. 925-3974
ENDEAVOR LODGE (4 blocks from center of town & lifts)
905 E. Hopkins Ave. 925-2847
FASCHING HAUS ((base of Aspen Mtn.)
747 S. Galena St. 925-2260
FIRESIDE LODGE (4 blocks from center of Aspen)
130 W. Cooper 925-6000
THE GANT (base of Aspen Mtn.)
610 West End, Box K-3 925-5000

HEARTHSTONE HOUSE (2 blocks from center of Aspen)
134 E. Hyman. 925-7632
HEATHERBED LODGE & GUEST RANCH
Box 530, base of Aspen Highlands 925-7077
HIGHLANDS INN
(Maroon Creek Valley, Aspen Tennis Ranch)
1650 Maroon Creek Rd., Box 4708. 925-5050
THE HISTORIC REDSTONE INN (45 miles from Aspen)
Located on Colorado Hwy. 133
0082 Redstone Bl., Redstone, CO 81623 . . .963-2526
HOLIDAY INN OF ASPEN
Foot of Buttermilk Mtn., Hwy. 82 925-1500
HOTEL JEROME (corner of Mill & Main)
330 E. Main St. 925-1040
INNSBRUCK INN
233 W. Main St. 925-2980
INVERNESS LODGE
122 E. Durant 925-8500
LIFT ONE (base of the mountain)
131 E. Durant 925-1670
LIMELITE LODGE (center of town)
228 E. Cooper Ave.. 925-3025
LITTLE RED SKI HAUS
118 E. Cooper Ave.. 925-3333
MAROON CREEK LODGE (Aspen Highlands)
1498 Maroon Creek Rd., Box 236 925-3491
THE MOLLY GIBSON LODGE
120 W. Hopkins. 925-2580
MOUNTAIN CHALET (1 block from Hyman St. Mall)
333 E. Durant St.. 925-7797
NORTH STAR LODGE (2 blocks from Aspen Mtn.)
914 Waters Ave.. 925-2946
NUGGET LODGE
110 W. Main, Box N 925-6760
PLUM TREE INN
22475 Hwy. 82, west of Aspen 925-2700
ST. MORITZ LODGE
334 W. Hyman 925-3220
SHADOW MOUNTAIN VILLAGE (on Aspen Mtn.)
809 S. Aspen St., P.O. Box DD 925-7055
SNOWFLAKE LODGE (1 block from center of town)
221 E. Hyman. 925-3221
SNOWMASS COTTAGES (on Roaring Fork River)
9461 Hwy. 82, 14 miles from Aspen,
Box 246, Snowmass, CO 81654. . .927-3273, 923-3146
SNOW QUEEN LODGE & CONDOMINIUMS
124 E. Cooper Ave., center of town
P.O. Box 4901. . . . . .925-2815, 925-9973
STIRLING HOMES (rentals throughout Aspen town)
600 E. Main St. 925-5757
T-LAZY-7 GUEST RANCH (Maroon Creek)
Maroon Creek Rd., Box 240. 925-7254
TIPPLE INN (next to Little Nell chairlift)
505 E. Dean St., P.O. Box 147 925-6580
TIPPLE LODGE (base of Little Nell, Aspen Mtn.)
620 S. Galena, P.O. Box 147 925-1116
ULLR LODGE
520 W. Main. 925-7696
VILCOR (condos - various locations)
555 N. Mill St.. . . . . (800) 525-4200, 925-1900
THE WOODSTONE (base of Little Nell near bus stop)
Durant at Sprint St., Box 617 925-6760

RECREATION

CHAIRLIFT RIDE

MID-JUNE THRU LABOR DAY 925-5300

CLIMBING

INSTRUCTION & GUIDES FOR ASCENTS ON SOPRIS, CAPITOL, GRIZZLY, & OTHER PEAKS IN THE 13,000 TO 14,000 FOOT RANGE
U.S. Forest Service 925-3445

FISHING

ROARING FORK AND FRYING PAN, LINCOLN RESERVOIR, HUNTER, CASTLE, MAROON & SNOWMASS CREEKS
Equipment & licenses at Chuck Fothergill's Outdoor Sportsman, corner of Copper & Hunter Streets & at the Miner's Bldg. on Main St.

GOLF

ASPEN CHAMPIONSHIP GOLF COURSE
Hwy. 82, west of town near Plum Tree Inn . . 925-2145
SNOWMASS COUNTRY CLUB
Just Below Snowmass 923-4012

HEALTH CLUBS

ASPEN ATHLETIC CLUB
720 E. Hyman. 925-2531
THE ASPEN CLUB
1450 Crystal Lake Rd. 925-8900
ASPEN HEALTH CENTER
The Meadows, 25 Meadows Rd.. 925-3586

HORSEBACK RIDING

T-LAZY-7 RANCH
Maroon Creek Rd. 925-7040
SNOWMASS STABLES
Snowmass Resort 923-3075
POMEGRANATE STABLES
West of Aspen, Hwy. 82 925-2700
ERICKSON RANCH
Red Mtn., a mile from town. 925-9861, 925-1659
HEATHERBED STABLES
Maroon Creek Rd. 925-6987

JEEPING

CHAMBER OF COMMERCE 925-1940

SWIMMING

THE JAMES E. MOORE POOL
Across from Aspen High School
Maroon Creek Rd. . . . . .925-2020 X 72
THE JEROME POOL
Hotel Jerome on Main St. 925-1040

TENNIS

ASPEN CITY COURTS
Plum Tree Inn, Hwy. 82 925-6984
Iselin Park, Maroon Creek Rd.. 925-2020
ASPEN MEADOWS
Meadows Rd., Aspen Institute. 925-7208
SNOWMASS COUNTRY CLUB
Below Snowmass 923-4011
ASPEN RACQUET CLUB (all-weather bubble)
Across from the Holiday Inn, Hwy. 82. 925-7794
ASPEN CLUB
1450 Crystal Lake Rd. 925-8900
HIGHLANDS INN TENNIS COURTS & RANCH
Base of Aspen Highlands Ski Area
Maroon Creek Rd. 925-5050

WATER SPORTS

KAYAKING & RAFTING TRIPS
Chamber of Commerce. 925-1940

RESTAURANTS

ABETONE RISTORANTE & BAR
(seafood, vegetarian, pasta)
620 E. Hyman. 925-9022
ANDRE'S (American, disco)
310 S. Galena 925-6200
ARTHUR'S CHINESE RESTAURANT
(Mandarin, Szechwan)
1st & Main Streets 925-7931
ARYA (Continental)
In the Aspen Inn 925-6266
ASPEN MINE COMPANY (American)
Hyman St. Mall 925-7766
ASPEN STEAK CO. (Cocktails)
420 E. Hyman. 925-1387
BAGEL NOSH (deli, catering, take-out)
7 a.m. till 3 a.m., except Sundays
533 E. Hopkins at Hunter St. 925-2121
THE CAPTAIN'S ANCHORAGE (American, seafood)
Spring St. 925-2485
COOPER STREET PIER (bar)
500 E. Cooper. 925-7758
COPPER KETTLE (international)
Between Little Nell & the Continental Inn. . . 925-3151
COUNTRY ROAD (seafood & cocktails, midnight menu)
Downstairs in the Mill & Main Bldg. 925-6556
CRYSTAL PALACE (cabaret, dinner)
300 E. Hyman. 925-1455
CRYSTAL VALLEY STEAK HOUSE (steaks, seafood)
Main St. in downtown Carbondale 963-1850
DUNNAVANT'S (American)
in the Highlands Inn 925-8886
EPICURE (breakfasts)
Corner of Mill & Main Streets 925-3202

GALENA ST. EAST (American, seafood)
Castle Creek Bridge 925-2333
GOLDEN HORN (Continental & Swiss, wine)
Downstairs at Cooper & Mill Streets 925-3373
HOMEPLATE (homecooked dinners)
Mountain Chalet 925-1986
HOTEL JEROME BAR
Hotel Jerome, Mill & Main. 925-1040
JOLLY JESTER (magic bar, theatre dinner magic show, Continental & vegetarian)
520 E. Cooper. 925-5335
LITTLE ANNIE'S (American)
517 E. Hyman Ave.. 925-1098
THE LITTLE KITCHEN (vegetarian)
Garden level, Mason & Morse Bldg. 925-1966
LITTLE NELL'S (bar, disco)
611 E. Durant 925-3636
MOTHER LODE (Italian)
314 E. Hyman Ave.. 925-7700
PABLO'S MEXICAN RESTAURANT
Downstairs in the Mountain Plaza Bldg. 925-6213
PADDY BUGATTI'S (Irish-Italian, live music)
Continental Inn 925-2717
PARLOUR CAR (French)
615 W. Hopkins 925-3810
POPPYCOCK'S (Creperie)
Brand Bldg. 925-1245
PRIMAVERA (Italian)
Brand Bldg. 925-6120
RED ONION (apres ski bar)
420 E. Cooper. 925-6853
ROCK 'N HORSE (rock 'n roll disco)
Below the Hotel Jerome 925-4230
SALLY'S SKI VIEW (steaks, view)
Snowmass Shopping Center 923-5885
SARDY FIELD RESTAURANT (made-to-order
Aspen Airport 925-6563
THE SHAFT (American)
Cooper Ave. at Hunter St 925-1483
SKIER'S CHALET & STEAKHOUSE
710 S. Aspen St. 925-3381
SOUPER PLACE TO EAT (homemade meals)
415 E. Hyman Mall 925-8266
THE FIREHOUSE TAVERN (lunch & dinner)
415 E. Hopkins 925-4670
TORO'S (Mexican, margaritas)
Downstairs on Hyman Ave. Mall 925-2134
UTE CITY BANQUE (Continental)
Hyman at Galena 925-4373

SERVICES

AUTOMOTIVE

CONNER CHEVRON
232 E. Main 925-7370
EMERGENCY AUTO SERVICE
Also snowplowing. 925-1266
THE ROARING FOR AUTO RENTAL LTD. (4-wheel drive)
Airport Business Center Bldg. 19 925-8574

BANKS

ASPEN SAVINGS & LOAN
225 N. Mill. 925-6400
BANK OF ASPEN
119 S. Mill 925-2500
FIRST NATIONAL BANK IN ASPEN
420 E. Main 925-1450
PITKIN COUNTY BANK & TRUST
534 E. Hyman. 925-6700

CAMPING

ASPEN - BASALT KOA
2 miles west of Basalt, Hwy. 82 927-3532

CATERING

ASPEN CATERERS
709 E. Main, 302 925-3901
MOM'S FOODS
Including cocktails 925-6661
THE CHEESE COMPANY
615 E. Cooper. 925-2977
LE CUISINER (gourmet, baked products)
Snowmass Shopping Center 923-5797, 925-7100

CHILD CARE

ASPEN BABYSITTING & ASPEN GOOD-TIMES DAY CAMP
0200 Lone Pine Rd. 925-4661
ASPEN CHILDREN'S CENTER
(ages 1 - 2, 3 - 5, Montessori program)
144 Baltic Ave. 925-6444
LITTLE RED SCHOOL HOUSE (2½ - 5, winter)
Box 5361, Snowmass Village 923-3756

LAUNDRY SERVICES

ASPEN LAUNDRY & CLEANERS
301 E. Hopkins 925-3444
THE WHALE OF A WASH (same-day service)
415 E. Main 925-9957

RENTAL SERVICES

ASPEN RENT-ALL
0197 Ventnor, Aspen Airport Business Ctr. . . 925-3285

TELEVISION RENTAL

HENRY'S ELECTRONIC CENTER
465 N. Mill. 925-2310

THEATERS

ISIS
406 E. Hopkins 925-7702
PLAYHOUSE
25 E. Main. 925-2050

TRANSPORT SERVICES

ROARING FORK EXPRESS (freight, local delivery)
0030 Mediterranean,
Aspen Airport Business Center 925-7744

TOURIST SERVICES

ASPENHOST (errands, picnics, stocking, babysitting & other services - any problem)
415 E. Hyman. 925-6442

TRANSPORTATION

HIGH MOUNTAIN TAXI & LIMOUSINE. 925-5245, 923-5245
MELLOW YELLOW TAXI CO.. 925-2282

TOURS

ASPEN SKI TOURS
Box 320, 300 S. Spring. 925-9500
FIRSTOURS
Courthouse Plaza, 530 E. Main 925-6900
OUTSIDE COLORADO . . . . (800) 525-9404

TRAVEL AGENTS

ASPEN TRAVEL
Park Central Bldg.. 925-3431
MEISSNER TRAVEL AGENCY
601 S. West End. 925-8996
ROCKY MOUNTAIN TRAVEL
311 W. Main. 925-8105

STORES & SKI SHOPS

ACCESSORIES

ASPEN UNLIMITED (gifts, accessories)
615 E. Cooper & 400 E. Cooper 925-2394
PATRICIA MOORE, INC. (gifts, accessories)
610 E. Hyman Ave.. 925-3523

ANTIQUES

BEST OF ALL WORLDS
505 E. Hyman. 925-2909
THE COUNTRY FLOWER
Hyman Mall 925-6522
MARJORIE'S BARN
By appointment. 925-7008
SORENSEN'S DANISH ANTIKS
724 W. Main 925-4253

BAKERIES

CHIP, CHIP HOORAY COOKIE CO.
Aspen A's, 550 E. Durant 925-9545

BEAUTY

AMELIA'S HAIRSTYLING
(haircuts, men & women, manicures, facials)
407 E. Hyman. 925-7112
THE BODY SHOP OF ASPEN (skin and hair care)
Durant Mall, 710 E. Durant / Brand Bldg., 203 S. Galena
THE COS BAR (make-up & skin care)
Aspen Plaza Bldg., 533 E. Hopkins 925-6249
GENO HAIRDRESSERS (haircutting)
Hunter Square Bldg. 925-4446
LA FEMME SKIN CARE BOUTIQUE
Aspen Arcade 925-8546
SHEAR HAPPENING (hair care)
710 E. Durant. 925-2272

BOOKSTORES

ASPEN BOOKSHOP
205 S. Mill. 925-7371
EXPLORE BOOKSELLERS
221 E. Main 925-5336

BOUTIQUES

ELLI OF ASPEN (men, women)
101 S. Mill. 925-3203
EVE DOVE (designer clothing)
105 S. Monarch 925-8222
GERANIUMS 'n Sunshine (also children's)
Mill St. Station 925-6134
INTERNATIONAL BOUTIQUE OF ASPEN
(ladies clothing)
203 S. Galen, Brand Bldg. 925-6592
THERAPY (designer fashions)
525 E. Cooper, Aspen Grove Mall. 925-7511

CLOTHING

ASPENGLO (men, women)
Aspen Square 925-4510
CRACKERS (infants to 7 years, gifts)
526 E. Hyman. 925-4913
FRANNY MARLEY'S (designer and sportswear)
412 E. Hyman. 925-6850
GREAT AMERICAN CLOTHING COMPANY
402 S. Hunter 925-6810
HEDGEHOG (children's)
101 S. Monarch 925-8412
LYTHIA NATURAL FIBER CLOTHING
Galena & Cooper
MUNCHKIN HOUSE (children's)
Aspen Arcade 925-9163
PEACHES EN REGALIA (men, women)
Aspen Plaza 925-5784
PITKIN COUNTY DRY GOODS (men, women)
308 S. Galena, Aspen Arcade 925-1681
RUANAS (alpaca)
450 S. Galena 925-7373
SMITH'S (Western, furs, boots)
525 E. Cooper. 925-5788

TOM MIX FLYING SCHOOL
(casual, Western - men's, ladies)
410 E. Hyman. 925-4550

DRUGSTORES

ASPEN DRUG (liquor, prescriptions)
Hyman & Galena 925-3311
CARL'S PHARMACY (all purpose), 306 E. Main. 925-3273
CROSSROADS DRUG & GENERAL STORE
Cooper at Galena 925-3976
THE DRUG COMPANY (also art supplies, toys)
North Mill Plaza. 925-3880

FLORISTS

INTERIOR GARDENS
720 E. Hyman. 925-1199
WILDFLOWERS AT THE JEROME
Mill St. entrance. 925-1173
PLANTIQUES
415 S. Spring 925-2210

GALLERIES

ANOTHER GALLERY
414 E. Hyman. 925-5290
APPLEQUIST GALLERY, LTD. (custom framing)
400 E. Main 925-7110
GALLERY 10
525 E. Cooper Ave.. 925-9044
GALLERY VIRTU
555 E. Durant. 925-7171
HIGH SOCIETY
Mill & Main Bl. 925-5571
THE PUTNEY GALLERY
Mesa Store Bldg., 500 W. Main 925-5086
PATRICIA MOORE, INC.
610 E. Hyman Ave.. 925-3423
SILVERMAN MUSEUM
620 E. Hyman. 925-7986
SQUASH BLOSSOM (Indian art)
450 S. Galena 925-3214
STEFAN'S FRAME STUDIO
433 N. Spring 925-8011

GIFTS

THE ASPEN TEA & SPICE CO.
(coffee, smoke shop, fruits, nuts, candies)
Brand Bldg., 203 S. Galena 925-4633
THE BAGGAGE CLAIM
307 S. Galena 925-8777
COLUMBINE OF ASPEN
(gemstones, minerals, antique guns)
408 E. Hyman. 925-2853
DAVIAN'S (handcrafted items)
523 E. Cooper. 925-8456
HOLIDAY INN GIFT SHOP
Holiday Inn 925-1500
KHALICHEH PARANDEH (imports)
427 E. Hopkins 925-4761

PYRAMID IMPORTS
Mason & Morse Bldg.. 925-7232

GLASSWORKS & STAINED GLASS

DUMERESQUE ENGRAVED GLASS
Box 8902, Aspen
HIGH SOCIETY (Colorado crafts, glassware)
Mill & Main Bldg. 925-5571

GROCERIES

BUTCHER'S BLOCK (meat & fish)
415 S. Spring 925-7554
CITY MARKET
Near Little Nell, 711 E. Cooper 925-2590
CLARK'S MARKET
300 Puppy Smith 925-8046
THE GROCERY
Airport Business Center 925-8162
TOM'S MARKET (home deliveries in Aspen & Snowmass)
Hyman at Galena 925-3215

HEALTH FOOD STORE

PITKIN COUNTY GRAINERY
716 E. Hyman. 925-6629

JEWELRY

ALPINE JEWELERS
409 E. Hopkins at bell tower 925-3292
ASPENIQUE
414 E. Hyman. 925-8087
ASPEN LEAF JEWELERS
207 S. Galena 925-5693
ASPEN SCIENTIFIC GEM LAB
620 Hyman Bldg. 925-6356
GOLDMAN OF ASPEN
525 E. Cooper. 925-3050
THE GOLDEN BOUGH
Aspen Arcades, Box 4998 925-2660
HWR JEWELRY
400 E. Hopkins 925-4610
JAMES OLSEN & ASSOCIATES (diamond brokerage)
Box 1904 925-1935
MATTERPLAY JEWELRY
420 E. Hyman. 925-2678
OPULENCE
315 E. Hyman. 925-5600
PATTI'S POTPOURRI
611 E. Cooper. 925-7203
SUNRISE, FIRE & WATER
308 S. Hunter 925-1998

KITCHENWARE

THE KITCHEN SHOP
The Durant Mall, 720 E. Durant 925-4654

ASPEN CITY CONT.

LE TUB
600 E. Hopkins 925-7161
THE FREUDIAN SLIP
308 S. Hunter 925-4427

LIQUOR

MAGNIFICO (wines & liquor)
210 S. Mill 925-7444
OF GRAPE & GRAIN (free delivery)
434 E. Cooper. 925-8600
GREAT WESTERN SPIRIT CO. (free delivery)
Next to Clark's Market - 300 Puppy Smith . . 925-8200
THE GROG SHOP (free delivery, next to City Market)
710 E. Durant 925-3000
UNCLE WILL'S SPIRIT HOUSE
413 E. Hyman. 925-3366

PARTY SUPPLIES

THE PAPER PIG
Durant Mall, 720 E. Durant 925-4654

LUGGAGE & LEATHER GOODS

THE BAGGAGE CLAIM
307 S. Galena 925-8777
H.T. YODER LEATHER GOODS
203 S. Galena 925-4115
LEATHER DRAGON (bags, wallets)
107 S. Monarch 925-7921

SHOES

FOOTLOOSE MOCCASINS
516 E. Hyman. 925-9155
LA PIUMA
605 E. Cooper, Aspen Sq. Arcade. 925-2150
OZZIE'S SHOES
312 S. Hunter 925-6271

SPORT SHOPS & SKI EQUIPMENT

ASPEN HIGHLANDS SKI SHOP (rental, repair)
Maroon Creek Rd. 925-2464
ASPEN MOUNTAIN SPORTS (rental, repair)
611 E. Durant 925-5773
ASPEN SKI SWAP (used ski equipment, repair)
415 E. Hyman. 925-1581
ASPEN SPORTS
(ski, bicycle & moped rental, racquet stringing)
408 E. Cooper. 925-6331
BELL MOUNTAIN SPORTS (overnight ski repairs)
312 E. Hyman. 925-4111
BOULDER MOUNTAINEER
315 E. Hyman. 925-2849
BREEZE, Inc.
555 E. Durant 925-1360
CRYSTAL SKI RENTALS (rental, overnight ski repair)
555 E. Durant, base of Aspen Mtn. 925-7748
JUNIOR MOUNTAIN SPORTS
(for toddlers through size 18)
555 E. Durant. 925-7889
KINDERSPORT, JUNIOR SKI & SPORTS OUTFITTERS
400 E. Hyman. 925-4900
L'EQUIPE
472 E. Hyman. 925-2222
ASPEN LID STORE
533 E. Cooper. 925-7576
THE MOGUL SHOP
Corner Durant & Galena, base of Little Nell. . 925-4220
THE MOUNTAIN LID (wool hats)
Cooper St. 925-8458
THE SKI CONNCECTION
408 Hunter 925-6910
P'NUTS (children's sports)
315 E. Hyman. 925-5599
POMEROY SPORTS
614 E. Durant 925-7875
SABBATINI SPORT (ski rental, overnight repair)
208 S. Mill 925-3626
SCANDINAVIAN DESIGN (handknit sweaters)
302 S. Galena, No. 5 925-7299
SHADOW MOUNTAIN SKI SHOP (rental)
Aspen A's 925-6740
SIRI & PETER'S (Scandinavian handknits)
400 E. Hyman. 925-5044
SPORTHAUS LINDNER
Hyman & Mill 925-7849
SPORT STALKER
428 E. Hyman. 925-9237
STEFAN KAELIN'S
425 E. Cooper, on the Mall 925-2987

STATIONERY & OFFICE SUPPLIES

IMPRESSIONS OF ASPEN (artist materials, posters)
Durant Mall Bldg., 720 E. Durant. 925-7620
SANDY'S OFFICE SUPPLY
E. Highland 925-1620

TOYS

HOBBY SHOP
Mason & Morse Bldg. on Hyman 925-1368
POCKETS
601 E. Hyman. 925-9331
THINK TOYS
7 days a week 925-9256

TRANSPORTATION

AIR

ASPEN AIRWAYS 925-3400, 925-7181
BONANZA AIRLINES. . . . . (800) 332-1402
COLORADO AIRLINES. . . . . (800) 349-5378
From Colorado . . . . (800) 332-1404

ROCKY MOUNTAIN AIRWAYS. 925-2352

AUTO

From Denver via U.S. 6 & Interstate 70 through the Eisenhower Tunnel, over Vail Pass to Glenwood Springs (exit 24). Then, Colorado State Highway 82 to Aspen, 205 miles. Eastern Approach via Independence Pass is open approximately the 2nd week of June through the summer, till the first heavy snowfall in November.

AUTO RENTAL

ASPEN AUTO
Airport Center. 926-6110
AVIS
Airport. 925-2355, (800) 331-1212
BUDGET
Pomegranate Inn 925-2151, (800) 228-9650
HERTZ
Airport. 925-7368, (800) 654-3131
NATIONAL
Airport. 925-1144, (800) 328-4567
ROARING FORK (4-wheel drive)
Airport Business Center, Bldg. 10. 925-8574
THRIFTY
Pomegranate Inn 925-8667, (800) 331-4200

BUS

CONTINENTAL TRAILWAYS
Aspen Airport. 925-1234
LOCAL BUS
Pitkin County .925-8484

LIMOS

HIGH MOUNTAIN CAB. 923-5245
MELLOW YELLOW CAB 925-2282
YELLOW CAB . . . . (303) 242-2542

TRAIN

AMTRAK
San Francisco Zephyr, between San Francisco, Denver & Chicago. . . . . (800) 421-8320
DENVER & RIO GRANDE WESTERN RAILROAD
Between Denver, Glenwood Springs, Grand Junction & Salt Lake City. From Denver . . . . . 629-5533 X 2298
Glenwood Springs. 945-5011

S N O W M A S S

P.O. BOX 1248, ASPEN, CO 81611 (303) 9251220

AREA INFORMATION

BASE ELEVATION
8,250 feet
HOURS
9:00 a.m. - 4:00 p.m.
LIFTS
12 chairlifts, 13,500 capacity per hour
LONGEST RUN
3½ miles
NURSERY
Information 923-2000
SEASON
Late November to early April, snowmaking
SNOW PHONE
8:30 a.m. - 5:00 p.m.. 925-1220
Other times 925-1221, 925-1222
TRAILS
10% beginner, 65% intermediate, 25% advanced
TRAVEL
From Denver, 205 miles, Grand Junction, 140 miles, via I-70 and Rt. 82; Colorado Springs, 260 miles via I-25, I-70 and Rt. 82. Aspen Airport: : Rocky Mountain and Aspen Airways from Denver; Bonanza Airlines, Grand Junction, Colorado Springs, Salt Lake City.
VERTICAL DROP
3,600 feet

EMERGENCY

AMBULANCE. 923-3333
FIRE 923-2222

LODGING

CENTRAL CONDO INFORMATION 923-2000

ASPENWOOD CONDOS. 923-2711
CARRIAGEWAY APTS.. 923-2000
CENTER WILLOW CONDOS. 923-2000
CRESTWOOD CONDO . . . . .923-2450 X 28
INNS AT SNOWMASS. . . . . .923-4310 X 48
INTERLUDE CONDOS 923-2000
LAURELWOOD CONDOS . . . . .923-3110 X 20
LICHENHEART CONDOS 923-2000
MOUNTAIN CHALET. . . . . .923-3900 X 38
POKOLDI LODGE 923-2000
SEASONS FOUR CONDOS. 923-2000
SHADOWBROOK CONDOS 923-2300
SILVER TREE / EL DORADO. . . . . . . .923-3520 X 49
SNOWMASS INN. 923-2000
STONEBRIDGE LODGE . . . . .923-2420 X 21
STONEBRIDGE CONDOS . . . . .923-4323 X 76
TAMARACK TOWNHOUSE 923-2000
TERRACE HOUSE. 923-2000
TOP OF THE VILLAGE. 923-3673
UPPER WILLOW CONDOS 923-2000
WILDWOOD INN. . . . . .923-3550 X 43

RECREATION

SNOWMASS COUNTRY CLUB
Tennis 923-4011
Golf. 923-4012

RESTAURANTS

CASA CHE RESTAURANT. 923-4648
COURSE & COURTS 923-3292
LA RESERVE. 923-4989

THE LAST RESORT 923-4581
PEPPERMILL RESTAURANT 923-2570
REFECTORY 923-3576
THE STEW POT 923-2263
STONEBRIDGE INN RESTAURANT 923-2420
TIMBERLINE RESTAURANT 923-4004
TIMBERMILL INN 923-4774
TOWER RESTAURANT 923-4650
VILLAGE DELI 923-3957
WINESKIN RESTAURANT 923-4992

STORES & SKI SHOPS

BRIGHT & SHINY THINGS (gifts) 923-4666
BRAE & BLARNEY BRITISH (sweaters, kilts) . . 923-5336
CAP 'N CORK (liquor) 923-4100
CROSSROADS STORE 923-4106
DESPERADO'S (Western wear) 923-2134
GENE TAYLOR'S (ski shop) 923-3660
H.T. YODER (leather goods) 923-3660
HILLIS OF SNOWMASS (furs) 923-4070
INSIDE OUTFITTERS (ski shop) 923-5290
INSIGNIA HOUSE (art) 923-2419
L'MAISON D'ART (art) 923-4794
SHIRT OFF MY BACK 923-3917
SHORT SPORT (ski shop) 923-5010
STEFAN KAELIN'S (ski shop) 923-2717
STEIN'S LITTLE SHOP (women's apparel) 923-3665
VILLAGE CHEESE SHOP 923-2597

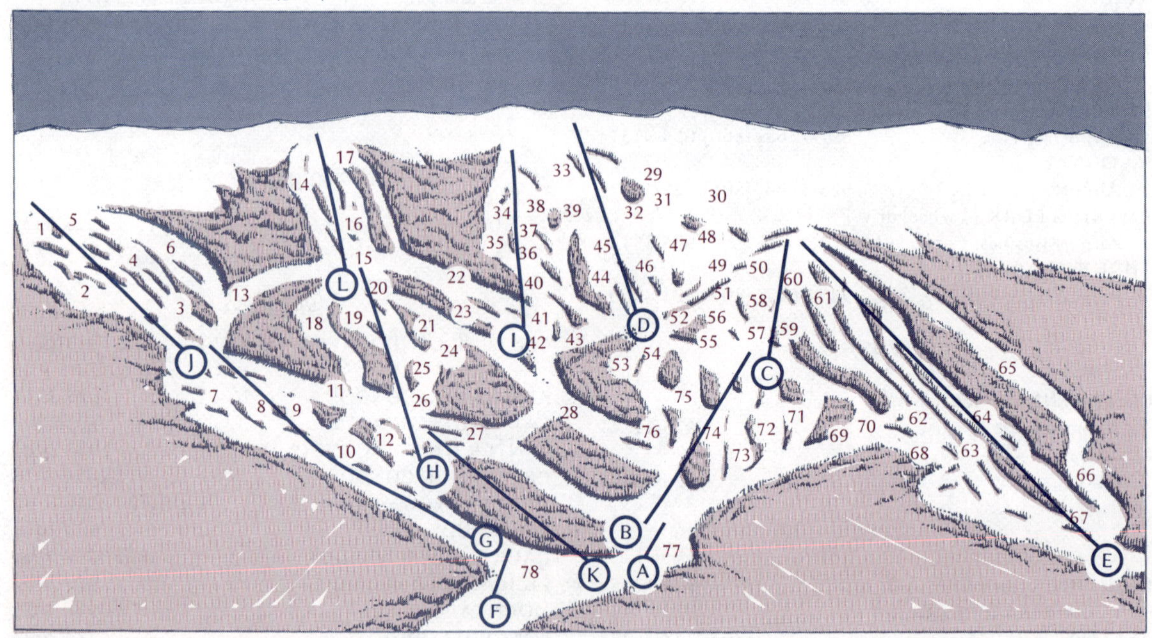

SNOWMASS RUNS

1 BULL RUN
2 SPIKE HOLLOW
3 GREY WOLF
4 BEAR BOTTOM
5 GUNNER'S VIEW
6 SANDY PARK
7 FUNNEL BYPASS
8 FUNNEL
9 BEELINE
10 BOTTOMS UP
11 SLIDER
12 LOWER SLIDER
13 TURKEY TROT
14 THE EDGE
15 SHOWCASE
16 REIDAR'S
17 EAST BOWL
18 NAKED LADY
19 LODGE POLE
20 LOG DECK
21 ART'S ULCER
22 GREEN CABIN
23 GRANITE
24 COFFEE POT
25 LUNKERVILLE
26 LOG DECK
27 VILLAGE BOUND
28 GREEN CABIN
29 CLIFFSIDE
30 UPPER POWDERHORN
31
32 LUPINE
33 TIMBERLINE
34 SHEER BLISS
35 EASTER ISLAND
36 SHEER BLISS
37 WEST FACE
38 COYOTE HOLLOW
39 GARRET GULCH
40 FREE FALL
41 GLISSADE
42 CAMP 3
43 TRESTLE
44 WHISPERING JESSE
45 BIG BURN
46 WINESKIN
47 DALLAS FREEWAY
48 MICK'S GULLEY
49 MAX PARK
50 PIPELINE
51 SUNNYSIDE
52 BANZAI
53 MONK'S HOOD
54 LUNCH LINE
55 CONEY GLADE
56 MOONSHINE
57 UTE CHUTE
58 FAST DRAW
59 PROMENADE
60 ZUGSPITZE
61 SLOT
62 WILDCAT
63 CAMPGROUND
64 BEAR CLAW
65 LOWER POWDERHORN
66 BELLY GRABBER PITCH
67 CATWALK
68 OPTION
69 DAWDLER CATWALK
70 DAWDLER
71 SCOOPER
72 HAL'S HOLLOW
73 VELVET FALLS
74 BLUE GROUSE
75 CABIN
76 BANZAI CUT-OFF
77 FANNY HILL
78 ASSAY HILL

SNOWMASS LIFTS

A VILLAGE
B BURLINGAME
C SAM'S KNOB
D BIG BURN
E CAMPGROUND
F ASSAY HILL
G FUNNEL
H ALPINE SPRINGS
I COULOIR
J ELK CAMP
K WOOD RUN TRIPLE CHAIR
L HIGH ALPINE

BEAVER CREEK

P.O. BOX 7, VAIL, CO 81657 (303) 949-6400

AREA INFORMATION

BASE ELEVATION
8,100 feet

HOURS
8:30 a.m. - 3:30 p.m.

LIFTS
6 chairs; upon completion, 15 chairs

SEASON
Mid-December to early April

TRAILS
25% easiest,
35% intermediate, 40% advanced
TRAVEL
I-70, 110 miles west of Denver, 130 miles east of Grand Junction. The Beaver Creek (Avon) exit 167 is 10 miles west of Vail. Rocky Mountain Airways flies into Avon, 1 mile from Ski Area entrance; bus service also available.
VERTICAL DROP
3,340 feet

UPON FULL BUILDOUT THERE WILL BE 15 LIFTS; ALSO, LODGING & STORES IN AVON. LODGING IS AVAILABLE THROUGH THE VAIL RESORT.

EMERGENCY

AVON POLICE 949-4280
EMERGENCY POLICE, FIRE, AMBULANCE 911
ROAD CONDITIONS 476-5323
STATE HIGHWAY PATROL 328-6343
VAIL POLICE. 476-5671

LODGING

VAIL RESORT ASSOCIATION
Central Reservations 476-5677

RESTAURANTS

GEORGES (lunch, dinner, reservations advised)
Hwy. 6 in Eagle-Vail 949-4229
HOLE-IN-THE-WALL (lunch, dinner)
Benchmark Shopping Center, Avon. 949-5463
RUBY'S (lunch, dinner)
Hwy. 6, Eagle-Vail 949-5212
SCORESHEET LOUNGE (burgers, sandwiches)
Eagle Valley Bowl. 949-5228
SUGAR & SPICE (breakfast & lunch)
Benchmark Shopping Center, Avon. 949-4322
WHISKEY CREEK STOCKMAN'S CLUB
(dinner, reservations advised)
Whiskey Creek, top of Eagle-Vail Golf Course 949-4942

SERVICES

AIR

ROCKY MOUNTAIN AIRWAYS
Denver 398-3896
Vail. 476-4750

AUTO RENTAL

AVIS 476-6611
HERTZ. 476-5133

BUS

BEAVER CREEK TRANSIT OFFICE 949-6121
Schedules & routes 949-6400
TRAILWAYS BUS 476-5137

BRECKENRIDGE

BOX 1901 | 1599 SUMMIT COUNTY RD. 3
BRECKENRIDGE, CO 80424 | (303) 453-2918, 453-2368

AREA INFORMATION

PEAK 8	PEAK 9
BASE ELEVATION 9,630 feet	BASE ELEVATION 9,630 feet
LIFTS 6 chairs, 2 pomas, 2 lifts	LIFTS 5 chairs
LONGEST TRAIL 1.6 miles	LONGEST TRAIL 2.6 miles
TERRAIN 440 acres	TERRAIN 360 acres
TOP ELEVATION 11,843 feet	TOP ELEVATION 11,460 feet
VERTICAL DROP 2,213 feet	VERTICAL DROP 1,830 feet

HOURS
9 a.m. to 3:45 p.m.
NURSERY
8:30 a.m. to 4:30 p.m., all ages, Peaks 8 & 9, D Base
SNOW PHONE 837-9907
SEASON
Late Nov. to early April
TRAVEL
From Denver, 85 mi. W. on I-70. From Stapleton Int'l. Airport, exit Frisco/Breckenridge, S. on Hwy. 9, 10 mi. to Breckenridge. From Vail, 30 mi. E. on I-70. By bus: Continental Trailways, daily, between Denver & Frisco, from downtown Denver and Stapleton Int'l. Airport. By air: 4,000 ft. landing strip at Breckenridge for twin-engine aircraft; no services.

EMERGENCY

EMERGENCY. 911
BRECKENRIDGE POLICE 453-2941
COLORADO STATE PATROL. 668-3133
FIRE 453-2474
ROAD/WEATHER REPORTS 453-1090
SUMMIT COUNTY AMBULANCE. 468-2805
SUMMIT COUNTY RESCUE 453-2232
SUMMIT COUNTY SHERIFF 453-2232

LODGING

CENTRAL RESERVATIONS. 453-2918

ALMAR & ASSOCIATES (3 condos)
500 Four O'Clock Rd. 453-6228
ARBUCKLE HOUSE
67 Moonstone Rd. 453-1321
ARMSTRONG HOUSE
0307 Moonstone Rd. 453-2025
BEAVER RUN
649 Village Rd. 453-6000
BEZDEK HOUSE
522 High Point Dr. 453-6185

BRECKENRIDGE CONT.

BLAZING SADDLES
200 W. Washington 453-2876
BLUE RIVER CONDOS
580 Colorado, Hwy. 9 453-2260
BOREAS PASS (2 properties)
0041 Summit County Rd., 518 453-6131
BRECKENRIDGE INN
600 S. Ridge. 453-2333
BRUSH HOUSE
Spruce Valley Ranch 453-1133
BUNTING HOUSE
Boreas Pass Rd. 453-6941
CLAUDE'S LODGE
Wagon Rd., County Rd., 11 453-2420
COCHRAN APARTMENTS
County Rd., 925, Peak 7. 453-1412
CRISPELL HOUSE
107 S. High St. 453-1412
CROFUTT'S NAPSACK LODGE & DORM
200 Ski Hill Rd.. 453-2420
FALLON
304 High St.. . . . . (800) 255-3456
FIRESIDE INN
212 Wellington Rd.. 453-6456
HIGH COUNTRY LODGE
5064 Summit County Rd., 3 453-2577
HOLIDAY INN AT LAKE DILLON
650 N. Main St., Frisco. 668-5000
BRYAN HOBBS (2 properties)
2920 S. Parker Rd., Aurora, CO 80014 (800) 455-1890
HORIZONS UNLIMITED (4 properties)
455 Village Rd. 453-1119
INNER CIRCLE CONDOS
820 Kinnikinick Dr. 453-2686
INTERNATIONAL TRADERS (5 properties)
325 S. Main 453-2863
LANCES WEST
835 Broken Lance Dr. 453-2856
LONGBRANCH ENYEART
107 N. Harris 453-1383
MC LEARY HOUSE
124 Royal Tiger. 453-2393
MOTHER LODE RENTALS
800 S. Columbine. 453-2918
NICHOLL'S LODGING
302 S. Ridge St.. 453-2392
PANDA BEARS
321 S. High St. 453-2386
PINE RIDGE
805 Columbine 453-6943
POOL'S PLACE
403 High St.. 453-6962
RESORT RENTALS (18 properties)
Bell Tower Mall 453-6060
RIDGE ST. INN
100 W. Lincoln 453-6065
SEAL HOUSE
0038 Summit County Rd., 904, Peak 7 453-2661
SITZMARK
207 E. Adams 453-6962
SUNDOWNER - GERRITY
0951 Summit County Rd., 400 . . . . . (800) 398-2490
SUNSET - WILKIN
Summit County Rd., 400 . . . . (800) 685-5212
TANNENBAUM BY THE RIVER
805 S. Columbine. 453-6380
TANNHAUSER
407 S. Ridge. 453-2136
TYROLLEAN TERRACE - COGBILL
0112 Overlook Dr. 453-2876
VAL D'ISERE - GALBREATH
French St. 453-6456
VALDORA VILLAGE - TARNUM
0406 Summit County Rd., 450 453-6108

RECREATION

BRECKENRIDGE NORDIC CENTER (cross country)
P.O. Box 1776. 453-6855
BRECKENRIDGE SKATING RINK
Maggie Pond, Bell Tower Mall 453-1460
BRECKENRIDGE STABLES
Maggie Pond, Bell Tower Mall 453-1460
COLORADO ADVENTURES LTD.
P.O. Box 851, Steamboat Springs, CO . (800) 879-2039
FOUR CORNERS EXPEDITIONS
Buena Vista, CO. . . . . (800) 395-8949
THE SKI TOURING EXPERIENCE
221 S. Main St. 453-2930
TIGER RUN
0050 Summit County Rd., 315 453-2231

RESTAURANTS

BRECKENRIDGE INN / EDELWEISS (entertainment)
600 S. Ridge. 453-2333
BRIAR ROSE (bar, American)
109 E. Lincoln St. 453-9948
CLAIMJUMPER
130 S. Main 453-6858
DEMETRI'S ON THE ROOF
Georgian Square. 453-2888
EL PERDIDO
306 N. French. 453-2928
H.P. CASSIDY'S (entertainment, American)
Peak 9 Parking Area, 200 Village Rd.. 453-6828
HORSE SHOE II
115 S. Main St. 453-9804
THE MAGGIE
Peak 9 Base Area 453-6223
MI CASA (Mexican)
100 Village Rd., Steinmark Bldg. 453-2071
MINERS CAMP (American, disco)
Bell Tower Mall 453-6848
SWEET SURRENDER
325 S. Main 453-6969
WHALE'S TAIL (American, cocktails)
323 S. Main 453-2221

SERVICES

AUTOMOTIVE
Minit Mart 453-6252

BANKS

Bank of Breckenridge, 301 S. Main 453-2521
Summit County Bank, Frisco, 120 S. 4th St. 668-3333

DRUGS & SUNDRIES

The Drug Store, Bly Bldg., Ski Hill Rd. 453-2362
The Grocery Store, 200 W. Washington 453-6129

FILM

Old West Photo, Bell Tower Mall 453-9861

LIQUOR

The Liquor Store, Bly Bldg., Ski Hill Rd. . . . 453-2253
Mountain Liquor, Bell Tower Mall 453-6499
Wine & Cheese Shop, 203 S. Main 453-2043

STORES & SKI SHOPS

BOOKSTORES

GREAT NORTHERN BOOK & POSTER

Bell Tower Mall 452-2444

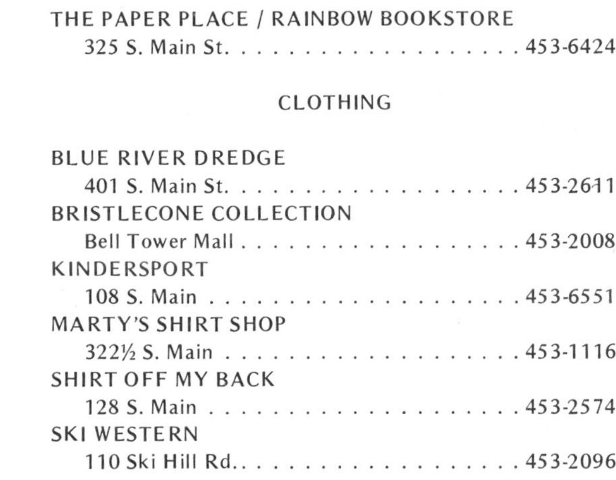

THE PAPER PLACE / RAINBOW BOOKSTORE

325 S. Main St. 453-6424

CLOTHING

BLUE RIVER DREDGE

401 S. Main St. 453-2611

BRISTLECONE COLLECTION

Bell Tower Mall 453-2008

KINDERSPORT

108 S. Main 453-6551

MARTY'S SHIRT SHOP

322½ S. Main 453-1116

SHIRT OFF MY BACK

128 S. Main 453-2574

SKI WESTERN

110 Ski Hill Rd. 453-2096

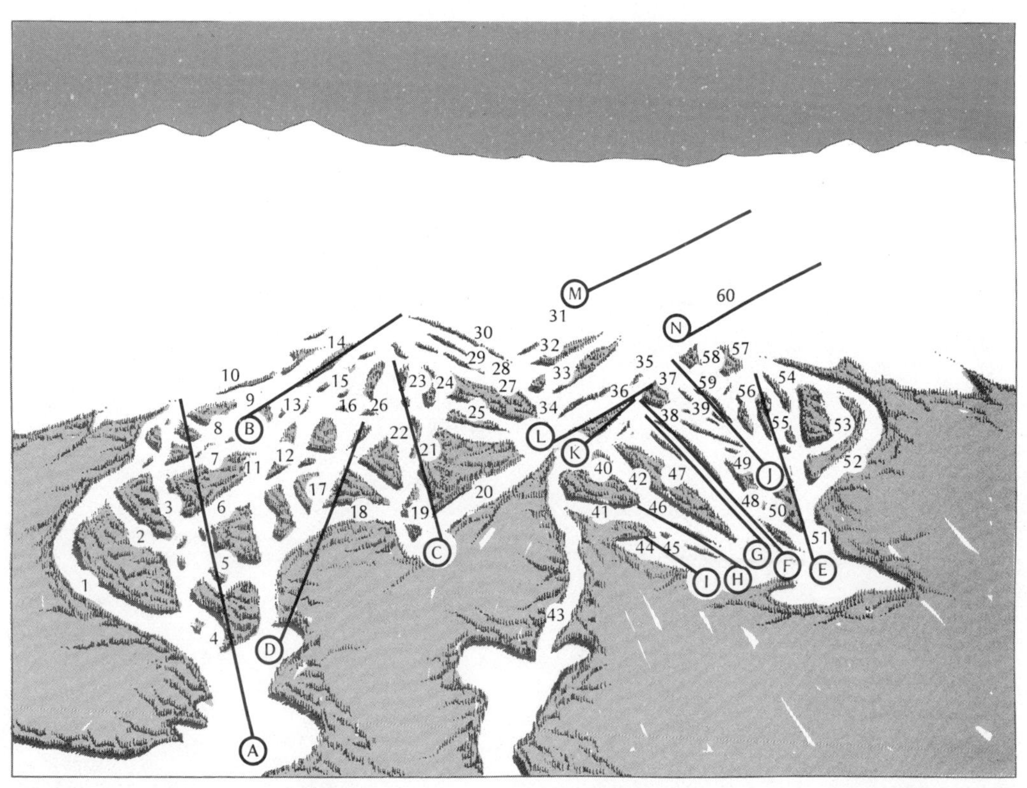

BRECKENRIDGE RUNS

1 LOWER LEHMAN
2 RED ROVER
3 SILVERTHRONE
4 UPPER LEHMAN
5 BRIAR ROSE
6 CASHIER
7 WELLINGTON
8 AMERICAN
9 LITTLE HARRY
10 MINNIE
11 COUNTRY BOY
12 BONANZA
13 SIZZLER
14 UPPER COLUMBIA
15 UNION
16 TOM'S BABY
17 INFERNO
18 DEVILS CROTCH
19 MINE SHAFT
20 GOLD KING
21 PEERLESS
22 SHOCK
23 SPUR
24 CORKSCREW
25 C TRANSFER
26 SUNDOWN
27 SAWMILL
28 FOUR O'CLOCK
29 PSYCHOPATH
30 SOUTHERN CROSS
31 TIGER
32 GOODBYE GIRL
33 MACH 1
34 TO PEAK 8
35 TO PEAK 9
36 1ST ACCESS
37 2ND ACCESS
38 FREEWAY
39 TWISTER
40 TRYGUE'S
41 PARKLANE
42 POWERLINE
43 SWINGER
44 BOREAS
45 SWINGER CUT-OFF
46 SPRINGMEIER
47 THE GLADE
48 CRESCENDO
49 CALLIE'S ALLEY
50 MAY DAY
51 SPRUCE
52 LITTLE JOHNNY
53 ROUNDER'S RUN
54 HIGH ANXIETY
55 EGO LANE
56 NORTH STAR
57 DUKE'S RUN
58 CONTEST BOWL
59 HORSESHOE BOWL
60 STEEP

BRECKENRIDGE LIFTS

A CHAIR 1
B CHAIR 2
C CHAIR 3
D CHAIR 4
E CHAIR 5
F CHAIR 6
G POMALIFT 1
H POMALIFT 2
I T-BAR 2
J T-BAR 3
K CHAIR A1
L CHAIR A2
M CHAIR B
N CHAIR C
O CHAIR D

SUMMIT SKIWEAR
100 Village Rd. 453-1010
TIGER RAGS
221 S. Main 453-2121
UNCLE JIM'S T-SHIRTS & GIFTS
101 S. Main 453-6008
WINTER SPORT
Georgian Square. 453-1300
YANKEE PEDDLER & KID STUFF
400 S. Main 453-2585

FLORIST

BRECKENRIDGE FLORISTS
Georgian Square. 453-2252

GIFT SHOPS

AU PETIT MARCHE
Bell Tower Mall 453-6564
BAY STREET COMPANY
232 S. Main 453-6303
GIFTS POURRI INC.
401 S. Main 453-6869
HANGIN' TREE LEATHER
Bell Tower Mall 453-1373
PRIZE BOX
204 S. Main 453-6229
SKINNY WINTER
123 S. Main 453-6300
TIGER RUN
0050 Summit Rd., 315. 453-2231
WHITE BUFFALO
Bell Tower Mall 453-2777
WILDFLOWER
124 S. Main 453-2574

JEWELRY

THE ASSAY OFFICE
330 S. Main 453-2148
BRISTLECONE CONNECTIONS
Bell Tower Mall 453-2008

SKI EQUIPMENT & RENTALS

A RACER'S EDGE
303 S. Main St. 453-6254
ADVANCE SKI SHOP & RENTALS
401 S. Main 453-6868
BREEZE SKI RENTALS
100 Village Rd., 600 S. Ridge 453-6405
FOR SKIERS ONLY
120 S. Main St. 453-6667
LONE STAR SKI RENTALS
111 Ski Hill Rd.. 453-2003
MAVERICK SKI SHOP
100 Ski Hill Rd.. 453-6720
MOUNTAIN HAUS
326 S. Main St. 453-6960
NORWAY HAUS
110 Lincoln St. 453-2375
RECREATION SPORTS & RENTALS
Bell Tower Mall 453-2194
THE SKI STOP
114 S. Main 453-1333
SKI WESTERN
110 Ski Hill Rd.. 453-2096

COPPER MOUNTAIN

P.O. BOX 1, COPPER MTN., CO 80443 (303) 668-2882

AREA INFORMATION

BASE ELEVATION
9,600 feet
CHILD CARE. 668-2882
HOURS
9 a.m. - 4 p.m., 8:30 a.m. - 4 p.m., weekends & holidays
LIFTS
10 double chairlifts, 2 surface lifts
LOCATION
75 miles west of Denver on I-70, exit 195.
From Stapleton Int'l. Airport, Denver.
LODGING
All lodging reservations, addresses & information are made through the Copper Mountain Resort Association, P.O. Box 3033, 80443. There are 18 condos plus club med, 1,828 rental beds. . . . . (303) 668-6477
Copper Mountain Lodging Services,
P.O. Box 3117, 80443 . . . . (303) 668-2220
LONGEST RUN
2½ miles
SNOWFALL
250 inches, snow making under F & G lifts
TRAILS
48, 20% beginner, 55% intermediate, 25% expert

RECREATION

COLORADO ADVENTURES (river rafting)
June thru Sept. 879-2039, (800) 332-3200
COPPER MOUNTAIN CORRAL (rides, fishing trips)
At entrance to Village 668-2200
DILLON YACHT BASIN (sailing)
June thru Sept. 468-2936
FOUR CORNERS EXPEDITION (river rafting)
June thru Sept. 395-8949, (800) 332-9254
TIGER RUN
Snowmobile & Jeep Tours. 453-2231

RESTAURANTS

THE CENTER (cafeteria, wine & beer) 668-2882
COPPER STILL (prime rib, seafood)
Snowbridge Square Bldg.. 668-2020
FARLEY'S (American)
Snowflake Bldg., base of B-lift 668-2577
MIKE & MIGUEL'S (Mexican, Steaks, bar)
Snowbridge Square Bldg.. 668-6481

MOUNTAIN STANDARD TIME
(live entertainment, cocktails)
Snowbridge Square Bldg.. 668-2070
PEZZINI'S CHOCOLAT HAUS (ice cream)
Mountain Plaza 668-6168
THE PLAZA RESTAURANT (Continental)
Mountain Plaza, main level. 668-2882
SOLITUDE STATION (cafeteria, beer & wine)
Top of F-lift 668-2882
TUSO'S (Continental, bar)
Snowflake Bldg.. 668-6090

ALL FACILITIES ARE LOCATED AT THE SKI AREA

STORES & SKI SHOPS

CHRISTY SPORTS (also rentals)
Copper Junction Bldg. 668-6250
COPPER MT. ETC. SHOP (essentials)
2nd floor of the Center
Solitude Station @ top of F-lift
Transportation Center 668-2882
COPPER MT. RENTAL & REPAIR
ground level of the Center 668-2882
COPPER SPIRITS (liquor, etc.)
Mountain Plaza 668-6426
THE FOOD BASKET (gourmet, natural foods)
Snowbridge Square Bldg.. 668-2937
MODERN TIMES (souvenirs, gifts)
Copper Junction Bldg. 668-2211
MOUNTAIN BOOKS & GIFTS
Mountain Plaza 668-2107
MOUNTAIN SHOP (rentals, sales)
Snowflake Bldg.. 668-6169
NUGGETS & NECESSITIES (film, drugs, etc.)
Mountain Plaza 668-6460
RECREATION SPORTS
Snowbridge Square Bldg.. 668-2919
SHIRT FACTORY
Snowbridge Square Bldg.. 668-6467
SUMMIT SKI RENTAL
Bridge End Bldg. 668-6499
ZAMBINI'S LIQUORS
Snowbridge Square Bldg.. 668-2323

CRESTED BUTTE

BOX 528, CRESTED BUTTE, CO 81224 (303) 349-6611

AREA INFORMATION

BASE ELEVATION
9,375 feet
HOURS
9:00 a.m. - 4:00 p.m., halfday begins at 12:30
LIFTS
7 chairs, 1 bar
LONGEST RUN
1½ miles
NURSERY
Ages 3 - 9, must be toilet trained, call Ski Area
SEASON
December 1st - Mid-April
SNOW PHONE 349-5327
TRAILS
20% beginner, 38% intermediate, 27% expert
TRAVEL
30 miles from Gunnison, 230 miles from Denver, via U.S. 285 & U.S. 50 to Hwy. 135 to Ski Area. The Mountain Express bus system service between Mt. Crested Butte and Ski Area; also, the Gunnison Airport, meeting all arriving and departing flights.
VERTICAL DROP
2,150 feet

LODGING

ALPINE CHALET RENTALS
Box 247 349-5386
CRESTED BUTTE LODGE
Box 206 349-5322
ELK MOUNTAIN LODGE
Box 148 349-5114
FOREST QUEEN HOTEL & RESTAURANT
Box 127 349-5336
IRWIN LODGE
Box 457 349-5140
NORDIC INN
Box 939 349-5542
ORE BUCKET LODGE
Box 427 349-5519
PURPLE MOUNTAIN LODGE
Box 897 349-5888
ROZMANS
Box 909 349-6669
SAN MORITZ CONDOMINIUMS
Box 169 349-5150
SKI CREST LODGE
Box 729 349-6629
VALLEY HI RESORT
Box 777 349-5887

ALL LODGING IS IN CRESTED BUTTE 81224

RESTAURANTS

ALPENHOF 349-5692
ANGELLO'S 349-5708
ARTICHOKE 349-5400
BACCHANALE 349-5257
EL DORADO CAFE 349-5737
FOREST QUEEN HOTEL & RESTAURANT. . . 349-5336
GRUBSTAKE OGMEG 349-9982
JEREMIAH'S RESTAURANT 349-5322
LE BOSQUET. 349-5808
OLD WORLD BAKERY. 349-6868
PENELOPE'S 349-5178
RAFTERS. 349-5713
THE ROCKING HORSE. 349-6193
SCHMOOZIES 349-5914
SOUPCON. 349-5448
STARGAZER. 349-5785
UPSTAIRS DOWNSTAIRS (restaurant & bar) . . 349-6474
VINEYARD. 349-5820
WAY STATION. 349-6573

CRESTED BUTTE CONT.

STORES & SKI SHOPS

ACME LIQUOR. 349-5709
BATTERIE DE CUISINE 349-5688
CRESTED BUTTE DRUG STORE. 349-5855
CRESTED BUTTE GROCERY 349-5675
CRESTED BUTTE SKI RENTAL
At the slopes, call Ski Area
FLATIRON SPORTS. 349-5543
ICE MOUNTAIN JEWELRY 349-6331
MOUNTAIN DRUG DEALER 349-5875
MT. CRESTED BUTTE GROCERY & DELI . . . 349-5246
MT. CRESTED BUTTE LIQUOR. 349-5246
NASTAR SKI RACING
At the slopes, call Ski Area
SNOWFLAKE GIFTS 349-5819
STEPHANIC'S GROCERY MARKET 349-5588

GENEVA BASIN

P.O. BOX 65, GRANT, CO 80448 (303) 789-1426

AREA INFORMATION

BASE ELEVATION
10,500 feet
HOURS
9:00 a.m. - 4:00 p.m.
LIFTS
2 chairs, 3 bars,
LONGEST RUN
1 mile
NURSERY
18 months to 7 years, Mon.- Fri., holidays, call Ski Area
SEASON
Mid-November to April, snowmaking
SNOW PHONE 789-1426
TRAILS
25% beginner, 45% intermediate, 30% expert
TRAVEL
Denver - 65 miles, Rt. 285; I-70 to Georgetown,
14 miles on Guenella Pass Rd.
VERTICAL DROP
1,250 feet

EMERGENCY

AMBULANCE SERVICE
Clear Creek County. 569-3232
Platte Canyon Rescue 838-4357
DR. FRANK REED 838-4686
FLIGHT FOR LIFE . . . . (800) 332-3123
POLICE
Clear Creek County. 571-5631
Park County 838-4441

LODGING

GEORGETOWN MOTOR INN
12 mi. N. of Geneva Basin via Guanella Pass Rd.
1100 Rose, Georgetown, 80444. 569-3201
GLEN ISLE RESORT (cabin)
18 mi. S.E. of Ski Area on U.S. 285
5 minutes west of Bailey
P.O. Box 128, Bailey, 80421 838-5461
LODGE AT GEORGETOWN
12 mi. N. of Geneva Pass Rd.
1600 Argentine, Georgetown, 80444. 569-3211
MOOREDALE VILLAGE
18 mi. S.E. of Geneva Basin on U.S. 285
P.O. Box 231, Bailey, 80421 838-5918
TUMBLING RIVER RANCH
U.S. 285 to Grant, then 4 miles on Park County Rd. 62
17 miles south of Ski Area. 838-5981

RESTAURANTS

DOS AMIGOS (Mexican, margaritas)
¼ mi. N. of Evergreen Lake, 4055 Hwy. 74 . . 674-5495
HI-LANDER (Mexican-American)
U.S. 285 at Conifer, Bailey 838-4003
THE INN PLACE (Mexican, cocktails)
U.S. 285, Grant 838-2325
KAREN'S EAT SHOPPE (also bakery, deli)
Downtown Bailey. 838-4673
KEY'S ON THE GREEN (steaks)
Upper Bear Creek Rd., W. of Evergreen Lake 674-4181
MOOREDALE VILLAGE (American, cocktails)
17 miles from Geneva, S.W. on U.S. 285. . . . 674-7076
PLATTE RIVER INN (American, bar)
U.S. 285 & City Rd. 62 838-4975

STORES & SKI SHOPS

ARVADA SKI & SPORT
9100 Ralston Rd., Arvada, 80002 421-5820
CANYON LIQUORS
Downtown Bailey. 838-4378
DICK SKI & SPORTS
2600 W. Main, Littleton, 80102. 794-4521
SKI RENTAL SHOP
At slope 789-1426

KEYSTONE / ARAPAHOE

BOX 2818, KEYSTONE, CO 80435 (303) 468-2316

AREA INFORMATION

AUTO RENTAL, Enterprise. 320-1120
BASE ELEVATION
Keystone, 9,300 feet; Arapahoe, 10,780 feet
BUS SERVICE
Daily from Frisco Airport.
Call Trailways 534-2291
CROSS COUNTRY RENTAL
Keystone's Touring Center, east of ice skating
rink in Keystone Village.
LIFTS
Keystone: 1 triple chair, 8 double chairs, 1 poma,
11,050 capacity per hr.
Arapahoe: 1 triple chair, 4 double chairs,
6,200 capacity per hr.

LIMOUSINES
American Limousines. 424-6930
LONGEST RUN
Keystone, 3 miles; Arapahoe, 1½ miles
NURSERY
Ages 1 - 12
OVERNIGHT SKI CHECK
Repair shop at base of Go-Devil lift at Keystone
RENTALS
At the base of both Keystone and Arapahoe
RESERVATIONS. 468-1234
SEASON
Keystone: Mid-Nov. to late April
Arapahoe- early Dec. to June
SNOW PHONE 572-SNOW
TOURS BY SNOWCAT
Daily from the Mountain Home at Keystone
TRAILS
Keystone: 32 - 20% beginner, 65% intermediate, 15% advanced. Arapahoe: 22 - 10% beginner, 50% intermediate, 40% advanced.
TRAVEL
Arapahoe Basin, 5 miles east, Hwy. 6. Breckenridge, 12 miles south, Hwy. 9. Copper Mountain, 14 miles south, Hwy. 6. Dillon, 5 miles west, Hwy. 6. Stapleton Int'l. Airport, Denver, 75 miles northeast, Hwy. 6 to I-70.
VERTICAL DROP
Keystone, 2,340 feet; Arapahoe, 1,670 feet

STORES, SHOPS, MEDICAL CLINIC, SECURITY LODGING, RESTAURANTS AND ALL SERVICES MAY BE REACHED BY DIALING THE KEYSTONE SWITCHBOARD . . . . (303) 468-2316

LODGING

ARGENTINE
East of the lake
DECATUR
Off Hwy. 6, west of the lake
EDGEWATER
East of the lake
FLYING DUTCHMAN
South of Soda Ridge Rd., east of Irishman Rd.
KEY CONDO
Keystone Rd., east side
KEYSTONE LODGE
Hwy. 6, across from tennis courts
LAKESIDE
Off Hwy. 6, south of the lake
LENAWEE
Off Hwy. 6, west of the lake
MONTEZUMA
Off Hwy. 6, west of the lake
QUICKSILVER
East of Tennis Courts
SUNRISE 1, 2 & 3
South of Hwy. 6, east of Husky Station
TENNIS TOWNHOUSES
South of Tennis Courts
WILD IRISHMAN
South of Irishman Rd., off County Rd. 4
WILLOWS
Off Hwy. 6, west of the lake

CONDO REGISTRATION & INFORMATION OFF HWY. 6, EAST OF KEYSTONE RD.

RESTAURANTS

ALF'S GASTHOF BAVARIA (European)
N. of Hwy. 6 overlooking Snake River 468-2702
BENTLEY'S (dinner, entertainment, cocktails)
Conference Center . . . . X 3862
BIGHORN STEAKHOUSE (cocktails)
Keystone Lodge. . . . . X 3740
BRASSERIE (breakfast & lunch)
Beside Conference Center, W. of lodge . . . . . . X 3825
ESTEBAN'S (Mexican, bar)
Overlooking the Snake River . . . . . 468-0020 X 3539
GARDEN ROOM (Continental, cocktails)
Overlooking Keystone Lake, in Lodge Bldg . . . X 3740
KEYSTONE RANCH (full service dinner)
Overlooking Golf Course. . . . . X 3901
LAST CHANCE SALOON (entertainment, dancing, bar)
East of the lake . . . . X 5329
THE NAVIGATOR (seafood, cocktails)
East of the Lake. . . . . X 3860
PEZZINI'S CHOCOLAT HAUS (ice cream, etc.)
Conference Center . . . . X 3793
SKI TIP RANCH (complete dinner)
¾ mi. W. of area via Montezuma Rd. 468-9928
SILVER SEED EMPORIUM (to go, catering)
Keystone Village 468-2774
SNAKE RIVER SALOON (Continental, entertainment)
Off Hwy. 6, W. of Montezuma Rd. 468-2788
TENDERFOOT LOUNGE
Keystone Lodge. . . . . X 3741
WESTERN BARBECUES (Wednesday evening cookouts)
S.E. end of Keystone Lake near Snake River . . X 3866

STORES & SKI SHOPS

ALASKAN ENCOUNTER (gifts)
B-BAR-K (clothes)
THE CHILDREN.S SHOP
FINGERPRINTS (crafts, gifts)
GLOBAL VILLAGE (gifts)
JOHN GARDINER'S TENNIS CLINIC (pro shop)
OTRAS COSAS (boutique)
PATHFINDER (cross-country store)
ROCKY MOUNTAIN HIGH (wine & liquor)
SPORT STALKER (equipment)
SUMMIT WESTERN WEAR
UNICORN'S DESIRE (jewelry & leather)

ALL STORES & SHOPS ARE LOCATED IN KEYSTONE VILLAGE, N.W. OF KEYSTONE LODGE, BETWEEN KEYSTONE RD. & HWY. 6.

PURGATORY

P.O. BOX 666, DURANGO, CO 81301 (303) 247-9000

AREA INFORMATION

BASE ELEVATION
8,950 feet
HANDICAPPED SKIERS 247-9000
HOURS
9 a.m. to 4 p.m.
GASOLINE AVAILABILITY NUMBER. 247-8900
NURSERY
Ages 2 - 6, 8:30 a.m. - 4:30 p.m.
LIFTS
5 double chairlifts, 2 rope tows (adult & child)
LONGEST RUN
2 miles
SEASON
November to early April
TRAILS
27% beginner, 44%, intermediate, 29% expert
TRAVEL
From Albuquerque, 212 miles, Hwy. 44 to U.S. 55 to U.S. 160. From Colorado Springs, 312 miles, Hwy. 24 to U.S. 285 to U.S. 160. From Denver, 384 miles, Hwy. 25 to U.S. 16 to U.S. 550. From Grand Junction, 150 miles, Hwy. 50 to U.S. 550.
VERTICAL DROP
1,600 feet

EMERGENCY

POLICE, FIRE, SHERIFF. 911
AMBULANCE. 565-7777
POISON CONTROL 247-9499
ROAD & WEATHER. 247-0007
STATE ROAD & WEATHER 565-4511

LODGING

ADOBE INN
2178 Main Ave. 247-2743
ALPINE NORTH MOTEL
3515 Main Ave. 247-4042
BASE LODGE & DAY LODGE. 247-8900
BEAR RANCH SKIERS' DORM
42570 Hwy. 550 247-0111
BEST WESTERN DURANGO INN
21382 State Hwy. 160 247-3251
BEST WESTERN LODGE AT PURGATORY
49617 Hwy. 550 247-9669
CABOOSE MOTEL
3363 Main Ave. 247-1191
DURANGO TRAVELODGE
150 - 5th St. 247-0955, (800) 255-3050
EDELWEISS MOTEL
689 County Rd. 203 247-5685
FOUR WINDS MOTEL
20797 West Hwy. 160 247-4512
FRONTIER MOTEL
3131 Main Ave. 247-5460
GENERAL PALMER HOUSE
567 Main Ave.. 247-4747
GYPSY MOTEL
3701 Main Ave. 247-9950
HIDDEN VALLEY MOTEL
2202 Main Ave. 247-0460
HOLIDAY INN
800 Camino Del Rio 247-5393
LANDMARK MOTEL
3030 Main Ave. 259-1333
MOUNTAIN SHADOWS MOTEL
3255 Main Ave. 247-5285
QUALITY INN SUMMIT
1700 County Rd. 203 259-1430
RAMADA INN & CONFERENCE CENTER
25926 Hwy. 550 259-1010
REDWOOD LODGE
763 County Rd. 203 247-3895
ROYAL MOTEL
2068 Main Ave. 247-3952
SIESTA MOTEL
3475 Main Ave. 247-0741
SILVER SPRUCE MOTEL
2929 Main Ave. 247-2202
SILVER SPUR MOTEL
3416 Main Ave. 247-5552
SLEEPY HOLLOW LODGE
2970 North Main Ave. 247-1741
STRATER HOTEL
699 Main Ave.. 247-4431
SUNSET MOTEL
2855 Main Ave. 247-2653
THUNDERBIRD LODGE
2701 Main Ave. 247-1663
WESTERN STAR MOTEL
3310 Main Ave. 247-4895

RESTAURANTS

THE ASSAY OFFICE (American, cocktails)
3206 Main Ave. 247-1316
BEAR RANCH (steak & fondue)
42570 U.S. Hwy. 247-0111
BELL CREEK RIG (beef, seafood)
1640 E. Main, Cortez. 565-3391
CHINA RESTAURANT (bar)
1525 Main Ave. 259-0868
THE COURT CLUB OF DURANGO (American, bar)
1600 Florida Rd. 259-2579
EDELWEISS RESTAURANT
689 Country Rd. 203. 247-5685
FARQUAHRT'S (rock'n roll, country)
725 Main Ave.. 247-9861
FORMERLY ZHIVAGO'S (American, cocktails)
1260 Empire, Silverton. 387-9902
FRANCISCO'S RESTAURANTE & CANTINA (rock)
619 Main Ave.. 247-4093
GOLD THIEVERS STEAK HOUSE (cook your own)
2811 Marcos Rd., Cortez. 565-4375
KATIE O'BRIEN'S EATING PARLOR
128 6th Ave.. 247-9083
LA COCINA (Mexican, beer)
509 8th Ave., on the College Plaza 247-8444

LOST PELICAN (steak, seafood, cocktails)
658 Main Ave.. 247-8502
MR. ROSEWATER'S DELI
552 Main Ave.. 247-8788
MOLLY GIBSON RESTAURANT & LOUNGE
(entertainment)
1100 E. Main, Cortez. 565-9550
ORE HOUSE
147 6th Ave.. 247-5707
PALACE RESTAURANT (American, bar)
1 Depot Pl.. 247-2018
PANHANDLER PIES
948 Main Ave.. 259-1365
THE RAM RESTAURANT & LOUNGE
25926 Hwy. 550 259-1010
SILVER SPUR (country & western music)
3416 Main Ave. 247-3662
STRATER HOTEL
669 Main Ave.. 247-4431
SWEENEY'S GRUBSTEAK
1644 Country Rd. 203 247-5236
TRAVELERS ORIENTAL CUISINE
303 W. Main, Cortez 565-7366
WARM FLOW RESTAURANT (espresso, beer & wine)
937 Main Ave.. 247-9748
WINDOWS ON THE WOODS RESTAURANT & CAFE
1000 Alpine Forest Dr., Bayfield 884-9019

STORES & SKI SHOPS

ALPINE SPORTS (ski shop)
707 Main Ave.. 247-1935
AL'S LIQUORS
3225 Hwy. 550 247-1115
BLYTHE SPIRITS
At the slopes, call Ski Area
CONCEPTS IN CLOTHING (women's)
758 Main Ave.. 259-1298
DOE'S DELI & GROCERIES
175 Beatrice Dr., Purgatory 259-0988
FOUR FACES OUTDOOR SPORTS (ski shop)
144 W. 10th 247-0500
GARDENSWARTZ L SPORTING GOODS
863 Main Ave 247-2660
THE GREENERY OF DURANGO (gifts)
801 Main Ave.. 259-0663
INFERNO SKI SHOP (rental, sales, service, apparel)
49348 Hwy. 550 247-0894
LIQUOR WORLD
695 Camino del Rio 259-0144
MAC'S HERMOSA SUPERMARKET
32223 Hwy. 550, Durango. 259-0666
NEEDLES COUNTRY STORE (liquor)
3 miles south of Purgatory. 247-1221
PACESETTERS (women's clothing)
945 Main Ave.. 247-4556
PINE NEEDLE MOUNTAINEERING
835 Main Ave.. 247-8728
PURGATORY SPORTS
528 Main Ave.. 259-1485
RIO GRANDE TRADING CO. (gifts)
519 Main Ave.. 259-1745
SAFEWAY STORES
26 Town Plaza. 247-5937
SEVEN TWO-ELEVEN FOOD STORE
732 6th. 247-3188
1854 Main Ave. 247-3224
SPIRITS OF DURANGO (wines)
501 Main Ave.. 247-8640
STUART'S OF DURANGO (women's clothing)
713 Main Ave.. 247-0136
TREASURE TUNNEL (gifts)
643 Main Ave.. 247-3704
THE SKI BARN
3690 Main Ave. 247-1923
WAGONWHEEL LIQUORS
30 Town Plaza. 247-1655

STEAMBOAT

BOX L, STEAMBOAT SPRGS., CO 80477 (303) 879-0880

AREA INFORMATION

BASE ELEVATION
6,900 feet
HOURS
9:00 a.m. - 4:00 p.m.
LIFTS
13 chairs, 4 tows, 1 gondola
18,660 capacity per hour
LONGEST RUN
2½ miles
NURSERY
6 months to 7 years. . . . . 879-2220 X 2119
RACES. 879-6111
SEASON
End of November to mid-April, no snowmaking
SNOW PHONE . . . . (800) 525-2501, 879-2220
TRAILS
23% beginner, 49% intermediate, 48% advanced
TRAVEL
From Denver, 157 miles, I-70 to Rt. 9 at Silverthorne, exit No. 205, north on Rt. 9 to US 40, west to Ski Area. From Grand Junction, 200 miles, I-70 E. to exit 157, Rt. 131 N. to Ski Area.
VERTICAL DROP
3,600 feet

CAMPGROUNDS

COLD SPRINGS
Yampa, Forrest Rt. 900
DRY LAKE
Steamboat, Buffalo Pass Rd.
DUMONT LAKE
Rabbit Ears Pass, U.S. 40
GORE PASS
Toponas, Hwy. 134
GRANITE
Steamboat, Buffalo Pass Rd.

STEAMBOAT CONT.

GRIZZLY CREEK
Steamboat, Buffalo Pass Rd. - Hebron
HAHN'S PEAK LAKE
Hahn's Peak Village, Co. Rd. 129
HIDDEN LAKES
Steamboat, Buffalo Pass Rd. - Hebron
HIMES PEAK
Oak Creek, Flat Tops Wilderness
HINMAN
Clark, Co. Rd. 64
HORSESHOE
Yampa, Forest Rt. 900
MARVINE
Oak Creek, Flat Tops Wilderness
MEADOWS
Rabbit Ears Pass, U.S. 40
NORTH FORK
Oak Creek, Flat Tops Wilderness
STILLWATER
Yampa, Forrest Rt. 900
SUMMIT LAKE
Steamboat, Buffalo Pass Rd.
TRAPPERS LAKE
Oak Creek, Flat Tops Wilderness
VAUGHN LAKE
Oak Creek, Flat Tops Wilderness
WALTON CREEK
Rabbit Ears Pass, U.S. 40

EVENTS

SUMMER

COWBOYS' ROUNDUP DAYS & RODEO
4th of July weekend (5 days)
SUMMER ARTS FESTIVAL
Mid-June to mid-July
HOBIE CAT POINTS RACE
REPERTORY THEATRE
June to September
ROUTT COUNTY FAIR
Hayden in early September
RABBIT EARS HILL CLIMB CLASSIC
Bike Race in August
N.W. COLORADO HORSE SHOW
August
JACKPOT RODEOS
Friday nights throughout Summer

FALL

AUTUMN FOLIAGE TOURS
Mid-September to Mid-October
WORLD CLASS 10,000 METER RUN
September

WINTER

STEAMBOAT NORDIC GAMES
Mid-January
REPERTORY THEATRE
Late-December thru mid-April
WINTER CARNIVAL
The 2nd week of February
COWBOYS' DOWNHILL RACES
Mid-January
N.W. COLORADO ART SHOW
February

SPRING

REPERTORY THEATRE
Thru mid-April
RABBIT EARS CROSS COUNTRY SKI CLASSIC
Mid-April
CARDBOARD CLASSIC SKI RACE
Mid-April

LODGING

ALPENGLOW MANAGEMENT
(customized vacation arrangements)
All properties located at the mountain 879-3676
ANCHOR MOTEL
½ block off Lincoln Ave.
adjacent to Yampa River 879-0675
BEAR CLAW CONDOMINIUMS
On Ski Trail Lane 879-1757
BEAR POLE RANCH
Strawberry Park, 2½ miles from town 879-0576
BEST WESTERN ALPINER
Downtown Steamboat 879-1430
BEST WESTERN PTARMIGAN INN
Base of Ski Area. 879-1730
BLACK MOUNTAIN RANCH
Off Hwy. 131, N.E. of McCoy. . . . 476-1200, 926-3478
BRONZE TREE (condominiums)
Box AAA, 80499 879-1035
BRISTOL MOTOR LODGE
917 Lincoln Ave. 879-1400
BURGESS CREEK TOWNHOUSES
In the pines along Burgess Creek Rd. 879-1035
D BAR K MOTEL
1½ miles east of Ski Area on US 40. 879-3377
ELK RIVER GUEST RANCH
Seedhouse Rd.—County Rd. 129 879-3843
FISH CREEK CAMPGROUND
1 mile east of Ski Area on US 40 879-5476
FOUR SEASONS CONDOMINIUMS
Apres Ski Way, just above Village Ctr. 879-4445
GLEN EDEN RANCH
18 miles N. of Ski Area, County Rd. 129 . . . 879-3906
HARBOR HOTEL AND MOTEL
703 Lincoln St. 879-1522
HAYSTACK (dormitory & private rooms)
2030 Walton Creek Rd. 879-0587
HOLIDAY INN
E. Hwy. 40, ¾ mile from Ski Area 879-2250
HOME RANCH
Clark, CO 879-1780, 879-0469
IRON HORSE INN
On City transit route 879-0340

LARSON'S SUBALPINE LODGE
2½ miles E. on US 40, 1 mile N. on Walton Creek
On Columbine Dr., just E. of Ski Area 879-2600
LICHEN LODGE – AT RABBIT EARS
25 miles S.E. of Ski Area on Hwy. 40 724-3450
THE LODGE AT STEAMBOAT
200 yards from Gondola 879-6000
THE MORAINE
¾ mile from lifts 879-1035
MOUNTAIN RESORTS (condo & apt. rentals)
Clock Tower Bldg. at Ski Area 879-3700
NITE'S REST MOTEL
601 N. Lincoln Ave. 879-1212
NORDIC LODGE
1036 Lincoln Ave. 879-0531
PARK MEADOWS CONDOMINIUMS
3295 Apres Ski Way 879-9940
PINE REAL ESTATE
Walton Creek, Stormwatch, Creekside Condos 879-4175
THE PROMONTORY
Directly across from the ski mountain
Apres Ski Way 879-5000
RABBIT EARS MOTEL (east end of town)
201 Lincoln Ave. 879-1150, 879-1151
RAINBOW COTTAGES
702 Oak Street 879-1834
RAMADA INN
Off Hwy. 40 between downtown & Ski Area . 879-2900
RENDEZVOUS
1590 Kinni Kinnick Lane 879-2399
SCANDINAVIAN LODGE AND CONDOMINIUMS
Near Thunderhead Lift 879-0517
THE SHADOWS (townhomes)
½ mile from gondola 879-1035
SHERATON STEAMBOAT RESORT
At the base of Mt. Werner 879-2220
SHERATON THUNDERHEAD INN
At the base of Mt. Werner 879-0303
SKI TOWN CAMPGROUND
2 miles W. of Ski Area on US 40 879-0273
SKI TRAIL CONDOMINIUMS
Under the gondola 879-2135
SKY VALLEY LODGE
7 miles E. of Mt. Werner, off US 40 879-5158
STEPHENS COLLEGE/PERRY MANSFIELD CAMP
1½ mi. from downtown, Strawberry Park Rd. 879-1060
STORM MEADOWS
On the mountain next to chairlifts 879-1035
SUNSPORT SOLAR CONDOMINIUMS
2 blocks from gondola 879-2057, 1-484-1371
THUNDER MOUNTAIN PROPERTIES (rentals)
Ski Time Square 879-4457
VISTA VERDE GUEST RANCH
Seedhouse Rd., Clark 879-3858

RECREATION

ADVENTURE BOUND
(raft trip, Colorado River, May 31st - July 12th)
Office in lobby, Sheraton Steamboat Resort 1-824-3967
ALL SEASONS RANCH
(pack trips, high country hunts, sleigh ride dinners)
Box 412 VG, Hayden, 81639 276-3463
BUGGYWHIP'S FISH & FLOAT SERVICE
Box 568, Oak Creek 736-2530
COLORADO ADVENTURES (raft trip, 4-wheel drive trip)
Box 851, 80477 879-2039
FLOATING, INC. (raft ride)
1104 Lincoln, Box 5143, 80499 879-2553
GAMES ROOM SUBMARINE SHOP & ARCADE
Off alley across parking lot from the Cameo. . 879-9847
H LAZY RANCH
(horseback riding, trail rides, sleigh rides, fishing, hunts)
Box 2013, 80477 879-3795
HOT WATER WORKS (hot tubs in private rooms)
Next to Cinema in Ski Time Square 879-0919
OUTRAGEOUS ADVENTURES RIVER CO.
(May thru July on the North Platte River)
Box 2825, 80477 879-3505
OPEN (bowling)
29585 West US 40 879-9840
SOMBRERO STABLES
(horseback rides, pack trips, hunting, June 1st–Oct 1st)
Mt. Werner Rd. at the base of the Ski Area &
in Clark on airport road, County Rd. 129 . . . 879-2306
STEAMBOAT ATHLETIC CLUB
Adjacent to the Gallery & Storm Meadows Condos
Storm Meadows Dr.. 879-1036
STEAMBOAT AVIATION (charter flights, scenic flights)
3 miles W. of town at Steamboat Airport . . . 879-1204
STEAMBOAT LAKE STATE PARK & MARINA
(ski-boats, party-boats, sail-boats, fishing-boats, canoes)
Steamboat Lake State Park 879-3845
STEAMBOAT SPRINGS
HEALTH & RECREATION ASSOCIATION
Box 1211, 136 Lincoln Ave.. 879-1828
STEAMBOAT SPRINGS
PARKS AND RECREATION DEPT.
Family recreation 879-4300
STEAMBOAT SPRINGS
WINTER SPORTS CLUB
Howelsen Hut 879-0695
TANGLEWOOD RANCH (big game hunting)
35 miles N. of Steamboat on County Rd. 129
Just east of Columbine, Box 5219, 80499 . . . 879-3353

RESTAURANTS

BEAR POLE RANCH (entertainment)
Strawberry Park, 2½ miles from town 879-0576
THE BLACKBIRD BAKERY
Downtown 879-5999
Foothills, 1 mi. W. of town 879-4342
BRANDYWINE (beef, seafood)
8th St., downtown 879-9939
THE BUTCHER SHOP RESTAURANT (steak house)
Ski Time Square 879-2484
C.J.'s CAFE & RESTAURANT (international cuisine, bar)
Lincoln Ave. near 9th St., downtown 879-9754
CAMEO BAR & RESTAURANT (American, bar)
600 Lincoln, next to Courthouse 879-4421
CANTINA (Mexican, bar)
818 Lincoln 879-0826
THE CLOCKTOWER RESTAURANT (barbecue)
Ski Area in Clocktower Square 879-3220

STEAMBOAT CONT.

CONSERVATORY LOUNGE (cocktail lounge)
Thunderhead Inn at base of Mt. Werner 879-0303
THE COVE RESTAURANT (Chinese, cocktails)
Downtown. 879-9955
DOS AMIGOS (Mexican)
Mt. Werner Rd., Base Area. 879-4270
EL RANCHO RESTAURANT & LOUNGE
(steaks, fish, Mexican)
425 Lincoln 879-9988
THE GALLERY RESTAURANT (international, bar)
Storm Meadows Drive,
Above Storm Meadows Athletic Club 879-0239
GLEN EDEN RANCH
(Western style food, lounge, entertainment weekends)
18 mi. N. on Hwy. 129 in Clark. 879-3906
THE GOLD MINE (Italian, bar)
In town. 879-0300
GOOD TASTE CREPE SHOPPE (bar)
Good News Bldg. at 5th & Lincoln 879-4106
HOLE-IN-THE-WALL (lounge, live entertainment)
Sheraton Steamboat Inn 879-2220
L'APOGEE (French)
810 Lincoln Ave. 879-1919
LA TRATTORIA (Italian, entertainment, cocktail lounge)
Base Area in Best Western Ptarmigan Inn . . . 879-1730
MATTIE SILKS (Continental/American, bar)
Ski Time Square. 879-2441
MAZZOLA'S ITALIAN RESTAURANT & LOUNGE
Steamboat Square. 879-2405
MOTHER'S DELI (take out, catering, beer)
Ski Time Square. 879-0798
MOTHER'S DELI TOO (also ice cream)
Good News Bldg., 5th & Lincoln 879-0398
OLD WEST STEAK HOUSE (also seafood)
Old West Bldg., 11th & Lincoln. 879-1441
PANTRY NATURAL FOODS & GRANARY
Under the big pine tree
Where the river meets the park 879-2552
PINE GROVE RESTAURANT (Western, cocktails)
US 40 between town & mountain. 879-1190
RAMADA INN RESTAURANT & LOUNGE
Ramada Inn off Hwy. 40. 879-2900
RIVER BEND INN (barbecue, steak)
4½ mi. W. of Steamboat Springs on Hwy. 40 879-1615
ROBBER'S ROOST RESTAURANT (American)
Base of Mt. Werner, Sheraton Steamboat Inn . 879-2220
SCANDINAVIAN LODGE DINING ROOM
(one entree nightly)
Base of the Thunderhead & Arrowhead Lifts . 879-0517
SHORT BRANCH SALOON (bar, entertainment)
8th & Lincoln 879-3555
THE SIDESTEP (Mexican food & cocktails)
738 Lincoln Ave., downtown 879-9933
SKY VALLEY LODGE
GOLDEN EAGLE RESTAURANT
(homemade, barbecues, cocktails)
8 mi. E. of Steamboat, ¼ mi. off Hwy. 40. . . 879-5158
STUBBEL GOOS CASTLE, LTD. (French, lounge)
Village Plaza above gondola terminal 879-4411
THUNDERHEAD INN RESTAURANT (American)
Across from Ski Time Sq., on Mt. Werner Rd.. 879-0303
TUBBOAT SALOON (western saloon, entertainment)
Mt. Werner Rd. 879-9990

SERVICES

AIR

FRONTIER AIRLINES
Yampa Valley Airport, Hayden
23 miles from Ski Area. 879-0103, 879-4076
Outside Colorado . . . . (800) 225-6680
ROCKY MOUNTAIN AIRWAYS
Steamboat Airport, 6 miles from Ski Area. . . 398-3896
Outside Colorado . . . . (800) 322-1199

BANKS

ALPINE FEDERAL SAVINGS & LOAN ASSOCIATION
8th & Lincoln 879-2450
ROUTT COUNTY NATIONAL BANK
320 & 802 Lincoln Ave. 879-0550
UNITED BANK OF STEAMBOAT SPRINGS
555 Lincoln Ave. 879-4040

BUS

STEAMBOAT SPRINGS TRANSIT 879-3717
STEAMBOAT STAGE COMPANY. 879-2032

CONVENTIONS

LES GOURMETS
P.O. Box 2021, 80477 879-2613
STEAMBOAT IMAGE MAKERS
P.O. Box 2530, 80477 879-1389
THE STEAMBOAT INSTITUTE
P.O. Box 717, 80477. 795-3000

PHARMACIES

BECKETT I
806 Lincoln Ave. 879-1620
BECKETT II
Ski Time Square. 879-0424
BECKETT III
Steamboat Village Plaza 879-3193
HEALTH CENTER PHARMACY
Across from hospital 879-3320
LYON MERIT DRUG (delivery service)
Downtown, 9th & Lincoln. 879-1114
SUNDANCE DRUG MART
Next to Safeway 879-4611

ROAD SERVICE

BAKER AUTO SUPPLY
Foothills Shopping Plaza, W. Hwy. 40 879-4200
BOB'S DOWNTOWN CONOCO
942 Lincoln Ave. 879-9735

J.W. BREWER TIRE COMPANY
Corner of Hwy. 40 & Airport Road,
1 mile west of town. 879-4225
FOUR SEASON AUTO PARTS & SUPPLY, INC.
West Hwy. 40 879-1175
GRAY AUTOMOTIVE, INC.
29575 West Hwy. 40, next to Snow Bowl II. . 879-1840
THE OPEN ROAD (auto parts & service)
U.S. 40 W., turn right at Ford dealership. . . . 879-4256
PARK CHEVRON
1008 Lincoln Ave., across from Post Office . . 879-1065
STEAMBOAT STANDARD (tow service, engine service)
345 Lincoln Ave. 879-1165

THEATRES

DOWNTOWN & SKI TIME SQUARE 879-0181
THE DEPOT (legitimate & revival) 879-4684

STORES & SKI SHOPS

ALLEN'S – A MAN'S STORE (clothing)
828 Lincoln Ave. 879-0351
ALTAMOUNT (ski & mountaineering shop)
737 Lincoln 879-2800
ARISTOS SOUTH AMERICAN IMPORTS
Ski Time Square, Box 5146, 80499. 879-4392
BARE NECESSITIES (gifts)
Ski Time Square. 879-2929
BARE SKIN LEATHER (clothing)
At the Gondola, Steamboat Village Plaza . . . 879-2555
BEDELL'S (24 hours, beer)
3rd & Lincoln 879-0395
BEYOND REPAIR SKI & SPORTS SHOPS
Ski Time Square. 879-2354
BILL BULLOCK'S (clothing)
745 Lincoln Ave. 879-2970
BLAKE JEWELRY
Harbor Hotel, downtown, 703 Lincoln. 879-3233
THE BOTTLENECK (liquor store)
Lincoln Ave. between 7th & 8th 879-1255
BOOMTOWN BOOKSTORE
Ski Time Square. 879-3510
THE BOOTLEGGER (shoe store)
912 Lincoln Ave., Thiesen Mall 879-1996
CITY MARKET
335 Lincoln Ave. 879-3284
CLARK GENERAL STORE & LIKKER
Clark & Hahn's Peak
County Road 129. . . . . 879-3849, 879-3900
CLOCK TOWER SPORTS (rental & repair)
Clocktower Square 879-1976
COWBOY'S MERCANTILE (western store)
1104 Lincoln Ave. 879-2205
THE DAMSEL (lingerie & intimate apparel)
Ski Time Square. 879-3010
DAN BYFORD'S FLY SHOP
In Ski Haus International 879-6836
DEL'S JEWELRY
837 Lincoln Ave. 879-0940
THE DOROTHY SHOP (ladies clothing)
821 Lincoln Ave. 879-0544
DREAM ISLAND LIQUOR
Off Hwy. 40, west of town 879-2462
DREAM ISLAND SPORTING GOODS & GROCERIES
West Hwy. 40 879-2467
THE ELEPHANT'S TRUNK (shoe & toy store)
Sundance Plaza between town & mountain . . 879-3468
THE FAIR EXCHANGE (used & new clothing, etc.)
9th & Lincoln, downtown 879-3511
FRONT PAGE (gifts, jewelry)
5th & Lincoln, Good News Bldg. 879-2180
GRANT'S JUNIORS (children's store)
807-811 Lincoln Ave. 879-4581
HARWIGS SADDLERY & WESTERN WEAR
911 Lincoln Ave. 879-0910
THE HOMESTEADER (gourmet, gift store)
127 11th St. 879-5880
INSIDE EDGE SPORTS
Centennial Mall in Craig 879-1250
F.M. LIGHT & SONS (Western clothing)
Clock Tower Square 879-1822
MOUNTAINCRAFT
Sundance Plaza next to Safeway 879-2368
810 Lincoln Ave. 879-2364
NAVAJO CRAFTSMAN (Indian arts shop)
Base Area 879-2707
PACKRAT MOUNTAINEERING
Steamboat Square. 879-4327
PADDLEWHEEL GIFT SHOP
Across from Gondola Parking lot 879-5485
PLAZA LIQUOR
Steamboat Village Plaza 879-3174
ROCKY MOUNTAIN GEM & JEWELRY
851 Lincoln Ave., downtown 879-3309
SKI HAUS INTERNATIONAL
845 Lincoln Ave. 879-0385
At Storm Meadows Athletic Club
Storm Meadows Dr.. . . . . 879-1035 X 147
SKYLINE JEWELERS
Ski Time Square. 879-4261
SPORT STALKER
Next to the Gondola 879-0371
STEAMBOAT BAGGAGE COMPANY
Steamboat Square. 879-3558
STEAMBOAT KIDS' INC. (children's clothing)
118 8th. 879-1318
STEAMBOAT SPRINGS SPORTING GOODS
908 Lincoln Ave. 879-1240
STEAMBOAT VILLAGE SKI SHOP & THE PIER
Ski Time Square. 879-2445
STRAIGHTLINE FLY & TACKLE SHOP
Harbor Hotel, 7th & Lincoln 879-9717
STARTING GATE (ski & sport shop, rentals)
Steamboat 879-4321
VILLAGE CENTER LIQUORS
2275 Ski Trail Lane. 879-3238
VILLAGE CENTER SKI RENTALS (repair)
Next to Base Area parking lots 879-3237
WERNER'S STORM HUT
Steamboat Village Plaza (rental & repairs). . . 879-1645
906 Lincoln Ave. (ski fashions) 879-0916
At Steamboat Ski Touring Center. . . 879-2220 X 2295

STEAMBOAT CONT.

WINE RACK (party planning)
Ski Time Square. 879-0485

WHATNOT SHELF (bookstore)
Sundance Plaza 879-5292

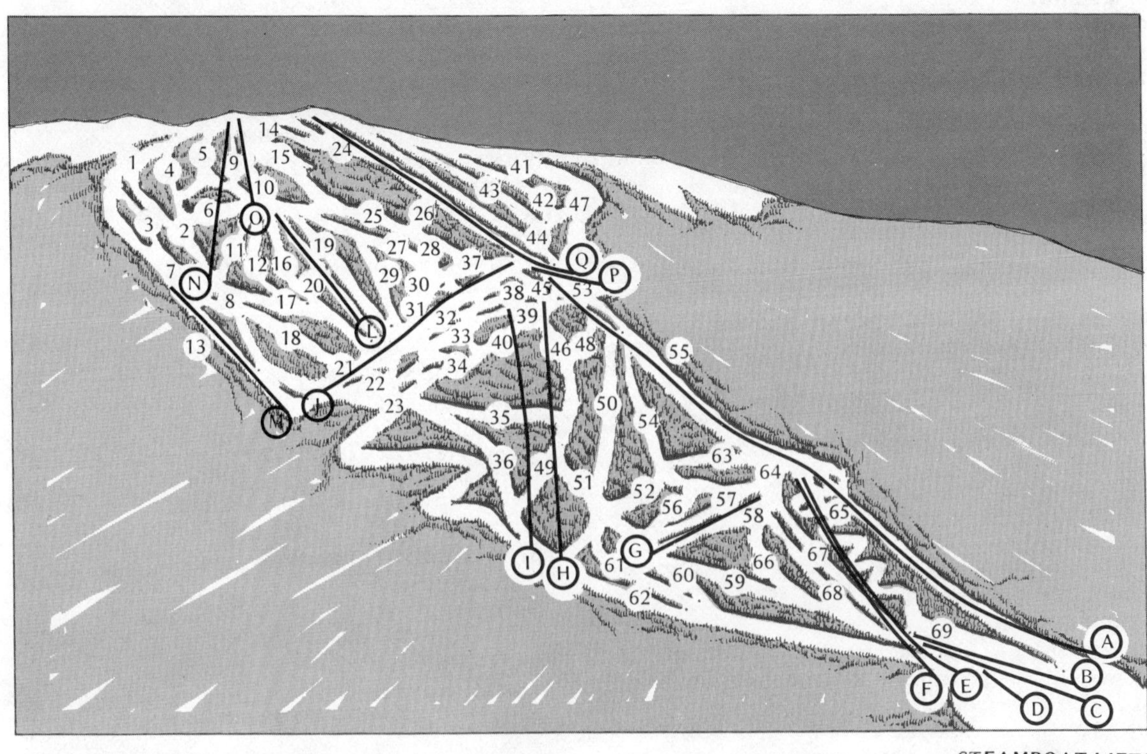

STEAMBOAT RUNS

1 BIG MEADOW
2 FLYING Z (1)
3 FLYING Z (2)
4 CROWTRACK
5 BUDDY'S RUN
6 MEADOW LANE
7 WAPITI
8 ROUNDUP
9 TRIANGLE
10 CALF ROPER
11 CYCLONE
12 TYPHOON
13 DROPOUT
14 TRAVERSE
15 STORM PEAK
16 TORNADO
17 TORNADE LOANE
18 LOWER CYCLONE
19 TWISTER
20 EGO
21 FLAT POINT
22 SUNRISE
23 SO WHAT
24 SHADOWS
25 SUNSET
26 DAWN
27 RAINBOW
28 DUSK
29 MOONLIGHT
30 PARK LANE
31 RAINBOW
32 BLIZZARD
33 LIGHTNING
34 WHY NOT
35 BETWIXT
36 VAGABOND
37 SKYLINE
38 NORTHER
39 CENTRAL PARK
40 VAGABOND
41 HIGH NOON
42 TWO O' CLOCK
43 TWILIGHT
44 DAYBREAK
45 TOWER
46 CONCENTRATION
47 LOWER HIGH NOON
48 OOPS
49 LOWER CONCENTRATION
50 TED'S RIDGE
51 EAGLE'S NEST
52 MAIN DRAG
53 SPUR RUN
54 VERTIGO
55 HEAVENLY DAZE
56 BIGFOOT
57 BEAR CLAW
59 SHORT CUT
60 GIGGLE GULCH
61 SWINGER
62 RIGHT-O-WAY
63 JESS CUT-OFF
64 SITZ
65 YOO HOO
66 VOGUE
67 SEE ME
68 VOODOO
69 HEADWALL

STEAMBOAT LIFTS

A STAGECOACH
B SOUTHFACE
C HEADWALL
D PREVIEW
E CHRISTIE II
F CHRISTIE III
G BASHOR
H THUNDERHEAD
I ARROWHEAD
J BURGESS CREEK
K (TO BE BUILT)
L FOUR POINTS
M WJW
N BAR UE
O SUMMIT
P ELKHEAD
Q PRIEST CREEK

T E L L U R I D E

BOX 307, TELLURIDE, CO 81435 (303) 728-3856

AREA INFORMATION

BASE ELEVATION
8,735 feet

HOURS
9 a.m. to 4 p.m.,
9:30 a.m. to 4:30 p.m. from March 15th

FACILITES (on slope)
2 restaurants, 2 bars, rental & repair. Restaurants are open 8:30 a.m. to 4 p.m. Call ski area for information.

LIFTS
6 double chairs, 6,426 capacity per hr.

LONGEST RUN
2.85 miles

NURSERY
Ages 1 - 7, 9 a.m. to 4 p.m.

SEASON
Nov. 27th to April 12th

SNOW PHONE 728-3856, 837-0793

TRAILS
455 acres, 23 miles, 21 intermediate, 15 advanced
34.5 acres beginner slopes.

TRAVEL
127 miles woutheast of Grand Junction, 67 miles from Montrose, 125 miles northwest of Durango, 79 miles north of Cortez, in the Uncompahgre National Forest.

From Grand Junction & Montrose take U.S. 50, 61 miles to Montrose; U.S. 550, 26 miles south to Ridgway; turn west on Colorado 62, 24 miles to junction with Colorado 145 at Placerville; turn east, 16 miles to Telluride. From Durango take U.S. 160 west to Cortez, 46 miles; turn north on Colorado 145, 76 miles to junction with spur at Colorado 145; turn east, 3 miles to Telluride.

LODGING

BROWN HOMESTEAD
BUSHWACKER INN
CORONET CREEK
DAHL HAUS
JOHNSTONE INN
LAST DOLLAR CONDOS
MANITOU LODGE
NEW SHERIDAN
TOMBOY INN
VICTORIAN INN

ALL FACILITIES ARE IN TOWN AT THE BASE OF COONSKIN LIFT. ALL RESERVATIONS, STREET ADDRESSES AND INFO. AVAILABLE THROUGH TELLURIDE CENTRAL RESERVATIONS (303) 728-4431

RESTAURANTS

BAKED IN TELLURIDE
127 N. Fir 728-9902
BREAKFAST AT THE JOHNSTONE
115½ N. Aspen 728-3316
CHINA MOON BAKERY
Fat Alley 728-4363
THE DELI
217 E. Colorado Ave.. 728-4254
EXCELSIOR CAFE
Missouri Boys Bldg.. 728-4250
FAR PAVILIONS
116 N. Oak 728-4441
FLORADORA
103 W. Colorado Ave. 728-9937
FLOUR GARDEN
119 S. Spruce 728-3502
ICE HOUSE
150 S. San Juan 728-4580
IRON LADLE
113 E. Colorado Ave.. 728-3337
LA PALOMA
Fir & San Juan Ave. 728-3580
MOON GYPSY
Colorado & Spruce
NEW SHERIDAN BAR
231 W. Colorado Ave.
POWDERHOUSE
226 W. Colorado Ave. 728-3622
ROMA BAR
133 E. Colorado. 728-9923
THE SENATE
123 S. Spruce 728-3683
THUNDERCHICKEN
Missouri Boys Bldg.. 728-3375

SERVICES

AIR
Frontier & Continental Airlines from Denver, United from L.A., Chicago, & San Francisco
AUTOMOTIVE
Boomerang Auto, west of Telluride. 728-3698
Chris' Towing, 200 E. Colorado. 728-3398
Mini-Mart Chevron, Hwy. 145. 728-3630
AUTO RENTALS
Boomerang Auto Service, west of Telluride . . 728-3698
BUS
Continental Trailways, daily
DAY CARE
Sally Bundy, call first. 728-4253
Rainbow Day Care, appointment suggested . . 728-3820
EMERGENCY
Clinic 728-3848
Fire. 728-3800
Sheriff 728-3931
LIMO
Tomboy Service. 728-3698
LIQUOR STORES
Rocky Mt. Spirits, 232 W. Colorado Ave. . . . 728-4400
Telluride Liquors, 219 W. Colorado Ave. . . . 728-3380
MARKET
Rose's Market, 335 W. Colorado 728-3977
PHARMACY
Sunshine Pharmacy, 236 W. Colorado 728-3601

STORES & SKI SHOPS

BETWEEN THE COVERS BOOKSTORE
218 W. Colorado Ave.
CHINA ROSE
306 W. Pacific 728-4169
THE EXAMINER (clothing)
232 W. Colorado Ave.
FINO BOUTIQUE
215 E. Colorado Ave.. 728-3567
MOTHERLODE MERCANTILE
221 W. Colorado Ave. 728-3367
OLYMPIC SPORTS
101 W. Colorado Ave. 728-4477
PACIFIC SKIS UNLIMITED
109 W. Colorado Ave. 728-3312
RITZY GYPSY
136 E. Colorado Ave.. 728-3629
SAN JUAN FLEA MARKET
206 E. Colorado Ave.. 728-4350
SMALL BUSINESS
217 E. Colorado Ave.
SMUGGLER MINE (gifts)
220 W. Colorado Ave. 728-3307
TELLURIDE SKI RENTALS
Coonskin Base, Day Lodge. 728-3856
TELLURIDE SPORTS
226 W. Colorado Ave. 728-3501
TELLURIDE TRAPPINGS & TOGGERY
109 E. Colorado Ave.. 728-3338
YOUNG'S SUPPLY
157 S. Fir 728-4196

V A I L

241 E. MEADOW DR., VAIL, CO 81657 (303) 476-1000

AREA INFORMATION

BASE ELEVATION
8,200 feet
HOURS
8:30 a.m. - 3:30 p.m.
LIFTS
17 chairs, 1 poma lift (children's),
1 gondola, 21,400 capacity per hour
LONGEST RUN
4½ miles
NURSERY
Ages 2 - 6, call Ski Area
SEASON
November - April, snowmaking
SNOW PHONE 476-4888
TRAILS
30% beginner, 40% intermediate, 30% advanced
TRAVEL
I-70, 100 miles west of Denver,
140 miles east of Grand Junction.
VERTICAL DROP
3,050 feet

EMERGENCY

AMBULANCE. 911
FIRE DEPARTMENT . . . . .476-2200 or 911
POLICE DEPARTMENT. 476-5671
VAIL VALLEY MEDICAL CENTER
181 W. Meadow Dr.. 476-2451

LODGING

CENTRAL RESERVATIONS. 476-5677

ANTLERS LODGE
680 W. Lionshead Pl. 476-2471
CHRISTIANIA AT VAIL
356 E. Hanson Ranch Rd. 476-5641
GASTHOF GRAMSHAMMER
231 East Gore Creek Dr. 476-5626
HOLIDAY INN / HOLIDAY HOUSE
13 Vail Rd. 476-5631
HOTEL SONNENALP
242 E. Meadow Dr.. 476-5656
INN AT WEST VAIL
2211 North Frontage Rd. West 476-3890
KIANDRA / TALISMAN LODGE
20 Vail Rd. 476-5081
LION SQUARE LODGE
660 West Lionshead Pl.. 476-2281
THE LODGE AT VAIL
174 E. Gore Creek Dr. 476-5011
MARIOTT'S MARK RESORT & CONVENTION CENTER
714 W. Lionshead Circle 476-4444
RAMS-HORN LODGE
416 Vail Valley Dr.. 476-5646
ROOST LODGE
1783 North Frontage Road West 476-5451
SANDSTONE CREEK CLUB
1020 Vail View Dr.. 476-4405
SITZMARK LODGE
183 Gore Creek Dr.. 476-5001
SUNBIRD LODGE
675 Lionshead Pl.. 476-5264
VAIL ATHLETIC CLUB HOTEL
352 East Meadow Dr.. 476-0700
VAIL HOME RENTALS
143 E. Meadow Dr.. 476-2221
VAIL VILLAGE INN
68 South Frontage Road East 476-5622
WESTWIND AT VAIL
548 South Frontage Road 476-5031

RESTAURANTS

ALAIN'S
223 E. Gore Creek Dr. 476-0152
ALFIE PACKERS (bar)
536 W. Lionshead Mall 476-2121
AMBROSIA
17 E. Meadow Dr.. 476-1964
BAXTER'S
278 Hanson Ranch Rd.. 476-5775
BEER & WINE STUBE
May be reached by non-skiers
via the Lionshead Gondola. . . . . . . 476-5601 X 4541
CAFETERIAS
At the slopes, Mid-Vail & Eagles Nest
CITY LIMITS (bar)
263 Gore Creek Dr.. 476-1877
COOK SHACK
At the slopes, Mid-Vail . . . . 476-5601 X 4550
CYRANOS, TOO
710 W. Lionshead Circle 476-5551
DONOVAN'S COPPER BAR
Bridge St. 476-5209
FRASIERS (bar)
Lionshead Gondola Bldg. 476-5601
GARTON'S BRIDGE STREET SALOON
285 Bridge St.. 476-2172
HONG KONG CAFE (bar)
227 E. Wall 476-1818
LOS AMIGOS (Mexican)
318 E. Hanson Ranch Rd. 476-5847
PEPI'S GASTHOF GRAMSHAMMER
(Continental restaurant & bar)
231 E. Gore Creek Dr.. 476-5626
PISTACHIOS
291 Bridge St.. 476-5070
PURCELLS (bar)
549 W. Lionshead Mall 476-2601
RED LION (bar)
304 E. Bridge St. 476-5740
SHADOWS (bar)
714 W. Lionshead Circle 476-4444
SHEIKA'S (bar)
220 E. Gore Creek Plaza 476-1515
THE SLOPE (apres ski bar)
278 Hanson Ranch Rd.. 476-5296

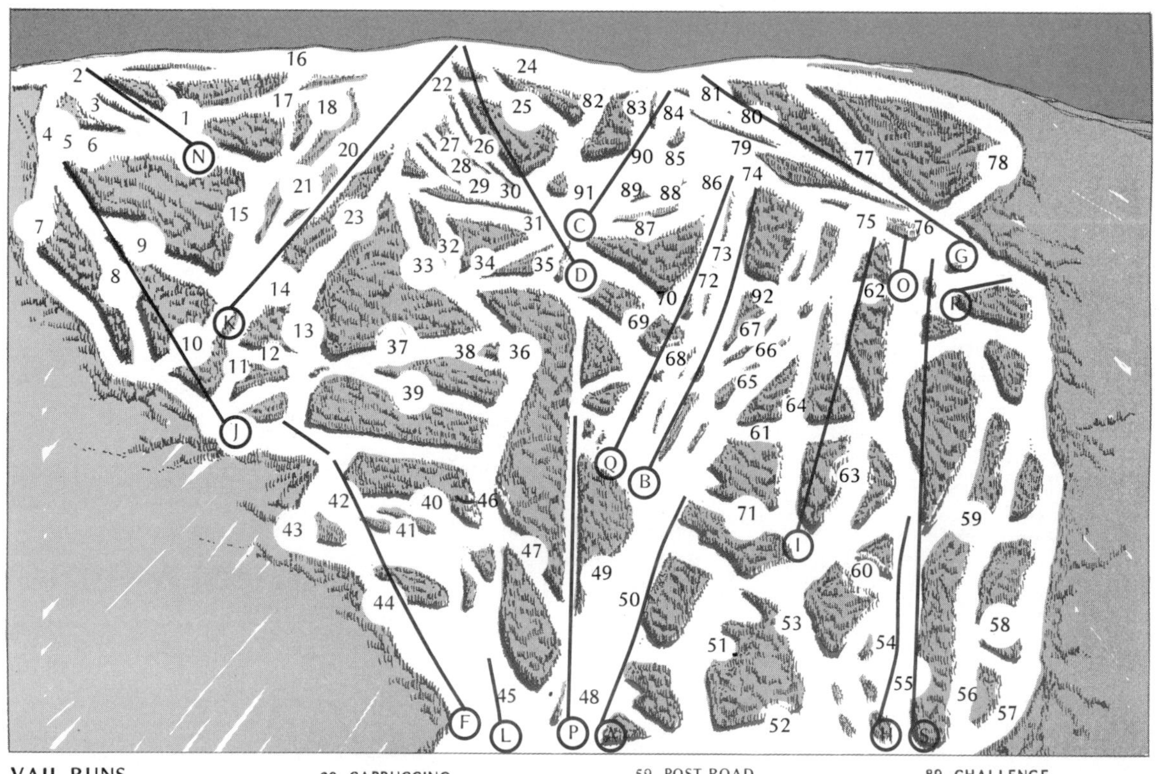

VAIL RUNS

1 WHISKEY JACK
2 SOUR DOUGH
3 BOOMER
4 TIN
5 PANTS
6 FLAP JACK
7 BLUE OX
8 HIGHLINE
9 ROGER'S RUN
10 CHOKER CUT-OFF
11 LOG CHUTE
12 FLAP JACK
13 PRIMA
14 PRONTO
15 FLAPJACK
16 SNAG PARK
17 TIMBERLINE CATWALK
18 NORTHWOODS
19 NORTHSTAR
20 GANDY DANCER
21 FIRST STEP
22 RIM RUNS
23 PRIMA
24 MINTURN MILE
25 RAMSHORN
26 ZOT
27 WHISTLE PIG
28 EXPRESSO
29 CAPPUCCINO
30 SWINGSVILLE
31 CHRISTMAS
32 RIVA GLADE
33 RIVA RIDGE
34 GITALONG ROAD
35 SPRUCE FACE
36 TOURIST TRAP
37 SKID ROAD
38 COMPROMISE
39 NORTHFACE CATWALK
40 ASPEN ALLEY
41 FOLLOW ME
42 RUDER'S RUN
43 BOO BOO
44 AFTERTHOUGHT
45 GOPHER HILL
46 FOLLOW ME ROAD
47 MILL CREEK ROAD
48 ADIOS
49 GIANT STEPS
50 INTERNATIONAL
51 BEAR TREE
52 VILLAGE CATWALK
53 BORN FREE
54 THE GLADE
55 BWANA
56 SAFARI
57 SIMBA
58 CHEETHA
59 POST ROAD
60 LION'S WAY
61 CUB'S WAY
62 OWL ROOST
63 MINNIE'S MILE
64 LEDGES
65 COLUMBINE
66 LODGE POLE
67 THE BERRIES
68 BLACK FOREST
69 SHORT CUT
70 COLD FEET
71 LIONS WAY
72 AVANTI
73 PICKEROON
74 EAGLE'S NEST RIDGE
75 OUZO
76 GAMETRAIL
77 THE WOODS
78 LOST BOY
79 FARO
80 DEUCES WILD
81 SHOWBOAT
82 THE SKIPPER
83 HUNKY DORY
84 K.C.
85 THE MEADOWS
86 JAKES JAUNT
87 MIDVALE EXPRESS
88 OVER EASY
89 CHALLENGE
90 LOOK MA
91 SOUTH LOOK MA
92 SURRENDER

VAIL LIFTS

A CHAIR 1
B CHAIR 2
C CHAIR 3
D CHAIR 4
E CHAIR 5
F CHAIR 6
G CHAIR 7
H CHAIR 8
I CHAIR 9
J CHAIR 10
K CHAIR 11
L CHAIR 12
M CHAIR 13
N CHAIR 14
O CHAIR 15
P CHAIR 16
Q CHAIR 17
R POMA
S GONDOLA

SERVICES

AIR

ROCKY MOUNTAIN AIRWAYS

Avon 949-5600
Denver 398-3896
Vail 476-4750

AUTO RENTAL

AVIS (Vail drop station)

Downtown Denver 839-1280
Vail 476-5405
Stapleton Int'l. Airport 398-3725

HERTZ (Vail drop station)

Downtown Denver 861-2128
Vail 476-5133
Stapleton Int'l Airport 398-3693

BUS

ALPINE CHARTER COACHES 668-3939

FREE SHUTTLE

Vail, Lionshead, East Vail &
Red Sandstone 476-5613, 476-2255

VAIL CONT.

LIMO

AIRPORT LIMOUSINE SERVICE. 893-6464
AMERICAN LIMOUSINE SERVICE. 424-6930

TAXI

VAIL GUIDES, INC.. .476-5387

STORES & SKI SHOPS

CHARLIES' GONDOLA SKI SHOP
482 W. Lionshead Mall. 476-1700
CHRISTY SPORTS
293 Bridge St.. .476-2244
COLORADO INSIGHT
492 E. Lionshead Circle 476-3689
GORSUCH LTD.
263 E. Gore Creek Dr. 476-2294
HEAD FIRST
227 Bridge St.. .476-3933
PEPI SPORTS
231 Bridge St.. .476-5206
SUNRISE AT VAIL LTD.
675 Lionshead Pl.. 476-1040
VAIL ASSOCIATES SKI RENTALS & REPAIRS
600 W. Lionshead Mall. . . . . 476-5601 X 4415
Gold Peak . . . . 476-5601 X 4410
VILLAGE INN SPORTS
17 E. Meadow Dr.. 476-4515
VAIL MOUNTAINEERING
500 Lionshead Mall. 476-1414

WINTER PARK MARY JANE

BOX 36, WINTER PARK, CO 80482 (303) 726-5514

AREA INFORMATION

BASE ELEVATION
9,000 feet
HOURS
8:30 a.m. to 4:00 p.m., staggered
LIFTS
12 chairs, 14,900 capacity per hour
LODGING
Central Reservations: 726-5588
LONGEST RUN
2 miles
NURSERY
6 months to 8 years, call ski area
SEASON
Late November to Late April, 20% snowmaking
SNOW PHONE
(303) 892-1453
TRAILS
52+ trails
25% beginner, 40% intermediate, 35% advanced
TRAVEL
67 miles from Denver via I-70 to Hwy. 40, Berthoud Pass
VERTICAL DROP
1,125 feet

CONNECTICUT

MOHAWK MTN.

CORNWALL, CT 06753 (203) 672-6100

AREA INFORMATION

BASE ELEVATION
1,000 feet
HOURS
9:30 a.m. to 4 p.m.
LIFTS
4 chairs, 1 poma, 6,200 capacity per hr.
LOCATION
West of Torrington, north of Litchfield and Danbury, I-8, Rt. 7 & NY 22 are fed from I-84 & Merritt Pkwy., a short drive off Rt. 4, Cornwall.
LODGING
Base Lodge includes Ticket Office, Ski Shop, Rentals, Cafeteria. Call ski area. Plenty of lodging in nearby towns. See "Location".
LONGEST RUN
1½ miles
SEASON
December to end of March
SNOWFALL
73 inches
SNOW PHONE
Cornwall 672-6100
N.Y. City. . . . . (212) 757-4455
New Haven. .467-3212
Hartford 987-6333
VERTICAL DROP
665 feet

LODGING

BONNIE BROOK MOTEL
Cornwall Bridge 672-6219
THE INN AT THE LAKE
New Preston .868-2168
INTERLAKEN INN
Lakeville 435-9878
LITCHFIELD HILL MOTEL
West Goshen. 491-3036

YANKEE PEDDLER INN
Torrington 489-9226

RESTAURANTS

THE DECK (entertainment)
West Cornwall 672-6765
YANKEE PEDDLER
Torrington 489-9926

POWDER RIDGE

MIDDLEFIELD, CT 06455 (203) 349-3454

AREA INFORMATION

BASE ELEVATION
450 feet
HOURS
9:30 a.m. to 10:30 p.m. Mon. - Thurs.,
Open until 2:30 a.m. Fridays,
6:30 a.m. to 10:00 p.m. Sat. & Sun.
LIFTS
4 chairs, 2 bars, 2 tows, 10,000 capacity per hour
LODGING
2 lodges at base, call ski area
LONGEST RUN
1½ miles
NURSERY
(800) 243-3760
(800) 622-3321 from CT
SEASON
Mid-Nov. to mid-April, 50% snowmaking
SNOW PHONE
(800) 243-3760
(800) 622-3321 from CT
TRAILS
12 trails, 30% beginner, 50% intermediate, 20% difficult
TRAVEL
20 miles from Hartford,
From N.Y. via I-95 to exit 48, I-91, to E. Main St., 2 miles to Rt. 147, right on Powder Hill Rd.
VERTICAL DROP
540 feet

IDAHO

BOGUS BASIN

1405 BOGUS BASIN RD. BOISE, ID 83702
TELEPHONE: (208) 336-4500

AREA INFORMATION

BASE ELEVATION
5,800 feet
HOURS
9:00 a.m. - 4:30 p.m.
4:30 - 10:00 p.m., night skiing - 3 chairs
LIFTS
6 chairs, 1 poma lift, 4 beginner's rope tows as needed
LONGEST RUN
Over 8,000 feet
NURSERY
Toilet trained, call Ski Area
SEASON
Late November to mid-April, no snowmaking
SNOW PHONE 342-2100
TRAILS
25% beginner, 50% intermediate, 25% advanced
TRAVEL
16 miles north of Boise. Frontier, Republic and United Airlines serve the Boise Municipal Airport. Ski Area bus or limousine will meet flights on a reservation basis.
VERTICAL DROP
1,800 feet

ALL LODGING, RESTAURANTS, SERVICES, STORES & SKI SHOPS ARE IN BOISE, 83702, UNLESS NOTED OTHERWISE.

EMERGENCY

IDAHO FIRE DEPT. 342-4561
IDAHO HIGHWAY PATROL 384-2900
POISON CONTROL . . . . (800) 632-8000
POLICE 345-8200

LODGING

BEST WESTERN SAFARI MOTOR INN
City Center 344-6556
BOISEAN MOTEL (apartments)
1300 So. Capitol Bl. 343-3645
HOLIDAY INN
(restaurant, cocktail lounge, indoor pool)
Boise Airport, I-80 & Vista Ave. 344-8365
IDANHA HOTEL
(historic landmark, dining, 1935 Rolls-Royce limousine)
10th & Main 342-3611
INTERNATIONAL DUNES
3031 Main 344-3521
OWYHEE PLAZA (2 restaurants & lounges)
11th & Main, near business district 343-4611
PIONEER INN
(restaurant, 2 outdoor whirlpools on heated deck)
At the slopes, call Ski Area
QUALITY INN
(restaurant, coffee shop)
1025 S. Capitol Bl. . . . . (800) 228-5151
RODEWAY INN (restaurant, 24 hour coffee shop)
2900 Chinden Bl. 343-1871
ROYAL INN (restaurant, lounge, indoor pool)
Boise 376-2700

THE RED LION DOWNTOWNER
(restaurant, coffee shop, bar, barber & beauty shops)
Downtown Boise 344-7691
STATEHOUSE TRAVELODGE
10th & Grove, downtown 342-4622
SUPER 8 LODGE
I-84 at Vista Ave. 344-8871

RECREATION

BOISE TOWN TRAIN (1 hour ride, summer)
4 departures daily from Museum, Julia Davis Park
THE COURTHOUSE
(racquetball, jacuzzi, saunas, excercise room, gym)
7211 Colonial 377-0040
INDIAN LAKE GOLF COURSE
4700 Umatilla Ave. 362-5771
PLEASANT VIEW RECREATION & PAR 3
(lighted driving range)
Near Airport 345-0230

RESTAURANTS

ANNABEL'S FISH RESTAURANT (reservations)
3107 Overland. 342-2602
CASA BLANCA (Mexican, live music nightly)
5200 Fairview, Mini Mall. 375-3333
THE CHART HOUSE (cocktails)
On the bank of the Boise River 336-9370
FIREWATER SALOON
Inside the Pioneer Lodge, call Ski Area
PETER SCHOTT'S CONTINENTAL
RESTAURANT & LOUNGE (entertainment nightly)
10th & Main 336-9100
RAY'S SEAFOOD RESTAURANT (steaks also)
9th & Main, Plaza Level, 1 Capital Center
SANDPIPER (entertainment in the lounge)
1100 West Jefferson 344-8911
TWIN DRAGON (Chinese-American)
2200 Fairview 344-2141
THE UPPER CRUST PIE & SANDWICH SHOPPE
109 N. 9th 344-9477

SERVICES

AUTO

GRANT'S TRUCK & CAR STOP (gas, food, 24 hours)
I-80 at Broadway, exit 54

AUTO RENTAL

BOB RICE FORD RENT-A-CAR & LEASING
3150 Main 342-6811
THRIFTY RENT-A-CAR
1801 Fairview Ave. 342-7726

BANKS

THE IDAHO FIRST NATIONAL BANK
10th St., downtown 383-7000

HOSPITALS

SAINT ALPHONSUS (24 hr. emergency/trauma center)
1055 N. Curtis Rd. 376-1211
ST. LUKE'S (24 hr. emergency outpatient dept.)
Boise 386-2344

STORES & SKI SHOPS

ANDREW BARR LTD. (men's clothing)
311 N. 8th St., Hoff Bldg., downtown 336-2737
BOISE BOOK MART (used books)
1810 W. State St. 342-3161
THE BOOK SHOP (specializing in Western Americana)
908 Main. 342-2659
OLD BOISE (over 25 shops & restaurants)
Main St., 4th thru 6th
OPEN AIR SPORTS
(equipment, cross country skiing, backpacking, running)
6899 Overland Rd. 376-4484
ORIENT EAST (jewelry & other items)
113 N. 11th. 344-6232
SKI SHOP (sales, rentals, repairs)
At the slopes, call Ski Area
SMALL SALES (Idaho handmade miniatures)
409 S. 8th St. 345-2281
WESTGATE SHOPPING COMPLEX (enclosed)
Fairview Ave. at Cole

MAGIC MTN.

P.O. BOX 158, ALBION, ID 83311 (208) 638-5555

AREA INFORMATION

BASE ELEVATION
7,400 feet
HOURS
10:00 a.m. - 4:30 p.m.
LIFTS
1 chair, 1 poma lift, 1 rope tow
1,600 capacity per hour
LONGEST RUN
1½ miles
SEASON
December to April, no snowmaking
SNOW PHONE 734-5700
TRAILS
3 easier runs, 2 more difficult, 6 most difficult
TRAVEL
Located 28 miles south of Hansen via I-80,
Kimberly/Twin Falls exit.
VERTICAL DROP
900 feet

POMERELLE

P.O. BOX 158, ALBION, ID 83311 (208) 638-5555

AREA INFORMATION

BASE ELEVATION
8,000 feet

HOURS
10:00 a.m. - 4:30 p.m., daily
4:30 - 10:00 p.m., nights - Mon. thru Sat.
LIFTS
2 chairs, 1 rope tow, 2,000 capacity per hour
SEASON
November to April, no snowmaking
SNOW PHONE 638-5555
TRAILS
16 ski runs, 4 - night skiing
TRAVEL
24 miles off I-80 via Idaho 77, Declo/Albion exit
VERTICAL DROP
1,000 feet

EMERGENCY

AMBULANCE. 678-1111
CITY POLICE. 678-1106
COUNTY SHERIFF 678-2251
FIRE DEPT.. 678-5511
HOSPITAL 678-4444

LODGING

BANNER MOTEL
917 E. Main St. 678-8393
BURLEY INN
At I-84 & Hwy. 74 678-3501
CARLOS MOTEL
803 E. Main St. 678-5534
EAST PARK MOTEL
507 E. Main St. 678-2241
EVERGREEN MOTEL
635 W. Main St.. 678-0356
GREENWELL MOTEL
904 E. Main St. 678-5576
LAMLITER MOTEL
304 E. Main St. 678-5591
PARISH MOTEL
721 E. Main St. 678-5505
PONDEROSA INN
At I-84 & Hwy. 74 678-9073
POWERS MOTEL
703 E. Main St. 678-5521
STARLITE MOTEL
500 Overland Ave. 678-7766
Y-DELL MOTEL
1331 E. Main St. 678-5542

RESTAURANTS

BURLEY INN (live music, dancing)
800 N. Overland Ave.. 678-3501
CONNERS CAFE
I-84 & Hwy. 27 678-9367
EDITH'S
E. Hwy. 30 South. 678-9859
EL MATADOR
130 W. Main St.. 678-9938
KENZO'S RESTAURANT
1242 Overland Ave.. 678-8659
NELSON'S CAFE & PILOTS CLUB (live music, dancing)
125 W. Main St.. 678-7171
PETE & MARIE'S
901 Overland Ave. 678-9393
PONDEROSA INN (live music, dancing)
North Overland 678-9073
PRICE'S CAFE
2444 Overland Ave.. 678-5149
SIX-TEN (Ben Ricks)
1054 Overland Ave.. 678-4514

STORES & SKI SHOPS

THE POWDERHORN
1336 Overland Ave.. 678-0661
SUNSET SPORTS CENTER
2159 Overland Ave.. 678-8381
VAN SANT'S YOGURT & DELI
300 E. 5th North 678-5700
VILLAGE SPORTS DEN
1061 Overland Ave.. 678-3998

ALL EMERGENCY LISTINGS, LODGING, RESTAURANTS, STORES & SHOPS ARE IN BURLEY, IDAHO 83318

SKI SCHWEITZER

BOX 815, SANDPOINT, ID 83864 (208) 263-5147

AREA INFORMATION

BASE ELEVATION
4,200 feet
HOURS
9 a.m. to 4 p.m.
LIFTS
7 chairs, 1 T-bar, 9,000 capacity per hr.
LONGEST RUN
2,000 feet
RESERVATIONS. 263-9555
SEASON
Late Nov. to April
SNOW PHONE 263-9555
TRAILS
39 runs, 20% beginner, 30% intermediate, 50% advanced
VERTICAL DROP
2,000 feet

LODGING

AT BASE

CENTRAL RESERVATIONS. 263-3331

THE ALPINE
Near the St. Bernard's Keg
BLUE BEETLES
5 minutes from lifts
THE DIE SCHMETTERLING
Next door to St. Bernard's Keg
RED CRICKET
Last stop on the main road
SCHWEITZER CREEK
On the mountain

SCHWEITZER CONT.

SCHWEITZER OVERNIGHTER
At the Ski Area
THE TAMARACKS
10 minute walk to day area

IN TOWN

CHALET MOTEL
Rt. 3, 2 miles north on Hwy. 95 263-3202
CONNIE'S MOTOR INN
323 Cedar St. 263-9581
EDGEWATER LODGE
56 Bridge St.. 263-3194
KANIKSU MOTEL
317 Cedar St. 263-8141
LAKE AIRE MOTEL
Hope, Idaho, 13½ miles east of town. 264-5512
LAKESIDE MOTEL
106 Bridge St. 263-3717
RAINBOW RESORT
Hope, Idaho, 13 miles east of town. 264-5412
SANDPOINT INN
2 miles south of town on Hwy. 95 263-4195
TRAVLRS MOTEL
807 N. 5th. 263-2111

RECREATION

BACKPACKING
Kaniksu National Forest
BOATING
Carefree Houseboating 263-5710
Page Charter Service 264-5559
Windbag 263-7811
FISHING
Lake Pend Oreille, Clark Fork River, Cocolalla Lake, Pack River, Round Lake, Big Lightning Creek, Shepherd Lake, Priest Lake
GOLF COURSE
Elks Lodge, north of town, open to public
HUNTING
Blacktail & whitetail deer, bears, elk, waterfowl
TENNIS
At city beach

RESTAURANTS

BACCALA HOUSE
Hwy. 200 East. 263-5193
CAPN'S TABLE (dinner, entertainment)
HCR 66, Garfield Bay 263-4481
CONNIE'S RESTAURANT & LODGE (family-style)
323 Cedar 263-3302
THE DONKEY JAW (steaks, Mexican)
212 Cedar 263-5337
EDGEWATER LOUNGE
56 Bridge St.. 263-3194
THE GARDEN RESTAURANT (Continental)
Sandpoint Marina 263-5187
GIBRONI'S (deli, gourmet, lunch)
2nd & Pine. 263-7423
HYDRA (cocktails, dinner)
115 Lake. 263-7123
KEG ROOM & LOUNGE (Continental)
At the area. 263-5147
THE LITEHOUSE (smorgasbord)
Off Hwy. 200, Hope 264-5514
MIDDLE EARTH TAVERN (entertainment, dancing)
1st at Church 263-3238
MOBY'S DEEP SIX (Chinese, live music)
202½ N. 1st 263-8955
P.J.'S BAR & GRILL
222 N. 1st St. 263-2313
THE PASTA HOUSE (Italian)
4th at Poplar. 263-6722
TRAVLRS RESTAURANT & LOUNGE
807 N. Fifth Ave.. 263-2111
TRUBY'S HEALTH FOOD
113 Main St.. 263-6513
WAGON BRIDGE (American, disco, live music)
U.S. 95, S. of Long Bridge 263-5013
WEIGHSIDE OMELET HAUS
202 N. Second Ave.. 263-5732

SERVICES

AUTO RENTALS

COCHRAN'S CHEVRON
5th & Cedar 263-2723
EVERGREEN FORD
4th & Cedar 263-3127

BANKS

BANK OF IDAHO, N.A.
201 E. Superior 263-2181
FIRST NATIONAL
201 Main. 263-6891

EMERGENCY

FIRE 263-2113
HOSPITAL 263-1441
POLICE 263-2114
SHERIFF 263-3136

PHARMACY

SANDPOINT DRUG
313 N. First 263-2102

STORES & SKI SHOPS

ALPINE SHOP
213 Church 263-5157
ATTIC TO CELLAR (gifts)
504 Oak St., Foster's Corner 263-5911
BARTHOLOMEW'S BOOKWORM
504 Oak, Foster's Corner 263-8122
FOUR SEASONS (women's apparel)
Downtown. 263-5522
THE GOODIE GALLERY (gifts, candies, nuts)
Gunning's Alley, ground floor. 263-2901

THE GREAT NORTHWEST FUR & TRADING POST
204 N. 1st 263-7941
THE HIDE AWAY (jewelry)
2nd at Church 263-7933
THE IMAGE MAKER (film)
320 N. 1st 263-5322
LARSON'S (clothing)
327 N. 1st.. 263-2414
LITTLE BITS (gifts)
504 Oak, Foster's Crossing. 263-4422
NORTH COUNTRY BIKE & SKI
North Boyer 263-6630
THE OUTDOOR CONNECTION (skiing, backpacking)
110 S. 1st 263-7723
SANDPOINT SADDLERY (western)
504 Oak, Foster's Crossing. 263-6112
VANDERFORD'S (books, gifts, etc.)
201 Cedar 263-2417

SUN VALLEY

SUN VALLEY, ID 83353 (800) 635-8261
TELEPHONE FROM ID: (208) 622-4111

AREA INFORMATION

BASE ELEVATION
5,800 feet
HOURS
9:00 a.m. - 4:00 p.m.
LIFTS
8 doubles, 8 triples, 22,500 capacity per hour
LONGEST RUN
3 miles
NURSERY
Call Ski Area
SEASON
Mid-December to early-April, snowmaking
SNOW PHONE
Call Ski Area
TRAILS
34% beginner, 46% intermediate, 20% advanced
TRAVEL
300 miles from Salt Lake City, north on I-15 to I-84 N.; west on I-84 to Hwy. 75 N. From Boise, 150 miles, I-84 E. to Rt. 20 N. to Hwy. 75 N. From Idaho Falls, 150 miles, I-15 S. to I-84 W. to Hwy. 75 N. From Twin Falls, 81 miles via Hwy. 75 N. Also see "Air" and "Bus" under Services.
VERTICAL DROP
3,400 feet

EMERGENCY

AMBULANCE. 726-8234
FIRE 726-8234
HOSPITAL 622-3323
POLICE 622-5345
SHERIFF 788-2271

LODGING

ATELIERS CONDOS
Studio suites & 2 bedroom units, daily maid service
COTTONWOOD CONDOS
Studio to 4 bedrooms, daily maid service
DOLLAR MEADOWS CONDOS
Studio to 4 bedrooms, daily maid service
LODGE APARTMENT
1 - 3 bedrooms, daily maid service
SNOWCREEK CONDOS
Studio to 4 bedrooms, daily maid service
SUN VALLEY INN
Dining, full service
SUN VALLEY LODGE
Dining, full service
VILLAGER I & II CONDOS
Studio to 4 bedrooms, daily maid service
WILDFLOWER CONDOS
1 - 3 bedrooms, daily maid service

ALL LODGING MAY BE REACHED BY CALLING (800) 635-8261; IN IDAHO, (208) 622-4111.

RECREATION

BOWLING
Lodge basement
HOCKEY
Sun Valley Suns, behind the Lodge
ICE SKATING
Behind the Lodge, rentals
JACUZZI
Olympic pool, near Wildflower Condos
MASSAGE
By appointment, main floor lodge
OPERA HOUSE
First run movies, dance performances
POOL
2, the Lodge & the Inn cocktail service at the Lodge
SAUNA
Men's & women's, near the pool at the Lodge
WOODSIDE RACQUET CLUB
Inside tennis. 788-3475

RESTAURANTS

BERT'S OTHER PLACE
Alcorn Village 622-4241
CABANA
312 E. Ave., Ketchum 726-3818
THE CHARTHOUSE
Elkhorn Village Mall 622-4533
THE CONTINENTAL (also take-out)
Sun Valley Inn 622-4111
THE CHRISTIANA
Sun Valley Rd. 726-3388
DUCHIN DINING ROOM (gourmet)
Sun Valley Lodge 622-4111
EAST AVE
Across from the Bank of Idaho 726-5639
KETCHUM FISH MARKET
312 East Ave. North 726-8360
THE KONDITOREA (PASTRIES)
Sun Valley Mall 622-4111
LA PROVANCE
Trail Creek Village 726-3032
THE HOBBIT INN
4th & Walnut 726-4303

LITTLE ANNIE'S (desserts)
Across from Louis' 726-5484
MULVANEY'S SALOON
Center of Ketchum 726-8251
THE ORE HOUSE (entertainment)
Sun Valley Mall 622-4363
PENGUINI'S (Italian)
Sun Valley Mall 622-4111
PIONEER SALOON
308 N. Main 726-3139
THE RAM (entertainment)
Sun Valley Mall 622-4111
SILVER CREEK RESTAURANT & BAR (entertainment)
271 N. Main St. 726-3314
THE RIVER STREET RETREAT
(fireside, wine cellar, reservations advised)
120 E. River St. 726-9914
SLAVEY'S
Sun Valley Rd. & Main 726-5083
SU CASA (Mexican)
2 blocks N. of Bank of Idaho 726-4210
TRAIL CREEK CABIN
Via Horsedrawn carriage 622-4111
WARM SPRINGS RESTAURANT
1 mile out on Warm Springs Rd. 726-8238

SERVICES

AIR

FRIEDMAN MEMORIAL AIRPORT
Hailey, is 12 miles from Ski Area. Runway elevation is 5,315 feet; length is 5,000 feet. VFR only, lighted runway, voluntary curfew - 10 p.m. to 6 a.m., tie downs.
FRONTIER AIRLINES
Boise, Salt Lake City
MAJOR AIRLINES
Salt Lake City
MOUNTAIN WEST
Commuter air service, Salt Lake City & Boise to Friedman Memorial Airport, Hailey 343-0990
REPUBLIC AIRLINES
Boise, Salt Lake City, Twin Falls
UNITED AIRLINES
Boise, Salt Lake City

AUTO RENTAL

AVIS
Hailey 788-2382
BUDGET
Sun Valley 622-8229
HERTZ
Sun Valley 622-3322
NATIONAL
,Sun Valley 622-8221

BEAUTY SHOP

BEAUTY SHOP (men & women by appointment)
In the Lodge, call Ski Area

BUS

BOISE-WINNEMUCCA STAGES
Service from Boise 336-3300
GREYHOUND
Service from Salt Lake City . . . . (801) 355-4684
LEWIS BROS
Service from Salt Lake City . . . . (801) 359-8677
STAR VALLEY JACKSON STAGES
Service from Idaho Falls 522-0210
SUN VALLEY STAGES
Service from Boise, Idaho Falls, Twin Falls . . 733-3921
TRAILWAYS
Service from Salt Lake City . . . . (801) 328-8121

CLEANERS

SUN VALLEY VALET SHOP (laundry, dry cleaning)
In the Village . . . . 622-4111 X 2447

DRUG STORES

CHATEAU DRUG
Giacobbi Square. 726-5696
KETCHUM DRUG & GIFT CENTER
Main St. 726-3411

LIMO

SUN VALLEY STAGES
From Twin Falls Airport. 733-3921

TAXI

SUN VALLEY TAXI-LIMO 726-3260

STORES & SKI SHOPS

ASPEN SPORTS (skiis, boots, winter clothing)
The Colonnade 726-3361
ATKINSONS' MARKET
(will deliver you & your groceries to your place)
Giacobbi Square. 726-5668
BACKWOOD MT. SPORTS
75 at Warm Springs 726-8818
CARROLL'S (ladies' clothing)
Giacobbi Square. 726-5055
CHATEAU DRUG & TRUE VALUE HARDWARE STORE
Giacobbi Square. 726-5696
EX LIBRIS BOOKS & UPSTAIRS GALLERY
Sun Valley Mall 622-8174
FIGA (fashions for men & women)
Sun Valley Mall, call Ski Area
F-STOP (film, cameras, 24 hr. color prints, loaners)
Sun Valley Mall, call Ski Area
FRIPPERY (children's clothing, toys)
In the Village, call Ski Area
KETCHUM DRY GOODS (men & women)
The Colonnade 726-9624
KID'S STUFF (toys, books, crafts & clothes)
Giacobbi Square, basement level 726-4301
KIVA (Indian jewelry, crafts, artifacts)
In the Village, call Ski Area

LODGE SHOP (gift shop, jewelry)
At the slopes, call Ski Area

MAGIC POSTER (Sun Valley posters, photography service)
In the Village, call Ski Area

NICKI'S HANG'UP (frame shop & Art Gallery)
Vargold Lane 726-5079

THE OUTER SHELL (natural shampoos, lotions, & oils)
100 Leadville Ave. 726-3962

THE PICKET FENCE (linens)

PETE LANE'S (ski equipment, repair, rental, ski clothes)
Sun Valley Mall, call Ski Area

RAGS TO RICHES (winter clothing)
4th & East Ave. 726-8386

THE SHEEPSKIN COAT FACTORY (rugs, quilts, toys)
4th St. 726-3588

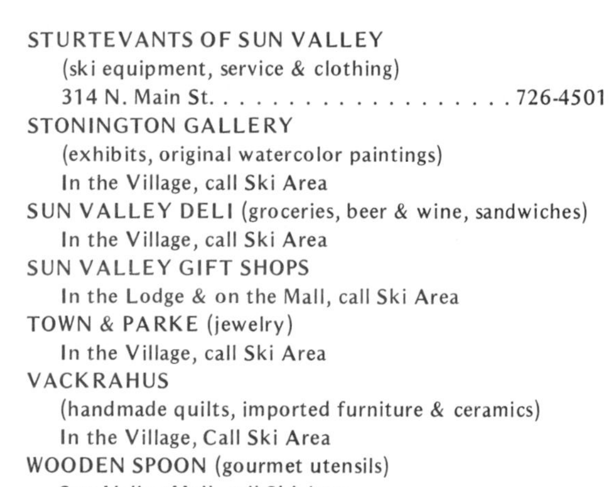

STURTEVANTS OF SUN VALLEY
(ski equipment, service & clothing)
314 N. Main St. 726-4501

STONINGTON GALLERY
(exhibits, original watercolor paintings)
In the Village, call Ski Area

SUN VALLEY DELI (groceries, beer & wine, sandwiches)
In the Village, call Ski Area

SUN VALLEY GIFT SHOPS
In the Lodge & on the Mall, call Ski Area

TOWN & PARKE (jewelry)
In the Village, call Ski Area

VACKRAHUS
(handmade quilts, imported furniture & ceramics)
In the Village, Call Ski Area

WOODEN SPOON (gourmet utensils)
Sun Valley Mall, call Ski Area

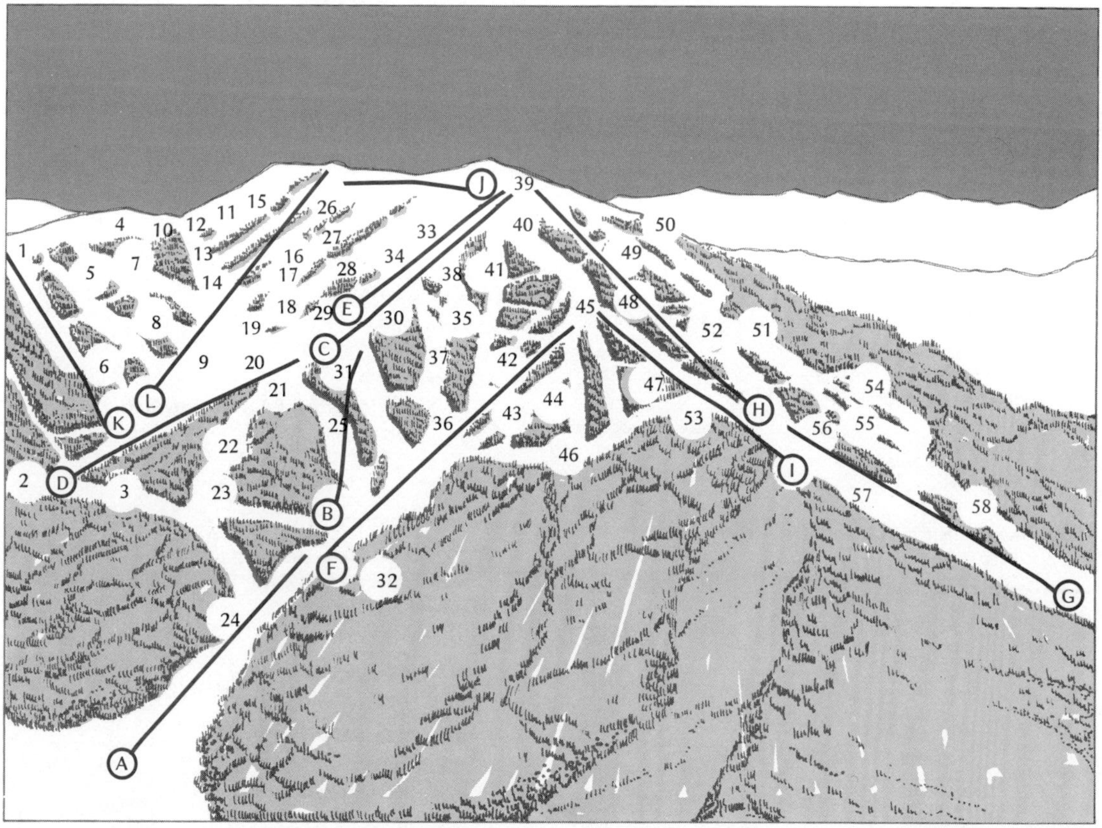

SUN VALLEY RUNS

1 GRETCHEN'S GOLD
2 LOWER BROADWAY
3 OLYMPIC RIDGE
4 SEATTLE RIDGE
5 SOUTHERN COMFORT
6 HOUR GLASS
7 SILVER FOX
8 BYRON'S PARK
9 COLD SPRINGS CUT OFF
10 BROADWAY
11 BROADWAY FACE
12 NO NAME BOWL
13 FAR OUT BOWL
14 LEFTY BOWL
15 MAYDAY BOWL
16 LOOKOUT BOWL
17 LITTLE EASTER BOWL
18 CHRISTMAS BOWL
19 GUN TOWER LANE
20 INHIBITION
21 ROUND HOUSE SLOPE
22 OLYMPIC
23 LOWER OLYMPIC
24 LOWER RIVER RUN
25 EXHIBITION
26 EASTERN BOWL
27 CHRISTMAS RIDGE
28 RIDGE
29 RIDGE SO SLOPES
30 ROUND HOUSE LANE
31 CANYON
32 CLIFF AREA
33 BLUE GROUSE
34 UPPER HOLIDAY
35 CUT OFF
36 LOWER HOLIDAY
37 MID RIVER RUN
38 UPPER RIVER RUN
39 BALD MOUNTAIN
40 UPPER COLLEGE
41 CENTRAL PARK
42 SUNNYSIDE 6
43 LOWER COLLEGE
44 GRADUATE
45 FLYING SQUIRREL
46 LILLY MARLANE
47 PLAZA
48 LIMELIGHT
49 WARM SPRINGS FACE
50 INTERNATIONAL
51 UPPER GREY HAWK
52 MID WARM SPRINGS
53 FLYING MAID
54 COZY
55 HEMINGWAY
56 MID GREYHAWK
57 LOWER WARM SPRINGS
58 LOWER GREYHAWK

SUN VALLEY LIFTS

A LOWER RIVER RUN
B EXHIBITION
C CHRISTMAS
D COLD SPRINGS
E RIDGE
F SUNNYSIDE
G LOWER WARM SPRING
H LIMELIGHT
I FLYING SQUIRREL
J LOOKOUT
K SEATTLE RIDGE
L MAYDAY

S U N D O W N

9000 ASBURY RD., DUBUQUE, IA 52001 (319) 556-6676

AREA INFORMATION

HOURS
Mon. thru Sun., 9 a.m. - 10 p.m.
LIFTS
1 double, 1 triple, 1 quad trail,
3 rope tows, 6,000 capacity per hr.
RENTALS
At the slope
SEASON
Dec. 1st thru Mar. 15th
SNOW PHONE
556-0100
TRAVEL
Hwy. 20 to JFK, N. on JFK to
Asbury Rd., Left (W.) on Asbury Rd.
5½ hrs. to ski area from Dubuque.

LODGING

CHATEAU MOTEL
3750 Central. 556-2120
CORRAL MOTEL
1280 Dodge 556-1551
DODGE HOUSE MOTEL
701 Dodge. 556-2231
DUBUQUE INN
U.S. 20 West. 556-7760
GLENVIEW MOTEL
1050 Rockdale Rd.. 556-2661
HOLIDAY INN
1111 Dodge 556-3340
JULIEN MOTOR INN
200 Main St.. 556-4200
MIDWAY MOTOR LODGE
3100 Dodge St. 557-8000
REGAL 8 INN
Hwy. 20 West 556-0880
SIESTA MOTEL
Hwy. 20 556-4411
SWISS INN
Hwy. 20, E. Dubuque 742-3136
TIMMERMAN'S MOTOR INN
East Dubuque 742-3181

ALL LODGING, RESTAURANTS & SERVICES ARE IN DUBUQUE, 5 MILES FROM THE SKI AREA, UNLESS OTHERWISE NOTED

RECREATION

ALPINE SLIDE

CHESTNUT MT. RESORT
Galena, Illinois

BICYCLING

Top of floodwall, 16th St. North to the Point

SUBMARINA SANDWICH SHOP (rentals)
3265 Central Ave.. 556-0310
TAYLOR RENTALS
3330 Asbury Rd. 557-1301

BOATING

ARROWHEAD MARINA
Mud Lake Rd.. 552-2303
DUBUQUE MARINA
Eagle Point. 582-3653
DUBUQUE YACHT BASIN
1630 E. 16th St. 556-7708
FRENTRESS ST. MARINA
Rt. 1, E. Dubuque . . . . (815) 742-3155

TENNIS

EAGLE POINT PARK (lighted)
Shiras Ave.
FLORA PARK (lighted)
2565 Green St.
MURPHY PARK
S. Grandview Ave.
VETERANS MEMORIAL PARK (lighted)
Kane & Northview

RESTAURANTS

AVALON SUPPER CLUB
Richardsville. 552-2121
THE BISTRO RESTAURANT & LOUNGE (entertainment)
951 Main St.. 588-3131
THE BRIDGE RESTAURANT & LOUNGE (entertainment)
31 Locust St. 557-7280
CHATEAU SUPPER CLUB (entertainment)
3750 Central Ave.. 588-2341
THE CIRCLE (entertainment)
90 Sinsinawa. 742-3812
COCK-N-BULL (entertainment)
701 Dodge. 556-2231
DEMETRI'S RESTAURANT
665 Dodge. 556-9460
THE DODGE HOUSE
3400 Dodge 556-7760
THE DUBUQUE MINING CO. (entertainment)
Kennedy Mall 557-1729
HOFFMAN HOUSE (night club)
3100 Dodge 557-8900
MARIO'S ITALIAN RESTAURANT
1928 Main St. 556-9424
THE MONTE CARLO
378 Main St.. 583-9532
THE MORACCO (entertainment)
1413 Rockdale Rd.. 582-2947

THE RYAN HOUSE
1375 Locust 556-9900
SFIKAS
401 Central 582-8140
THE VILLAGE INN
1940 J.F.K. Rd.. 556-0893

SERVICES

AIRLINES

BEYER AVIATION, Municipal Airport 556-7300
MISSISSIPPI VALLEY AIRLINES, Airport. . . . 556-5910
MUNICIPAL AIRPORT 582-1715
OZARK AIRLINES 588-1471

AUTO RENTAL

AVIS, Airport. 556-0656
HERTZ
285 Locust St.. 588-2005
LINCOLN-MERCURY RENTAL
245 Railroad Ave.. 556-3281
NATIONAL, Airport 583-6729

BUS LINES

GREYHOUND
Union Bus Depot 583-3397
IOWA COACHES, INC.
1180 E. Roosevelt 556-5385

SHOPPING AREAS

ASBURY SQUARE
Asbury & Kennedy Rds.
CENTURY PLAZA
Along Century Dr.
HILLCREST SHOPPING AREA
Kennedy Rd. & Hillcrest St.
INN PLAZA
Hwy. 20 West by Dubuque Inn
KENNEDY MALL
Kennedy Rd. & Hwy. 20
PLAZA 20
Hwy. 20 at Devon St.
TOWN CLOCK PLAZA
Downtown
WARREN PLAZA
Hwy. 20 West

TAXI

A-OK YELLOW CAB. 582-1818

TRAIN

AMTRAK (daily from Chicago)
Iowa & Jones St. 556-8797
Reservations & Information . . . . (800) 621-0353

MAINE

SUGARLOAF/USA

CARRABASSET VALLEY KINGFIELD, ME 04947
TELEPHONE (207) 237-2000 RESERVATIONS 237-2361

AREA INFORMATION

BASE ELEVATION
1,637 feet
HOURS
9:00 a.m. - 4:00 p.m.
LIFTS
5 chairlifts, 5 T-bars, 1 gondola, 9,300 capacity per hour
LONGEST RUN
3 miles
NURSERY
Age 3 & cup, call Ski Area
SEASON
Mid-November to mid-April, snowmaking
SNOW PHONE
Call Ski Area, 4 a.m. to 12 midnight
TRAILS
30% beginner, 40% intermediate, 30% advanced
TRAVEL
From points south, I-95 N. to Maine Turnpike, exit 12, Rt. 4 N. to Rt. 27 N. through Kingfield to Ski Area. From Montreal and points west, east on Rt. 10 to Sherbrooke to Lennoxville, Rt. 212 S./E. to Woburn and border, Rt. 27 S. to Ski Area. From Maritimes – from Calais, Rt. 1 or Rt. 9 to Bangor, I-95 to Rt. 2 to Skowhegan, Rt. 201 to Rt. 148 to Madison, Rt. 16 to Kingfield to Ski Area.
VERTICAL DROP
2,637 feet

LODGING

CENTRAL RESERVATIONS
8:30 a.m. to 5:00 p.m.. 237-2861

ARNOLD TRAIL INN (family dining)
Stratton, 04982 246-2000
BLUE OX LODGE (apartments, maid service)
Kingfield, 04947 237-2200
CAPRICORN LODGE (nightly entertainment)
Kingfield, 04947 237-2801
COUNTRY CUPBOARD (guest house, meals)
Kingfield, 04947 265-2193
FARMINGTON MOTEL (next to restaurant)
Farmington, 04938 . . . . .778-4680, 778-2805
HOTEL CARRABASSET / LEFT BANK CONDOS
Kingfield, 04947 235-2115

JUDSON'S SUGARLOAF MOTEL
Kingfield, 04947 235-2641
LAMPLIGHTER MOTEL
(restaurant, entertainment weekends)
Downtown Stratton, 04982 246-2911
LUMBERJACK LODGE
At the base of Sugarloaf 237-2141
MOUNTAINSIDE CONDOMINIUMS (studio - 5 bedrooms)
On the mountain 237-2000
MOUNTAIN VIEW MOTEL
Rt. 27, Stratton, 04982 246-2033
THE PALACE IN THE WILDERNESS
(whirlpool, sauna, steamroom in an indoor solarium)
Kingfield, 04947 265-4000
RED STALLION (pub, dining, dancing, entertainment)
Kingfield, 04947 235-2791
STRATTON MOTEL (across from restaurant)
Stratton, 04982. 246-4171
SUGARLOAF INN / BIRCHWOOD CONDOMINIUMS
(dining, lounge, entertainment)
On the mountain 237-2701
VILLAGE SOUTH
Village Square, Ski Area 237-2000
WINTER'S INN (hilltop mansion)
Kingfield, 04947 265-5421

RESTAURANTS

ARNOLD TRAIL INN (breakfast, dinner, cocktails)
Stratton 246-2000
BUTCHER BLOCK II (hot & cold deli, take-out)
On the mountain, Village West, downstairs
CAPRICORN LODGE (cocktails, live music)
At the slopes. 237-2801
CARBUR'S (cocktails)
158 Court St., Auburn 782-2795
CHICK-A-DEE
Rt. 4 at the Auburn-Turner line. 225-3523
CHUCK WAGON (open all day)
Livermore Falls 897-4031
COUNTRY CUPBOARD (breakfast, lunch, Sat. dinner)
Across the Lord Bridge on Rt. 27, Kingfield. . 265-2193
COUNTRY MILE (Continental, wine)
Stratton 246-2131
FIDDLEHEAD'S
(cocktails, entertainment in Bauer's Back Room)
23 Pleasant St., Farmington 778-9259
GEPETTO'S
(open all day, Italian food at dinner, bar, entertainment)
On the mountain, Village West 237-2192
JAKE CASSIDY'S (lunch, dinner, cocktails)
On the mountain 237-2175
THE LAMPLIGHTER
(open all day, full bar, weekend entertainment)
On the mountain 246-2911
LONGFELLOW RESTAURANT (lunch, dinner, full bar)
Downtown Kingfield 265-4394
MA JUDSON'S (open all day, full bar)
Judson's Sugarloaf Motel, Carrabassett Valley 235-2641
MACHO'S (Mexican, steaks, seafood)
On the highway, Carrabassett Valley 235-2421
MAXWELL'S
(soups/sandwiches, full bar, apres-ski, entertainment)
Upstairs in the Base Lodge. 237-2000
ONE STANLEY AVENUE (Continental)
Kingfield 265-5541
PIONEER HOUSE (open all day, full bar)
U.S. Rt. 2, 2 mi. E. of Farmington 778-4845
RED STALLION
(steaks/seafood, full bar, after 9, rock & roll bands,)
SUGARLOAF INN (full bar, lounge, reservations advised)
On the mountain 237-2701
TRAIL'S END (steak & seafood house, lunch & dinner)
Eustis. 246-9431
THE TRUFFLE HOUND (European, wine cellar)
On the mountain, Village West 237-2355
TUFULIO'S (Italian, full bar, entertainment)
At the Valley Crossing 235-2465
THE WILDERNESS CAFE
(Continental, cocktails, also breakfast)
The Palace in The Wilderness, Kingfield 265-4000
WINTER'S INN (French, full bar)
On the hill in Kingfield. 265-5421

SERVICES

AIR

BANGOR AIRPORT (2 hr. driving time)
Bar Harbor & Delta Airlines from Boston
CARRABASSET VALLEY AVIATION
2,800 ft. runway, airport service,
fuel, car rentals, ski shuttle 235-2288
PORTLAND AIRPORT (2½ hr. driving time)
Air New England, Bar Harbor & Delta from Boston
WATERVILLE AIRPORT (1¼ hr. driving time)
Air New England from Boston

AUTO RENTAL

AVIS . . . . (800) 331-1212

AUTO SERVICE

ARNOLD TRAIL SERVICE STATION (gas, repairs)
Stratton 246-2653
SUGARLOAF SHELL (gas, repairs, tune-ups)
Access Rd., Ski Area 237-2591
VFR EXXON (full service)
North Anson. 635-2303

BANKS

FIRSTBANK
Downtown Kingfield 265-2502
KINGFIELD SAVINGS BANK
On the mountain 237-2181
Kingfield 265-2181

DRUG STORE

HOWARD'S REXALL DRUGS
Farmington 778-2695

GROCERIES

BUDS MARKET (beer, wine)
Kingfield 265-5451
BUTCHER BLOCK II (beer, wine, deli)
Village West 237-2400
NADEAU'S STORE
Stratton 246-2551
NORTHLAND CASH SUPPLY (beer, wine)
Stratton 246-2376

LAUNDROMAT

VALLEY CROSSING LAUNDROMAT
(self-service or drop-off)
At the Crossing or on the mountain 235-2274

LIQUOR

AYOTTE'S COUNTRY STORE (Agency Liquor Store)
The Valley 235-2443

TAXI

SUGARWHEELS
(shuttle & taxi service, by reservation
between Ski Area, airports, & terminals)
Ski Area 237-2133, 237-2861

STORES & SKI SHOPS

EMERY'S (clothing)
On Broadway in Farmington 778-4787
EVERYDAY MUSIC (tapes, records, sheet music)
Rt. 2 & 4, Mt. Blue Center, Farmington 778-3483
FERRARI BROS. (men's clothing)
Farmington 778-4866
GAIL'S GARB (women's clothing, accessories)
On the mountain, Village West 237-2112
HANGING LOCKER (casual & outdoor clothing)
On the mountain, Village South. 237-2657
JACKMAN'S CRAFT SHOP (slate & pewter gifts)
Valley Crossing 235-2961
NORTHERN LIGHTS (Alpine & Nordic skiing equipment)
Farmington 778-6566
ONCE UPON AN ISLAND (gifts)
On the mountain, Village West 237-2293
THE SKI RACK (full service ski shop)
Sugarloaf Access Road, Livermore Falls 237-2792
THE SKI SHOP AT SUGARLOAF (full service)
On the mountain, Village Center 237-2000
THAYER-DIGGERY (Western clothing)
Valley Crossing 235-2459
TRANTEN'S GENERAL STORE
Kingfield 265-2202

SUNDAY RIVER

BETHEL, ME 04217 (207) 826-2187

AREA INFORMATION

BASE ELEVATION
980 feet
HOURS
9:00 a.m. - 4:00 p.m., Mon. - Fri.
8:00 a.m. - 4:00, weekends & holidays
LIFTS
1 chair, 3 T-bars, 1 poma lift
4,350 capacity per hour
LONGEST RUN
3 miles
NURSERY
Ski school, ages 2 & up, call Ski Area
SEASON
Mid-November to early May, snowmaking
SNOW PHONE
Call Ski Area
TRAILS
25% beginner, 50% intermediate, 25% advanced
TRAVEL
Just north of Bethel, on U.S. 2 E. on the way to Newry and Rumford. Turn left approximately 3 miles north of the road interchange at Bethel.
VERTICAL DROP
1,630 feet

LODGING

BETHEL INN & COUNTRY CLUB (restaurant)
Broad & Main Streets. 824-2175
BETHEL SPA MOTEL
Main St. 824-4989
CONRAD'S TOURIST HOME
Main St. 824-2505
FRIENDSHIP INN - LINNELL MOTEL
Rt. 2, Rumford, 04276. 364-4511
GOODWIN'S MOTEL
Main St., South Paris, 04281 743-5121
JOMAR MOTEL & RESTAURANT
Rt. 2, Shelburne, NH 03581. . . . . . . (603) 466-9491
KIMBALL'S MOTEL
Rt. 2, Rumford Center, 04278 364-4495
L'AUBERGE
Mill house 824-2774
MADISON MOTOR INN (restaurant)
Rt. 2, East Rumford, 04276. 364-7973
MOLLYOCKET MOTEL (indoor pool)
Rt. 2, West Paris, 04289 674-2345
NORSEMAN INN
Route 2 824-2002
PHILBROOK FARM INN (dining, reservations only)
North Rd., Shelburne, NH 03581. . . . (603) 466-3831
SHELBURNE BIRCHES MOTOR INN
Rt. 2, Shelburne, NH 03581. . . . . . . (603) 466-3941
SOUTH RIDGE CONDOMINIUMS (1 - 3 bedrooms)
On the mountain, call Ski Area

SUNDAY RIVER CONT.

TOWN & COUNTRY LODGE (restaurant, entertainment)
Rt. 2, Gorham, NH 03581 . . . . (603) 466-3315

ALL LODGING IS IN BETHEL, 04217, UNLESS NOTED OTHERWISE.

RESTAURANTS

BETHEL SPA RESTAURANT (open all day)
Main St., Bethel 824-2810

BOILER ROOM (German)
Bryant Pond . . . . . Ask Operator for Bryant Pond 100

BULL DOG DINER (breakfast, lunch)
Railroad St., Bethel. 824-2295

JORDAN'S (open all day, closed Weds.)
Locke Mills 875-3515

MOTHER'S
(sandwiches, quiches, homemade soups, full bar)
Main St., Bethel 824-2589

SUNDAY RIVER CAFETERIA & CASCADES LOUNGES
(breakfast, lunch, full bar, til 4, lounge til 5:30)
Main Lodge at the Ski Area

MASSACHUSETTS

BERKSHIRE EAST

S. RIVER RD. CHARLEMONT, MA 01339
TELEPHONE (413) 339-6617

AREA INFORMATION

LIFTS
4 chairs, 1 T-bar, 1 J-bar, 2 tows

LONGEST TRAIL
2 miles

NURSERY
1 - 7 years, between Ticket Office & Main Lodge

SNOW PHONE . . . . (800) 628-5030

TRAILS
19, 6 easy, 4 intermediate, 9 difficult

TRAVEL
Minutes from I-91 on Rt. 2, 63 miles from Albany, 77 miles from Hartford, 35 miles from Pittsfield, MA

VERTICAL DROP
1,180 feet

EMERGENCY

AMBULANCE. 339-4460
FIRE 339-4460
MEDICAL CENTER 625-9717
POLICE 625-2390
STATE POLICE. 625-6311

LODGING RESTAURANTS

CHARLEMONT INN (food, lodging)
Route 2 339-4910

HILLTOP (lodging)
Route 2, Shelburne Falls. 635-2587

OLDE WILLOW (food, lodging)
Route 2, East Charlemont 339-4483

OXBOW (food, lodging)
Route 2, East Charlemont 625-6729

RED ROSE (lodging)
Route 2, East Charlemont 636-2666

BRODIE MTN.

RT. 7, NEW ASHFORD, MA 01237 (413) 443-4752

AREA INFORMATION

BASE ELEVATION
11,450 feet

EMERGENCY
Ambulance. 458-3719
Fire 445-4559
Hospital 499-4161
Police. 443-4107

HOURS
9 a.m. - 11 p.m., open all week

LIFTS
3 double chairs, 6,000 per hr. capacity

LONGEST RUN
1½ miles

NURSERY
6 months to 8 years, call ski area

SEASON
November thru April

SNOWPHONE. 443-4751

TRAILS
17 miles, 30% beginner, 50% intermediate, 20% difficult

TRAVEL
From Boston 130 miles west on Rt. 2, south on Rt. 7. From New York, 160 miles north on Taconic Pkwy., east on Rt. 295, Rt. 22 N. to Rt. 43 E. to Brodie Mt. Rd., east to Rt. 7 N.

VERTICAL DROP
1,250 feet

LODGING

ADAMS

ADAMS BERKSHIRE INN
Commercial St., Rt. 8 743-2960

NEW ASHFORD

BASE LODGE
Brodie Mountain 443-4752

CARRIAGE HOUSE
Route 7 458-5359
DUBLIN HOUSE
Route 7, Brodie Mountain 443-4752
NEW ASHFORD INN
Route 7 458-8041
SPRINGS MOTOR INN
Route 7 458-5945

NORTH ADAMS

AIRPORT TOURIST HOME
861 State Rd. 663-5272
REDWOOD MOTEL
915 State St.. 664-4351
SHERATON INN
40 Main St. 664-4561

WILLIAMSTOWN

BERKSHIRE HILLS MOTEL
Junction Routes 2 & 7 458-3950
CHIMNEY MIRROR MOTEL
Route 2 458-5202
COZY CORNER MOTEL
1 Sand Springs Rd. 458-5677
1896 MOTEL
Cold Spring Rd.. 458-8125
FOUR ACRES MOTEL
Rt. 2, State Rd. 458-8158
GREYSTONE LODGE
28 Southnorth St.. 458-3948
LE JARDIN INN
Cold Spring Rd.. 458-8032
MAPLE TERRACE MOTEL
555 Main St.. 458-8108
NORTHSIDE MOTEL
45 North St.. 458-8107
SWISS MEADOWS
Rt. 43, Hancock Rd. 458-8111
TREADWAY / WILLIAMS INN
Routes 2 & 7 N.. 458-9371
THE VILLAGER MOTEL
Route 7 N.. 458-4046
WILLOWS MOTEL
State Rd.. 458-5768

RECREATION

ALPINE SLIDE

JIMINY PEAK RESORT. 548-5771

BOATING

HOSSAC LAKE
Cheshire
MAUSERT'S POND
Clarksburg State Park
NORTH POND
Savoy Mtn. State Forest
WINDSOR LAKE
N. Adams

CAMPING - PRIVATE

CHARLEMONT
Mohawk Park, off Rt. 2 339-4470
FLORIDA
Chilson's Pond, Tilda Hill Rd.. 664-6001
NEW ASHFORD
Brodie Mtn. Campground, Rt. 7. 443-4754
NORTH ADAMS
Historic Valley Park, Windsor Lake. 664-9228
SAVOY
Shady Pines, Loop Rd.. 743-2694
WILLIAMSTOWN
Privacy Campgrounds, Rt. 43 458-3125

GOLF

FOREST PARK COUNTRY CLUB
Forest Park Ave., Adams. 743-9771
GREYLOCK GLEN
Base of Mt. Greylock, Adams 743-2960
NORTH ADAMS COUNTRY CLUB
Rt. 8, Clarksburg 664-9011
STANFORD VALLEY GOLF COURSE
The Lane off Rt. 8 . . . . (802) 694-9144
TACONIC GOLF CLUB
Meachum St.. 458-3997
WAUBEEKA SPRINGS GOLF LINKS
Routes 7 & 43. 458-5869

HIKING

THE APPALACHIAN MOUNTAIN CLUB
5 Joy St., Boston, MA 02108
THE WILLIAMS OUTING CLUB TRAIL & GUIDE MAP
Lamb Stationery, 85 Main St., N. Adams
Renzi's, 36 Spring St., Williamston

HORSEBACK RIDING

CLOVER HILL FARM
Adams Rd., Williamstown 458-8500
SHADOWBROOK STABLES
Northwest Hill, Pownal. . . . . (802) 823-5572

ICE SKATING

LANSING CHAPMAN RINK
Williams College, Williamstown 597-2433
MEMORIAL INDOOR RINK
S. Church St., N. Adams 664-9474

TENNIS

BERKSHIRE INDOOR TENNIS CLUB
Rt. 7, New Ashford. 458-9577
MINICIPAL COURTS
Noel Field, State St., N. Adams & Greylock
Field, Protection Ave., N. Adams
WILLIAMS COLLEGE COURTS
Lynde Lane, Williamstown

RESTAURANTS

ADAMS

ADAMS BERKSHIRE INN (entertainment)
Commercial St. 743-2960
BOUTI - FARE (American, entertainment)
200 Howland Ave., Rt. 8. 743-0193

NEW ASHFORD

MILL ON THE FLOSS (Continental)
Route 7 458-9123
NEW ASHFORD INN (Italian, American)
Route 7 458-8041
SPRINGS RESTAURANT (Continental)
Route 7 458-3465

NORTH ADAMS

SHERATON INN (American, entertainment)
40 Main St. 664-4561

WILLIAMSTOWN

THE BRITISH MAID (French, entertainment, bar)
State Rd., Rt. 2 458-4961
COUNTRY RESTAURANT (Continental)
52 North St., Rt. 7 458-4000
FOUR ACRES (Continental)
State Rd., Rt. 2 458-5436
GOURMET EAST (Chinese, entertainment)
State Rd., Rt. 2 485-9386
LE JARDIN (French)
Cold Spring Rd., Routes 2 & 7 458-8032
TACONIC PARK RESTAURANT (Continental)
Cold Spring Rd., Routes 2 & 7 458-3090
TREADWAY WILLIAMS INN
Junction of Routes 2 & 7 458-9371

STORES & SKI SHOPS

THE HOOSUCK GUILD STORE (gifts, crafts)
Windsor Mall, Rt. 2 664-6383
THE WIGWAM & WESTERN SUMMIT (gifts)
North Adams 663-3205
COLLEGE BOOK STORE
Spring St., Williamstown. 458-4808
ARCADIAN SHOP (backpacking gear)
Water St., Williamstown 458-3670
KRAZY QUILTS (camping equipment)
249 Union St., North Adams

MALLS

ARTERY ARCADE
Veterans' Memorial Dr., Rt. 2, N. Adams
COLONIAL SHOPPING CENTER
State Rd., Rt. 2, Williamstown
DOWNTOWN NORTH ADAMS
Summer St. & Park St.
NORTH ADAMS PLAZA
Curran Hwy., Rt. 8
THE VILLAGE BEAUTIFUL
Spring St. & Water St., Williamstown

B U T T E R N U T

GREAT BARRINGTON, MA 01230 (413) 528-2000

AREA INFORMATION

BASE ELEVATION
800 feet
HOURS
8:30 a.m. - 4:00 p.m., weekends & holidays
9:00 a.m. - 4:00 p.m., weekdays
LIFTS
5 chairs, 1 T-bar, 6,800 capacity per hour
LONGEST RUN
1½ miles
NURSERY
Ages 3 - 6, weekends & holidays beginning December 26th - call Ski Area.
SEASON
December 4th thru March 28th
SNOW PHONE 528-2000, (800) 628-5030
TRAILS
15% beginner, 60% intermediate, 25% advanced
TRAVEL
From Great Barrington, 2 miles via Rt. 23 E.
From Boston, 135 miles via I-90, Rt. 7 & Rt. 23.
From New York City, 126 miles via Tacomic State Parkway & Rt. 23 E.
By air: Great Barrington Airport, 5 miles from Butternut, with a 2700 foot runway with instrument approach 528-1010
By bus: From New York City via Resort or Bonanza Lines. From Hartford via Arrow Lines.
VERTICAL DROP
1,000 feet

LODGING

ACORN ACRES MOTEL
2½ mi. N. on Rt. 7, Great Barrington. 528-9111
BERKSHIRE MOTOR INN
3 mi. S. on Rt. 7, Great Barrington 528-3150
BRIARCLIFF MOTOR LODGE
3½ mi. N. on Rt. 7 between
Great Barrington & Stockbridge. 528-3000
DAFFERS MT. INN & RESTAURANT
12 miles from Great Barrington, Rt. 57 258-4453
ELLING'S "GUEST HOUSE"
4 miles west on Rt. 23, Great Barrington
1746 Colonial Homestead 528-4103
FRIENDSHIP INN MONUMENT MOUNTAIN MOTEL
2¼ mi. N. on Rt. 7, Great Barrington. 528-3272
HOLIDAY HOUSE MOTEL
11mi. W. on Rt. 23, Hillsdale, NY . . . (518) 325-3030
INTERLAKEN INN
2 mi. E. of junction of Routes 44 & 112
Lakeville, CT . . . . (203) 435-9878

IVANHOE COUNTRY HOUSE
10 mi. S. on Rt. 41, Sheffield 229-2143
JUG END RESORT
8½ mi. W. on Jug End Rd., S. Egremont 528-0434
LANTERN HOUSE MOTEL
2½ mi. N. on Rt. 7, Great Barrington. 528-2350
MOUNTAIN VIEW MOTEL
½ mi. W. on Rt. 23, Great Barrington 528-0250
PLEASANT VALLEY MOTEL
10 mi. N. on Rt. 7, left on Rt. 102
West Stockbridge 232-4216
RED LION INN
7 mi. N. on Rt. 7, Stockbridge 298-5545
SEEKONK PINES "GUEST HOUSE"
5 mi. W. on Rt. 23, Great Barrington. 528-4192
THE 1780 EGREMONT INN
5 mi. W. in S. Egremont, just off Rt. 23 528-2111
WILLIAMSVILLE INN
5 mi. N. on Rt. 41, West Stockbridge. 274-6580

RESTAURANTS

AUGUST MOON RESTAURANT
(Szechuan, Mandarin, Cantonese, International)
1½ mi. S. on Rt. 7, Great Barrington 528-9363
CILDARA HOUSE RESTAURANT (French, American)
[mi. W. on Rt. 23, Great Barrington 528-0017
ELM COURT INN
3 mi. W. on Rt. 71 off Rt. 23, N. Egremont . . 528-0325
FAIRFIELD INN (fireside tavern)
6 mi. W. on Rt. 23, Great Barrington. 528-2720
HANS' RESTAURANT (international, seafood, bar)
7 mi. S. on Rt. 7, Great Barrington. 528-0710
SHED RESTAURANT (lunch & dinner, steaks, seafood)
6 mi. S. on Rt. 7, Sheffield 229-8774
THE OLD MILL (Bar Parlor)
7 mi. W. on Rt. 23, S. Egremont 528-1421

JIMINY PEAK

COREY RD. HANCOCK, MA 01237 (413) 738-5431

AREA INFORMATION

BASE ELEVATION
1,300 feet
HOURS
9:00 a.m. - 10:30 p.m., weekdays
8:30 a.m. - 10:30 p.m., Saturdays
8:30 a.m. - 4:00 p.m., Sundays
Night skiing, 6:00 - 10:30 p.m., Mon. - Sat.
LIFTS
4 chairs, 1 tow, 5,000 capacity per hour
3 chairs at night
LONGEST RUN
2 miles
NURSERY
2 years & up, call Ski Area
SEASON
Mid-November to April 1st
SNOW PHONE 738-5431
Toll free, inside Mass.. . . . . (800) 292-6633
TRAILS
30% beginner, 30% intermediate, 40% advanced
TRAVEL
Massachusetts Turnpike to Rt. 7 N., east on Brodie Mountain Rd., then follow signs to Ski Area. Or, Rt 22 in NY to Rt. 43 east & north, then west on Brodie Mountain Rd., follow signs.
VERTICAL DROP
1,200 feet

EMERGENCY

FIRE 738-5660
STATE POLICE. 445-5511

LODGING

BERKSHIRE HILLS MOTEL
Routes 2 & 7, Williamstown 458-3950
CHIMNEY MIRROR MOTEL
U.S. Rt. 2, Williamstown. 458-5202
CLIFFSIDE MOTOR INN (Restaurant)
Rt. 7 S. , Bennington, VT 05201 . . . . (802) 442-8547
COUNTRY VILLAGE (condos)
Write Ski Area or call. . . . . (800) 628-6178, 738-5025
THE DALTON HOUSE (room, private baths)
955 Main St., Dalton, 01226 684-3854
THE 1896 MOTEL (restaurant)
Routes 2 & 7, Williamstown, 01267 458-8125
ELWAL PINES MOTOR INN
Routes 2 & 7, 811-J Cold Spring Rd.
Williamstown, 01267 458-8161
THE HANCOCK INN
Rt. 43, 2 mi. S. of Ski Area, Hancock Village 738-5873
JERICHO VALLEY MOTEL
Rt. 43, Hancock Rd., Williamstown, 01267 . . 458-5406
MILLHOF INN
Rt. 43, Stephentown, NY 12168 . . . . (518) 733-5606
MOTEL BLU-STONE
Box 417, East Greenbush, NY 12061 (518) 477-6515
MT. VERNON MOTEL
Routes 9 & 20, Columbia Turnpike
East Greenbush, NY 12061 . . . . (518) 477-9352
Outside New York . . . . (800) 328-5511
NORTH ADAMS INN (restaurant)
40 Main St., North Adams, 01247 664-4561
THE PILGRIM MOTEL
Housatonic St., Lee, Mass. Pike, exit 2 243-1328
SOUTH GATE MOTEL
Rt. 7, 2 mi. S. of Bennington, VT 05201(802) 447-7525
THE SPRINGS RESTAURANT & MOTOR INN
Rt. 7, New Ashford, 01237 458-5945
SUNSET MOTEL
114 Housatonic St., Lee, exit 2, MA Pike . . . 243-0302
SUSSE CHALET MOTOR LODGE (coffee shop)
Routes 7 & 20, Lenox, 01240. 637-3560
Toll free . . . . (800) 258-1980

RESTAURANTS

CAPTAIN'S TABLE (steaks, seafood)
Routes 2 & 7, Williamstown 458-5645

THE CHEFS TACONIC RESTAURANT
(American / Continental)
Williamstown . . . . (413) 458-3090, 458-5683

HEADLESS HORSEMAN RESTAURANT
Cliffside Motor Inn, Rt. 7 S.
Bennington, VT . . . . (802) 442-8547

ITALIAN VILLAGE (steaks, prime rib, seafood)
579 Fenn St., near East St. 443-9851

LES PYRENEES (French Provincial)
Queechy Lake, Canaan, NY . . . . (518) 781-9994

THE NEW RAINBOW RESTAURANT
(varied menu, seafood)
109 First St., Pittsfield 442-3270

THE SPRINGS (Continental, motor inn)
Rt. 7, New Ashford 458-3465

WEST STOCKBRIDGE
("Yankee Market Village" - 5 restaurants, shopping, and entertainment after dark)
Massachusetts Pike, exit 1 & Rt. 22, B3 exit

STORES & SKI SHOPS

AZIMUTH, LTD. (ski shop)
At slopes, call Ski Area
897 New Loudon Rd., Latham, NY . . (518) 783-7750

BESSE-CLARKE (ski & sport shop)
North & Summer St., downtown Pittsfield . . 499-1090

TONON'S SKI HAUS (sales, rentals, repairs)
247 North St., Pittsfield 443-0671

WEST STOCKBRIDGE
("Yankee Market Village" - shopping, restaurants, and entertainment after dark)
Massachusetts Pike, exit 1 & Rt. 22, B3 exit

MT. TOM

P.O. BOX 1158, HOLYOKE, MA 01040 (413) 536-0416

AREA INFORMATION

BASE ELEVATION
700 feet

HOURS
9:00 a.m. - 5:00 p.m., Mon. - Fri.
8:30 a.m. - 5:00 p.m., Sat. & Sun.
5:00 - 10:00 p.m., night skiing

LIFTS
3 chairs, 3 bars, 2 tows, 7,770 capacity per hour

LONGEST RUN
3,600 feet

NURSERY
9:00 - 12:00 & 1:00 - 2:00, Mon. - Fri.
Until 4:00 on weekends

SEASON
December 15th to end of March, snowmaking

SNOW PHONE 536-0416
Toll free in NY, NJ, CT, RI, VT, NH . . (800) 628-5030
In Massachusetts . . . . (800) 292-6633

TRAILS
30% beginner, 60% intermediate, 10% expert

TRAVEL
North of junction of I-90 & I-91. I-91 to Rt. 5 to Mt. Tom Access Rd. Ski Area is 2 miles from Holyoke.

VERTICAL DROP
680 feet

EMERGENCY

BAYSTATE AMBULANCE SERVICE. 536-8951
POLICE 536-0111
HOLYOKE HOSPITAL 536-5221

LODGING

AUTUMN INN (breakfast & lunch)
259 Elm St., Northampton, 01060 584-7660

BEST WESTERN – BLACK HORSE
500 Riverdale Rd., West Springfield, 01089 . . 733-2161

CHALET MOTOR LODGE
Johnny Cake Hollow Rd., Chicopee, 01021 . . 592-5141

COLLEGE INN (lunch & dinner)
29 College St., South Hadley, 01075 533-7119

COLONIAL HILTON INN (restaurant, cocktail lounge)
I-91 at Rt. 5 exit, Northampton, 01060 586-1211

FAIRFIELD INN & CONFERENCE CENTER (restaurant)
Massachusetts Turnpike, exit 5
450 Memorial Dr., Chicopee, 01021 592-7722

FEDERAL PLAZA MOTOR INN (restaurant, lounge)
50 Federal St., Springfield 781-8090

HOLIDAY INN OF HOLYOKE (restaurant, lounge)
Exit 15 on I-91 at Ingleside exit
Holyoke, 01040. 534-3311

HOLIDAY INN OF SPRINGFIELD (restaurant, lounge)
I-91 & I-291 junction, Springfield. 781-0900

HOSPITALITY MOTOR INN (2 restaurants, lounge)
Exit 49 off I-91, 1 Bright Meadowview Bl.
Enfield, CT 06082 . . . . (203) 741-2211

HOWARD JOHNSON'S MOTOR LODGE
(restaurant, cocktail lounge)
Riverdale Rd., West Springfield, 01089 739-7261

MARRIOTT HOTEL (restaurant, 3 cocktail lounges)
Take Columbus Ave. - Springfield Center, exit off I-91
1500 Main St., Springfield 781-7111

MEDALLION MOTEL
13 River St., at Memorial Ave., Rt. 147
West Springfield, 01089 781-3260

NORTHAMPTON INN & WIGGINS TAVERN (restaurant)
36 King St., Northampton, 01060 584-3100

QUALITY INN / STONEHAVEN (restaurant, 2 lounges)
70 Chestnut St., Springfield, 01103 781-8030

RAMADA INN (pancake house serving all meals, lounge)
Exit 6, Massachusetts Pike
At junction of Rt. 291 592-9101

RIVIERA MOTEL
Rt. 5, Smiths Ferry, Holyoke, 01040. 536-3377

RODEWAY INN (International restaurant)
Exit 6 off Massachusetts Pike
Burnett Rd., Chicopee, 01020. 592-7751

SHERATON INN, SPRINGFIELD WEST
(restaurant, cocktail lounge, nightly entertainment)
1080 Riverdale Rd., West Springfield, 01089 781-8750

SPRINGFIELD TRAVELODGE
700 State St., Springfield, 01109 739-2161

STEARNS MOTOR LODGE
½ mile north of exit 21 off I-91
Rt. 5, West Hatfield, 01088 247-5601

SUSSE CHALET (Howard Johnson's Restaurant)
4 miles north of exit 4, Massachusetts Pike
Rt. 5, Holyoke 536-1980

TOWN HOUSE MOTOR LODGE (adjoining restaurant)
Rt. 5, Northampton, 01060 586-1500

WEST SPRINGFIELD MOTEL
437 Riverdale St., West Springfield, 01089 . . 785-5365

YANKEE PEDLAR INN (restaurant)
Holyoke, at junction of Routes 5 & 202 532-9494

RESTAURANTS

SEE LODGINGS FOR OTHER RESTAURANTS

TOM'S TAVERN
Mt. Tom Lodge, Ski Area

SKI SHOPS

MT. TOM SKI SHOP
Ski Area 536-0712
Enfield, CT . . . . (203) 745-5060

MT. TOM RENTAL SHOP
Ski Area 536-2602

M I C H I G A N

BIG POWDERHORN

BESSEMER, MI 49911 (906) 932-4838
LODING TELEPHONE: (906) 932-3100

AREA INFORMATION

BASE ELEVATION
1,218 feet

HOURS
9:00 a.m. - 4:00 p.m.
Wed. & Sat., 7:00 - 10:00 p.m.

LIFTS
5 chairlifts, 2 rope tows, 7,500 capacity per hour

LONGEST RUN
1 mile

NURSERY
Sitters available, advance notice, call Ski Area

SEASON
End of November to early-April, no snowmaking

SNOW PHONE
Call Ski Area, or, outside Michigan . . . (800) 338-1246
In Michigan 932-4870

TRAILS
41% novice, 35% intermediate, 24% expert

TRAVEL
Near Lake Superior & Northern Wisconsin, 2 miles north of Hwy. U.S. 2 on Powderhorn Rd. By air to Iron-Gogebic County Airport, 2 miles away, Republic Airlines. See Indianhead "Services".

VERTICAL DROP
Over 600 feet

EMERGENCY

AMBULANCE. 932-4140, 932-2323
BESSEMER POLICE 667-0203
FIRE 667-0203
GRAND VIEW HOSPITAL 932-2525
IRONWOOD POLICE 932-1234
MICHIGAN STATE POLICE 224-9691

LODGING

BIG POWDERHORN LODGING ASSOCIATION
(chalet accomodations, maid service, kitchen)
At the slopes. 932-3100

BLUFF'S VIEW MOTEL
West U.S. 2, Bessemer 667-0311

POWDERMILL INN (up to 8 persons, kitchenettes)
Powderhorn Rd., Box 194, Bessemer. 932-0800

SCHROEDER CHALETS (up to 20 people)
Bessemer . . . . (612) 475-3723

TRAVELERS' MOTEL
East U.S. 2, Bessemer. 667-0243

12 FLAGS / CHALET d'OEX (accomodate 12 & 10)
Bessemer . . . . . days (414) 258-1234, nights 538-4029

WIN-FALL HOUSE
(2 apartments, accomodate up to 6 & 9)
115 Sellar St., Bessemer . . . 667-0032, (312) 761-7470

BIG POWDERHORN CONT.

RESTAURANTS

ALPENINN (cocktails)
At the slopes. 667-0211
CARIBOU LODGE (cocktail lounge, entertainment)
At the slopes. 932-4714
CIRCLE HILLS RESTAURANT & COCKTAIL LOUNGE
Between Big Powderhorn & Copper Peak
CT 513, Ironwood 932-3857
DON 'N SUDS FAMILY RESTAURANT (from 6 a.m.)
U.S. 2, Bessemer 663-4513
SNOWFLAKE DINING ROOM (live music in adjacent bar)
Main Lodge at the slopes, call Ski Area
STONEGATE FARM SUPPER CLUB (cocktail lounge)
Black River Rd., 2 mi. N. of Bessemer 667-0219

SERVICES

AUTO

C & M OIL COMPANY (gas, tires)
U.S. 2, Bessemer 667-0222
COUNTRY CORNER PARTY STORE (self-service gas)
U.S. 2, Ramsey turnoff,
between Bessemer & Wakefield 667-0334

BANKS

THE BESSEMER NATIONAL BANK
Bessemer 667-0246
THE FIRST NATIONAL BANK
Wakefield 224-9581
FIRST NATIONAL BANK OF IRONWOOD
Downtown. 932-1620
East Cloverland Dr. 932-0102

DRUG STORE

BESSEMER PHARMACY
Downtown Bessemer 667-0215, 663-4543

GROCERIES

COUNTRY CORNER PARTY STORE (beer, wine)
U.S. 2, Ramsey turnoff
between Bessemer & Wakefield 667-0334
HIWAY 2 SUPER VALU
U.S. 2, Bessemer
STAN'S BIG DOLLAR
Downtown Bessemer

STORES & SKI SHOPS

BEN FRANKLIN STORE (variety)
Sophie St., downtown Bessemer 663-4222
BIG POWDERHORN MOUNTAIN SKI SHOP
At the slopes, call Ski Area
HULSTROM'S CITY NEWS & AGATE SHOP
221 S. Suffolk St., downtown Ironwood. . . . 932-4440
J.C. PENNEY COMPANY (ski apparel)
100 W. Aurora St., Ironwood 932-3240
LEATHER & GIFT
West U.S. 2, Bessemer 667-0500
TREK & TRAIL (cross-country skis, rentals)
U.S. 2, Bessemer 663-4791

B L A C K J A C K

P.O. BOX 66, BESSEMER, MI 49911 (906) 229-5115
LODGING TELEPHONE: (906) 229-5915

AREA INFORMATION

FOR LODGING, RESTAURANT, SERVICE, STORE & SKI SHOP LISTINGS, SEE INDIANHEAD

HOURS
9:00 a.m. - 4:00 p.m.
LIFTS
3 chairs, 2 rope tows, 3,600 capacity per hour
LONGEST RUN
5,300 feet
NURSERY
Call Ski Area
SEASON
Late November to early April, no snowmaking
SNOW PHONE
Call Ski Area
TRAILS
20% novice, 55% intermediate, 25% expert
TRAVEL
Near the Northern Wisconsin border and Lake Superior, 1 mile north of U.S. 2 on Blackjack Rd. Located between Big Powderhorn Mountain and Indianhead. Air and bus service, see Indianhead.
VERTICAL DROP
465 feet

C A B E R F A E

CADILLAC, MI 49601 (616) 862-3400

AREA INFORMATION

BASE ELEVATION
740 feet
HOURS
9:30 a.m. - 4:30 p.m., 4:30 - 9:30 p.m. nights
LIFTS
2 chairs, 6 T-bars, 14 rope tows
LONGEST RUN
¾ mile
NURSERY
2 - 6 years, call Ski Area
SEASON
Thanksgiving to Easter
SNOWMAKING
Yes
SNOW PHONE 862-3303
TRAILS
30% beginner, 50% intermediate, 20% advanced
TRAVEL
From Cadillac, 12 miles west via M-55

VERTICAL DROP
350 feet

LODGING

ALL LODGING, RESTAURANTS, ETC., ARE LOCATED IN OR NEAR CADILLAC, UNLESS INDICATED.

BIRCHWOOD RESORT (housekeeping)
6545 E. M-115 775-9101
BU-T-REST MOTEL
9628 Mackinaw Trail 775-7948
BILL OLIVER'S CABERFAE MOTOR INN (restaurant)
M-55 West, P.O. Box 327 775-2458
CADILLAC SANDS MOTOR INN (restaurant, lounge)
M-115 & M-55 West. 775-2407
DRIFTWOOD LODGE
M-55 West 775-2932
EDELWEISS LODGE (restaurant, lounge)
Ski Area 862-3302
GARLETS CORNER
M-55 & M-37, 10 miles W. of Ski Area 862-3500
GREEN MILL MOTEL
U.S 131, north side of Manton 824-3504
LOST PINES LODGE (restaurant, lounge)
3846 W. 38 Mile Rd., Harrietta, 49638. 389-2222
MAPLE HILL MOTEL
U.S. 131, S. of Cadillac. 775-0164
MAR-LYN'S RESORT (housekeeping cabins)
1749 North Bl. 775-3732
MC GUIRE'S MOTOR LODGE & RESORT
7880 Mackinaw Trail South 775-9947
MUSHROOM CAP MOTEL
Mesick, 49668. 885-1222
OLSON'S MOTEL
U.S. 131, N. of Cadillac 775-7281
PILGRIM'S VILLAGE RESORT
On Lake Mitchell, M-115 & M-55 775-5412
PINE CHATA MOTEL & SKI SHOP
523 S. Lake Mitchell Dr. (M-55) 775-4677
PINE KNOLL MOTEL
8072 Mackinaw Trail. 775-9471
SOUTH SHORE MOTEL & RESORT
1236 Sunnyside Dr.. 775-7641
SUN 'N SNOW LODGE
301 S. Lake Mitchell Dr.. 775-9961
SUNNYSIDE MOTEL
1011 Sunnyside Dr.. 775-3170
SUNSET POINT CABINS (housekeeping cabins)
On Lake Mitchell 775-9163
WATT MOTEL
Mackinaw Trail, Box 331 775-9494

RECREATION

BOWLING
Caberfae Lanes, West M-55 775-9959
ICE FISHING
Ice Shanty Rental, Mar-Lyn's Lakeside Resort
1749 North Blvd. 775-3732
ICE SKATING
Artificial ice rink, Wexford County Fairgrounds
N. Mitchell at 13th St. 775-0621
RACQUETBALL
Cadillac Racquet Club, 725 Seneca Pl. 775-5642
Pine Grove Racquetball, 8179 Mackinaw Trail 775-9908
ROLLER SKATING
The Spot Roller Rink, 2592 N. Lake Mitchell 775-9056
SNOWMOBILE RENTAL
Four Seasons Recreation, 1566 N. Mitchell St. 775-4491
Lost Pines Lodge, 3846 W. 38 Mile Rd. 389-2222
SNOWSHOE RENTAL
At Ski Area 862-3301
TENNIS (indoor)
Cadillac Racquet Club, 725 Seneca Pl. 775-5642
THEATRE
Cinema Theatre 1 & 2, 202 S. Mitchell St.. . . 775-4357

RESTAURANTS

KING'S TABLE RESTAURANT (dancing, entertainment)
Bill Oliver's Caberfae Motor Inn, M-55 W. . . . 775-2458
BONANZA FAMILY RESTAURANT
621 S. Mitchell 775-2561
CADILLAC PARTY LOUNGE (cocktails)
516 N. Mitchell 775-9073
CLIPPER ROOM RESTAURANT & LOUNGE
Cadillac Sands, M-115 & M-55. 775-2407
CROSSROADS BAR (sandwiches, chicken, steaks)
8996 W. 30 Rd., Harrietta 389-2272
ELIAS BROTHERS BIG BOY (breakfast, dinner & lunches)
1310 S. Mitchell St.. 775-7125
GARLETS CORNER
Hoxeyville, M-55 at M-37 862-3500
HARVEST TABLE
1034 N. Mitchell 775-1861
HILLCREST RESTAURANT (breakfast, lunch, dinner)
1250 S. Mitchell St.. 775-4191
LITTLE CAESAR'S PIZZA PARLOR
6184 E. M-115, Cadillac West Mall 775-9725
LOST PINES LODGE (cocktails)
3846 W. 38 Mile Rd., Harrietta 389-2222
MARINA RESTAURANT & LOUNGE (Italian, seafoods)
M-55 & M-115. 775-9322
MC GUIRE'S RESTAURANT
1 mi. S. of Cadillac, Mackinaw Trail 775-9947
SUN 'N SNOW RESTAURANT & LOUNGE
301 S. Lake Mitchell Dr.. 775-5332
SWEITZER'S FAMILY RESTAURANT (Salad bar, lounge)
101 E. Harris St. 775-1071
WATERFRONT RESTAURANT
M-115 near M-55 775-7555

SERVICES

CLEANERS

BRITE 'N CLEAN
131 Paluster 775-0851
WELLINGTON CLEANERS & FURRIERS
113 E. Chapin. 775-2141

HAIR STYLING

STEVE FOWLER'S BEAUTY SALON (men & women)
114 S. Mitchell 775-7609

LIQUOR

G & D LIQUOR STORE
223 S. Mitchell St. 775-5251
MIDGET MARKET
830 N. Mitchell St. 775-5741

STORES & SKI SHOPS

CABERFAE SKI SHOP
Ski Area 862-3302
MIDGET MARKET
830 N. Mitchell St. 775-5741
PBS PARTY STORE
1010 S. Mitchell St.. 775-9157
PINE CHATA SKI SHOP - MOTEL
523 S. Lake Mitchell 775-3657

INDIANHEAD

WAKEFIELD, MI 49968 (906) 229-5181

AREA INFORMATION

BASE ELEVATION
1,297 feet
HOURS
9:00 a.m. - 4:30 p.m.
LIFTS
4 chairs, 2 T-bars, 1 poma lift, 8,550 capacity per hour
LONGEST RUN
1 mile
NURSERY
Age 2 & up, call Ski Area
SEASON
End of November to early April, snowmaking
SNOW PHONE . . . . (800) 338-1243
TRAILS
25% novice, 50% intermediate, 25% expert
TRAVEL
Near Lake Superior & Northern Wisconsin, 1 mile west of Wakefield on U.S. 2. See "Services"
VERTICAL DROP
638 feet

EMERGENCY

AMBULANCE. 932-4140, 932-2323
FIRE 224-8591
Ironwood 932-1235
GRAND VIEW HOSPITAL 932-2525
POLICE 224-8311
Ironwood 932-1234

LODGING

DIRECT RESERVATIONS 229-5133

ADVANCE MOTEL
East U.S. 2, Ironwood, 49938. 932-4511
BINGO'S MOTEL
M-28, Wakefield, 49968 229-5593
BLUE CLOUD MOTEL
West U.S. 2, Ironwood, 49938 932-0920
THE CEDAR MOTEL
U.S. 2, Ironwood, 49938. 932-4376
CIRCLE HILLS RESORT MOTEL & CONDOMINIUMS
(restaurant, cocktail lounge)
Rt. 1, Box 238B, Ironwood, 49938. 932-3857
CRESTVIEW MOTEL
West U.S. 2, Ironwood, 49938 932-4845
DAVEY'S MOTEL
U.S. 2, Ironwood, 49938. 932-2020
THE FISHERMAN RESORT (restaurant)
On M-64, Rt. 1, Box 175, Marenisco, 49947 842-3366
GOGEBIC LODGE (restaurant, bar)
8 mi. N. of Hwy. 2 on M-64
Star Rt. Box 125, Marenisco, 49947 842-3321
GRANATO MOTEL & RESTAURANT (24 hr. restaurant)
Near junction of Hwy. U.S. 2 & M-28
Wakefield, 49968 224-8091
INDIANHEAD MOTEL
At the slopes. 229-5133
IRONWOOD MOTEL (restaurant next door)
West U.S. 2, Ironwood, 49938 932-5520
KESKEN KAIKKI (2-story home)
302 E. Arch, Ironwood, 49938 932-0209
MT. ZION MOTEL
On U.S. 2, 1 mi. E. of junction of U.S. 51
Ironwood, 49938 932-3632
RAVENHURST
Near Ski Area, Box 138, Wakefield, 49968 . . 229-5249
THE REGAL MOTEL
East U.S. 2, Wakefield, 49968. 229-5122
THE ROYAL MOTEL (next to restaurant)
U.S. 2, Ironwood, 49938. 932-4230
SANDPIPER MOTEL
East U.S. 2, Ironwood, 49938. 932-2000
SUN-E-SIDE COTTAGES (2 to 6 people)
West U.S. 2, Ironwood, 49938 932-3012
TOWNE HOUSE MOTOR INN
(group lodging, dining room & entertainment)
215 S. Suffolk St., Ironwood, 49938. 932-2101
TWILITE MOTEL (restaurant next door)
East U.S. 2, Ironwood, 49938. 932-3010
WAKEFIELD MOTOR LODGE
(restaurant, cocktail lounge, indoor heated pool)
500 Lakeshore Dr., Wakefield, 49968 224-9661
WESTERN'S MOTEL
2 mi. W. of Bergland on M-28
Box 46, Bergland, 49910. 575-3545
WONDERLAND MOTEL (across from restaurant)
Box 346-C, Bergland, 49910. 575-3434

RESTAURANTS

CHAMONIX (reservations)
At the slopes. 229-5181
CHINA SEA PALACE
Intersection of U.S. 2 & M-28
202 Sunday Lake St. 224-8511

THE FISHERMAN RESORT
On Lake Gogebic, Hwy. M-64, Marenisco . . . 842-3366
GOGEBIC LODGE
8 mi. N. of Hwy. 2 on M-64, Marenisco 842-3321
THE LODGE
At the slopes in the Main Lodge. 229-5181
SUN-N-SNO RESTAURANT
U.S. 2, Ironwood 932-4530
WAKEFIELD MOTOR LODGE,
RESTAURANT & LOUNGE (live music weekends)
500 Lakeshore Dr. 224-9661

SERVICES

AIR

IRON / GOGEBIC COUNTY AIRPORT
(Courtesy pickup with advance notice, call Ski Area)
8 miles from the slopes. 932-3121
REPUBLIC AIRLINES. 932-1920

AUTO

BESSEMER AUTO COMPANY (service, rentals)
U.S. 2, Bessemer 667-0291
CORMIER'S STANDARD SERVICE
912 Putnam St., Wakefield. 224-9751
EDDY PARK SHELL (24 hr. tow service)
M-28, Wakefield. 224-8011
HERTZ RENT-A-CAR
Iron/Gogebic County Airport, Ironwood . . . 932-2501
PENROSE SKELLY (tow service)
McLeod & Suffolk St., Ironwood . .932-4501, 932-0745
SASS TIRE & AUTO SERVICENTER
300 E. McLeod, Ironwood. 932-2100

BUS

COURTESY PICKUP
From Bus Terminal - advance notice, call Ski Area
GREYHOUND BUS LINES
108 S. Moore, Bessemer 667-0402
WISCONSIN-MICHIGAN COACHES (for Greenbay)
118 W. Aurora, Ironwood 932-4221
ZEPHYR BUS LINES (for Minneapolis)
118 W. Aurora, Ironwood 932-4221

DRUG STORE

BESSEMER PHARMACY (closed Sunday)
Downtown Bessemer 667-0215, 663-4543

GROCERIES

LOPEZ I.G.A. FOODLINER
½ block S. of U.S. 2, Lake St., Ironwood . . . 932-0632

STORES & SKI SHOPS

BLACK BEAR SPORTING GOODS
(cross-country equipment, snow shoes, ice fishing gear)
U.S. 2, Ironwood 932-5213
CHALET PARTY STORE (beer, wine & liquor)
408 Sunday Lake St., Wakefield 224-6351
RIGGS HALLMARK GIFT SHOP
Downtown Ironwood. 932-4432
ROYAL BAKERY
U.S. 2, Ironwood 932-1931
SMEETH'S SPORTING CENTER
(downhill & cross-country ski, apparel)
U.S. 2, Ironwood 932-4210

N U B S N O B

RURAL RT. 2 HARBOR SPRINGS, MI 49740
TELEPHONE: (616) 526-2131

AREA INFORMATION

AIR
From Pellston
BASE ELEVATION
870 ft.
BUS
Greyhound daily to Petoskey
HOURS
9:30 a.m. to 4:30 p.m.
LIFTS
1 quad, 1 triple & 3 double chairs,
pomalift & rope tow
LONGEST RUN
3/4 of a mile
NURSERY
Call ski area
SEASON
Dec. 15th to April 1st
SNOW PHONE 526-2131
TRAILS
20 runs, 30% novice, 40% intermediate, 30% expert
TRAVEL
10 miles from Petoskey, 5 miles from Harbor Springs
VERTICAL DROP
425 ft.

EMERGENCY

FIRE 526-6211
HOSPITAL
Little Traverse. 347-7373
Lockwood MacDonald 347-5000
POISON CONTROL 347-0555
SHERIFF 347-2032
STATE POLICE. 347-8101

LODGING

BEST WESTERN INN
U.S. 131 South, Petoskey . . . . (800) 528-1234
BIRCHWOOD INN
Little Traverse Bay 526-2151
GOLFVIEW MOTEL
1011 U.S. 31 North, Petoskey. 347-8281
HARBOR HILLS MOTOR LODGE
514 M-131, Harbor Springs 347-5121

NUBS NOB CONT.

HARBOUR INN
Little Traverse Bay 526-2168

HAYNER'S MOTEL
Junction U.S. 31 & 131 South 347-8717

HOLIDAY INN
U.S. 131 South, Petoskey 347-6041

THE INN ON THE HILL
U.S. 131 South, Petoskey 347-4193

LODGE
At ski area 526-2131

PETOSKEY MOTEL
Junction U.S. 31 & 131 347-8177

THE RUSTLERS' DEN
Harbor Springs 526-2871

SUNDOWN MOTEL
U.S. 31 & 131, Petoskey 347-2561

THIS OLE HOUSE
M-31 on Crooked Lake. 347-8127

RESTAURANTS

ARBORETUM (dining & cocktails)
Harbor Springs 526-6291

THE BOOTLEGGERS (4 dining rooms)
U.S. 131 South, Petoskey 347-1651

COUNTRY HEARTH (dining & cocktails)
U.S. 31 North & M-131 347-5940

DUFFY'S (Oriental)
On road to Nubs Nob. 526-2189

FLYING DUTCHMAN (American, cocktails)
M-131 btwn. Petoskey & Harbor Springs. . . . 347-2941

THE NEW YORK (French, Continental)
Downtown Harbor Springs. 526-5901

PARK GARDENS CAFE (American, seafood, cocktails)
425 E. Lake St., Petoskey 347-8251

THE PIER (American, cocktails)
Petoskey 347-2771

VIC'S OF PETOSKEY
U.S. 131, 1 block S. of U.S. 31 347-8383

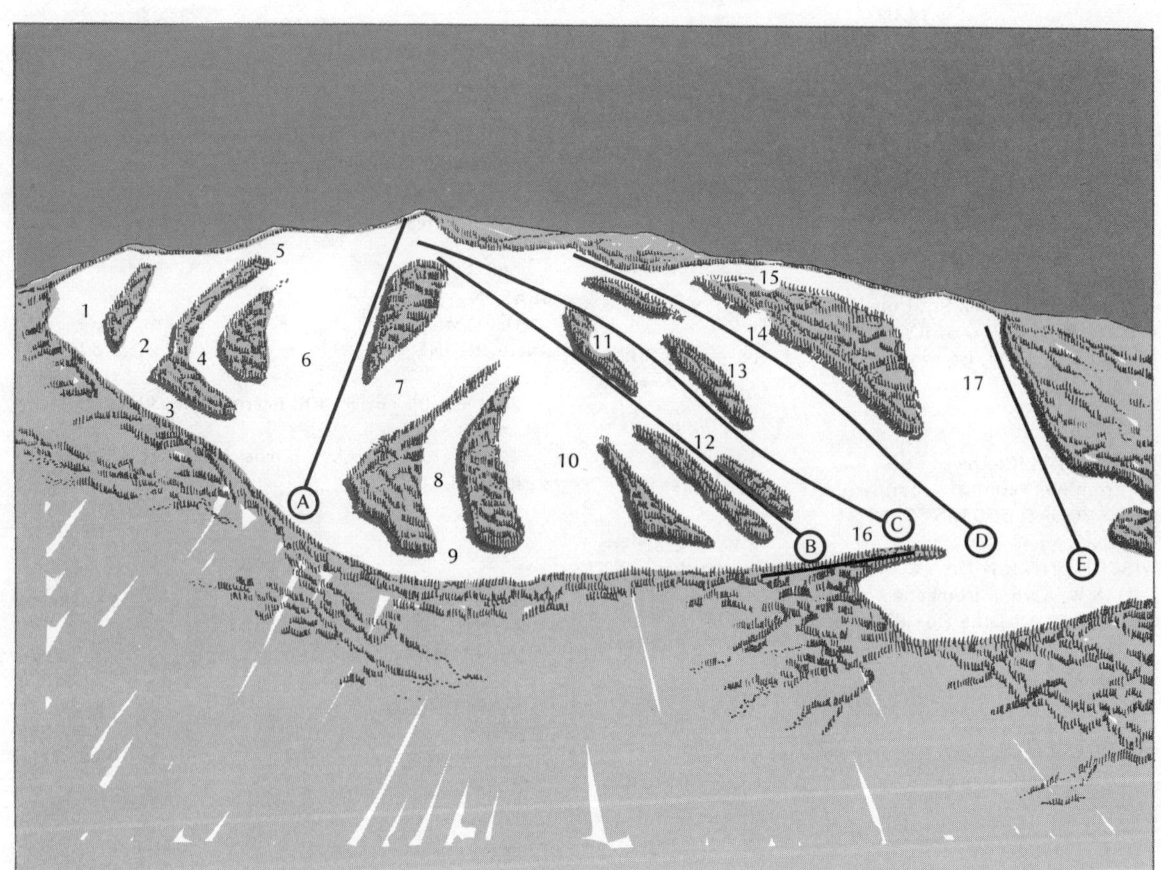

NUBS NOB LIFTS

1 FUN BOWL
2 EASY MILE
3 EASY MILE TRAIL
4 AMES LANE
5 THE RIDGE
6 DORIES BOWL
7 REVELRY
8 BIRCH RUN
9 EASY MILE TRAIL
10 SMOOTH SAILING
11 OLD SMOKEY
12 VALLEY
13 SCARFACE
14 CHUTE
15 NORTHWEST PASSAGE
16 PRACTICE AREA
17 MISTER CHARLIE

NUBS NOB RUNS

A DORIES LIFT
B BLUE LIFT
C GREEN LIFT
D YELLOW LIFT
E POMA LIFT

MINNESOTA

SPIRIT MTN.

9500 SPIRIT MT. PL DULUTH MN 55810 (218) 628-2891

AREA INFORMATION

CAMPING
Spirit Mountain Campground . . . . . . (218) 628-2891
HOURS
Mon., 10 a.m. - 5 p.m.
Tues. - Fri., 10 a.m. - 10 p.m.
Sat. & Sun., 9 a.m. -10 p.m.
LIFTS
2 triple, 3 double chairs, 7,000 per hr. capacity
LONGEST SLOPE
3,800 feet
RENTAL
At ski area
SEASON
Thanksgiving to April 1st
TRAILS
14 runs, 65 acres
25% beginner, 50% intermediate, 25% advanced
2 slalom runs, night skiing, snowmaking
TRAVEL
10 min. S. of Duluth on I-35, Baundary Ave. exit.;
150 mi. N. of Minneapolis/St. Paul.
By bus: Greyhound via Duluth Depot daily.
By air: Republic Airlines to Duluth Int'l. Airport.
By train: Amtrak daily from Minneapolis/St. Paul to the Duluth Depot.
VERTICAL DROP
610 feet

LODGING

THERE ARE 15 PRIVATE MOUNTAIN VILLAS AT THE SKI AREA. THE SPIRIT MOTOR INN IS ONE MILE FROM THE AREA. FOR INFORMATION AND RESERVATIONS CALL . . . . (218) 628-2891

FOR MORE DULUTH LODGING AND DINING INFORMATION . . . (218) 728-4285, 24 hr. no. 724-0872

DOWNTOWN

BEST WESTERN
131 W. Second St. 727-6851
HOLIDAY INN
250 S. First Ave., E. 722-8821
NORMANDY- BEST WESTERN
207 W. Superior ST. 722-1202
RADISSON DULUTH HOTEL
Fifth Ave. W. & W. Superior St.. 727-8981

EAST

EDGEWATER EAST - BEST WESTERN
2330 London Rd.. . . . . . . 728-3601, (800) 232-1333
LAKE AERIE MOTEL
2416 London Rd.. 724-8513

WEST

ALLYNDALE MOTEL
516 N. 66th Ave., W. 628-1061
DULUTH MOTEL
4415 Grand Ave. 628-1008
SPIRIT MOTOR INN
Across I-35 from Spirit Mountain. 628-3691

NORTH SHORE

SHORECREST SUPPER CLUB & MOTEL
10407 N. Shore Scenic Drive 525-2286

RESTAURANTS

THESE RESTAURANTS ARE IN DULUTH. THERE ARE 2 RESTAURANTS & 2 LODGES AT THE SPIRIT MT. CHALET

THE BELLOWS (Continental, American, entertainment)
2230 London Rd.. 728-4471
THE BLACK STEER (steaks, seafood, cocktails)
319 W. Superior St.. 722-7568
CHINESE LANTERN (Chinese, entertainment)
402 W. First St. 722-7481
COUNTRY KICHEN (American, open 24 hrs.)
1810 Miller Trunk 722-9883
9305 Westgate Bl.. 624-9591
THE EATING EMPORIUM (Syrian)
19 W. Superior St.
GRANDMA'S SALOON & DELI
522 Lake Ave. S. @ foot of Aerial Lift Bridge 727-7809
HIGHLAND SUPPER CLUB (American, dancing, band)
1301 Miller Trunk Hwy. 722-7713
THE JOLLY FISHER (seafood, cocktails)
10 W. Superior St. 722-4305
NATCHIO'S (Greek, belly-dancers)
109 N. 2nd Ave. W.
NORMANDY VILLAGE (American, dancing, band)
207 W. Superior St.. 722-1202
PERKINS CAKE & STEAK HOUSE (open 24 hrs.)
14th Ave. E. & London Rd. 728-3619
PICKWICK (char-broiled dishes)
508 E. Superior St. 727-8901
RADISSON DULUTH MOTEL (rooftop dining)
Fifth Ave. W. & Superior St.. 727-8981
SIR BENEDICTS TAVERN ON THE LAKE (sidewalk cafe)
805 E. Superior St. 728-1192
WILLIAM'S NORTH SHORE (American, entertainment)
2502 London Rd.. 728-3671

STORES & SKI SHOPS

ALL STORES & SHOPS LISTED ARE IN DULUTH. SKI RENTAL & REPAIR SHOP AT THE SKI AREA.

SPIRIT MTN. CONT.

APPLETREE (S. American, gifts)
1092 London Rd.. 724-5024

CANAL COMPANY (books, gifts, etc.)
Canal Park 727-5244

DAISY GIFT SHOP
St. Scholastica Priory. 728-3631

DULUTH TENT & AWNING (camping supplies)
1610 W. Superior St. 722-3898

KEG 'N MILL (health foods & aids)
1826 London Rd.. 724-0861

LIFESTYLE (gifts)
Normandy Mall, downtown

TWEED MUSEUM GIFT SHOP
Ordean Ct., Univ. of Minnesota 726-8527

WINSLOW'S GIFTS & PLAZA SHOP
Normandy Mall 722-3631
1231 E. Superior St. 724-0919

MONTANA

BIG MTN.

P.O. BOX 1215, WHITEFISH, MT 59937 (406) 862-3511

AREA INFORMATION

BASE ELEVATION
4,750 feet

HOURS
9:30 a.m. to 4:30 p.m., night skiing

LIFTS
3 chairs, 1 bar, 1 tow, 3,000 capacity per hour

LODGING
Central Reservations: 862-3511

LONGEST RUN
2.5 miles

NURSERY
Call ski area

SEASON
Late November to mid-April

SNOW PHONE
Call Ski Area

TRAILS
25 runs, 20% Beginner, 60% Intermediate, 20% Difficult

VERTICAL DROP
2,000 feet

BIG SKY

P.O. BOX 1, BIG SKY, MT 59716 (406) 995-4211

AREA INFORMATION

BASE ELEVATION
7,500 feet

HOURS
9 a.m. to 4 p.m.

LIFTS
1 gondola, 3 double chairs, 1 triple chair,
1 rope tow, 6,400 capacity per hr.

LONGEST RUN
3 miles

NURSERY
At slope, all day

SEASON
Thanksgiving thru April

SNOW PHONE
Outside Montana . . . . (800) 548-4486
In Montana 995-4211

TRAILS
35 miles, 24 slopes, 25% beginner,
50% intermediate, 25% advanced

VERTICAL DROP
2,300 feet

EMERGENCY

AMBULANCE. 587-0911
FIRE & MEDICAL EMERGENCY 587-0671
SHERIFF 586-2315

LODGING

ALL RESERVATIONS
Outside Montana . . . . (800) 548-4486
Within Montana 995-4211

CAMPING 995-4407

MEADOW VILLAGE
Broadwater Condos
Glacier Condos
Meadow Motel (economy lodging)
Silver Bow Condos
Yellowstone Condos

MOUNTAIN VILLAGE
Deer Lodge Condo
Hill Condo
Huntley Lodge (204 rooms, skating rink)
Stillwater Condo

RESTAURANTS

GALLATIN CANYON
Buck's T-4 (2 bars, game room, dancing)
Hunter's Inn (also bar)

HUNTLEY LODGE
Chet's Bar (entertainment)
Fondue Stake (dinner)
Main Dining Room (breakfast, lunch, dinner)
Steak House (dinner)

MEADOW VILLAGE
Yellow Mule (breakfast, lunch, dinner)

MOUNTAIN MALL
Ernie's Deli
Jimmer's Brass Bell (also bar)

SERVICES

AIR

Frontier Airlines, Bozeman's Gallatin Field 586-4711

Northwest Airlines, Bozeman's Gallatin Field 587-4591

AUTO RENTAL

Avis, at airport 587-0204

Hertz, at airport. 388-6939

National 388-6694

BUS

Yellowstone Park Bus Co.

TAXI

City Taxi, Bozeman. 586-2341

STORES & SKI SHOPS

THE COUNTRY STORE (groceries)

Meadow Village

ERNIE'S GENERAL STORE

In the Mall. 995-4376

LONE MOUNTAIN SPORTS

In the Mall. 995-4471

MOUNTAIN DRY GOODS (clothing)

In the Mall. 995-4141

T-s ON TOP (clothing)

In the Mall. 995-4347

VILLAGE REXALL DRUG

In the Mall. 995-4649

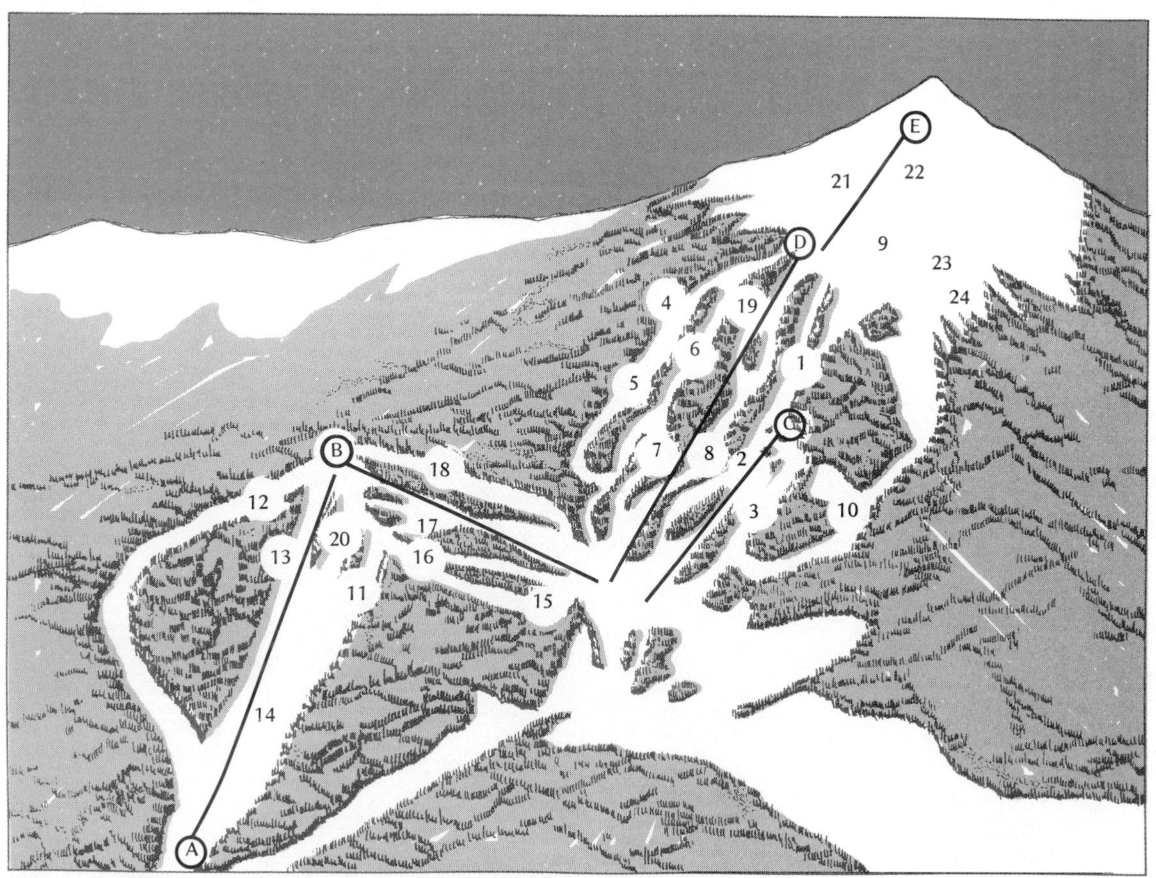

BIG SKY RUNS

1 K
2 LONE WOLF
3 WHITE WING
4 THE MEADOWS
5 LOBO
6 CALAMITY JANE
7 HUNTLEY HOLLOW
8 CRAZY HORSE
9 MORNING STAR
10 BOZEMAN TRAIL
11 ELK PARK RIDGE
12 BIG HORN
13 BROKEN ARROW
14 ELK PARK MEADOWS
15 SILVER KNIFE
16 TIPPY'S TUMBLE
17 AMBUSH
18 HANGMAN'S
19 BUFFALO JUMP
20 MAD WOLF
21 SUNDOWN
22 NEVER SWEAT
23 LITTLE ROCK TONGUE
24 BIG ROCK TONGUE

BIG SKY LIFTS

A MAD WOLF CHAIR
B RAMS HEAD CHAIR
C EXPLORER CHAIR
D GONDOLA
E LONE PEAK CHAIR

NEW HAMPSHIRE

BRETTON WOODS

BRETTON WOODS, NH 03575 (603) 278-5000

AREA INFORMATION

BASE ELEVATION
2,000 feet
HOURS
9:00 a.m. - 4:00 p.m.
LIFTS
2 chairs, 1 bar, 3,400 capacity per hour
LONGEST RUN
Over 6,300 feet
NURSERY
Toilet trained, call Ski Area
SEASON
Mid-December to mid-April, snowmaking
SNOW PHONE 278-5051
TRAILS
30% beginner, 45% intermediate, 25% advanced
TRAVEL
I-93 to Rt. 3 to Rt. 302 E. to Ski Area. North Conway is 30 miles beyond Bretton Woods on Rt. 302
VERTICAL DROP
1,100 feet

LODGING

CENTRAL RESERVATIONS. 278-1000

BRETTON WOODS MOTOR INN
Near Ski Area, shuttle bus provided
MOUNT WASHINGTON HOTEL
Near Ski Area, shuttle bus provided
TOWNHOUSES
At the Slopes

RESTAURANTS

DARBY'S TAVERN (Continental)
Bretton Woods Motor Inn 278-1000
FABYANS STATION (pub)
Bretton Woods 846-2222
MT. WASHINGTON HOTEL
Bretton Woods 278-1000
SKI SIDE
2 restaurants, 2 cafeterias, 3 cocktail lounges

DARTMOUTH SKIWAY

P.O. BOX 246, LEBANON, NH 03766 (603) 763-2301

AREA INFORMATION

BASE ELEVATION
1,000 feet
INFORMATION
75 E. Wheelock St. Hanover, 03755 643-3903
LIFTS
2 double chairs, T-Bar, 2,500 capacity per hr.
LODGING
Base Lodge with cafeteria, shop
LONGEST RUN
1 mile
SNOWPHONE. 795-2143
TRAILS
12, 1 slope
TRAVEL
Hanover, off Rt. 10, 3 miles E. of Lyme.
VERTICAL DROP
900 feet

KING RIDGE

P.O. BOX 246, LEBANON, NH 03766 (603) 763-2301

AREA INFORMATION

BASE ELEVATION
1,000 feet
LIFTS
1 triple & 1 double chair, 6,700 capacity per hr.
LODGING
New London 03257 763-2301
LONGEST RUN
1 mile
NURSERY
Base Lodge
SEASON
Dec. 29th - March 6th (peak)
SNOW PHONE 526-6966
TRAILS
12.4 slopes
TRAVEL
I-89, exit 11, New London
VERTICAL DROP
800 feet

MT. SUNAPEE

P.O. BOX 246, LEBANON, NH 03766 (603) 763-2301

AREA INFORMATION

LIFTS
5 double chairs, T-bar, 5,500 capacity per hr.
LODGING
Base & Summit Lodge, Ski Shop,
Mt. Sunapee 03772 763-2356
LONGEST RUN
1¾ miles
SNOW PHONE 763-4020
TRAILS
20

TRAVEL
I-89, Rt. 103 in Newbury
VERTICAL DROP
1,500 feet

RAGGED MTN.

P.O. BOX 246, LEBANON, NH 03766 (603) 763-2301

AREA INFORMATION

BASE ELEVATION
1,100 feet
LIFTS
Double chair, T-bar, 1,800 capacity per hr.
LODGING
Base Lodge, Cocktail Lounge, Ski Shop,
Danbury 03230 768-3971
LONGEST RUN
1½ miles
TRAILS
12
TRAVEL
Rt. 104, Danbury
VERTICAL DROP
1,400 feet

WHALEBACK

P.O. BOX 246, LEBANON, NH 03766 (603) 763-2301

AREA INFORMATION

BASE ELEVATION
1,200 feet
LIFTS
Double chair, 1,800 capacity per hr.
LODGING
Base Lodge, Ski Shop, Cocktails, Nursery,
P.O. Box 266, Lebanon 03766 448-2607
LONGEST RUN
1 mile
TRAILS
9, 3 slopes
TRAVEL
4 miles south of Lebanon, I-89, exit 16
VERTICAL DROP
670 feet

DARTMOUTH/ LAKE SUNAPEE

LODGING

ANDOVER MEADOW
Rt. 11, Andover 03216. 735-5224
ARNOLD'S MOTOR LODGE
Rt. 11 & 103 between Newport & Claremont,
R.F.D. 1, Box 267, Claremont 03743 542-2511
BACK SIDE INN
Rand Pond, R.F.D. 2, Box 541, 03773. 863-5161
THE BRADFORD INN
Near Junction 103 & 114,
Main St., Bradford 03221 938-5309
FAMILY CREST
Route 4-A, Enfield 03748 448-4007
FOLLANSBEE INN, North Sutton
Exit 10, I-89, Rt. 114, 03260 927-4221
THE HANOVER INN, Dartmouth College
Hanover 03755 643-4300
HOLIDAY'S LAKESIDE LODGE, New London
Rt. 103 A, 03257 763-5541
THE INN AT SUNAPEE
Burkehaven Rd., 03782 763-4444
KNOLWOOD INN
Box 44-D, Newbury 03255 763-2916
LAKEVIEW HOUSE
Box 164D, 03782. 863-2361
LAMPLIGHTER MOTOR INN
Newport Rd., New London, 03257. 526-6484
THE LEDGES FARM
Exit 13, I-89, Rt. 10, Grantham 03753 863-1002
LOCH LYME LODGE & COTTAGES
Lyme, 03768 795-2141
MASCOMA LAKE LODGE RESORT HOTEL
Enfield 03748 632-9378
MOOSE MOUNTAIN LODGE
Etna 03750 643-3529
MOUNT SUNAPEE HOTEL
Rt. 103, 03772 763-5592
MT. KEARSARGE INN & COUNTRY CLUB
North Sutton 03260 927-4246
NEWPORT MOTEL
Newport 03773 863-1440
OCCOM INN
35 N. Main St., Hanover 03755 643-2313
PLEASANT LAKE
N. Pleasant St., New London 03257 526-6271
SHERATON NORTH
I-89, exit 20, W. Lebanon 03784 298-5906
SUNAPEE WEST
P.O. Box 31, W. Springfield 03284 763-5945
SUNSET MOTEL
West Lebanon 03784. 298-8721
WHITE BIRCH MOTEL
Mount Sunapee 03772 763-2701

RECREATION

CAMPGROUNDS

CROW'S NEST
Newport, exit 9, I-90. 863-4030
RAND POND
Goshen, Rand Pond Rd., Rt. 103. 863-3350
SUNAPEE WEST (West Springfield)
Exit 13, I-89, left @ Grantham Store 763-5945

SNOWMOBILING

OSBORNE MARINE
Sunapee 763-2611

SNO-BUG VILLAGE
Danbury, 48 North Rd. 768-3901

SKI TOURING

DEXTER'S INN
9 Stagecoach Rd., Sunapee 763-5571
EASTMAN SKI TOURING
Grantham 863-4500
LA SALETTE SKI TOURING
Enfield, I-89, exit 17, Rt. 4 A 632-5533
THE LEDGES FARM
Grantham, exit 13, I-89, Rt. 10. 863-1002
NORS SKI TOURING (New London)
1½ miles east of I-89, exit 11, Rt. 11. 526-4685

RESTAURANTS

ANNIE MC CASSAR'S (jazz, disco, dinner)
163 Pleasant St., Claremont 542-9289
THE BISTRO - BEERGARDEN
AT CHEESE, ETC. (also take-out)
11 Lebanon St., Hanover. 643-2690
FOLLANSBEE INN (American)
Exit 10, I-89, Rt. 114, N. Sutton 927-4221
THE HANOVER INN (cocktails, dinner)
Dartmouth College, Hanover 643-4300
THE INN AT SUNAPEE (American)
Burkehaven Rd.. 763-4444
JESSE'S RESTAURANT (steak & seafood)
Hanover 643-4111
LANDERS RESTAURANT (Syrian)
Rt. 120, exit 18 off I-89 448-1243
THE LEDGES (beef raised on own farm, cocktails)
Grantham 863-1002
NEW LONDON INN (American, tavern)
New London. 526-2791
OLDE BRICK HEARTH STEAK HOUSE(cocktails)
Rts. 11 & 103, Newport 863-2665
PLEASANT LAKE INN (Continental)
N. Pleasant St., New London 526-6271
SHERATON NORTH
COUNTRY INN (Continental, bar, entertainment)
Airport Rd., West Lebanon 298-5906
SUGAR HOUSE RESTAURANT (American)
Off Rt. 89, exit 19, Colonial Plaza 298-7950

SERVICES

AIR

AIR NEW ENGLAND
Between Lebanon - Boston & New York
New York . . . . (800) 225-3640
Boston . . . . (617) 569-5510
Lebanon . . . . (800) 225-3640

AUTO RENTAL

AVIS
Lebanon Regional Airport. 643-3725

AUTO REPAIR

THE CAR STORE
Hanover 649-1603

BANKS

DARTMOUTH NATIONAL BANK
51 Lyme Rd., Hanover. 643-6321
FIRST CITIZENS NATIONAL BANK
55 Main St., Newport. 863-1750
Main St., Sunapee. 763-5400
Warner 456-2272

BUS

VERMONT TRANSIT
Daily from Boston, New York, Hartford, Montreal
Departs from Greyhound Terminals. . . (802) 295-3011

STORES & SKI SHOPS

BOB SKINNER'S SKI SHOPS (also rentals)
Mt. Sunapee Traffic Circle 763-2303
11 School St., Claremont 542-8412
BROWNS OF BERMUDA (European sportswear)
Main St., Hanover. 643-5005
CAMPION'S
Main St., Hanover. 643-4220
CARROLL REED (also rentals)
Mt. Sunapee Ski Area
37 S. Main St., Hanover 643-2206
THE COLLEGE SPORT SHOP (women's)
Main St., New London 526-2271
CROSSROAD OF SPORTS (also tennis, rentals)
King Ridge Ski Area 526-4220
New London, Main St. 526-4071
DARTMOUTH BOOKSTORE
Main St., Hanover. 643-3616
LEAGUE OF NEW HAMPSHIRE CRAFTSMEN
13 Lebanon St., Hanover. 643-5050
LEATHER 'N THINGS
Rt. 12 A, West Lebanon 298-8094

G U N S T O C K

P.O. BOX 336, LACONIA, NH 03246 (603) 293-4341

AREA INFORMATION

BASE ELEVATION
900 feet
HOURS
9:00 a.m. - 4:00 p.m.
8:30 a.m. - 4:00 p.m., weekends
LIFTS
3 chairlifts, 3 T-bars, 1 tow, 5,200 capacity per hour
LONGEST RUN
2½ miles
NURSERY
9:00 a.m. to 4:00 p.m., call Ski Area
SEASON
Mid-December to April 1st, snowmaking

SNOW PHONE 293-4341
TRAILS
25% beginner, 50% intermediate, 25% advanced
TRAVEL
I-93 to Rt. 3 to Rt. 11A to Ski Area
VERTICAL DROP
1,400 feet

LODGING

LACONIA SHERATON INN (restaurant, lounge)
Rt. 3, Laconia 5248000
LAURANNE VILLAGE (housekeeping cottages)
Route 11B 366-5589
MAE DENNY'S EATING,
DRINKING & LODGING ESTABLISHMENT
Junction of Routes 11 & 11B 293-4351
MARGATE RESORT (2 restaurants, lounge)
Rt. 3, Laconia 524-5210
MATTERHORN MOTOR LODGE
Rt. 25, Moultonboro Neck Rd., Moultonboro 253-4314
THE NASWA INN (near restaurants, lounges)
Rt. 3, Weirs Blvd., Laconia. 366-4341
RIVERVIEW MOTEL (near restaurants, lounges)
Alton Traffic Circle. 875-5001
TWIN LANTERN MOTEL (near restaurants, lounges)
Rt. 3, Weirs Blvd., Laconia. 366-4412
WINNISQUAM HOUSE MOTOR INN (restaurant, lounge)
3 mi. N. on U.S. Rt. 3 from exit 20, I-93 . . . 524-2708

RESTAURANTS

COLONIAL HOUSE OF PANCAKES (all day menu)
Rt. 11, Gilford, across from Shopping Plaza. . 524-9871
GANDY DANCER SALOON - HOWARD JOHNSON'S
Weirs Beach, Rt. 3 366-4766
THE GRIDDLE (breakfast, lunch)
Off I-93, Tilton 286-7105
MAE DENNY'S EATING,
DRINKING & LODGING ESTABLISHMENT
Junction of Routes 11 & 11B 293-4351
TIME OUT RESTAURANT & LOUNGE
Italian, American, seafood
644 Union Ave., Laconia. 524-1198
UNION HOUSE AND GRANITE PUB (lunch, dinner)
Downtown Laconia. 524-5783

STORES & SKI SHOPS

ARLBERG SKI SHOP
Opposite Ski Area entrance 293-7781
AUSTRIAN SKI SHOP
Rt. 11, opposite Laconia Airport 524-7445
GUNSTOCK SKI SHOP
Lower level, main lodge, Ski Area. 293-4341
LAKES REGION SHOPPING PLAZA
Rt. 11, Gilford
PICHE'S SKI SHOP INC.
Rt. 11A, Gilford & Bedford Aves., Laconia . . 524-2068

LOON MTN.

LINCOLN, NH 03251 (603) 745-8111

AREA INFORMATION

BASE ELEVATION
950 feet
HOURS
9:00 to3:30 p.m.
LIFTS
5 chairs, 1 gondola, 4,600 capacity per hour
LONGEST RUN
2¼ miles
NURSERY
Full services at The Inn, call Ski Area
SEASON
December to mid-April, snowmaking
SNOW PHONE 745-8100
TRAILS
20% novice, 50% intermediate, 30% expert
TRAVEL
I-93, "Mile 100" exit 32 to Loon Mountain Road, 2 miles to Ski Area – 2 hours from Boston, 3 hours from Providence, 3½ hours from Montreal, 4 hours from Hartford, 6½ hours from New York City.
VERTICAL DROP
1,800 feet

LODGING

BEACON MOTEL (restaurant & lounge)
Lincoln. 745-8118
THE INN AT LOON MOUNTAIN
(restaurant, apres & evening live entertainment)
Ski Area 745-8111
KANCAMAGUS MOTOR LODGE (1 mile)
Lincoln. 745-3365

RESTAURANTS

THE BARN AT LOON
(light suppers, live dancing, entertainment)
Ski Area, weekdays, 3:00 p.m. to 1:00 a.m.
Weekends, 11:00 a.m. to 1:00 a.m.
THE INN AT LOON MOUNTAIN
(apres & evening live entertainment)
Ski Area 745-8111
THE OCTAGON BASE LODGE (breakfast, lunch, snacks)
Ski Area, 8:00 - 4:30,
Upstairs - beer & wine, 11:30 a.m. - 5:30 p.m.
TRUANT'S TAVERN (lunch, light dinners)
North Woodstock 745-2239

STORES & SKI SHOPS

SPORT THOMA (ski shop)
Lincoln. 745-8151
Ski Area 745-8111
LOON MOUNTAIN POTTERY
Resident potters open throughout Lincoln

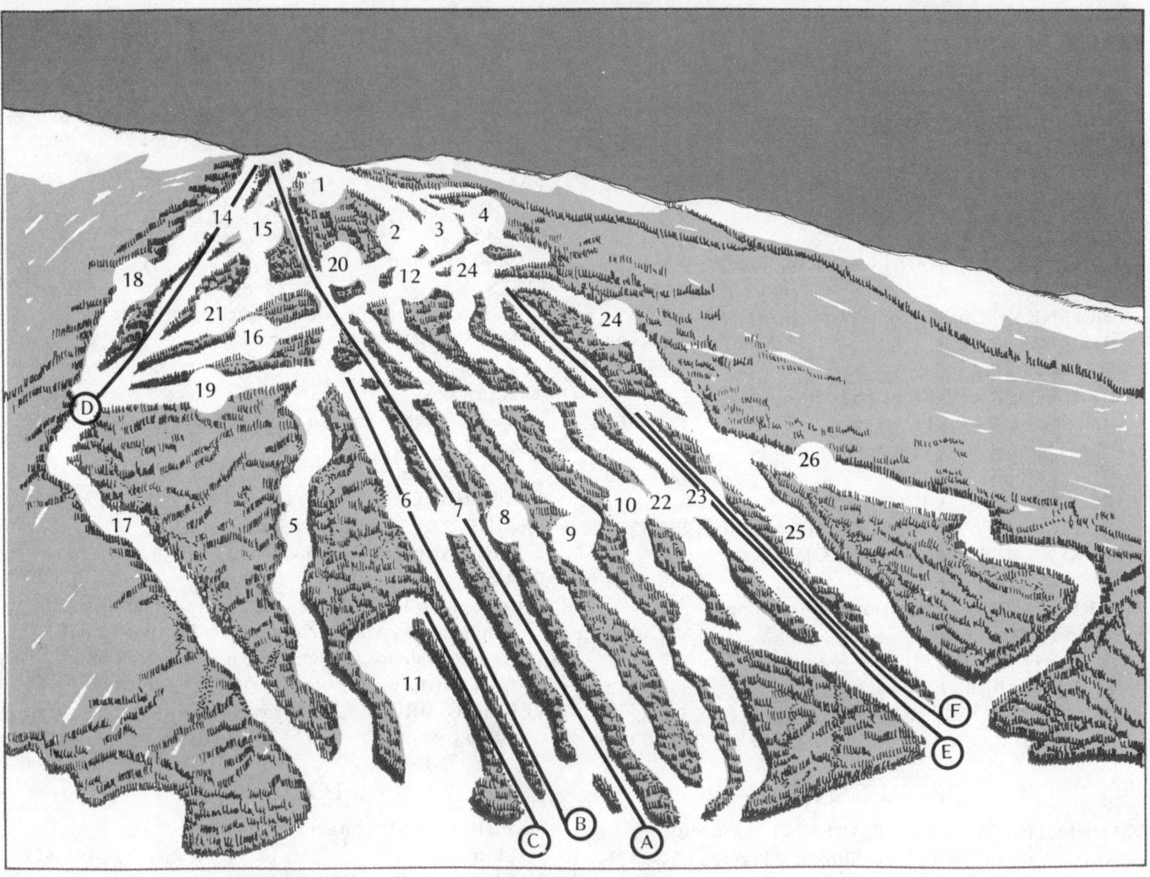

LOON MTN.

RUNS

1 EXODUS
2 UPPER FLYING FOX
3 UPPER PICKED ROCK
4 UPPER BEAR CLAW
5 LOWER BEAR CLAW
6 SEVEN BROTHERS
7 PICKEROON
8 LOWER FLYING FOX
9 LOWER PICKED ROCK
10 BLUE OX
11 LITTLE SISTER
12 GRAND JUNCTION
14 BIG DIPPER
15 ANGEL STREET
16 ROLLING BEAR
17 BROOKWAY
18 TRIPLE TROUBLE
19 THE LINK
20 CROSSCUT
21 LOWER BASIN STREET
22 RAMPASTURE
23 NORTHSTAR
24 RUMRUNNER
25 COOLIDGE STREET
26 SPEAKEASY

LIFTS

A GONDOLA
B SEVEN BROTHERS CHAIR
C LITTLE SISTER CHAIR
D EAST BASIN CHAIR
E WEST BASIN CHAIR I
F WEST BASIN CHAIR II

MT. WASHINGTON VALLEY

ATTITASH

RT. 302, BARTLETT, NH 03812 (603) 374-2369

AREA INFORMATION

BASE ELEVATION
793 feet

HOURS
9:00 a.m. - 4:30 p.m.

LIFTS
4 chairs

LONGEST RUN
2 miles

NURSERY
Open 7 days, 12 months & up, call Ski Area

SEASON
December 25th thru the winter, no snowmaking

SNOW PHONE 374-2369, (800) 258-0316

TRAILS
15 novice, 19 intermediate, 5 expert

TRAVEL
From the North, Routes 2, 16 and 302. From the South, I-95 & Rt. 16 to Rt. 302; 8 miles northwest of North Conway.

VERTICAL DROP
1,550 feet

BLACK MTN.

RT. 16B, JACKSON, NH 03246 (603) 383-4490

AREA INFORMATION

BASE ELEVATION
1,353 feet

HOURS
9:00 a.m. to 4:30 p.m.

LIFTS
1 chair, 2 T-bars, 1 J-bar, 2,900 capacity per hour
LONGEST RUN
1 mile
SEASON
Mid-December to Late March
SNOW PHONE 383-4490
Night 383-6886
TRAILS
3 novice, 6 intermediate, 5 expert, 2 practice
TRAVEL
From the North, Routes 2, 16 to 16B. From the South, I-95 & Rt. 16 to Rt. 16 B; 2 miles north of the Covered Bridge in Jackson.
VERTICAL DROP
1,200 feet

MT. CRANMORE

P.O. BOX 640, N. CONWAY, NH 03860 (603) 356-5544

AREA INFORMATION

BASE ELEVATION
500 feet
HOURS
9:00 a.m. - 4:00 p.m.
LIFTS
2 tramways, 3 chairs, 1 poma lift
5,000 capacity per hour
LONGEST RUN
1½ miles
SEASON
December to early April, snowmaking
SNOW PHONE
Call Ski Area
TRAILS
1 novice, 4 novice/intermediate,
7 intermediate, 5 expert
TRAVEL
From the North, Routes 2 & 16; from the South, I-95 to Rt. 16; then 1 mile from North Conway.
VERTICAL DROP
1,500 feet

PATS PEAK

RT. 114, S. HENNIKER, NH 03242 (603) 428-3241

AREA INFORMATION

BASE ELEVATION
690 feet
HOURS
9:00 a.m. - 4:00 p.m., weekdays
8:30 a.m. - 4:30 p.m., weekends
LIFTS
3 chairs, 2 T-bars, 1 J-bar,
1 rope tow, 6,000 capacity per hour
LONGEST RUN
¾ mile
NURSERY
1 to 5 years, call Ski Area
SEASON
Late November to early April, snowmaking
SNOW PHONE 428-3245
In Boston . . . . (617) 262-5454
TRAILS
37% novice, 39% intermediate, 24% expert
TRAVEL
On Flanders Rd. off Rt. 114 S., 3 miles south of Henniker Center, 15 miles west of Concord, exit 5 off I-89; 26 miles north of Manchester, on Rt. 114.
VERTICAL DROP
710 feet

LODGING

BRADFORD INN (full breafast & dinner)
20 minutes from Ski Area, Bradford 938-5309
BRICK TOWER MOTEL (dining room, cocktail lounge)
25 minutes from Ski Area, Concord 224-9565
COLBY HILL INN
(adults only, dining room, breakfast & dinner)
5 minutes from Ski Area, Henniker. 428-3281
CONCORD COACH MOTEL
25 minutes from Ski Area, Concord 224-2511
HENNIKER MOTEL (walk to lifts)
Opposite Ski Area. 428-3536
HIGHWAY HOTEL (dining room, cocktail lounge)
25 minutes from Ski Area, Concord 225-6687
HOWARD JOHNSONS MOTOR LODGE
(dining room, cocktail lounge)
25 minutes from area, Concord 224-4011
RAMADA INN (dining room, cocktail lounge)
25 minutes from Ski Area, Concord 224-9534
SHERATON WAYFARER (dining room & cocktail lounge)
30 minutes from Area, Bedford 622-3766
THE INN AT THE PEAK (bunk house, restaurant)
Across from Ski Area. 428-3228, 428-9407

RESTAURANTS

RESTAURANTS ARE LISTED UNDER LODGINGS

SKI SHOP

PATS PEAK SKI SHOP (rental, sales, service, repair)
At slopes, call Ski Area

TYROL

P.O. BOX 129, JACKSON, NH 03846 (603) 384-4315

AREA INFORMATION

BASE ELEVATION
1,450 feet
HOURS
8:30 a.m. to nightfall
LIFTS
1 T-bar, 1 poma lift, 1,200 capacity per hour
LONGEST RUN
1 mile

TYROL CONT.

NURSERY
Near the slopes, call Ski Area
SEASON
December to mid-April
SNOW PHONE 383-4315, 356-3171
TRAILS
2 novice, 5 intermediate, 3 expert
TRAVEL
From the North, Rt. 2 & 16 to 16B. From the South, Rt. I-95 to Rt. 16 to Ski Area; Jackson, 2 miles; and Conway, 8 miles.
VERTICAL DROP
1,000 feet

WATERVILLE VALLEY

MT. TECUMSEH, NH 03223 (603) 236-8311

AREA INFORMATION

BASE ELEVATION
1,850 feet
EMERGENCY
Ambulance & Fire 524-1545
Hospital 536-1120
Police. 236-4732
HOURS
9 a.m. to 4 p.m.
INFORMATION . . . . (603) 236-8311
LIFTS
4 double chairs, 3 triple chairs,
1 T-bar, 1 J-bar, 9,302 per hr. capacity
LONGEST RUN
3 miles
NURSERY
Daily
SEASON
Mid-Nov. thru April
SNOW PHONE
From MA, CT, RI, NY, NJ,
PA, DE, DC, MA, MI . . . . (800) 258-8983
From New Hampshire . . . . (800) 552-0388
TRAILS
7 beginners, 13 intermediate, 12 advanced
TRAVEL
130 miles north of Boston, 2½ hours, up I-93.,
6 hours from New York City.
VERTICAL DROP
2,020 feet

ALL LODGING, RESTAURANTS & FACILITIES ARE WITHIN WALKING DISTANCE TO THE SLOPE, OR ARE ACCESSIBLE VIA FREE SHUTTLEBUS.

LODGING

CENTRAL RESERVATIONS. 236-8371
BUNKHOUSE
The Waterville Valley Bunkhouse 236-8326
CONDOS
Mad River Condos 236-8211
Osceola Townhouses 236-8211
Settler's Waterville Condos. 236-8211
Snow's Brook Condominium 236-8211
Village Condos 236-8301
Windsor Hill Condos 236-8321
INNS
Landmark East & West. 236-8355
Silver Squirrel Inn. 236-8366
Snowy Owl Inn 236-8383
The Valley Inn & Tavern. 236-8336

RESTAURANTS

BASE LODGE RESTAURANT & LOUNGE . . .236-8311
FINISH LINE RESTAURANT & LOUNGE. . . .236-8800
FOURWAYS RESTAURANT. 236-8331
LOGGER'S BAR AT THE FOURWAYS. 236-8331
RUSTIC NAIL LOUNGE 236-8331
THE VALLEY INN & TAVERN 236-8669

SERVICES

AUTO SERVICE
Waterville Valley Mobil. 236-8604
CONVENTIONS
White Mt. Conference Center 236-8331
GROCERIES
Jugtown Country Store 236-8662
POST OFFICE
Jugtown Country Store 236-8204
SNACK BAR
Starting Gate 236-8311
TENNIS
The Valley Inn 236-8336

STORES & SKI SHOPS

FEMROCK ANTIQUES (at Snowy Owl Inn) . . . 236-8383
MT. TECUMSEH SKI SHOP. 236-8311
NORDIC SKI SHOP (at Ski Touring Center) . . . 236-8311
THE PARTRIDGE SHOPPE (at Finish Line) . . . 236-8881
THE RUFFLED GROUSE SHOP. 236-4747

WILDCAT MTN.

RT. 16, PINKHAM NOTCH JACKSON, NH 03846
TELEPHONE: (603) 466-3326

AREA INFORMATION

BASE ELEVATION
1,950 feet
HOURS
8:30 a.m. - 3:30 p.m.
LIFTS
3 chairlifts, 1 gondola, 1 T-bar, 5,000 capacity per hour
LONGEST RUN
2¾ miles

SEASON
Mid-November to late April, snowmaking
SNOW PHONE . . . . (800) 258-8902
From NH. . . . . (800) 552-8952
TRAILS
7 novice, 7 intermediate, 8 expert
TRAVEL
From the North, Rt. 2 to Rt. 16, about 10 miles south of Gorham. From the South, I-95, then Rt. 16, about 10 miles north of Jackson.
VERTICAL DROP
2,100 feet

CAMPGROUNDS

BLACKBERRY CROSSING (1st come, 1st served)
6 mi. W. of Conway, Kancamagus Hwy.
COVERED BRIDGE, SWIFT RIVER (1st come, 1st served)
6 mi. W. of Conway, Kancamagus Hwy.
CRAWFORD NOTCH STATE PARK (1st come, 1st served)
12 mi. from Bartlett, Rt. 302
DOLLY COPP, PEABODY RIVER (1st come, 1st served)
6 mi. S. of Gorham, Rt. 16
DUGWAY (1st come, 1st served)
4 mi. from Conway, Dugway Rd.
JIGGER JOHNSON (trailers, 1st come, 1st served)
13 mi. W. of Conway, Kancamagus Hwy.
MOAT VIEW TERRACE
W. Side Rd., N. Conway 356-5578
MOOSE BROOK STATE PARK (1st come, 1st served)
2 mi. W. of Gorham, U.S. 2 - swimming
N. CONWAY PINES
W. Side Rd., N. Conway 356-3305
SACO RIVER
Rt. 16, N. Conway 356-3360
SILVER SPRINGS
Rt. 302, Bartlett 374-2221
SIT 'N BULL
Rt. 302, Conway 427-8905, 447-5065
TUCKERMAN RIVER (1st come, 1st served)
16 mi. S. of Gorham, Rt. 16, AMC Permit
WHITE LEDGE (1st come, 1st served)
5 mi. S. of Conway, Rt. 16

LODGING

ADORA MOTOR INN &
OLD SCHOOL HOUSE DINING ROOM
(breakfast, dinner, full liquor license)
1 mi. S. of the Village, Rt. 16, N. Conway. . . 356-2601
ATTITASH MOUNTAIN VILLAGE (ski from your door)
Rt. 302, Bartlett 374-2386, 374-2752
BEECHWOOD MOTEL
Rt. 302, Glen 383-9680
BERNERHOF INN
Rt. 302, Glen 282-4414
BEST WESTERN NORTH CONWAY INN
(walking distance to the Village)
Rt. 16, N. Conway 356-5447, (800) 528-1234
BLAKE HOUSE
4 mi. N. of Jackson Village in Pinkham Notch
Box 246V, Jackson, 03846 383-9057
CHRISTMAS FARM INN (1778 Colonial Inn)
Rt. 16B, Jackson 383-4313
CLOVER MOTEL
Rt. 16, N. Conway 356-2871
THE COUNTRY INN & MOTEL
Rt. 302, Bartlett 374-2353
COVERED BRIDGE MOTEL
Rt. 16, , Box M277, Jackson, 03846 383-6630
CRANMORE INN
Kearsarge St., N. Conway 356-5502
CRANMORE MT. LODGE
1 mi. N. of Mt. Cranmore Inn
Kearsarge Rd., Box 1194, N. Conway, 03860 356-2044
CRESTWOOD MOTOR LODGE
Rt. 16, N. Conway 356-5492
DANA PLACE INN
Rt. 16, Jackson 383-6822
THE DARBY FIELD INN
Bald Hill, Conway. 447-2181
EAGLE MOUNTAIN HOUSE
Rt. 16B, Box E, Jackson, 03846 383-4264
EASTERN SLOPES LODGE
Main St., N. Conway 356-3686
FOX RIDGE RESORT
Rt. 16, N. Conway 356-3151
GATEWAY MOTEL & COTTAGES
Rt. 16, on the Saco River,
¼ mi. N. of Conway Village 447.2645
GREEN GRANITE MOTEL & APARTMENTS
Adjacent to entrance of Mt. Valley Shopping Mall
Routes 16 & 302, N. Conway 356-3960
HITCHING POST MOTEL
Rt. 16, Box M537, Conway 447-5919
THE HOLIDAY INN
Rt. 16A, Intervale. 356-9772
IRON MOUNTAIN HOUSE
Rt. 16, Jackson 383-9020
LABNON'S MOTOR LODGE
Junction of Routes 16 & 113, Conway. 447-3395
LEDGEWOOD INN
Rt. 16, N. Conway 356-3666
MARTINS MOTEL
Rt. 16, Conway 447-5366
MOTEL ON THE RIVER
Rt. 16, Jackson 383-4241
MOUNTAIN VALLEY MOTEL
Rt. 16A, Intervale. 356-2858
MOUNTAIN VALLEY RENTAL SERVICES
(private homes & condos)
Box 1255, N. Conway 356-2858, 356-6038
NANCY GRANT REALTY (condos, chalets, cottages)
Box 268, N. Conway 356-5371
NERELEDGE INN
¼ mi. from N. Conway Village 356-2831
NEW ENGLAND INN
Rt. 16A, Intervale. 356-5541
NORDIC VILLAGE RESORT (cottages)
Rt. 16, Jackson 383-4265
NORTH COLONY MOTEL
Rt. 302, Bartlett 374-6679
OLD FIELD HOUSE MOTOR LODGE
Rt. 16A, Intervale. 356-5478

OXEN YOKE INN & MOTEL
Kearsarge St., N. Conway 356-2931
PALMER HOUSE INN
Rt. 153, Eaton Center 447-2120
PARKA PLACE
Rt. 302, Glen 383-4303
PERRY'S MOTEL & COTTAGES
Rt. 16A, Box MWV80, Intervale, 03845 356-2214
POOL'N PINE MOTOR INN
Rt. 16, N. Conway 356-2811
PRESIDENTIAL WATERBED MOTEL
Rt. 16, N. Conway 356-9744
PUSS'N BOOTS MOTEL
Rt. 302E & 113E, 5 mi. E. of Conway 447-8905
RED JACKET MT. VIEW MOTOR INN
Rt. 16, N. Conway 356-5411
RIVER RUN MOTEL CONDOMINIUMS
Rt. 302, Bartlett 374-2386
SKY VALLEY MOTEL & CHALETS
Rt. 302, Bartlett 374-2322
SNOWVILLAGE LODGE
Snowville. 447-2818
STONE FOX LODGE
Tin Mine Rd., Jackson 383-6636
STONEHURST MANOR
Rt. 16, N. Conway 356-3113
STORYBOOK MOTOR INN
Routes 16 & 302
Box 100 MWC, Glen, 03838. 383-6800
SUNNY-SIDE LODGE
Seavey St., N. Conway 356-6239
SWANWIER MOTOR COURT
W. Main St., Conway 447-2471
SYLVAN PINES MOTEL
Route 16 & 302, N. Conway 356-2878
THORN HILL LODGE
Box MWV, Jackson. 383-4242, 383-9797
TUCKERMAN'S INN & TAVERN
Scenic Vista, Intervale 356-2752
VILLAGE HOUSE
Jackson Village 383-6666
WHITNEYS' VILLAGE INN
Jackson. 383-6886
Toll free, except Mass. . . . . (800) 225-2550
WILDCAT INN & TAVERN
Jackson Village 383-4245
WILDERNESS CABINS
Bear Notch Rd., Box 1289, Conway, 03818
WILDFLOWERS GUEST HOUSE
Rt. 16, N. Conway 356-2224
Toll free, except Mass. . . . . (800) 225-2550

RECREATION

ALPINE SLIDE, ATTITASH
Route 302, Bartlett. 374-2369
CANOEING & KAYAKING
Rt. 302, 2 mi. E. of the Conway 447-2177
CONWAY (auto toll road, summit view)
Pinkham Notch, Rt. 16, Mt. Washington. . . . 466-3988
FISHING
A New Hampshire license is required. Saco and Ellis Rivers: brook, rainbow and brown trout. Moose, Peabody, Swift, Wild and Wildcat Rivers: rainbow and Brown trout. East Branch River: brook and occasional brown trout. Crystal Lake: pickerel, splace and brook trout. Silver Lake: bass, pickerel, lake trout and salmon. Conway Lake: bass, pickerel, and lake trout. Falls, Hatch, Long, Mountain, Saco and Sawyer Ponds: trout.
GONDOLA TRAMWAY, WILDCAT MOUNTAIN
Rt. 16, Pinkham Notch. 466-3326
HERITAGE NEW HAMPSHIRE (exhibits, etc.)
Rt. 16, Glen 383-9775
HOME PORT (miniature golf, roller skating arcade)
Sunset Hill Rd. & Routes 16/302
HUNTING
For deer season dates. 356-3171
ROLLERSKATING
Brennan's House of Wheels
Rt. 302, Redstone 356-2478
SKI TOURING
Black Mountain, Jackson. 383-4490
Carroll Reed Touring Center
North Conway Country Club 356-3121
Mt. Cranmore, N. Conway 356-5544
Dana Place Inn, Jackson 383-6822
Jackson Ski Touring Foundation,
Box 90VA, Jackson, 03846 383-9355
Tyrol, Jackson. 383-4315
Wildcat Mt., Rt. 16, Pinkham Notch 466-3326
SKIMOBILE - MT. CRANMORE
Off Rt. 16, N. Conway 356-5544
STORY LAND (Kiddie amusement park)
Rt. 16, ¼ mi. N. of Rt. 302 383-4293
TENNIS & GOLF
Jack Frost Shop (tennis, 2 courts)
Rt. 16A, Jackson 383-4391
Mc Donald's Pro Shop (golf)
Main St., N. Conway 356-9700
Mountain Valley Court Club (health club, racquet ball)
Routes 16 & 302, N. Conway 356-5774
Mt. Cranmore Tennis Club (health club)
N. Conway. 356-3164
N. Conway Country Club (golf)
Main St. 356-9700
Wentworth Hall Golf & Tennis Club
Rt. 16A, Jackson 383-6659

RESTAURANTS

BARNABY'S (shows, dance entertainment)
Rt. 16, N. Conway 356-5781
THE BERNERHOF INN (European)
Rt. 302, Glen 383-4414
BIG PICKLE (home cooking, deli, wine & beer)
Seavey St., N. Conway 356-3954
BRADSTREET'S BEEF & BEVERAGE
(steak, seafood, dancing)
Rt. 16, 1 mile north of N. Conway 356-3996

CHEZ ALAIN (French)
Kearsarge St., N. Conway 356-5295
DAISY'S EATING & DRINKING ESTABLISHMENT
Eastern Slopes Inn, Main St., N. Conway . . . 356-5680
DANA PLACE INN (Continental, piano weekends)
Rt. 16, Jackson, Pinkham Notch 383-6822
DUNKIN DONUTS (bakery products, soup, 24 hours)
Rt. 16, N. Conway 356-5676
HEARTHSTONE (cocktails)
Crestwood Motor Lodge, Rt. 16, N. Conway 356-5492
THE HOMESTEAD RESTAURANT (salad bar)
Rt. 16, N. Conway 356-5900
HORSEFEATHERS (homemade food, bar)
Main St., N. Conway 356-2687
THE LOBSTER TRAP RESTAURANT
(B.Y.O.B. drinking privilege)
West Side Rd., N. Conway 356-5578
THE MAD HATTER RESTAURANT (Italian)
Rt. 302, Glen 374-6667
MERLINO'S STEAK HOUSE
Rt. 16, N. Conway 356-9705
RED PARKA PUB (steak house, seafood, entertainment)
Rt. 302, Glen 383-4344
THE SCOTTISH LION
1 mi. N. of town on Main St.
Rt. 16, N. Conway 356-2482
STORYBOOK INN (American, cocktails)
Routes 16 & 302, Glen. 383-6800
WILDCAT INN & TAVERN
Through the covered bridge, Jackson Village 383-4245

SERVICES

AIR

BERLIN
Milan Airport 448-2251
FRYEBURG, MAINE
Eastern Slope Airport . . . . (207) 935-2466
LACONIA
Winnipusankee Airlines. . . . . (800) 864-6811
MANCHESTER
Precision 623-7201
PORTLAND, MAIN
Delta . . . . (207) 774-3941
WHITE MT. AIRPORT. 356-2930

AUTO RENTAL

NATIONAL
N. Conway. 356-5718
PRESIDENTIAL MOTORS
Intervale 356-3136

BANKS

NORTH CONWAY BANK
S. Main St., N. Conway. 356-5466
Rt. 16, Glen 383-6813
WHITE MOUNTAIN NATIONAL BANK
Conway, N. Conway, Glen. 356-5451

DENTIST

EUGENE M. KUYSMAN
Pine Professional Bldg., N. Conway. 356-3355

HOSPITAL

N. CONWAY, RT. 16. 356-5461

TAXI

HARRIS TAXI
N. Conway. 356-5577

TELEGRAMS

WESTERN UNION. 356-5744

TRAVEL AGENT

SACO VALLEY TRAVEL
Gibson Block, Main St., N. Conway 356-5555

WEATHER

CONWAY 447-5252
N. CONWAY 356-3636

STORES & SKI SHOPS

BITTERSWEET GREENHOUSE
Rt. 16, N. Conway 356-3944
CARROLL REED SKI SHOP (rental, repair service)
Main St., N. Conway 356-3121
THE COUNTRY PEDDLER (cheeses, teas, jellies, gifts)
So. Main St., N. Conway. 356-3696
BOB DUNCAN CAMERA & RECORD SHOP (film)
Main St., N. Conway 356-2714
INTERNATIONAL MT. EQUIPMENT
(cross-country ski equipment)
Main St., N. Conway 356-5287
JACK FROST SHOP
(ski equipment, rentals, repairs, clothing, gifts)
Jackson. 383-4391
JOE JONES SHOP (skis, rentals, ski apparel)
Main St., N. Conway 356-2891
THE LANDFALL COLLECTION (gifts)
Main St., N. Conway 356-2743
NANTUCKET MODEL T'S (T-shirts)
Main St., N. Conway 356-5296
NORTH COUNTRY FAIR - SILVER STUDIO
(handcrafts, jewelry)
Theater district, Main St., N. Conway 356-5819
NORTH COUNTRY PHOTO (cameras, accessories, film)
Main St., N. Conway 356-5018
THE PENGUIN (home furnishings, glassware, houseware)
Main St., N. Conway 356-2340
QUODDY MOCCASIN FACTORY OUTLET
(leather, handsewn, also other lines of footwear)
Rt. 16, N. Conway 356-3237
RED CARPET SKI SHOP (accessories & rentals)
Bartlett. 374-6600

RIND & VINE CHEESE SHOP
Routes 16 & 302 356-6295
ROBBINS & KOLLN (fashion clothing)
Main St., N. Conway 356-2611
SCHATZI'S (fashion boutique)
S. Main St., N. Conway. 356-2022
SHAW'S (supermarket, deli)
Northway Plaza, Routes 16 & 302
N. Conway. 356-5471
SPORTS OUTLET SKI SHOPS (sales, rental, fashions)
N. Conway. 383-9641
Jackson. 356-2295
THE STARTING GATE SKI & GIFT SHOP
(full ski rental & service)
Base of Mt. Cranmore, N. Conway 356-3167
TOUCH OF CLASS
(goose down items, bath accessories, gifts)
Mechanic St., N. Conway 356-6301
WILDCAT VALLEY COUNTRY STORE
(old-time country store)
Rt. 16A, Jackson 383-9612
YIELD HOUSE (gifts, decorative accessories)
Rt. 16, N. Conway 356-5338

NEW JERSEY

HIDDEN VALLEY

P.O. BOX 433, VERNON, NJ 07462 (201) 827-2000

AREA INFORMATION

BASE ELEVATION
780 feet
HOURS
9:00 a.m. - 6:00 p.m.
6:00 - 10:30 p.m., night skiing
LIFTS
2 chairs, 1 tow, 2,800 capacity per hour
LONGEST RUN
3,600 feet
NURSERY
Ages 2 - 6, call Ski Area
SEASON
Early December to late March, snowmaking
SNOW PHONE 764-4200
TRAILS
25% beginner, 50% intermediate, 25% advanced
TRAVEL
I-80 to Rt. 23 N. to Rt. 515
to Breakneck Rd. to Ski Area.
VERTICAL DROP
620 feet

LODGING

APPALACHIAN MOTEL
Rt. 94, Vernon, 07462. 764-7127
FOUR SEASONS MOTEL
Rt. 23, Franklin, 07416 827-7890
HIGH POINT MOTOR LODGE
Rt. 23, Colesville, 07461. 875-4529
HOLIDAY MOTEL
Rt. 206, Andover, 07821 786-5260
PLAYBOY RESORT & COUNTRY CLUB
Great Gorge, Rt. 517, McAfee, 07428 827-6000
SUXXEX MOTEL
Rt. 23, Sussex, 07461 . . . . 875-4191, 875-7700
VALLEY VIEW MOTOR LODGE
Rt. 15, Sparta, 07871 729-3144
WARWICK MOTEL
Rt. 17-A South, Warwick, 10990 . . . . (914) 986-4822
94 MOTEL
Rt. 94, McAfee, 07428. 827-4666
ROLLING HILLS MOTEL
Rt. 23, Sussex, 07461 875-9923

RESTAURANTS

THE GEORGE INN
Rt. 94, McAfee 827-5758
HANNIBAL'S INN
Rt. 284, Westtown, NY . . . . (914) 726-3571
HIDDEN VALLEY BASE LODGE
Restaurant, cafeteria & cocktail lounge at the slopes
ST. CHARLIE'S INN
Rt. 23, Oak Ridge. 697-5151
WARWICK GARDENS
Galloway Rd., Warwick, NY. . . . . . . (914) 986-4383

VERNON VALLEY/ GREAT GORGE

BOX 848, MC AFEE, NJ 07428 (201) 827-2000

AREA INFORMATION

BASE ELEVATION
440 feet
HOURS
8:30 a.m. - 10:45 p.m., weekends & holidays
9:00 a.m. - 10:45 p.m., weekdays
LIFTS
14 chairlifts, 4 rope tows, 12,000 capacity per hour
LONGEST RUN
7,920 feet
NURSERY
2 - 6 years, call Ski Area
SEASON
Thanksgiving to April, snowmaking
SNOW PHONE 827-3900

TRAILS
50, 6% beginner 22% novice
42% intermediate, 28% expert
TRAVEL
From New York City, Lincoln Tunnel, Rt. 3 W. to Rt. 46 W. to Rt. 23 N. to Rt. 94 (Hamburg). Right on Rt. 94 E. for 3 miles. George Washington Bridge, Rt. 80 W. to Rt. 23 N. From New Jersey Turnpike & Pkwy., exits for Rt. 80 W. to Rt. 23 N. to Rt. 94 E.
VERTICAL DROP
1,040 feet

LODGING

CENTRAL RESERVATIONS. 827-2000

APPALACHIAN MOTEL 764-7127
HIGH POINT MOTOR LODGE. 875-4529
PLAYBOY RESORT & COUNTRY CLUB 827-6000
ROLLING HILLS MOTEL 875-9923
ROUTE 94 MOTOR LODGE 827-4666
SUSSEX MOTEL 875-4191
VALLEY VIEW MOTOR LODGE 729-3144
WARWICK MOTEL . . . . (914) 986-4822
HOLIDAY MOTEL. 786-5260

RESTAURANTS

CAFETERIAS
2 at slope
GASLIGHT ROOM AND BARNSTUBE
Great Gorge South
HEXAGON LOUNGE AT VERNON VALLEY
Overlooking ski slopes

NEW MEXICO

ANGEL FIRE

DRAWER B, ANGEL FIRE, NM 87718 (505) 377-2301

AREA INFORMATION

BASE ELEVATION
8,500 feet
HOURS
9 a.m. to 4:30 p.m., no night skiing
LIFTS
2 triple chairs, 4 double chairs, 3,200 per hr. capacity
LONGEST RUN
3½ miles
RENTALS (Call Ski Area)
Winter Sports, Day Lodge
Village Ski Shop, Ltd. (near main parking lot)
SEASON
Thanksgiving to Easter
SERVICES
Angel Fire Mini Mart & Pharmacy (groceries, gasoline, rent-a-car), at ski area. 377-2345
SNOWFALL
120 inches
SNOW PHONE 377-2301
TRAVEL
26 miles east of Taos, U.S. 64 to New Mexico 38.
By plane: private airstrip, 6,700 ft., altitude 8,370 ft., (Unicom 122.8).
Commercial flights daily to Albuquerque.
VERTICAL DROP
2,180 feet

LODGING

THE COMMONS AT ANGEL FIRE (jacuzzi, fireplace, etc.)
P.O. Box 121 377-2312
STEEN'S BEST WESTERN MOTEL
(clothing store, sauna, laundromat)
Hwy. 38, NM 87718 377-2301
THE STARFIRE LODGE (pool, laundry)
P.O. Drawer B. 377-2301
THE SNOWBIRD LODGE (sauna, game room)
P.O. Box 174 377-2393
THE WREN (Whirlpool, kitchens)
P.O. Box 48 377-2393

RESTAURANTS

ANGEL FIRE COUNTRY CLUB (entertainment)
1 mile past ski area, Hwy. 38 377-2301
FALLEN ANGEL LOUNGE
At Ski Area . . . . Call Ski Area

EAGLE CREEK

P.O. Box 1417, Ruidoso, NM 88345 (505) 336-4211
In state (800) 432-9031 Out of state (800) 545-5135

AREA INFORMATION

BASE ELEVATION
7,400 feet
HOURS
8:00 a.m. - 4:00 p.m., daily
6:00 - 10:00 p.m., Thursday thru Sunday, holidays
LIFTS
1 chair, 2 tows, 1 bar, 1,800 capacity per hour
SEASON
Late November to mid-April, snowmaking
SNOW PHONE
Call Ski Area
TRAILS
35% beginner, 55% intermediate, 10% advanced
TRAVEL
From Ruidoso, 7 miles northwest on Hwy. 37 to Ski Run Rd. to Ski Area.
VERTICAL DROP
500 feet

POWDER PUFF

P.O. BOX 786, RED RIVER, NM 87558 (505) 754-2941

AREA INFORMATION

BASE ELEVATION
8,600 feet
HOURS
9:00 a.m. - 4:00 p.m.
LIFTS
2 chairs, 3 tows, 5,000 capacity per hour
LONGEST RUN
500 feet
NURSERY
Call Ski Area
SEASON
Early November to Late March, snowmaking
SHOW PHONE
Call Ski Area
TRAILS
50% beginner, 40% intermediate, 10% advanced
TRAVEL
¼ mile west of Red River, 105 miles north of Santa Fe via Rt. 68 to Rt. 3 to Rt. 38 to Ski Area. From Denver, I-25 S. to Rt. 64 to Eagle Nest, Rt. 38 to Ski Area.
VERTICAL DROP
100 feet

LODGING

ALPINE LODGE
(restaurant, tavern, ski shop, rentals, beauty salon)
At base of Red River Big Lift, Box 137 754-2952
ARROWHEAD LODGE (rooms, apartments)
Close to Red River Ski Area, Box 261-C 754-2255
EDELWEISS CONDOMINIUMS (2 bedrooms)
P.O. Box 320 754-2942
EISENHUT CONDOMINIUMS
(3 - 4 bedrooms, daily maid service)
P.O. Box 305 754-2326
EL WESTERN LODGE (rooms, apartments)
Center of town, on the river, Box 301 754-2272
FOXFIRE LODGE (walking distance, both Ski Areas)
P.O. Box 203 754-2540
GOLDEN EAGLE LODGE (rooms, deluxe apartments)
P.O. Box 866 754-2227
THE LAZY BEAR LODGE (cabins & apartments)
P.O. Box 104 754-2981
THE LODGE AT RED RIVER (dining, cocktails, dancing)
P.O. Box 188 754-2213
PONDEROSA LODGE (2 bedroom apartments)
Center of town, Box 338. 754-2988
RED RIVER INN & RESTAURANT
(art gallery-gift shop, Avis Rental Cars)
Across from main chairlift, P.O. Box 818 . . . 754-2930
RIVER RANCH
Close to Powder Puff Ski Area, Box 300. . . . 754-2293

RESTAURANTS

RED ONION RESTAURANT
Alpine Lodge 754-2952
RED RIVER INN & RESTAURANT
Across from Red River main chair lift 754-2930
THE MOTHERLODE
(family-style dining, cocktails, dancing)
The Lodge at Red River 754-2213
TEXAS RED'S STEAKHOUSE, ETC.
Red River 754-2964

SERVICES

AUTO RENTAL

AVIS
Red River Inn 754-2930

BEAUTY SALON

BEAUTY SALON
Alpine Lodge 754-2952

STORES & SKI SHOPS

ART GALLERY - GIFT SHOP
Red River Inn 754-2930
RENTAL SHOPS
Powder Puff, call Ski Area
Red River, call Ski Area
SITZMARK SKI SHOP (and rentals)
Alpine Lodge 754-2952

RED RIVER

P.O. BOX 303, RED RIVER, NM 87558 (505) 754-2223

AREA INFORMATION

BASE ELEVATION
8,750 feet
HOURS
8:00 a.m. - 4:30 p.m.
LIFTS
4 chairs, 2 tows, 5,350 capacity per hour
LONGEST RUN
2½ miles
SEASON
Late November to mid-April, snowmaking
SNOW PHONE
Call Ski Area
TRAILS
35% beginner, 45% intermediate, 20% advanced
TRAVEL
North of Santa Fe, 105 miles via Rt. 68 to Rt. 3 to Rt. 38 to Ski Area. From Colorado, I-25 S. to Rt. 64 to Eagle Nest, Rt. 38 to Ski Area.
VERTICAL DROP
1,524 feet

RUIDOSO
SIERRA BLANCA

P.O. Box 220, Ruidoso, NM 88345 (505) 336-4356

AREA INFORMATION

BASE ELEVATION
9,700 feet
HOURS
8:45 a.m. - 4:00 p.m.
LIFTS
1 gondola, 6 chairlifts, 2 tows, 8,100 capacity per hour
LONGEST RUN
2½ miles
SEASON
Late November to mid-April, snowmaking
SNOW PHONE 257-9001
TRAILS
40% beginner, 40% intermediate, 20% advanced
TRAVEL
From El Paso, Texas, 180 miles northeast via US 54 to US 70 to Ruidoso, then 16 miles northwest via Rt. 37 to Rt. 532 to Ski Area.
VERTICAL DROP
1,700 feet

LODGING & RESTAURANTS

ALL LODGINGS ARE IN RUIDOSO
UNLESS OTHERWISE INDICATED

RESERVATION SERVICES 257-4947, 257-5081
Toll free . . . . (800) 545-5133, 545-5135

A FRAME CABINS
Box 1403 257-7474
ALPINE LODGE
Drawer M 257-4423
ALTO ALPS CONDOS
Box 130, Alto 88312. 336-4379
ALTO CREST CABINS
Box 2709 258-3535
AMERICAN MOTEL
Box 3639 HS 378-4825
APACHE MOTEL
Box 3914 HS 257-2986
APACHE VILLAGE
Box 488 257-2435
ALTO ALPS CONDOS
Box 130 336-4379
ASPEN LODGE APARTMENTS
Box 2625 257-2978
BLUE SPRUCE LODGE
Box 190 257-4451
BURCH'S FOX CAVE APARTMENTS (restaurant)
Ruidoso Downs 88346. 378-4781
CABIN RENTAL SERVICE
Box 1860 257-5511
CANYON CABINS
Box 1022 257-2076
CARRIZO LODGE
Drawer A. 257-2375
CASEY'S CABINS
Box 396 257-2804
CHAPPARAL HOTEL (restaurant)
Box 306 378-4461
CREE MANOR MOTEL
Box 3559 257-4058
CRO'S NEST MOTEL (restaurant)
Box 883 257-2773
DAN DEE CABINS
Box 844 257-2165
DOWNS MOTEL (restaurant)
Box 839, Ruidoso Downs 88346 378-4134
EL ALTO LODGE
Box 255 257-2521
FAIRWAY MEADOWS CONDOS
Box 2102 257-4019
FOREST HOME CABINS
Box 2068 257-4504
HIGH COUNTRY LODGE
Box 137 336-4321
HOLIDAY HOUSE (lodging, restaurant)
310 Sudderth 257-4003
HOLIDAY INN (restaurant)
Box 3830 HS 378-4051
HORSESHOE INN
Box 684 257-2870
IDLEHOUR LODGE
Box 576 257-2711
INN OF THE MOUNTAIN GODS (lodging, restaurant)
Box 259, Mescalero 88340. 257-5141
INNSBROOK VILLAGE CONDOS
Box A 257-4646
LA JUNTA GUEST RANCH
Box 139, Alto 88312. 336-4361
LAMPLIGHTER MOTEL
Box 1369 257-2327
LAZY T MOTEL
Box 442 257-4301
LOOKOUT ESTATES CONDOS
Box 1135 257-4542
MARK APARTMENTS
Box 2863 357-2771
MITCHEL MOTEL
Box 643, Ruidoso Downs 88345 378-4098
MOUNTAIN AIR CABINS
Box 2474 257-5600
NOB HILL LODGE
Box 3605 HS 257-4018
PINECLIFF CONDOMINIUM VILLAGE
Box 716 378-4427
PINES MOTEL
Box 3182 257-4334
PINON PARK CONDO RENTALS
Box 606 257-4995
PONDEROSA COURTS
Box 513 257-2631

RUIDOSO CONT.

RESORT PROPERTIES (management)
Drawer 2200. 257-9212

ROSEBUD CABINS
215 Main. 257-7989

RUIDOSO LODGE
Box 134 257-2510

SHAW'S APARTMENTS
Box 246 257-4455

SHERWOOD FOREST
Drawer U. 257-2424

SIERRA BLANCA CABINS
Box 458 257-2103

SITZMARK CHALET
Box 1235 257-4140

SKYLINE MOTEL
Drawer 936, Ruidoso Downs 88346 378-4220

SMOKEY BEAR MOTEL (restaurant)
US Hwy. 380, Capitan 88316 354-2253

STAGECOACH MOTEL
137 Sudderth 257-2610

STARLITE CABINS
Box 657 257-2255

STEWART MOTEL
Box 253 257-2504

STORY BOOK CABINS
Box 472 257-2115

SWISS CHALET MOTEL (restaurant)
Box 759, Alto 88313. 336-4392

THUNDERBIRD LODGE
Box 1421 257-2525

TIMBERLINE MOTEL
Box 3867 HS 378-4706

TOMAHAWK LODGE
Box 460 257-4078

TWENTY-NINE PINES
Box 1255 257-4249

TOWNHOUSE LODGE
Box 849 257-2511

VANTAGE POINTS APARTMENTS
Box 356 258-3100

VILLA INN (restaurant)
Box 3329 HS 378-4471

VILLAGE LODGE AT INNSBROOK
Box 2301 257-9021

WHISPERING PINES (lodging, restaurant)
Box 316 257-4311

WEST WINDS LODGE
Box 1458 . . . . 257-4031, (800) 238-2552

WINNER'S INN
Box 2733 257-5886

WORTLEY HOTEL (restaurant)
Box 55, Lincoln 88338. 653-4381

SKI SHOPS

A FRAME SKI SHOP
Hwy. 37, Box 1403. 257-7474

ADOBE SKI RENTAL
Adobe Shopping Center, Box 62 257-2684

ALPINE SKI SHOP
Sudderth Dr., Box 758 257-4505

ALTO SKI SHOP
Hwy. 37, Box 215, Alto 88312 336-4386

EAGLE CREEK SKI AREA
Ski Area Rd., Box 1417 336-4211

RAY HEID'S SKI SHOP
Sudderth Dr., Box 370. 257-7357

INN OF THE MOUNTAIN GODS
Hwy. 70 W., Box 259, Mescalero 88340. . . . 257-5141

MORGAN'S MOUNTAIN SPORTS
Hwy. 37, Box 1556, Alto 88312 257-5061

MOUNTAIN SKI SHOP
Sudderth Dr., Box 340. 257-4695

PERFORMANCE SKI SHOP
Sudderth Dr., Box 2370 257-5066

PRO SKI SHOP
Sudderth Dr., Box 2854 257-5096

RUSH SKI RENTAL
Mechem Dr., Box 2370. 257-4772

SIERRA BLANCA SKI SHOP
Sudderth Dr., Box 340. 257-4696

SKI TECHNIQUE
Sudderth Dr., Box 2844 257-9396

SKI WEST SPORTS
Ski West Shopping Court, Box 4582 257-7165

SKINNERS SKI RENTALS
Hwy. 37, Box 885 257-4275

ASPEN TRAILS SKI SHOP
Hwy. 37, Box 2713, Ruidoso 258-3610

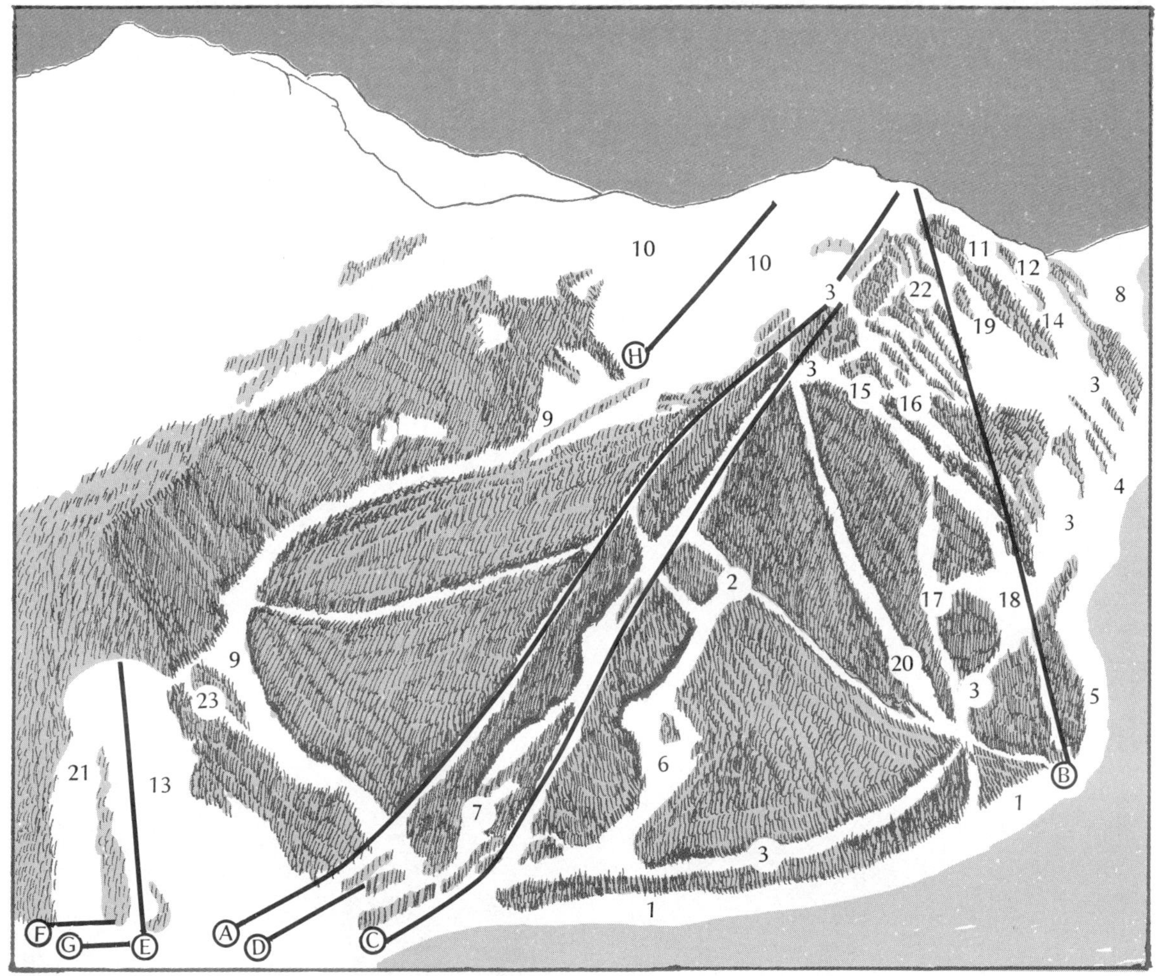

SIERRA BLANCA

RUNS

1 LOWER SPRUCE
2 UPPER SPRUCE
3 SIERRA BLANCA TRAIL
4 MOONSHINE
5 LOWER MOONSHINE
6 SNOW PARK
7 SMOKEY BEAR
8 AMBUSH
9 DEEP FREEZE
10 APACHE BOWL
11 MEADOWS
12 CHINO
13 CAPITAN
14 EAST MEADOWS
15 INCREDIBLE
16 THE TERRIBLE
17 PEEBLES
18 CHUTE
19 GERONIMO
20 CALIENTE
21 SLALOM HILL
22 ROVER
23 TOP NOTCH

LIFTS

A GONDOLA
B CHAIR NO. 1
C CHAIR NO. 2 (LINCOLN)
D CHAIR NO. 3
E CHAIR NO. 4 (CAPITAN, TRIPLE)
F POMA
G MIGHTEY MITE

SANDIA PEAK

10 TRAMWAY LOOP, N.E. ALBUQUERQUE, NM 87122
TELEPHONE: (505) 296-9585

AREA INFORMATION

BASE ELEVATION
8,500 feet

LIFTS
3 chairs, 2 pomas, 1 pony lift, 2,600 capacity per hr.

LOST & FOUND
Ticket desk

SEASON TICKETS. 296-9585

SKI RENTALS
Tramway, lower terminal & Ski Area, lower terminal

SNOW PHONE 296-9585

TRAILS
24, 10% beginner, 80% intermediate, 10% difficult

TRAVEL
2 miles northeast of Albuquerque,
I-40, N.M. 14, N.M. 44 or tram.

LODGING

AIRPORT MARINA HOTEL
2910 Yale Bl., S.E. 843-7000

BEST WESTERN FOUR SEASONS MOTOR INN
2500 Carlisle, N.E. 265-1211

HILTON INN
1901 University Bl., N.E. 243-8661

HOWARD JOHNSON'S MOTOR LODGE
900 Medical Arts Ave., N.E. 243-5693
PLAZA HOTEL
125 Second St., N.W.. 243-1321
RAMADA INN
25 Hotel Circle, N.E. 296-5472
SHERATON OLD TOWNE INN
800 Rio Grande Bl., N.W. 843-6300

RESTAURANTS

AL MONTE'S (Continental)
1306 Rio Grande Bl., N.W. 243-3709
ALFALFA'S (live rock, bar)
5001 Lomas Bl., N.E.. 268-9855
BIRD OF PARADISE (Mexican, dancing)
5211 Gibson Bl., S.E.. 255-1736
CARAVAN EAST (country music, dancing)
7707 Central Ave., N.E. 265-7877
COCINA DE CARLOS (Mexican)
4901 Lomas Bl., N.E.. 255-5079
THE ESTABLISHMENT (AMerican, bar, dancing)
275 Montgomery Plaza, N.E. 883-2560
FAR WEST CLUB (live entertainment, dancing)
10205 Central Ave., N.W. 831-4811
FRIARS CLUB (live entertainment, dancing)
6825 Lomas Bl., N.E.. 266-6605
HIGH FINANCE (bar, American)
Upper Tramway Terminal
LA FARIGOULE (French)
Guadalupe Trail, N.W. 898-1171
LIQUID ASSETS (American, bar)
6910 Montgomery Bl., N.E. 881-6476
OLE HENRY'S DINNER THEATRE
9704 Montgomery Bl., N.E. 293-5060
ORE HOUSE (American, bar)
7100 Central Ave., S.E. 266-5564
PELICAN'S (American, seafood, bar)
9800 Montgomery Bl., N.E. 298-7678
SUMMIT HOUSE (atop Sandia Peak)
Via Aerial Tramway
VICTOR'S GOOD TIMES (Cont., bar, entertainment, etc.)
4410 Wyoming Bl., N.E. 293-9363

SERVICES

ALL SERVICES ARE IN ALBUQUERQUE

AUTO RENTALS
Avis. 842-4080
Budget 243-2888
Hertz 842-4235
National 766-6827
BUS LINES
Greyhound. 243-4435
Shuttlejack (from airport) 243-2244
Trailways. 842-5511
EMERGENCY
Fire/Police 911
St. Joseph's Hospital, 400 Walter St., N.E.. . . 243-8811
TAXICABS
Albuquerque Cab 255-8623
Checker Cab 243-7777
Yellow Cab 247-8888

TRAMWAY
Sandia Peak, Tramway Rd., N.E.,
4 miles from city 298-8518

S A N T A F E

BOX 2287, SANTA FE, NM 87501 (505) 982-4429

AREA INFORMATION

BASE ELEVATION
10,400 feet
HOURS
9:00 a.m. - 4:30 p.m.
LIFTS
2 chairs, 3 poma lifts, 4,400 capacity per hour
LONGEST RUN
3 miles
SEASON
Late November to early April, snowmaking
SNOW PHONE 983-9155
TRAILS
20% beginner, 40% intermediate, 40% advanced
TRAVEL
16 miles northeast of Santa Fe on Rt. 475. Stop at a service station before you start - quite a climb.
VERTICAL DROP
1,650 feet

LODGING

ALAMO LODGE
1842 Cerrillos Rd. 982-1841
BISHOP'S LODGE (restaurant)
3 mi. N. of Plaza on Bishop's Lodge Rd. 983-6377
COTTONWOOD COURT
1742 Cerrillos Rd. 982-5571
EL REY MOTEL
1862 Cerrillos Rd. 982-1931
GARRETT'S DESERT INN (2 dining rooms - one, buffet)
311 Old Santa Fe Trail 982-1851
HILTON INN - SANTA FE (restaurant)
100 Sandoval 988-2811
HOLIDAY INN (restaurant)
2900 Cerrillos Rd. 471-8072
INN OF THE GOVERNORS (restaurant)
234 Don Gaspar. 982-4333
INN AT LORETTO (restaurant)
Old Santa Fe Trail & Alameda. 988-5531
LA CASA JUDY MOTEL
2325 Cerrillos Rd. 471-8273
LA FONDA HOTEL (restaurant)
100 E. San Francisco 982-5511
LAMPLIGHTER MOTEL (restaurant)
2405 Cerrillos Rd. 471-8987
LA PAZ COURT
725 Cerrillos Rd. 982-5952
LA POSADA INN
330 E. Palace Ave. 983-6351
LINDA MOTEL
2505 Cerrillos Rd. 471-8471
RANCHO ENCANTADO (restaurant)
State Rd. No. 22, Rt. 4, Box 570 982-3537

SANTA FE CONT.

RODEWAY INN (restaurant & lounge)
3011 Cerrillos Rd. 471-1211
SHERATON SANTE FE INN (restaurant)
750 N. St. Francis Dr., P.O. Box 2347 982-5591
THUNDERBIRD MOTEL
1821 Cerrillos Rd. 983-4397
TRAVELODGE
646 Cerrillos Rd. 982-3551
WESTERN SCENE
1608 Cerrillos Rd. 983-9893

RESTAURANTS

FOR ADDITIONAL RESTAURANTS, SEE LODGINGS

THE BULL RING
(2 restaurants, bar & lounge, entertainment 5 nights)
Continental (gourmet cuisine)
Cantina (New Mexican)
414 Old Santa Fe Trail 983-3328
THE CAPTAIN'S TABLE (cocktails, casual dress)
3364 Cerrillos Rd. 471-1919
CARROW'S HICKORY CHIP
FAMILY RESTAURANT (24 hours)
1718 St. Michael's Dr. 471-7856
CASA BLANCA (American food, happy hour, dancing)
La Fonda Hotel 983-2024
THE COMPOUND (lunch, dinner, Sunday brunch)
653 Canyon Rd.. 982-4353
DE ARCO'S MONK'S RETREAT
(Kosher sandwiches, noon to 7 p.m., entertainment, dancing, Fri. & Sat., 8 p.m. - 1 a.m.)
3397 Cerrillos Rd. 471-1991
THE DILI DELI
(sandwiches & dinner entrees, 11:30 a.m. - 7 p.m.)
On the Plaza
EL CAMINO REAL RESTAURANT (Mexican)
Airport Rd., ½ mi. from Airport
turn-off, on left 471-9971
EL GACHO INN (international, cocktails, entertainment)
Old Las Vegas Hwy. 983-9808
EL NIDO EN TESUQUE (prime rib, seafood, dancing)
5 miles north of the Plaza 982-8719
EL PARAGUA (Mexican, steaks, seafood, margaritas)
1 block E. of Taos Hwy. on Rt. 76, Espanola 753-3211
ERNIE'S (Swiss-trained chef, reservations advised)
731 Canyon Rd., Camino Cyn. Compound . . 982-4274
JIMMIE'S "TINY'S" RESTAURANT & LOUNGE
(Mexican, steaks, sandwiches)
1015 Pen Rd. Shopping Center 983-9817
LA PALOMA (native New Mexican, American)
225 East Devargas. 982-8182
LA TERTULIA
(century old adobe, native New Mexican food, cocktails, reservations)
416 Agua Fria 988-2769
TINNIE'S LEGAL TENDER
(American, wine list, cocktails)
I-25 to exit 290, Lamy 982-8425
THE PALACE (lunch in bar, dinner)
140 W. Palace 982-9891
THE PINK ADOBE (cocktails)
406 Old Santa Fe Trail 983-9976
PLAZA ORE HOUSE
(steak, seafood, entertainment in lounge)
50 Lincoln Ave, upstairs 983-8687
PLAZA RESTAURANT (Mexican, seafood, cocktails)
54 Lincoln Ave. 983-9918
THE SHED (lunch, native New Mexican)
113½ E. Palace, in Prince Patio 982-9030
SHOHKO CAFE (Japanese, Chinese)
At Jefferson & West Water behind Hilton Inn
409 W. Water St. 983-7288
SPANISH INN
(New Mexican, steak, seafood, piano lounge)
1611 Calle Lorca 983-3889
STEAKSMITH (cocktails, reservations advised)
210 Don Gaspar. 988-3333
TIA SOPHIA'S RESTAURANT
(Mexican, American, breakfast, lunch)
125 W. San Francisco. 983-9880

SERVICES

AUTO

CAPITOL FORD (service)
301 N. Guadalupe. 983-6316

BANK

FIRST NATIONAL BANK
The Plaza. 983-2782

STORES & SKI SHOPS

ALPINE SPORTS (cross-country & alpine)
121 Sandoval 983-5155
ARTESANOS IMPORTS
222 Galisteo St. 983-5563
BASE CAMP (cross-country)
121 W. San Francisco. 982-9707
THE CAMERA SHOP (1 day service on printing)
109 E. San Francisco 983-6591
JACKALOPE POTTERY
2820 Cerrillos Road 983-7430
SKI RENTAL SHOP
At the slopes, call Ski Area
TIANO SPORTING GOODS (complete rentals)
228 Galisteo 982-2518

SKI CLOUDCROFT

BOX 14, CLOUDCROFT, NM 88317 (505) 682-2587

AREA INFORMATION

BASE ELEVATION
8,600 feet
HOURS
9 a.m. to 4 p.m., night skiing
LIFTS
3, 1,000 per hr. capacity

LOCATION
2.2 miles E. of Cloudcroft, 20 miles E. of Alamogordo on U.S. Hwy. 82
LONGEST RUN
½ mile
TRAILS
16
SEASON
Thanksgiving to Easter
VERTICAL DROP
450 feet

LODGING

ASPEN MOTEL
P.O. Box 375 682-2526
BOYLAND'S TOWNHOUSE No. 4
Cloudcroft 682-2577
CLOUD COUNTRY LODGE
P.O. Box 287 682-2511
CLOUDCROFT INN
P.O. Box 493 682-2928
DE WITT'S END TOWNHOUSE
2847-B Quay Loop 479-2855
LAZY DAY CABINS
Mayhill, 88339 687-3693
MOUNTAIN CABIN REFERRAL SERVICE
2828 Quay Loop 479-2579
RENT A CABIN
P.O. Box 455 682-2631
TALL TIMBER CABINS
P.O. Box 402 682-2031

SERVICES

EMERGENCY
Ambulance/Police. 682-2090
Hospital 437-3770
Medical Facility 682-2542
BANK
First National 682-2531
GAS (also grocery)
Gulf, 8 mi. W. of town on Hwy. 82. 682-2955
GROCERY
Bradley's, 8 a.m. to 9 p.m.. 682-2128

S U G A R I T E

P.O. BOX 1043, RATON, NM 87740 (505) 445-5000

AREA INFORMATION

ELEVATION
8,000 feet
LIFTS
1 chair, 1 poma lift
SEASON
Thanksgiving to Easter, snowmaking Open Thursday thru Sunday and every day during the Christmas Holidays.
TRAVEL
12 miles from Raton, which is on I-25 & U.S. 64/87, a few hours drive from Albuquerque, Amarillo, and Denver. Check with Amtrak and Greyhound for schedules. Facilities for charter & private aircraft: see services.

LODGING

CAPRI MOTEL
304 Canyon Drive. 445-3641
COLT MOTEL
1160 S. 2nd St. 445-2732
CRYSTAL MOTEL
1021 S. 2nd St. 445-3681
EL KAPP MOTEL
200 Clayton Rd. 445-2791
EL PORTAL HOTEL
101 N. 3rd St.. 445-3631
EL RANCHO MOTEL
1005 S. 2nd St. 445-2291
GRANDVIEW MOTEL
312 Canyon Dr.. 445-8191
HOLIDAY INN
Clayton Rd. 445-5555
MAVERICK MOTEL
1510 S. 2nd St. 445-3792
MELODY LANE MOTEL
136 Canyon Dr.. 445-3655
MESA VISTA MOTEL
726 E. Cook 445-3611
MOTEL 6
Clayton Rd. 445-9666
OASIS MOTEL
S. 2nd St. 445-2766
ROBIN HOOD MOTEL
1354 S. 2nd St. 445-5577
SANDS MANOR MOTEL
Clayton Rd. 445-2737
TEXAN MOTEL
201 Clayton Rd. 445-3892
TRADEWINDS MOTEL
Clayton Rd. 445-2754
VIC MON MOTEL
305 Clayton Rd. 445-2763
VILLAGE INN MOTEL
1297 S. 2nd St. 445-3617
WESTERNER MOTEL
1460 S. 2nd St. 445-3101

RESTAURANTS

ALL SEASONS FAMILY RESTAURANT (open all day)
Hwy. 87 445-9889
CAPRI RESTAURANT
304 Canyon Dr.. 445-9755
COLT RESTAURANT
1160 S. 2nd St. 445-2457
CRYSTAL CAFE & LOUNGE (open all day)
1021 S. 2nd St. 445-9461
HOBO JOE'S (Fri. & Sat. to 3 a.m.)
Dona Anna Plaza 445-5256

SUGARITE CONT.

JOHNNY'S BAKERY & COFFEE SHOP
(breakfast & lunch, closed Sunday)
134 N. 2nd St.. 445-8131
LA COSINA CAFE (open all day, closed Tuesday)
745 S. 3rd. St.. 445-9675
LOREAN'S RESTAURANT & PANCAKE HOUSE
(Fri. & Sat., 24 hours)
Hwy. 87 445-9924
MARIA'S CAFE (open all day, closed Monday)
445 S. 2nd St.. 445-9575
MELODY LANE RESTAURANT (open all day)
136 Canyon Dr.. 445-3461
OASIS CAFE (open all day)
South of Raton 445-2766
RENO'S CAFE (24 hours)
140 Clayton Rd. 445-9919
SANDS RESTAURANT (open all day)
Hwy. 87 445-9777
SUGARITE STEAK HOUSE
At the slopes. 445-5000
SWEET SHOP (coffee shop / dining room in evening)
1201 S. 2nd St. 445-9811
TINNIE'S PALACE (open all day)
1st St. & Cook Ave.. 445-3285
UNCLE LOUIE'S (open all day)
255 Sugarite Ave.. 445-9931

SERVICES

AIR

RATON MUNICIPAL AIRPORT 445-3076, 445-3689

AUTO

JIM'S EXXON (service calls)
Raton. 445-9721

BANK

FIRST NATIONAL BANK IN RATON
2nd & Park Ave.. 445-2735

HAIR STYLING

BONNEE UNISEX STYLING SALON
Raton Realty Bldg., 139 S. 2nd 445-3221

STORES & SKI SHOPS

CARY-JO GIFTS
Dona Anna Plaza 445-8542
HAVEN COLLECTABLES
1st St., next to museum 445-9434
SUGARITE SKI & RENTAL SHOP
At the slopes, call Ski Area
TADUS JEWELRY
137 Cook Ave. 445-9731

TAOS SKI VALLEY

TAOS, NM 87571 (505) 776-2291

AREA INFORMATION

BASE ELEVATION
9,207 feet
HOURS
9:00 a.m. - 4:00 p.m.
LIFTS
6 chairs, 2 cable lifts, 5,200 capacity per hour
LONGEST RUN
5¼ miles
NURSERY
Ages 3 - 7, call Ski Area
SEASON
Saturday before Thanksgiving to mid-April
SNOW PHONE 776-2291
TRAILS
25% beginner, 25% intermediate, 50% expert
TRAVEL
Albuquerque to Santa Fe on I-25, Santa Fe to Taos on Rt. 68. Turn right onto Rt. 150 about 4 miles from Taos, then 15 miles to Ski Area.
VERTICAL DROP
2,612 feet

LODGING

ABOMINABLE SNOW-MANSION (dining room)
9 miles from the lifts
P.O. Box 3271. 776-8298
ADOBE WALL MOTEL
3½ blocks east of Plaza, Box 1081 758-3972
AMIZETTE INN (shuttle service)
2 miles from the slopes. 776-2451
EL PUEBLO MOTOR LODGE & CONDOMINIUMS
Near the plaza & Indian Pueblo
P.O. Box 92 758-8641
HOLIDAY INN
(coffee shop, dining room, cocktail lounge, entertainment, shuttle service)
HONDO LODGE
At the slopes. 776-2277
HOTEL EDELWEISS
At the slopes. 776-2301
HOTEL ST. BERNARD
At the slopes. 776-2251
KACHINA LODGE & MOTEL
(coffee shop, dining room, lounge, entertainment)
Near Indian Pueblo, P.O. Box NN. 758-2275
KANDAHAR CONDOMINIUMS
At the slopes. 776-2226
LA FONDA HOTEL (transportation to Ski Area)
On the Plaza, P.O. Box 1447 758-2211
RIO HONDO CONDOMINIUMS
At the slopes, base of Strawberry Hill 776-2646
SAGEBRUSH INN
(Continental, Mexican food, cocktails, entertainment)
P.O. Box 1566. 758-2254

SIERRA DEL SOL CONDOMINIUMS
At the slopes, 70 yards from lifts 776-2981

TENNIS RANCH OF TAOS (condo-hotel)
(restaurant, cocktail lounge, shuttle, indoor tennis)
P.O. Drawer BBB 776-2211

THUNDERBIRD LODGE & CHALETS
At the slopes. 776-2280

WAYFARER'S INN (restaurant, cocktail lounge)
Just east of the Taos Plaza, P.O. Box 604 . . . 758-2071

RESTAURANTS

APPLE TREE RESTAURANT (breakfast thru dinner)
Center of Taos. 758-1900

CASA CORDOVA (Continental, cocktails, wines)
Arroyo Seco, 10 miles from slopes 776-2200

DON PABLO GOMEZ (Mexican, American)
2 miles south of Plaza 758-9281

HONDO LODGE DINING ROOM (breakfast thru dinner)
At the slopes, call Ski Area

LA DONA LUZ (Continental, wines)
Just east of the Plaza 758-3332

MICHAEL'S KITCHEN (coffee shop & bakery)
North of the Plaza 758-4178

ROBERTO'S (Spanish)
East of the Plaza 758-2434

ROLF'S RESTAURANT & LOUNGE (Swiss)
14 miles from Ski Area. 776-2649

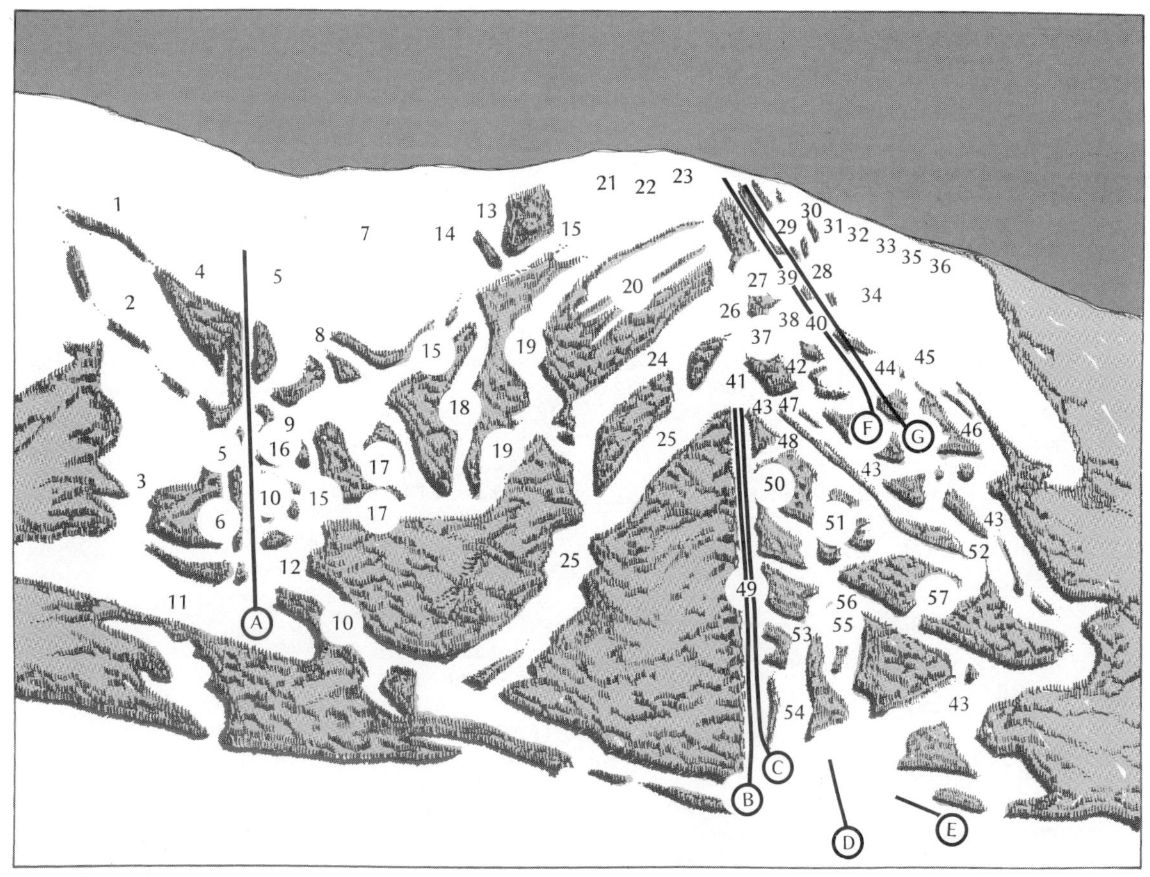

TAOS

RUNS

1 NASTAR CHUTE
2 HUNZIKER BOWL
3 EL FUNKO
4 SHALAKO
5 PATTON
6 LOWER PATTON
7 TWIN TREES CHUTE
8 JAPANESE FLAG
9 BABY BEAR
10 RUBEZAHL
11 SCHWENDI
12 STREET CAR
13 CORNER CHUTE
14 TRESKOW
15 HONEY SUCKLE
16 PAPA BEAR
17 WINKELRIED
18 TOTEMOFF
19 WALKYRIES
20 WALKYRIES CHUTE
21 NINOS HEROES
22 JUAREZ
23 HILDAGO
24 LORELEI
25 LONGHORN
26 BAMBI
27 CAMINO
28 SINUOSO
29 BLITZ
30 SPITFIRE
31 OSTER
32 FABIAN
33 STAFFENBERG
34 WEST BASIN
35 ST. BERNARD
36 THUNDER BIRD
37 CASTOR
38 POLLUX
39 REFORMA
40 BONANZA
41 ZAGAVA
42 UPPER POWDERHORN
43 WHITE FEATHER
44 MUCHO GUSTO
45 LOWER STAFFENBERG
46 FIRLEFANZ
47 PSYCHO-PATH
48 PORCUPINE
49 AL'S/RUN
50 RHODA'S INFERNO
51 SPENCER BOWL
52 BAMBI GLADE
53 SNAKEDANCE
54 SHOWDOWN
55 EDELWEISS GLADE
56 LOWER INFERNO
57 JEAN'S GLADE

LIFTS

A KACHINA
B EL CAPITAN
C CHILI LINE
D LITTLE TOOT
E POMA

BELLEAYRE

P.O. BOX 313, HIGHMOUNT, NY 12441 (914) 254-5601

AREA INFORMATION

BASE ELEVATION
2,540 feet
CHILDCARE
In the Novice Lodge - call Ski Area
EMERGENCY - FIRST AID AT AREA
HOURS
9:00 a.m. to 4:00 p.m.
LIFTS
4 chairs, 2 T-bars, 1 J-bar, 6,500 capacity per hour
LODGING
From NewYork . . . . (800) 942-6910
From Eastern U.S. . . . . (800) 431-6010
3 lodges at slope
LONGEST RUN
10,000 feet
RENTALS
At base - call Ski Area
SEASON
Thanksgiving to the end of March
SNOWPHONE. 254-5600
From New York. . . . . (800) 942-6904
From Eastern U.S. . . . . (800) 431-6012
TRAILS
25, 8 novice, 17 intermediate & difficult
TRAVEL
In the catskills, 37 miles west of Kingston, in Pine Hills, off Route 28.
VERTICAL DROP
1,265 feet

LODGING

ALL LODGINGS HAVE RESTAURANTS ON THE PREMISES, UNLESS OTHERWISE NOTED.

THE ALPINE INN
Alpine Rd., Oliverea 254-5026
AUBERGE DES 4 SAISONS (French)
Shandaken 688-2223
COLD SPRING LODGE
Oliverea Rd., Big Indian 254-5711
FLAGSTONE INN (coffee shop & lounge)
Fleischmanns 254-5101
KASS INN & MOTEL (entertainment)
Margaretville 586-4841
MERRITT'S MOTEL (no restaurant)
Rt. 28, Margaretville 586-4464
MT. GATE INN
McKinley Hollow Rd., Oliverea 254-9815
MT. VALLEY LODGE
Oliverea Rd., Big Indian 254-5300
PINE HILL ARMS
Main St., Pine Hill. 254-9811
STARLITE MOTEL (no restaurant)
Rt. 28, Pine Hill. 254-4449
THE WHITE HOUSE LODGE
Pine Hill 254-4200
WILDACRES MOTEL
Highmount. 254-9868

RESTAURANTS

OTHER RESTAURANTS ARE AT LODGINGS

AL'S (seafood, prime rib)
Rt. 28, Phoenicia 688-5880
THE PALMERS WOODLAND VALLEY INN (seafood)
Rt. 28, Phoenicia 688-5711
ROXBURY RUN (Swiss-American, entertainment)
Denver . . . . (607) 326-7577

BIG TUPPER

TUPPER LAKE, NY 12986 (518) 359-3651

AREA INFORMATION

BASE ELEVATION
2,000 feet
EMERGENCY
Ambulance. 359-9111
Hospital 359-3355
HOURS
9 a.m. to 4:30 p.m.
LIFTS
3 chairs, 1 T-bar
NIGHT SKIING
Trails 4, 5, 6, 7, 8, 13, & 14
SEASON
Mid-Dec. thru Easter
SNOW PHONE
359-3651
SNOWFALL
125 inches
TRAILS
10 novice, 9 intermediate, 4 expert
TRAVEL
From Albany, 150 miles; Lake Placid, 30 miles.
From Watertown, 95 miles; Lake Clear Airport, 35 miles.
VERTICAL DROP
1,152 feet

LODGING

ALL MAILING ADDRESSES ARE TUPPER LAKE UNLESS OTHERWISE INDICATED.
ZIP CODE - 12986, AREA CODE - 518

ADAMS GUEST HOUSE
39 Park St.. 359-3497
ADIRONDACK HOTEL ON LONG LAKE
Long Lake, NY 12847 624-4700

ALPINE MOTEL & MARINA
Overlooking Big Tupper Lake, Rt. 30 359-9553
AMERICAN HOUSE
72 Lake St. 359-7450
BAILEY'S LAKEVIEW MOTEL
24 Demars Blvd.. 359-9882
BARTLETT PAIR MOTEL
Box 35 Childwold, NY 12922. 359-2489
BULL POINT MOTEL & COTTAGES
On Upper Saranac Lake, P.O. Box 1089 359-2012
CRANBERRY LAKE INN
Box CC, Cranberry Lake, NY 12927 . . (315) 848-3301
CURTIGAY COVE
On Little Wolf Lake, 444 Park St. 359-3300
EMPERIAL MOTEL
Overlooking Big Tupper Lake, Moody Rd.. . . 359-9040
FAUST MOTEL
151 Main St.. 359-9088
GREENWAY TERRACE MOTEL
Box 1123, Moody Rd. 359-3660
HAUSER'S HAVEN
Little Wolf Rd., 103 Washington St. 359-9007
IRENE'S CAMPSITE & COTTAGE
Across from Little Wolf, Beach 359-9907
JAY'S STORM COVE
On Lake Simond, Lake Simond Rd. 359-9560
MT. ARAB LODGE & COTTAGES
Eagle Crag Lake, Box 786 359-9300
MT. MORRIS VIEW MOTEL
Star Route 2. 359-3286
NORTHWOOD CABINS
Sara-Tupper Hwy.. 359-9606
PANTHER POINT COTTAGE (On Upper Saranac Lake)
Box 928, Racquette River Dr.. 359-9383
PARK MOTEL
Routes 3 & 30, 336 Park St.. 359-3600
PINE TERRACE MOTEL & TENNIS CLUB
On Big Tupper Lake, Moody Rd 359-9258
PLAZA HOTEL
On Routes 3 & 30, 179 Park St.. 359-9840
QUINN COTTAGE (On Little Wolf)
Write: Nov. 1st to May 1st - 733 Willowhead Dr., Naples, FL 33940; May 1st to Nov. 1st - 840 E. Lake Rd. Canandaigua Lake, Rushville, NY 14544.
RED TOP MOTEL & COTTAGES
Overlooking Big Tupper Lake, Moody Rd.. . . 359-9209
SHAHEEN'S MOTEL, INC.
310 Park St.. 359-3384
SUNSET PARK MOTEL
On Tupper Lake, Rt. 3, 71 Demars Bl. 359-3995
THREE PILLARS ON TUPPER LAKE (Summer)
Moody Rd.. 359-3093
TIMBER LODGE MOTEL
Overlooking Big Tupper Lake, Moody Rd.. . . 359-2320
TOP NOTCH MOTEL
315 Park St.. 359-9467
TUPPER LAKE MOTEL
259 Park St.. 359-3381
WAUKESHA COTTAGES
On Big Tupper Lake, Moody Rd. 359-2650
WAUKESHA MOTEL
On Big Tupper Lake, Moody Rd. 359-2072

THE WAWBEEK (On Upper Saranac Lake)
Rt. 30 one mi. N. of Rt. 3, Summer (518) 359-3800
Winter . . . . (315) 386-8522
WHISPERING WOODS CAMPSITE & COTTAGES
Walker Rd., Long Lake, NY 12847 624-5121

RESTAURANTS

THE BARNSIDER
Moody Rd., Rt. 30 359-2234
BIG TUPPER COCKTAIL LOUNGE
Ski Area . . . . Call Ski Area
CANALI'S RESTAURANT/LOUNGE
320 Park St.. 359-9848
KADELI'S (deli)
Park St.. 359-2710
MASON'S RESTAURANT/LOUNGE
337 Park St.. 359-2181
OVILLA'S CLUB (disco)
Cliff Ave.. 359-9839
PINE GROVE RESTAURANT
166 Main St.. 359-3669
PLAZA HOTEL
179 Park St.. 359-9840

SERVICES

BANKS

FARMER'S NATIONAL
402 Park St.. 359-2917
TUPPER LAKE NATIONAL
75 Park St.. 359-3344

BUS

TRAILWAYS
Miss Tupper Diner, Cliff Ave. 359-9621

CLEANER

CORNELL DRY CLEANING
24 High St.. 359-2261

GROCERS, DELIS

GRAND UNION
Demars Bl.. 359-9825
LE BOUEF'S MARKET
17 Broad St.. 359-9875
SLIM'S MARKET
35 Wawbeek Ave.. 359-2274

LIQUOR STORE

RAY'S
Demars Blvd. Shopping Center 359-3450

LOCKSMITH

GERY'S LOCK & KEY
200 Main St.. 359-9430

BIG TUPPER CONT.

PHARMACY

MONAKEY & MEADER
82 Park St.. 359-3378

WESTERN UNION

TIP TOP SPORTS SHOP
40 Park St.. 359-9222

STORES & SKI SHOPS

AMERICAN MEROUN CLOTHING
22 Main St. 359-9393
AMES DEPT. STORE
Demars Bl 359-3325
GINSBERG'S DEPT. STORE
81 Park St.. 359-3301
JOHN MAROUN SPORTING GOODS
24 Main St. 359-3500
LARKIN'S GINGERBREAD HOUSE
68 Park St.. 359-3644
LA ROCQUE'S DEPT. STORE
87 Park St.. 359-3091
LA VALLEY'S WOODSHED (gifts)
Rt. 3, Demar's Bl.. 359-9440
MARY'S BOUTIQUE & DRESS SHOP
97 Park St.. 359-2121
MC CARTNEY'S MEN'S SHOP
96 Park St.. 359-2131
PUFF-N-STUFF (gifts)
72 Park St.. 359-3439
SHAW'S CRAFTS & HOBBIES
95 Park St.. 359-3369
SKI & SPORT SHOP
Ski Area
SUN SPORTS
53 High St.. 359-3886
TIP TOP SPORTS SHOPS
40 Park St.. 359-9222

B L U E M O N T

YORKSHIRE, NY 14173 (716) 496-6041

AREA INFORMATION

BABYSITTING
1 yr. & up, Non-holidays, Tues. thru Fri.
HOURS
Open 8 a.m., night skiing
LIFTS
2 rope tows, 2 T-bars, 1 double chair
SEASON
Late Nov. thru late March
TRAILS
2, 5 slopes, 3 difficult runs
TRAVEL
45 minutes from Buffalo, 1 hr. from Canada. From Buffalo, Rt. 400 S. to Rt. 16, right at Yorkshire Corners
VERTICAL DROP
110 feet

EMERGENCY

FIRE & AMBULANCE. 492-2522
HOSPITAL 592-2871
POLICE 373-2550

LODGING

NICHOLS BROOK MOTEL (3 miles from slope)
Routes 16 & 39, Sardinia 496-7226
JOHNNY'S MOTEL & RESTAURANT (5 miles from slope)
572 Main St., Arcade. 492-3600
ZOAR MOTEL (10 miles from slope)
Rt. 219, Box 35, Springfield. 592-2839

RESTAURANTS

NICHOUS BROOK
Olean Rd., Routes 16 & 39, Chaffee 496-9898
THE CRYSTAL INN
242 Main St., Arcade. 492-4392
THE ARCADIAN RESTAURANT
249 Main St., Arcade. 492-4010
LELAND HOUSE (also motel)
Main St., Springville 592-7631
MAMA'S RESTAURANT (Italian)
Olean Rd., Rt. 16, Chaffee. 496-8229

C O R T I N A V A L L E Y

HAINES FALLS, NY 12436 (518) 589-6500

AREA INFORMATION

BASE ELEVATION
1,925 feet
HOURS
9:00 a.m. - 4:00 p.m.
LIFTS
2 chairs, 1 tow, 3,400 capacity per hour
LONGEST RUN
5,200 feet
SEASON
Thanksgiving - April
SNOWMAKING
Yes
SNOW PHONE 589-6500
TRAILS
20% beginner, 60% intermediate, 20% expert
TRAVEL
From the South, N.Y. State Thruway, exit 20 to Rt. 32 to Rt. 32A to Rt. 23A. From the North, N.Y. Thruway exit 21 to Rt. 23 west to Rt. 296.
VERTICAL DROP
625 feet

EMERGENCY

AMBULANCE. 589-9700
FIRE 589-5151

HOSPITALS

Benedictine Hospital, Kingston . . . . . (914) 338-2500
Greene County Memorial Hospital, Catskill . . 943-2000
Kingston City Hospital . . . . (914) 331-3131

HUNTER POLICE 589-9700

SKI PATROL

Call Ski Area. . . . . 589-6500 X 25

LODGING

CENTRAL RESERVATIONS FOR ALL LODGING INCLUDING CONDOS & CHALETS 263-4208

ALFREDO'S SUNSHINE VILLA
Restaurant, cocktails

ANTONIO'S INN
Night club, meals cooked to order

COLONEL'S TABLE INN - O'SHEA'S
Dining, cocktails, entertainment

CORTINA VALLEY GUEST LODGE
Cocktail lounge

EGGERY LODGE
Full country breakfast

THE FORESTER
Walking distance to restaurants

FRIAR TUCK INN
Dining, cocktails

GREENE MOUNTAIN VIEW INN
Dining, cocktails

HANS COUNTY LINE MOTEL
Dining, cocktails

HERITAGE INN
1865 Colonial Inn

HUNTER HOUSE
Restaurant, cocktail lounge

THE KANE'S
Continental breakfast

THE REDCOAT'S RETURN
Full breakfast

RED RANCH MOTEL
Adjacent to restaurant

SCRIBNER HOLLOW MOTOR LODGE
Dining

SUN LAND FARM MOTEL
Dining

TERRACE GARDEN MOTEL
Restaurants nearby

VILLAGGIO RESORT HOTEL
Entertainment, dancing

VILLA VOSILLA
Cocktail lounge, night club, dancing

WASHINGTON IRVING LODGE
Dining, cocktails

RESTAURANTS

ALFREDO'S SUNSHINE VILLA (steaks, seafood, bar)
Main St., Hunter 263-4271

ALPINE RESTAURANT (breakfast thru dinner, cocktails)
Main St., Hunter 263-4448

BLUE STONE DINING ROOM (breakfast, dinner)
O'Shea's, Ski Bowl Rd., Hunter 263-4104

THE COOKERY (breakfast thru dinner)
Main St., Hunter 263-9940

CORTINA VALLEY GUEST LODGE (dining, cocktails)
At Ski Area

CRISTY'S (lunch, dinner)
Main St., Hunter 263-9940

ELEPHAS NORTH (3-level disco, no food)
Main St., Hunter 263-4217

FIRESIDE RESTAURANT (Sun. brunch, ski season)
Rt. 23A, Hunter. 263-4216

GANNON'S INN (cocktails)
Rt. 296, Jewett 263-9969

HANS COUNTY LINE RESTAURANT (all day menu)
Rt. 32A, Palenville 678-2264

HERITAGE INN (seafood)
Main St., Hunter 263-4333

LA GRIGLIA RISTORANTE (Northern Italian)
Rt. 296, Windham 734-4499

LEVITY'S CAFE (cocktails)
Main St., Tannersville. 589-9908

RUSTIC INN (breakfast thru dinner, open til 6 a.m.)
Main St., Tannersville. 589-9811

TANNERSVILLE YACHT CLUB
Rear of A & P Parking lot, Tannersville 589-5495

THE REDCOAT'S RETURN (country gourmet)
County Rd. 16, Platte Clove. 589-9858

STILLWATER
Fieldstone Fireplace Lounge, Pub room, sandwiches, steaks & snacks
Rt. 23A, Tannersville. 589-9903

SUGAR MAPLES DISCO LOUNGE (no food)
Live entertainment on weekends, Maplecrest . 734-4000

UNCLE'S (Live bands, dance floor, two large bars)
No food except Buffet & Happy Hours on weekends
Rt. 23A, Tannersville. 589-5551

VESUVIO RESTAURANT (Neopolitan)
Goshen Rd., Hensonville 734-3663

VILLAGGIO RESORT (Italian-American)
Rt. 23A, Haines Falls. 589-5000

VILLA VOSILLA (Italian-American)
Rt. 23A, Tannersville. 589-5240

GORE MTN.

RT. 28, N. CREEK, NY 12853 (518) 251-2411

AREA INFORMATION

BASE ELEVATION
1,500 feet

HOURS
9:00 a.m. - 4:30 p.m.

LIFTS
5 chairs, 1 gondola, 1 T-bar,
1 J-bar, 6,500 capacity per hour

LONGEST RUN
3½ miles

NURSERY
Ages 2 - 6 years 251-2612

SEASON
Early December to late March, snowmaking

GORE MTN. CONT.

TRAILS
20% beginner, 50% intermediate, 30% advanced
TRAVEL
Rt. 87 to exit 26, Pottersville, or exit 23, Warrensburg; continue on to North Creek, then 2 miles to Ski Area.
VERTICAL DROP
2,100 feet

LODGING

CHAMBER OF COMMERCE
Lake George 668-5755
North Creek 251-2612

RECREATION

SKATING RINK
SKI TOURING & SNOWSHOE TRAILS
TOBOGGAN & SLED SLOPE

GREEK PEAK

RD. 2, CORRAND, NY 13045 (607) 835-6111

AREA INFORMATION

BASE ELEVATION
1,320 feet
HOURS
Weekdays, 10:00 a.m. - 10:30 p.m.
Saturday & holidays, 8:00 a.m. - 10:30 p.m.
Sunday, 8:00 a.m. - 5:00 p.m.
LIFTS
6 chairlifts, 1 twin T-bar, 1 Poma lift
6,400 capacity per hour
LONGEST RUN
1½ miles
NURSERY
Open daily, Base Lodge - call ski area
SEASON
November to April, snowmaking
SNOW PHONE
Inside New York State . . . . (800) 252-9927
Outside New York State . . . . (800) 847-6727
TRAILS
48% beginner, 42% intermediate, 10% expert
TRAVEL
North-bound traffic on I-81, exit at Marathon exit 9 to Rt. 11 N. to Rt. 90 W. to Ski Area. South-bound traffic on I-81, exit at McGraw exit 10 to Rt. 11 S. to Rt. 90 W. to Ski Area.
VERTICAL DROP
780 feet

LODGING

ARCADIA (condos & homes across from slopes)
Mark J. Hamlet Real Estate, RD 2
Cortland 13045. 835-6111
BEST WESTERN DINKLER MOTOR INN
1100 James St., Syracuse . . . . (315) 472-6961
BROOKPINE SKI LODGE
Rt. 90, Virgil 849-6211
COLLEGETOWN MOTOR LODGE
312 College Ave., Ithaca, 14850 273-3542
CORTLAND HOLIDAY INN
2 River St., Cortland 756-7543
HOLIDAY INN - ARENA
2 Hawley St., Binghamton. 722-1212
HOLIDAY INN - SUNY
4105 Vestal Pkwy., Binghamton 729-6371
IMPERIAL 400 MOTEL
28 Port Watson St., Cortland 753-3383
ITHACA HOLIDAY INN
310 N. Triphammer Rd., Ithaca. 257-3100
ITHACA RAMADA INN
222 S. Cayuga St., Ithaca 272-1000
OWEGO TREADWAY INN
Upper Fifth Ave., Owego 687-4500
POINT MOTEL
Rt. 11, Whitney Point 692-4451
QUALITY INN
Upper Court St., Binghamton 775-7443
RIVERSIDE MOTEL
4408 Homer Ave., Cortland 753-3388
SEVEN VALLEY MOTOR LODGE
46 Tompkins St., Cortland. 753-1515
SHERATON ITHACA INN
One Sheraton Dr., Ithaca. 257-2000
THOMPSON'S MOTEL
390 Tompkins St., Cortland 756-7286
THREE BEAR INN
Exit 9 on I-81, Marathon. 849-3258
WONDERLAND LODGE
654 Elmira Rd., Ithaca 272-5252

RESTAURANTS

COMANDO'S RESTAURANT
3 Comando Ave., Cortland. 756-9666
CORINTHIAN TRAPEZARIA
At Ski Area 835-6111
FOUR FLAGS
10 South West St., Homer 749-3058
GOLDEN GARTER
Rt. 281 - West Rd., Cortland 753-6383
HOLIDAY INN - STONE BRIDGE MILL
Clinton Ave. & River St., Cortland 756-7543
HOWARD JOHNSON'S
Locust Ave., Cortland 756-9948
J. P.'s PLACE
91 North St. Ext., Dryden 844-9490
KELLY'S REEF
294 Tompkins St., Cortland 753-9397
L'AUGERGE ALPINE
34 Main St., McGraw 836-8984
LIDO RESTAURANT
152 Port Watson St., Cortland. 756-9679
LITTLE ITALIAN KITCHEN
Rt. 281 - West Rd., Cortland 756-9405
OLD PORT HARBOUR
702 W. Buffalo St., Ithaca 272-6550
PONDEROSA
Rt. 13, Cortland. 756-2383

TAVERNA
At Ski Area 835-6111
TERRACE RESTAURANT
Tompkins St. Ext., Cortland. 753-1151
THE RUSTY NAIL
Rt. 281 - West Rd., Cortland 753-7238
THREE BEAR INN
Cortland St., Marathon. 849-9618
TURBACK'S
919 Elmira Rd., Ithaca. 272-6484

SERVICES

SERVICE STATIONS

CANFIELD'S AMERICAN
W. Main St., Dryden 844-8608
DEMA AGORA (gas only)
Greek Peak. 835-6111
JOHN'S GROCERY STORE (gas only)
Rt. 90, Virgil 835-6780
KELLEY & SONS REPAIR SERVICE
77 Cortland St., Marathon 849-3003
GORDON'S GULF STATION
Clinton Ave., Cortland 756-9753
RT. 281 MOBIL
Rt. 281 & Madison St., Cortland 756-9561
VIRGIL GARAGE (no gas)
Rt. 90, Virgil 835-6713

THEATRES

CINEMA III
S. Main St., Cortland 753-8153
PLAZA THEATRE
Tompkins & Glenwood. 753-7386

STORES & SKI SHOPS

CORTLANDVILLE MALL
Rt. 13, Cortland
EUREKA CAMPING CENTER
625 Conklin Rd., Binghamton. 722-1212
JOHN'S GROCERY STORE
4 Corners in Virgil, 2 mi. from Ski Area 835-6780
NORDIC SPORTS
31 Main St., Downtown Cortland. 753-9553
OAKDALE MALL
Harry L Dr., Binghamton
SHOPPINGTOWN DEWITT
Erie Blvd. E., Syracuse
FAYETTEVILLE MALL
Syracuse/Fayetteville

HOLIDAY VALLEY

ELLICOTVILLE, NY 14731 (716) 699-2345

AREA INFORMATION

HOURS
Days, 9:30 a.m. - 4:30 p.m.
Weekends, holidays, 11 a.m. - 4:30 p.m.
Night, 4 p.m. - 10 p.m.
LIFTS
3 chairs, 3 T's, 2 tows
NURSERY
Pool house by Main Chalet, ages 2 - 9, 9 a.m. - 5 p.m.
SEASON
November to April
SNOW PHONE 699-2644
TRAILS
18; 13 lighted for night skiing
18 miles of cross-country
TRAVEL
45 miles south of Buffalo, Rt. 219 S.
VERTICAL DROP
750 feet

EMERGENCY

AMBULANCE. 699-2312
FIRE .699-2312, 699-2739
POLICE 699-2120

LODGING

EDELWEISS
Route 219 699-2734
ELLICOTTVILLE INN
Washington 699-2373
HOLIDAY HAUS
Route 219 . . . . .699-2151, 699-4809
HOLIDAY VALLEY MOTEL
Route 219 699-2160
KELLY HOUSE
39 E. Washington 699-4515
THE SKIER'S INN
Route 219 699-2391

RESTAURANTS

THE BARN (American, cocktails)
9 Monroe. 699-8991
BIRDWALK
Ashford Station 699-2749
BLUE DENIM (home style, sandwiches)
Route 219 699-2638
CARSON'S (American)
34 Washington. 699-8966
ELLICOTTVILLE DEPOT
Route 219 699-4774
ELLICOTTVILLE INN (cocktails, sandwiches)
10 Washington. 699-2373
GIN MILL
24 Washington. 699-8980
HABBITT'S HAUS (to go)
25 Washington. 699-4758
HARNESS SHOP (American, cocktails)
44 Washington. 699-8969
PEE WEE'S (tavern, American)
55 Washington St.. 699-8968
RUSTY NAIL (disco)
Route 219 699-4693
SILVER FOX
Hughey Alley 699-4622

HOLIDAY VALLEY CONT.

SERVICES

AUTO REPAIR

CITY GARAGE
48 Washington. 699-2334
GOLLEY'S
Washington & Mill 699-2878
SPAULDING
Route 219 699-4811

BANKS

M & T TRUST CO.
Washington St. 699-2341
SALAMANCA BANK
54 Washington St.. 699-2366

BUS

ELLICOTTVILLE TRANSIT 699-2105
TRAILWAYS
7 Washington 699-2384

DOCTOR / DENTIST

DR. DUSZYNSKI
E. Health Center 699-2371
STEPHEN ILLIG, DDS
3½ Washington St. 699-2354

DRUGS

HOLIDAY SHOP
7 Washington 699-2384

LIQUOR

GAY SPIRITS
17 Washington St.. 699-2293

LAUNDROMAT

DEPOT
Route 219, behind E. Depot

LODGING INFORMATION

CHAMBER OF COMMERCE
Tourist & Recreation 699-2722

STORES & SKI SHOPS

ADVENTUREBOUND (skiing)
16 Washington. 699-2364
DEKDEBRUNS (skiing)
Washington St. 699-2754
DOWN UNDER (clothing, gifts)
Washington & Monroe 699-2666
EARTH ARTS (gifts)
Washington & Monroe
ELDER CRAFT (clothing)
28 Washington. 945-3448
HOLIDAY SHOP (gifts)
7 Washington 699-2384
LIMITED EDITION (gifts, clothes)
27 Washington. 699-4064
MOUNTAIN SKI SHOP
Clubhouse Chalet at slope
NORTHRUP STYLE SHOP (clothing)
Washington St.
PRO SHOP
Holiday Valley

HUNTER MOUNTAIN

HUNTER, NY 12422 (818) 263-4223

AREA INFORMATION

BASE
1600 feet
CHILD CARE 263-4223
HOURS
9 a.m. - 4 p.m.
LIFTS
Capacity: 15,000 per hr., 1 triple chair, 8 double chairs, 1 T-bar, 2 poma lifts, 2 rope tows, 1 pony lift
SEASON
Thanksgiving thru Easter
SNOWFALL
125 inches
SNOW PHONE . . . . (212) 683-4933
TRAILS & SLOPES
Beginner 10, intermediate 16, advanced 11
TRAVEL
Catskill - ½ hour, N.Y. City - 2½ hrs., N.Y. Thruway, exit 20, Rts. 32 N. to 32 A to 23 A. From the North, N.Y. Thruway exit 21, E. on Rt. 23 & Rt. 23 A West.
VERTICAL DROP
1600 feet.

EMERGENCY

AMBULANCE. 589-9700
FIRE, Hunter 943-3333
GREENE COUNTY HOSPITAL 943-2000
POLICE 589-9700
RESCUE SQUAD. 589-5252
STATE POLICE. 263-4808

LODGING

HUNTER AREA HOTEL SERVICE 263-4723

ALFREDO'S SUNSHINE VILLA, Hunter. 263-4271
AUBERGE DES 4 SAISONS, Shandaken 688-2223
BAVARIAN MANOR, Purling 622-3261
CLOVER LODGE, Hunter. 263-4219
DOMENICK'S HOTEL, Tannersville 589-5950
EGGERY LODGE, Tannersville. 589-5363
EVERGREEN COTTAGES, Hunter 263-4932
THE FORESTER MOTOR LODGE, Hunter . . . 263-4555

HILLSIDE LODGE, Tannersville 589-5544
HUNTER HIGHLANDS, Hunter 263-3606
HUNTER HOUSE, Hunter. 263-4611
HUNTER'S VILLAGE INN, Hunter 263-4788
LEXINGTON HOTEL, Lexington 989-9797
THE MAPLES, Hunter 263-4497
MARICHKA MOTEL, Hunter. 263-4660
NIELSEN'S LODGE, Hensonville. 734-3749
NOTCH MOUNTAIN HOUSE, Hunter. 263-4936
O'SHEA'S COLONEL'S TABLE, Hunter 263-4104
PRATTSVILLE HOUSE, Pratsville 299-8571
RAINBOW CABINS, Catskill 678-3349
RED RANCH MOTEL, Palenville. 678-3380
ROSA DEL MONTE, Haines Falls 589-9796
SCRIBNER HOLLOW, Hunter 263-4211
SUN-LAND FARM MOTEL, Hunter. 263-4811
TERRACE GARDEN, Hunter. 263-4422
VILLAGIO RESORT, Haines Falls. 589-5000
VILLA VOSILLA, Tannersville. 589-5240
WERNER'S SWISS CHALET, Tannersville 589-5445
WINDHAM MT. INN, Windham. 734-4270

RESTAURANTS

ALFREDO'S SUNSHINE VILLA, Hunter. 263-4271
ALPINE RESTAURANT, Hunter. 263-4448
AUBERGE DES 4 SAISONS, Shandaken (914) 688-2223
CHATEAU BELLEVIEW (French), Tannersville 589-5525
THE CLUB (bar), Hunter 263-4480
DOMENICK'S, Tannersville 589-5950
EGGERY LODGE, Tannersville. 589-5363
FIRESIDE LOUNGE, Hunter 263-4216
GOLDEN ROOSTER, Hunter. 263-9984
HERITAGE INN, Hunter 263-4333
HUNTER HOUSE, Hunter. 263-4611
LA GRIGLIA (Italian), Windham. 734-4499
REDCOAT'S RETURN (English), Elka Pk. 589-6379
THETFORD'S SIR SIRLOIN (Continental, American)
Windham. 734-3322
VESUVIO (Italian), Hensonville 734-3663
WERNER'S SWISS CHALET (German)
Tannersville 589-5445

SERVICES

AUTOMOTIVE
Byrne's Garage, Tannersville. 589-6440
P & G Auto Body, Hunter 263-9916
Schaller's Automotive, Kingston . . . . (914) 338-4714
AUTO RENTAL
Avis, Lucas Ave., Kingston. . . . . (914) 338-5137

STORES & SKI SHOPS

CRAZYHORSE SKI & SPORT, Hunter 263-4249
FUN-TYME SKI & SPORT, Hunter 263-4400
HUNTER MOUNTAIN SKI SHOP, at area 263-4666
SNOW BIRD SKI SHOPS, Hunter 263-4433

WHITEFACE

WHITEFACE, NY 12997 (518) 946-2223

AREA INFORMATION

BASE ELEVATION
1,220 feet
HOURS
9:00 a.m. - 4:30 p.m.
LIFTS
5 chairs, 1 T-bar, 1 J-bar,
1 poma lift, 2,000 capacity per hour
LONGEST RUN
2½ miles
NURSERY
At the slopes, call Ski Area
SEASON
Mid-December to late March, snowmaking
SNOW PHONE 946-7171
TRAILS
35% beginner, 45% intermediate, 20% advanced
TRAVEL
In upstate New York, on Rt. 86, in Wilmington, about 35 miles from exit 30 of the Adirondack Northway, I-87. Follow signs to the Ski Area.
VERTICAL DROP
3,216 feet

EMERGENCY

AMBULANCE. 523-9511
FIRE 523-2535
PLACID MEMORIAL HOSPITAL 523-3311
POLICE 523-3306

LODGING

ADIRONDACK INN (restaurant, cocktail lounge)
Opposite the Olympic Center, Lake Placid. . . 523-2424
ADIRONDACK LOJ (family meals, cross country trails)
Box 867, Lake Placid. 523-3441
ALPINE MOTOR INN (restaurant)
Wilmington Rd., Rt. 86 523-2180
ARK LODGE (restaurant & cocktail lounge)
Rt. 9N, just N. of Keene, Upper Jay 946-2276
ART DEVLIN'S OLYMPIC MOTOR INN
2 blocks from Olympic Center 523-3700
BEST WESTERN GOLDEN ARROW MOTOR INN
(restaurant, cocktail lounge)
137 Main St., Lake Placid 523-3353
CARRIAGE HOUSE MOTOR INN
1 mi. from Lake Placid, Rt. 73 523-2260
EDELWEISS MOTEL
14 Wilmington Rd., Rt. 86, Lake Placid 523-3821
EDGE OF THE LAKE MOTEL
56 Saranac Ave., Lake Placid 523-9430
FAIRWAY INN (opposite restaurant)
Rt. 73, Lake Placid 523-3619
HAWKEYE MOTEL
(near restaurant, cross country trails)
Rt. 86, 1 mi. E. of Wilmington 946-2347

HOLIDAY LODGE & RESTAURANT (cocktail lounge)
At the foot of Whiteface Mtn., North Pole. . . 946-2251
HOLIDAY INN (restaurant, bar, entertainment)
Olympic Dr., Lake Placid 523-2556
HOLLY HILL MOTEL
Saranac Ave., Lake Placid 523-9231
HOWARD JOHNSONS MOTOR LODGE
(restaurant, bar & lounge)
Rt. 86, Saranac Ave., Lake Placid. 523-9555
HUNGRY TROUT MOTEL (restaurant & cocktail lounge)
Rt. 86, 9 mi. NE of Lake Placid. 946-2217
INN AT WHITEFACE (restaurant, cocktail lounge)
At the slopes. 946-2232
INTERLAKEN LODGE (restaurant, cocktail lounge)
Interlaken Ave., Lake Placid. 523-3180
LAKE PLACID HILTON
(restaurant, lounge, entertainment)
Saranac Ave., Lake Placid 523-4411
LAKE PLACID CLUB RESORT (restaurant)
Shore Dr., Lake Placid 523-3361
LAKESHORE MOTEL
54½ Saranac Ave., Rt. 86, Lake Placid 523-2261
LANDMARK MOTOR LODGE & RESTAURANT
At entrance to Whiteface Mtn. 946-2247
LEDGEROCK MOTOR INN (near restaurant, reservations)
Placid Rd., Wilmington. 946-2302
MC KELLEN'S PINE LODGE
4 Greenwood St., Lake Placid. 523-3070
MAPLE LEAF MOTOR INN
Village at Lake Placid. 523-2471
MIRROR LAKE INN (restaurant, 2 cocktail lounges)
Mirror Lake Dr., Lake Placid 523-2544
MON AMOUR (restaurant, cocktail lounge)
Saranac Ave., Lake Placid 523-2711
MOUNTAIN VIEW COTTAGE
59 Sentinel Rd., Lake Placid. 523-3053
NORTH COUNTRY MOTOR INN
Whiteface Mtn. 946-2488
NORTHWAY MOTEL
5 Wilmington Rd., Lake Placid 523-3500
OLYMPIC HEIGHTS
Cascade, Lake Placid 523-9328
PINES RESORT (housekeeping cottages)
46 Saranac Ave., Lake Placid 523-2800
PLACID BAY MOTOR INN
70 Saranac Ave., Lake Placid 523-2001
PRAGUE INN
Rt. 73, Lake Placid 523-3410
RAMADA INN
Saranac Ave., Lake Placid 523-2587
ST. MORITZ HOTEL (dining room, cocktail lounge)
Saranac Ave., Lake Placid 523-9240
SAMARINA MOTEL (next to restaurant)
34 Saranac Ave., Lake Placid 523-2750
SCHULTE'S MOTOR INN
Rt. 73, Lake Placid 523-3532
SKATE & SKI MOTEL
Saranac Ave., Lake Placid 523-3176
SWISS ACRES MOTOR INN (restaurant & lounge)
Saranac Ave., Lake Placid 523-3040
THUNDERBIRD MOTOR INN
Main St., Lake Placid 523-2439
TOWN & COUNTRY MOTEL
Whiteface Mtn. 946-2263
TOWN & COUNTRY MOTOR INN
65-67 Saranac Ave., Lake Placid 523-9268
TOWN HOUSE MOTOR INN
40 Saranac Ave., Lake Placid 523-2532
VILLAGE MOTEL
(next to restaurant & cocktail lounge)
The Village at Lake Placid, Rt. 73 523-2150
WHITEFACE INN COTTAGES
Whiteface Inn Rd., Lake Placid 523-2551
WHITEFACE CHALET
(restaurant, bar, lounge, cross country trails)
2 mi. from Whiteface Mtn.. 946-2207
WHITE SLED MOTEL (next to restaurant)
Rt. 73, Lake Placid 523-9314
WILDWOOD ON THE LAKE
88 Saranac Ave., Lake Placid 523-2624
WINTERSET INN (restaurant & cocktail lounge)
12 Lake Shore Dr., Lake Placid 523-4485

RESTAURANTS

ALPINE CELLAR (German)
Wilmington Rd., Lake Placid 523-2180
ANCIENT MARINER (seafood & Italian)
Main St., Lake Placid 523-9405
ARK LODGE (breakfast, dinner)
Upper Jay 946-2276
ART DEVLIN'S OLYMPIC MOTOR INN COFFEE SHOP
Main St., Lake Placid 523-3700
BENCHMARK RESTAURANT (lunch, dinner)
Saranac Ave., Lake Placid 523-9615
BURGERMEISTER (German)
Main St., Lake Placid 523-4326
BLACK STALLION ROOM
(Swiss, German & Italian, cocktail lounge)
Main St., Lake Placid 523-2424
CAPTAIN BILLY'S WHIZ BANG DELI
Main St., Lake Placid 523-2682
CASCADE INN
Cascade Rd., Lake Placid. 523-2130
CASK & CLEAVER (breakfast, lunch, dinner)
Ramada Inn, Saranac Ave., Lake Placid 523-2587
CHALET
Mirror Lake Dr., Lake Placid 523-3339
CHARCOAL PIT (cocktail lounge)
Saranac Ave., Lake Placid 523-3050
CHARLIE'S
Whiteface Inn Rd., Lake Placid 523-9955
CHUBB RIVER TAVERN
Main St., Lake Placid 523-9919
THE COTTAGE (full bar)
Mirror Lake Dr., Lake Placid 523-9845
COUNTRY KITCHEN (breakfast, lunch & dinner)
137 Main St., Lake Placid 523-3970

FREDERICK'S (entertainment weekends)
Signal Hill, Lake Placid 523-2310
HOLIDAY INN (live entertainment)
Olympic Dr., Lake Placid 523-2556
HOLIDAY LODGE (breakfast, dinner)
Base of Whiteface Mtn. Hwy. &
Santa's Workshop, Wilmington 946-2551
INN AT WHITEFACE (German & American)
Rt. 86, Wilmington 946-2232
INTERLAKEN LODGE (Swiss & French)
Interlaken Ave., Lake Placid 523-3180
JEREMIAH'S RESTAURANT & LOUNGE
(breakfast & lunch; dinner with a Continental menu)
Shore Dr., Lake Placid 523-4485
JIMMY'S 21 (lunch & dinner)
21 Main St., Lake Placid 523-2353
LAKE PLACID HILTON (entertainment in lounge)
Saranac Ave., Lake Placid 523-4411
LAKE PLACID CLUB RESORT
(cocktail lounge, entertainment, dancing)
Shore Dr., Lake Placid 523-3361
LUMS (family style menu)
Main St., Lake Placid 523-1706
MIRROR LAKE INN
(cocktail lounge, reservations requested)
Mirror Lake Dr., Lake Placid 523-2544
MON AMOUR
Saranac Ave., Lake Placid 523-2711
RINGERS ICE CREAM & SANDWICH SHOP
Alpine Mall, Lake Placid 523-9587
SWISS ACRES (Swiss & American, seafood)
Saranac Ave., Lake Placid 523-3040
VILLA VESPA (Italian)
Saranac Ave.. 523-9959
WHITEFACE CHALET (family style dining)
Wilmington 946-2207

SERVICES

AIR

ADIRONDACK Flying Service
Cascade Rd. 523-2473
AIR NORTH
Saranac Lake 891-0715
U.S. AIR
Saranac Lake . . . . (800) 245-2200

AUTO RENTAL

AVIS RENT A CAR
47 Hillcrest Ave. 523-3506
HERTZ RENT A CAR
Lake Placid Airport. 523-2473
NATIONAL CAR RENTAL
249 Main St.. 523-3377

AUTO REPAIR

AIRPORT MOTORS
Cascade Rd. 523-4322
DON'S SUNOCO SERVICE
417½ Main St.. 523-3878
GENE'S SHELL
211 Main St.. 523-9975
RAY'S EXXON
359 Main St.. 523-3434

BANKS

BANK OF LAKE PLACID
81 Main St. 523-9544
FARMERS NATIONAL
32 Saranac Ave.. 523-9535
MARINE MIDLAND
Saranac Lake 891-3711
SARANAC FEDERAL SAVINGS & LOAN
Saranac Lake 891-2323

BARBER / BEAUTY SHOPS

CARLO'S
Saranac Ave.. 523-2020
GILLIS HAIRCUTTERS
Alpine Mall 523-9736
HAIR DEN
322 Main St.. 523-3520
LAKE PLACID BEAUTY SHOP
Lake Placid Resort Hotel. 523-2828

BUS

ADIRONDACK SITESEEING
Hilton Plaza 523-4431
ADIRONDACK TRAILWAYS / GREYHOUND
89 Main St. 523-2950
HOYT'S TOURS
Saranac Lake 891-1473
SHOW & TELL TOURS
Cascade Rd. 523-3154

CLEANERS

AMERICAN VILLAGE
Coldbrook Plaza. 523-3811
EUGENE'S CLEANERS
River St. 523-3161

DRUG STORES

PLAZA PHARMACY
Cold Brook Plaza 523-2011
LAKE PLACID DRUG
Main St. 523-3385

GROCERIES

LAKE PLACID IGA
Main St. 523-2251
POTLUCK
Main St. 523-3106

WHITEFACE

RUNS

1 FOX
2 WOLF
3 BEAR
4 DEER
5 BUTTER CUP
6 APPLEKNOCKER
7 TRILLIUM
8 LOWER VALLEY RUN
9 LOWER NORTH WAY
10 BOREEN
11 BURTON'S CUT OFF
12 CALAMITY LANE
13 THRUWAY
14 MOUNTAIN RUN
15 VALLEY RUN
16 BROADWAY
17 EASY STREET
18 DARKWAY
19 APPROACH
20 WILDERNESS
21 MC KENZIE
22 EMPIRE
23 NORTHWAY
24 ESSEX
25 EXCELSIOR
26 DOWNHILL
27 CLOUDSPIN

LIFTS

A CHAIR 1A
CHAIR 1B
B CHAIR 2
C T-BAR
D J-BAR
E CHAIR 5
F CHAIR 6A
CHAIR 6B

WHITEFACE CONT.

CORNER GROCERY
Sentinel Rd. 523-3752

LIQUOR STORES

LAZY A LIQUOR
Main St. 523-9072

MIRROR LAKE LIQUOR
Main St. 523-3812

WINE & SPIRIT SHOPPE
Cold Brook Plaza 523-2333

LAKE PLACID LIQUOR
Sentinel Rd. 523-9222

TAXI

DABY'S LIMOUSINE
McKinley St.. 523-3611

EDDIE'S TAXI
River St. 523-2024

GENE'S TAXI
River St. 523-3161

PAT'S TAXI
Cascade Acres 523-3210
ROY'S TAXI
Hurley Ave. 523-2303

STORES & SKI SHOPS

ANTIQUE CLOSET (gift shop)
Crestview Plaza, Lake Placid. 523-3672
ARTHUR VOLMRICH (jeweler)
Main St., Lake Placid 523-2970
BARK EATER (ski shop)
Keene. 576-2221
BELL STORE (clothing)
Coldbrook Plaza, Lake Placid 523-3020
CASCADE SKI TOURING
Cascade Rd., Lake Placid. 523-9605
CRESTVIEW GIFT GALLERY
Main St., Lake Placid 523-3672
DARRAH COOPER JEWELERS
Hilton Plaza, Lake Placid. 523-2774
EASTERN MOUNTAIN SPORTS (ski equipment)
Main St., Lake Placid 523-2505
EQUIPE SPORTS (ski equipment)
Main St. 523-2909
ETCETRA (gift shop)
Main St., Lake Placid 523-9622
E-MAGA-ZEE (clothing, gifts)
Main St., Lake Placid 523-3560
HIGH PEAKS WESTERN GIFTS
Alpine Mall, Lake Placid 523-2571
HOCUS POCUS (clothing)
8 Main St., Lake Placid. 523-2111
ORMSBY'S NEWS & GIFTS
Main St., Lake Placid 523-3012
PLACID CREATIONS (gift shop)
Alpine Mall, Lake Placid 523-9541
QUILTED TURTLE (clothing)
Main St., Lake Placid 523-4448
SWISS SHOP (ski equipment)
Main St., Lake Placid 523-3772
VILLAGE STORE (clothing)
117 Main St., Lake Placid 523-2830

NORTH CAROLINA

CATALOOCHEE

RT. 1, BOX 500, MAGGIE, NC 28751 (704) 926-0285

AREA INFORMATION

BASE ELEVATION
4,660 feet
HOURS
9:30 a.m. - 4:30 p.m., daily
7:00 p.m. - 10:00 p.m.Wed. & Fri. nights (after Jan. 1st)
LIFTS
1 chair, 2 tows, 1 T-bar, 1,500 capacity per hour
LONGEST RUN
With snowmaking, 5,300 feet
SEASON
December 1st to March 1st
SNOWMAKING
Yes
SNOW PHONE 926-1401
TRAILS
1 novice, 1 ski school, 2 advanced, 4 intermediate
TRAVEL
Four miles off U.S. 19 at Maggie Valley, connecting with I-40 & I-26; 35 miles west of Asheville, 20 miles east of Cherokee. United & Piedmont Airlines to Asheville's all weather airport. Fixed base operator, Asheville Flying Service. Rental cars at airport.
VERTICAL DROP
740 feet

LODGING

CENTRAL RESERVATIONS (24 hr. service) 926-0455
COOL WATER COTTAGES & MOTEL
Hwy. 19, Maggie Valley 926-1516
THE HERITAGE COTTAGES
Hwy. 19, Maggie Valley . . . (800) 438-0821, 926-1450
HOLIDAY INN
Hwy. 19 & 276, Maggie Valley 926-0201
LAUREL PARK INN
Rt. 1, Box 130, Maggie Valley, 28751 926-1700
THE LODGE
118 Ninevah, Waynesville, 28786 456-9073
MAGGIE VALLEY COUNTRY CLUB & MOTOR LODGE
Box 126, Maggie Valley, 28751 926-1616
MOUNT VALLEY LODGE
Hwy. 19, Box 94, Maggie Valley, 28751 926-1521
MOUNTAIN BROOK COTTAGES
Rt. 2, Box 301 (U.S. 441), Sylva 586-4329
MOUNTAIN JOY COTTAGES
Rt. 1, Box 466, Maggie Valley, 28751 926-1257
PIONEER VILLAGE RESORT (log cabins)
Rt. 1, Box 405, Maggie Valley, 28751 926-1881
SCOTTISH INN
Maggie Valley . . . . (800) 251-1962, 926-1251
SKYVIEW MOTEL
U.S. 19, 1½ mi. W. of Ghost Town
Rt. 1, Box 545, Maggie Valley, NC 28751 . . 926-1188
SMOKEY SHADOWS SKI LODGE
Near Resort, Box 444, Maggie Valley, 28751 926-0001
STONY CREEK MOTEL
P.O. Box 215, Maggie Valley, 28751 926-1996
TWINBROOK RESORT (kitchenette cottages)
Box 683, Maggie Valley, 28751 926-1388

CATALOOCHEE CONT.

RESTAURANTS

BAR-B-QUE SHAK'
Stony Creek Motel, Maggie Valley 926-1996
HOLIDAY INN
Hwy. 19 & 276, Maggie Valley 926-0201
THE LODGE (Viennese, American)
118 Ninevah, Waynesville, 28786. 456-9073
MOUNT VALLEY LODGE & RESTAURANT
Hwy. 19, Maggie Valley 926-1521
THE NEW ALFREDO'S (Italian & American)
Center of Downtown Maggie Valley 926-1820
SPRINGHOUSE RESTAURANT (Rathskeller Lounge)
Hwy. 19, Maggie Valley 926-1516

SERVICES

FITNESS CENTER

NAUTILUS FITNESS CENTER (hot tubs)
Hwy. 19, Dellwood Section, Maggie Valley . . 926-3628

PHARMACY

MAGGIE VALLEY PHARMACY (film, magazines, books)
Hwy. 19, Stallard Mall 926-0263

STORES & SKI SHOPS

THE CABIN DOOR (furniture, toys, gifts)
Maggie Valley Shopping Center 926-3201
THE HORNET'S NEST (gifts, jams & jellies)
Maggie Valley Shopping Center 926-0794
THE LEATHER SHOP
Maggie Valley 926-0797
MAGGIE IGA MARKET (Meat, groceries, wine)
Maggie Valley
REPAIR SHOP
Call Ski Area
THE SHOP ON THE MOUNTAIN
Call Ski Area

O H I O

SNOW TRAILS

BOX 63, POSSUM RUN RD., MANSFIELD, OH 44901
TELEPHONE: (419) 522-7393

AREA INFORMATION

BASE ELEVATION
990 ft.
HOURS
10 a.m. to 11 p.m., weekdays
9 a.m. to 10 p.m., weekends & holidays
LIFTS
3 chairs, 2 bars, 5,900 capacity per hr.
LONGEST RUN
2,000 ft.
NURSERY
Call ski area
RENTAL
At ski area
SEASON
Dec. thru Mid-March
SNOW PHONE
Call ski area
TRAILS
easy 1, intermediate 5, difficult 2
TRAVEL
Cleveland & Columbus, 1 1/2 hrs., I-71 to Rt. 13
VERTICAL DROP
300 ft.

EMERGENCY

AMBULANCE. 525-3311
FIRE DEPT.. 525-2121
HIGHWAY PATROL. 524-3841
SHERIFF 524-2412
TOWING (Daugherty's) 756-3729

LODGING

CARROUSEL'S PARK PLACE (also dinner)
191 Park Ave., West 522-3662, (800) 543-4036
LK RESTAURANTS & MOTELS
Ski Center at ski area (800) 282-5711, (800) 848-5767
LODGE AT SKI CENTER (also restaurant)
At the slope 522-7393
MANSFIELD'S BEST WESTERN (also restaurant)
800 Laver Rd.. 589-2200
MOHICAN STATE PARK & LODGE
Rt. 2, Perrysville 938-5411

RESTAURANTS

ADAMS RIB
777 Lexington Ave., Mansfield
BAR N
779 Laver Rd., Mansfield
CASTLE KEEP
3 S. Walnut, Mansfield
DAUGHERTIES (also grocery, tow rig)
I-71, exit 169, Rt. 13. 756-3729
GOURMET ROOM
1313 S. Main St., Mansfield
THE LAST RUN
The Lodge at Snow Trails
PARK PLACE
191 Park Ave., West Mansfield
ROCKY'S PUB
22 S. Park, Mansfield

OREGON

MT. BACHELOR

P.O. BOX 103, BEND, OR 97701 (503) 382-2442

AREA INFORMATION

BASE ELEVATION
6,000 feet

HOURS
9:00 a.m. - 4:00 p.m.,
extended to 4:30 in mid-February

LIFTS
8 chairs, 1 rope tow, 8,460 capacity per hour

LONGEST RUN
1 mile

NURSERY
Call Ski Area

SEASON
November 1st to June 22nd

SNOW PHONE 382-7888
Washington . . . . (206) 634-0071
California . . . . (415) 982-5864
Toll free in Oregon . . . . (800) 452-6872

TRAILS
11 beginners' runs, 10 intermediate, 11 advanced

TRAVEL
Hwy. 20 & Hwy. 97 to Bend, then Cascade Lakes Hwy., 22 miles southwest to Ski Area. By air, private planes to Bend, Redmond & Sunriver airports. Major carriers to Portland. Hughes Airwest or Air Oregon to Redmond.

VERTICAL DROP
1,700 feet

LODGING

ALL LODGING IS IN BEND, UNLESS OTHERWISE NOTED. ZIP - 97701.

CENTRAL RESERVATIONS 382-8334

BEND RIVERSIDE
1565 N.W. Hill 382-3802

BEND'S 97 HOST MOTEL
61440 S. Hwy. 97. 382-1951

CASCADE LODGE
420 S.E. Third. 382-2612

CHALET MOTEL
510 S.E. Third St.. 382-6124

CHAPARRAL MOTEL
1500 S. Hwy. 97 389-1448

CIMMARON MOTEL
201 N.E. Third St. 382-8282

CITY CENTER MOTEL
509 N.W. Franklin Ave. 382-5321

DUNES MOTEL
1515 N.E. Third St.. 382-6811

EDELWEISS MOTOR INN
2346 N.E. First St. 382-6222

HILLCREST MOTEL
61405 S. Hwy. 97. 389-5910

HOLIDAY MOTEL
880 S.E. Third St.. 382-4620

INN OF THE SEVENTH MOUNTAIN
Century Dr., P.O. Box 1207 382-8711
Toll free, in Oregon. . . . . (800) 542-6810
Outside Oregeon . . . .(800) 547-55668

KAH-NEE-TA LODGE
Warm Springs 553-1112

MAVERICK MOTEL
437 N.E. Third St. 382-7711

MOTEL WEST
216 N.E. Irving 389-5577

MT. BACHELOR MOTEL
2359 N.E. 1st St. 382-6365

MT. BACHELOR VILLAGE (condos)
19717 Century Dr. 389-5900

PILOT BUTTE MOTOR INN
1236 N.W. Wall St. 382-1411

PIONEER MOTOR INN
215 N.W. Greenwood. 382-2381

PLAZA MOTEL
1430 N.W. Hill St. 382-1621

POPLAR MOTEL
163 S.E. Third St.. 382-6571

RAINBOW MOTEL
154 N.E. Franklin. 382-1821

RED LION MOTEL
849 N.E. Third St. 382-8384

RIVERHOUSE MOTOR INN
3075 N. Hwy. 97 . . . . . . .in Oregon, (800) 452-6878
Outside Oregon . . . . (800) 547-3928

ROCK SPRINGS GUEST RANCH
64201 Tyler Rd. 382-1957

ROYAL GATEWAY
475 S.E. Third St.. 382-5631

SKYLARK MOTEL
450 S.E. Third St.. 382-4891

SPORTSMAN'S MOTEL
3705 N. Hwy. 97 382-2211

SUN COUNTRY MOTEL
52560 Hwy. 97, La Pine 536-1735

SUNRIVER LODGE
Sunriver, 97701 593-1221
Toll free, in Oregon. . . . . (800) 452-6874
Other Western States . . . . (800) 547-3922

THUNDERBIRD MOTEL
1415 N.E. Third St.. 382-7011

TOM-TOM MOTOR INN
3600 N. Hwy. 97 382-4734

WEST VIEW MOTEL
Hwy. 97, La Pine 536-2115

WESTWARD HO MOTEL
904 S.E. 3rd St.. 382-2111

WOODSMAN MOTEL
Hwy. 97, Crescent 433-2710

RESTAURANTS

THE ALBATROSS (cocktail lounge)
61363 S. Hwy. 97. 388-2517
BEEF & BREW (cocktail lounge)
3194 N. Hwy. 97 388-4646
BEND WOOLEN MILL PUB
(beer & wine, entertainment, dancing)
1854 N.E. First St. 382-6767
BLACK FOREST INN & LOUNGE
25 S.W. 14th St. & Century Dr. 389-3138
CINDERS RESTAURANT & LOUNGE
(entertainment, dancing)
197 N.E. Third St. 389-2664
COUNTRY KITCHEN
2115 N.E. Third St.. 389-1131
CYRANO RESTAURANT (wine)
828 N.W. Wall St.. 389-6276
DEJOLA'S RESTAURANTE (beer, wine)
61 N.W. Oregon Ave.. 388-1288
DESCHUTES STATION TAVERN
(beer & wine, entertainment, dancing)
61219 S. Hwy. 97. 389-7574
DILLON'S RESTAURANT & LOUNGE
63011 N. Hwy. 97 388-3545
EARTH & SKY, AN EATING PLACE (beer, wine)
111 N.W. Oregon Ave. 388-2153
ELMER'S COLONIAL PANCAKE & STEAK HOUSE
(cocktail lounge)
415 N.E. Third St. 382-7778
EYVETTE'S EATING & GATHERING PLACE
(beer, wine)
815 S.E. Third St.. 389-0094
FRIEDA'S RESTAURANT & LOUNGE
1955 N.E. First St. 382-3790
HONG KONG RESTAURANT & LOUNGE
530 S.E. Third St 389-8880
JOSIAH'S RESTAURANT & LOUNGE
(entertainment, dancing)
Inn of the Seventh Mountain, Century Dr.. . . 382-8711
KOPPER KITCHEN & LOUNGE (24 hours)
1415 N.E. Third St.. 382-7627
LE BISTRO (cocktails)
1203 N.E. Third St.. 389-7274
MEXICALI ROSE (beer, wine)
301 N.E. Franklin. 389-0149
ORIGINAL JOE'S RESTAURANT & LOUNGE
1033 N.W. Bond St. 382-8028
THE RIVERHOUSE RESTAURANT & LOUNGE
(entertainment, dancing)
3075 N. Hwy. 97 389-3111
SUNRIVER LODGE RESTAURANT & LOUNGE
(entertainment, dancing)
Sunriver 593-1221
SUNSPOT RESTAURANT
Sunriver 593-1988
TOM-TOM RESTAURANT (24 hours)
3650 N. Hwy. 97 382-1391
THE TRAIL RESTAURANT
1070 N.W. Bond St. 382-3254
TUMATO EMPORIUM RESTAURANT & LOUNGE
(entertainment)
64619 Hwy. 20 382-2202

SERVICES

AUTO RENTAL

PORTLAND OR REDMOND AIRPORTS
Hertz . . . . (800) 654-3131
National . . . . (800) 328-4517

BUS

PARK-AND-RIDE
(Resort Bus leaves Resort Terminal daily for Ski Area)
1223 N.E. 1st St. 389-7755
TRAILWAYS (Portland to Bend, Bend to Ski Area)
Depot in Bend. 382-2151

TRAIN

AMTRAK
Check with your local Amtrak agent

STORES & SKI SHOPS

BLUE LODGE SKI SHOP
At the slopes, call Ski Area
BLUE SKY ART GALLERY
1900 N.E. First St. 389-6623
MAIN LODGE SKI SHOP
At the slopes, call Ski Area
RENTAL SHOP
At the base of Blue Lodge, call Ski Area
SKJERSAA SKI SHOP
On the way to Ski Area in Bend. 382-2154
STOWELL'S SPORT HAUS
926 N.E. Greenwood Ave.. 382-5325

MT. HOOD

P.O. BOX 47, MT. HOOD, OR 97041 (503) 337-2222

AREA INFORMATION

BASE ELEVATION
4,520 feet
HOURS
9:00 a.m. to 4:30 p.m., night skiing
LIFTS
6 chairs, 3 tows, 3,000 capacity per hour
LODGING
11 miles away, at Government Camp
LONGEST RUN
1.5 miles
SEASON
Mid-November to late June
SNOW PHONE
(503) 227-7669
TRAILS
25% Beginner, 40% Intermediate, 35% Difficult

TRAVEL
67 miles from Portland via I-80 and Hwy. 35,
Bus available from Portland
VERTICAL DROP
2,975 feet

SKI ASHLAND

P.O. BOX 220, ASHLAND, OR 97520 (503) 482-2897

AREA INFORMATION

BASE ELEVATION
6,600 feet
EMERGENCY. . . . . Call 911
Police. 482-5211
Sheriff 776-7111
Hospitals. 773-6281, 482-2441
HOURS
9 a.m. to 4 p.m.
LIFTS
2 chairs, 3 surface lifts
LONGEST RUN
1 mile
SKI SHOP
Call ski area.
SNOW PHONE 482-2754
TRAILS
Wooded, open slopes, 4 shutes, 22 runs
TRAVEL
Ashland is 20 miles away, S. on I-5, exit at Mt. Ashland
VERTICAL DROP
1,150 feet

LODGING

CENTRAL RESERVATIONS. 488-1011

ASHLAND HILLS INN
Ashland 482-8310, (800) 547-4747
ASHLAND MAIN STREET HOUSE
Ashland 488-0969
BARDS INN
3 blocks from City Center, Ashland 482-0049
BASE LODGE
At ski area 482-2897
BAVARIAN INN
N. of Ashland, Phoenix exit 535-1678
CEDARWOOD INN
1801 Siskiyou Bl.,Ashland. 488-2000
FRONTIER LODGE
4361 S. Pacific Hwy., Phoenix 535-1047
HOLIDAY INN
I-5 & Crater Lake Hwy., Medford. 779-3141
KNIGHT'S INN
I-5 at Hwy. 66, Ashland 482-5111
THE MANOR
N. end of Ashland on Main 482-2246
MARK ANTONY HOTEL
Downtown Ashland. 482-1721
THE PALM MOTEL
1065 Siskiyou Bl., Ashland 482-2636
THE RED LION
200 N. Riverside, Medford. 779-5811
THE TIMERS
1450 Ashland St., Ashland. 482-4242
VALLEY ENTRANCE
1103 Siskiyou Bl., Ashland 482-2641
VISTA 6 MOTEL
I-5 at Hwy. 66. 482-4423
WHITE MOTEL
1520 Siskiyou Bl., Ashland 482-2626

TIMBERLINE

GOVERNMENT CAMP, OR 97028 (503) 272-3311

AREA INFORMATION

BASE ELEVATION
5,250 feet
HOURS
9:30 a.m. to 9:30 p.m.
LIFTS
4 chairs, 2 tows
LODGING
Call ski area
LONGEST RUN
2 miles
NURSERY
Weekends only, call ski area
SEASON
Year round
SNOW PHONE
Call ski area
TRAILS
23 trails,
25% Beginner, 50% Intermediate, 25% Difficult
TRAVEL
1.5 hours from Portland via Hwy. 5 to Hwy. 80 North, to Woodville Exit to Hwy. 26. Bus & limo service available, call ski area
VERTICAL DROP
1,750 feet

PENNSYLVANIA

BLUE KNOB

P.O. BOX 247, CLAYSBURG, PA 16625 (814) 239-5111

AREA INFORMATION

BASE ELEVATION
2,100 feet
HOURS
9:00 a.m. - 4:30 p.m.; weekends, 9:00 a.m. - 5:00 p.m.
Twilight, 3:00 p.m. - 10:00 p.m.
Night, 6:00 p.m. - 10:00 p.m.
LIFTS
3 chairs, 2 platter pulls, 3,000 capacity per hour
LONGEST RUN
9200 feet
NURSERY
Any age, call Ski Area
SEASON
December to Mid-March
SNOW PHONE . . . . (800) 458-3403
TRAILS
15% beginner, 70% intermediate, 15% advanced
TRAVEL
Pittsburgh, 100 miles via Pennsylvania Turnpike to exit 11 (Bedford), Rt. 220 N. to Rt. 869 W. to Pavia & follow ski signs, 20 miles from Turnpike exit.
VERTICAL DROP
1,052 feet

LODGING

CONDOMINIUM INFO. & RESERVATIONS. . . 239-8253

BENNETT'S MOTEL
Bedford 623-5108
FT. BEDFORD INN
Bedford 623-8181
COTTAGE INN
Ebensburg 472-8002
HAVEN REST MOTEL
Rt. 220, East Freedom 695-4401
HILLCREST INN
Bedford 623-5174
HOLIDAY INN
Altoona 944-4581
Bedford 623-9006
MIDWAY MOTEL
Bedford 623-8107
PENN MANOR
Bedford 623-8177
QUALITY INN
Bedford 623-5188
RAMADA INN
Breezewood 735-4005
SHERATON INN
Altoona 946-1631

RESTAURANTS

ARENA RESTAURANT
300 yards north of Turnpike interchange . . . 623-8074
COACH ROOM
118 South Richard St. 623-6815
ED'S STEAK HOUSE
¼ mile north of turnpike on U.S. 220 623-8894
LANDMARK RESTAURANT
131 South Juliana St.. 623-5488
East Penn St. 623-6762

CAMELBACK

BOX 168, TANNERSVILLE, PA 18372 (717) 629-1661

AREA INFORMATION

LODGING, RESTAURANTS, SERVICES, ETC.
SEE "THE POCONOS"
BABY SITTING
Late Dec. thru early March
BASE ELEVATION
1,200 ft.
CONDO PHONE 629-3661
HOURS
8:30 a.m. to 10 p.m., open 8 a.m. Sat. & Sun.
LIFTS
4 chairs, 2 T-bars, 5000 per hr. capacity
LONGEST RUN
6,500 ft.
RENTAL
At area
SEASON
Dec. to late March
SNOW PHONE
PA . . . . (800) 532-8201
NY, NJ, MD, DEL, VA. . . . . (800) 233-8100
TRAILS
16 novice, 8 intermediate, 4 expert
VERTICAL DROP
730 ft.

MOUNT AIRY

Mount Pocono, PA 18344 (717) 839-8811

AREA INFORMATION

LODGING, RESTAURANTS, SERVICES, ETC.
SEE "THE POCONOS", PAGE
LIFTS
2 chairs
LODGING (for lodging nearby, see page)
Mount Airy 839-8811
Pocono Gardens 595-7431
Toll free from area codes 215 & 717 . . (800) 532-8271
From NY, NJ, MD, DEL. . . . . (800) 233-8116

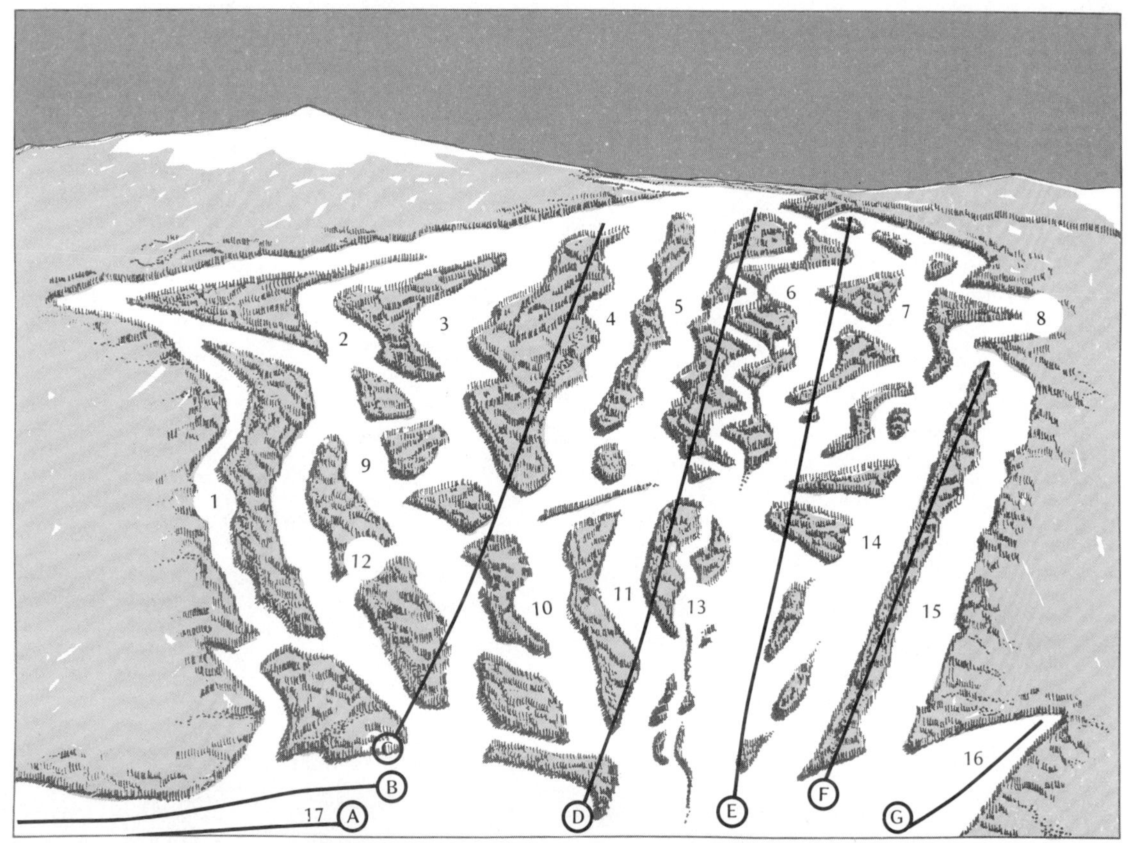

CAMELBACK RUNS

1 MARK ANTONY
2 CLEOPATRA
3 BIG POCONO RUN
4 MARJIE'S DELIGHT
5 THE ROCKET
6 THE ASP
7 THE HUMP
8 KING TUT
9 HONEYMOON LANE
10 THE SPHINX
11 SULLIVAN'S TRAIL
12 MAIN LINE
13 JOHN BAILEY
14 THE INTERSTATE
15 LAUREL GLADE
16 RHODODENDRON GROVE
17 THE SUNBOWL

CAMELBACK LIFTS

A SUNBOWL T-BAR
B SUNBOWL CHAIR
C CLEOPATRA CHAIR
D SULLIVAN CHAIR
E BAILEY CHAIR
F GLADE T-BAR
G J-BAR

P O C O N O S

POCONOS - INFORMATION FOR ALL POCONOS RESORTS

EMERGENCY

HOSPITAL, STROUDSBURG 421-4000
POLICE, TANNERSVILLE 421-4651

LODGING

ANTLER'S LODGE & COTTAGES
Swiftwater 3. 839-7243
BROOKDALE ON THE LAKE
Scotrun 40. 839-8843
BUDGET MOTEL
Rt. I-80, Exit 51, Stroudsburg. 424-5451
CAMELTOP LODGE
At the slope 662-1661
CRESCENT LODGE
Cresco 4 595-7486
HOLIDAY GLEN
Swiftwater. 839-7015
HOLIDAY INN
Rts. 611 & 33, Stroudsburg 426-6100
MEMORYTOWN, U.S.A.
Mt. Pocono 839-7176
MOUNTAIN SPRINGS LAKE
Reeders. 629-0251
MOUNTAINTOP COTTAGES & MOTEL
Swiftwater. 839-9755
PENN'S WOOD
Box 77, Tannersville 629-0131
THE POCAMONTAS RESORT
Bartonsville 629-0234
POCONO ESTATES
Exit 46N, I-80, Stroudsburg. 421-4881
RIMROCK COUNTRY
Box 5368, R.D. 5 629-2360
SHERATON POCONO INN, Stroudsburg
I-80, exit 48 . . . . 424-7930, (800) 325-3535
STRICKLAND'S
Mt. Pocono 839-7155

RECREATION

BOATS

DOUBLE W RESORT
4 mi. W. of Hawley 226-3118
KITTATINNY CANOES
Drigman's Ferry Bridge
LEISURE LAKE
Rt. 611, Swiftwater
THE POCONO BOATHOUSE
Old Rt. 940, Lake Naomi 646-2728
PEP'S INN & VILLAGE
Rt. 507, Tafton
POINT PLEASANT CANOES
Rt. 209, Bushkill
P.P. & L. CAMPGROUND
On Lake Wallenpaupack

CAMPGROUNDS

HICKORY RUN STATE PARK
White Haven
LAKE WALLENPAUPACK
Star Rt. Box 60, Lakeville
MAGIC VALLEY PARK
Rt. 209, Bushkill

GOLF

CANADENSIS GOLF COURSE
Next to Catholic Church, Canadensis
EVERGREEN
Penn Hills Lodge, Analomink
FERNWOOD
Rt. 209, Bushkill
MERGAGEL'S
Rt. 611, 2 mi. S. of Mt. Pocono
TANGLWOOD
Off I-84, Exit 6, 10 mi. N. on Rt. 507, Tafton

HIKING EQUIPMENT

TOM & DON'S LAKE STORE
Rt. 390, Promised Land 676-3741

HORSEBACK RIDING

DOUBLE "W" FARM
4 mi. from Hawley Post Office 226-3816
E-J RIDING STABLE
Rt. 940, E. of Mt. Pocono, Paradise Valley 839-8725

ICE SKATING

FERNWOOD
Rt. 209, Bushkill
MOUNT AIRY LODGE
Mt. Pocono
POCONO ICE-A-RAMA
Rt. 191, Analomink

RAFTING

KITTATINNY CANOES
Dingmans Ferry 828-2700
PT. PLEASANT CANOE OUTFITTERS
Rt. 209, Bushkill 558-6776
WHITE WATER RUBBER RAFT RIDES
Double "W" Farm 226-3551

TENNIS

FERNWOOD
Rt. 209, Bushkill
MOUNT AIRY LODGE
Mt. Pocono
SHAWNEE RACQUET CLUB
Eagle Valley Corners, Rt. 209, E. Stroudsberg

RESTAURANTS

AT THE SLOPE

CAMELTOP
At ski area 629-9893
THE PADDOCK
Camelback Rd. 629-2640

BARTONSVILLE

FLORENTINO'S (Italian)
Rt. 611. 424-1923

BLAKESLEE

BLAKESLEE INN (Italian, American, bar)
Junction Rts. 115 & 940. 646-2037
THE TUDOR INN (Continental, entertainment)
Junction Rts. 115 & 903. 646-2950

BUSHKILL

POCMONT (American, entertainment)
Off Rt. 209 588-6671
TOP OF THE WORLD AT
SAW CREEK (American, entertainment)
Off Rt. 209 588-9444

CANADENSIS

HIDDEN LAKE RESTAURANT (dinner)
Dutch Hill Rd., off Rt. 447 595-2862
THE OVERLOOK INN (Continental, French, cocktails)
Dutch Hill Rd. off Rt. 447. 595-7519
PINEKNOB INN & LOUNGE (American)
Rt. 447, S. of Village 595-2532
PUMP HOUSE INN (French, cocktails)
Skytop Rd., Rt. 390 595-7501

CRESCO

THE HOMESTEAD INN (American, cocktails)
¼ mi. behind Garden Gate, Sand Springs Dr. 595-3171

DELAWARE WATER GAP

SAYRE'S (Italian, French)
Rt. 611 476-0025

EAST STROUDSBERG

THE ALTERNATIVE (Chinese, Polynesian)
Bus Rt. 209 476-0454
BIRCHWOOD (Dining, entertainment)
Cherry Lane, near Analomink 629-0222

HAWLEY

THE SETTLER'S INN (American, bar)
108 Weldwood 226-2993
TANGLWOOD MOTOR LODGE (entertainment)
Rts. 507 & 6 266-4515

MOUNTAINHOME

DIAMOND JIM'S (seafood, steaks)
Rt. 390 595-2533
UGUCCIONI'S (Italian, lounge)
Rt. 390 595-2431

MOUNT POCONO

HIGHLAND INN (American, cocktails)
Rt. 611, S. of Mt. Pocono 839-9281
MOUNT AIRY LODGE (Continental, entertainment)
Off Rt. 611 839-8811
POCONO GARDENS LODGE (Continental, entertainment)
Rt. 940 595-7431

PARADISE VALLEY

CRESCENT LODGE (American, lounge)
Junction Rts. 191 & 940 595-7486

POCONO LAKE

ALPINE PUB STEAKHOUSE
Rt. 940 646-9865

POCONO SUMMIT

JOHNNIE'S POCONO SUMMIT INN (Italian, Continental)
Rt. 940 839-7401

PROMISED LAND

OLD RANGER'S INN (Steak)
Rt. 390, 2 mi. S. of I-84 676-3561
WILSON INN (American)
Rt. 390 676-3429

SNYDERSVILLE

SNYDERSVILLE DINER (open 24 hrs.)
Rt. 209 992-4003

STROUDSBURG

ATHENS BY NIGHT (Greek, lounge)
745 Main St. 431-9368
BEAVER HOUSE (seafood, steak)
Rt. 611 424-1020
HOUSE OF MING (Cantonese)
Foxtown Hill, Rt. 611 S. 424-0950
WYCOFF'S TEA ROOM
Main St. 421-1400

SWIFTWATER

AMBER CLUB (American)
Rt. 611 839-7352
FANUCCI'S (Italian, entertainment)
Rt. 611 839-7097
THE OLD HEIDELBERG (German)
Rt. 611 839-9954

TANNERSVILLE

ALFREDA'S (supper club)
Autumn View Lodge, Rt. 715 N. 629-4388
THE INN AT TANNERSVILLE (saloon, steak)
Rt. 611 629-9893
THE RED ROOSTER (American, Continental, cocktails)
Rt. 715, ½ way to Henryville 629-9859
THE SUMMIT RESORT (entertainment)
Exit U.S., I-80 & Rt. 715 629-0203

SERVICES

AIRPORTS

BIRCHWOOD-POCONO AIRPARK
E. Stroudsburg, W. on Rt. 447 at Analomink
or E. on Rt. 611, Tannersville Inn 629-0222
STROUDSBURG AIRPARK LTD.
Stroudsburg - Pocono Airport, off Bus. Rt. 209
Lear jet service 421-8900

MARKETS

KINSLEY'S
Rt. 611, Tannersville
BELMONT SHOPPING PLAZA
Rt. 611 N., Mt. Pocono
QUICK SHOP FOOD MART
Belmont Shopping Plaza
POCONO SHOPPING CENTER
Rt. 940 btwn. Mt. Pocono & Blakeslee Corners
JACK'S DELI
Rt. 611 N., Mt. Pocono 839-8780
HANDY'S VARIETY STORE
Buck Hill Forks
LEWIS SUPERMARKET
Rt. 390, Mountainhome
VILLAGE MARKET
2 mi. E. of Blakelee 646-9742
MT. POCONO BEVERAGE CO.
Rt. 611, N. of Rt. 940 839-7403

PHARMACY

MT. POCONO PHARMACY
Rt. 611 N., Belmont Shopping Plaza 839-9810
POCONO PINES PHARMACY
Pocono Pines 646-8111

PHOTO SUPPLIES

B G PHOTO SHOP
Pocono Village Mall. 839-8512

STORES & SKI SHOPS

BIG PINE GIFT SHOP
Lake Wallenpaupack, Rt. 507, Paupack 857-1139
THE CHEESE BOARD
354 N. 9th St., Stroudsburg 424-8612
COOKS TOUR (Gourmet Shop)
Pocono Village Mall. 839-6033
DUNKELBERG'S (sporting goods)
Quaker Plaza, Stroudsburg. 421-7950
FRANCES BURROWS (women's clothing)
718 Main, Stroudsburg
GENERATIONS (clothing, arts & crafts)
Pocono Village Mall. 839-8140
HAMPTON HOUSE (gifts)
Pocono Village Mall, Rts. 611 & 940. 839-9323
HESS'S (dept. store)
Stroud Mall, Rt. 611 & Bridge St.
HOLIDAY GIFT CENTER
770 Main St.. 421-2119
THE HOUSE OF CANDLES
Rt. 715, btwn. Henryville & Tannersville . . . 629-1953
KRETSCHMER'S GIFT SHOP
617 Main St., Honesdale
LA PINATA (gifts)
Rt. 940, Blakeslee. 646-2325
MAY'S (men's apparel)
Stroud Mall 421-0226
MOUNTAIN LAUREL GIFT SHOPPE
1 mi. off Rt. 435 & I-380 842-9779
THE PINES SKI & SPORT (ski shop & rentals)
Camelback Rd. & Sullivan Trail
ROCKING CHAIR GIFT SHOP
Rt. 390, Mountainhouse 595-7241
ROSANA (gifts)
Main St., Mt. Pocono 839-7893
SOLITARY MAN (men's sportswear)
Stroud Mall 424-1221
THE SPORTSMAN'S DEN
Rt. 940, Pocono Lake 646-2203
WOEHRLE'S BAIT SHOP
Rt. 940, Mt. Pocono 839-7448

S E V E N S P R I N G S

CHAMPION, PA 15622 (814) 352-7777

AREA INFORMATION

BASE ELEVATION
2,075 feet
HOURS
9:00 a.m. - 4:30 p.m.,
4:30 - 11:00 p.m., night skiing
LIFTS
9 chairs, 1 poma lift, 3 rope tows
15,000 capacity per hour
LONGEST RUN
1½ miles
NURSERY
Ski Area . . . . X 7629
SEASON
Early December to early April, snowmaking
SNOW PHONE
Call Ski Area
TRAILS
15% beginner, 65% intermediate, 20% advanced
TRAVEL
From the West, Pennsylvania Turnpike, exit 9, turn left off the exit ramp, Rt. 711 about 2 miles to Champion, turn left at the Gulf Station, follow signs to Ski Area, about 8 miles. From the East, take Turnpike exit 10, Somerset, turn right off the exit ramp; at the 3rd traffic light, turn right, Rt. 31 W. for about 7 miles, turn left at Pioneer Park, go about 4 miles to the first stop, turn right, 5 miles to Ski Area. From the South, PA Routes 711, 53, 653 or 219. From the North, PA Routes 119, 219, then Rt. 31 to 711.
VERTICAL DROP
865 feet

EMERGENCY

AMBULANCE
New Centerville 445-4133
Saltlick 455-2900
Somerset 445-9711
Stahlstown. 593-2200
FIRE
New Centerville 445-4133
Normalville Area 455-3000
Saltlick Township. 455-2900
Somerset 445-4600
Springfield Township. 455-3211
Stahlstown. 593-2200
HOSPITALS
Connellsville 628-1500
Mt. Pleasant 547-3502
Somerset 443-2626
MEDICAL CLINIC
Ski Area . . . . X 7022
SKI PATROL
Ski Area . . . . X 7814
SOMERSET SHERIFFS OFFICE. 443-3679

STATE POLICE

Greensburg. 834-4400
Uniontown. 437-1555
Somerset, County Detail 445-4104
Somerset, Turnpike Detail 445-9606

LODGING

CENTRAL RESERVATIONS
Hotel rooms, suites, chalets, condos 352-7777
OVERFLOW ACCOMODATIONS
Donegal - 12 miles W. / Ligonier - 22 miles N.W.
Somerset - 17 miles E. / New Stanton - 35 miles W.

COBBLER'S MOTEL
Turnpike exit 10, Somerset 445-4121
COLEMAN MOTEL
Turnpike exit 10, Somerset 445-4144
DONEGAL MOTEL
Turnpike exit 9 . . . . (412) 593-2828
HIGHLANDER MOTEL
Turnpike exit 10, Somerset 445-7988
HOLIDAY INN
Ligonier, Turnpike exit 9 to Rt. 711 N. (412) 238-9445
New Stanton, Turnpike exit 8. . . . . . (412) 925-3571
Somerset, Turnpike exit 10 445-9611
INN AMERICA
Turnpike exit 8, New Stanton. . . . . . (412) 925-3591
LAUREL HIGHLANDS
Turnpike exit 9, Donegal. . . . . (412) 593-7222
LAUREL MOTEL
Turnpike exit 10, Somerset 445-7919
MONTIQUE'S
Turnpike exit 9, Donegal. . . . . (412) 593-2461
RAMADA INN
Turnpike exit 10, Somerset 443-4646

RECREATION

BOWLING
Convention Center, ground level . . . . X 7922
CROSS COUNTRY SKIING
Golf Course
HANDBALL. . . . . X 7796
HEALTH SPA (jacuzzi & sauna)
Convention Center, ground level . . . . X 7796
MINI-GOLF (indoors)
Convention Center, ground level . . . . X 7626
SWIMMING (indoor skiside pool)
Center Lodge, Ground level . . . . X 7724
RACQUETBALL (indoor)
Convention Center, ground & mid level . . . . . X 7796
TENNIS (indoor)
Convention Center, top level . . . . X 7984, 7796

RESTAURANTS

THE BAVARIAN LOUNGE (occasional entertainment)
Center Lodge, top level
CAFETERIAS
Two, at the Ski Area
COFFEE SHOP
Center Lodge, top level
THE CHAR-N-GRILL ROOM (salad bar)
Center Lodge, top level
FOGGY GOGGLE (bar, weekend entertainment)
Ski Lodge
MATTERHORN LOUNGE (bands)
Center Lodge, mid level
THE OAK ROOM
Top level
RATHSKELLAR (bar, occasional entertainment)
Ski Lodge

STORES & SKI SHOPS

ART GALLERY (paintings, framed prints, gifts)
Center Lodge, mid level . . . . X 7625
FUDGE SHOP
Assortment of fudge, candies, jellies
GIFT SHOP (souvenirs, magazines, sundries)
Center Lodge, mid level . . . . X 7627
THE LEATHER SHOP
(hand-crafted items, belt buckles)
Center Lodge, mid level . . . . X 7577
SKI RENTAL SHOP . . . . X 7823
T'S SHOE DEPOT & JEANERY
Center Lodge, ground level . . . . X 7527
TREASURE HAUS (costume jewelry, 14 K gold)
Center Lodge, top level. . . . . X 7685
WILLI'S CROSS COUNTRY SKI CENTER
(equipment, clothing, rentals)
Golf Course
WILLI'S SKI SHOP
Ski equipment, repairs, clothing, accessories. . . X 7919

TANGLWOOD

BOX 56, TAFTON, PA 18464 (717) 226-9500

FOR OTHER LODGINGS, RESTAURANTS, STORES & SKI SHOPS, SEE POCONOS, PAGE

BASE ELEVATION
1,335 feet
HOURS
9:00 a.m. - 4:15 p.m., Sun., Mon. & Tues.
9:00 a.m. - 10:00 p.m., Weds. thru Sat., after Dec. 21st
LIFTS
1 chair, 2 T-bars, 1 beginners lift
SNOW PHONE 226-9500
TRAILS
8 trails & slopes
TRAVEL
From Northern New Jersey & New York, New York Thruway, Harriman exit, Rt. 17 W. to exit 121 W., to I-84 W. From Central & Southern New Jersey, I-80 W. to exit 34B (Spart), Rt. 15 N. to Rt. 206 N. to I-84 W. From Philadelphia, Northeast extension of Pennsylvania Turnpike to exit 35 (Pocono), I-80 E. to 380 W. to exit 6 (Gouldsboro), then 507 N. From Scranton & Wilkes Barre, I-81 N. to 380 E. to I-84 E.
VERTICAL DROP
415

EMERGENCY

AMBULANCE
Hawley 226-4601
Honesdale 253-3482
Tafton 226-9221
FIRE
Blooming Grove. 775-7122
Hawley 226-3855
Honesdale 253-2822
Tafton 226-9221
HOSPITAL
Wayne County Hospital 253-1300
POLICE
Hawley 253-5752
Honesdale 253-1900
Tafton 775-7374
STATE POLICE
Honesdale 253-2130
Lords Valley. 296-6451

LODGING

TANGLWOOD MOTOR LODGE (restaurant)
R.D. 2, Hawley 226-4515, 226-4545

RESTAURANTS

PERDY'S
Rt. 6, Hawley 226-9295
THE SETTLERS INN
108 Welwood Ave., Hawley 226-2993
SUNSET GROVE RESTAURANT
Rt. 507, Hawley. 226-2200
WHITE BEAUTY VIEW
Rt. 507, Greentown 857-0234
WOODEN SPOON
Rt. 507, Greentown 676-9291

STORES & SKI SHOPS

HAWLEY DEPARTMENT STORE. 226-9205
HAWLEY HAIR DRESSING SHOP 226-9880
HAWLEY HEALTH FOOD CENTER 226-4702
HAWLEY NEWS & NOVELTY STORE 226-2360
SKI RENTAL SHOP
At the slopes, call Ski Area

U T A H

A L T A

ALTA, UT 84070 (801) 742-3333

AREA INFORMATION

Alta, Utah 84040 (801) 742-3333, 742-2040

AREA INFORMATION

BASE ELEVATION
8,500 feet
HOURS
9:30 a.m. - 4:30 p.m.
LIFTS
8 chairlifts, 1 transfer tow, 7,000 capacity per hour
LONGEST RUN
Over 4 miles
SEASON
Mid-November to May, no snowmaking
SNOW PHONE
Call Ski Area
TRAILS
25% beginner, 45% intermeidate, 30% advanced
TRAVEL
From Salt Lake City, 25 miles S.E. via Wasatch Blvd. to Rt. 210, or Salt Lake City Airport to I-15 S. and Rt. 90 S. to Rt. 210 to Ski Area.
VERTICAL DROP
2,000 feet

LODGING & RESTAURANTS

ALTA LODGE (restaurant, liquor store)
Walk to lifts 742-3500
ALTA PERUVIAN (restaurant, liquor store)
Walk to lifts 742-3000, (800) 453-8488
BLACKJACK CONDOMINIUM LODGE
Walk to lifts 742-3200
GOLDMINER'S DAUGHTER LODGE
(restaurant, bar-lounge, ski shop/rentals, satellite TV)
Base Area 742-2300, (800) 453-4573
HELLGATE CONDOS (cross-country trails to slopes)
Walk to lifts 742-2020
RUSTLER LODGE (restaurant, liquor store)
Ski or walk to Base Area. 742-2200
SNOWPINE LODGE (ski shop, lunch cafeteria)
Near lifts. 742-3274

STORES & SKI SHOPS

ALTA LODGE (sundries store)
Base Area 742-3580
JOAN COLLINS (skis)
Alta. 742-2994
DEEP POWDER HOUSE SKI SHOP
Alta. 742-2400
GOLDMINER'S DAUGHTER LODGE (ski shop)
Base Area 742-2300
SKI RACK (sales, rentals)
Peruvian Lodge, Alta 742-3350
SNOW PINE LODGE (ski sale, rental, repair, gifts)
Alta. 742-3274

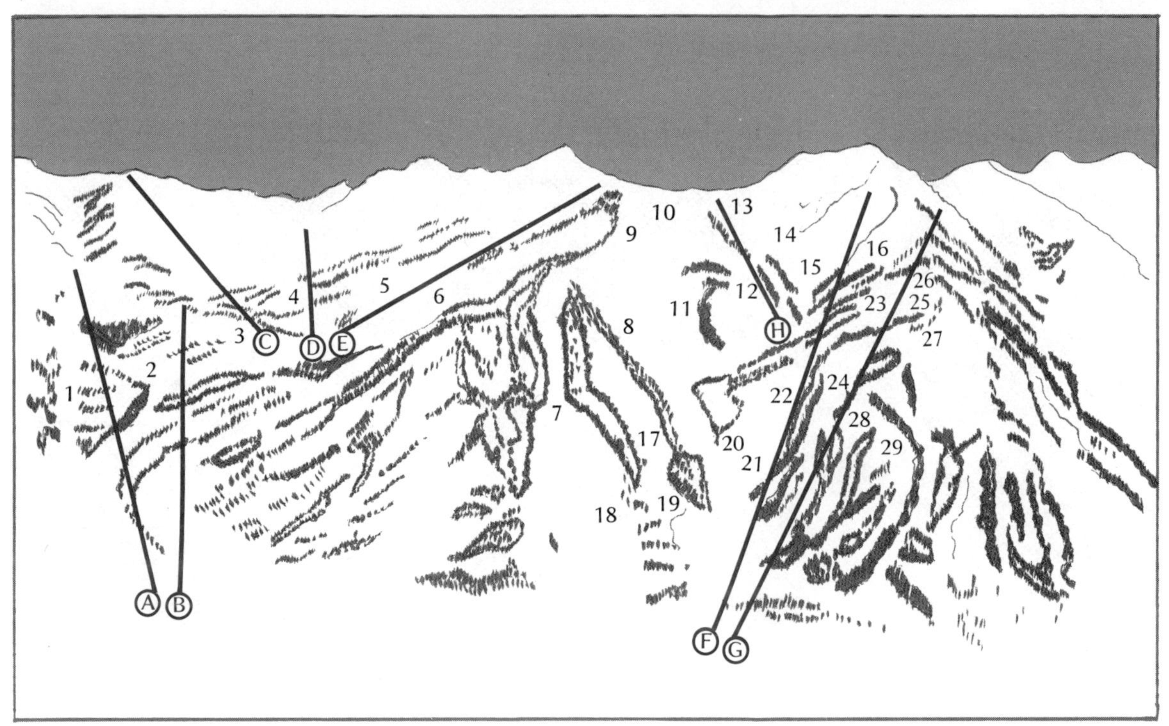

ALTA

RUNS

1 PATSEY MARLEY
2 CROOKED MILE
3 SUNNYSIDE
4 DEVIL'S ELBOW
5 ROLLER COASTER
6 EXTROVERT
7 ALF'S HIGH RUSTLER
8 STONE CRUSHER
9 SUN SPOT
10 RACE COURSE
11 RACE COURSE SADDLE
12 LOWER SUNSPOT
13 MAMBO
14 BALLROOM
15 MAIN STREET
16 AGGIE'S ALLEY
17 MEADOW
18 CAT TRACK
19 CORKSCREW
20 NINA CURVE
21 SCHUSS GULLY
22 COLLINS FACE
23 MIDWAY
24 BEAR PAW
25 WARMUP
26 PERUVIAN RIDGE
27 PUNCH BOWL
28 ROCK GULLY
29 WILDCAT FACE

LIFTS

A ALBION
B SUNNYSIDE
C SUPREME
D CECRET
E SUGARLOAF
F COLLINS
G WILDCAT
H GERMANIA

BRIANHEAD

P.O. BOX 38, CEDAR CITY, UT 84720 (801) 586-4636

AREA INFORMATION

BASE ELEVATION
9,700 feet
HOURS
9 a.m. to 4 p.m.
LIFTS
Capacity - 4,000 per hr.
2 double chairs, 3 triple chairs
LONGEST TRAIL
1¾ miles
RENTALS
3 shops at the area
TRAILS
31, 20% beginner, 60% intermediate, 20% advanced
TRAVEL
Las Vegas, 190 miles northeast via I-15.
Los Angeles, 470 miles via I-15.
By air: Sky West Airlines from Las Vegas;
By bus: Greyhound to Cedar City & Parowan.
SEASON
Nov. to May 1st
SNOW PHONE 586-4636
VERTICAL DROP
1,280 feet

EMERGENCY

AMBULANCE. 586-6587, 586-9445
FIRE 586-9421
HIGHWAY PATROL. 586-9445
HOSPITAL 586-6587
POLICE 586-6531
SHERIFF 586-6531

LODGING

THE ASPENS
P.O. Box 76 586-3166
BRIAN HEAD VILLAGE CONDOS
P.O. Box 55 586-6662
CHALET VILLAGE
P.O. Box 88 586-6778
EDELWEISS CONDOS
P.O. Box 48 586-3042

RESTAURANTS

BRIAN HEAD INN (breakfast & lunch)
At the slope
FERDINANDS (Mexican, American)
At the slope
MINNIE'S MANSION (American, dinner)
At the slope

STORES & SKI SHOPS

APPLE ANNIE'S COUNTRY STORE
Brian Head Inn
BRIAN HEAD NORDIC SKI CENTER
Bristlecone Hostel, Box 30. 586-8825
BRIAN HEAD SPORTS
Next to Minnie's Mansion 586-7462
GEORG'S SKI SHOP & LODGE
Bottom of Lift 1 586-3134

B R I G H T O N

BRIGHTON, UTAH 84121 (801) 359-3283

AREA INFORMATION

ALL LODGINGS, RESTAURANTS & SERVICES ARE IN SALT LAKE CITY, UNLESS OTHERWISE NOTED.
BASE ELEVATION
8,730 feet
HOURS
9:00 a.m. - 4:30 p.m.
5:00 - 10:00 p.m., Mon. - Sat., night skiing, 2 chairs
LIFTS
3 chairs for intermediate & advanced
1 chair for beginners, 4,000 capacity per hour
LONGEST RUN
1¼ miles
SEASON
Mid-November to May, no snowmaking
SNOW PHONE
Call Ski Area
TRAILS
25% beginner, 50% intermediate, 25% advanced
TRAVEL
30 miles from Salt Lake Int'l. Airport, I-80 E. to I-250 S. along Wasatch Bl., then east to the top of Big Cottonwood Canyon.
VERTICAL DROP
1,100 feet

LODGING

BRIGHTON CHALETS
Close to lifts. 278-3888
HILTON INN
150 W. 5 South St. 532-3344
HOLIDAY INN - DOWNTOWN
230 W. 6 South St. 532-7000
HOTEL UTAH
S. Temple & Main Sts. 531-1000
INTERNATIONAL DUNES HOTEL
206 S. West Temple St.. 521-9500
LITTLE AMERICA HOTEL
500 S. Main St. 363-6781
MT. MAJESTIC LODGE - MOTEL
(cafeteria, dining room, state liquor store, ski shop)
Adjoining day lodge 364-3382
ROYAL EXECUTIVE INN
121 N. 300 West St. 521-3450
SILVER FORK LODGE (family-style meals)
3 minute drive from lifts. 649-9551
TRAVELODGE
161 W. 6 South St. 521-7373

RESTAURANTS

BALSAM EMBERS (Continental)
2350 Foothill Dr.. 466-4496
BILL & NADA'S (open 24 hours)
479 S. 6th East 359-6984
CASA DEL SOL (Mexican, entertainment)
Trolley Square. 531-8228
CATTLE BARON (steak)
2110 Emigration Canyon 582-8991
CHINA VILLAGE
7334 S. Main 355-5507
FINN'S (American, Continental)
2675 Parley's Way 466-4682
HEATHER (entertaiment)
2832 E. 6200 South 272-4468
HIBACHI (Japanese)
238 E. South Temple. 364-5456
HOTEL UTAH RESTAURANT (American)
S. Temple & Main Streets 531-1000
TAYLOR'S CAFE (soul food)
244 W. South Temple 532-9272
LA CAILLE AT QUAIL RUN (French, Basque)
9565 S. Wasatch Bl.. 942-1751
LA FLEUR DE LIS (French)
338 S. State 359-5753
LAMB'S GRILL
169 S. Main 364-7166
LE PARISIEN (French)
417 S. 3rd East 364-5223
RISTORANTE DELLA FONTANA (Italian)
336 S. 400 East 328-4243

BRIGHTON CONT.

ROYAL PALACE (Continental, American)
249 S. 4th East 359-5000
THE TOWNE HALL
Salt Lake Hilton, 151 W. 5th South 532-3344

SERVICES

AUTO RENTALS

AMERICAN INT'L. 322-2488
AVIS . . . . (800) 331-1212
BUDGET. 363-1500
HERTZ. 328-2088
NATIONAL 539-0200

BUS

GRAY LINE (charter & limos) 521-6070
GREYHOUND 355-4684
LAKE SHORE MOTOR COACH 328-3361
LEWIS BROS.. 359-8677
TRAILWAYS 328-8121
UTAH TRANSIT DISTRICT 531-8600

STORES & SKI SHOPS

VILLAGE STORE (groceries, gifts)
At the slopes, call Ski Area
SKI RENTAL & REPAIR SHOP (ski clothing)
At the slopes, call Ski Area

PARK CITY

P.O. BOX 39, PK. CITY, UT 84060 (801) 649-8111

AREA INFORMATION

ALL LODGINGS, RESTAURANTS, SERVICES, STORES & SKI SHOPS ARE IN PARK CITY UNLESS NOTED OTHERWISE. ZIP - 84060.

BASE ELEVATION
6,900 feet
HOURS
9:00 a.m. - 4:00 p.m., daily
4:00 - 10:00 p.m., 7 nights a week
LIFTS
11 chairs, 1 gondola, 14,500 capacity per hour
LONGEST RUN
3½ miles
NURSERY
Ages 3 to 6, call Ski Area
SEASON
End of November to beginning of May, snowmaking
SNOW PHONE 649-9571
TRAILS
11 novice, 30 intermediate, 24 expert
TRAVEL
27 miles east of Salt Lake City via I-80
VERTICAL DROP
3,100 feet

LODGING

ALPINE PROSPECTOR LODGE (restaurant, private club)
P.O. Box 1388. 649-9975
THE BLUE CHURCH LODGE
P.O. Box 1720. 649-8009
CHAMONIX
3865 So., 3500 E.
Salt Lake City, 84109 . . . . .277-5072, 262-1299
CHATEAU APRES LODGE (close to resort)
P.O. Box 579 649-9372
THE CLAIM JUMPER (restaurant & club)
P.O. Box 939 649-8825
COPPERBOTTOM INN (restaurant & lounge)
P.O. Box 2460. 649-5111
EDELWEISS HAUS (close to resort)
P.O. Box 495 649-9342
THE INNSBRUCK (1 block to the lifts)
P.O. Box 222 649-9829
JACKHAMMER CHALET (apartment complex)
c/o 3409 Mile High Drive
Salt Lake City, 84117 278-3241
JUPITER (rentals)
P.O. Box 2045. 649-8186
KING CON RENTALS
P.O. Box 155 649-7791
MINE CAMP (condo apartments, close to resort)
P.O. Box 1147. . . . . .649-8222, 649-9611
MOTHERLODE CONDOMINIUMS
P.O. Box 1825. 649-6372
PARK CITY RACQUET CLUB
P.O. Box 1360. . . . . 649-8200, (800) 453-5731
PARK CITY RESERVATIONS
P.O. Box 1330. 649-9598
PARK CITY RESORT LODGING
P.O. Box 1846. 649-6368
PARK STATION (rentals)
P.O. Box 905 649-7717
PARKWEST
At Park West Ski Resort, 3 miles from Park City
P.O. Box 1598. . . . . 649-9663, (800) 453-5757
PROSPECTOR SQUARE
HOTEL & CONFERENCE CENTER
P.O. Box 1698. . . . . 649-7100, (800) 453-3812
THE SKIERS LODGE
(rooms & apartments, close to resort & lifts)
P.O. Box 778 649-8800
SNOWFLOWER (rentals)
P.O. Box 957 649-6400
THREE KINGS (units on golf course)
P.O. Box 217 649-6305
TRAMWAY LODGE (140 yards from gondola & lifts)
P.O. Box 9. 649-8443
WASATCH CONDO
P.O. Box 1088. 649-6606
THE YARROW – HOLIDAY INN
(restaurant, pub, state liquor store)
P.O. Box 1840. . . . . 649-7000, (800) 238-8000

RESTAURANTS

ADOLPH'S (mini-bottle license)
On the Golf Course 649-7177

BAGEL NOSH
592 Main St.. 649-6674
BROTHER CHRISTOPHER
(Italian, American, mini-bottle license)
1492 Park Ave. 649-9300
CAR 19 (mini-bottle license)
438 Main St.. 649-9474
THE CARBIDE LAMP (mini-bottle license)
596 Main St.. 649-6466
CHINA BRIDGE (Cantonese)
Holiday Village Shopping Center 649-5757
THE CLAIM JUMPER
(mini-bottle store & private club on premises)
573 Main St.. 649-8051
COPPERBOTTOM INN (liquor store & bar on premises)
Shortline Rd. 649-5111
THE CORNER STORE (deli, happy hour)
Plaza level at the Resort Center 649-8600
COWBOY BAR & RESTAURANT
(barbecue, steaks, liquor store on premises)
268 Main St.. 649-4146
THE EATING ESTABLISHMENT
317 Main St.. 649-8284
EL PAPAGAYO (Mexican)
430 Main St.. 649-6900
FINNEY'S (a gathering place, sandwiches)
136 Heber Ave. 649-9536
GRUB STEAK (prime rib, seafood, state liquor store)
Prospector Square. 649-8060
JANEAUX'S (mini-bottle license & private club)
306 Main St.. 649-6800
JODY'S (Italian, private club, live band, dancing)
350 Main St.. 649-6793
MAIN STREET DELICATESSEN
525 Main St.. 649-6498
MC WILLY'S (sandwiches, salads, soups, natural ice cream)
Holiday Village Mall 649-9687
MILETI'S (Italian, private club on premises)
412 Main St.. 649-8211
MINER'S DELIGHT (ice cream)
442 Main St.. 649-8001
MOUNTAIN FISHERY
(mini-bottle store, private club on premises)
368 Main St.. 649-4006
MT. AIR CAFE
Junction of Hwy. 224 & Park Ave. 649-9868
PARK CITY YACHT CLUB
(seafood, beef, vegetarian, mini-bottle license)
PROSPECTOR'S SIRLOIN (wine service, cocktail lounge)
Top of Main St. 649-7482
ROYCE'S OF PARK CITY
(liquor store on premises, mini-bottle license)
In the Holiday Inn 649-8659
RICHARD'S
(imported coffees & teas, pocket bread sandwiches)
Plaza Level at Resort Center. 649-9791
SHANNON'S (mini-bottle license)
438 Main St.. 649-9474

SERVICES

AUTO RENTAL

AMERICAN INTERNATIONAL OF PARK CITY
P.O. Box 126 649-8741
AMERICAN INTERNATIONAL OF SALT LAKE
1355 West North Temple St.
Salt Lake City, 84116 . . . . 322-2488, (800) 527-0202
OTHERS AT SALT LAKE AIRPORT
Avis, Budget, Hertz, National & Dollar Rent-A-Car

BUS

LEWIS BROTHERS EXPRESS BUS SERVICE
Regular scheduled shuttle service to and from Salt Lake City Int'l. Airport, downtown Salt Lake City and Park City.

HELICOPTER

HOSKING HELICOPTER SERVICE
P.O. Box 351, Bountiful, 84010 295-3402
Salt Lake Airport / Park City Shuttle
Park City Ski Corp.. 649-8111
HELICOPTER SKIING
Information & reservations taken at The Powder Room
Plaza Level at Resort Center. 649-6967

LIMO

LEWIS BROTHERS STAGES
Between Salt Lake Airport & Park City
Salt Lake City 359-8677
Park City. 649-6778

PHARMACY

ALPHA BETA
Holiday Village Mall 649-6134

SNOWMOBILING

SNOW MACHINE RENTALS
P.O. Box 2745, Highways 40 & 248 649-6554

TAXI

PARK CITY TAXI 649-8567
UTE CAB COMPANY
Salt Lake City 359-7788
YELLOW CAB COMPANY
Salt Lake City 521-2100

THEATRES

HOLIDAY CINEMAS THREE
Holiday Village Mall 649-6541
SILVER WHEEL THEATRE
(melodrama, Fri. & Sat. nights at 8:00 p.m.)
328 Main St.. 649-9361

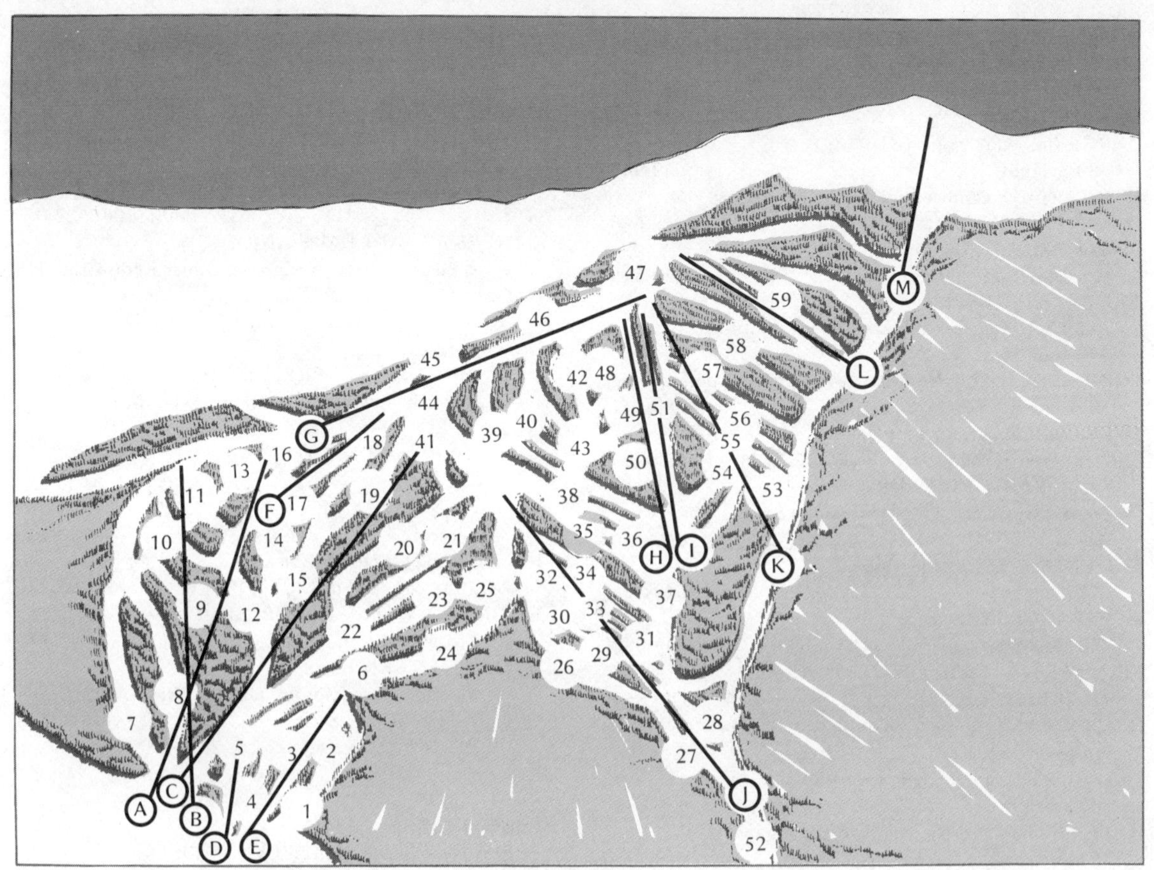

PARK CITY RUNS

1 CLEMENTINE
2 PICK N SHOVEL
3 QUICK SILVER
4 THREE KINGS
5 KINGS CROWN
6 SILVER HOLLOW
7 NASTAR
8 PAY DAY
9 BLANCHE
10 NAIL DRIVER
11 WIDOWMAKER
12 TREASURE-HOLLOW
13 DIVIDEND
14 WATERFALL
15 SIDEWINDER
16 SILVER QUEEN
17 CRESCENT
18 SILVER SKIS
19 SHAFT
20 LADIES GS
21 MENS GS
22 MENS SL
23 LADIES SL
24 GOTCHA
25 GOTCHA CUT-OFF
26 SELDOM SEEN
27 HOT SPOT
28 COMBUSTION
29 CLIMAX
30 MONITOR
31 EUREKA
32 LIBERTY
33 SHAMUS
34 SITKA
35 CHANCE
36 HIGH GARD
37 BROADWAY
38 KING CON
39 CLAIM JUMPER
40 ASSESSMENT
41 POWDER KEG
42 HIDDEN SPLENDOR
43 HALF LOAD
44 QUARTER LOAD
45 BONANZA
46 BELMONT
47 BLUESLIP
48 NEWPORT
49 LOST PROSPECTOR
50 DYNAMITE
51 PROSPECTOR
52 THAYNES CANYON
53 CARBIDE CUT
54 PARLEY'S PARK
55 SUNNYSIDE
56 GLORY HOLE
57 FORD COUNTRY
58 SINGLE JACK
59 DOUBLE JACK
60 THAYNES
61 THE HOIST
62 KEYSTONE
63 JUPITER ACCESS
64 WEST FACE
65 INDICATOR
66 6 BELLS
67 SILVER CLIFF
68 FORTUNE TELLER
69 SHADOW RIDGE
70 PORTUGESE GAP
71 SCOTT'S BOWL

PARK CITY LIFTS

A GONDOLA
B PAY DAY
C VICTORIA STATION
D FIRST TIME
E THREE KINGS
F TRACK ONE
G ANGLE STATION
H LOST PROSPECTOR
I PROSPECTOR
J KING CONSOLIDATED
K FORD COUNTRY
L THAYNES
M JUPITER CHAIR

PARK CITY CONT.

STORES & SKI SHOPS

B BAR G CUSTOM LEATHER
541 Main St.. 649-8638

BLOOM'S (gifts)
363 Main St.. 649-9853

CANYON DESIGNS (jewelry)
438 Main St.. 649-8662

CARTIER'S (handmade dolls, weaving, gifts)
355 Main St.. 649-7087

THE CLOTHES STORE
354 Main Street 649-7988

DOLLY'S BOOKSTORE & BOUTIQUE
510 Main St.. 649-8062

THE ELIZABETH SHOPPE (clothing, women & children)
531 Main St.. 649-6112

STEIN ERIKSEN (ski rental & sport shop)
Plaza at Resort Center 649-8110

THE FAMILY JEWELS (gift shop, art gallery, framing)
591 Main St.. 649-8594

THE HAT STORE (cowboy hats)
354 Main St.. 649-9132

HOLIDAY TOPS (tee-shirt shop, western hats, gift items)
Holiday Village Mall 649-6955

INDIAN ARTS CENTER & GIFT EMPORIUM
Parking level at Resort Center 649-7620

JOHNSON GALLERY (custom framing)
Parking level at Resort Center 649-8102
KARLYNN'S (women's fashions & gifts)
Holiday Village Mall 649-7079
KIMBALL ART CENTER
638 Park Ave. 649-8882
KINDERSPORT (ski rentals & sales)
580 Main St.. 649-8338
LIGNELL'S P.C.M.I. (jeans, slacks)
408 Main St.. 649-7350
MADAME GOODSHOT'S
(photos from the past, costumes over street clothes)
517 Main St.. 649-7781
THE MAIN STREET PHOTOGRAPHER
(film processing, camera supplies)
523 Main St.. 649-9431
MEYER GALLERY
305 Main St.. 649-8160
MINORS ONLY (children's clothing & accessories)
Holiday Village Mall 649-5074
PARK CITY LEATHERWORKS (western wear)
324 Main St.. 649-9424
PARK CITY PHOTO / STATUS GALLERY
(action sport photography)
Holiday Village Mall 649-9494
THE POWDER ROOM
(mountain photography & helicopter skiing)
Plaza Level at Resort Center. 649-6967
ROOT SELLER (natural food store)
465 Main St.. 649-8337
SUMMIT COUNTY T-SHIRTS
562 Main St.. 649-6433
SUNSET SPORT CENTERS (ski shop)
Park West Ski Resort 649-9589
TIMBER HAUS (ski & sport)
628 Park Ave. 649-9712
TOMMY KNOCKERS GIFTS & JEWELRY
Holiday Village Mall 649-8482
TUCK BOX (imported copper & brass)
438 Main St.. 649-8662
THE VILLAGE IDIOT (from t-shirts to tobacco to records)
511 Main St.. 649-5988
THE VILLAGE STORE (souvenirs, film, sundries)
Plaza Level at Resort Center. 649-8306
THE WOODHAUS (sports shop)
1240 Park Ave. 649-9123
WOLFE'S (ski & sporting goods store)
Plaza at Resort Center 649-9852

P A R K W E S T

P.O. BOX 1598, PK. CITY, UT 84060   (801) 649-9663

AREA INFORMATION

FOR ADDITIONAL LODGINGS, RESTAURANTS, SERVICES & SHOPS, SEE PARK CITY,

BASE ELEVATION
7,000 feet
HOURS
9:00 a.m. - 4:30 p.m., daily
5:00 - 10:00 p.m., Tues. thru Sat.
LIFTS
7 chairs, 7,200 capacity per hour
LONGEST RUN
2¼ miles
SEASON
End of November to mid-April, snowmaking
TRAILS
20% beginner, 45% intermediate, 35% expert
TRAVEL
24 miles east of Salt Lake City via I-80, exit Park City turnoff.
VERTICAL DROP
2,000 feet

LODGING

RED PINE CHALETS
Base Area 649-9663, (800) 453-5757

RESTAURANTS

BRANDING IRON RESTAURANT & SALOON
At slopes, call Ski Area

SERVICES

HELICOPTER SKIING

UTAH POWDERBIRDS
Advance reservations 649-9663

TRANSPORTATION

RENTAL CAR
Check with Park West reservation office.
SHUTTLE
Skiers lodging in Park City, skiing Park West may ride the courtesy shuttle from town to Park West and return.

SKI SHOP

PARK WEST SPORTS SHOP
(equipment, attire, accessories, rentals)
At slopes, call Ski Area

S N O W B A S I N

Box 200, HUNTSVILLE, UT 84317   (801) 621-2234

AREA INFORMATION

BASE ELEVATION
6,400 feet
FOOD SERVICE
Cafeteria at base of lodge
EMERGENCY
Call resort or operator
LIFTS
2 triple lifts, 4 double lifts, 6,400 capacity per hr.
SEASON
Late Nov. to mid-April

SNOWBASIN CONT.

SERVICES
All services, shops, etc., are located in Ogden, 17 miles west of Snowbasin.
SKI SHOP
At base lodge
SNOW PHONE 621-7691
TRAILS
1,300 acres, 40 runs, 20% beginner, 45% intermediate, 35% expert.
TRAVEL
55 miles from Salt Lake City Int'l. Airport, via I-15 N., exit E. at Ogden's 12th St. to Ogden Cyn., follow signs 17 miles east to ski area.
VERTICAL DROP
2,400 feet

LODGING

ALL ACCOMODATIONS ARE IN OGDEN, 17 MILES WEST OF SNOWBASIN.

BIG Z MOTEL
1123 West, 2100 South 394-6632
CIRCLE R MOTEL
5223 South, 1900 West 773-7432
COLONIAL MOTEL
1269 Washington Bl. 399-5851
FLYING J MOTEL
1206 West, 2100 South 393-8644
HOLIDAY INN
3306 Washington Bl. 399-5671
IMPERIAL 400 MOTEL
1956 Washington Bl. 393-8667
LAZY J MOTEL
951 W. Riverdale Rd.. 621-2990
MILLSTREAM MOTEL
1450 Washington Bl. 394-9425
MOONLIGHT INN
1825 Washington Bl. 621-8350
MOUNTAIN VIEW MOTEL
563 W. 24th St. 394-1414
RAMADA INN
2433 Adams Ave.. 394-4503
TRAVELODGE
2110 Washington Bl. 394-4563

RESTAURANTS

ALL RESTAURANTS ARE IN OGDEN

BRATTEN'S SEA FOOD GROTTO
3376 Harrison Bl.. 394-0567
EL MATADOR
2564 Ogden Ave. 393-3151
GRAYCLIFF LODGE
508 Ogden Canyon 392-6775
THE GREENERY RESTAURANT
Mouth of Ogden Canyon. 392-1777
LEE'S BAR-B-Q
2866 Washington Bl. 621-9120
LION'S DEN RESTAURANT
3607 Washington Bl. 399-5804
OGDEN VALLEY INN
7345 East, 900 South 745-2481
PRAIRIE SCHOONER STEAK HOUSE
445 Park Bl. 392-2712
WAREHOUSE RESTAURANT
337 31st St. 393-3040
ZITO'S FIRESIDE SUPPER CLUB
7695 S. Hwy. 89, Weber Cyn. 479-4640

SNOWBIRD

SNOWBIRD, UT 84070 (801) 742-2222

AREA INFORMATION

BASE ELEVATION
8,100 feet
CENTRAL NUMBER
Reservations, restaurants, stores & shops. . . . 742-2000
CHILD CARE
3 years & up, Cliff Lodge 742-3300
HELICOPTER SKIING
1st level, Wasatch Guides
HOURS
9:30 a.m. to 4:30 p.m.
LIFTS
7 chairs, 1 tramway
LONGEST RUN
2.5 miles
MEDICAL CLINIC
At slope
SEASON
Late November to May 1st
SNOW PHONE 742-2222, (800) 521-6050
TRAILS
20% beginner, 40% intermediate, 40% expert
TRAVEL
Southeast, 31 miles from Salt Lake City Int'l. Airport via I-80 E., then I-215 to Hwy. 210 to Alta; then, 1 mile to Ski Area.
VERTICAL DROP
2,900 feet

LODGING

ALL LODGING IS AT THE SLOPE
CENTRAL RESERVATIONS. 742-2000

CLIFF LODGE 742-3300
IRON BLOSAM LODGE. 742-3100
LODGE AT SNOWBIRD. 742-2100
TURRA MURRA LODGE. 742-2500

RESTAURANTS

ALL RESTAURANTS ARE AT SKI AREA. . . . 742-2000

BIRDFEEDER
Light fare
EAGLE'S NEST
Private lounge
FORKLIFT
Dinner
PLAZA
Breakfast & lunch
STEAK PIT
Seafood & steak
TRAM ROOM BAR
Dancing, entertainment

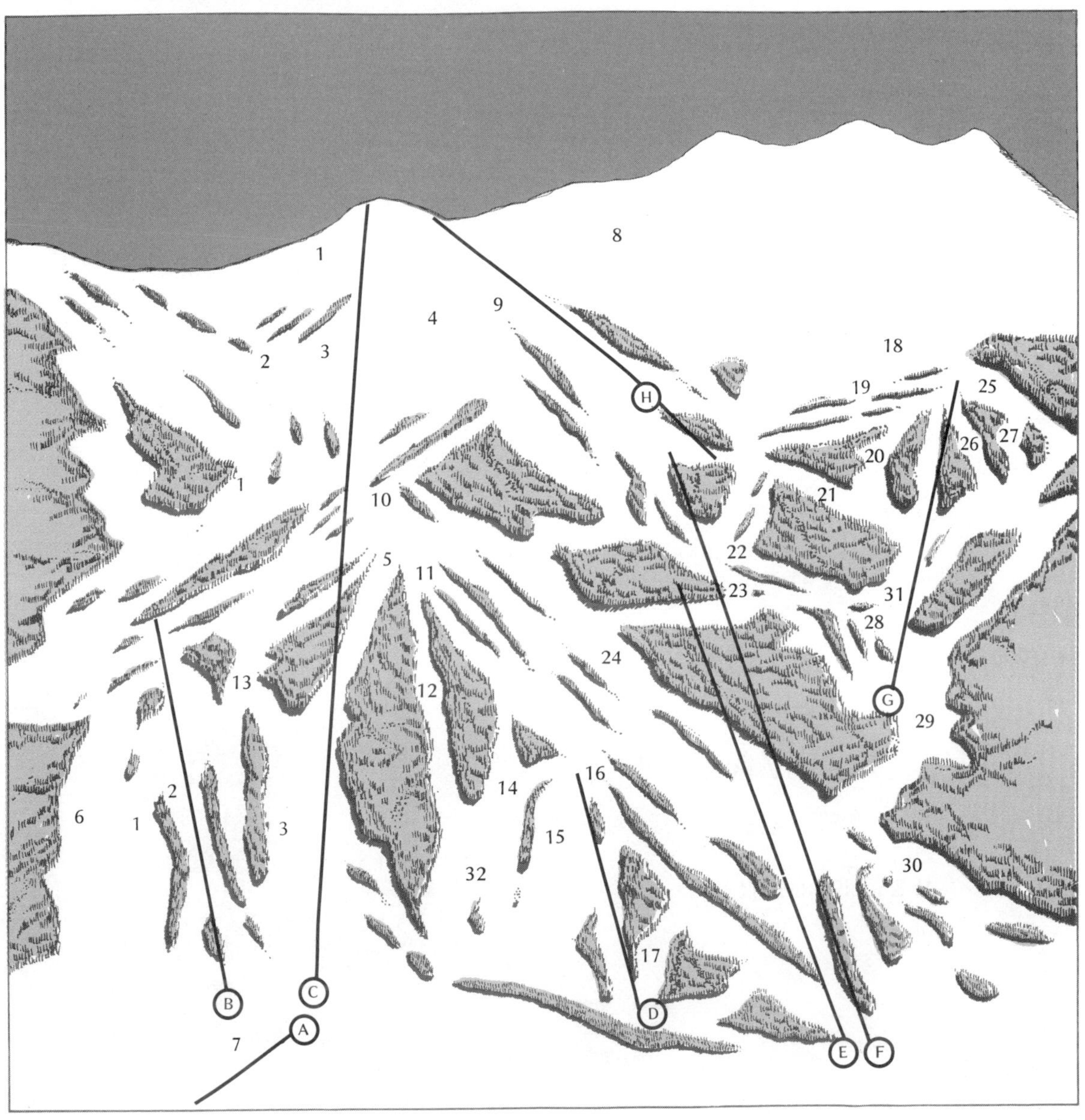

SNOWBIRD

RUNS

1 CHIP'S RUN
2 PRIMROSE PATH
3 SILVER FOX
4 PERUVIAN CIRQUE
5 DALTON'S DRAW
6 BLACKJACK
7 CHICKADEE
8 LITTLE CLOUD
9 REGULATOR JOHNSON
10 WILBERE BOWL
11 WILBERE CHUTE
12 MACH SCHNELL
13 EASIEST ROUTE
14 HARPER'S FERRY EAST
15 HARPER'S FERRY
16 WILBERE RIDGE
17 WILBERE CUTOFF
18 BASSACKWARDS
19 ELECTION
20 S.T.H.
21 BLACK FOREST
22 ORGAN GRINDER
23 BICARBONATE
24 BIG EMMA
25 BANANAS
26 GADZOOKS
27 BANANA SPLIT
28 CARBONATE
29 LOWER BASSACKWARDS
30 WEST SECOND SOUTH
31 CAT TRACK
32 BASS HIGHWAY

LIFTS

A PERUVIAN DOUBLE CHAIR
B CHICKADEE DOUBLE CHAIR
C AERIAL TRAMWAY
D WILBERE RIDGE DOUBLE CHAIR
E MID-GAD DOUBLE CHAIR
F GAD I DOUBLE CHAIR
G GAD II DOUBLE CHAIR
H LITTLE CLOUD DOUBLE CHAIR

SERVICES

UNLESS OTHERWISE LISTED 742-2000

AUTO RENTALS

American International. 322-2488
Avis (drop at Iron Blosam Lodge). . . . (800) 331-1212
Budget 363-1500
Hertz 328-2088
National 539-0200

BUSES

Bonneville Van Service 364-6520

SNOWBIRD CONT.

Gray Line (charter & limos) 521-6070
Lake Shore Motor Coach. 328-3361
Lewis Bros. 359-8677
Trailways. 328-8121
Utah Transit District 531-8600

GROCERIES
General Gritts (1st level)

LAUNDRY
In each lodge

PHARMACY
Snowbird Pharmacy (2nd level)

POST OFFICE
9 a.m. - 7 p.m., at Snowbird Pharmacy

TAXI
City Cab 363-5014
Ute Cab 359-7000
Yellow Cab 521-2100

STORES & SKI SHOPS

ALL STORES & SHOPS ARE AT THE SKI AREA AND MAY BE REACHED BY CALLING 742-2000

CANYON DESIGN
Jewelry, 2nd level

GENERAL GRITTS
Deli, 1st level

THE GIFTHAUS
1st level

MARIPOSA
Alterations, 1st level

MORROW'S NUT HOUSE
2nd level

NORSK LEATHER SHOP
2nd level

POWDERHOUND BOUTIQUE
3rd level

SPORT STALKER SKI SHOP
3rd level

TIMBERHAUS SKI SHOP
2nd level

THE TUCK BOX
Gifts, 1st level

V E R M O N T

BOLTON VALLEY

BOLTON VALLEY, VT 05477 (802) 451-3220

AREA INFORMATION

BASE ELEVATION
2,150 ft.

EMERGENCY
Fire Dept. 434-3497
Hospital 656-2345
Police. 655-3435
Ski Patrol . . . . 434-2131, ext. 323

GIFTS
4 double chairs

HOURS
9 a.m. to 4 p.m.

NURSERY
Full day, toilet trained only

TRAILS
25 Alpine, 12 cross country (½ intermediate, ½ beginner), 17 miles expert trail to Stowe.

TRAVEL
By car, from Boston, 3½ hrs., Rt. 93 toExit 10 Rt. 89, Rt. 2 W. to ski area. Auto rental at Burlington Int'l. Airport 434-2131
By air, U.S. Air, Delta, Air North, Air New England from Burlington Int'l. Airport.
By bus, Vermont Transit at Waterbury, VT 434-2131
By train, The Montrealer, Amtrak, Waterbury 434-2131

SEASON
Thanksgiving thru mid-April

VERTICAL DROP
1,100 ft.

LODGING

THE BLACK BEAR
300 yards from lifts. 434-2126

BOLTON VALLEY LODGE
At the slope 434-2131, (800) 451-3220

TRAILSIDE CONDOS
At the slope 434-2953, (800) 434-2769

RESTAURANTS

FIRESIDE DINING ROOM
In the lodge . . . . 434-2131, ext. 357

JAMES MOORE TAVERN (entertainment)
In the Lodge. . . . . 434-2131, ext. 358

LAST RUN CAFE
In the Lodge. . . . . 434-2131, ext. 238

PAPPA D'S ITALIAN RISTORANTE
In the Lodge. . . . . 434-2131, ext. 252

STORES & SKI SHOPS

ALL STORES CAN BE REACHED AT 434-2131 AND ARE LOCATED IN THE HOTEL

THE GROCERIE . . . . .ext. 158
SKI SHOP . . . . .ext. 355
WINE & CHEESE SHOP. . . . . .ext. 156

BROMLEY MOUNTAIN

BOX 1130 MANCHESTER CENTER, VT 05255
TELEPHONE: (802) 824-6915

AREA INFORMATION

BASE ELEVATION
1,950 feet
HOURS
9:00 a.m. - 4:00 p.m.
Beginning 8:30 on weekends & holidays
LIFTS
5 chairs, 1 J-bar, 1 pony lift, 6,330 capacity per hour
LONGEST RUN
2½ miles
NURSERY
1 month to 6 years, call Ski Area
SEASON
Late November to mid-April, snowmaking
SNOW PHONE 297-2211
TRAILS
20% advanced, 60% intermediate, 20% beginner
TRAVEL
Rt. 7 to Manchester Center, Rt. 11 E. to Ski Area.
Air service to Keene, NH, Rutland or Springfield. See "Services" for local airlines, car rental, and bus service.
VERTICAL DROP
1,334 feet

LODGING

CENTRAL RESERVATIONS. 824-6915

THE ASPEN MOTEL
Television
THE BARN LODGE
Family/game room
THE BARNSTEAD MOTEL
Television, family/game room
BLUE GENTIAN LODGE
Family/game room
BROMLEY SUN LODGE
Television, indoor pool, sauna, pets allowed
CHALET MOTEL
Phone, television, sauna
COLD SPRING MOTEL
Television, pets allowed
EDDMAN'S EYRIE
Television
HAIG'S
Television, entertainment
IRON KETTLE MOTEL
Connecting rooms, televison, pets allowed
JO-MARY'S MOTEL
Television
LIFTLINE LODGE / BERGHAUS
Phone, connecting rooms
MAGIC VIEW MOTEL
Television, family/game room, pets allowed

BROMLEY MTN. CONT.

MANCHESTER VIEW MOTEL
Television
MARBLEDGE MOTEL
Television, connecting rooms
NORDIC INN
Entertainment
NORTH SHIRE MOTEL
Television
OLYMPIA MOTOR LODGE
Television
PALMER HOUSE MOTEL
Phone, television, sauna, whirlpool
THE POST HORN INN
Connecting rooms, television, pets allowed
RED SLED MOTEL
Phone, television
SNOW BOUND MOTEL
Television
SNOWDON MOTEL
Television, connecting rooms
STAMFORD MOTEL
Television, pets allowed, connecting rooms
STRATTON MOUNTAIN INN
Phone, television, entertainment
SUNDERLAND MOTEL & LODGE
Television, sauna, pets allowed, connecting rooms
SWISS INN
Television, family/game room, connecting rooms
VALHALLA MOTEL
Television
WHITE PINE LODGE
Television, family game room, pets allowed

RESTAURANTS

THE BUTTERY
(quiches, crepes, sandwiches, cocktails til 4)
The Jelly Mill, Rt. 7, Manchester 362-3544
BIRKENHAUS (Continental, by reservation only)
Rt. 7, 3½ mi. N. of Manchester 362-1616
CHESTER INN
Rt. 11 on the Village Green, Chester 875-2444
GARLIC JOHN'S (Italian)
Bromley Mountain Rd.. 362-9843
HAIG'S (dancing)
Foot of Stratton Mtn., Bondville 297-1300
THE HEARTHSTONE
(seafood, cocktails, reservations suggested)
Rt. 100, South Londonderry 824-3505
THE HIND QUARTERS (lounge)
On the Green, Chester 875-2400
KANDAHAR (Continental)
Routes 11 & 30 824-5531
LIFTLINE LODGE (Austrian, reservations requested)
Stratton Mountain 297-2600
THE LONDONDERRY INN (cocktails, reservations only)
Londonderry 824-5226
THE MAD BATTER (restaurant & bakery)
3 mi. N. of Rt. 30,
Rt. 100, South Londonderry 824-5050
THE QUALITY RESTAURANT (extensive salad bar)
Manchester Center 362-1317
RED FOX INN (reservations requested)
Winhall Hollow Rd., Bondville 297-2543
STRATTON MOUNTAIN INN (entertainment)
Stratton Mountain 297-2500
THEODORE'S (lunch, cocktails)
Stratton Base Lodge, 1st floor, call Ski Area
VILLAGE AUBERGE
Rt. 30, Dorset 867-5715

SERVICES

AIR

AIR NEW ENGLAND
To Keene, NH, Rutland or Springfield (800) 225-3640
PRECISION VALLEY AIRWAYS
To Keene, NH, Rutland or Springfield 357-3761

AUTO RENTAL

AVIS
Albany, NY . . . . (518) 482-4421
Keene, NH. 352-8525
Lebanon 298-7753
Rutland 775-2933

BUS

GREYHOUND
To Brattleboro & Manchester, VT
NEW ENGLAND SHUTTLE SERVICE
From Keene, Hartford, Boston &
N. Y. City Airports, by reservation 464-2276

BEAUTY SHOP

BIRKENHAUS BEAUTY SHOP
Stratton Mountain 297-2202

GROCERIES

WINHALL MARKET
Bondville. 297-1933
JAMAICA GENERAL STORE
Jamaica. 874-4151
R-D SUNOCO & GROCERY
Routes 30 & 100, Rawsonville 297-2165
WEST RIVER COUNTRY STORE
(wine, cheese, natural foods)
Garden Complex, Londonderry 824-5091

THEATRE

DERRY TWIN CINEMA
Londonderry Shopping Center 824-3331

TRAIN

AMTRAK
To Brattleboro & Manchester, VT

SKI SHOPS

THE FIRST RUN (ski sales, rental, repair, skiwear)
Bromley, call Ski Area

BURKE MTN.

EAST BURKE, VT 05832 (802) 626-3305

AREA INFORMATION

BASE ELEVATION
1,200 feet
HOURS
9 a.m. - 4 p.m.
LIFTS
Capacity per hr., 3,480
1 double chair, 1 double lift
2 poma lifts, 1 T-bar
LONGEST RUN
3½ miles
NURSERY
4 mo. to 7 yrs., all day
SEASON
Thanksgiving to Easter
SNOW PHONE 626-3305
TRAILS
24 trails, 3 open slopes, 130 acres, 15 miles
TRANSPORTATION
7 mi. from I-91, 20 mi. from I-93; 2½ hrs. from Montreal, Rt. 10 E. from Rt. 55 S. to I-91 S. to Lyndonville, Exit 24 to Rt. 114. From Boston, 3½ hours, I-93 N. to Littleton, Rt. 18 W. to St. Johnsbury I-91 N. to Exit 23, Rt. 5 N. & 114.
VERTICAL DROP
2,000 feet

EMERGENCY

FIRE 626-3211
E. BURKE FIRE & RESCUE SQUAD 626-5554
HOSPITAL 748-8141
LSC RESCUE 626-5053
POLICE 748-3111

LODGING

ANCHOR WAY MOTEL
Route 5, Lyndon 626-5832
BAKER FARMHOUSE
West Burke. 626-3305
BURKE MOUNTAIN CONDOS
Burke Mountain. 626-3305
BURKESIDE CONDOS
By Sherburne Farm Chairlift 626-3305
HERITAGE CHALETS
Box 41, East Burke. 626-9009
HIGH MEADOWS CONDOS
Near Willoughby Lodge 626-3305
HOLIDAY MOTEL (15 minutes away)
25 Hastings St., St. Johnsbury. 748-8192
HOUSE IN THE WOODS
Kirby Rd., East Burke 626-9243
LYNBURKE MOTEL
Lyndonville 626-3346
LYNDON MOTEL
Route 5, Lyndon 626-5505
NELSON FARMHOUSE (6 miles away)
Madigan Lane, Harvard, MA 01451 456-8823, 485-1664
SPRUCE WOODS CONDOS
Near Willoughby Lodge 626-3305
YANKEE TRAVELER MOTEL (15 minutes away)
65 Portland St., St. Johnsbury 748-3156

RECREATION

BOATING
State beaches & boat landings at Lake Willoughby and Crystal Lake. Sunfish Races, Joe's Pond in Danville weekly in the summer.
CAMPING
10,000 acres, full facilities
Write to ski area for information.
FISHING
Dish Mill Brook, East Branch of Passumpsic River, Newark Pond, Center Pond, Crystal Lake
GOLF
St. Johnsbury Country Club, Rt. 5 north of St. Johnsbury, 9 holes. Orleans Country Club, I-91 North, Orleans, 18 holes.
HIKING
1 hr. drive from Appalachian Trail, Mt. Burke Trails from the Base Lodge & from the summit—marked trails
HORSEBACK RIDING
West Burke, call Kay Switzer, 467-3380
SWIMMING
Beaches at Joe's Pond, Crystal Lake, Island Pond, Lake Willoughby, Maidstone State Park
TENNIS
Lyndonville, Powers Park & Lyndon State College (night tennis). St. Johnsbury, Rt. 2 west by pool
TOLL ROAD
Scenic drive from ski area, 360 degree view
3,267 ft. elevation

RESTAURANTS

EAST BURKE VILLAGE FARE
East Burke. 626-8782
LUIGI'S (Italian, American, bar)
Main St., Lyndonville. 626-9202
OLD CUTTER INN
East Burke. 626-5152
OSCAR'S BAKERY & COFFEE SHOP
Church St., Lyndonville
SLICE & SPICE (take-out)
Main St., Lyndonville. 626-9888
WILLY'S (American, bar)
East Burke. 626-8475

STORES & SKI SHOPS

COUNTRY HEARTH SKI SHOP
Upper Lodge at ski area 626-5800
EAST BURKE VILLAGE STORE (general store)
East Burke. 626-9618
EAST BURKE MARKET
East Burke
RECREATION PLUS
Depot St., Lyndonville. 626-5011

KILLINGTON

KILLINGTON, VT 05751 (802) 422-3333

AREA INFORMATION

BASE ELEVATION
1,060 feet
HOURS
9:00 a.m. - 4:00 p.m., weekdays
8:00 a.m. - 4:00 p.m., weekends & holidays
LIFTS
11 chairs, 1 gondola, 1 poma lift
18,200 capacity per hour
LONGEST RUN
5 miles
NURSERY
1st floor of Snowshed Lodge
8:30 a.m. - 4:00 p.m., call Ski Area
SEASON
End of October to end of May
SNOW PHONE 422-3261
Toll free from New England or New York,
except for 802 & 716 areas . . . . (800) 451-4301
TRAILS
41% beginner, 25% intermediate,
34% advanced, snowmaking
TRAVEL
Located in Central Vermont at the junction of U.S. 4 & Vt. 100, 16 miles east of Rutland. From N.Y. City, I-95 to I-91 to exit 6, Rutland, onto Vt. 103 to Vt. 100 to U.S. 4 to Ski Area. Or, N.Y. Thruway to exit 24 at Albany to I-87 N. to Fort Anne/Rutland exit, to N.Y. 149 E. to U.S. 4 E. to Killington. From Boston, I-93 to I-89 N. to U.S. 4 to Ski Area.
VERTICAL DROP
3,060 feet

LODGING

ALL LODGINGS ARE IN KILLINGTON
UNLESS OTHERWISE NOTED.
ZIP - 05751, AREA CODE - 802.

CENTRAL RESERVATIONS. 422-3711

ALPENHOF (1 mile)
Killington Rd., Box 75 422-9787
THE ALPINE INN (3 miles)
Killington Rd.. 422-3485
THE ARCHES (9 miles)
U.S. 4 W., R.D. 2, Mendon, 05701 773-6644
BASIN LODGE (1 mile)
Killington Rd.. 422-3377
CHALET INTERNATIONAL (2 miles)
Killington Rd.. 422-3481
CHALET KILLINGTON (1 mile)
Killington Rd., Box 144 422-3451
CHALET ROEDIG (3 miles)
South View Path, off Killington Rd. 422-3810
CHALET SALZBURG (3 miles)
Killington Rd.. 422-3315
CORTINA INN (8 miles)
U.S. 4 West 773-3331
FLEUR DE LIS LODGE (11 miles)
Vt. 100 N., Pittsfield, 05762 746-8949
THE FRACTURED ROOSTER (2 miles)
Telefon Trail. 422-3288
THE FRIENDSHIP INN – TYROL MOTEL
U.S. 4 West 773-7485
GREY BONNET INN (4 miles)
Vt. 100 North 775-2537
GRINDELWALD GUEST HAUS (7 miles)
Stage Rd., off Vt. 100 N. 422-3474
THE INN AT LONG TRAIL (5 miles)
Box 267, U.S. 4 W. at Sherburne Pass 775-7181
KILLINGTON GATEWAY CONDOMINIUMS (9 miles)
U.S. 4 W., Mendon, 05701. 773-2301
KILLINGTON COUNTRY RESORT (10 miles)
Vt. 100 N., Pittsfield, 05762 . . . .775-1779, 746-8981
KILLINGTON - PICO MOTOR INN (9 miles)
U.S. 4 West 773-9716
KILLINGTON RESORT LODGE & APT'S. (2 miles)
Killington Rd.. 422-3417
KILLINGTON VILLAGE (walking distance)
100 Killington Rd. 422-3613
KILLINGTON VILLAGE INN (1 mile)
Killington Rd., Box 153 422-3301
LITTLE BUCKHORN LODGE (2 miles)
Killington Rd.. . . . . .422-3314, 775-3189
MENDON MOTEL & CHALETS (11 miles)
R.D. 2, U.S. 4 W., Mendon, 05701 773-2424
MOUNTAIN MEADOWS LODGE (4 miles)
Thundering Brook Rd., off U.S. 4 E. 775-1010
THE MOUNTAIN INN (walking distance)
One Killington Rd. 422-3595
MOUNTAIN SIDE MOTOR COURT (12 miles)
U.S. 4 E., Bridgewater, 05035 672-3370
NORTHBROOK CONDOMINIUMS (2 miles)
Telefon Trail, Box 172 422-3737
PICO PEAK LODGE (6 miles)
U.S. 4 West 773-6331
PIKES LODGE (1 mile)
Killington Rd.. 422-9782
RED CLOVER INN (9 miles)
Woodward Rd., off U.S. 4 W., Mendon, 05701 775-2290
RED ROB INN (1 mile)
Killington Rd.. 422-3303
SHERBURNE - KILLINGTON MOTEL (4 miles)
U.S. 4 West 773-9535
SKOL HAUS MOTOR LODGE (2 miles)
Killington Rd.. 422-3305
SNOBIRD LODGE (9 miles)
Vt. 100 N., Pittsfield, 05762 746-8073
SNOWED INN (2 miles)
Miller Brook Rd., off Killington Rd. 422-3407
STRATTON'S LODGE (8 miles)
U.S. 4 West, Mendon, 05701 775-4739
SUMMIT LODGE (3 miles)
Killington Rd., Box 119A 422-3535
SWISS FARM LODGE (3 miles)
Killington Rd., Box 119A 422-3535
TRAILSIDE LODGE (6 miles)
Coffeehouse Rd., off Vt. 100 N., Box 205. . . 422-3532

TURN OF RIVER LODGE (6 miles)
U.S. 4 E., Box 257 422-3317
VAL ROC MOTEL (8 miles)
U.S. 4 East. 422-3881
THE VERMONT INN (9 miles)
U.S. 4 West 773-9847
WHIFFLETREE CONDOMINIUMS (½ mile)
100 Killington Rd. 422-3101
WHISPERING PINES LODGE (3 miles)
South View Path, off Killington Rd. 422-3014
WHITE STONE MOTEL (11 miles)
U.S. 4 W., Mendon, 05701. 773-2155

RESTAURANTS

ALPINE INN (breakfast, dinner, cocktail lounge)
Killington Rd.. 422-3485
ANGUS TAVERN & SKI VACATION CENTER LOUNGE
(lunch, dinner, service bar)
Snowshed Area at Ski Area 422-3333
BACK BEHIND STEAK SALOON
(seafood specials, cocktail lounge)
U.S. 4 E. & Vt. 100 S., W. Bridgewater. 422-9907
BARBER'S RESTAURANT
(breakfast, lunch, dinner, cocktail lounge)
U.S. 4 West, Mendon 773-6424
BASIN LODGE
(breakfast, dinner, cocktail lounge, happy hour)
Killington Rd.. 422-3377
BILBO'S (deli, cocktail lounge, live band/disco)
Killington Rd.. 422-3686
CHALET KILLINGTON
(dinner, cocktail lounge, hors d'oeurves,
live entertainment, 4 - 6 p.m.)
Killington Rd.. 422-3451
CHARITY'S 1887 TAVERN
(lunch, dinner, cocktail lounge)
Killington Rd.. 422-3800
CHURCHILL'S RESTAURANT (dinner, cocktail lounge)
U.S. 4 W., Mendon 775-3219
CORTINA INN (dinner a la carte, cocktail lounge, disco)
U.S. 4, Mendon 773-3331
GREY BONNET INN
(breakfast, dinner a la carte, cocktail lounge)
Vt. 100 North 775-2537
KILLINGTON - PICO MOTOR INN
(dinner, cocktail lounge, happy hour)
U.S. 4 W., Mendon 773-9716
KILLINGTON VILLAGE INN (dinner, cocktail lounge)
Killington Rd.. 422-3301
KINGS FOUR
(dinner, breakfast - midnight to 3 a.m., cocktail
lounge, live entertainment - Fri. & Sat.)
Killington Rd.. 422-3594
LAKESIDE LOUNGE & RESTAURANT
(dinner, light menu, cocktail lounge)
Snowshed Area at Ski Area 422-3333
LAUREN'S GRACIOUS COUNTRY DINING
(Continental, wine cellar, cocktail lounge)
U.S. 4 East. 422-3886
NORTHBROOK INN
(breakfast, dinner, cocktail lounge, happy hour)
U.S. 4 East. 422-3737
PASTA POT (Italian, cocktail lounge)
U.S. 4 East. 422-3004
PICKLE BARREL
(cocktail lounge, snacks, happy hour, rock band)
Killington Rd.. 422-3035
RED ROB INN
(breakfast, dinner, cocktail lounge, live entertainment)
Killington Rd.. 422-3303
SIRLOIN SALOON (lunch dinner, cocktail lounge)
U.S. 7 S., Rutland. 773-7900
SNOWSHED LOUNGE
(Deli, wine & cheese shop, cocktail
lounge, folk singer, closes at 6 p.m.)
Snowshed Area at Ski Area 422-3333
STEAKS & THINGS (coffee shop, coctail lounge)
U.S. 4 West 775-1575
SUMMIT LODGE
(breakfast, dinner, cocktail lounge, live entertainment)
Killington Rd.. 422-3535
THE VERMONT INN
(dinner a la carte, children's menu, cocktail lounge)
U.S. 4 W., Mendon 773-9847
WOBBLY BARN
(dinner, cocktail lounge, happy hour, rock band)
Killington Rd.. 422-3392
ZORBA'S TAVERN
(Greek, Italian, lunch Sat. & Sun., cocktail lounge)
Killington Rd.. 422-3600

SERVICES

AIR

ALBANY AIRPORT
110 miles, 2¼ hours
BOSTON AIRPORT
158 miles, 3¼ hours
Connecting to Lebanon, NH & Rutland, VT Airports
BURLINGTON AIRPORT
84 miles, 1¾ hours
Connecting to Lebanon, NH Airport
HARTFORD AIRPORT
162 miles, 3¼ hours
Connecting to Lebanon, NH Airport
LEBANON, NH AIRPORT
39 miles, 1 hour
NEW YORK – LA GUARDIA AIRPORT
250 miles, 5½ hours
Connecting to Lebanon, NH Airport
RUTLAND, VT AIRPORT
20 miles, ½ hour

AUTO

AVIS RENT-A-CAR
Albany Airport . . . . (518) 869-8404
Burlington Airport . . . . (802) 864-0411
Lebanon, NH Airport. . . . . (603) 298-7753
Rutland, VT Airport . . . . (802) 775-2933

KILLINGTON RUNS

1 SNOWSHED SLOPE
2 YODELER
3 HIGHLANDER
4 IDLER
5 SKI SCHOOL SLOPE
6 GREAT EASTERN
7 SNOWSHED CROSSOVER
8 NORTHBROOK CROSSOVER
9 EASIER WAY TO GREAT EASTERN
10 SOUTH RIDGE LINK
11 NORTHBROOK TRAIL
12 CARPENTER'S RUN
13 4-MILE TRAIL
14 HIGH ROAD
15 NEEDLE'S EYE
16 SKYE LARK
17 SUPERSTAR
18 VALLEY PLUNGE
19 FROSTLINE
20 SHAGBACK
21 RIDGEVIEW
22 OUTERLIMITS
23 WILDFIRE
24 BOOMERANG - UPPER
25 PIPE DREAM - UPPER
26 ESCAPE
27 WANDERER
28 HOMERUN
29 THE JUG - UPPER
30 ECHO WOODS (GLADES)
31 BOOMERANG (LOWER)
32 PIPE DREAM (LOWER)
33 THE JUG (LOWER)
34 JUG HANDLE
35 ROUNDABOUT
36 BREAKAWAY
37 GOAT PATH
38 CASCADE
39 ESCAPADE
40 FLUME
41 CAT WALK
42 EAST FALL
43 DOWN DRAFT
44 BIG DIPPER
45 RIM RUN
46 RACER'S EDGE
47 WEST GLADE
48 EAST GLADE
49 RIME
50 HIGH TRAVERSE
51 KILLINK
52 UPPER MOUSE RUN
53 UPPER ROYAL FLUSH
54 SKID WAY
55 THE VALE
56 UPPER BUNNY BUSTER
57 LOWER MOUSE RUN
58 THE CHUTE
59 MOUSE TRAP
60 CONCLUSION
61 GREAT BEAR
62 NORTH STAR
63 LOWER BUNNY BUSTER
64 HIGH LINE RACING TRAIL
65 LOWER ROYAL FLUSH
66 HORN
67 RH ROAD
68 CAPER
69 TIMBERLINE
70 HEADER
71 VAGABOND
72 SWIRL

KILLINGTON LIFTS

A SNOWSHED DOUBLE CHAIR 1
B SNOWSHED DOUBLE CHAIR 2
C SNOWSHED DOUBLE CHAIR 3
D SNOWDON DOUBLE CHAIR
E SNOWDON TRIPLE CHAIR
F UPPER SNOWDON POMA LIFT
G GLADES TRIPLE CHAIR
H KILLINGTON DOUBLE CHAIR
I RAMS HEAD DOUBLE CHAIR
J BEAR MOUNTAIN TRIPLE CHAIR
K SOUTH RIDGE TRIPLE CHAIR
L GONDOLA SECTION 1
M GONDOLA SECTION 2
N GONDOLA SECTION 3
O NEEDLE'S EYE DOUBLE CHAIR

LIMO

NEW ENGLAND LIMO SERVICE
Roundtrip transfers from Lebanon, NH
Airport to Killington lodges . . . . (603) 643-5558

SHUTTLE SERVICE

ARK TRANSPORTATION
Rutland airport, bus depot, rental car agencies,
daily service from lodges to slopes 422-3054

TAXI

RED'S TAXI
Rutland 773-3377

GREEN MOUNTAIN TAXI
Rutland 773-3694

STORES & SKI SHOPS

GONDOLA BASE LODGE (Ski Area)
Limited ski, rental & repair shops under terminal

KILLINGTON LODGE (Ski Area)
Major ski & repairs shops - 1st floor
SNOWSHED LODGE (Ski Area)
Major ski shop - 1st floor
SKI VACATION CENTER AT SNOWSHED (Ski Area)
Major ski rental & repair shops - both on 1st floor, overnight ski tuning

MAD RIVER GLEN

WAITSFIELD, VT 05673 (802) 496-3551

AREA INFORMATION

FOR EMERGENCY LISTINGS, RESTAURANTS, LODGING, SERVICES, STORES & SKI SHOPS, SEE SUGARBUSH VALLEY

BASE ELEVATION
1,600 feet
HOURS
9:00 a.m. - 4:00 p.m.
LIFTS
4 chairs, 3,000 capacity per hour
LONGEST RUN
2 miles
NURSERY
The Cricket Club Nursery, call Ski Area
SEASON
December to mid-April, snowmaking
SNOW PHONE 496-3551
In Montreal . . . . (514) 845-9840
In N.Y., New England Vacation Council (212) 757-4455
Vermont Snow Line (not toll free) . . . (802) 229-0531
TRAILS
7 easy, 9 intermediate, 9 expert
TRAVEL
Vermont Route 17, also known as the McCullough Turnpike on the Ap Gap (Appalachian Gap) Road, 5 miles west of the Route 17 & 100 intersection.
VERTICAL DROP
2,000 feet

MOUNT SNOW

Mount SNOW, VT 05356 (802) 464-8501

AREA INFORMATION

BASE ELEVATION
1,900 feet
HOURS
8:00 a.m. - 4:00 p.m., weekends
From 9:00 a.m. on weekdays
LIFTS
11 chairs, 2 gondolas
LONGEST RUN
2½ miles
NURSERY
Ages 2 - 8, call Ski Area
SNOW PHONE 464-2151
TRAILS
20% beginner, 70% intermediate, 10% advanced
TRAVEL
In West Dover in Southern Vermont, 10 miles north of Wilmington, on Rt. 100. I-91 to Rt. 9, Brattleboro, then Rt. 100 to Ski Area. See "Services" for air and shuttle service and car rental.
VERTICAL DROP
1,680 feet

LODGING

LODGING IS IN WEST DOVER, 05356, UNLESS OTHERWISE NOTED.

ABROAD MOTOR INN (indoor pool, dining)
West Dover, 05356 464-3911
ALP-HOF (menu dining)
Handle Rd.. 464-3344
ANDIRONS LODGE
(restaurant, 2 lounges, entertainment, happy hour)
Rt. 100. 464-2114
BERKLEY & VELLER REAL ESTATE
(chalets, condos, farm-houses, duplexes)
Rt. 100, Wilmington, 05363. 464-8585
BROOK BOUND LODGE (family-style dining)
Coldbrook Rd., Wilmington, 05363 464-5267
CHALET WALDWINKEL (dining)
Box 364 464-5281
COOPER HILL LODGE (home cooked meals)
Box 146, East Dover, 05341. 348-6333
DALEM'S CHALET
(dining, full liquor license, indoor pool)
16 South St., Brattleboro, 05301 254-4323
DEERHILL INN (dinner)
Box 397 464-9382
ENCORE AT THE SLOPES (menu dining, cocktail lounge)
Box 385 464-3392
FOUR SEASONS INN (restaurant, cocktail lounge)
Rt. 100. 464-8303
GOLDEN EAGLE MOTEL (home cooked food, full bar)
R.D. 4, Box 184, W. Brattleboro, 05301. . . . 464-5540
HANDLE HOUSE (home-cooked meals served family style)
Handle Rd.. 464-5449
THE HERMITAGE INN
(Continental, cocktail lounge, entertainment)
Coldbrook Rd., Wilmington, 05363 464-3759
HORIZON MOTOR INN
(dining, cocktail lounge, indoor pool)
Rt. 9, Wilmington, 05363 . . . . . .464-2131, 464-3726
INN AT SAWMILL FARM (dining)
Box 8. 464-8131
IRONSTONE LODGE (menu dining, cocktail lounge)
Box 308LB 464-3796
KENYON REALTY
(private chalets, condos, 2 - 5 bedrooms)
Rt. 100. 464-2101
KITZHOF (family-style meals served)
West Dover, 05356 . . . . .464-8310, 464-2675
THE LODGE AT MOUNT SNOW
(menu dining, indoor/outdoor heated pool, whirlpool, lounge, entertainment)
Box 755 . . . . 464-5112, (800) 451-4289

MT. SNOW CONT.

LONGWOOD FARMS INN (dining)
Box 116, Marlboro, 05344. 257-1545
MOTEL ON THE MOUNTAIN (family style dinners)
Rt. 9, Searsburg, 05363 464-5628
MOUNT SNOW VALLEY REAL ESTATE (chalets/condos)
Rt. 100, Wilmington, 05363. . . . .464-2147, 464-5154
MOUNTAINEER LODGE
Handle Rd.. 464-5404
NORDIC HILLS LODGE
Coldbrook Rd., Wilmington, 05363 464-5130
NORTH BRANCH CLUB (dining, wine)
Star Route 464-3319
NORTH REAL ESTATE (chalets)
Box 761 . . . . .464-2196, 464-2090
NORWAY LODGE (cocktail lounge)
West Dover, 05356 464-3377
NUTMEG INN (dining)
Box 818LG, Wilmington, 05363 464-3351
OLD RED MILL (dining, near downtown shops)
Box 787, Wilmington, 05363 464-3700
ON THE ROCKS LODGE (dining, wine cellar)
Smith Rd., Wilmington, 05363 464-8364
RED CRICKET INN & CONDOMINIUMS (menu dining)
Box 338MS 464-8817
RED SHUTTER LODGE (meals)
Box 792, Wilmington, 05363 464-3768
SCHRODER HAUS (dining)
Higley Hill Rd., Wilmington, 05363 464-5574
SHIELD LODGE (home cooked meals)
Box 366 464-3984
SNOW DEN INN (meals)
Box 615 464-9355
SITZMARK LODGE (home cooked meals, entertainment)
East Dover Rd., Wilmington, 05363 464-3384
SLALOM LODGE (dining)
Shafter St., Wilmington, 05363 464-3783
SNOWBROOK AT MOUNT SNOW (walk to lifts)
West Dover, 05356 464-5154
SNOW LAKE LODGE (dining, cocktail lounge)
300 Mountain Rd.,
Mount Snow. 464-3333, (800) 451-4211
TAMARACK AT MOUNT SNOW (menu dining)
West Dover, 05356 464-8850
THUNDERBIRD INN (dining, entertainment)
Box 66 464-5550
TRAIL'S END LODGE (dining, 4 miles to slopes)
Smith Rd., Wilmington, 05363 464-9396
VIKING MOTEL (fireside dining, bar, lounge)
Box 236, Wilmington, 05363 464-5608
THE VINTAGE MOTEL (near restaurants, shops)
Box 222MS, Wilmington, 05363 464-8824, 464-3709
WEATHERVANE LODGE (Swiss-styled inn)
Dorr Fitch Rd. 464-5426
WEST DOVER INN (dining, lounge)
West Dover, 05356 464-5207
WHIPPLETREE LODGE (full breakfast)
Tannery Rd.. 464-5485
THE WHITE HOUSE OF WILMINGTON
(turn of the century mansion, international cuisine)
Box 757, Wilmington, 05363 464-2135

WILDYRIE INN (breakfasts, dinners)
Rt. 100. 464-5652
YANKEE DOODLE LODGE (dining, entertainment)
Rt. 100. 464-5591

RESTAURANTS

ANDIRONS LODGE
(2 lounges, entertainment, happy hour)
Rt. 100, West Dover 464-2114
FOUR SEASONS INN (cocktail lounge)
Rt. 100, West Dover 464-8303
MOUNT SNOW LODGE (cafeterias, restaurants, bars)
At the slopes, call Ski Area

SERVICES

AIR

AIR NEW ENGLAND
To Keene, NH. . . . . (800) 225-3640
PRECISION VALLEY AIRWAYS
To Keene, NH. 357-3761

AUTO RENTAL

AVIS
Albany, NY . . . . (518) 482-4421
Keene, NH. 352-8525

BUS

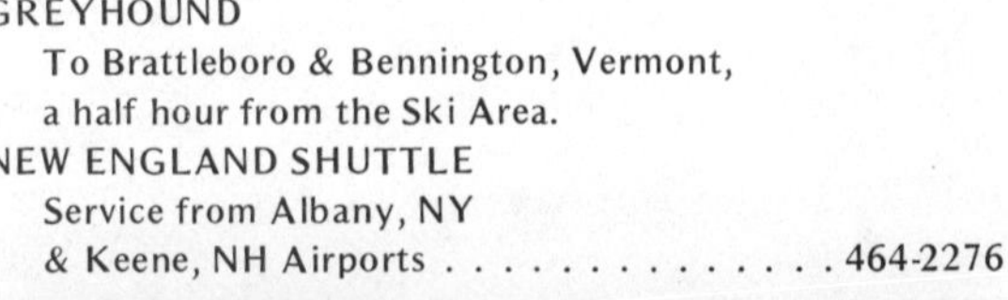
GREYHOUND
To Brattleboro & Bennington, Vermont,
a half hour from the Ski Area.
NEW ENGLAND SHUTTLE
Service from Albany, NY
& Keene, NH Airports 464-2276

MOUNT SNOW RUNS

1 SUNBROOK AREA
2 MOONWALK
3 COLDBROOK
4 BEARTRAP
5 LONG JOHN
6 CUTOFF
7 LONG JOHN
8 DEER RUN
9 UNCLE'S
10 RIDGE RUN
11 POWER LINE
12 UPPER EXIBITION
13 SOUTH BOWL
14 LIFT LINE 7
15 HOP
16 UPPER SUNDANCE
17 DEER RUN
18 SWITCHBACK
19 LINK
20 TRAMLINE
21 UPPER LODGE
22 UPPER LEDGE
23 COMMITTED
24 UPPER CANYON
25 PLUMMET
26 UPPER OVERBROOK
27 EGO ALLFY
28 BACK TO MIDSTATION
29 CHOKE
30 DROP
31 LOWER LODGE
32 BYPASS
33 LOWER SUNDANCE
34 BEAVER HILL
35 STANDARD
36 ILLUSION
37 LOWER CANYON
38 LOWER OVERBROOK
39 SOMERSET ROAD
40 SNOWDANCE
41 ONE MORE TIME
42 NORTH FACE
43 MIXING BOWL
44 LOWER EXIBITION

MOUNT SNOW LIFTS

A LITTLE BEAVER
B MIXING BOWL
C SAP BUCKET
D SUNDANCE
E BEAVER
F SNOWDANCE
G NORTH FACE
H GONDOLA
I GONDOLA
J SUNBROOK
K CANYON
L SKI SCHOOL
M SUMMIT
N CHILDREN'S

S T O W E

106 Mountain Rd., Stowe, VT 05672 (802) 253-7321

AREA INFORMATION

BASE ELEVATION
1,300 feet

HOURS
9:00 a.m. - 4:00, weekdays
8:30 a.m. - 4:00 p.m., weekends & holidays

LIFTS
1 enclosed gondola, 8 chairlifts, 3 bars
8,000 capacity per hour

LONGEST RUN
4½ miles

NURSERY
At the slopes, call Ski Area

SEASON
Mid-November to late April, snowmaking

SNOW PHONE . . . . (802) 253-8521
Canada . . . . (802) 253-7321

TRAILS
10% beginner, 70% intermediate, 20% advanced

TRAVEL
I-89 to Rt. 100 N. to Rt. 108 at Stowe to Ski Area.
Airport at Burlington; Amtrak services Waterbury.

VERTICAL DROP
2,100 feet

LODGING

ALPINE MOTOR LODGE (dining, cocktails)
Rt. 108. 253-7700
ANDERSENS' (Austrian food)
Rt. 108. 253-7336
BOTTOM NOTCH LODGE & PUB (dining)
Rt. 108. 253-8905
BUCCANEER MOTEL & SKI LODGE (breakfast, snacks)
Rt. 108. 253-4772
BUTTERNUT INN & CHALETS
Rt. 108. 253-4277
CHARBONNEAU'S (guest house)
Rt. 100 N.. 253-7701
THE CHARDA (Austrian-Hungarian fcuisine)
Rt. 100 N.. 253-4598
COUNTRY SQUIRE
Rt. 100 S. 253-4207
DIE ALPENROSE (near restaurant)
Rt. 108. 253-7277
EDSON HILL MANOR (dining)
Edson Hill Rd.. 253-7371
THE 1860 HOUSE (guest lodge)
School St. 253-7351, 253-8544
FIDDLER'S GREEN INN (dining)
Rt. 108. 253-8124
FOUR WINDS
Tabor Hill Rd.. 253-4543
FOXFIRE INN (Italian food)
Rt. 100 N.. 253-8459
THE GABLES INN (dining)
Rt. 108. 253-7730
GOLDEN EAGLE MOTOR INN & APARTMENTS
(coffee shop, near restaurant)
Rt. 108. 253-4811
GOLDEN KITZ LODGE & MOTEL (breakfast)
Rt. 108. 253-4217
GREY FOX INN (dining, salad bar)
Rt. 108. 253-8921
GUEST HOUSE "CHRISTEL HORMAN"
Rt. 108. 253-4846
HADLEIGH HOUSE (one room cottages)
Rt. 100 N.. 253-7703
HIGH HILLS (country lodge)
Stowe Hollow Rd. 253-4210
HOB KNOB INN (adjacent restaurant)
Rt. 108. 253-8549
THE INN AT THE MOUNTAIN (European cuisine)
Rt. 108. 253-7311
INNSBRUCK MOTOR INN (dining, bar)
Rt. 108. 253-8582
LOGWOOD INN (lodge, apartment, chalets, dining)
Edson Hill Rd.. 253-7354
LOWER VILLAGE INN (home cooking)
Rt. 100 S. 253-7787
MANSFIELD MOTEL (Continental breakfast)
Rt. 108. 253-4124
MT. MANSFIELD TOWNHOUSES & LODGE CONDOS
(dining, Fireside Tavern)
Rt. 108. 253-7311

MOUNTAIN ROAD MOTEL ("Dine Around" Ski Package)
Rt. 108. 253-4566
MOUNTAIN VIEW CONDOMINIUMS (1 & 2 bedrooms)
Rt. 108. 253-4144
NOTCHBROOK RESORT (single rooms to 3 bedrooms)
Notchbrook Rd.. 253-4882
NICHOLS LODGE & GOLDBROOK CAMPING AREA
(rooms, dorms, family-style meals)
Rt. 100 S. 253-7683
PEACOCK MOTEL
Rt. 100 S. 253-7244
THE PUB AT STOWE (traditional English food, lounge)
Rt. 108. 253-8669
ROCKY RIVER LODGE (near restaurants)
Rt. 108. 253-7643
ROUND HEARTH (dormitory for small or large groups)
Rt. 108. 253-7223
SANS COUCI INN (dining)
Rt. 108. 253-7558
THE SALZBURG INN (American-Continental restaurant)
Rt. 108. 253-8541
SCANDINAVIA INN & CHALETS (dining)
Rt. 108. 253-8555
SIEBENESS LODGE (dining)
Rt. 108. 253-8942
SKI INN (dining)
Next to Ski Area, Rt. 108 253-4050
SNOWDRIFT MOTEL & EFFICIENCIES (mountain view)
Rt. 108. 253-7305
SPRUCE POND INN (dining, cocktails, ice skating)
Rt. 100 S. 253-4828
STOWE-AWAY LODGE (country inn, dining, lounge)
Rt. 108. 253-8972
STOWE-BOUND LODGE (guest house on sheep farm)
Rt. 100 S. 253-4515
STOWE COTTAGE CLUB (daily maid service, view)
Cottage Club Rd. 253-4206
STOWEFLAKE RESORT (restaurant, bar & lounge)
Rt. 108. 253-7355
STOWEFLAKE TOWNHOUSE APARTMENTS
(mountain views, restaurant, lounge)
Rt. 108. 253-7355
STOWEHOF INN (view, European cuisine)
Edson Hill Rd.. 253-9722
THE STOWE MOTEL (view, kitchenettes)
Rt. 108. 253-7629
SUN & SKI MOTEL ("Dine Around" Ski Package)
Rt. 108. 253-4818
TEN ACRES LODGE (dining, rooms & guest houses)
Luce Hill & Barrows Rd.. 253-7638
TIMBERHOLM INN (country inn, breakfast)
Cottage Club Rd. 253-7603
TOPNOTCH AT STOWE (dining, bar, entertainment)
Rt. 108. 253-8585
TOWN & COUNTRY MOTOR LODGE (dining, lounge)
Rt. 108. 253-7595
TRAPP FAMILY LODGE
(dining, oldest major Cross Country Ski Center)
Luce Hill Rd. 253-8511
WINTERHAUS (dorms, family-style meals, lounge)
Rt. 108. 253-7731

RESTAURANTS

BOTTOM NOTCH PUB (entertainment, weekends)
Rt. 108. 253-8905
THE CHARDA (Austrian-Hungarian)
Rt. 100 N. 253-4598
EDSON HILL MANOR (licensed lounge)
Edson Hill Rd.. . . . . .253-7371, 253-9797
FOXFIRE INN (Italian)
Rt. 100 N. 253-8459
GOLDEN EAGLE COFFEE SHOP
Rt. 108. 253-4811
THE GREENERY (International)
Depot St.. 253-9380
HAPELTON'S WEST BRANCH CAFE (seafood)
Main St. 253-4653
HOB KNOB INN (gourmet)
Rt. 108. 253-8549
THE PATRIDGE INN RESTAURANT (seafood)
Rt. 108. 253-8000
THE PUB AT STOWE (English)
Rt. 108. 253-8669
RESTAURANT SWISSPOT (Swiss wines)
Main St. 253-4622
THE SALZBURG INN (American, Continental)
Rt. 108. 253-8541
THE SHED (restaurant, pub)
Rt. 108. 253-4364
SPRUCE POND INN (gourmet)
Rt. 100 S. 253-4828
STEEN'S (cocktails)
Rt. 108. 253-7269
THE THREE GREEN DOORS (American)
Rt. 108. 253-8979
TOPNOTCH AT STOWE (Continental)
Rt. 108. 253-8585
WHISKERS (American, cocktails)
Rt. 108. 253-8996

SERVICES

AUTO REPAIR

BUCKY'S AUTO REPAIR
Rt. 100 S. 253-7538
COLLINS AUTO PARTS
Rt. 100 S. 253-4848
STOWE AUTO SERVICE
Rt. 108. . . . . .253-7608, 253-8194

BANKS

FRANKLIN-LAMOILLE BANK
Main St. 253-7368
MOUNTAIN TRUST COMPANY
Rt. 108. 253-8525
THE UNION BANK
Park St.. 253-7348

RECREATION

STOWE CINEMA & PROJECTION ROOM LOUNGE
Stowe Center (cocktail lounge in theatre) . . 253-4678
STOWE HOT TUBS (private tubs and spas)
Rt. 100 S. 253-9365
STOWE TOURS
Begin & end at Ski Area 253-7321

TRANSPORTATION

DOLLAR RENT A CAR
Burlington Int'l Airport 863-1666
HERTZ RENT A CAR
Burlington Int'l Airport 864-7409
RUSSELL'S STOWE TAXI SERVICE
Rt. 100 S. 253-7224

TRAVEL SERVICES

STOWE TRAVEL SERVICE
Main St. 253-7752, 253-4581
TRAVEL UNLIMITED, INC.
Rt. 108. 253-8576

STORES & SKI SHOPS

A.J.'S SKI SHOP
Rt. 108. 253-4593
BOOTS 'N BOARDS (skis & clothing)
Rt. 108. . . . . .253-4225, 253-8460
THE CAMERA STORE
Rt. 108. 253-4842
CUISINE CORNER (cookware, utensils)
Rt. 108. 253-9690
FASHIONS AT STOWE, LTD. (women's clothing)
Rt. 108. 253-9294
FOOD FOR THOUGHT (natural food)
Rt. 100 S. 253-4733
FRONT FOUR SPORTS (ski shop)
Rt. 108. 253-9690
HARRINGTON'S OF VERMONT
(cob-smoked products, cheese, gifts)
Rt. 100 S. 253-4121
JIM SHEPHARD SKI SHOP
Rt. 108. 253-4760
LACKEY'S VARIETY STORE
Main St. 253-7624
MT. MANSFIELD SKI & RENTAL SHOPS
Rt. 108. 253-7311
MOUNTAIN CHEESE & WINE
Rt. 108. 253-8606
MOUNTAIN ROAD MARKET (groceries, beer & wine)
Rt. 108. 253-8123
SHAW'S GENERAL STORE (ski sales & rentals)
Main St. 253-4040
STAFFORDS PHARMACY & GIFT SHOP
Main St. 253-7361
STOWARE GIFT SHOP
Rt. 100 S. 253-4075
THE STOWE COUNTRY SHOP (cheese, wine, deli)
Rt. 108. 253-4044
STOWE HARDWARE
Main St. 253-7205
STOWE WOOLENS, LTD. (hand-knitted sweaters & hats)
Rt. 108. 253-8052

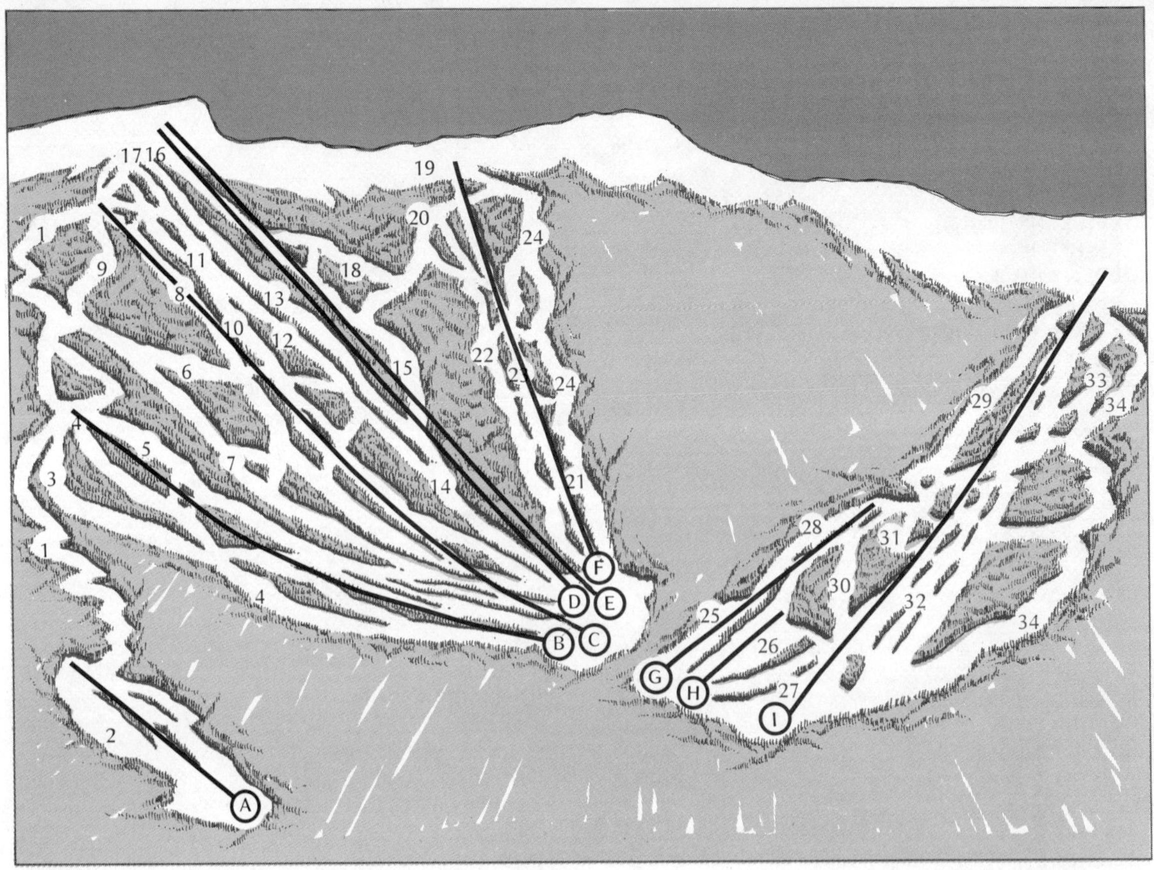

STOWE

RUNS

1 TOLL ROAD
2 TOLL HOUSE SLOPES
3 LULLABY LANE
4 TYRO
5 STANDARD
6 CROSS OVER
7 GULCH
8 NORTH SLOPE
9 SKIMEISETER
10 HAYREIDE
11 SR
12 LOOKOUT
13 STAR
14 LIFTLINE
15 NATIONAL
16 GOAT
17 LORD
18 NOSE DIVE
19 RIMROCK
20 CLIFF TRAIL
21 SWITCHBACK
22 PERRY MERRIL
23 GONDOLIER
24 CHIN CLIP
25 WEST SLOPE
26 EAST SLOPE
27 RICK'S RUN
28 WEST RUN
29 SMUGGLERS
30 EAST RUN
31 RIDGE RUN
32 MAIN STREET
33 WHIRLAWAY
34 STERLING

LIFTS

A TOLL HOUSE T-BAR
B MT. MANSFIELD T-BAR
C LOOKOUT DOUBLE
D MT. MANSFIELD SINGLE
E MT. MANSFIELD DOUBLE
F GONDOLA
G LITTLE SPRUCE DOUBLE
H LITTLE SPRUCE T-BAR
I BIG SPRUCE DOUBLE

SUGARBUSH VALLEY

WARREN, VT 05674 (802) 583-2381
SUGARBUSH NORTH (802) 496-3301

AREA INFORMATION

BASE ELEVATION

Sugarbush, 1,483 feet
Sugarbush North, 1,450 feet

HOURS

Sugarbush, 9:00 a.m. - 4:00 p.m.
Sugarbush North, 8:30 a.m. - 4:00 p.m.

LIFTS

9 chairs, 2 Poma lifts, 1 T-bar, 1 tramway. Capacity per hour - 13,700. Both mountains may be skied for the price of a Sugarbush ticket.

LONGEST RUN

2.5 miles

SUGARBUSH VALLEY CONT.

NURSERY
6 weeks & up, call Ski Area, Sugarbush
SEASON
Mid-November to May, snowmaking
SNOW PHONE
Vermont conditions (24 hours) . . . . . (802) 229-0531
From Montreal - Vermont Info.. . . . . (514) 845-9840
In N.Y., New England Vacation Council (212) 757-4455
TRAILS
17 easy, 33 intermediate, 23 expert
TRAVEL
From New York City & Connecticut, N.Y. Thruway to exit 24 to I-87 to exit 20 to Fort Ann.; Rt. 149 to Rt. 4 to Rt. 100 to Rt. 17 to Sugarbush Access Rd. From Montreal, Auto Route to exit 9 & Rt. 7 to I-89 in Vt., south to Waterbury, Vt., exit 10; Rt. 100 S. to Rt. 17 to Sugarbush Access Rd. From Boston, Rt. I-93 to I-89, exit 9, south on Rt. 100B to Rt. 100 to Rt. 17 to Sugarbush Access Rd.
VERTICAL DROP
Sugarbush - 2,400 feet
Sugarbush North - 2,600 feet

EMERGENCY

CENTRAL VERMONT HOSPITAL
Berlin 229-9121
FAYSTON FIRE NUMBER 496-2400
GAME WARDEN 496-2475
MAD RIVER AMBULANCE 496-3600
MORETOWN FIRE DEPT. 496-3731
PHARMACY 496-2345
STATE POLICE 496-2262
VALLEY ANIMAL HOSPITAL 496-3006
VALLEY AREA ASSOCIATION 496-3409
VALLEY DENTAL ASSOCIATES 496-2524
VALLEY MEDICAL CENTER 496-3838
VERMONT MEDICAL CENTER
Burlington 656-2345
WAITSFIELD FIRE DEPT. 496-2400
WARREN FIRE DEPT. 496-3661

LODGING

QUITTNER'S STARK VIEW LODGE
(private rooms & dorms, home cooking)
P.O. Box 1830, So. Starksboro, 05487 453-2045
SGT. PEPPER'S CAMP A.W.O.L.
Box 78, RR1, Warren, 05674 583-2255
THE SCHULTZ'S (private rooms, semiprivate baths)
Moretown Village, 05660 496-2366
SCHNEIDER HAUS (chalet, rooms)
Rt. 100, Box 283A, Duxbury, 05660 244-7726
SEASONS AT SUGARBUSH VALLEY
(private rooms, dorm rooms, efficiency apartments)
Wm. & Patricia Minnerly, Warren, 05674 . . . 496-3112
'SNOHOUSE (private & bunkrooms)
Bill & Deedie Iler, Waitsfield, 05673 496-3646
THE SNUGGERY (rooms, tavern)
J. Callahan & R. Pacilli, R.R. 46A,
Waitsfield, 05673 496-2322
THE SUGARBUSH INN (restaurants)
Warren, 05674. 583-2301
SUGARHOUSE MOTOR INN (restaurant)
P.O. Box 525, Middlebury, 05753 388-2770
THE SUGARTREE (country inn)
Warren, 05674. 583-3211
TUCKER HILL LODGE (country inn, cuisine, bar)
Waitsfield, 05673 496-3983
VALLEY INN
Rt. 100, Box 8, Waitsfield, 05673 496-3450
WAIT FARM MOTOR INN
R.D. 1, Box 381, Waitsfield, 05673. 496-2033
THE WHITE HORSE INN
(country inn, private rooms & dorm rooms)
P.O. Box 232, Waitsfield, 05673 496-2476

RESTAURANTS

LODGING BUREAU. . . . . (800) 451-5030

ALPEN INN (restaurant, lounge)
Rt. 100, Waitsfield, 05673. 496-3416
BAGATELLE TAVERN & INN
Waitsfield, 05673 496-3979
BIRCHWOOD LODGE & CHALETS
German Flats Rd., Waitsfield, 05673 583-2100
BRISTOL MOTOR INN
Box 535, Bristol, 05443 453-2326
CAMEL'S HUMP VIEW FARM
(guest house, family style meals)
Jerry & Wilma Maynard, Moretown, 05660 . . 496-3614
CARPENTER FARM SKI LODGE
(private rooms & dorms)
Moretown, 05660 496-3433
CHRISTMAS TREE INN (country inn, lounge)
Box 23, Warren, 05674. 583-2211
THE GARRISON (condos, 1¼ miles to Mad River Glen)
Lisle Gilber, Rt. 17, Waitsfield, 05673 496-2352
GOLDEN HORSE LODGE
Warren, 05674. 583-3200
GOLDEN LION INN
Box 336, Warren, 05674. 496-3084
HIGH & DRY MOTEL (restaurant, bar)
Rt. 100, Waitsfield, 05673. 496-3937
HOLIDAY INN (restaurant, lounge)
Blush Hill Rd., Waterbury, 05676. 244-7822
HOTEL SUGARBUSH
Warren, 05674. 583-2311
JOSLIN'S ROUND BARN FARM (private rooms, dorms)
Mr. & Mrs. Ralph Joslin, Waitsfield, 05673 . . 496-3834
KNOLL FARM COUNTRY INN
(guest farm, family style meals)
Bragg Hill, Waitsfield, 05673 496-3939
THE LODGE (2 single beds per room, hall baths)
Sugarbush Rd., Warren, 05674 583-2474
MADBUSH CHALET MOTOR INN
Rt. 100, Waitsfield, 05673. 496-3966
MAD RIVER BARN (home cooking)
Rt. 17, Waitsfield 496-3310
MILLBROOK INN & RESTAURANT
Rt. 17, Waitsfield 496-2405

BAGETELLE TAVERN & INN (traditional New England)
Rt. 100, Waitsfield 496-3979
THE BLUE TOOTH (cocktails, entertainment)
Sugarbush Access Rd. 583-2656
CHEZ HENRI (French, lunch, apres ski, dancing)
Sugarbush Village 583-2600
CHINA BARN (Szechuan, Mandarin, Cantonese)
Rt. 17, Fayston 496-3579
COLONIAL ROOM & ONION PATCH
(Continental - upstairs, seafood & steaks - downstairs)
Sugarbush Inn, Warren 583-2301
THE COMMON MAN (Continental)
German Flats Rd. 583-2800
THE DEN (steak house & pub)
Routes 17 & 100, Waitsfield. 496-8880
DOWNSTREET STEAKHOUSE RESTAURANT
(cocktails, dance music)
Sugarbush Access Rd., Warren. 583-3100
FOX HILL – LAS CUEVAS (Spanish)
Sugarbush Access Rd., Warren. 583-2626
GOLDEN HORSE LODGE (Continental, lounge)
Sugarbush Access Rd., Warren. 583-3200
HIGH & DRY (Italian, cocktails)
Routes 17 & 100, Waitsfield. 496-3937
MILL RESTAURANT (Italian, seafood, steaks)
Rt. 100B, Moretown 496-3181
MILLBROOK INN & RESTAURANT
Rt. 17, Waitsfield 496-2405
THE PHOENIX (Continental)
Sugarbush Village, Warren 583-2777
ROGO'S PUB & INN
Near Sugarbush Ski Area, Warren 583-9951
SAM RUPERT'S RESTAURANT
(veal, chicken, seafood, vegetarian)
Sugarbush Access Rd., Warren. 583-2421
TUCKER HILL
Rt. 17, Waitsfield 496-3983
VALLEY HIDEAWAY RESTAURANT & LOUNGE
(Continental)
Alpen Inn, Rt. 100, Waitsfield. 496-3416

SERVICES

AIR

U.S. AIR
Burlington . . . . (800) 448-2970
DELTA
Burlington . . . . (800) 225-3600
AIR NEW ENGLAND
Burlington & Montpelier. 223-5282
VALLEY FLYING SERVICE. 496-3720

AUTO RENTAL

AVIS
Burlington 864-0411
HERTZ
Burlington 864-7409
Montpelier 223-3815
NATIONAL
Burlington 864-7441
BUDGET
Burlington 658-1211

AUTO SERVICE

BONNETTE'S - TEXACO 496-3698
HAP'S - TEXACO & ESSO 496-3948
KINGSBURY - SHELL. 496-3366
SUGARBUSH - TYDOL 496-3977
VILLAGE GROCERY - SHELL 496-2045
VILLAGE SQUARE - MOBIL. 496-3333

DOCTORS

VALLEY MEDICAL CENTER 496-3838
VALLEY DENTAL CENTER. 496-2524

TAXI

ALPINE TAXI
Waterbury 244-8697
BON VOYAGE SKI TAXI
Waitsfield 496-2442

TRAIN

AMTRAK
Montpelier & Waterbury . . . . (800) 523-5720

STORES & SKI SHOPS

APPALACHIAN GAP (clothing)
Village Square Shopping Center, Waitsfield . . 496-2009
CABIN FEVER QUILTS & PILLOWS
(original & custom designed)
Rt. 100, The Old Church, Waitsfield 496-2287
GREEN MOUNTAIN COFFEE ROASTERS
(coffees, nuts, teas)
Village Square, Waitsfield 496-4357
INVERNESS SKI SHOP
Mad River Glen 496-3343
JANY BOUTIQUE (men & women)
Mad River Green, Waitsfield 496-3274
NORTH VERMONT SKI SHOPS
Sugarbush Access Rd., Warren. 583-2511
Mad River Glen, Fayston. 496-2309
OWL'S BASKET (wines, gourmet foods, breads)
Village Square, Waitsfield 496-3420
ROSIE BOREL'S L'ESCALIER
(hand-blocked fabrics, antiques)
Sugarbush Village, Warren 583-2666
SIGI SPORTS (specialty ski shops)
Sugarbush, Sugarbush North &
Sugarbush Village. 583-2795
THE STORE (gifts, wrapped & mailed)
Sugarbush Village. 583-2288
Rt. 100, Waitsfield 496-4465
THE TOY STORE
Village Sq. Shopping Ctr., Rt. 100, Waitsfield 496-3270
TRILLIUM'S PAST TIMES CLOTHING SHOPPE
Bridge St., Waitsfield 496-3918
TROLL SHOP (ski & sportwear)
Rt. 100, Waitsfield 496-2171

STRATTON

VERMONT, 05155 (802) 297-2200

AREA INFORMATION

BASE ELEVATION
Sun Bowl, 1,872 feet; North Face, 2,125 feet
HOURS
9:00 a.m. - 4:30 p.m.
LIFTS
8 chairlifts, 10,500 cpacity per hour
LONGEST RUN
Over 3½ miles
NURSERY
Ages 1 - 3, call Ski Area
SEASON
Mid-November to mid-April, snowmaking
SNOW PHONE 297-2211
TRAILS
45% beginner, 30% intermediate, 25% advanced
TRAVEL
Southern Vermont, I-91 to Rt. 30 N. to Bondville to Ski Area. From Northern Vermont, I-91 S. to Rt. 11 to Rt. 30 to Bondville to Stratton Mountain – not the town of Stratton. Air service to Keene, NH, Rutland and Springfield. See "Services" for local airlines, car rental and bus service.
VERTICAL DROP
Sun Bowl, 2,003 feet; North Face, 1,750 feet

STRATTON & BROMLEY ARE 10 MILES APART WITH A SHUTTLE SERVICE BETWEEN. BOTH MOUNTAINS CAN BE SKIED ON THE SAME LIFT TICKET.

SUICIDE SIX

WOODSTOCK, VT 05091 (802) 583-2381

AREA INFORMATION

BASE ELEVATION
550 feet
HOURS
9:00 a.m. - 4:00 p.m.
LIFTS
2 chairs, 1 J-bar, 2,200 capacity per hour
LONGEST RUN
5,700 feet
SEASON
Mid-December to March, snowmaking
SNOW PHONE 457-1622
TRAILS
35% beginner, 45% intermediate, 20% advanced
TRAVEL
I-89 to Rt. 4 to Rt. 12 N. Ski Area is 3 miles north of Woodstock..
VERTICAL DROP
650 feet

EMERGENCY

AMBULANCE. 457-1234
FIRE 457-2323
OTTAUQUECHEE HEALTH CENTER 457-3030
POLICE 457-1420
SKI PATROL 457-1666

LODGING

BARNARD VALLEY VIEW MOTEL & DRIFTWIND RESTAURANT (cocktails)
5 miles N. of Woodstock on Rt. 12. 457-2123
KEDRON VALLEY INN & MOTEL & STABLES
South Woodstock 457-1473
THE NEW ENGLAND INN (breakfast & dinner)
41 Pleasant St., Rt. 4, east of Village 457-9804
RIVERSIDE LODGE (breakfast & dinner to guests)
3 miles west of Woodstock. 457-2250
SHIRE MOTEL
46 Pleasant St., U.S. 4, east of Village 457-2211
THE WOODSTOCK INN
(dining room, cocktail lounge, coffee shop)
Set back from the Village Green 457-1100
WOODSTOCK MOTEL
East of Village on Rt. 4 457-2500

RESTAURANTS

DRIFTWIND RESTAURANT (cocktails)
In Barnard Valley View Motel
5 miles north on Rt. 12 456-2123
THE NEW ENGLAND INN (breakfast & dinner)
41 Pleasant St., Rt. 4, east of Village 457--9804
THE PRINCE & THE PAUPER (lounge)
Across Dana Lane from Historical Society
Just off Elm St. 457-1818
RUMBLE SEAT RATHSKELLER
Woodstock East, in the 1834 Stone House. . . 457-3609
SUICIDE SIX BASE LODGE
The lounge, call Ski Area
THE WOODSTOCK INN
(dining room, cocktail lounge, coffe shop)
Set back from the Village Green 457-1100

STORES & SKI SHOPS

DESIGN ASSOCIATES / WINDSOR GALLERIES
(antiques, made-to-order rugs)
47 Central Street 457-1702
MAC HUGH, INC. (men's & women's clothing)
No. 1 The Green 457-2720
THE RED CUPBOARD (Vermont-made products)
Rt. 4, 2 miles west of Woodstock Village . . . 457-3722
SHIRE APOTHECARY (drug store)
13 Elm St. 457-2707

SOUTH WOODSTOCK COUNTRY STORE
(groceries, wine & beverages, gas)
5 miles south of Woodstock, Rt. 106. 457-3050
WESTENFELD DELICATESSEN & MEATS
Woodstock East 457-1062
WOODSTOCK INN GIFT SHOP
Set back from the Village Green 457-1100
WOODSTOCK SPORTS (ski equipment & clothing)
30 Central Street 457-1568
THE YANKEE BOOKSHOP
12 Central Street 457-2411
THE YOUNG CHEESE SHOP (cheese & wines)
Central St. 457-1715

WASHINGTON

CRYSTAL MTN.

CRYSTAL MTN., WA 98022 (206) 663-2255

AREA INFORMATION

BASE ELEVATION
4,400 feet
HOURS
8:30 a.m. - 4:00 p.m., daily
Night skiing, 2:00 - 10:00 p.m., except Monday
LIFTS
7 chairlifts, 1 T-bar & 10 rope tows
8,680 capacity per hour
LONGEST RUN
3½ miles
NURSERY
6 years & under, call Ski Area
SEASON
November thru mid-May, no snowmaking
SKI & RENTAL SHOP
At Ski Area 663-2239
SNOW PHONE 634-3771
STORE
At Ski Area, mini supermarket, wine shop
TRAILS
10% beginner, 20% intermediate
40% advanced, 30% expert
TRAVEL
From Seattle-Tacoma Int'l. Airport, 70 miles (major airlines); 76 miles from Boeing Int'l Airport (West Coast Airlines). From Enumclaw, follow Hwy. 410 for 33 miles. Just before the Rainier National Park entrance, turn left and travel 7 miles up Crystal Mtn. Blvd. Airstrip, 1.4 miles WSW of Enumclaw, 2,000 ft. gravel East-West runway. Elev., 740 Ft. above sea level.
VERTICAL DROP
3,102 feet

LODGING

ALPINE INN (restaurant)
At Base Area. 663-2262
CRYSTAL CHALETS (condo)
Near Ski Area 663-2311
CRYSTAL INN (restaurant, lounge, dancing)
Near Base Area 663-2330
CRYSTAL HOUSE
Near Base Area 663-2236
SILVER SKIS CHALET (condos)
Near Ski Area 663-2245

RESTAURANTS

ALPINE INN RESTAURANT
Near Base Area 663-2262
CRYSTAL INN RESTAURANT
Near Base Area 663-2330
DAY LODGE
Cafeteria service, main floor
Lunch room & snack bar, lower level
SNORTING ELK CELLAR (snacks, refreshments, dancing)
At Ski Area
SUMMIT HOUSE
At the crest of Crystal Mountain

MISSION RIDGE

BOX 1765, WENATCHEE, WA 98801 (509) 633-6543

AREA INFORMATION

BASE ELEVATION
4600 feet
HOURS
9:30 a.m. - 4:30 p.m., daily
5:00 - 10:00 p.m., Wed. thru Sat. & holidays
LIFTS
4 chairs, 3 rope tows, 3,710 capacity per hour
LONGEST RUN
5 miles
SEASON
December to April, snowmaking
SNOW PHONE 663-7631
TRAILS
30% beginner, 50% intermediate, 20% advanced
TRAVEL
Near U.S. 97, south of Wenatchee. Ski Area is 13 miles from Wenatchee.
VERTICAL DROP
2,140 feet

LODGING

ALL LODGINGS ARE IN WENATCHEE, UNLESS OTHERWISE NOTED. ZIP - 98801.
AVENUE MOTEL
720 N. Wenatchee Ave.. 663-7161

MISSION RIDGE CONT.

BEL AIR MAGIC KEY MOTEL
1405 N. Wenatchee Ave.. 663-8165
BEST WESTERN RIVERS INN
580 Valley Mall Parkway
East Wenatchee . . . . (800) 523-1234, 884-1474
CAMPBELL'S LODGE
Foot of Lake Chelan 682-2561
CANNON'S RESORT & MOTEL
Downtown Lake Chelan, 98816. 682-2932
CHIEFTAIN MOTEL
1005 N. Wenatchee Ave.. . . . (800) 572-4456, 663-8141
CRESCENT BAR RESORT MOTEL
Quincy, 98840 787-1511
DER RITTERHOF MOTOR INN
190 Hwy. 2, Leavenworth, 98826 548-5845
EDDIE MAYS FLAG INN
11 W. Grant Rd.
East Wenatchee . . . . (800) 552-7388, 884-6611
EDELWEISS HOTEL & RESTAURANT
Leavenworth, 98826 548-7015
HAUS ROHRBACH PENSION
Leavenworth, 98826 548-7024
HOLIDAY LODGE
610 N. Wenatchee Ave.. . . . (800) 453-4511, 663-8167
HOTEL TYROL
Leavenworth, 98826 548-7032
IMPERIAL 400 MOTEL
700 N. Wenatchee Ave.. . . . (800) 531-5300, 663-8133
THE INN AT WAPATO POINT
Wapato Pt., Manson, 98831 (800) 572-9531, 687-9511
LYLE'S MOTEL
924 N. Wenatchee Ave.. 663-5155
MOTEL LYON
1836 N. Wenatchee Ave.. 662-6121
ROONEY'S COFFEE SHOP & MOTOR LODGE
821 N. Wenatchee Ave.. . . . . . . .662-2602, 662-8208
SCOTTY'S MOTEL
1004 N. Wenatchee Ave.. 662-8165
STARLITE MOTEL
1640 N. Wenatchee Ave.. 663-8115
THUNDERBIRD MOTOR INN
1225 N. Wenatchee Ave.. . . (800) 547-8010, 663-0711
TOWN & COUNTRY MOTEL
2921 School St. at U.S. Routes 2 & 97. 663-5157
TRAVELERS MOTEL
Center of Town, Chelan, 98816. 682-4215
TRAVELODGE MOTEL
232 N. Wenatchee Ave.. . . . (800) 255-3050, 663-7121
THE UPTOWNER MOTEL
101 N. Mission St. 663-8516
VILLAGE INN MOTEL
Cashmere, 98815 782-3522

RESTAURANTS

APPLE INN (live music)
Hwy. 2, Cashmere. 782-2006
CAFE CHRISTA (German)
Leavenworth. 548-5074
CAMPBELL HOUSE RESTAURANT
Foot of Lake Chelan 682-2441
CHIEFTAIN RESTAURANT (lounge, entertainment)
1005 N. Wenatchee Ave.. 663-7188
COACHMAN INN (lounge, entertainment)
Cashmere. 782-3213
COLUMBIA RIVER KITCHEN (homestyle & natural)
400 Ninth 663-8318
COVEY'S (live entertainment, dancing)
800 N. Wenatchee Ave.. 662-8183
DAS BERGHAUS
Leavenworth. 548-7313
DAVID BROWN'S LA COCINA (Mexican)
1650 Grant Rd. 884-6915
EDDIE MAYS FLAG INN
(prime rib/steaks, open 24 hours, lounge, dancing)
11 W. Grant Rd.. 884-6611
EDELWEISS RESTAURANT & HOTEL
Leavenworth. 548-7015
ELLOWEE BEACH RESTAURANT
Wapato Point, Manson 687-9511
HENSON'S HITCHING POST TAVERN
Hwy. 2, Cashmere. 782-3250
HOTEL TYROL
Leavenworth. 548-7032
LITTLE PEDRO'S (cocktails)
1211 N. Mission. 662-9812
LITTLE VIKING (cocktails)
280 Grant Rd., E. Wenatchee 884-9911
MANDARIN RESTAURANT
Valley North Shopping Center 663-5801
PEPPERMINT SQUARE (old fashioned ice cream parlour)
23 S. Wenatchee Ave.. 663-2211
RIVER'S HAVEN
560 N. Main, E. Wenatchee 884-2427
ROY'S CHUCK WAGON
Valley North Shopping Center 663-8323
SIRACO'S RESTAURANT (Greek, American)
17 S. Mission 663-7985
THUNDERBIRD MOTOR INN
(live entertainment, dancing nightly)
1225 N. Wenatchee Ave.. 663-0711
WOLFGANG'S TUMWATER INN (lounge, entertainment)
Leavenworth. 548-7835

SERVICES

AIR

WENATCHEE AERO (air charter)
Northwest 884-0533

BANKS

CENTRAL WASHINGTON BANK
501 North Mission 663-0733
SEATTLE-FIRST NATIONAL BANK
Wenatchee Ave. at Orondo St.. 662-8121
SECURITY BANK
Wenatchee Valley Mall 884-7111

DRUG STORES

OSCO DRUG
Wenatchee Valley Mall 884-5421

OWL DRUG
39 S. Wenatchee Ave.. 662-7133
PAY LESS DRUG STORE
Valley North Mall Store 663-1695
VALU PLUS PHARMACY
Fifth Street Mall, 5th & Mission. 663-8771

DRY CLEANING

NANCEKIVELL'S CLEANERS
2nd & Chelan 663-0791

FLORIST

VALLEY FLORAL
1050 Orondo St. 662-2186

HAIR SALON

WAVELENGTHS (men & women)
15 Palouse 663-2731

STORES & SKI SHOPS

ARLBERG MOUNTAIN SHOP
(rentals, repairs, & sales - 7 days a week)
At slopes, call Ski Area
THE CELLAR (deli)
Mission Square 662-1722
THE CLOCK SHOP
Leavenworth. 548-7725
COURTESY CONVENIENCE MARKET
(delivery service, groceries, beer, gas)
116 N. Chelan 662-2830
MILLER'S CAMERA
Downtown Wenatchee 663-2511
7 ELEVEN (groceries, party mixers, beer)
Mission & Ferry 662-1044
Miller & Springwater 662-3266
J. STEVENS (gift boutique)
Palouse & Mission. 663-1575
TINY'S OF CASHMERE (gifts)
Cashmere. 782-1850
TANNENBAUM GIFTS & GALLERIE
Leavenworth. 548-7014

STEVENS PASS

BOX 98, LEAVENWORTH, WA 98826 (206) 973-2500

AREA INFORMATION

BASE ELEVATION
4,000 feet
HOURS
Wed. thru Sun., 9 a.m. to 10 p.m.
LIFTS
8 chairs, 2 triple
LONGEST RUN
6,047 feet
SEASON
Mid-Nov. thru Mid-April
SKI RENTAL & REPAIR
At ski area
SNOW PHONE 634-0200
TRAVEL
Seattle, I-5 to U.S. 2 east, 70 miles
Leavenworth, U.S. 2 west, 36 miles
VERTICAL DROP
1,800 feet

LODGING

ALL LODGING IS IN NEARBY LEAVENWORTH
CENTRAL RESERVATIONS. . . . . (206) 973-2500

CRYSTAL HOTEL
917 Commercial St.. 548-5798
DER RITTERHOFF MOTOR INN
Highway 2 548-5845
EDELWEISS HOTEL & RESTAURANT
843 Front St. 548-7015
EVERGREEN SCHOENTAL MOTEL
1127 Front St. 548-5515
HAUS ROHRBACH PENSION
12882 Ranger Rd. 548-7024
ICICLE RIVER RANCH CAMPGROUND
3 mi. out, Rt. 1, Box 123 548-5420
PINE VILLAGE KOA CAMPGROUND
Hwy. 2 on Riverbend Rd. 548-7709
RIVERS EDGE MOTEL
Rt. 1, Box 60 548-7612
SQUIRREL TREE INN
Coles Corner, Star Route. 763-3124
TYROL HOTEL & RESTAURANT
633 Front St. 548-7032

RESTAURANTS

BURGER HAUF
701 Hwy. 2 548-7791
CAFE CHRISTA (German)
Front & 8th Sts.. 548-5074
DAS BERGHAUS (Sandwiches, salads)
Hwy. 2 at Front St.. 548-7313
DAS SPEISHAUS
Hwy. 2 548-7130
ENCHANTMENT DELI
894 Hwy. 2 548-5345
HANSEL & GRETEL DELI
Front St.. 548-7721
ICICLE CREAM SHOP
819 Front St.
ICICLE TAVERN
829 Front St. 548-5713
KATZENJAMMER RESTAURANT (steak & seafood)
8th St. 548-5826
RATSKELLER TAVERN
629 Front St. 548-7111
SKI TAVERN
841 Front St. 548-7013
SUSSWAREN (ice cream)
733 Front St. 548-5755
TUMWATER INN (American, dancing)
9th & Commercial 548-7835

SERVICES

AUTOMOTIVE

DICK'S AUTOMOTIVE
Hwy. 2 548-7134
DIE ARCO TANKSTELLE
Hwy. 2 548-5523
DON'S SALES & SERVICE
Hwy. 2 548-7912
JIM'S CHEVRON
Hwy. 2 548-7714
JOE'S REPAIR
76 E. Leavenworth Rd.. 548-5453
KAR KARE 66
1133 Hwy. 2. 548-7732

BANKS

CASHMERE VALLEY BANK
Hwy. 2 548-5231
SEATTLE FIRST NATIONAL BANK
715 Front St. 548-5821

CLEANERS

HONEYSET CLEANERS & LAUNDROMAT
707 Front St. 548-5620

EMERGENCY

AMBULANCE. 548-7011
CLINIC
821 Commercial. 548-5812
FIRE DEPT.. 548-7711
RANGER STATION (fire). 548-5817
SHERIFF 548-7931

LIQUOR STORES

SCHNAPS SHOP
894 Hwy. 2 548-7822
VILLAGE WINE CELLAR
Front St.

PHARMACY

LARSON DRUG
821 Front St. 548-9731

STORES & SKI SHOPS

ALPEN HANSEL (woodcarving)
224 8th St.. 548-7811
ALPEN HAUS
807 Front St. 548-7407
BAVARIAN BOUQUET (flowers)
207 10th St.. 548-5612
BUCKLADEN FINE BOOKS
120 9th St.. 548-5911
DER LOWE (gifts)
833 Front St. 548-7407
DER MARKT PLATZ
801 Front St. 548-7422
DER SPORTSMANN
837 Front St. 548-5623
DIANA'S PLACE
819 Front St. 548-4101
FRAU JOAN (clothing)
222 9th St.. 548-5141
ITHACA BOOKSTORE
Hwy. 2 548-5098
MAXINE'S ARTS & CRAFTS
140 9th St.. 548-7411
THE OAK SHOP
Motteler Bldg.
THE RARE FIND (gifts)
Hwy. 2 548-4123
SPLENDORED THINGS (gifts)
219 8th St.. 548-5131
TANNENBAUM GIFT SHOP
645 Front St. 548-7014
THE TREASURE CHEST
Motteler Bldg. 548-5714
TYROLEAN SHOP (Men's clothing)
827 Front St. 548-5622
VILLAGE FASHIONS
827 Front St. 548-5622

WEST VIRGINIA

CANAAN VALLEY

RT. 1, BOX 39, DAVIS, WV 26260 (304) 866-4121

AREA INFORMATION

AIRLINE
Allegheny to Elkins & Clarksburg from Baltimore/Wash., Charleston, Pittsburgh, & Columbus
BASE ELEVATION
3,430 feet
EMERGENCY
Nurse on duty at resort. Hospitals in Elkin (32 miles)
Dairs Hospital 636-3300
Memorial General 636-2900
Police. 478-3101
HELICOPTER CHARTER. 636-6803
HOURS
9 a.m. to 4 p.m.
LIFTS
2 chairs, 1 poma, 1,200 per hour

NURSERY
6 months to 6 years
SEASON
Dec. 15th to March 15th
SNOW PHONE 866-4121
TRAILS
10 easy, 11 intermediate, 6 difficult
TRAVEL
From Baltimore & Washington D C., Rt. 70 W. to 40 W. At Cumberland MD, Rts. 40 & 48 W. to Rt. 219 S. at Keyser's Ridge into Thomas, WV to Rt. 32 S.
From Charleston, Rt. 79 N. to Rt. 33 E. at Weston To Harman, 33 N. to ski area.
From Pittsburgh, Rt. 79 S. to 48 E. at Westover, to Rt. 219 S. at Keyser's Ridge, MD, Rt. 219 S. into Thomas, WV where Rt. 32 S. goes into Canaan Valley.
From Cleveland, Rt. 77 S. to Rt. 50 E. at Parkersburg to 219 S. at Redhouse, MD to Thomas WV, Rt. 32 S. to ski area.
VERTICAL DROP
860 feet

ALL LODGINGS & RESTAURANTS ARE AT THE SKI AREA AND MAY BE REACHED BY DIALING (304) 866-4121, UNLESS OTHERWISE NOTED

LODGING

CABIN MOUNTAIN VIEW
Rt. 1, Davis, 1 mile away. 866-4102
CABINS
15, with housekeeping
CAMPSITES
34, with hookups
CANAAN VALLEY LODGE
250 rooms, full service
MOUNTAIN VIEW MOTEL
Rt. 1, Davis, 3 miles away 866-4166

RESTAURANTS

ASPEN ROOM (American)
With view of the Valley
DISCO
At the ski area
HIGHLANDER CHINA HOUSE (supper club)
Rt. 32, Davis. 259-5221
LAUREL LODGE (cocktails)
In the lodge
MONTWOOD (Italian, lounge)
Rt. 32, Thomas 463-4291
THE NO LE HACE SOCIAL CLUB (drinks, entertainment)
Rt. 32, Davis. 259-5533
THE PUB
Ski Center
WEISS HOUSE (home-style)
Foot of Slope A

STORES & SKI SHOPS

A.J.'S GIFT SHOP
No. 2 Kel-Mat Mini Mall 463-4442
CABIN MOUNTAIN SPORT & SKI RENTALS
At the area. 866-4107
CONASTOGA WESTERN WEAR
No. 4 Kel-Mat Mini Mall 463-4545
THE COUNTRY STORE (camping, hunting, etc.)
In the campground
GENERAL STORE (groceries, gas, liquor)
Rt. 32, 2 mi. N. of resort. 866-4252
THE GOLF SHOP
At the area
MT. STATE MUSEUM & GIFT GALLERY
William Ave., Davis 259-5323
SKI-DOO SNOWMOBILES
Kel-Mat Mini-Mall, Thomas 423-4545
SKI SHOP
In the Valley Haus

S N O W S H O E

BOX 10, SNOWSHOE, WV 26209 (304) 799-6600
RESERVATIONS: (304) 799-6762

AREA INFORMATION

BASE ELEVATION
3,250 feet
HOURS
8:30 a.m. - 4:15 p.m.
LIFTS
4 chairs, 5,000 capacity per hour
LONGEST RUN
8,200 feet
NURSERY
Ages 2 - 8 . . . . 799-6600 X 189
SEASON
Mid-November to Mid-April, snowmaking
SNOW PHONE 799-6630
West Virginia Ski Conditions, in WV . . (800) 642-3638
Outside WV . . . . (800) 624-8633
TRAILS
10% beginner, 50% intermediate, 40% advanced
TRAVEL
On U.S. 219, 42 miles south of Elkins, or 60 miles north of Lewisburg. Jet service via Piedmont Airlines to Greenbrier Vallery Airport in Lewisburg, with limo and car rental available. Allegheny Airlines connects out of Elkins with major airlines.
VERTICAL DROP
1,598 feet

EMERGENCY

EMERGENCY MEDICAL AID (24 hours). . . . . .Dial 400
EMERGENCY POLICE . . . . Dial 192 or "0"
FIRE . . . . .Dial 500

LODGING

CENTRAL RESERVATIONS. 799-6762

LANDS END TOWNHOUSES
Atop the mountain, 4 & 5 bedrooms
LEATHERBARK CONDOMINIUMS
1 - 3 bedrooms

SNOWSHOE CONT.

SPRUCE LODGE
Economy lodge
SUNDOWN VILLAGE
Hutch Chalets, 3 bedrooms
TIMBERLINE LODGE
Deluxe rooms
TREETOP CONDOMINIUMS
2 & 3 bedrooms
WABASSO CONDOMINIUM
2 bedrooms

RESTAURANTS

BURGER SLOPE
Resort Center
CAFETERIA
Resort Center
THE CARRY-OUT (sandwiches)
Summit Lobby .Dial 128
FUNKY'S EMPORIUM (cocktails, live music, no food)
Resort Center, upper level
GOOD TIME BOBBY'S (steak, seafood & specialties)
Resort Center, main level . . . . .Dial 246
THE SKIDDER (cocktails, live entertainment - 5 nights)
Adjoining Skidder Slope & Ticket Center . . . .Dial 131
THE SUMMIT
(cocktail lounge, reservations & proper attire for dinner)
Adjoining Timberline Lodge. . . . . .Dial 126

SERVICES

AMOCO GAS & CAR SERVICE
(gas & emergency car service)
8:00 a.m. - 6:00 p.m., Mon - Fri.
9:00 p.m., Sat. & Sun. . . . . .Dial 446
U.S. POST OFFICE
2 - 5:00 p.m., Tues. thru Sat. . . . . .Dial 245

STORES & SKI SHOPS

EDELWEISS SKI SHOP (sales, repair)
Ticket Center Bldg. Dial196
SKI RENTAL DEPARTMENT
Slopeside level, Spruce Lodge
WHY NOT! SHOP (stationery, sundries, gifts)
Resort Center . . . . .Dial 239

WISCONSIN

DEVIL'S HEAD

P.O. BOX 38, MERRIMAC, WI 53561 (608) 493-2251
(312) 236-0891 MILWAUKEE (414) 342-2040

AREA INFORMATION

HOURS
10:00 a.m. - 5:30 p.m., Mon. - Fri.
9:00 a.m. - 5:30 p.m., Sat. & Sun.
6:00 - 11:00 p.m., night skiing
6:00 p.m. closing, Dec. 24th
LIFTS
8 chairs, 3 rope tows, 11,000 capacity per hour
LONGEST RUN
4,500 feet
NURSERY
Baby sitters available, call Ski Area
SNOW PHONE
Call Ski Area
TRAILS
20% beginner, 60% intermediate, 20% advanced
TRAVEL
35 miles north of Madison, 9 miles south of Baraboo; west of I-90 off Wisconsin Hwy. 78 & CTH "DL"
VERTICAL DROP
495 feet

ALL LODGING, RESTAURANTS, STORES & SKI SHOPS ARE AT THE SLOPES. CALL SKI AREA FOR INFORMATION.

LODGING

CONDOMINIUMS
Maid service
DEVIL'S INN
Room service menu, restaurant & lounge
DEVIL'S HEAD LODGE
Room service, dining room cafeteria, 2 lounges, ski shop indoor swimming pool, whirlpool, sauna, & game room
DEVIL'S HOSTEL
Dormitory-style

RESTAURANTS

THE CORNUCOPIA ROOM
Breakfast, lunch, & dinner
THE DEVIL'S DEN
Cocktails, no food, dancing
THE DOMINO LOUNGE
Cocktails, no food
FRIAR MINGEN'S ROOM
Buffet-style breakfast, lunch & dinner
LIFT HAUS RESTAURANT
Between lifts 3½ & 4
SUMMIT RESTAURANT & LOUNGE
Devil's Inn, 6th floor, breakfast, lunch & dinner

STORES & SKI SHOPS

LOKI'S LAIR
Ski equipment, sportswear, repairs
WINE & CHEESE SHOP
Main Lobby

HIDDEN VALLEY

1815 MAPLE ST. MANITOWOC, WI 54220
TELEPHONE: (414) 863-2813

AREA INFORMATION

HOURS
Tues., Thurs., Fri., 10 a.m. to 4 p.m.
Tues., Thurs. nights, 6:30 to 10 p.m.
Sat., Sun., 9:30 a.m. to 4:30 p.m.
Holidays, Dec. 20th to Jan. 1st,
9:30 a.m. to 4:30 p.m., no night skiing
LIFTS
1 double chair, 1200 per hr.; 4 rope tows
LOCATION
13 mi. N. of Manitowoc, WI, 18 mi. S. of Green Bay
U.S. Hwy. I-43 to Exit 91 to Hwy. 147 to
County Rd. 141, turn S. to Hidden Valley Rd.
LONGEST RUN
3,600 ft.
SEASON
Dec. 10th to end of March
SKI RENTALS
Alpine Ski Shop at ski area, also at
4326 W. Michigan Ave.. 684-1552
SNOWFALL
4 ft., 100 % snowmaking
SNOW PHONE 863-2713
TRAILS
4 trails, 3 open slopes
VERTICAL DROP
200 ft.

LODGING & RESTAURANTS

ALL LODGINGS HAVE DINING FACILITES

CARLTON INN (entertainment), Two Rivers
T515 Memorial Dr., 4 mi. away 793-4524
FOX HILLS INN (pool, sauna), Mishicot
P.O. Box 129, 4 mi. away 755-2376
GUEST HOUSE INN (entertainment), Manitowoc
9th & Washington St., 15 mi. away 682-8271
LEFT END (cocktails), Manitowoc
N. 8th St., 15 mi. away. 684-7179
PINES MOTEL, Manitowoc
Hwy. 141, City Rt. 4. 682-9377
THRIFTEE SCOT MOTEL, Manitowoc
4604 Calumet Ave. 684-7841

PLAYBOY RESORT

LAKE GENEVA, WI 53147 (414) 248-8811
(800) 621-1116 IN ILLINOIS (800) 972-6727

AREA INFORMATION

BASE ELEVATION
1,085 feet
HOURS
9:00 a.m. - 5:00 p.m.
3:00 - 11:00 p.m., night skiing
LIFTS
3 chairs, 2 bars
NURSING
Babysitters, call Ski Area
SEASON
Early December to mid-March, snowmaking
SNOW PHONE
Call Ski Area
TRAILS
20% beginners, 60% intermediate, 20% advanced
TRAVEL
2 miles east of Lake Geneva at the junction of
Routes 50 & 12.
VERTICAL DROP
211 feet

LODGING

COUNTRY MOTEL
2½ mi. W. of Lake Geneva on Rt. 50 245-6115
HILTON INN (restaurant)
300 Wrigley Dr. 248-9181
INTERLAKEN LODGE
3½ mi. W. of Lake Geneva on Rt. 50 248-9121
PLAYBOY RESORT
Complete resort facilities, call Ski Area

RECREATION

BICYCLING
BOATING
Canoes, sailboats, paddleboats, paddlewheeler
CROSS COUNTRY SKIING
GOLF
2 18-hole courses
HEALTH CLUB
Men's & women's steam room, sauna, whirlpool
HORSEBACK RIDING
SKEET & TRAP SHOOTING
SNOWMOBILING
RACQUETBALL & HANDBALL
Indoor courts
TENNIS
Indoor & outdoor courts

RESTAURANTS

THE CABARET (show room)
At the Resort
GLEN NELSON'S
812 Main St.. 248-1500
THE LIVING ROOM (buffet dining)
At the Resort
SILVANO'S (Italian, American)
1 Mi. N. of Lake Geneva on County H 248-8117
SKI CHALET (cafeteria style)
At the Resort
THE SWEET TOOTH (ice cream, desserts)
At the Resort
VIP ROOM (exquisite cuisine)
At the Resort

PLAYBOY RESORTS CONT.

YACHT CLUB
Hilton Inn, 300 Wrigley Dr. 248-9181

S K Y L I N E

RT. 3, FRIENDSHIP, WI 53934 (608) 339-3421

AREA INFORMATION

HOURS
Thurs./Fri., 10:00 a.m. - 4:30 p.m.
Sat./Sun., 9:00 a.m. - 4:30 p.m.
Weds. thru Sat., 5:30 a.m. - 10:00 p.m.

LIFTS
2 chairs, 2 rope tows

LONGEST RUN
½ mile

SEASON
Mid-December to early April, closed Dec. 25th
Open daily, mid-December to early January

SNOW PHONE
Call Ski Area

TRAILS
6 slopes, plus cross-country trails

TRAVEL
I-90 to Hwy. 13, 80 miles north of Madison

VERTICAL DROP
335 feet

LODGING

CAMELOT MOTEL & CABINS
Rt. 2, Friendship 339-9948

DELLS CLUB CONDOMINIUMS & DEER RUN CABINS
Rt. 1, Oxford, 53952. 586-4191

DELLWOOD PINES COTTAGES
Friendship 339-6888

FRIENDSHIP HOTEL
Friendship 339-3112

OAK CREST MOTEL
Adams, 53910. 339-3369

PRESTONAIRE MOTEL
Friendship 339-7295

ROCHE-A-CRI MOTEL
Friendship 339-3269

SHERMALOT MOTEL
1148 Queens Way, Nekoosa, 54457
Hwy. 13, Lake Sherwood . . . . (715) 325-2626

S U N B U R S T

P.O. BOX 546, KEWASKUM, WI 53040 (414) 626-4605

AREA INFORMATION

BASE ELEVATION
886 feet

HOURS
Mon. - Fri., 3:30 p.m. - 10 p.m.
Sat. & Holidays, 10 a.m. - 10 p.m.
Sun., 10 a.m. - 5 p.m.

LIFTS
1 chair, 4 tows, 3 T-bars

LONGEST RUN
1500 feet

RENTALS
Full service, at slope

SEASON
Dec. 1st to March 8th

SNOW PHONE 352-9005

TRAILS
7.35 acres

TRAVEL
5 miles north of West Bend, west of U.S. 45
30 miles north of Milwaukee

VERTICAL DROP
214 feet

EMERGENCY

CLINIC. 626-4616
FIRE 338-4411
POLICE 626-2323
RESCUE. 626-2411

LODGING

ACE MOTEL
West Bend 334-4816

BONNE BELL MOTEL
Kewaskum. 626-2186

HOLIDAY INN
West Bend 338-0636

WEST BEND MOTOR INN
West Bend 334-2312

RESTAURANTS

THE BINKERY
West bend 338-3360

CAMPBELLS
Kewaskum. 626-8100

GLACIER INN
Kewaskum. 626-2711

HOMESTEAD SUPPER CLUB
Kewaskum. 626-4447

SCHMIDSELHAUS
West Bend 334-3203

T-BAR (entertainment)
At slope 626-4605

WASHINGTON HOUSE
West Bend 338-8884

T E L E M A R K

CABLE, WI 54821 (715) 798-3811

AREA INFORMATION

HOURS
9 a.m. to 4:30 p.m.

LIFTS
Capacity, 13,000 per hr.
2 bars, 3 chairs, 4 tows

SEASON
Thanksgiving thru mid-April
SNOW PHONE 798-3811
TRAILS
176 kilometers, beginner 40%, intermediate 40%, difficult 20%
TRAVEL
Minneapolis/St. Paul, 3 hrs., Hwy. 35 N. to Hwy. 70 E. to 63 N. to Cable, west 2 miles.
By air: Midstate Airlines to Hayward from
Chicago & Milwaukee. . . . . (800) 472-2321
Outside Wisconsin. . . . . (800)826-2343
Fly direct to Telemark, Cable Union Airport, 3,700 ft., lighted, Lat. 46*11', long. 91*15', elevation 1,351 ft..
By bus: Zephyr Lines, from Minneapolis.
VERTICAL DROP
370 feet

EMERGENCY

AMBULANCE. 798-2300
FIRE 798-3790
HOSPITAL 634-8911
SHERIFF 373-5405

LODGING

ALPINE RESORT
Lake Owen. 798-3603
BON NUIT L'HOTEL
Cable 798-3792
HAYWARD LAKES RESORT ASSOC.
Hwys. 63 & 27 634-4801
LAKE HAYWARD MOTEL
Hwy. 27, Hayward 634-2646
LAKE OWEN LODGE
Lake Owen. 798-3785
THE LAKEWOODS
County M, Cable 794-3785
RIVERSIDE MOTEL
Hayward 634-2661
TELEMARK LODGE (full services)
Cable 798-3811

RESTAURANTS

CRAZY HORSE (sandwiches & pizza)
County M, Cable 798-3474
HILLTOP INN
County D, Cable 794-2130
KARABALIS' (lunch & dinner)
212 Iowa Ave., Hayward. 634-2462
TELEMARK LODGE (full service)
At slope 798-3811
TURK'S INN (dinner)
Hwy. 63, Hayward 634-2957

STORES & SKI SHOPS

CABLE LIQUOR
Highway M. 798-3404
MARKET PLACE 16A
Highway 63 634-8996
RONDEAU'S SHOPPING CENTER
Highway M. 798-3211

W H I T E C A P

MONTREAL, WI 54550 (715) 561-2227

AREA INFORMATION

HOURS
9:00 a.m. - 4:00 p.m.
Night Skiing, Saturday
LIFTS
4 chairs, 1 T-bar, 4 rope tows
over 6,000 capacity per hour
LONGEST RUN
5,000 feet
NURSERY
Call Ski Area
SEASON
End of November to early-April, no snowmaking
SNOW PHONE
Call Ski Area
TRAILS
34% novice, 33% intermediate, 33% expert
TRAVEL
Northern Wisconsin, near the Michigan border and Lake Superior, 3 miles west of Hwy. 77 on County Trunk E. By Air to Iron - Gogebic Airport, Ironwood, Michigan, Republic Airlines. Bus service provided by Wisconsin-Michigan Coaches, Greyhound & Zephyr Bus Lines.
VERTICAL DROP
400 feet

FOR ADDITIONAL LODGINGS, RESTAURANTS, SERVICES, STORES & SHOPS, SEE INDIANHEAD MOUNTAIN, MICHIGAN, PAGE

LODGING

ANDERSON'S CHEQUAMEGON MOTEL
U.S. Hwy. 2 & 13
West end of Ashland, 54806. 682-4658
ARROWHEAD RESORT (bar)
2 miles north of Mercer
Box 187, Mercer, 54547 476-2324
ASHLAND MOTEL FRIENDSHIP INN
Hwy. U.S. 2, west end of Ashland, 54806 . . . 682-5503
BADGER MOTEL
3 miles from Ski Area on Hwy. 77
Box 128, Iron Belt, 54536. 561-3840
BELL MOTEL (restaurant)
U.S. 2, 407 E. Front St., Ashland, 54806 . . . 682-4109
THE CARRIAGE HAUS
Base of the mountain, call Ski Area
THE COACH HAUS (kitchenettes)
Base of the mountain, call Ski Area
CLUB 51 (bar, restaurant)
Hwy. 51, 1½ mi. N. of Mercer, 54547 476-9951
THE EQUINOX LODGE (2 & 3 bedroom cottages, chalets)
20 minutes from Ski Area,
Box BSC, Winchester, 54567 686-2525

WHITECAP CONT.

HOLIDAY INN (dining room, bar)
U.S. 2, Hurley, 54534 561-3030
HURLEY INTERSTATE BUDGET INN
100 Silver St., Hurley, 54534 561-2901
LAKE AIRE MOTEL
Junction of U.S. 2 & 13,
downtown Ashland, 54806 682-4551
MC COY'S RESORT
¼ mi. E. of Hwy. 51, Mercer, 54547 476-2217
MC COY'S RESORT (modern homes)
¼ mi. E. of Hwy. 51, Mercer, 54547 476-2217
NATURE'S WORLD MOTEL
U.S. Hwy. 51, Mercer, 54567 476-2421
REST VALLEY MOTEL
3 minutes W. of Ironwood on U.S. 2 561-5221
THE STABLES
Base of the mountain, call Ski Area
VITTONE'S MOTEL
U.S. 2 & 51 W., ½ mi. from Ironwood
Hurley, 54534. 561-4840

RESTAURANTS

THE BLUE BAYOU INN
U.S. 51, Manitowish Waters 543-2537
BONAVENTURE SUPPER CLUB
404 Silver St., Hurley. 561-9800
BRANDING IRON (pub & steak house)
Silver St., Hurley 561-9943
CONNIE'S SUPPER CLUB (Italian, cocktails)
Silver St., Hurley 561-9807
DING-A-LING SUPPER CLUB (cocktails)
Hwy. 51 & 47, Manitowish 476-2270
EVERGREEN SUPPER CLUB (bar)
Hwy. 51, 7 mi. S. of Mercer 543-2111
LIBERTY BELL CHALET (Italian, cocktails)
109 5th Ave. S., Hurley 561-3653
PETRUSHA'S SUPPER CLUB (Italian, cocktails)
Hwy. 51, ½ mi. S. of Hurley. 561-9888
PIER 10 SUPPER CLUB & THE RIVERBOAT LOUNGE
At the border, Silver St., Hurley 561-2179
SKY LAWN SUPPER CLUB (cocktails)
Hwy. 51, 7 mi. S. of Hurley 561-3545

SERVICES

BANK

IRON EXCHANGE BANK
310 Silver St., Hurley. 561-2662

GROCERIES

COPPS FOOD STORE
Hwy. 51 N., next to Holiday Inn, Hurley . . . 561-3000
ERSPAMER SUPERMARKET
Business U.S. 2 & Hwy. 51 S., Hurley 561-5195

LIQUOR

GEORGE'S SPIRITS
Silver St., near Hwy. 51, Hurley. 561-4300
TOWN & COUNTRY LIQUORS
Hwy. 51 N., next to Holiday Inn, Hurley . . . 561-3252

STORES & SKI SHOPS

AVE'S SPORT CENTER (snowmobiles)
Hwy. 51 N., Hurley. 561-2720
GIOVANONI'S TRUE VALUE HARDWARE
(sporting goods, gifts)
Downtown Hurley 561-4141
WHITECAP MOUNTAINS
Ski Shop & Repair Shop, call Ski Area

WYOMING

GRAND TARGHEE

ALTA, WY, VIA DRIGS, ID 83422 (307) 353-2304
OUT OF STATE PHONE: (800) 443-8146

AREA INFORMATION

BASE ELEVATION
8,000 feet
HOURS
9:30 a.m. to 4:00 p.m.
LIFTS
3 chairs, 1 surface tow, 3,600 capacity per hour
LONGEST RUN
2½ miles
NURSERY
Toilet trained, call Ski Area
SEASON
Mid-November to mid-April, no snowmaking
TRAILS
10% beginner, 70% intermediate, 20% expert
TRAVEL
12 miles east of Driggs, Idaho, just inside the Wyoming border on the western side of the Teton Mountains. Jackson Hole is 42 miles east; Idaho Falls, 87 miles southwest: Salt Lake City, 290 miles south.
VERTICAL DROP
2,200 feet

LODGING

TARGHEE LODGE
40 yards from lifts
TEEWINOT LODGE
50 yards from lifts

SIOUX LODGE APARTMENTS
50 yards from lifts

RESTAURANTS

PIONEER CAFETERIA
Base Area
STEAK HOUSE
Base Area

STORES & SKI SHOPS

SKI RENTAL SHOP
At the slopes
SPORT SHOP
At the slopes

SERVICES

AIR

IDAHO FALLS AIRPORT
Western & Republic Airlines
JACKSON HOLE AIRPORT
Frontier Airlines
RED BARON FLYING SERVICE
Driggs Teton Peaks Airport, 13 miles from Ski Area.
Will meet all flights at other 2 airports.
Advance reservations . . . . (208) 354-8131

AUTO RENTAL

AVIS
Idaho Falls. . . . . (800) 331-1212
Jackson Hole 733-3422
HERTZ
Idaho Falls. . . . . (800) 654-3131
NATIONAL
Idaho Falls. . . . . (800) 654-3131

BUS

SHUTTLE BUS (48 hour advance notice)
Will meet incoming or outgoing flights, pick-up at Avis Counter; fee, minimum: 2 passengers 353-2304
TARGHEE EXPRESS
Tues. & Fri., leave Jackson Hole, 8:00 a.m., arrive at Grand Targhee, about 9:30; leave Grand Targhee for Jackson Hole at 4:30 p.m. Call Ski Area.

JACKSON HOLE

P.O. BOX 290 — TETON VILLAGE, WY 83025
TELEPHONE: (307) 733-2292, (800) 443-6931

AREA INFORMATION

BASE ELEVATION
6,311 feet
CENTRAL RESERVATIONS. . 733-4005, (800) 443-6931
CHILD CARE
Pooh Corner, basement of the Hostel. 733-9901
CUSTOMER SERVICE
Call Ski Area in Teton Village
EMERGENCY. 911
HOURS
9 a.m. - 4 p.m., no night skiing
LIFTS
6 triple chairs, 1 tram (63 capacity), 5,500 capacity per hr.
LONGEST RUN
7 miles
RENTAL
At slope, See also "Stores & Ski Shops"
SEASON
Early Dec. to mid-April
SECURITY (24 hours). 733-2331
SKI PATROL . . . . .733-2292 X 50
SNOWFALL
38 feet
SNOW PHONE 733-2291
TRAILS
2 mountains: Rendezvous & Apres Vous, 60 runs & trails, 6 novices, 39 intermediate, 36 expert
TRAVEL
12 miles from Jackson via State Hwy. 75, 250 miles from Salt Lake City, 81 miles from Twin Falls
VERTICAL DROP
Apres Vous, 2,170 feet; Rendezvous, 4,139 feet

LODGING

THE ANTLER MOTEL
43 W. Pearl St., Box 575, 83001 733-2535
THE ANVIL MOTEL
1 bl. from Town Sq., Box 486, 83001 733-3668
G PAR K HOTEL
5 minute walk from downtown
Box 955H, 83001. 733-2364
THE GRAND VU MOTEL
Broadway, 3 blocks west of Town Square
P.O. Box 1787, 83001 733-2324
THE HORSESHOE MOTEL
N. Cache St., 2 blocks from Town Square
Box 97, 83001 733-2287
THE RAMADA SNOW KING INN
Base of Snow King Mtn., Box SKI, 83001. . . 733-5200
RANCHO INN
Downtown Jackson, Box 596, 83001 733-6363
THE RAWHIDE MOTEL
75 S. Hillward, Box 581, 83001. 733-2893
THE TRAPPER MOTEL
1½ blocks from Town Sq., Box 1712, 83001 733-2648

TETON VILLAGE

CENTRAL RESERVATIONS. . . . . (800) 443-6931
VILLAGE TRAVEL 733-7182

ALPENHOF
Pool, restaurant, entertainment 733-3242
CRYSTAL SPRINGS INN
Near the aerial tramway 733-4423
HOSTEL
Lounge, recreation room, nearby tennis 733-3415
THE INN AT JACKSON HOLE
Heated pool 733-2311

JACKSON HOLE CONT.

SOJOURNER INN
Restaurants, entertainment, pool, sauna 733-3657
VILLAGE CENTER
Restaurant, ski shop 733-3155

CONDOMINIUMS

CENTRAL RESERVATIONS. . . . . (800) 443-6931

EAGLE'S REST, pool saunas view
FOUR SEASONS, fireplaces, saunas
GROS VENTRE / TENSLEEP
JACKSON HOLE RACQUET CLUB
7 miles from Jackson 733-3990
LA CHOUMINE, efficiency apartments
NEZ PERCE
RENDEZVOUS
SLEEPING INDIAN
SNOWRIDGE, saunas, covered parking
TIMBER RIDGE, 4 bedrooms, 3 baths
WHITERIDGE, 2 bedrooms, garages

RECREATION

DIAL-A-PARK
Grand Teton Information 733-3220

BOATING & FISHING

BAKER - EWING FLOAT TRIPS
Box 1243R, Jackson 83001 733-3410
CHARLIE SANDS' TRIPS
"Wildwater," Box 290, Jackson 83001. 543-2545
FT. JACKSON FLOAT TRIPS (also fishing)
310 W. Broadway, Jackson 83001 733-2583
GRAND TETON LODGE CO. TRIPS (also fishing)
P.O. Box 240, Moran 83013. 733-2855
JACK DENNIS WHITEWATER (also fishing)
Box 328, Jackson 83001. 733-3270

GOLF

JACKSON HOLE GOLF & TENNIS CLUB
8 miles north of Jackson. 733-3111
JACKSON HOLE RACQUET CLUB
Foot of Teton Mtn. Range
7 miles from Jackson 733-3990

ICE SKATING

ADJACENT TO AERIAL TRAM, NO RENTALS

RESTAURANTS

JACKSON

THE BAR J. CHUCKWAGON
(ranch hand supper, entertainment)
1 mile up Teton Village Rd., call 1st 733-3370
THE BLUE LION (French)
N. of Fred's Market on Millward 733-3912
THE ORIGINAL ROCKY MOUNTAIN OYSTER
Stagecoach bar, Wilson 733-6610
THE OVERLOOK (Continental)
At Ramada Snow King Inn 733-5200
THE RANCHER BAR & LOUNGE
20 E. Broadway 733-3886
R.J. BAR & LIQUOR STORE
Broadway, 4 blocks west of Town Sq. 733-3853
SHADY LADY SALOON
Ramada Snow King Inn 733-5200
THE SILVER SPUR
West side of the Town Sq. 733-3279
THE STEAK PUB
U.S. 89, 3 miles south of Jackson
THE STRUTTING GROUSE
Jackson Hole Golf & Tennis Club
8 miles north of Jackson. 733-3111
THE VIRGINIAN (dancing)
Hwy. 187, West Jackson 733-2792
VISTA GRANDE (Mexican)
Midway to Teton Village, Village Rd. 733-6964

TETON VILLAGE

ALPENHOF RESTAURANT (Continental)
Closest to all lifts 733-3242
THE INN RESTAURANT
100 yards from chairlifts. 733-2311
LA FONDUE HOUSE
The Inn at Jackson Hole 733-2311
MANGY MOOSE RESTAURANT (entertainment)
Bar & other restaurants downstairs 733-4913
THE STOCK MAN'S RESTAURANT
Sojourner Inn 733-3657
THE TAVERN (entertainment)
Sojourner Inn 733-3657
WHAT'S UP
The Village Center 733-3155

SERVICES

AIR

CHARTER AIRCRAFT
Imeson Aviation. 733-4767
Village Travel 733-7182
DAILY SERVICE
From Denver via Frontier 733-3100
Western & Republic into Idaho Falls from Salt Lake City
IDAHO FALLS AIRPORT SHUTTLE
Saturdays only from Idaho Falls Airport

AUTO RENTALS

BELDEN RENT-A-CAR (airport & pickup)
Snow King Inn 733-3970
HERTZ
Call for locations 733-2270, (800) 654-3131
THRIFTY (airport pickup)
Union 76, Grand Teton Plaza 733-4295

STORES & SKI SHOPS

ANNELIESE SPORT FASHION
Alpenhof Lodge. 733-6838

HIDEOUT LEATHER & GIFTS
In the Village Center 739-9580

JACK DENNIS OUTDOOR SHOP
Cache Creek Sq., Jackson

JACKSON HOLE SKI & SPORTS
North side of Town Sq., Jackson 733-4449

JACKSON SPORTING GOODS
38 W. Broadway, Jackson 733-3461

MANGY MOOSE LIQUOR STORE
At the Mangy Moose 733-4913

RENDEZVOUS MT. GIFT SHOP
At the top of the tram

TETON VILLAGE SPORTS
Crystal Springs Inn 733-2181

THE VILLAGE SHIRTWORKS
Downstairs in the Mangy Moose. 733-6559

THE VILLAGE STORE (full service)
In the Village Center 733-4733

WILDERNESS SPORTS
Next to the tram 733-4297

WYOMING OUTFITTERS
Town Sq., Jackson 733-3877

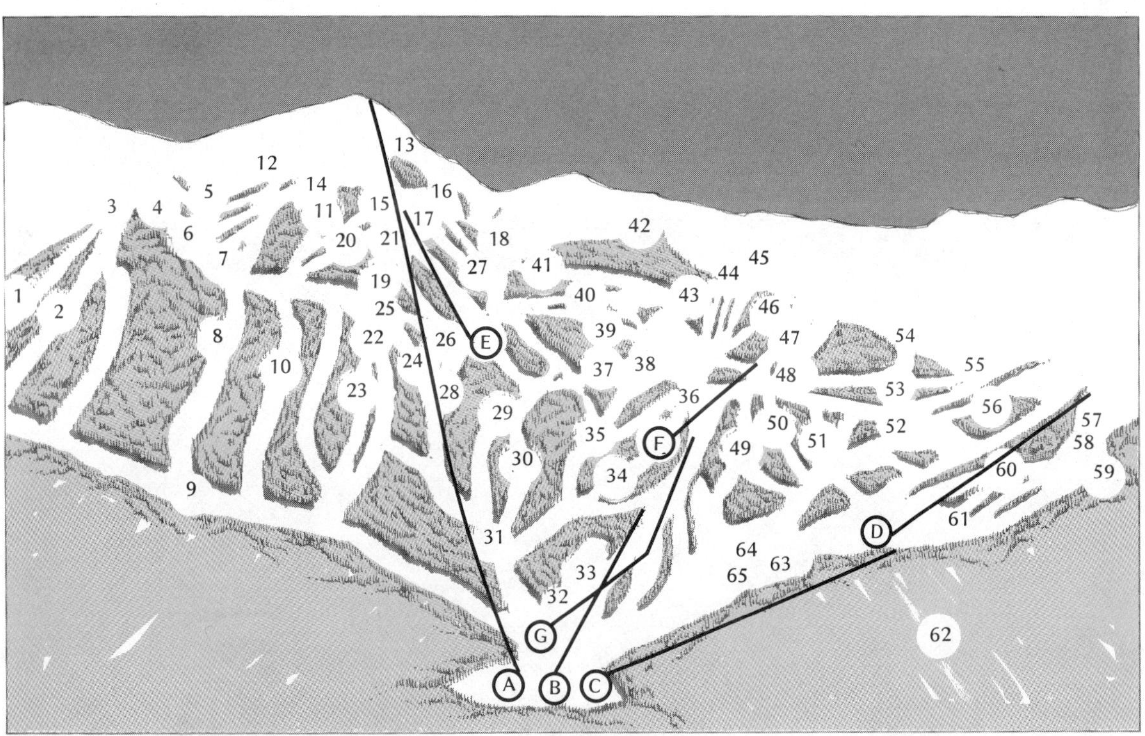

JACKSON HOLE RUNS

1 SOUTH HOBACK
2 NORTH HOBACK
3 RENDEZVOUS TRAIL
4 BIVOUAC
5 CHEYENNE BOWL
6 BIRD IN THE HAND
7 PEPI'S RUN
8 LOWER SUBLETTE RIDGE
9 UNIOUN PASS TRAVERSE
10 RAWLING'S BOWL
11 ALTA CHUTES
12 RENDEZVOUS BOWL
13 CORBET'S COULOIR
14 GROS VENTRE TRAVERSE
15 LARAMIE BOWL
16 EAST RIDGE TRAVERSE
17 EXPERT CHUTES
18 GROS VENTRE
19 GRAND
20 SOUTH PASS
21 GANNETT
22 SOUTH COLTER RIDGE
23 BUFFALO BOWL
24 NORTH COLTER RIDGE
25 LANDER BOWL
26 RIVERTON
27 THUNDER
28 LOWER TRAMLINE
29 GROS VENTRE TRAIL
30 SLALOM
31 SUNDANCE GULLY
32 EAGLE'S REST CUT OFF
33 SESAME STREET RUN
34 JACKSON FACE
35 NEZ PERCE
36 BLACKTAIL
37 AVALANCHE
38 SURPRISE
39 AMPHITHEATER TRAVERSE
40 NEZ PERCE TRAVERSE
41 CIRQUE
42 HEADWALL
43 CAMPGROUND
44 TIMBERED ISLAND
45 EASY DOES IT
46 LIFT LINE
47 SLEEPING INDIAN
48 WIDE OPEN
49 BEAVERTOOTH
50 ASHLEY RIDGE
51 SOLITUDE
52 SOLITUDE TRAVERSE
53 TOGWOTEE PASS TRAVERSE
54 MORAN FACE
55 MORAN
56 WERNER
57 TEEWINOT
58 ST. JOHN'S
59 BOUNDARY
60 SECRET SLOPE
61 TEEWINOT GULLY
62 CROSS COUNTRY TRAIL
63 LOWER WERNER
64 ANTELOPE FLATS
65 LOWER TEEWINOT

JACKSON HOLE LIFTS

A AERIAL TRAM
B EAGLE'S REST DOUBLE CHAIR
C TEEWINOT DOUBLE CHAIR
D APRES VOUS DOUBLE CHAIR
E THUNDER DOUBLE CHAIR
F CASPER BOWL TRIPLE CHAIR
G CRYSTAL SPRINGS CHAIRLIFT

CANADA

FORTRESS MTN.

BOX 7220, STAT. E, CALGARY, ALBERTA T3C 3M1
(403) 264-4626

AREA INFORMATION

BASE ELEVATION
6,700 feet

HOURS
9:00 a.m. - 4:00 p.m., daily
8:30 a.m. - 4:00 p.m., weekends & holidays

LIFTS
3 chairs, 2 T-bars, 5,000 capacity per hour

LONGEST RUN
1.2 miles

NURSERY
Ages 2 - 6, call Ski Area

SEASON
Late November to mid-May, no snowmaking

SNOW PHONE 288-1411

TRAILS
30% beginner, 40% intermediate, 30% advanced

TRAVEL
From Calgary to Kananaskis Pass, forty miles, then thirty miles to Ski Area, located in Kananaskis Valley Provincial Park. Daily bus from Calgary, returning at 4:00 p.m. Information. 264-4626

VERTICAL DROP
1,100 feet

FORTRESS MOUNTAIN (CANADA) RUNS
1 FRIAR'S TUCK
2 PALISADE PARK
3 WATCH ME
4 PORTCULLIS
5 THE CANADIAN
6 RIDGE RUN
7 DOWN THE GARDEN PATH
8 GARDEN PATH
9 COURTYARD
10 SLOE GIN
11 RAMPART
12 TURKISH DELIGHT
13 ROOKIE
14 PALISADE
15 BIG SCOOP
16 SORCERER
17 BURNT OUT
18 SHOW OFF
19 ENCHANTED FOREST
20 ROLLER COASTER
21 WALL STREET
22 EASY OUT
23 CANTERBURY TRAIL
24 JOLLY JESTER
25 GETAWAY
26 PITCHFORK
27 FLYING FORTRESS
28 GOOD KNIGHT
29 COLISEUM
30 CAULDRON
31 SHERWOOD FOREST

FORTRESS MOUNTAIN (CANADA) LIFTS
A THE CANADIAN TRIPLE CHAIR
B BACKSIDE DOUBLE CHAIR
C FORTRESS DOUBLE CHAIR
D BEGINNER'S T-BAR
E CURVED T-BAR SOUTH
F CURVED T-BAR NORTH
G NEW T-BAR NORTH

SKI LAKE LOUISE

BOX 5 LAKE LOUISE, ALBERTA TOL 1E0
(403) 522-3555

AREA INFORMATION

BASE ELEVATION
5,400 feet

HOURS
8:45 a.m. - 4:00 p.m.

LIFTS
5 chairlifts, 1 gondola, 1 poma lift, 2 T-bars, 1 beginner's rope tow, 7,600 capacity per hour

LONGEST RUN
5 miles

NURSERY
Ages 2 - 6, call Ski Area

SEASON
Early December to late April, no snowmaking

SNOW PHONE
Calgary 244-6665
Outside Alberta . . . . (800) 661-6446

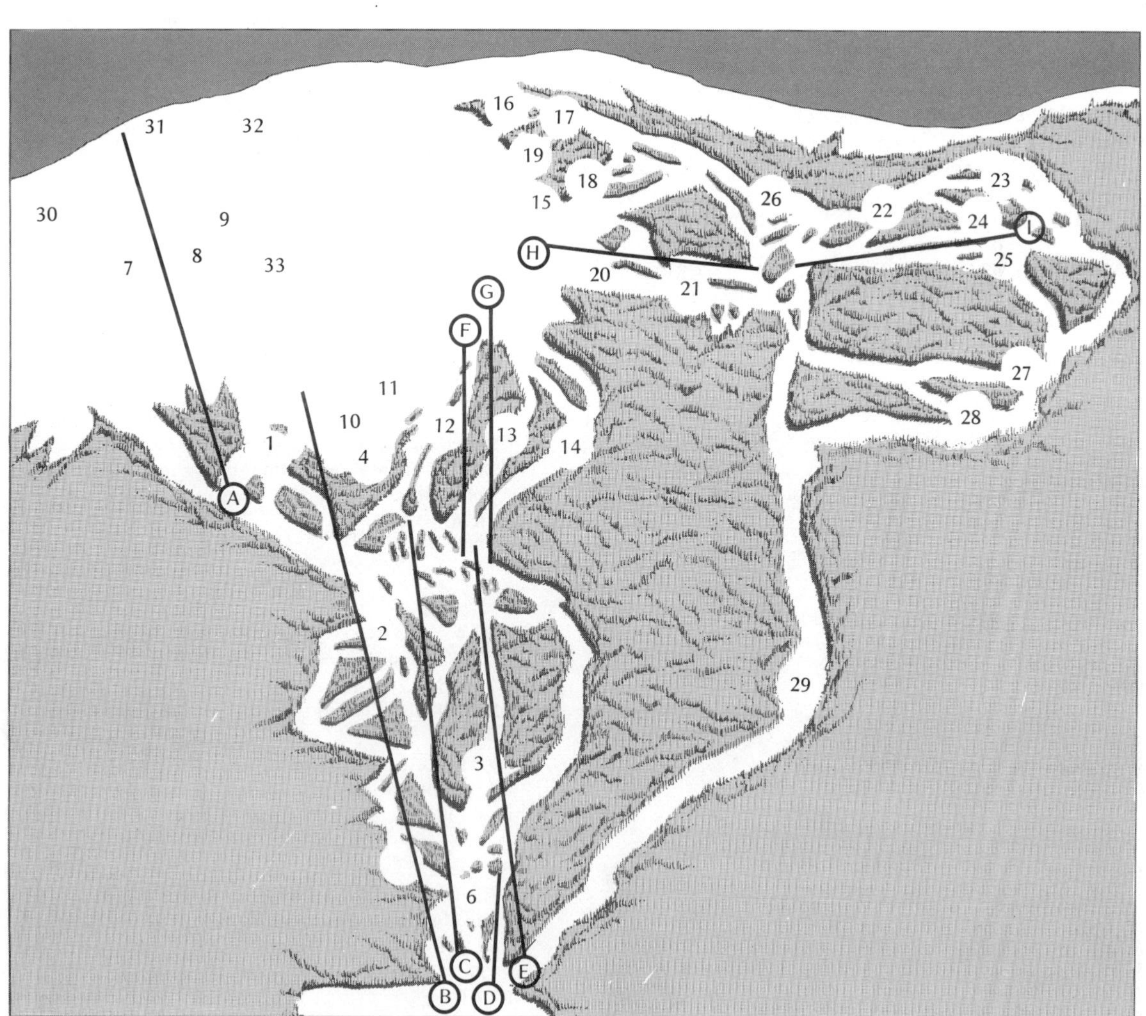

SKI LAKE LOUISE RUNS

1 WIWAXY
2 MEN'S DOWNHILL
3 LADIES' DOWNHILL
4 GRIZZLY BOWL
5 JUNIPER
6 SUNNYSIDE
7 OUTER LIMITS
8 SUNSET
9 SKYLINE
10 GULLY
11 UPSHOOT TRAIL
12 EAGLE FLIGHT
13 WAPTA
14 EAGLE MEADOWS
14aMEADOWLARK
15 PIKE
15aPIKABOO
16 ALLEY
17 OLD PTARMIGAN
18 PTARMIGAN
19 NEW PTARMIGAN
20 EXHIBITION
21 PTARMIGAN CHUTES
22 MARMOT
23 WOLVERINE
24 LYNX
25 LARCH
26 PRUNEPICKER
27 BOBCAT
28 LOOK-OUT
29 THE SKI OUT
30 BOOMERANG
31 SHOULDER ROLL
32 RIDGE RUN
33 SADDLEBACK

SKI LAKE LOUISE LIFTS

A SUMMIT T-BAR
B OLYMPIC CHAIR
C GLACIER TRIPLE CHAIR
D SUNNY T-BAR
E GONDOLA
F EAGLE POMA
G EAGLE CHAIR
H PTARMIGAN CHAIR
I LARCH CHAIR

LAKE LOUISE CONT.

RESTAURANTS
1 restaurant, 3 cafeterias, 1 lounge, at the slopes
TRAILS
20% beginner, 45% intermediate, 35% advanced
TRAVEL
From Calgary, 115 miles via Trans-Canada Highway 1.
VERTICAL DROP
3,250 feet

LODGING

THE KINGS DOMAIN
The Domain Apartments (resort-condo style)
The Hostelry
Lake Louise Inn (restaurant, bars, indoor pool)
Temple Chambers (adjacent to the Inn)
Box 209, Lake Louise 522-3791
PIPESTONE LODGE (bar, next to restaurant)
Box 69, Lake Louise 522-3989
THE POST HOTEL (dining, bar)
Box 69, Lake Louise 522-3989, 522-3877

ADDITIONAL LODGINGS & RESTAURANTS ARE IN BANFF, SEE SUNSHINE VILLAGE, PAGE

MARMOT BASIN

BOX 1300, JASPER, AL T0E 1E0 (403) 853-3816

AREA INFORMATION

BASE ELEVATION
5,680 feet
HOURS
9:00 a.m. - 4:00 p.m.
LIFTS
3 chairlifts, 2 T-bars, 4,600 capacity per hour
LONGEST RUN
3½ miles
NURSERY
Jasper Day Care Centre, Box 1595
Ages 2 - 5, toilet trained, reservations 852-4666
SEASON
Early December to late April, no snowmaking
SNOW PHONE
Call Ski Area
TRAILS
35% beginner, 35% intermediate, 30% advanced
TRAVEL
North of Calgary and Lake Louise via Highway 93; west of Edmonton via Highway 16. Daily rail service from Vancouver and Edmonton. Major airlines to Vancouver, Calgary and Edmonton with interconnecting bus service. Chartered flights from Edmonton to the Jasper-Hinton Airport, 40 miles east of Ski Area.
VERTICAL DROP
2,300 feet

LODGING

ANDREW MOTOR LODGE (dining, lounge)
2 blocks from CNR Station, Box 850 852-3394
ASTORIA MOTOR INN
(dining lounge, coffee shop, bar, entertainment)
Box 850 852-3351
THE ATHABASCA HOTEL
(dining lounge, coffee shop, tavern, entertainment)
Box 1420 852-3386
DIAMOND MOTEL
Box 757 852-3143
JASPER INN MOTOR LODGE
(individual ski lockers, waxing room, indoor pool)
Box 879 852-4461
LOBSTICK LODGE (dining room, indoor pool)
Box 1200 852-4431
MARMOT LODGE
(dining, cocktails, cabaret, waxing facilities)
Box 687 852-4471
MOUNT ROBSON
3 blocks to VIA train station &
Greyhound bus depot, Box 88 852-3327
THE WHISTLERS MOTOR HOTEL
Across from VIA train station &
Greyhound bus depot, Box 250. 852-3361
PYRAMID LAKE BUNGALOWS
4 miles northwest of town, Box 388 852-3536

RESTAURANTS

AMETHYST DINING ROOM
2 blocks from CNR Station 852-4577

ASTORIA RESTAURANT
1 block from CNR depot. 852-4132

LOBSTICK DINING LOUNGE
East end of town 852-4703

MARMOT DINING ROOM
East end of town 852-4544

WHISTLER'S RESTAURANT
Across from VIA train station. 852-4046

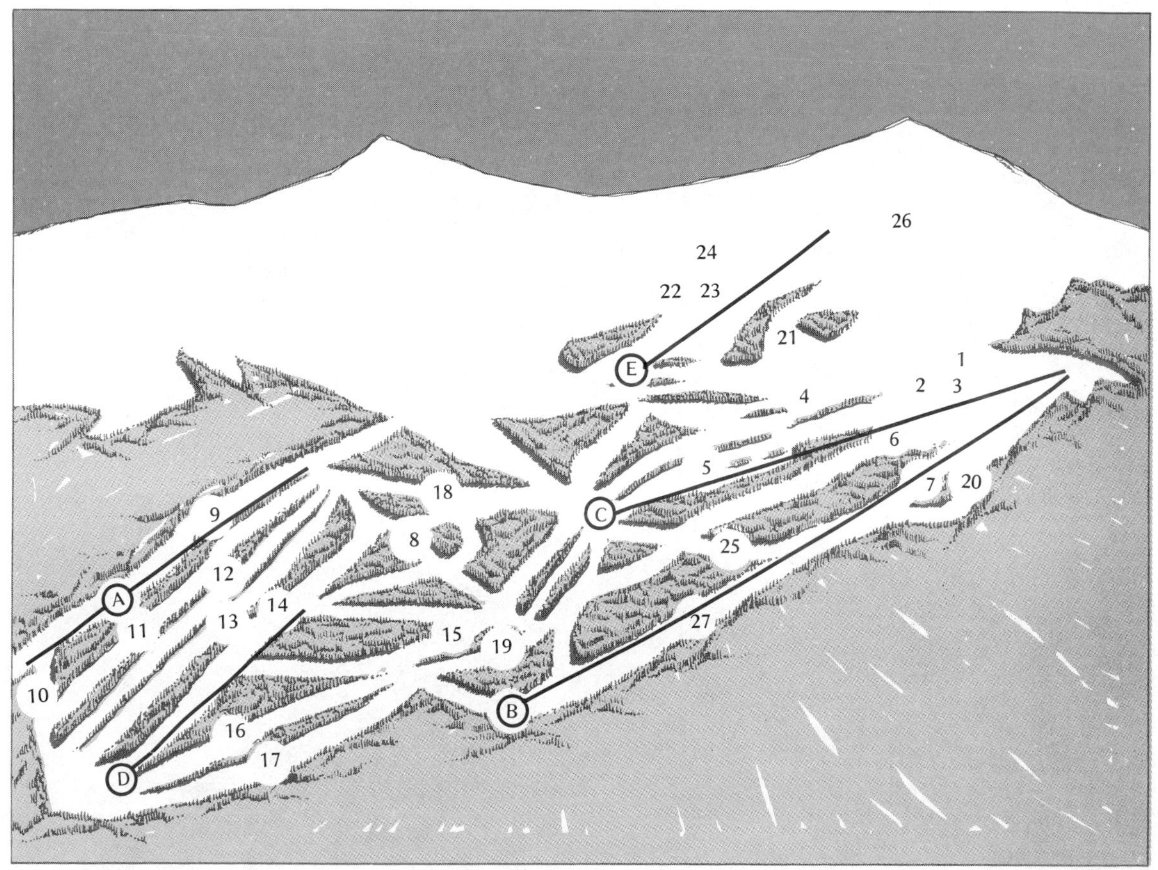

MARMOT BASIN

RUNS
1 BASIN RUN
2 PARADISE
3 PUNCH BOWL
4 MILK RUN
5 HIGHWAY 16
6 SHOW OFF
7 EXHIBITION
8 BUNNY HOP
9 SLASH
10 DEAD FALL
11 SPILLWAY
12 LIFTLINE
13 DROMEDARY
14 TRANQUILIZER
15 SLOW POKE
16 SCHOOL HOUSE
17 HOME RUN
18 SLEEPY HOLLOW
19 OLD ROAD
20 KIEFERS DREAM
21 DUPRES
22 MADISON AVENUE
23 KNOB HILL
24 MC CREADY'S CHOICE
25 BALLROON
26 PEAK RUN
27 RIDGE RUN

LIFTS
A YELLOW CHAIRLIFT
B RET T-BAR
C YELLOW T-BAR
D CARIBOU CHAIRLIFT
E KNOB CHAIRLIFT

MT. NORQUAY

BOX 1258, BANFF, AL TOL 0C0 (403) 762-4421

AREA INFORMATION

BASE ELEVATION
5,700 feet

HOURS
9:00 a.m. - 4:00 p.m.

LIFTS
2 chairlifts, 2 T-bars, 1 beginner platter lift, 1 rope tow, 4,860 capacity per hour

LONGEST RUN
8,248 feet

SEASON
Mid-November to early April, no snowmaking

SNOW PHONE
Call Ski Area

TRAILS
35% beginner, 15% intermediate, 50% advanced

TRAVEL
4 miles from Banff, 75 miles from Calgary and Calgary Int'l. Airport. Brewster Transport from Banff twice daily to Ski Area; and from airport to Banff, once daily.

MOUNT NORQUAY CONT.

VERTICAL DROP
1,300 feet

LODGINGS & RESTAURANTS IN BANFF, SEE SUNSHINE VILLAGE, PAGE

SUNSHINE VILLAGE

BOX 1510, BANFF, ALBERTA T0L 0C0 (403) 762-3383

AREA INFORMATION

BASE ELEVATION
7,082 feet

NORQUAY (CANADA) RUNS
1 BUNNY SLOPE
2 LONE PINE PRACTICE SLOPE
3 STONEY SQUAW NO. 1
4 STONEY SQUAW NO. 2
5 THE PROMENADE
6 WISHBONE NO. 1
7 WISHBONE NO. 2
8 WISHBONE NO. 3
9 WISHBONE CUTBACK
10 WISHBONE SCHUSS
11 LOWER GULLEY
12 LONE PINE
13 BOWL
14 NORTH AMERICAN
15 PRUNE PICKER'S CUTBACK
16 MEMORIAL SLOPE
17 SKI OUT TO TIMBERLINE LODGE

NORQUAY (CANADA) LIFTS
A BEGINNERS' PLATTER LIFT
B LONE PINE DOUBLE CHAIR LIFT
C STONEY SQUAW T-BAR
D WISHBONE T-BAR
E MEMORIAL ROPE TOW
F NORQUAY DOUBLE CHAIRLIFT

HOURS
8:30 a.m. - 4:30 p.m.
LIFTS
5 chairlifts, 1 gondola, 3 T-bars,
1 rope tow, 6,500 capacity per hour
LONGEST RUN
2¼ miles
NURSERY
Age 2 & up, call Ski Area
SEASON
Mid-November to late May, no snowmaking
SNOW PHONE
Call Ski Area
TRAVEL
18 kilometers west of Banff in the Banff National Park. Flashing light over the Trans-Canada Highway indicates exit. Arrange indoor parking at the Banff Springs Hotel, 762-2211. Transportation through Brewster Transport to and from Banff. The last 4.5 kilometers to the village are by gondola only; therefore, use warm clothing and foot wear. By air to Calgary International Airport, then airporter service to Banff where Ski Area, upon advance confirmation, will provide transportation.
VERTICAL DROI
1,848 feet

LODGING

ALPINE MOTEL
Box 279, 521 Banff Ave.. 762-2332
ARCHWAY MOTEL
Box 684, Minnewanka 762-2507
ASPEN LODGE(next to restaurant)
Box 1018, 501 Banff Ave.. 762-4418
BANFF MOTEL
Box 279, 519 Banff Ave.. 762-2713
BANFF PARK LODGE (restaurant, bar)
Box 2200, Lynx St.. 762-4433
BANFF SPRINGS HOTEL (restaurant, bar)
Box 960, Spray Ave. 762-2211
BANFFSHIRE INN (next to restaurant)
Box 489, 537 Banff Ave.. 762-2201
BEL PLAZA
Box 189, Minnewanka Rd.. 762-3455
BIG HORN MOTEL (next to restaurant & bar)
Box 1328, Marmot St. 762-3386
BOW VIEW MOTOR LODGE (restaurant)
Box 339, 228 Bow Ave. 762-2261
CASCADE INN (restaurant, bar)
Box 790, 124 Banff Ave.. 762-3311
CHARLTON'S CEDAR COURT
Box 1478, 513 Banff Ave.. 762-2527
CHARLTON'S EVERGREEN COURT (next to restaurant)
Box 1478, 459 Banff Ave.. 762-3307
DRIFTWOOD INN
Box 1016, 340 Marten St. 762-3727
HOMESTEAD INN (restaurant)
Box 669, 218 Lynx St.. 762-4471
IRWIN'S MOTOR INN (restaurant)
Box 1198, 429 Banff Ave.. 762-4188
KING EDWARD HOTEL (restaurant, bar)
Box 250, 137 Banff Ave.. 762-2251
MOUNT ROYAL HOTEL (restaurant, bar)
Box 550, 138 Banff Ave.. 762-3331
PINEWOODS MOTEL
Box 610, 720 Banff Ave.. 762-2248
PTARMIGAN INN
Box 1840, 337 Banff Ave.. 762-2207
RED CARPET INN (restaurant)
Box 1800, 425 Banff Ave.. 762-4184
RIMROCK INN (restaurant, bar)
Box 1110, Upper Hot Springs Rd. 762-3356
RUNDLE MANOR APT. HOTEL
Box 489, 348 Marten St.. 762-2707
SPRUCE GROVE MOTEL
Box 471, 545 Banff Ave.. 762-2112
SUNSHINE INN (dining room, lounge, sauna, hot tubs)
At the slopes, call Ski Area
SWISS VILLAGE LODGE
Box 1077, 556 Banff Ave.. 762-2256
TIMBERLINE HOTEL (restaurant, bar)
Box 69, Mt. Norquay Rd. 762-2281
TRAVELLER'S INN
Box 1017, 401 Banff Ave.. 762-4401
TUNNEL MOUNTAIN CHALETS
Box 1137, Tunnel Mountain Rd. 762-4515
VOYAGER INN (restaurant, bar)
Box 1540, 555 Banff Ave.. 762-3301
WOODLAND VILLAGE
Box 398, 449 Banff Ave.. 762-5521

RESTAURANTS

ALPINE STEAK HOUSE (bar)
Upstairs, 212 Buffalo St.. 762-2712
BANFF CAFE (bar, dancing, entertainment)
129 Banff Ave. 762-2553
BANFF PARK LODGE (bar, dancing, entertainment)
222 Lynx St. 762-4433
BANFF SPRINGS HOTEL (bar, dancing, entertainment)
Spray Ave. 762-2211
BOW VIEW RESTAURANT (bar)
228 Bow Ave. 762-3651
BUMPER'S THE BEEF HOUSE (bar, entertainment)
Marmot St. & Banff Ave.. 762-2622
CABOOSE STEAK & LOBSTER (bar)
Elk & Lynx St. 762-3622
CORIANDER NATURE FOODS
215 Banff Ave. 762-2878
DELI CORNER
215 Banff Ave. 762-4321
DRIFTERS INN (bar)
215 Banff Ave. 762-4525
EAGLE'S NEST (bar)
Rimrock Inn, Upper Hot Springs 762-3356
EL TORO (bar)
429 Banff Ave. 762-2520
GREAT EXPECTATIONS (bar, dancing, entertainment)
209 Banff Ave. 762-5122
GRIZZLY HOUSE (bar, dancing, entertainment)
207 Banff Ave. 762-4055
GUIDO'S SPAGHETTI FACTORY (bar)
Upstairs, 116 Banff Ave.. 762-4002

SUNSHINE VILLAGE CONT.

JOSHUA'S RESTAURANT (bar)
204 Caribou St. 762-2833

MAGPIE & STUMP FOOD & BEVERAGE EMPORIUM (bar, entertainment)
203 Caribou St. 762-2014

MELISSA'S MISSTEAK (bar, entertainment)
218 Lynx St. 762-4471

MOUNT ROYAL DINING LOUNGE (bar)
130 Banff Ave. 762-3331

MOUNTAIN GREENERY (bar)
120 Banff Ave. 762-5444

OMI OF JAPAN (bar)
124 Banff Ave. 762-2922

PARIS RESTAURANT (bar)
114 Banff Ave. 762-3554

RUNDLE RESTAURANT
319 Banff Ave. 762-3223

SAMO'S BROILER (bar)
137 Banff Ave. 762-3171

SILVER CITY (bar, dancing, entertainment)
Clock Tower Village 762-3337

TICINO'S (Swiss, Italian, bar)
Townhouse on Wolf St. 762-3848

MONT ORFORD

BOX 248, MAGOG, QU J1X 3W8 (819) 843-6548
LODGING: (819) 843-4200

AREA INFORMATION

BASE ELEVATION
1,200 feet

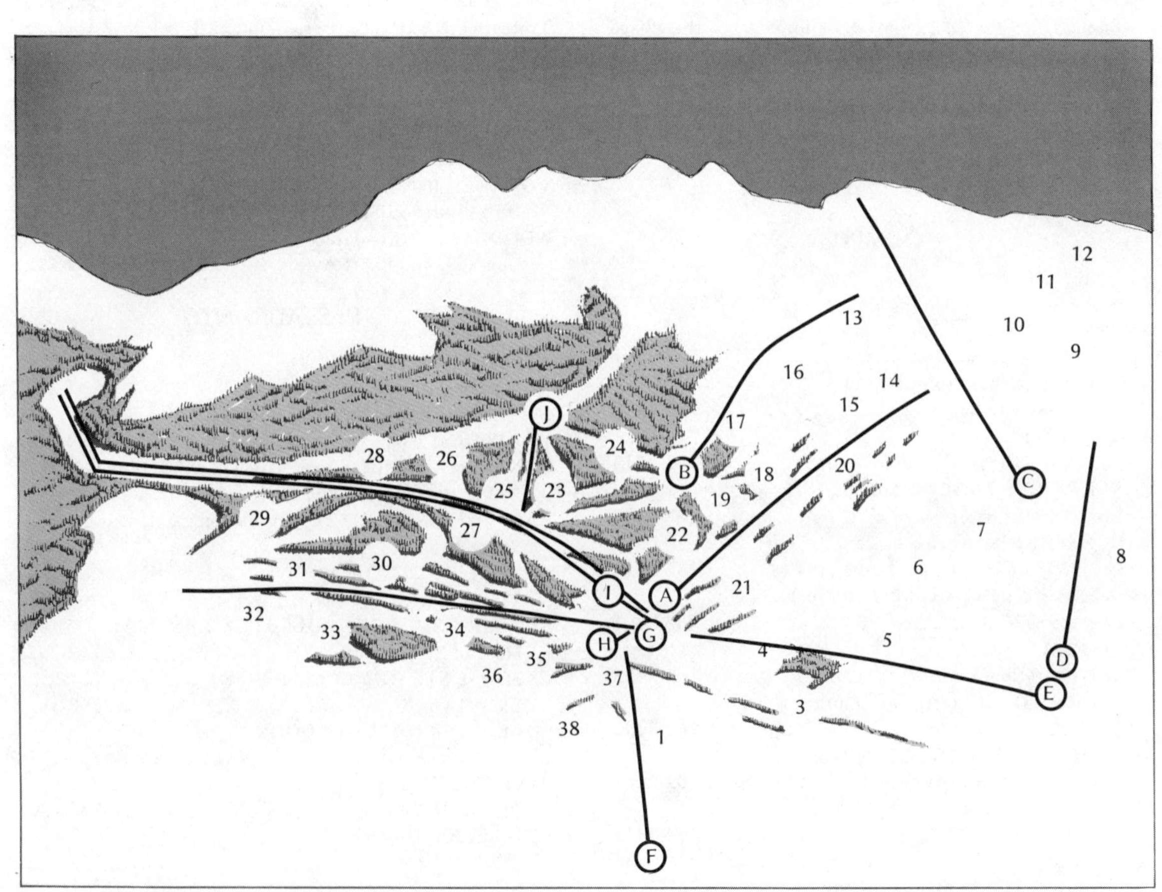

SUNSHINE VILLAGE RUNS

1 JERRY'S RUN
2 HEADWALL
3 DELL VALLEY
4 STRAWBERRY HILL
5 ROCK ISLE ROAD
6 SPRING HILL
7 HIGHWAY ONE
8 ASSINIBIONE TRAIL
29 MEADOW LARK
30 TIN CAN ALLEY
31 WA WA BOWL
32 TRAVERSE
33 PARIS BASIN
34 BIRD CAGE
35 WATERFALL
36 LITTLE BUNKER'S BOWL
37 DONKEY'S TAIL
38 GREEK RUN
9 PISTE NOIR
10 BOUNDARY BOWL
11 ABOMINABLE BENCH
12 BYE BYE BOWL
13 GREAT WHITE WAY
14 BREWSTER ROCK
15 BIG ANGEL
16 LITTLE ANGEL
17 TEEPEE TOWN
18 BARNER'S BOWL
19 PACKER'S TRAIL
20 WHITE WAY
21 PANDEMONIUM
22 PILGRIM'S TRAIL
23 SHORT & SWEET
24 MISS GRATZ
25 JACK RABBIT
26 EMMALINE
27 BORGEA TRAIL
28 RIDGE RUN

SUNSHINE VILLAGE LIFTS

A ANGEL CHAIRLIFT
B TEEPEE TOWN CHAIRLIFT
C GREAT DIVIDE CHAIRLIFT
D ASSINIBOINE T-BAR
E STRAWBERRY CHAIRLIFT
F STANDISH CHAIRLIFT
G WA WA T-BAR
H MITEY MITE
I GONDOLA
J FIREWEED T-BAR

HOURS

8:30 a.m. - 4:00 p.m.

LIFTS

3 chairs, 3 T-bars, 1 tow, 5,700 capacity per hour

LONGEST RUN

2½ miles

NURSERY

Toilet trained, call Ski Area

SEASON

Late November to April, no snowmaking

SNOW PHONE

Call Ski Area

TRAILS

40% beginner, 35% intermediate, 25% advanced

TRAVEL

67 miles from Montreal via Rt. 10 to Eastman to Ski Area in Mont Orford Provincial Park.

VERTICAL DROP

1,650 feet

LODGING

L'AUBERGE CHERIBOURG (dining, lounge)
C.P. 336, Magog 843-3308

AUBERGE DE L'ETOILE (dining)
1133 Main Street West, Magog 843-6521

L'AUBERGE DES GOUVERNEURS DE SHERBROOKE
(dining, wine cellar, piano bar)
3131 ouest, rue King, Sherbrooke 565-0464

AUBERGE ORFORD (dining)
Autoroute 10, exit 118
20 Merry south, Magog. 843-9361

Le BARON (2 dining rooms, lounge)
3200 ouest, rue King, Sherbrooke 567-3941

HOLIDAY INN SHERBROOKE (restaurant, lounge)
3535 ouest, rue King 563-2941

HOTEL WELLINGTON
(dining room, bars, cabaret with orchestra music)
68 sud, rue Wellington, Sherbrooke. 567-5261

MOTEL FLEURS DE LYS
Exit 115 of Autoroute 843-5508

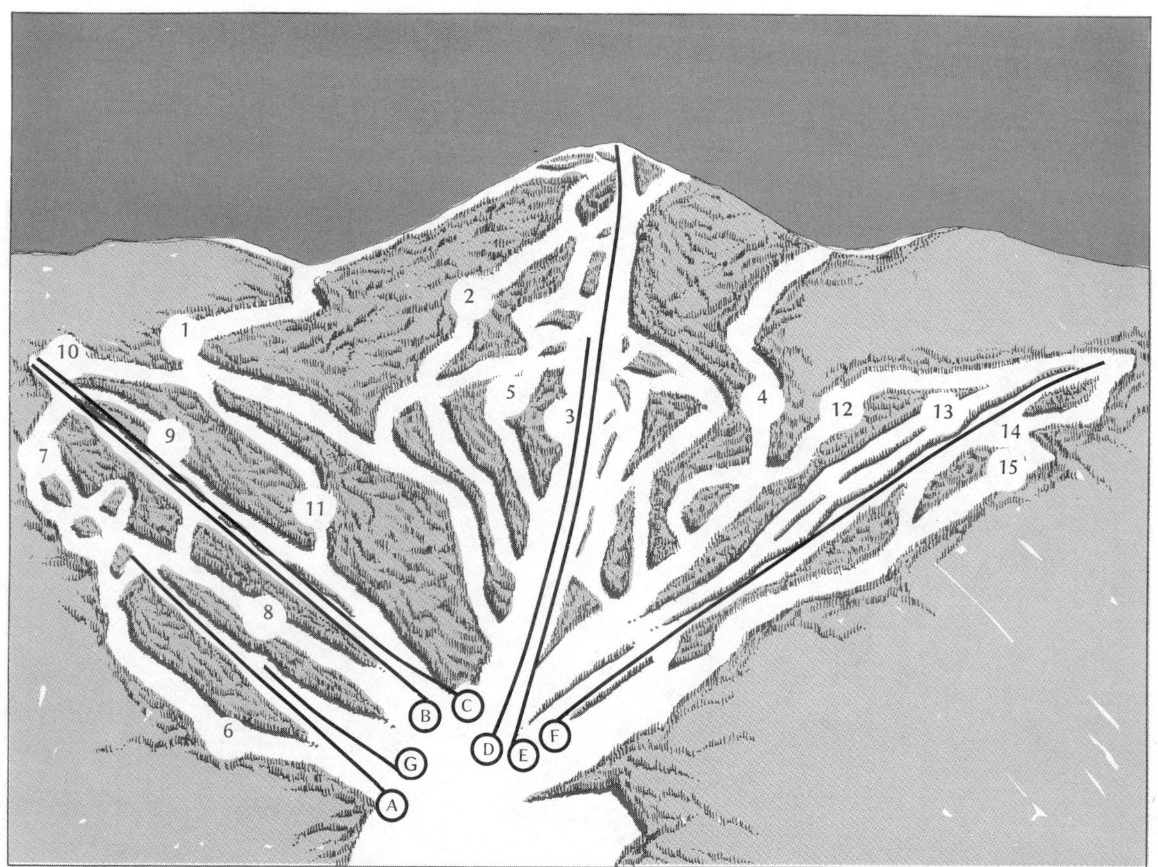

ONT ORFORD (CANADA) RUNS

1 TELE 7
2 CONTOUR
3 SUPER
4 GRANDE COULEE
5 TROIS-RUISSEAUX
6 ADAMS
7 LA 45
8 PENTE DOUCE
9 BOWEN
10 GAGNON
11 FAMILIALE
12 TOUSSISKI
13 CASCADES
14 GRANDE ALLEE
15 OOKPIC

MONT ORFORD (CANADA) LIFTS

A ARBALETE, 1,700 ft.
B ARBALETE, 3,300 ft.
C ARBALETE, 3,300 ft.
D TELESIEGE, 3,000 ft.
E TELESIEGE, 5,700 ft.
F TELESIEGE, 4,700 ft.
G MONTE PENTE DEBUTANTS, 700 ft.

MONT STE—MARIE

LAC STE.-MARIE, QU J0X 1Z (819) 467-5200

AREA INFORMATION

BASE ELEVATION
617 feet

HOURS
9:00 a.m. - 4:30 p.m.

LIFTS
3 chairs, 1 poma lift, 4,500 capacity per hour

LODGING
Auberge l'Abri, call Ski Area

LONGEST RUN
2.45 miles

NURSERY
All ages, call Ski Area

SEASON
Late November to late April, snowmaking

SNOW PHONE
Call Ski Area

TRAILS
25% beginner, 65% intermediate, 10% advanced

TRAVEL
55 miles north of Ottawa via Hwy. 105.
By air to Ottawa International Airport.

VERTICAL DROP
1,250 feet

MONT—SUTTON

SUTTON, QUEBEC J0E 2K0
(514) 538-2545 MONTREAL 866-5156

AREA INFORMATION

BASE ELEVATION
1,400 feet

HOURS
9:00 a.m. - 4:00 p.m.

LIFTS
5 chairlifts, 1 T-bar, 1 poma lift,
6,300 capacity per hour

LONGEST RUN
2¼ miles

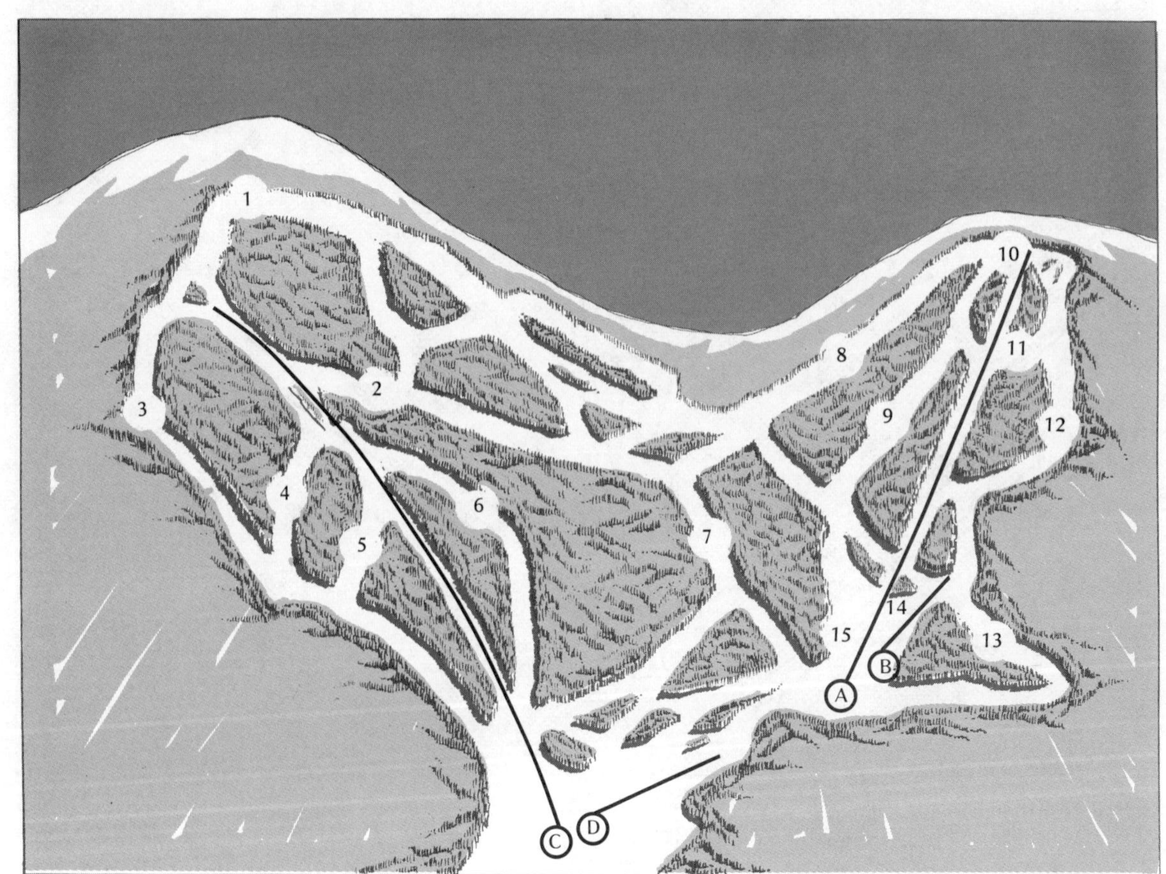

MONT STE. MARIE RUNS

1 RUE RADAR
2 CALYPSO
3 CARROUSEL
4 FORMIDABLE
5 BETSY
6 OUTAOUAIS
7 CRESCENDO
8 CHANSON
9 BELLEVUE
10 HEADWALL
11 TRAVERSE
12 SERENADE
13 DEBUTANTE
14 PREMIERE
15 EXHIBITION
16 PROMENADE

MONT STE. MARIE LIFTS

A TELESIEGE DOUBLE DOUBLE CHAIR, 4,700 ft.
B TELESIEGE DOUBLE DOUBLE CHAIR, 1,200 ft.
C TELESIEGE, 4,900 ft.
D POMA, 1,100 ft.

NURSERY
Age 2 & up, call Ski Area

SEASON
Late November to early May, snowmaking

SNOW PHONE 866-7639

TRAILS
30% beginner, 40% intermediate, 30% advanced

TRAVEL
From Montreal, Rt. 10 to Rt. 68 South to Rt. 104 East to Rt. 139 to Sutton, then 3 miles to Ski Area.

VERTICAL DROP
1,550 feet

LODGING

RESERVATIONS. . . . . (514) 538-2646, 538-2537

AUBERGE DE SUTTON (restaurant, bar, dancing)
Rd. 139, Sutton, J0F 2K0

AUBERGE DU BOURG (restaurant, bar, dancing)
Rue Maple, Sutton, J0E 2K0

HOTEL HORIZON (restaurant, bar, dancing)
Rue Maple, Sutton, J0E 2K0

HOTEL LE CASTEL DE L'ESTRIE
(restaurant, bar, dancing)
901 Main St., Granby, J2G 2Z5

LA PAIMPOLAISE (restaurant, bar, dancing)
Rue Maple, Sutton, J0E 2K0

RESTAURANTS

AUBERGE LA FONTAINE (French)
Main Street, Sutton

LA BROCHETTE (Chinese)
Rue Maple, Sutton

CAFE MOCADOR
17 Main North, Sutton

LE REFUGE (crepes)
Rue Maple, Sutton

SERVICES

TOWING SERVICE (24 hours) 538-2102, 538-2728

MONT SUTTON

RUNS
1 ST-BERNARD
2 SUTTON-IK
3 A-B-C
4 DYNAMIQUE
5 ALPINE
6 CAPUCINE
7 CENDRILLON
8 CASCADE
9 ALOUETTE
10 SOUS-BOIS II
11 MOHAWK
12 SOUS-BOIS IV
13 YOUPPE-YOUPPE
14 TORTUE
15 ALLEGANYS
16 ESCAPADE
17 MIRACLE
18 TRAVERSE
19 BARCAROLE
20 STARLET
21 STADE DE SLALOM
22 EXIL
23 CAPRICE
24 SURPRISE
25 SOUS-BOIS POMA

LIFTS
A T-BAR
B POMA
C DOUBLE CHAIR
D DOUBLE CHAIR
E DOUBLE CHAIR
F DOUBLE CHAIR
G DOUBLE CHAIR

MONT TREMBLANT

QUEBEC J0T 1Z0 (819) 425-2711

AREA INFORMATION

BASE ELEVATION
870 feet

HOURS
9:00 a.m. - 3:45 p.m.

LIFTS
7 chairlifts, 2 T-bars, 2 J-bars, 9,470 capacity per hour

LONGEST RUN
3½ miles

SEASON
Early December to early April, snowmaking

SNOW PHONE . . . . (514) 861-1925
French . . . . (514) 861-0792

TRAILS
15% beginner, 55% intermediate, 30% advanced

TRAVEL
From Montreal, 80 miles via Rt. 15 and Highway 117.

VERTICAL DROP
2,131 feet

LODGING

CENTRAL RESERVATIONS
Ontario, call collect. . . . . (416) 889-7734
U.S., toll free . . . . (800) 343-6768
Massachusetts . . . . (800) 272-2550

CUTTLE'S TREMBLANT CLUB (dining, piano bar)
Facing Mont-Tremblant's south side 425-2731

LE MANOIR PINOTEAU
(cocktails, wine parties, swiss fondues)
Overlooking Lac Tremblant & ski runs. 425-2795

MONT-TREMBLANT LODGE
(Base Area/cafeterias, bars, stores, ski shop, rental)
Call Ski Area, or in Montreal . . . . . . (514) 861-6165

VILLA BELLEVUE
(French & Continental dining, dancing, entertainment)
Near Ski Area 425-2734
Toll free, Quebec/Eastern Ontario . . . (800) 567-6744

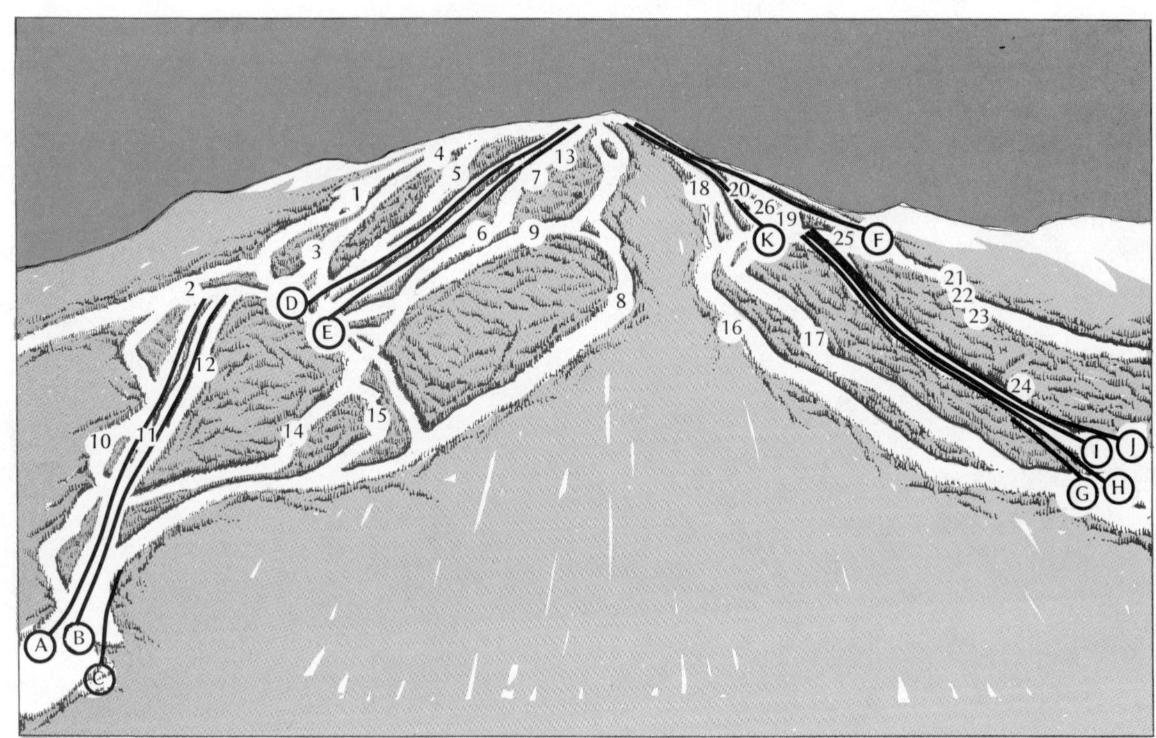

MONT TREMBLANT

RUNS

1 NANSEN
2 LA PASSE
3 ALPINE
4 BEAUVALLON
5 GRAND-PRIX
6 MC CULLOCH
7 KANDAHAR
8 RYAN
9 CHARRON
10 CURE DESLAURIERS
11 PROMENADE
12 FLYING MILE
13 DUNZEE
14 STANDARD
15 DESERRES
16 DEVIL'S RIVER
17 DUNCAN
18 MARIE CLAUDE ASSELIN
19 LOWELL THOMAS
20 ANDY MOE & AXEL
21 BEAUCHEMIN
22 FUDDLE DUDDLE
23 SISSY SCHUSS
24 EXPO
25 GAGNON
26 ROPE TOW

LIFTS

A DOUBLE CHAIR
B TRIPLE CHAIR
C POMA
D DOUBLE CHAIR
E DOUBLE CHAIR
F TRIPLE CHAIR
G POMA
H DOUBLE CHAIR
I DOUBLE CHAIR
J SINGLE CHAIR
K T-BAR

BIG WHITE

DRAWER 2039, STN. R — KELOWNA, BC V1X 4K5
TELEPHONE: /604 765-4111

AREA INFORMATION

BASE ELEVATION
5,450 feet

HOURS
9:00 a.m. - 3:30 p.m.
Free from 7:00 - 9:00 p.m., Tues., Fri., & Sat. night

LIFTS
4 chairs, 3 T-bars, 9,000 capacity per hour

LONGEST RUN
2 miles

VERTICAL DROP
1,900 feet

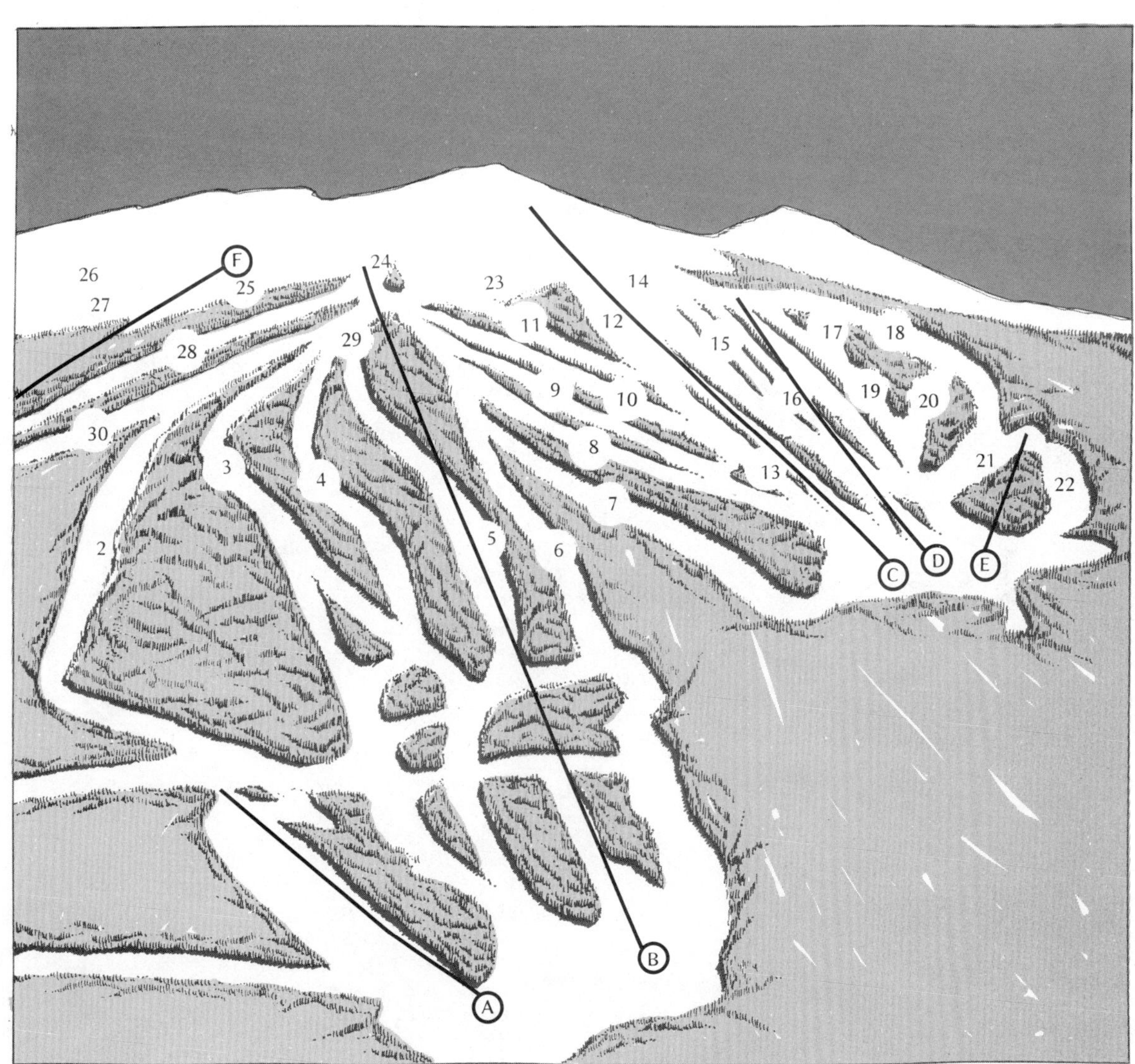

BIG WHITE SKI VILLAGE (CANADA) RUNS

1 ROOKIE
2 GOAT'S KICK
3 DRAGON'S TONGUE
4 PARADISE
5 EXHIBITION
6 PERFECTION
7 VILLAGER
8 SPECULATION
9 ROLLER COASTER
10 SQUIRREL
11 EASY OUT
12 HIGHWAY 33
13 SECRET
14 PAIGE'S RAGE
15 SPRUCE TRAIL
16 AL'S RETREAT
17 EASTER GULLY
18 POOFSTER'S PUFF
19 MERVYN'S CHOICE
20 KYLE'S CONNECTION
21 BUNNY BASIN
22 FREEWAY
23 ENCHANTED FOREST
24 THE CONNECTION
25 HAUTE ROUTE
26 WHITE FOOT TRAIL
27 FLAGPOLE
28 POWDER GULCH
29 PARADISE GLADES
30 SERWA'S SALUTE

BIG WHITE SKI VILLAGE (CANADA) CHAIRS/LIFTS

A 1,600 ft. CHALET T-BAR
B 6,000 ft. RIDGE CHAIR
C 5,500 ft. MAIN T-BAR
D 3,300 ft. EASTER TRIPLE CHAIR
E 1,600 ft. BUNNY T-BAR
F 3,500 ft. CHAIRLIFT

LODGING

DAS HOFBRAUHAUS
Condos, dining room & lounge
PONDEROSA INN (sauna, jacuzzi)
1 - 3 bedroom condos
PTARMIGAN INN (mixed sauna, hot & cold pools)
1 - 3 bedroom condos
WHITEFOOT LODGE (sauna, hot & cold pools)
Hotel, studio & 1 - 3 bedrooms, underground parking

RESTAURANTS

COPPER KETTLE DINING ROOM (Continental)
Breakfast, lunch, dinner / reservations advised for dinner
THE DAMFINO FIRESIDE NOOK (lunch, cocktails)
Entertainment nightly, except Fridays
DAS HOFBRAUHAUS (breakfast, lunch, dinner)
Dinner reservations advised
THE PEPPERMINT STICK (persons 18 & under)
Soda bar, dance floor, T.V. Room, games area
PINOCCHIO'S (Village Chalet)
Cafeteria style breakfast & lunch / family style dinner
SNOWSHOE SAM'S (breakfast, lunch, dinner)
Bear Trap Dining Room, pub and dancing
YOSEMITE'S RESTAURANT (breakfast, lunch, dinner)
Outdoor hot tubs for apres-ski

GIBSON PASS

DISTRICT SUPER. MANNING PROVINCIAL PARK
MANNING PARK, BC, V0X 1R0 (604) 840-8836

AREA INFORMATION

BASE ELEVATION
4,339 feet
HOURS
9:00 a.m. - 3:45 p.m.
LIFTS
2 chairlifts, 1 T-bar, 1 rope tow,
3,650 capacity per hour
LODGING
Manning Park Lodge (restaurant) 840-8822
SEASON
Mid-December to April, no snowmaking
SNOW PHONE 929-2358, 840-8836
TRAILS
30% beginner, 50% intermediate, 20% advanced
TRAVEL
Midway between Hope and Princeton on Hwy. 3, near the U.S. border, about 135 miles east of Vancouver.
VERTICAL DROP
1,388 feet

KIMBERLEY

BOX 40, KIMBERLEY, BC V1A 2Y5 (604) 427-4881

AREA INFORMATION

BASE ELEVATION
4,200 feet
HOURS
9:00 a.m. - 4:00 p.m.
9:00 a.m. - 3:30 p.m., North Bowl
5:00 - 10:00 p.m., Weds. thru Sat.
LIFTS
2 chairlifts, 1 T-bar, 2 rope tows,
4,200 capacity per hour
LONGEST RUN
4 miles
NURSERY
Out of diapers, arrangements can be made for babysitter to sit at your place of lodging; call Ski Area.
SEASON
December to April, snow making
SNOW PHONE
Call Ski Area
TRAILS
15% beginner, 60% intermediate, 25% expert
TRAVEL
On Highway 95A, 20 miles north of Cranbrook, 70 miles north of the U.S. border and 80 miles south of Radium Hot Springs.
VERTICAL DROP
2,300 feet

LODGING

ALPINE MOTEL (ski wax room)
1730 Warren Ave., V1A 1R8 427-3101
KIMBERLEY CABINS COURT
1 mi. N. on Hwy. 95A
Site 9, Box 1, SS No. 1, V1A 2Y3 427-3034
KIMBROOK INN
(dining room, coffee shop, lounge, pub, dancing)
2665 Warren Ave.. 427-4855
NORTH STAR MOTEL
1 mi. N. on Hwy. 95A
Box 6, V1A 2Y5 427-3813
PURCELL CHALET
Hwy. 95A South
Box 259, S. Kimberley V0B 1Z0 427-3181
PURCELL RESORT HOTEL
At the slopes, call Ski Area
ROCKY MOUNTAIN CONDOMINIUM RESORT HOTEL
(dining room, lounge)
At the slopes, call Ski Area
SYLVIA MOTEL
455 Ross St., V1A 2C5. 427-2203
TRAVELLAIRE MOTEL
2660 Warren Ave., V1A 1T5 427-2252

RESTAURANTS

AIKMAN'S RESTAURANT
175 Deer Park Ave. 427-3626

GAUSTHAUS DINING
240 Spokane St.. 427-4851
KIMBERLEY GARDEN RESTAURANT
(Oriental, Western)
190 Spokane St., in the Plaza 427-3366

TOD MTN.

BOX 865, KAMPLOOPS BC V2C 5M8
TELEPHONE: (604) 372-5757

AREA INFORMATION

BASE ELEVATION
3,963 feet
HOURS
9:00 a.m. - 3:15 p.m., through February 14th
9:00 a.m. - 3:30 p.m., through April
LIFTS
3 chairs, 2 platter lifts, 1 rope tow,
3,200 capacity per hour
LONGEST RUN
7 miles
NURSERY
Age 3 & up, call Ski Area
SEASON
Early December to late April, no snowmaking
SNOW PHONE 578-7151
TRAILS
25% beginner, 25% intermediate, 50% advanced
TRAVEL
Highways 1, 5 or 97, 33 miles northeast of Kamloops, which is serviced by Canadian National and Canadian Pacific Railways, Pacific Western Airlines and by Greyhound Bus Lines.
VERTICAL DROP
3,100 feet

TOD MOUNTAIN (CANADA) RUNS
1 5 MILE
2 CRYSTAL RUN
3 TRANS CANADA
4 CAHILTY
5 DYNAMITE
6 5-MILE CAT TRACK
7 LOWER EXHIBITION 1
8 OVER YONDER
9 MINI HEADWALL
10 LOWER CHIEF
11 WEST BOWL
12 TRAIL TO MID-STATION
13 7 MILE TRAIL
14 CARIBOO
15 UPPER EXHIBITION
16 THE ALLEY
17 SHORTCUT
18 SUNNY SIDE
19 THE RIDGE
20 ROLLER COASTER
21 EXPO
22 CHALLENGER
23 RIDGE BY-PASS
24 HIDDEN VALLEY
25 CHUTE
26 BIG "HEADWALL"
27 CHIEF

TOD MOUNTAIN (CANADA) LIFTS
A BURFIELD CHAIR
B SHUSWAP CHAIR
C CRYSTAL CHAIR
D BIG PLATTER LIFT
E LITTLE PLATTER LIFT
F HANDLE TOW

CARIBOU HELICOPTER SKIING LTD.

BOX 1824, BANFF, AL T0L 0C0 (403) 762-4171

AREA INFORMATION

AREA

Helicopters are based in Blue River, British Columbia, and fly into the Cariboos going west and the Monashees to the east, a region about 60 miles long and 20 miles wide, with a variety of terrain from glaciers, ridges, steep drop-offs to wide and narrow gullies. Average slopes: 1,500 to 3,000 feet, up to a length of 6,000 ft.

GROUPS

Formed by choice and experience. A maximum of 4 groups per helicopter, and a maximum of 11 guests per group, or by arrangement.

GUIDES & PILOTS

Are familiar with the skiing places and are very skillful and safety conscious. Guides speak English, German and French.

SAFETY

Radio communication between each guide, helicopter and base. Each guest is supplied with an avalanche piep. Each guide carries a first aid kit, crevasse and avalanche rescue equipment; the helicopter carries the same, as well as equipment such as tents, food, stove, and oxygen.

SEASON

Mid-January to early May

TRAVEL

Blue River is 140 miles northeast of Kamloops via the Yellowhead Highway No. 5. A charter bus is arranged to pick up guests Saturday morning at the airport in Kamloops, returning the following Saturday afternoon. Serviced by Pacific Western Airlines and the Canadian National Railway. Blue River offers a 5,600 ft. asphalt air strip, altitude: 1,800 feet; check for snow clearance conditions before approach.

WEATHER

High country weather; however, going by the last ten years, excellent skiing 70 to 80% of the time.

KOOTENAY HELICOPTER SKIING

805 9TH ST., NELSON, BC V1L 3C1 (604) 352-2111

AREA INFORMATION

AREA

Skiers flown into regions of the Selkirk Mountains, according to ability. Combined heli-skiing and downhill skiing, or exclusive heli-skiing are offered.

SEASON

J nuary to April

TRAVEL

Junction of Highways 3A & 6 in Southeast British Columbia.

WEATHER & AVALANCHE CONDITIONS

When the guide or pilot feel there is a hazard, slopes are available at Rossland's Red Mountain and Nelson's Whitewater Ski Area nearby.

PURCELL HELICOPTER SKIING

BOX 1530, GOLDEN, BC V0A 1H0
TELEPHONE: (604) 344-5410

AREA INFORMATION

AREA

5 minute flight directly from the hotel to area south and east of Golden and north of the Bugaboos; over 150 runs, most between 4,000 and 9,000 feet with every type of exposure and terrain—on glaciers, open slopes and in the trees.

GUIDES

Members of Canadian & Int'l. Mountain Guides Assoc.

GROUPS

Maximum of 3 groups per helicopter, one guide for each group of 9 guests.

SAFETY

Radio communication between guides, pilot and base. All skiers are equipped with an Avalanche Beacon, and each slope is checked by the guides before skiers begin. Avalanche forecasting is a joint effort with the Snow and Avalanche Research Centre nearby.

SEASON

December 20th - January 30th, Low Season
January 31st - May 24th, High Season

TRAVEL

Junction of Hwy. 95 and Trans-Canada Hwy., 50 miles west of Lake Louise. Aircraft: 4,000 ft. paved landing strip on banks of Columbia River, radio unicom 122.8. Greyhound east and west daily; Cranbrook/Bugaboo Buslines south daily. Also, Canadian Pacific Rail has service east and west twice daily.

WEATHER

When cloudy or snowing, skiing is mostly below the treeline; marginal weather, in the trees. If there is bad visibility, a mini bus will take skiers to Lake Louise.

ADDENDA

UNITED STATES

ALABAMA

CLOUDMONT

Mentone, AL 35984 (205) 634-3841

AREA INFORMATION

BASE ELEVATION
1,650 feet
HOURS
9:00 a.m. - 4:00 p.m.
6:00 - 10:00 p.m.
LIFTS
3 tows, 1,500 capacity per hour
SEASON
Mid-December to mid-March
Poly-snow slope, summer
SNOW PHONE
Call Ski Area
TRAVEL
40 miles from Chattanooga via I-24, I-59 & Rt. 117
VERTICAL DROP
150 feet

ALASKA

ARCTIC VALLEY

2710 Juneau St., Anchorage, AK 99504 (907) 272-7767

AREA INFORMATION

BASE ELEVATION
2,500 feet
HOURS
9:30 a.m. - 4:30 p.m., or until dark
LIFTS
2 chairlifts, 1 bar, 3 tows, 3,100 capacity per hour
SEASON
Early December to late April, no snowmaking
SNOW PHONE
Call Ski Area
TRAILS
20% beginner, 60% intermediate, 20% advanced
TRAVEL
Northeast of Anchorage, 15 miles.
VERTICAL DROP
1,400 feet

CLEARY SUMMIT

Fairbanks, AK 99701 (907) 456-5520

AREA INFORMATION

HOURS
Open weekends
LIFTS
3 bars, 2,400 capacity per hour
LONGEST RUN
6,000 feet
SEASON
November to May
SNOW PHONE
Call Ski Area
TRAILS
20% beginner, 65% intermediate, 15% advanced
TRAVEL
20 miles north of Fairbanks, Steese Highway
VERTICAL DROP
1,200 feet

EAGLECREST

490 S. Franklin St., Juneau, AK 99801 (907) 586-3700

AREA INFORMATION

BASE ELEVATION
1,200 feet
HOURS
10:00 a.m. - 3:00 p.m., Wed. thru Sun.
Until 4:00 p.m., March & April
Fri. & Sat., night skiing
LIFTS
2 chairlifts, 1 bar, 1 tow, 1,150 capacity per hour
LONGEST RUN
2 miles

SEASON
Late November to late April,
About 1 inch of snow daily
SNOW PHONE 586-6464
TRAILS
10% beginner, 20% intermediate, 70% advanced
VERTICAL DROP
1,400 feet

MT. EYAK

Box 267, Cordova, AK 99574 (907) 424-7455

AREA INFORMATION

BASE ELEVATION
250 feet
HOURS
Weekends, day only
LIFTS
1 chairlift, 2 tows, 500 capacity per hour
SEASON
December to May
SNOW PHONE
Call Ski Area
TRAILS
15% beginner, 50% intermediate, 25% advanced
TRAVEL
By plane or ferry.
VERTICAL DROP
900 feet

VIKING

Petersburg, AK 99833 (907) 772-3508

AREA INFORMATION

BASE ELEVATION
500 feet
HOURS
9:00 a.m. - 5:00 p.m., weekends & holidays
LIFTS
1 tow, 250 capacity per hour
LONGEST RUN
1,800 feet
NURSERY
Child care in Petersburg, call Ski Area
SEASON
November to mid-March
TRAILS
1 beginner, 1 intermediate, 2 advanced
VERTICAL DROP
500 feet

A R I Z O N A

ARIZONA SNOW BOWL

Box 158, Flagstaff, AZ 86002 (602) 774-0562

AREA INFORMATION

BASE ELEVATION
9,500 feet
HOURS
9:00 a.m. - 4:00 p.m.
LIFTS
1 chairlift, 1 bar, 5 tows, 1,500 capacity per hour
LONGEST RUN
1½ miles
NURSERY
Call Ski Area for information, child care in town
SEASON
Mid-November to April
SNOW PHONE 779-4577
TRAILS
30% beginner, 30% intermediate, 40% advanced
TRAVEL
14 miles from Flagstaff via Rt. 180 N.
VERTICAL DROP
2,100 feet

MT. LEMMON

Mt. Lemmon, AZ 85619 (602) 791-9791

AREA INFORMATION

BASE ELEVATION
8,130 feet
LIFTS
1 tow, 750 capacity per hour
SEASON
Mid-December to mid—April
TRAILS
20% beginner, 45% intermediate, 35% advanced
TRAVEL
26 miles northeast of Tucson, Catalina Hwy.
In Coronado National Forest
VERTICAL DROP
870 feet

SUNRISE

McNary, AZ 85930 (602) 334-2122

AREA INFORMATION

BASE ELEVATION
9,300 feet
HOURS
9:00 a.m. - 4:00 p.m.

LIFTS
3 chairlifts, 1 tow, 3,500 capacity per hour
LONGEST RUN
3 miles
NURSERY
By day or hour 334-2144
SEASON
Mid-November to mid-April, snowmaking
SNOW PHONE
Call Ski Area
TRAILS
30% beginner, 45% intermediate, 25% advanced
TRAVEL
On Hwy. 60; Pinetop, 30 miles; Phoenix, 210. Airstrip, 6,000 feet long, at Springerville.
VERTICAL DROP
1,440 feet

WILLIAMS

Williams, AZ 86046 (602) 635-2633

AREA INFORMATION

BASE ELEVATION
7,600 feet
HOURS
9:30 a.m. - 4:00 p.m., weekends & holidays
LIFTS
1 tow, 150 capacity per hour
SEASON
Mid-December to mid-April
SNOW PHONE
Call Ski Area
TRAILS
20% beginner, 70% intermediate, 10% advanced
TRAVEL
32 miles from Flagstaff, I-40
VERTICAL DROP
450 feet

C A L I F O R N I A

BADGER PASS

Yosemite, CA 95389 (209) 372-4611

AREA INFORMATION

BASE ELEVATION
7,200 feet
HOURS
9:00 a.m. - 4:30 p.m.
LIFTS
3 chairs, 2 T-bars, 1 tow, 4,700 capacity per hour
LODGING 373-4171
LONGEST RUN
1 mile
SEASON
Mid-November to mid-April, no snowmaking
SNOW PHONE 372-4808
TRAILS
30% beginner, 50% intermediate, 20% expert
TRAVEL
San Francisco, via Rt. 120 E., 220 miles; Los Angeles, via I-5 & Rt. 41, 313 miles; Las Vegas via Rt. 395 & Rt. 120 E., 340 miles; Reno, Rt. 120 W., 314 miles.
VERTICAL DROP
900 feet

EMERGENCY NUMBERS

MEDICAL CLINIC 372-4637
PARK SERVICE DISPATCHER 372-4461
TOWING SERVICE . . . . 372-4611 X 221

RECREATION

MOUNTAINEERING
Yosemite Park & Curry Co.,
Yosemite National Park, CA 95389 . . 372-4611 X 244
RENTAL STABLES/TOURS 372-4611

SERVICES

AUTO RENTAL

AT FRESNO AIRPORT
Avis, Budget, Hertz, Thrifty

BUS

GREYHOUND & TRAILWAYS
From San Francisco & Los Angeles, connects with Yosemite Transportation System in Merced.
YOSEMITE TRANSPORTATION SYSTEM
Between Merced & Yosemite Valley, direct connection with Amtrak & Golden Gate Airlines.

BOREAL

Truckee, CA 95734 (916) 426-3666

AREA INFORMATION

BASE ELEVATION
7,200 feet
HOURS
9:00 a.m. - 4:30 p.m.
4:30 - 10:00 p.m.
LIFTS
8 chairlifts, 8,400 capacity per hour, 4,000 daily maximum
LONGEST RUN
1 mile
SEASON
Late November to mid-April, snowmaking
SNOW PHONE 982-1771

TRAILS
20% beginner, 60% intermediate, 20% advanced
TRAVEL
I-80, 10 miles from Truckee; Reno, 45 miles; Sacramento, 90 miles.
VERTICAL DROP
600 feet

COPPERVALE

Susanville, CA 96130 (916) 257-6181

AREA INFORMATION

BASE ELEVATION
5,400 feet
HOURS
1:00 - 4:00 p.m., Tues. & Thurs.
9:00 a.m. - 4:00 p.m., weekends
LIFTS
1 bar, 1 tow, 1,200 capacity
LONGEST RUN
1,600 feet
SEASON
Late November to mid-April
SNOW PHONE
Call Ski Area
TRAILS
25% beginner, 50% intermediate, 25% advanced
TRAVEL
Between Susanville & Westwood
15 miles from Susanville

DODGE RIDGE

Pinecrest, CA 95364 (209) 965-3474

AREA INFORMATION

BASE ELEVATION
6,600 feet
HOURS
9:00 a.m. - 4:00 p.m.
LIFTS
6 chairlifts, 6 tows, 10,800 capacity per hour
LONGEST RUN
4,200 feet
NURSERY
Ages 2 - 8, call Ski Area
SEASON
Late November to mid-April, no snowmaking
SNOW PHONE 982-1771
TRAILS
20% beginner, 60% intermediate, 20% advanced
TRAVEL
Rt. 108 to Rt. 49, 30 miles from Sonora; 170 miles from San Francisco. Airport at Columbia, nearby.
VERTICAL DROP
1,000 feet

GRANLIBAKKEN

Tahoe City, CA 95730 (916) 583-4242

AREA INFORMATION

BASE ELEVATION
6,330 feet
HOURS
9:00 a.m. - 4:30 p.m.
LIFTS
1 bar, 450 capacity per hour
SEASON
Early December to Late April
TRAILS
Open slope, 50% beginner, 50% intermediate
TRAVEL
From I-80, take Rt. 89 S.
VERTICAL DROP
280 feet

HORSE MOUNTAIN

Eureka, CA 95501 (707) 443-6464

AREA INFORMATION

BASE ELEVATION
4,400 feet
HOURS
Wednesday afternoon, Saturday, Sunday
LIFTS
4 tows, 2,500 capacity per hour
LONGEST RUN
4,000 feet
SEASON
Early January to early April, snowmaking
SNOW PHONE
Call Ski Area
TRAILS
Open and tree-lined runs
TRAVEL
From Eureka, 40 miles, Rt. 299
to ten mile access route
VERTICAL DROP
600 feet

JUNE MOUNTAIN

June Lake, CA 93529 (714) 648-7733

AREA INFORMATION

BASE ELEVATION
7,650 feet
HOURS
8:00 a.m. - 4:30 p.m., weekdays
7:30 a.m. - 4:30 p.m., weekends
4:30 - 10:00 p.m., night skiing

LIFTS
5 chairlifts, 1 bar, 6,000 capacity per hour
LONGEST RUN
2 miles
SEASON
Mid-November to mid-April, snowmaking
SNOW PHONE 648-7545
TRAILS
30% beginner, 45% intermediate, 25% advanced
TRAVEL
15 miles from Mammoth Lakes; from Los Angeles, 330 miles via I-15 to U.S. 395; Reno, 145 miles via U.S. 395 N. Airport at Mammoth Lakes.
VERTICAL DROP
2,560 feet

KRATKA RIDGE

Box 186, La Canada, CA 91011 (213) 790-4683

AREA INFORMATION

BASE ELEVATION
6,800 feet
HOURS
8:30 a.m. - 4:30 p.m.
LIFTS
1 chairlift, 6 tows, 500 capacity per hour
LONGEST RUN
3,000 feet
SEASON
Mid-December to mid-April
SNOW PHONE
Call Ski Area
TRAVEL
35 miles from La Canada via Rt. 2
VERTICAL DROP
700 feet

LASSEN NATIONAL PARK

Mineral, CA 96063 (916) 595-3306

AREA INFORMATION

BASE ELEVATION
6,600 feet
HOURS
9:00 a.m. - 4:00 p.m.
Fri., Sat., Sun., & school holidays
LIFTS
1 bar, 2 tows, 1,200 capacity per hour
LONGEST RUN
¾ miles
SEASON
Late November to mid-April
SNOW PHONE
Call Ski Area
TRAILS
5 slopes
TRAVEL
49 miles from Red Bluff, I-5, Rt. 36 E.
VERTICAL DROP
600 feet

MT. REBA AT BEAR VALLEY

Bear Valley, CA 95223 (209) 753-2301

AREA INFORMATION

BASE ELEVATION
6,400 feet
HOURS
9:00 a.m. - 4:00 p.m.
LIFTS
7 chairlifts, 8,900 capacity per hour
LONGEST RUN
3 miles
SEASON
November to late April, no snowmaking
SNOW PHONE 982-1771
TRAILS
25% beginner, 50% intermediate, 25% advanced
TRAVEL
From Sacramento, Rt. 49 S. to Rt. 4 N. to Bear Valley. From Stockton, 105 miles via Routes 12 N., 49 S. and 4 N. Airports at Sacramento and Stockton.
VERTICAL DROP
2,100 feet

MT. WATERMAN

817 Lynnhaven Lane, La Canada,CA 91011 (213) 790-2002

AREA INFORMATION

BASE ELEVATION
7,200
HOURS
8:00 a.m. - 5:00 p.m.
LIFTS
2 chairlifts, 2,200 capacity per hour
LONGEST RUN
4,000 feet,
SEASON
November to May
SNOW PHONE
Call Ski Area
TRAVEL
35 miles northeast of La Canada via Angeles Crest Hwy.
VERTICAL DROP
800 feet

PLUMAS-EUREKA SKI BOWL

Quincy, CA 95971 (916) 836-2317

AREA INFORMATION

BASE ELEVATION
5,550 feet
HOURS
10:00 a.m. - 4:30 p.m.
Wed., Sat., Sun. & holidays
LIFTS
2 pomas, 1 tow, 950 capacity per hour
LONGEST RUN
1 mile
SEASON
Mid-December to mid-March
SNOW PHONE
Call Ski Area
TRAILS
Open and tree-lined runs
TRAVEL
30 miles west of Quincy, Rt. 70
VERTICAL DROP
650 feet

POWDER BOWL

Tahoe City, CA 95730 (916) 583-4373

AREA INFORMATION

BASE ELEVATION
5,450 feet
LIFTS
2 bars, 1 tow, 1,200 capacity per hour
SEASON
November to April
SNOW PHONE
Call Ski Area
TRAILS
Beginner and intermediate
TRAVEL
Between Alpine Meadows and Tahoe City, Rt. 89
VERTICAL DROP
850 feet

SHIRLEY MEADOWS

Wofford Heights, CA 93285 (714) 379-2871

AREA INFORMATION

HOURS
10:00 a.m. - 4:00 p.m., weekends
LIFTS
3 tows, 1,400 capacity per hour
LONGEST RUN
3,000 feet
SEASON
December to April
SNOW PHONE
Call Ski Area
TOP ELEVATION
7,000 feet
TRAILS
40% beginner, 30% intermediate, 30% advanced
TRAVEL
8 miles west of Wofford Heights, Evans Rd.

SIGNAL HILL

Norden, CA 95724 (916) 426-3632

AREA INFORMATION

BASE ELEVATION
7,500 feet
HOURS
9:30 a.m. - 4:00 p.m., weekends, holidays
LIFTS
1 tow, 400 capacity per hour
SEASON
Late November to mid-April
SNOW PHONE
Call Ski Area
TRAILS
Beginner and intermediate
TRAVEL
From Soda Springs, 4 miles east, I-80
VERTICAL DROP
350 feet

SKI GREEN VALLEY

Green Valley Lake, CA 92341 (714) 867-2338

AREA INFORMATION

BASE ELEVATION
7,200 feet
HOURS
9:00 a.m. - 4:30 p.m., weekends & holidays
LIFTS
2 bars, 2 tows
SEASON
December to mid-April
SNOW PHONE
Call Ski Area
TRAVEL
From San Bernardino, 22 miles, Rt. 330
VERTICAL DROP
300 feet

SKI SUNDOWN

Kirkwood, CA 95646 (209) 258-8543

AREA INFORMATION

BASE ELEVATION
6,450 feet
HOURS
9:00 a.m. - 4:00 p.m.
LIFTS
3 chairlifts, 1 tow
LONGEST RUN
Just under 2 miles
SEASON
Late November to mid-April, no snowmaking
SNOW PHONE
Call Ski Area
TRAILS
14 runs
TRAVEL
Rt. 88, 12 miles west of Kirkwood;
Tahoe City, 45 miles.
VERTICAL DROP
1,200 feet

STOVER

Chester, CA 96020 phone unlisted

AREA INFORMATION

HOURS
9:00 a.m. - 4:00 p.m.
LIFTS
1 bar, 1 tow, 900 capacity per hour
LONGEST RUN
½ mile
SEASON
Late November to mid-April
SNOW PHONE
Call Ski Area
TRAILS
25% beginner, 35% intermediate, 40% advanced
TRAVEL
4 miles west of Chester; Chico, 70 miles
VERTICAL DROP
500 feet

TAHOE SKI BOWL

Homewood, CA 95718 (916) 525-5224

AREA INFORMATION

BASE ELEVATION
6,250 feet
HOURS
9:00 a.m. - 4:30 p.m.
LIFTS
2 chairlifts, 1 tow, 3,200 capacity per hour
LONGEST RUN
1½ miles
SEASON
Late November to mid-April, snowmaking
SNOW PHONE
Call Ski Area
TRAILS
40% beginner, 40% intermediate, 20% advanced
TRAVEL
7 miles south of Tahoe City via
Rt. 89; Reno Airport, 50 miles.
VERTICAL DROP
1,600 feet

WOLVERTON

Sequoia Nat'l. Park, CA 93262 (209) 565-3381

AREA INFORMATION

BASE ELEVATION
7,220 feet
HOURS
9:30 a.m. - 4:00 p.m., weekends, holidays
LIFTS
3 tows, 900 capacity per hour
LONGEST RUNS
1,000 feet
SNOW PHONE
Call Ski Area
TRAILS
Open and tree-lined runs
Beginner to advanced
TRAVEL
20 miles from Three Rivers
Rt. 198 & Generals Highway
VERTICAL DROP
170 feet

COLORADO

BERTHOUD PASS

Box 520, Idaho Springs, CO 80452 (303) 569-9885

AREA INFORMATION

BASE ELEVATION
11,022 feet
HOURS
9:00 a.m. - 4:00 p.m., Tuesday thru Sunday
LIFTS
1 chairlift, 1 T-bar, 1 tow, 1,100 capacity per hour
LONGEST RUN
6,000 feet
SEASON
Late October to early June
SNOW PHONE
Call Ski Area
TRAILS
40% beginner, 40% intermediate, 20% advanced
TRAVEL
From Denver, 57 miles via I-70 and U.S. 40.
VERTICAL DROP
993 feet

CONQUISTADOR

601 Yale Pl., Canon City, CO 81212 (303) 275-2049

AREA INFORMATION

BASE ELEVATION
9,000 feet
HOURS
9:00 a.m. - 4:00 p.m., Thursday thru Sunday
LIFTS
2 pony lifts, 700 capacity per hour
LONGEST RUN
¼ mile
SEASON
Early December to early April, snowmaking
SNOW PHONE
Call Ski Area
TRAILS
100% beginner
TRAVEL
From Denver, 130 miles via I-25.
VERTICAL DROP
250 feet

ELDORA

Box 430, Nederland, CO 80466 (303) 258-3211, 447-8012

AREA INFORMATION

BASE ELEVATION
9,300 feet
HOURS
9:00 a.m. - 5:30 p.m.
5:30 - 9:30 p.m.
LIFTS
4 chairlifts, 1 T-bar, 6,000 capacity per hour
LONGEST RUN
1 mile
NURSERY
1 month to 5 years, call Ski Area
SEASON
Early November to early April, snowmaking
SNOW PHONE 447-8011
TRAILS
15% beginner, 65% intermediate, 20% advanced
TRAVEL
From Denver, Rt. 36 for 24 miles to
Boulder, then 21 miles via Rt. 119.
VERTICAL DROP
1,100 feet

HESPERUS

Durango, CO 81301 (303) 385-4555

AREA INFORMATION

HOURS
9:00 a.m. - 4:00 p.m., Tues. thru Sun.
LIFTS
1 T-bar, 1 tow
RESTAURANT
At the slopes, call Ski Area
SEASON
December to mid-April
TRAVEL
11 miles from Durango, Rt. 16
VERTICAL DROP
600 feet

HIDDEN VALLEY

Box 98, Estes Park, CO 80517 (303) 586-4165, 586-4887

AREA INFORMATION

BASE ELEVATION
9,400 feet
HOURS
9:00 a.m. - 4:00 p.m.
LIFTS
2 pomas, 2 T-bars, 3,200 capacity per hour
LONGEST RUN
1¼ miles
SEASON
Late November to early April

SNOW PHONE
Call Ski Area
TRAILS
30% beginner, 40% intermediate, 30% advanced
TRAVEL
From Denver, 75 miles via I-25, Routes 66 and 36.
VERTICAL DROP
2,000 feet

LODGING

ANDERSON'S WONDERVIEW (kitchen)
Box 427 586-4158
ASPEN GROVE COTTAGES (kitchen)
258 E. Riverside Drive 586-4584
BIG BEND MOTEL
Big Thompson Ave.. 586-3875
BRADSHAW'S BLUE CHIP COTTAGES (kitchen)
257 E. Riverside Drive 586-5881
BRANDING IRON MOTEL
1010 S. St. Vrain 586-4108
CARIBOU CHALET
1450 Big Thompson Ave. 586-2358
CASTLE MOUNTAIN LODGE (kitchen)
1700 Fall River Rd 586-3664
CIRCLE A LODGE (kitchen)
1889 Fall River Road. 586-4385
DEER CREST CHALETS
1400 Fall River Road. 586-2324
EIKER'S MOTOR LODGE
Spruce Drive. 586-3151
FAWN VALLEY INN (restaurant, kitchen)
2760 Fall River Road. 586-2388
4 SEASONS INN
1130 W. Elkhorn Ave. 586-5693
FOUR WINDS MOTOR LODGE
1120 Big Thompson Ave. 586-3313
HIGH COUNTRY MOTEL
321 South St. Vrain Hwy. 586-3443
HOBBY HORSE MOTOR LODGE
800 Big Thompson Ave. 586-3336
HOLIDAY INN RESORT (restaurant, lounge)
101 S. St. Vrain Hwy. 586-2332
THE HOMESTEAD (kitchen)
Box 1178 586-3426
THE INN AT ESTES (restaurant, lounge)
1701 Big Thompson Ave. 586-5363
LAZY H GUEST RANCH (29 miles from Area)
Allenspark 80510. 747-2532
LAZY R COTTAGES (kitchen)
891 Moraine 586-3708
MARK TWAIN MANOR (kitchen)
248 E. Riverside Drive 586-4100
MILES COTTAGES (kitchen)
1250 S. St. Vrain Hwy.. 586-3185
MOUNTAIN 8 INN
1220 Big Thompson Ave. 586-4421
MOUNTAIN MEADOW MOTEL & CABINS (kitchen)
381 S. St. Vrain Hwy. 586-3480
NICKY'S MOTOR LODGE (restaurant, kitchen)
1350 West U.S. 34 586-2123
OLYMPUS LODGE (kitchen)
2365 Big Thompson Ave. 586-3223
PEAK TO PEAK MOTOR LODGE (kitchen)
760 S. St. Vrain Hwy. 586-4451
PONDEROSA LODGE (kitchen)
1820 Fall River Road. 586-4233
RAM'S HORN COTTAGES (kitchen)
Spur 66. 586-4338
ROCKY MOUNTAIN MOTEL
945 Moraine Ave.. 586-3485
ROCKY SPUR COTTAGES (kitchen)
2121 Moraine Park Route 586-2392
SADDLE & SURREY MOTEL (kitchen)
1341 S. St. Vrain Hwy.. 586-3326
SHALAKO RESORT LODGE (kitchen)
Hwy. 36 E.. 586-2275
SILVER SADDLE MOTOR LODGE (kitchen)
1260 Big Thompson Ave. 586-4476
SKYLINE COTTAGES (kitchen)
Moraine Park Route 586-2886
STERLING COTTAGES (kitchen)
1241 High Drive. 586-4637
STONY KNOB COTTAGES (kitchen)
Moraine Park Route 586-4343
SUNNYSIDE KNOLL MOTEL & CABINS (kitchen)
1675 Fall River Road. 586-5759
SUNSET MOTEL (kitchen)
481 W. Elkhorn Ave.. 586-4237
SUNWATCH TOWNHOMES (kitchen)
Black Canyon Hills 226-9204
THATCHTOP MOUNTAIN CHALETS (kitchen)
Aspen Ave.. 586-2003
TINY TOWN COTTAGES (kitchen)
830 Moraine Ave.. 586-4249
TRAIL'S WEST COTTAGES (kitchen)
1710 Fall River Road. 586-4629
TRIPLE R COTTAGES (kitchen)
1000 E. Riverside Drive 586-4379
VACATION INN (kitchen)
Black Canyon Hills 586-2737
VALHALLA COTTAGES (kitchen)
Highways 36 & 66 586-3284
THE VILLAGER MOTEL
295 W. Elkhorn Ave.. 586-3557
WATER WHEEL LODGES (kitchen)
1750 Fall River Road. 586-3100
YMCA OF THE ROCKIES (kitchen)
Spur, Hwy. 66. 586-3341

HOWELSEN

Steamboat Springs, CO 80477 (303) 879-4300

AREA INFORMATION

BASE ELEVATION
6,690 feet

HOURS
12:00 - 6:00 p.m., 7:00 - 9:00 p.m., Tues. - Sun.
LIFTS
1 poma lift, 1 tow, 850 capacity per hour
LONGEST RUN
1 mile
SEASON
Mid-December to early April
SNOW PHONE
Call Ski Area
TRAILS
3 slopes, 37 degree grade
TRAVEL
Area is in Steamboat, 155 miles from Denver, I-70 W., Rt. 9 N., U.S. 40 W.
VERTICAL DROP
440 feet

LOVELAND

Box 455, Georgetown, CO 80444 (303) 569-2288, 571-5580

AREA INFORMATION

BASE ELEVATION
10,800 feet
HOURS
9:00 a.m. - 4:00 p.m.
8:30 a.m. - 4:00 p.m., weekends
LIFTS
6 chairlifts, 2 pomas, 8,200 capacity per hour
LONGEST RUN
1½ miles
NURSERY
Ages 5 - 12, call Ski Area
SEASON
Mid-October to early-May, snowmaking
SNOW PHONE
Call Ski Area
TRAILS
25% beginner, 50% intermediate, 25% advanced
TRAVEL
From Denver, 56 miles via I-70 W.
VERTICAL DROP
1,430 feet

LODGING

DILLON HOLIDAY INN (restaurant, lounge)
Box 428, Dillon 80435 668-5000
GEORGETOWN MOTOR INN (restaurant, lounge)
Box 277 569-3201
LAURITAS (restaurant, lounge)
Box 488 569-2931
THE LODGE AT GEORGETOWN (restaurant, lounge)
Box 278 569-3211
RAMADA INN
Box 368, Silverthorne 80498 468-6200

MONARCH

Garfield, CO 81227 (303) 539-4060

AREA INFORMATION

BASE ELEVATION
11,000 feet
HOURS
9:00 a.m. - 4:00 p.m.
LIFTS
2 chairlifts, 1 poma, 2,700 capacity per hour
LODGING (child care, restaurant, lounge)
Ramada Inn, U.S. 50 539-2581
LONGEST RUN
1½ miles
SEASON
November to April
SNOW PHONE
Call Ski Area
TRAILS
20% beginner, 65% intermediate, 15% advanced
TRAVEL
From Denver, 160 miles via Rt. 285; 3 miles west of Garfield in the San Isabel National Forest.
VERTICAL DROP
1,000 feet

PIKES PEAK

96 Raven Hills Ct., Colo. Springs, CO 80901 (303) 684-9868

AREA INFORMATION

BASE ELEVATION
10,500 feet
HOURS
9:30 a.m. - 3:30 p.m.
LIFTS
2 pomas, 1 rope tow, 1,000 capacity per hour
LODGING 635-1551
LONGEST RUN
1 mile
SEASON
Early November to early April
SNOW PHONE
Call Ski Area
TRAILS
75% beginner, 20% intermediate, 5% advanced
TRAVEL
From Denver, 80 miles via I-25 and U.S. 24.; 20 miles from Colorado Springs via U.S. 24.
VERTICAL DROP
1,000 feet

POWDERHORN

Box 1826, Grand Junction, CO 81501 (303) 242-5637

AREA INFORMATION

BASE ELEVATION
8,200 feet
HOURS
9:30 a.m. - 4:00 p.m., weekdays
8:30 a.m. - 4:00 p.m., weekends
LIFTS
2 chairlifts, 1 poma, 2,200 capacity per hour
LONGEST RUN
2 miles
SEASON
Late November to mid-April, snowmaking
SNOW PHONE
Call Ski Area
TRAILS
15% beginner, 65% intermediate, 20% advanced
TRAVEL
From Denver, 250 miles via I-70 and Rt. 65.
VERTICAL DROP
1,600 feet

LODGING

BAR-X MOTEL (restaurant, lounge, Area - 40 miles)
1600 North Ave. 243-1311
HOLIDAY INN (restaurant, lounge, Area - 40 miles)
Box 1725, 755 Horizon Dr. 243-6790
HOWARD JOHNSON'S (restaurant, lounge, Area - 40 miles)
752 Horizon Dr.. 243-5150
LE CHALET (restaurant, lounge, near Area - shuttle)
Box 150, Mesa 81643 268-5410

SHARKTOOTH

1721 13th Ave., Greeley, CO 80631 (303) 352-2565

AREA INFORMATION

BASE ELEVATION
4,600 feet
HOURS
7:00 - 10:00 p.m., Tuesday thru Friday
10:00 a.m. - 5:00 p.m., Sundays & holiday season
LIFTS
1 pony lift, 400 capacity per hour
LONGEST RUN
1,000 feet
SEASON
Mid-December to early March
SNOW PHONE
Call Ski Area
TRAILS
Beginner and intermediate
50% easiest, 30% more difficult, 20% most difficult
TRAVEL
From Denver, 50 miles via I-25 N., U.S. 34 E.
VERTICAL DROP
150 feet

SKI BROADMOOR

Box 1439, Colorado Springs, CO 80901 (303) 634-7711

AREA INFORMATION

BASE ELEVATION
6,200 feet
HOURS
10:00 a.m. - 10:00 p.m., Tues. thru Sat.
10:00 a.m. - 5:30 p.m., Sundays
LIFTS
1 chairlift, 1 tow, 600 capacity per hour
LONGEST RUN
2/3 mile
SEASON
Late November to mid-April, snowmaking
SNOW PHONE . . . . 634-7711, X 5460
TRAILS
60% beginner, 20% intermediate, 20% advanced
TRAVEL
From Denver, 66 miles via I-25; Colorado Springs, 4 miles via U.S. 85, U.S. 87 and Rt. 122.
VERTICAL DROP
600 feet

LODGING

BROADMOOR HOTEL (restaurant, lounge)
Colorado Springs 634-7711
4 SEASONS INN (restaurant, lounge)
Colorado Springs 576-5900
HOLIDAY INN (restaurant, lounge)
Colorado Springs 473-5530
HOWARD JOHNSON'S (restaurant, lounge)
Colorado Springs 598-1700

SKI COOPER

Box 973, Leadville, CO 80461 (303) 486-2277

AREA INFORMATION

BASE ELEVATION
10,500 feet
HOURS
9:00 a.m. - 4:00 p.m., Friday thru Sunday
Open daily during holidays
LIFTS
1 chairlift, 1 T-bar, 1 poma, 2,000 capacity per hour
LONGEST RUN
1¼ mile
SEASON
Late November to mid-April
SNOW PHONE
Call Ski Area
TRAILS
40% beginner, 50% intermediate, 10% advanced

SKI COOPER CONT.

TRAVEL
From Denver, 110 miles via I-70, Rt. 91 and U.S. 24
VERTICAL DROP
1,200 feet

LODGING

ALPS MOTEL
207 Elm St. 486-1223
BEL-AIR HOTEL
Spruce & Elm 486-0881
DELAWARE HOTEL
700 Harrison. 486-1155
MOUNTAIN PEAKS MOTEL
Harrison Ave. & Elm 486-3178
SILVER KING BEST WESTERN (restaurant, lounge)
2020 Poplar 486-2610

SKI IDLEWILD

Box 3, Winter Park, CO 80482 (303) 726-5562, 572-9523

AREA INFORMATION

BASE ELEVATION
8,700 feet
HOURS
9:00 a.m. - 4:00 p.m.
LIFTS
1 chair, 1 poma, 1,000 capacity per hour
LONGEST RUN
½ mile
SEASON
Late November to early April
SNOW PHONE
Call Ski Area
TRAILS
60% beginner, 40% more difficult
TRAVEL
From Denver, 72 miles via I-70 to U.S. 40, exit 232.
VERTICAL DROP
400 feet

LODGING

ALPENGLO MOTOR LODGE (rooms & kitchenettes)
Box 35 726-5294
ARAPAHOE LODGE (restaurant, lounge)
Box 44 726-8222
BRENNER'S SKI CHALET (¼ mile from area)
Box 15 726-5416
BROOKSIDE INN (restaurant, lounge)
Box 33 726-5944
LION'S GATE PINES LODGE (condos)
Box 113 726-8026
MILLERS IDLEWILD INN (restaurant, lounge)
Box 53. 726-5313
OLYMPIA MOTOR LODGE
Box 204 726-5539
SITZMARK LODGE (chalets, lounge)
Box 65 726-5453
SUNDOWNER MOTEL
Box 221 726-5452
TABERNASH LODGE (kitchenettes)
Box 576, Tabernash 80478 726-8264
VALLEY HI MOTEL
Box 11 726-5266
WINTER HAVEN SKI LODGE (restaurant, lounge)
Box 26 726-5353
WINTER PARK MEADOWS LODGE (condos)
Box 7. 726-5942

SKI SAN ISABEL

114 N. McCandless, Florence, CO 81226 (303) 275-1069

AREA INFORMATION

BASE ELEVATION
8,750 feet
HOURS
9:00 a.m. - 4:00 p.m., Friday thru Sunday
Open daily during holidays
LIFTS
1 pony lift, 2 rope tows, 1,400 capacity per hour
LONGEST RUN
1/5 mile
SEASON
Late November to early April
SNOW PHONE
Call Ski Area
TRAILS
85% beginner, 15% intermediate
TRAVEL
From Denver, 154 miles via I-25, Routes 96 and 165.
VERTICAL DROP
250 feet

SKI SUNLIGHT

Box 1061, Glenwood Springs, CO 81601 (303) 945-7491

AREA INFORMATION

BASE ELEVATION
8,150 feet
HOURS
9:00 a.m. - 4:00 p.m.
LIFTS
2 chairlifts, 1 bar, 1,500 capacity per hour
LONGEST RUN
4 miles

NURSERY
6 months and up, call Ski Area
SEASON
Late November to early April
SNOW PHONE
Call Ski Area
TRAILS
40% beginner, 30% intermediate, 30% advanced
TRAVEL
From Denver, 140 miles via I-70
VERTICAL DROP
1,580 feet

STONER

Cortez, CO 81321 (303) 882-4437

AREA INFORMATION

BASE ELEVATION
8,500 feet
HOURS
10:00 a.m. - 4:00 p.m., Sat., Sun., holidays
LIFTS
2 bars, 1 tow, 350 capacity per hour
LONGEST RUNS
4,000 feet
SEASON
Mid-December to early April
SNOW PHONE
Call Ski Area
TRAILS
10% beginner, 40% intermediate, 50% advanced
TRAVEL
26 miles northeast of Cortez, Rt. 145
VERTICAL DROP
1,250 feet

WOLF CREEK

Box 1036, Pagosa Springs, CO 81147 (303) 264-2533

AREA INFORMATION

BASE ELEVATION
10,650 feet
HOURS
9:00 a.m. - 4:00 p.m.
LIFTS
1 chairlift, 2 pomas, 1,900 capacity per hour
LONGEST RUN
1½ miles
SEASON
Mid-November to mid-April
SNOW PHONE
Call Ski Area
TRAILS
25% beginner, 45% intermediate, 30% advanced

TRAVEL
From Denver, 249 miles via I-25 and U.S. 160
VERTICAL DROP
1,125 feet

LODGING

THE ADOBE INN & MUD PUB (restaurant, lounge)
Box 1394 264-5404
CHINOOK MOTEL
Box 128, South Fork 81154. 873-9993
FOOTHILLS LODGE
Box 264, South Fork 81154. 873-5969
GASTHOF GRAMSHAMMER (Pepi's Restaurant, bar)
231 E. Gore Creek Dr. @ Bridge St.. 476-5626
HARVEY'S MOTEL
Box 67 264-5715
INN AT THE PASS (restaurant, lounge)
Box 1569 264-5385
INN MOTEL
Box 96, South Fork 873-5514
LOG HAVEN LODGE
Box 100, South Fork. 873-5321
PAGOSA LODGE (restaurant, lounge)
Box 245 . . . . 264-2271, (800) 528-1234
RAINBOW MOTEL (restaurant)
Box 41-C, South Fork 81154 873-5571
RELAY STATION (restaurant, lounge)
Box 205 264-2435
RIVER BEND RESORT
Box 172, South Fork 81154. 873-5344
RIVIERA MOTEL (restaurant, lounge)
Box 126, South Fork 81154. 873-5561
SAN JUAN MOTEL
Box 729 264-2262
SKY VIEW MOTEL
Box 74 264-5803
SPRING INN (restaurant, lounge)
Box 326 . . . . 264-2287, (800) 528-1234
SPRUCE LODGE
Box 181, South Fork 81154. 873-9980
WOLF CREEK RANCH
Box 40, South Fork 81154 873-5371

CONNECTICUT

MT. SOUTHINGTON

Southington, CT 06489 (203) 628-0954

AREA INFORMATION

BASE ELEVATION
100 feet
HOURS
9:30 a.m. - 10:30 p.m., weekdays
9:00 a.m. - 10:30 weekends
Night skiing from 5:00 p.m.
LIFTS
2 chairlifts, 1 J-bar, 3 T-bars,
1 tow, 4,800 capacity per hour
LONGEST RUN
1 mile
NURSERY
Ages 2 - 6, call Ski Area
SEASON
Late November to mid-March, snowmaking
SNOW PHONE
Call Ski Area
TRAVEL
From Hartford, 17 miles via I-84
VERTICAL DROP
420 feet

OHOHO

Woodstock, CT 06281 (203) 974-1040

AREA INFORMATION

BASE ELEVATION
600 feet
HOURS
1:00 - 9:00 p.m., weekdays
10:00 a.m. - 10:00 p.m., night skiing
5:00 - 10:00 p.m., night skiing
LIFTS
1 bar, 3 tows, 4,500 capacity per hour
LONGEST RUN
3,000 feet
SEASON
Early December to early April, snowmaking
SNOW PHONE
Call Ski Area
TRAILS
5 tree-lined slopes
TRAVEL
9 miles from Putnam, Rt. 171
VERTICAL DROP
300 feet

SKI SUNDOWN

New Hartford, CT 06057 (203) 379-0610

AREA INFORMATION

BASE ELEVATION
500 feet
HOURS
9:30 a.m. - 5:30 p.m., weekdays
8:30 a.m. - 4:30 p.m., weekends
6:30 - 10:00 p.m., nightly except Sunday
LIFTS
2 chairlifts, 1 bar, 1 tow, 3,500 capacity per hour
LONGEST RUN
Almost 1 mile
NURSERY
Ages 2 - 6, call Ski Area
SEASON
Early December to early April
SNOW PHONE
Call Ski Area
TRAILS
20% beginner, 60% intermediate, 20% advanced
TRAVEL
From Hartford, 22 miles via Rt. 44
to New Hartford; 2 miles via Rt. 219
VERTICAL DROP
540 feet

WOODBURY

Woodbury, CT 06798 (203) 263-2203

AREA INFORMATION

BASE ELEVATION
550 feet
HOURS
10:30 a.m. - 10:00 p.m., weekdays
9:00 a.m. - 10:00 p.m., Saturday
9:00 a.m. - 5:00 p.m., Sunday
LIFTS
1 chairlift, 1 bar, 1 tow, 2,300 capacity per hour
LONGEST RUN
¾ mile
SEASON
Early December to mid-March
SNOW PHONE
Call Ski Area
TRAVEL
From Waterbury, 17 miles; Woodbury, 4
VERTICAL DROP
300 feet

G E O R G I A

SKY VALLEY

Dillard, GA 30537 (404) 746-5301

AREA INFORMATION

HOURS
9:00 a.m. - 4:30 p.m., daily
6:00 - 10:00 p.m., Monday thru Friday
LIFTS
1 chairlift, 1 tow
SEASON
Mid-December to mid-March
SNOW PHONE
Call Ski Area
TRAILS
Two slopes, seven acres
TRAVEL
From Ashville, North Carolina, 50 miles
VERTICAL DROP
250 feet

I D A H O

BALD MOUNTAIN

Orofino, ID 83544 (208) 476-4942

AREA INFORMATION

HOURS
Weekends & holidays
LIFTS
1 T-bar, 1 tow, 1,200 capacity per hour
LONGEST RUN
1 mile
SEASON
Mid-December to mid-April
SNOW PHONE
Call Ski Area
TRAILS
Open runs
TRAVEL
6 miles north of Pierce, Rt. 11
VERTICAL DROP
970 feet

BEAR GULCH SKI BASIN

St. Anthony, ID 83445 (208) 527-3359

AREA INFORMATION

HOURS
Open weekends
LONGEST RUN
1 mile
SEASON
December to March
SNOW PHONE
Call Ski Area
TRAILS
1 trail, 6 open slopes
TRAVEL
In Targhee National Forest, 10 miles
northeast of Ashton, Route 47
VERTICAL DROP
1,240 feet

BLIZZARD SKI AREA

Moore, ID 83255 (208) 527-3359

AREA INFORMATION

BASE ELEVATION
5,700 feet
HOURS
10:00 a.m. - 4:00 p.m., weekends
LIFTS
1 bar, 1 tow
LONGEST RUN
¾ mile
SEASON
Late December to early March
SNOW PHONE
Call Ski Area
TRAILS
Open slopes
TRAVEL
20 miles west of Arco, U.S. 93A
VERTICAL DROP
800 feet

BRUNDAGE MOUNTAIN

McCall, ID 83638 (208) 634-2244

AREA INFORMATION

BASE ELEVATION
6,000 feet
HOURS
10:00 a.m. - 4:00 p.m.

LIFTS
2 chairlifts, 1 bar, 1 tow
SEASON
Mid-November to mid-April
SNOW PHONE
Call Ski Area
TRAVEL
From Boise, 105 miles via I-80
VERTICAL DROP
1,600 feet

CARIBOU SKI AREA

Pocatello, ID 83201 (208) 233-6134

AREA INFORMATION

HOURS
Wednesday to Sunday, days
Wednesday to Friday, nights
LIFTS
1 chairlift
SEASON
Early December to February
SNOW PHONE
Call Ski Area
TRAILS
Open slopes
TRAVEL
6 miles east of Pocatello
VERTICAL DROP
670 feet

COTTONWOOD BUTTE

Cottonwood, ID 83522 (208) 962-3624

AREA INFORMATION

BASE ELEVATION
4,820 feet
HOURS
10:00 a.m. - 4:00 p.m., weekends & holidays
7:00 - 10:30 p.m., Thursdays
LIFTS
1 bar, 1 tow, 500 capacity per hour
LONGEST RUN
3,000 feet
SEASON
Mid-December to late March
SNOW PHONE 962-3166
TRAVEL
7 miles from Cottonwood
U.S. 95 to access route
VERTICAL DROP
640 feet

KELLY CANYON

Idaho Falls, ID 83401 (208) 538-6261

AREA INFORMATION

BASE ELEVATION
5,600 feet
HOURS
10:00 a.m. - 4:00 p.m.
4:30 a.m. - 10:00 p.m.
LIFTS
3 chairlifts, 3 tows, 2,100 capacity per hour
LONGEST RUN
6,800 feet
NURSERY
Call Ski Area
SEASON
December to April
SNOW PHONE
Call Ski Area
TRAILS
7 runs, over 300 acres
TRAVEL
From Idaho Falls, 25 miles via Rt. 26
VERTICAL DROP
900 feet

LOOKOUT PASS

Wallace, ID 83873 (208) 744-1301

AREA INFORMATION

BASE ELEVATION
4,700 feet
HOURS
9:00 a.m. - 4:00 p.m., weekends & holidays
7:00 - 10:00 p.m., Fridays
LIFTS
2 pomas, 2 tows, 800 capacity per hour
LONGEST RUN
¾ mile
SEASON
Mid-December to early April
SNOW PHONE
Call Ski Area
TRAVEL
6 miles from Mullan, I-90
VERTICAL DROP
700 feet

MONTPELIER

909 Washington St. Montpelier, ID 83254 (208) 847-1133

AREA INFORMATION

HOURS
Weekends & holidays
11:00 a.m. - 5:00 p.m.
LIFTS
1 tow
LONGEST RUN
1,800 feet
SEASON
December to March
SNOW PHONE
Call Ski Area
TRAILS
1 slope, 100% beginner
TRAVEL
At the end of town
VERTICAL DROP
300 feet

NORTH-SOUTH BOWL

Emida, ID 83843 (509) 335-2651

AREA INFORMATION

BASE ELEVATION
3,350 feet
HOURS
1:00 - 10:00 p.m., Friday
9:00 a.m. - 10:00 p.m., Saturday
9:00 a.m. - 5:00 p.m., Sunday
LIFTS
1 chairlift, 2 tows, 1,200 capacity per hour
LONGEST RUN
1,500 feet
SEASON
Mid-December to mid-March
SNOW PHONE
Call Ski Area
TRAILS
Beginner and intermediate
TRAVEL
Rt. 95A from Moscow
VERTICAL DROP
450 feet

PEBBLE CREEK

Box 1056, Pocatello, ID 83204 (208) 775-3744, 775-4451

AREA INFORMATION

LIFTS
2 chairlifts, 2 pomas
LONGEST RUN
1 1/5 miles
SNOW PHONE
Call Ski Area
TRAILS
1 beginner, 4 intermediate, 9 advanced
TRAVEL
From Pocatello, 15 miles southeast
VERTICAL DROP
2,000 feet

SILVERHORN SKI AREA

Kellogg, ID 83837 (208) 786-9521

AREA INFORMATION

BASE ELEVATION
4,100 feet
HOURS
9:00 a.m. - 3:30 p.m., 5 day week
LIFTS
1 chairlift, 2 tows
LONGEST RUN
2 miles
NURSERY
Call Ski Area
SEASON
Mid-November to mid-April
SNOW PHONE 786-7661
TRAVEL
From Spokane, 65 miles
VERTICAL DROP
1,900 feet

SKYLINE

Pocatello, ID 83201 (208) 775-3744

LIFTS
1 chairlift, 3 bars, 1,100 capacity per hour
SEASON
December to May
SNOW PHONE
Call Ski Area
TRAILS
50% beginner, 50% intermediate
TRAVEL
15 miles from Pocatello
VERTICAL DROP
1,600 feet

SNOW HAVEN

Grangeville, ID 83530 (208) 983-2155

AREA INFORMATION

BASE ELEVATION
4,800 feet
HOURS
Weds., weekends, holidays
10:00 a.m. - 4:00 p.m.
LIFTS
1 T-bar, 2 tows, 1,400 capacity per hour
LONGEST RUN
1/3 mile
SEASON
December to April
SNOW PHONE
Call Ski Area
TRAILS
30% beginner, 70% intermediate
TRAVEL
7 miles from Grangeville, Fish Creek Rd.
VERTICAL DROP
400 feet

SOLDIER MOUNTAIN

Fairfield, ID 83327 (208) 764-2260

AREA INFORMATION

BASE ELEVATION
5,800 feet
HOURS
10:00 a.m. - 4:00 p.m., Wed. thru Fri.
9:30 a.m. - 4:00 p.m., Sat., Sun. & holidays
LIFTS
2 chairlifts, 1 bar, 2 tows, 2,000 capacity per hour
LONGEST RUN
2 miles
SEASON
Late November to April
SNOW PHONE
Call Ski Area
TRAILS
Beginner to advanced, 36 runs
TRAVEL
70 miles from Twin Falls
VERTICAL DROP
1,400 feet

TAMARACK

Troy, ID 83871 (208) 835-4714

AREA INFORMATION

BASE ELEVATION
3,500 feet
HOURS
1:00 p.m. - 4:00 p.m., Thursdays
9:00 a.m. - 4:00 p.m., Sat. & Sun.
LIFTS
1 T-bar, 1 tow, 600 capacity per hour
LONGEST RUN
4,000 feet
SEASON
Mid-December to early April
SNOW PHONE
Call Ski Area
TRAILS
3 slopes
TRAVEL
6 miles north of Troy
VERTICAL DROP
600 feet

TAYLOR MOUNTAIN

Idaho Falls, ID 83401 (208) 524-0202

AREA INFORMATION

HOURS
1:00 a.m. - 4:00 p.m.
6:00 - 10:00 p.m.
LIFTS
1 chairlift, 1 bar
LONGEST RUN
Over ½ mile
SEASON
Mid-December to April
SNOW PHONE
Call Ski Area
TRAVEL
13 miles from Idaho Falls
VERTICAL DROP
750 feet

I L L I N O I S

BUFFALO MOUNTAIN

Algonquin, IL 60102 (312) 426-7328

AREA INFORMATION

HOURS
2:00 - 10:30 p.m., weekdays
9:30 a.m. - 10:30 p.m., weekends
LIFTS
6 tows, 2,800 capacity per hour
LONGEST RUN
1,000 feet
SEASON
Mid-December to late March
SNOW PHONE
Call Ski Area
TRAILS
Beginner to advanced, 4 slopes
TRAVEL
From Chicago, 30 miles via
Northwest Tollway & Rt. 31 N.
VERTICAL DROP
200 feet

CHESTNUT MOUNTAIN

Galena, IL 61036 (815) 777-1320

AREA INFORMATION

HOURS
9:00 a.m. - 4:30 p.m., daily
6:00 - 10:00 p.m., Tues. thru Sat.
LIFTS
3 chairlifts, 7 tows, 4,500 capacity per hour
LONGEST RUN
3,200 feet
SEASON
Mid-December to early March, snowmaking
SNOW PHONE
Call Ski Area
TRAVEL
From Chicago, Northwest Tollway to U.S. 20 W.
VERTICAL DROP
460 feet

FOUR LAKES

Lisle, IL 60532 (319) 964-2550

AREA INFORMATION

HOURS
12:00 - 10:00 p.m., weekdays
9:00 a.m. - 10:00 p.m., weekends
LIFTS
6 tows
LONGEST RUN
1,000 feet
SEASON
Mid-December to early March, snowmaking
SNOW PHONE
Call Ski Area
TRAILS
20% beginner, 80% intermediate
TRAVEL
Outskirts of Chicago near Lisle, U.S. 53
VERTICAL DROP
130 feet

HOLIDAY PARK

Ingleside, IL 60041 (312) 546-8222

AREA INFORMATION

BASE ELEVATION
650 feet
HOURS
11:00 a.m. - 11:00 p.m., weekdays
9:00 a.m. - 11:00 p.m., weekends & holidays
Night skiing from 5:00 p.m.
LIFTS
1 chairlift, 5 tows, 2,800 capacity per hour
LONGEST RUN
1,400 feet
SEASON
December to March
SNOW PHONE
Call Ski Area
TRAILS
Beginner & intermediate
TRAVEL
40 miles from Chicago; 2 miles
from Fox Lake, Rt. 134 W.
VERTICAL DROP
200 feet

JAMES PARK WINTER SPORTS

Evanston, IL 60202 (312) 869-9449

AREA INFORMATION

HOURS
4:00 - 10:00 p.m., weekdays
10:00 a.m. - 10:00 p.m., weekends
LIFTS
1 tow
LONGEST RUN
300 feet
SEASON
Early December to early April, snowmaking

SNOW PHONE
Call Ski Area
TRAILS
Open slope; other sections of this area include tobogganing, tubing, sledding, ice skating rinks
TRAVEL
Located at Dodge & Oakton Streets
VERTICAL DROP
300 feet

MARRIOTT'S LINCOLSHIRE RESORT

Lincolnshire, IL 60115 (312) 634-0100

AREA INFORMATION

HOURS
5:00 p.m. - 11:00 p.m., Wednesday to Friday
11:00 a.m. - 11:00 p.m., Saturday & Sunday
LIFTS
1 bar
SEASON
Mid-December to late February
TRAILS
Beginner area
TRAVEL
Near O'Hare Airport, 30 miles from Chicago, I-294 to Deerfield Road
VERTICAL DROP
50 feet

PLUMTREE

Shannon, IL 61078 (815) 493-2881

AREA INFORMATION

HOURS
12:00 - 10:00 p.m., weekdays
9:00 a.m. - 10:00 p.m., weekends
Night skiing from 5:30 p.m.
LIFTS
1 chairlift, 1 bar, 2,000 capacity per hour
SEASON
Early December to early March
SNOW PHONE
Call Ski Area
TRAILS
50% beginner, 40% intermediate, 10% advanced - open slopes
TRAVEL
50 miles from Rockford via Routes 20, 26 & 72
VERTICAL DROP
180 feet

VILLA OLIVIA

Bartlett, IL 60103 (312) 742-5200

AREA INFORMATION

HOURS
11:00 a.m. - 11:00 p.m., weekdays
9:00 a.m. - 11:00 p.m., weekends, holidays
LIFTS
1 chairlift, 12 tows
LONGEST RUN
¼ mile
NURSERY
Ages 6 - 10
SEASON
Early December to mid-March
SNOW PHONE 695-SNOW
TRAVEL
Under one hour from Chicago
Rt. 20 W. to Ski Area
VERTICAL DROP
180 feet

I N D I A N A

BENDIX WOODS COUNTY PARK

New Carlisle, IN 46552 (219) 654-3155

AREA INFORMATION

BASE ELEVATION
890 feet
HOURS
6:00 - 10:00 p.m., Mon., Tues., Thurs.
1:00 - 10:00 p.m., Wed., Fri.
10:00 a.m. - 10:00 p.m., Sat., holidays
10:00 a.m. - 5:00 p.m., Sundays
LIFTS
4 tows, 600 capacity per hour
LONGEST RUN
1,000 feet
SEASON
December to March
SNOW PHONE
Call Ski Area
TRAILS
Beginner to advanced, open slopes
TRAVEL
10 miles west of South Bend
Rt. 2, access route posted
VERTICAL DROP
100 feet

MT. WAWASEE

New Paris, IN 46553 (219) 831-4112

AREA INFORMATION

HOURS
1:00 - 10:00 p.m., Mon., Weds., Fri.
11:00 a.m. - 10:00 p.m., Tues., Thurs.
9:00 a.m. - 10:00 p.m., Saturdays
9:00 a.m. - 6:00 p.m., Sundays
LIFTS
1 bar, 8 tows, 3,200 capacity per hour
LONGEST RUN
1,500 feet
SEASON
Mid-December to mid-March
SNOW PHONE
Call Ski Area
TRAILS
1 trail, 8 slopes
TRAVEL
10 miles from Goshen, near
Rt. 15 & U.S. 6 junction
VERTICAL DROP
150 feet

NASHVILLE ALPS

Nashville, IN 47448 (812) 988-6638

AREA INFORMATION

HOURS
8:00 a.m. to midnight
LIFTS
2 chairlifts, 2 tows, 4,000 capacity per hour
LONGEST RUN
2,000 feet
SEASON
Early December to March, snowmaking
SNOW PHONE
Call Ski Area
TRAVEL
Southwest of Indianapolis; four
miles from Nashville via Rt. 46
VERTICAL DROP
240 feet

PINES SKI AREA

Valparaiso, IN 46383 (219) 462-4179

AREA INFORMATION

HOURS
12:00 - 10:00 p.m., weekdays
10:00 a.m. - 10:00 p.m., weekends
LIFTS
4 bars, 6 tows, 9,000 capacity
LONGEST RUN
¼ mile
SEASON
Early December to early March
Artificial ramp skiing, off season
SNOW PHONE
Call Ski Area
TRAILS
7 slopes
TRAVEL
5 miles from Valparaiso, near
Route 49 & U.S. 6 junction
VERTICAL DROP
135 feet

PLEASANT RUN

Greencastle, IN 46135 (317) 653-5994

AREA INFORMATION

BASE ELEVATION
820 feet
HOURS
12:00 p.m. - 10:30 p.m., weekdays
9:30 a.m. - 11:00 p.m., weekends, holidays
LIFTS
4 tows
LONGEST RUN
900 feet
SEASON
December to March, snowmaking
SNOW PHONE
Call Ski Area
TRAILS
5 slopes, beginner and intermediate
TRAVEL
2 miles from Greencastle, Rt. 231
Access route signs posted
VERTICAL DROP
125 feet

SKI PAOLI PEAKS

Paoli, IN 47454 (812) 723-4696

AREA INFORMATION

BASE ELEVATION
600 feet
HOURS
Weekdays: 10:00 a.m. - 5:00 p.m., 6:00 - 10:00 p.m.
Weekends & holidays: 8:00 a.m. - 5:00 p.m., 6:00 -
10:00 p.m., 12:00 - 6:00 a.m.
LIFTS
2 chairlifts, 4 tows, 5,500 capacity per hour

SKI PAOLI CONT.

LONGEST RUN
3,200 feet
NURSERY
Near the slopes, call Ski Area
SEASON
Early December to March, snowmaking
SNOW PHONE 723-4698
TRAVEL
85 miles from Indianapolis via Rt. 37
VERTICAL DROP
300 feet

SKI STARLITE

Sellersburg, IN 47172 (812) 246-5471

AREA INFORMATION

HOURS
9:00 a.m. - 11:00 p.m.
LIFTS
2 chairlifts, 2 J-bars, 4,600 capacity per hour
LONGEST RUN
7,000 feet
SEASON
Mid-December to mid-March, snowmaking
SNOW PHONE
Call Ski Area
TRAVEL
Short drive from Clarksville
VERTICAL DROP
580 feet

SKI VALLEY

La Porte, IN 46350 (219) 362-1212

HOURS
6:00 - 10:00 p.m., Mon. - Fri.
10:00 a.m. - 10:00 p.m., Sat.
10:00 a.m. - 6:00 p.m., Sun.
LIFTS
1 T-bar, 5 tows
LONGEST RUN
800 feet
SEASON
Early December to mid-March, snowmaking
SNOW PHONE
Call Ski Area
TRAILS
Open slopes, beginner to advanced
TRAVEL
5 miles west of La Porte
Rt. 2 to Forrester Road
VERTICAL DROP
120 feet

I O W A

CRESCENT HILLS

Crescent, IA 51526 (712) 328-9547

AREA INFORMATION

BASE ELEVATION
1,200 feet
HOURS
11:00 a.m. - 9:00 p.m., weekdays
9:00 a.m. - 9:00 p.m., Sat., Sun. & holidays
LIFTS
1 T-bar, 1 poma, 1 tow, 3,000 capacity per hour
LONGEST RUN
1,800 feet
SEASON
Early December to early March
SNOW PHONE
Call Ski Area
TRAVEL
17 miles from Omaha, Nebraska via I-29
VERTICAL DROP
200 feet

DEER RUN

Dexter, IA 50079 (515) 789-4574

AREA INFORMATION

HOURS
9:00 a.m. - 9:00 p.m.
LIFTS
3 tows, 1,200 capacity per hour
LONGEST RUN
800 feet
SEASON
Mid-December to mid-March, snowmaking
SNOW PHONE
Call Ski Area
TRAILS
Beginner Area
TRAVEL
I-80 W. from Des Moines
VERTICAL DROP
200 feet

DUCK CREEK

Mt. Duck Park, Davenport, IA 52803 (319) 326-7814

AREA INFORMATION

HOURS
4:00 a.m. - 10:00 p.m., weekdays
12:00 - 10:00 p.m., Sundays, holidays

LIFTS
1 tow, 400 capacity per hour
LONGEST RUN
700 feet
SEASON
Early December to early February
SNOW PHONE
Call Ski Area
TRAILS
1 beginner slope
TRAVEL
In Davenport, E. Locust and Marlo Streets

FUN VALLEY

Montezuma, IA 50171 (515) 623-3456

AREA INFORMATION

HOURS
12:00 - 9:00 p.m., daily
10:00 a.m. - 9:00 p.m., Saturday
LIFTS
3 bars, 5 tows, 2,700 capacity per hour
LONGEST RUN
1,500 feet
SEASON
Mid-December to early March
SNOW PHONE
Call Ski Area
TRAVEL
2½ miles from Montezuma
60 miles from Des Moines
VERTICAL DROP
240 feet

HOLIDAY MOUNTAIN

Box 102, Estherville, IA 51334 (712) 362-2264

AREA INFORMATION

HOURS
9:30 a.m. - 9:30 p.m., Fri., Sat., holidays
12:00 - 9:30 p.m., Wednesday
10:00 a.m. - 5:00 p.m., Thursday
9:30 a.m. - 7:30 p.m., Sunday
LIFTS
2 T-bars, 2 tows, 2,600 capacity per hour
LONGEST RUN
1,200 feet
SEASON
December to March, snowmaking
SNOW PHONE
Call Ski Area
TRAILS
5 slopes
TRAVEL
In Estherville, Rt. 9, I-90
VERTICAL DROP
200 feet

HORSESHOE BEND

Millford, IA 51351 (712) 338-4007

AREA INFORMATION

HOURS
4:00 - 9:30 p.m., Monday - Friday
1:00 - 9:30 p.m., Saturday & Sunday
LIFTS
2 tows, 900 capacity per hour
LONGEST RUN
650 feet
SEASON
December to February
TRAILS
2 slopes
TRAVEL
5 miles outside of Milford
VERTICAL DROP
150 feet

NOR-SKI RUNS

Decorah, IA 52101 (319) 382-4158

AREA INFORMATION

HOURS
6:30 a.m. - 9:00 p.m., Tues. & Thurs.
10:00 a.m. - 4:30, Sat., Sun. & holidays
LIFTS
1 bar, 4 tows
LONGEST RUN
1,200 feet
SEASON
Mid-December to mid-March, no snowmaking
SNOW PHONE
Call Ski Area
TRAVEL
70 miles from Waterloo; under 2 miles
from junction of U.S. 52 & Route 9
VERTICAL DROP
240 feet

SKI VALLEY

Boone, IA 50036 (515) 432-2423

AREA INFORMATION

HOURS
1:00 - 5:00 p.m., Mon., Thur. & Fri.
1:00 - 10:00 p.m., Tues., Wed.
9:30 a.m. - 5:00 p.m., Sat., Sun.
LIFTS
3 tows
LONGEST RUN
1,800 feet
SEASON
Mid-December to mid-March
SNOW PHONE
Call Ski Area
TRAILS
Beginner to advanced
TRAVEL
3 miles west of Boone, Rt. 30
VERTICAL DROP
180 feet

SKI VILLA

Waverly, IA 50677 (319) 352-9922

AREA INFORMATION

HOURS
12:00 - 5:30 p.m., Mon., Wed., Fri.
12:00 - 10:00 p.m., Thursday
10:00 a.m. - 10:00 p.m., Sat. & holidays
10:00 a.m. - 6:00 p.m., Sunday
LIFTS
6 tows, 2,500 capacity per hour
SEASON
Mid-December to February, snowmaking
SNOW PHONE
Call Ski Area
TRAILS
2 slopes
TRAVEL
Northwest section of Waverly

SUNSET SKI SLOPE

Pella, IA 50219 (515) 626-3291

AREA INFORMATION

HOURS
2:30 - 9:00 p.m., Monday thru Saturday
LIFTS
5 tows
LONGEST RUN
1,000 feet
SEASON
Early January to early March, snowmaking
SNOW PHONE
Call Ski Area
TRAILS
Beginner to advanced
TRAVEL
From Pella, Rt. 163 E. to Rt. 4
Access route signs posted
VERTICAL DROP
150 feet

VETERAN'S MEMORIAL SKI HILL

Dubuque, IA 52001 (319) 582-9312

AREA INFORMATION

HOURS
6:00 a.m. - 9:00 p.m., weekdays
1:00 - 5:00 p.m., weekends
LIFTS
2 tows
SEASON
January to March, snowmaking
TRAILS
Beginner & intermediate
TRAVEL
Veteran's Memorial Park, Bunker Hill
VERTICAL DROP
120 feet

WINTER WORLD

Hardy, IA 50545 (515) 332-3329

AREA INFORMATION

HOURS
12:00 - 5:00 p.m., daily
9:30 a.m. - 5:00 p.m., holidays
6:00 - 10:00 p.m., Wednesday
LIFTS
2 cable cars, 2 rope tows
LONGEST RUN
1,400 feet
SEASON
Late November to mid-March, snowmaking
SNOW PHONE
Call Ski Area
TRAILS
1 beginner, 2 intermediate, 1 advanced
TRAVEL
3 miles east of Humboldt, Route 3
VERTICAL DROP
130 feet

KANSAS

MONT BLEU

R.R. 2, Box 335, Lawrence, KS 66044 (913) 842-3460

AREA INFORMATION

LIFTS
1 chairlift, 1 rope tow
LONGEST RUN
2,000 feet
SEASON
Late November to mid-March, snowmaking
SNOW PHONE
Call Ski Area
TRAILS
1 beginner, 1 intermediate, 1 advanced
TRAVEL
Kansas Rt. 10, 4 miles southeast of Lawrence
VERTICAL DROP
300 feet

MAINE

BAKER MOUNTAIN

Bingham, ME 04920 (207) 672-9369

AREA INFORMATION

BASE ELEVATION
380 feet
HOURS
9:30 a.m. - 4:30 p.m., weekends & holidays
LIFTS
1 bar, 500 capacity per hours
LONGEST RUN
3,500 feet
SEASON
Mid-December to mid-April
SNOW PHONE
Call Ski Area
TRAILS
Open slope
TRAVEL
25 miles from Skowhegan, U.S. 201
VERTICAL DROP
500 feet

BIG ROCK

Mars Hill, ME 04758 (207) 425-6711

AREA INFORMATION

HOURS
Night skiing
LIFTS
3 bars, 1 tow
SEASON
December to April
SNOW PHONE
Call Ski Area
TRAVEL
In Mars Hill, south of Presque Isle, U.S. 1
VERTICAL DROP
900 feet

BURNT MEADOWS

Brownfield, ME 04010 (207) 935-3636

AREA INFORMATION

HOURS
9:00 a.m. - 4:00 p.m.
LIFTS
1 bar, 1 tow, 800 capacity per hour
SEASON
November to April
SNOW PHONE
Call Ski Area
TRAVEL
45 miles from Portland, Routes 302 & 160
VERTICAL DROP
670 feet

CAMDEN SNOW BOWL

Camden, ME 04843 (207) 236-3438

AREA INFORMATION

BASE ELEVATION
100 feet
HOURS
10:00 a.m. - 5:00 p.m., weekdays
9:00 a.m. - 5:00 p.m., weekends
5:00 - 9:00 p.m., Mon. thru Sat.
LIFTS
1 chairlift, 2 bars, 2,000 capacity per hour
LONGEST RUN
1¼ mile
NURSERY
At the slopes, call Ski Area
SEASON
Mid-December to mid-March, snowmaking
SNOW PHONE
Call Ski Area

TRAILS
20% beginner, 60% intermediate, 20% advanced
TRAVEL
3 miles from Camden, U.S. 1, John St.
VERTICAL DROP
900 feet

CARIBOU SKI SLOPE

U.S. 1, Caribou, ME 04736 (207) 492-0891

AREA INFORMATION

HOURS
6:30 - 10:00 p.m., Fridays
1:00 - 5:00 p.m., weekends
LIFTS
1 bar, 1 tow, 200 capacity per hour
LONGEST RUN
500 feet
SEASON
December to March
SNOW PHONE
Call Ski Area
TRAVEL
Along U.S. 1, near New Brunswick
North of Mars Hill & Presque Isle
VERTICAL DROP
1,000 feet

CHISHOLM WINTER PARK

Rumford, ME 04276 (207) 364-8977

AREA INFORMATION

BASE ELEVATION
1,000 feet
HOURS
9:00 a.m. - 5:00 p.m., weekends
6:00 a.m. - 9:00 p.m., Mon. - Sat.
LIFTS
1 bar, 650 capacity per hour
LONGEST RUN
½ mile
SEASON
Mid-December to late March
SNOW PHONE
Call Ski Area
TRAILS
Open and tree-lined runs
TRAVEL
40 miles from Auburn, Routes 4 & 108
VERTICAL DROP
520 feet

COLBY

Waterville, ME 04901 (207) 872-9890

AREA INFORMATION

HOURS
Afternoons and evenings, Tues. - Sun.
LIFTS
1 T-bar, 700 capacity per hour
SEASON
December to March
SNOW PHONE
Call Ski Area
TRAVEL
20 miles from Augusta, Rt. 104
VERTICAL DROP
250 feet

EATON MOUNTAIN

Skowhegan, ME 04976 (207) 474-2666

AREA INFORMATION

BASE ELEVATION
1,670 feet
HOURS
6:00 a.m. - 10:00 p.m., Tues. - Sat.
9:00 a.m. - 10:00 p.m., weekends, holidays
LIFTS
1 chairlift
SEASON
December to March
TRAILS
30% beginner, 40% intermediate, 30% advanced
TRAVEL
24 miles from Waterville, U.S. 201 & 2
VERTICAL DROP
520 feet

EVERGREEN VALLEY

R.D. 1, E. Stoneham 04231 (207) 928-3300

AREA INFORMATION

BASE ELEVATION
600 feet
HOURS
9:00 a.m. - 4:00 p.m., weekdays
9:00 a.m. - 4:00 p.m., weekends
4:30 - 10:00 p.m., Saturday nights
Call Ski Area for holiday hours
LIFTS
3 chairlifts, 3,000 capacity per hour

LONGEST RUN
1¾ miles
SEASON
Late November to early April, snowmaking
SNOW PHONE
Call Ski Area
TRAILS
20% beginner, 50% intermediate, 30% advanced
TRAVEL
From Portland, U.S. Rt. 202 and Rt. 25
to Norway, then Rt. 118 & 5 to Ski Area
VERTICAL DROP
1,050 feet

LONESOME PINE TRAILS – FT. KENT

Fort Kent, ME 04743 (207) 834-5202

AREA INFORMATION

HOURS
1:00 p.m. - 4:30 & 7:00 - 10:00 p.m., Wed.
9:30 a.m. - 4:30 p.m., Friday thru Sunday
LIFTS
2 tows, 900 capacity per hour
LONGEST RUN
2,000 feet
SEASON
December to April
SNOW PHONE
Call Ski Area
TRAILS
Beginner & intermediate
TRAVEL
Northern tip of Maine, Rt. 2 or 11
VERTICAL DROP
500 feet

LOST VALLEY

Auburn, ME 04210 (207) 784-1561

AREA INFORMATION

HOURS
9:00 a.m. - 6:00 p.m.
6:00 - 11:00 p.m.
LIFTS
2 chairlifts, 1 bar, 1 tow, 1,200 capacity per hour
LONGEST RUN
¾ mile
NURSERY
From Age 2, call Ski Area
SEASON
Early December to mid-March, snowmaking
SNOW PHONE
Call Ski Area
TRAILS
40% beginner, 30% intermediate, 30% advanced
TRAVEL
4 miles from Auburn, Turnpike
VERTICAL DROP
240 feet

MAY MOUNTAIN

Island Falls, ME 04747 (207) 463-2101

AREA INFORMATION

BASE ELEVATION
500 feet
HOURS
5:00 a.m. - 10:00 p.m., Friday
10:00 a.m. - 10:00 p.m., Saturday
10:00 a.m. - 4:00 p.m., Sunday
LIFTS
1 bar, 700 capacity per hour
LONGEST RUN
¾ mile
SEASON
Late December to mid-March
SNOW PHONE
Call Ski Area
TRAILS
Beginner to advanced
TRAVEL
28 miles from Houlton, I-95, Rt. 2
VERTICAL DROP
520 feet

MT. ABRAM SKI SLOPE

Locke Mills, ME 04255 (207) 875-2601, 875-3314

AREA INFORMATION

BASE ELEVATION
960 feet
HOURS
9:00 a.m. - 4:00 p.m.
LIFTS
1 chairlift, 3 bars, 3,000 capacity per hour
LONGEST RUN
2 miles
SEASON
Early December to April, snowmaking
SNOW PHONE
Call Ski Area
TRAILS
Beginner to advanced
TRAVEL
75 miles from Portland, Turnpike N., Rt. 26
VERTICAL DROP
1,020 feet

MT. HERMON

Box 664, Hermon, ME 04401 (207) 848-5192

AREA INFORMATION

HOURS
Night skiing, Monday thru Saturday
LIFTS
2 bars, 1 tow
SEASON
December to March, snowmaking
SNOW PHONE
Call Ski Area
TRAVEL
10 miles from Bangor, U.S. 2
VERTICAL DROP
400 feet

MT. JEFFERSON

Lee, ME 04455 (207) 738-2177

AREA INFORMATION

LIFTS
1 bar, 1 tow, 1,000 capacity per hour
SEASON
December to March
SNOW PHONE
Call Ski Area
TRAILS
Beginner to advanced, ski jumping
TRAVEL
14 miles from Lincoln, Rt. 6
VERTICAL DROP
350 feet

PLEASANT MOUNTAIN

Bridgton, ME 04009 (207) 647-2022, 647-2604

AREA INFORMATION

BASE ELEVATION
650 feet
HOURS
9:00 a.m. - 4:00 p.m.
LIFTS
3 chairlifts, 3 T-bars, 4,000 capacity per hour
LONGEST RUN
5,200 feet
NURSERY
At the slopes, call Ski Area
SEASON
December to April, no snowmaking
SNOW PHONE
Call Ski Area
TRAILS
25% beginner, 45% intermediate, 30% expert
TRAVEL
Northwest of Portland, U.S. 302,
six miles west of Bridgton
VERTICAL DROP
1,256 feet

SADDLEBACK MOUNTAIN

Box 490, Rangeley, ME 04970 (207) 864-3380

AREA INFORMATION

BASE ELEVATION
2,500 feet
HOURS
9:00 a.m. - 4:00 p.m.
LIFTS
2 chairlifts, 3 T-bars, 3,200 capacity per hour
LONGEST RUN
2½ miles
SEASON
Late November to mid-April
SNOW PHONE
Call Ski Area
TRAILS
30% beginner, 30% intermediate, 40% advanced
TRAVEL
7 miles southeast of Rangeley,
Turnpike to Rt. 4 to Access Rd.
VERTICAL DROP
1,800 feet

SPRUCE MOUNTAIN

Greenville, ME 04441 (207) 897-2796

AREA INFORMATION

HOURS
7:00 a.m. - 10:00 p.m., Wed. - Fri.
10:00 a.m. - 4:00 p.m., Saturday
1:00 p.m. - 4:00 p.m., Sunday
LIFTS
4 tows, 1,200 capacity per hour
LONGEST RUN
1,600 feet
SEASON
Mid-December to early March
SNOW PHONE
Call Ski Area
TRAILS
Beginner to advanced, ski jumping
TRAVEL
10 miles from Greenville, Routes 6 & 15
VERTICAL DROP
400 feet

SQUAW MOUNTAIN AT MOOSEHEAD

Box D, Greenville, ME 04441 (207) 695-2272

AREA INFORMATION

BASE ELEVATION
1,350 feet
HOURS
9:15 a.m. - 4:00 p.m.
LIFTS
1 chairlift, 2 T-bars, 1 pony lift, 2,500 capacity
LONGEST RUN
2½ miles
NURSERY
At the slopes, call Ski Area
SEASON
Late November to mid-April
SNOW PHONE
Call Ski Area
TRAILS
30% beginner, 40% intermediate, 30% advanced
TRAVEL
6 miles west of Greenville, Rt. 15
VERTICAL DROP
1,750 feet

MARYLAND

BRADDOCK HEIGHTS SKI-WAY

Braddock Heights, MD 21714 (301) 371-7131

AREA INFORMATION

BASE ELEVATION
900 feet
HOURS
10:00 a.m. - 10:00 p.m.
LIFTS
1 bar, 2 tows, 1,500 capacity per hour
LONGEST RUN
1,250 feet
SEASON
Mid-December to mid-March, snowmaking
SNOW PHONE
Call Ski Area
TRAVEL
Under 50 miles from Washington, D.C.
and Baltimore, I-70, U.S. 40 Alternate
VERTICAL DROP
250 feet

WISP

Rt. 219, Oakland, MD 21550 (301) 387-4911

AREA INFORMATION

BASE ELEVATION
2,470 feet
HOURS
9:30 a.m. - 4:30 p.m., weekdays
9:00 a.m. - 4:30 p.m., Sat. & Sun.
12:30 - 4:30 p.m., holiday season
6:00 - 10:00 p.m., Jan./Feb., Tues. - Fri.
LIFTS
2 chairlifts, 1 T-bar, 1 poma
1 tow, 4,000 capacity per hour
LONGEST RUN
2½ miles
NURSERY
Call Ski Area
SEASON
Mid-December to early March, snowmaking
SNOW PHONE 387-4000
TRAILS
20% beginner, 55% intermediate, 25% advanced
TRAVEL
12 miles north of Oakland, U.S. 50 to 219
VERTICAL DROP
610 feet

MASSACHUSETTS

AMESBURY SKI TOWS

Amesbury, MA 01913 (617) 388-9205

AREA INFORMATION

HOURS
7:00 a.m. - 10:00 p.m., Mon. - Sat.
9:00 a.m. - 4:30 p.m., Sundays
LIFTS
3 bars, 1 tow
SEASON
Mid-December to March, snowmaking
SNOW PHONE
Call Ski Area
TRAILS
Open slopes, beginner & intermediate
TRAVEL
Forty miles from Boston
I-95, I-495 to Rt. 107 A
VERTICAL DROP
320 feet

BERKSHIRE SNOW BASIN

W. Cummington, MA 01265 (413) 634-8808

AREA INFORMATION

BASE ELEVATION
1,175 feet
HOURS
Weekends & holidays, day & night skiing
LIFTS
3 T-bars, 1 rope tow, 2,500 capacity per hour
LONGEST RUN
1 mile
SEASON
Late December to early April, snowmaking
SNOW PHONE
Call Ski Area
TRAILS
8 trails, 3 slopes, beginner to advanced
TRAVEL
25 miles west of Northampton,
18 miles east of Pittsfield
VERTICAL DROP
550 feet

BLUE HILLS

Milton, MA 02186 (617) 828-7490

AREA INFORMATION

HOURS
9:30 a.m. - 4:30 p.m., weekends
7:00 - 10:00 p.m., Mon. - Thurs.
7:00 - 12:00 p.m., Fri. and Sat.
LIFTS
1 chairlift, 2 bars, 2 tows
3,200 capacity per hour
LONGEST RUN
3,000 feet
SEASON
Early December to late April, snowmaking
SNOW PHONE
Call Ski Area
TRAILS
Beginner to advanced
TRAVEL
10 miles from Boston
Routes 128 N. & 64 N.
VERTICAL DROP
300 feet

BOSQUET

Tamarack Rd., Pittsfield, MA 01210 (413) 442-2436

AREA INFORMATION

BASE ELEVATION
1,125 feet
HOURS
12:00 - 10:00 p.m., weekdays
8:30 a.m. - 4:00 p.m., weekends & holidays
6:00 - 10:00 p.m., night skiing
LIFTS
2 chairlifts, 1 T-bar, 2 pomas, 5 rope tows
LONGEST RUN
1½ miles
NURSERY
Age 2 to 6, call Ski Area
SEASON
Early December to early April, snowmaking
SNOW PHONE
Call Ski Area
TRAILS
35% beginner, 35% intermediate, 30% advanced
TRAVEL
From Pittsfield, 2 miles southwest,
Massachusetts Turnpike, exit 2
VERTICAL DROP
750 feet

BOSTON HILLS

North Andover, MA 01845 (617) 683-2733

AREA INFORMATION

BASE ELEVATION
100 feet

HOURS
10:00 a.m. - 4:30 p.m., weekdays
9:00 a.m. - 4:30 p.m., holidays
6:30 - 10:00 p.m., Mon. - Fri.
LIFTS
1 chairlift, 3 tows, 4,500 capacity per hour
LONGEST RUN
2,100 feet
SEASON
Mid-December to mid-March, snowmaking
SNOW PHONE
Call Ski Area
TRAILS
Seven slopes
TRAVEL
From Boston, 20 miles
Rt. 93 N., 125, 114 E.
VERTICAL DROP
340 feet

BOXBORO HILLS

Boxboro, MA 01810 (617) 263-9005, 263-3967

AREA INFORMATION

HOURS
1:00 - 5:00 p.m., Mon. - Fri.
9:00 a.m. - 5:00 p.m., Sat., Sun.
7:00 - 10:00 p.m., Tues. - Sat.
LIFTS
1 T-Bar, 2 tows, 2,800 capacity per hour
LONGEST RUN
1,000 feet
SEASON
Mid-December to mid-March, snowmaking
SNOW PHONE
Call Ski Area
TRAILS
Beginner and intermediate
TRAVEL
Outskirts of Boston near Andover
VERTICAL DROP
130 feet

BRADFORD

Haverhill, MA 01830 (617) 373-0071

AREA INFORMATION

HOURS
3:00 - 10:00 p.m., weekdays
9:00 a.m. - 10:00 p.m., weekends
LIFTS
2 bars, 3 tows
LONGEST RUN
1,200 feet
SEASON
December to March
SNOW PHONE
Call Ski Area
TRAILS
Open slopes
TRAVEL
30 miles from Boston

CHICKLEY ALP SKI CENTER

Charlemont, MA 01339 (413) 339-4802

AREA INFORMATION

HOURS
Wed., weekends & holidays
9:00 a.m. - 4:00 p.m.
LIFTS
1 bar, 3 tows, 1,000 capacity per hour
LONGEST RUN
1 mile
SEASON
Mid-December to mid-March
SNOW PHONE
Call Ski Area
TRAVEL
3 miles south of Charlemont, Rt. 8A
VERTICAL DROP
500 feet

GROTON HILLS

Groton, MA 01450 (617) 448-5951

AREA INFORMATION

HOURS
9:30 a.m. - 4:30 p.m., weekends, holidays
LIFTS
1 bar, 5 tows
SEASON
December to March
SNOW PHONE
Call Ski Area
TRAILS
Beginner to advanced
TRAVEL
35 miles from Boston, Rt. 119, 3 & 40
VERTICAL DROP
150 feet

HAMILTON SKI SLOPES

Hamilton, MA 01936 (617) 468-4804

AREA INFORMATION

HOURS
Day & night skiing
LIFTS
1 bar, 5 tows
SEASON
December to March
SNOW PHONE
Call Ski Area
TRAVEL
24 miles from Boston
Rt. 128 N. to Rt. 1A

HARTWELL HILL

Littleton, MA 01460 (617) 486-4546

AREA INFORMATION

BASE ELEVATION
300 feet
HOURS
9:30 a.m. - 4:30 p.m., weekends, holidays
LIFTS
4 tows
LONGEST RUN
1,000 feet
SEASON
Mid-December to mid-March
SNOW PHONE
Call Ski Area
TRAVEL
30 miles from Boston, I-495, Rt. 2 A & 110
VERTICAL DROP
100 feet

HIDDEN VALLEY

Ashburnham, MA 01474 (617) 827-6032

AREA INFORMATION

HOURS
9:00 a.m. - 4:00 p.m., weekends
7:00 - 10:00 p.m., Wed. & Fri.
Day & night skiing, holiday weeks
LIFTS
1 bar, 5 tows, 1,200 capacity per hour
Lift tickets limited to 1,200
LONGEST RUN
1 mile
SEASON
December to March
SNOW PHONE
Call Ski Area
TRAVEL
30 miles from Worcester, Rt. 12
VERTICAL DROP
250 feet

JERICHO HILL

Marlboro, MA 01752 (617) 485-9730

AREA INFORMATION

HOURS
Weekends, holidays, skiing every night
LIFTS
2 tows
SEASON
December to March
SNOW PHONE
Call Ski Area
TRAVEL
30 miles from Boston, Routes 20 & 85
VERTICAL DROP
800 feet

JUG END

South Egremont, MA 01258 (413) 528-0434

AREA INFORMATION

HOURS
Day and night skiing
LIFTS
1 bar, 2 tows
SEASON
December to March
SNOW PHONE
Call Ski Area
TRAILS
Beginner to advanced,
TRAVEL
Halfway between Boston and
New York City, Route 23
VERTICAL DROP
500 feet

KLEIN INNSBRUCK

Franklin, MA 02038 (617) 528-5660

AREA INFORMATION

HOURS
6:30 a.m. - 10:00 p.m., daily
10:00 a.m. - 5:00 p.m., weekends & holidays

LIFTS
2 chairlifts
SEASON
December to March, snowmaking
SNOW PHONE
Call Ski Area
TRAILS
1 trail, 5 slopes
TRAVEL
From Providence, 15 miles
Rt. 495, King Street exit
VERTICAL DROP
200 feet

MERRIMAC VALLEY

Methuen, MA 01844 (617) 686-2021

AREA INFORMATION

HOURS
Open all week, day & night skiing
LIFTS
2 bars, 1 tow
SEASON
December to March, snowmaking
SNOW PHONE
Call Ski Area
TRAILS
2 open slopes
TRAVEL
2 miles west of Pelham
Hampshire Rd., Rt. 93
VERTICAL DROP
200 feet

MT. MOHAWK

Shelburne, MA 01370 (413) 625-2643

AREA INFORMATION

HOURS
Open every day
LIFTS
2 bars
SEASON
December to March
SNOW PHONE
Call Ski Area
TRAILS
Beginner to advanced
TRAVEL
45 miles from Springfield
Route 2 near Greenfield
VERTICAL DROP
400 feet

MT. WATATIC

Ashby, MA 01431 (617) 386-7921

AREA INFORMATION

BASE ELEVATION
1,250 feet
HOURS
10:00 a.m. - 10:00 p.m., weekdays
9:00 a.m. - 4:30 p.m., weekends
6:00 - 10:00 p.m., night skiing
LIFTS
2 bars, 2 tows, 2,500 capacity per hour
LONGEST RUN
¾ mile
SEASON
Mid-December to April
SNOW PHONE
Call Ski Area
TRAVEL
50 miles from Boston, Routes 2 & 119
VERTICAL DROP
550 feet

NASHOBA VALLEY

Westford, MA 01886 (617) 692-3033

AREA INFORMATION

BASE ELEVATION
200 feet
HOURS
9:00 a.m. - 4:30 p.m., 6:30 - 10:00 p.m.
LIFTS
2 chairlifts, 1 bar, 7 tows
LONGEST RUN
1,400 feet
SEASON
Mid-December to mid-March, snowmaking
SNOW PHONE
Call Ski Area
TRAILS
1 trail, 7 slopes
TRAVEL
From Boston, about 25 miles via
Routes 2 & 119 to Power Road
VERTICAL DROP
240 feet

OTIS RIDGE

Rt. 23, Otis, MA 01253 (413) 269-4444

OTIS RIDGE CONT.

AREA INFORMATION

HOURS
9:00 a.m. - 4:30 p.m.
LIFTS
1 T-bar, 1 J-bar, 1 poma, 1 pony lift
3 rope tows, 3,500 capacity per hour
LONGEST RUN
¾ mile
SEASON
Early December to early April, snowmaking
SNOW PHONE
Call Ski Area
TRAILS
40% beginner, 40% intermediate, 20% advanced
TRAVEL
From Boston, Mass. Turnpike
exit 3, Routes 20 W. & 23 W.
VERTICAL DROP
400 feet

PINE RIDGE

Barre, MA 01005 (617) 882-3000, 355-4396

AREA INFORMATION

BASE ELEVATION
850 feet
HOURS
Days: Saturday, Sunday, holiday weeks
Night skiing: Monday thru Saturday
LIFTS
2 bars, 1,800 capacity per hour
SEASON
Mid-December to mid-March, snowmaking
SNOW PHONE
Call Ski Area
TRAVEL
Rt. 122 to Rt. 32
VERTICAL DROP
200 feet

PROSPECT HILL

Waltham, MA 02154 (617) 893-4837, 893-4046

AREA INFORMATION

HOURS
Weekends & nights, Tues. thru Sun.
LIFTS
2 bars
SEASON
Mid-December to mid-March
SNOW PHONE
Call Ski Area
TRAILS
Beginner and intermediate
TRAVEL
10 miles from Boston
Rt. 128 to Winter St.
VERTICAL DROP
90 feet

WACHUSETT MOUNTAIN

Princeton, MA 01541 (617) 464-2355

AREA INFORMATION

BASE ELEVATION
1,025 feet
HOURS
9:00 a.m. - 4:00 p.m., 4:00 - 10:00 p.m.
LIFTS
1 tow, 2 bars, 2,500 capacity per hour
LONGEST RUN
4,000 feet
SEASON
Early December to early April
SNOW PHONE
Call Ski Area
TRAVEL
15 miles from Worcester
Rt. 2, 14 S., Mountain Rd.
VERTICAL DROP
660 feet

WARD HILL

Shrewsbury, MA 01545 (617) 842-6346

AREA INFORMATION

HOURS
10:00 a.m. - 5:30 p.m., 7:00 - 10:00 p.m.
LIFTS
2 bars, 5 tows, 1,100 capacity per hour
LONGEST RUN
2,000 feet
NURSERY
From age 2, Call Ski Area
SEASON
Late November to early March, snowmaking
TRAILS
Beginner to advanced
TRAVEL
30 miles from Boston, Turnpike, Rt. 9 & 20
VERTICAL DROP
200 feet

M I C H I G A N

ADVENTURE MOUNTAIN

Wakefield, MI 49968 (906) 883-3208

AREA INFORMATION

HOURS
Weekends
LIFTS
1 tow, 200 capacity per hour
SEASON
December to March
TRAILS
2 runs, also togoggan run & ice skating
TRAVEL
Near Mass City, U.S. 45

ALPINE VALLEY

6775 E. Highland Rd., Milford, MI 48042 (313) 887-2180

AREA INFORMATION

BASE ELEVATION
900 feet
HOURS
10:00 a.m. - 6:00 p.m., weekdays
9:00 a.m. - 6:00 p.m., weekends
6:00 - 11:00 p.m., night skiing
LIFTS
9 chairlifts, 13 tows, 10,500 capacity per hour
LONGEST RUN
One-third mile
SEASON
December to mid-March, snowmaking
SNOW PHONE 887-4183
TRAILS
30% beginner, 40% intermediate, 30% advanced
TRAVEL
Northeast of Detroit, I-96, U.S. 23 N., Rt. 59 E.
VERTICAL DROP
250 feet

AL QUAAL RECREATION AREA

Ishpeming, MI 49849 (906) 486-6181

AREA INFORMATION

HOURS
1:00 - 4:30 p.m., Saturday & Sunday
6:00 - 9:30 p.m., Tuesday & Thursday
LIFTS
3 tows, 350 capacity per hour
LONGEST RUN
1,000 feet
SEASON
Late December to mid-March
SNOW PHONE
Call Ski Area
TRAILS
50% beginner, 50% intermediate
TRAVEL
Northern section of Ishpeming

BIG VALLEY

Newbury, MI 49869 (906) 293-8785

AREA INFORMATION

BASE ELEVATION
140 feet
HOURS
1:00 - 5:00 p.m., weekends
LIFTS
3 tows, 450 capacity per hour
LONGEST RUN
800 feet
SEASON
Mid-December to mid-March
SNOW PHONE
Call Ski Area
TRAILS
Beginner to advanced
TRAVEL
2 miles from Newbury, Rt. 123
VERTICAL DROP
140 feet

BINTZ APPLE MOUNTAIN

Freeland, MI 48623 (517) 781-0170

AREA INFORMATION

HOURS
10:00 a.m. - 4:30 p.m., 5:00 - 10:30 p.m.
LIFTS
10 tows, 5,500 capacity per hour
LONGEST RUN
800 feet
SEASON
Early December to mid-March, snowmaking
SNOW PHONE
Call Ski Area
TRAVEL
8 miles from Saginaw, Rt. 58 W., 47 N.
VERTICAL DROP
200 feet

BOYNE HIGHLANDS

Harbor Springs, MI 49740 (616) 526-2171

AREA INFORMATION

BASE ELEVATION
800 feet
HOURS
9:00 a.m. - 4:30 p.m.
LIFTS
7 chairlifts, 1 T-bar, 1 tow
15,000 capacity per hour
LONGEST RUN
1 mile
NURSERY
Ages 2 to 7, call Ski Area
SEASON
Late November to mid-April, snowmaking
SNOW PHONE
Call Ski Area
TRAILS
35% beginner, 30% intermediate, 35% advanced
TRAVEL
4 miles north of Harbor Springs, Rt. 119
VERTICAL DROP
520 feet

BOYNE MOUNTAIN

U.S. 131, Boyne Falls, MI 49713 (616) 549-2441

AREA INFORMATION

BASE ELEVATION
720 feet
HOURS
9:00 a.m. - 4:30 p.m.
LIFTS
8 chairlifts, 3 rope tows
14,000 capacity per hour
LONGEST RUN
1 mile
NURSERY
Ages 3 to 6, call Ski Area
SEASON
Late November to mid-April, snowmaking
SNOW PHONE
Call Ski Area
TRAILS
20% beginner, 40% intermediate, 40% advanced
TRAVEL
Canadian Hwy. 17 in Ontario,
U.S. I-75, Rt. 32 W., U.S. 131 N.
VERTICAL DROP
450 feet

CANNONSBURG

Cannonsburg, MI 49317 (616) 874-6711

AREA INFORMATION

HOURS
10:00 a.m. - 5:00 p.m., weekdays
9:30 a.m. - 5:00 p.m., weekends
5:00 - 10:30 p.m., night skiing
LIFTS
3 chairlifts, 2 bars, 15 tows
11,000 capacity per hour
LONGEST RUN
One-third mile
NURSERY
At the slopes, call Ski Area
SEASON
Late November to mid-March, snowmaking
SNOW PHONE
Call Ski Area, outside state . . . . (800) 253-8748
TRAILS
30% beginner, 50% intermediate, 20% advanced
TRAVEL
Near Grand Rapids, I-96, Rt. 44
VERTICAL DROP
250 feet

CLIFFS RIDGE

Box 487, Marquette, MI 49855 (906) 225-1155

AREA INFORMATION

BASE ELEVATION
1,200 feet
HOURS
9:00 a.m. - 5:00 p.m., daily
6:00 - 9:00 p.m., Mon. - Fri.
LIFTS
1 chairlift, 2 T-bars, 2 tows
3,500 capacity per hour
LONGEST RUN
1¼ miles
NURSERY
Motels near Ski Area
SEASON
Early December to mid-April, snowmaking
SNOW PHONE
Call Ski Area
TRAILS
25% beginner, 50% intermediate, 25% advanced
TRAVEL
Ski Area is in Marquette near airport
VERTICAL DROP
600 feet

CRYSTAL MOUNTAIN

Thompsonville, MI 49683 (616) 378-2911

AREA INFORMATION

BASE ELEVATION
750 feet
HOURS
10:00 a.m. - 10:00 p.m., weekdays; 11:00 p.m., Fri.
8:00 a.m. - 11:00 p.m., weekends; 10:00 p.m., Sun.
LIFTS
4,500 capacity per hour
LONGEST RUN
½ mile
NURSERY
At the slopes, call Ski Area
SEASON
Late November to early April, snowmaking
SNOW PHONE
Call Ski Area
TRAILS
25% beginner, 40% intermediate, 35% advanced
TRAVEL
Northwest of Cadillac, 40 miles via Rt. 115 N. to Thompsonville, then 2½ miles to Ski Area
VERTICAL DROP
370 feet

GLADSTONE SPORTS PARK

Gladstone, MI 49837 (906) 428-9130

AREA INFORMATION

HOURS
11:00 a.m. - 5:00 p.m., weekends
6:00 - 10:00 p.m., Mon., Tues., Thurs.
LIFTS
1 bar, 4 tows
LONGEST RUN
400 feet
SEASON
Late December to mid-March
SNOW PHONE
Call Ski Area
TRAILS
Beginner and intermediate
TRAVEL
2 miles from downtown Gladstone
VERTICAL DROP
100 feet

GRAND VALLEY STATE COLLEGES

Allendale, MI 49401 (616) 895-6611 X 662

AREA INFORMATION

HOURS
Day & night skiing
LIFTS
1 tow
SEASON
Early January to mid-March
SNOW PHONE
Call office
TRAILS
One slope
TRAVEL
12 miles west of Grand Rapids

HANSON RECREATION AREA

Grayling, MI 49738 (517) 348-9266

AREA INFORMATION

HOURS
10:00 a.m. - 4:30 p.m., Sat. & Sun.
7:00 - 10:00 p.m., Thurs., Sat. & Mon.
LIFTS
1 bar, 4 tows
LONGEST RUN
2,500 feet
SEASON
Mid-November to March, snow making
SNOW PHONE
Call Ski Area
TRAVEL
1½ miles west of Grayling, Routes 72 & 93
VERTICAL DROP
200 feet

HICKORY HILLS

Traverse City, MI 49684 (616) 947-8566

AREA INFORMATION

BASE ELEVATION
280 feet
HOURS
2:00 - 9:00 p.m., weekdays
10:00 a.m. - 9:00 p.m., weekends
LIFTS
5 tows
LONGEST RUN
1,700 feet
SEASON
Late December to mid-March
SNOW PHONE
Call Ski Area
TRAVEL
Outskirts of Traverse City
VERTICAL DROP
250 feet

HILTON SHANTY CREEK

Box 355, Bellaire, MI 49615 (616) 533-8621

AREA INFORMATION

BASE ELEVATION
670 feet
HOURS
10:00 a.m. - 10:00 p.m.
LIFTS
3 chairlifts, 1 rope tow, 4,000 capacity per hour
LONGEST RUN
2,700 feet
NURSERY
At the slopes, call Ski Area
SEASON
Early December to mid-March, snowmaking
SNOW PHONE
Call Ski Area
TRAILS
35% beginner, 45% intermediate, 20% advanced
TRAVEL
40 miles from Traverse City, Rt. 88
VERTICAL DROP
300 feet

LOST PINES LODGE

Harrietta, MI 49638 (616) 389-2222

AREA INFORMATION

HOURS
9:30 a.m. - 4:30 p.m., 7:00 - 10:00 p.m.
LIFTS
1 tow
LONGEST RUN
1,000 feet
SEASON
Late November to early April
SNOW PHONE
Call Ski Area
TRAILS
Beginner and intermediate
TRAVEL
13 miles west of Cadillac, Rt. 55
VERTICAL DROP
100 feet

MAPLE MOUNTAIN

Munising, MI 49862 (906) 387-2754

AREA INFORMATION

BASE ELEVATION
300 feet
HOURS
10:00 a.m. - 6:00 p.m., weekends & holidays
LIFTS
1 tow
SEASON
Early December to early March
SNOW PHONE
Call Ski Area
TRAILS
Beginner to advanced
TRAVEL
In town
VERTICAL DROP
200 feet

MAPLEHURST

Kewadin, MI 49648 (616) 264-9675

AREA INFORMATION

HOURS
9:30 a.m. - 4:30 p.m., weekends & holidays
LIFTS
1 poma, 3 tows
LONGEST RUN
2,500 feet
SEASON
Mid-December to mid-March
SNOW PHONE
Call Ski Area
TRAILS
Beginner and intermediate
TRAVEL
8 miles from Elk Rapids; 20, Traverse City
VERTICAL DROP
250 feet

MICHAWAYE SLOPES

Gaylord, MI 49735 (517) 939-8719

AREA INFORMATION

HOURS
Weekends; daily, holiday season
LIFTS
1 chairlift, 2 pomas, 2 tows
LONGEST RUN
1,200 feet
SEASON
December to March
SNOW PHONE
Call Ski Area
TRAILS
9 slopes
TRAVEL
7 miles south of Gaylord, U.S. 27
VERTICAL DROP
210 feet

MIDDLEVILLE

Middleville, MI 49333 (616) 795-9872

AREA INFORMATION

HOURS
Day & night skiing, daily
LIFTS
1 bar, 5 tows, 4,000 capacity per hour
LONGEST RUN
1,000 feet
SEASON
Mid-December to mid-March, snowmaking
SNOW PHONE
Call Ski Area
TRAVEL
20 miles from Grand Rapids, Rt. 37

MIO MOUNTAIN

Ferndale, MI 48220 (517) 826-5569

AREA INFORMATION

HOURS
10:00 a.m. - 4:30 p.m., Fri. - Mon., holidays
Night skiing, Fridays and Saturdays
LIFTS
4 tows
LONGEST RUN
1,500 feet
SEASON
Mid-December to early April
SNOW PHONE
Call Ski Area
TRAVEL
In Huron National Forest, Routes 72 & 33
VERTICAL DROP
250 feet

MONT RIPLEY

Houghton, MI 49931 (906) 487-2340

AREA INFORMATION

BASE ELEVATION
700 feet
HOURS
1:00 - 5:00 p.m., weekdays
9:30 a.m. - 4:30 p.m., weekends
6:30 - 9:45 p.m., Wednesday
LIFTS
1 chairlift, 1 bar, 2,100 capacity per hour
LONGEST RUN
2,200 feet
SEASON
December to late March
SNOW PHONE
Call Ski Area
TRAILS
Open slopes
TRAVEL
215 miles from Green Bay, U.S. 41
VERTICAL DROP
420 feet

MOTT MOUNTAIN

Farwell, MI 48622 (517) 588-2945

AREA INFORMATION

HOURS
10:00 a.m. - 5:00 p.m., daily
7:00 - 10:00 p.m., Wed., Fri., Sat.
LIFTS
1 chairlift, 4 tows, 3,500 capacity per hour
LONGEST RUN
1,800 feet
SEASON
Mid-December to mid-March, snowmaking
SNOW PHONE
Call Ski Area
TRAVEL
1½ miles south of Farwell, U.S. 10
VERTICAL DROP
200 feet

MT. BRIGHTON

Brighton, MI 48116 (313) 229-9581

AREA INFORMATION

BASE ELEVATION
1,100 feet
HOURS
10:00 a.m. - 5:00 p.m., 6:00 - 11:00 p.m., weekdays
9:00 a.m. - 5:00 p.m., 6:00 - 11:00 p.m., weekends
LIFTS
6 chairlifts, 9 tows
LONGEST RUN
1,500 feet
SEASON
November to middle of March
SNOW PHONE 227-1451
TRAVEL
West of Detroit via I-96 W.
VERTICAL DROP
220 feet

MT. GRAMPIAN

Oxford, MI 48051 (313) 628-2450

AREA INFORMATION

HOURS
12:00 - 11:00 p.m.
LIFTS
1 chairlift, 1 J-bar, 6 tows
LONGEST RUN
1,800 feet
SEASON
Early December to mid-March, snowmaking
SNOW PHONE
Call Ski Area
TRAILS
Open skiing, 12 slopes
TRAVEL
35 miles From Detroit, U.S. 75, Rt. 24
VERTICAL DROP
200 feet

MT. HOLLY

13536 St. Dixie Hwy., Holly, MI 48442 (313) 634-8269

AREA INFORMATION

HOURS
10:00 a.m. - 6:00 p.m.
6:00 - 11:00 p.m., night skiing
LIFTS
7 chairlifts, 10 tows, 8,000 capacity per hour
LONGEST RUN
One-third mile
SEASON
Early December to mid-March, snowmaking
SNOW PHONE
Call Ski Area
TRAILS
25% beginner, 35% intermediate, 40% advanced
TRAVEL
South of Flint via I-75 to Holly exit
VERTICAL DROP
320 feet

MT. MANCELONA

Mancelona, MI 49659 (616) 587-9271

AREA INFORMATION

HOURS
9:30 a.m. - 4:30 p.m., Sat., Sun., & holidays
LIFTS
1 T-bar, 2 pomas, 3 tows
LONGEST RUN
¾ mile
SEASON
Mid-December to mid-March
SNOW PHONE
Call Ski Area
TRAVEL
155 miles from Grand Rapids, Route 131
VERTICAL DROP
300 feet

MT. MARIA SKI LODGE

Spruce, MI 48762 (517) 736-8377

AREA INFORMATION

HOURS
10:00 a.m. - 10:00 p.m., Mon. - Sat.
10:00 a.m. - 5:00 p.m., Sunday
LIFTS
1 chairlift, 3 tows, 3,600 capacity per hour
LONGEST RUN
4,500 feet
SEASON
December to April, snowmaking
SNOW PHONE
Call Ski Area
TRAILS
Tree-lined runs
TRAVEL
Rt. 72 to Hubbard Lake Road
VERTICAL DROP
280 feet

MT. ZION

Ironwood, MI 49938 (906) 932-9879

AREA INFORMATION

BASE ELEVATION
1,510 feet
HOURS
12:00 - 5:00 p.m., Tues. - Fri.
9:00 a.m. - 4:00 p.m., Saturday
11:00 a.m. - 4:00 p.m., Sunday
LIFTS
1 chairlift, 2 tows, 1,200 capacity per hour
LONGEST RUN
¾ mile
SEASON
Mid-December to mid-March
SNOW PHONE
Call Ski Area
TRAILS
Beginner to advanced
TRAVEL
Near Wisconsin border, U.S. 2
VERTICAL DROP
300 feet

PANDO

Rockford, MI 49341 (616) 874-8343

AREA INFORMATION

HOURS
4:00 - 10:00 p.m.
LIFTS
6 tows
SEASON
Mid-December to early March, snowmaking
SNOW PHONE
Call Ski Area
TRAILS
30% beginner, 40% intermediate, 30% advanced
TRAVEL
12 miles from Grand Rapids, Rt. 44

PETOSKEY WINTER SPORTS PARK

Petoskey, MI 49770 (616) 347-5550

AREA INFORMATION

HOURS
4:00 - 10:00 p.m., Monday - Friday
10:00 a.m. - 10:00 p.m., Saturdays
12:00 p.m. - 10:00 p.m., Sundays
LIFTS
1 tow
SEASON
Mid-December to early March
SNOW PHONE
Call Ski Area
TRAILS
30% beginner, 70% intermediate
TRAVEL
30 miles from Gaylord, U.S. 31

PINE KNOB

Clarkston, MI 48016 (313) 394-0880

AREA INFORMATION

BASE ELEVATION
1,000 feet
HOURS
10:00 a.m. - 5:00 p.m., 3:00 - 11:00 p.m., weekdays
9:00 a.m. - 5:00 p.m., 3:00 - 12:00 p.m., weekends
LIFTS
5 chairlifts, 7 tows
LONGEST RUN
¾ mile
SEASON
Mid-November to mid-March, snowmaking
SNOW PHONE
Call Ski Area
TRAVEL
From Pontiac, 8 miles, I-75 N. to Sashabaw Road
VERTICAL DROP
300 feet

PINE MOUNTAIN

Pine Mtn. Rd., Iron Mtn., MI 49801 (906) 774-2747

AREA INFORMATION

BASE ELEVATION
1,400 feet
HOURS
9:30 a.m. - 4:30 p.m.
LIFTS
3 chairlifts, 1 rope tow, 4,000 capacity per hour
LONGEST RUN
½ mile
NURSERY
Under 5 years, call Ski Area
SEASON
Late November to Late March, snowmaking
SNOW PHONE
Call Ski Area
TRAILS
20% beginner, 60% intermediate, 20% advanced
TRAVEL
2½ miles north of Iron Mountain, off U.S. 2 & 141
VERTICAL DROP
375 feet

LODGING

DOWNTOWNER MOTEL
700 S. Stephenson Ave. 774-5500
DUVAL'S RESORT (housekeeping cottages)
Star Rt. 1, Box 63, near Ski Area. 774-1689
EDGEWATER RESORT (log cabins)
Star Rt. 2, Box 348, 2 mi. from Ski Area . . . 774-6244
HILLCREST MOTEL
3 mi. E. of Iron Mtn., U.S. 2, Quinnesec 774-6866
THE HOLIDAY MOTEL (dining, cocktail lounge)
U.S. 2 & 141, Box 177. 774-6220
LAKE ANTOINE MOTEL
North U.S. 2. 774-6797
MILLIMANS DICKINSON INN (restaurant)
Iron Mountain. 774-5000
THE RANCHO MOTEL
North U.S. 2. 774-1848

PORCUPINE MOUNTAINS STATE PARK

Ontonagon, MI 49953 (906) 884-4735

AREA INFORMATION

HOURS
9:00 a.m. - 4:15 p.m.,
LIFTS
1 chairlift, 3 T-bars, 2 rope tows
3,500 capacity per hour
LONGEST RUN
6,000 feet
SEASON
Mid-December to early April
SNOW PHONE . . . . (800) 338-1246
In Michigan 932-4870
TRAILS
3 beginner, 7 intermediate, 3 expert
TRAVEL
Near Lake Superior, M-28 to Bergland,
north 9 miles beyond White Pines
VERTICAL DROP
600 feet

LODGING

FERN'S MOTEL & CABINS
Rt. 1, Box 10F 884-4522
HOKANS CHALET COTTAGES
Box C45, Lakeshore Rd.. 884-4230
JOHNSON'S MOTEL & FAMILY COTTAGES
Star Route, Box 162B 884-2653
RAINBOW MOTEL CHALETS & CONDOS
Box 286B, Silver City 49953 885-5329
Toll free . . . . (800) 541-9312
SUNSHINE MOTEL & CABINS
R. & S. Shamion, Box 109Z. 884-4406
TALLMAN'S MOTEL
On M-64, Box 8 884-4242

ROYAL VALLEY

R.R. 1, Box 434, Buchanan, MI 49107 (616) 695-3847

AREA INFORMATION

BASE ELEVATION
600 feet
HOURS
3:00 - 10:00 p.m., Monday thru Thursday
1:00 - 10:00 p.m., Tuesday, starting Jan. 1st
11:00 a.m. - 10:00 p.m., Friday
10:00 a.m. - 9:00 p.m., Saturday
10:00 a.m. - 6:00 p.m., Sunday
Call Ski Area for hours for holidays
LIFTS
2 chairlifts, 2 T-bars, 7 tows, 9,000 capacity per hour
LONGEST RUN
1,800 feet
SEASON
Late November to mid-March, snowmaking
SNOW PHONE 695-5862
TRAILS
20% beginner, 45% intermediate, 35% advanced
TRAVEL
South Bend, Indiana, 12 miles, I-94, U.S. 12
VERTICAL DROP
210 feet

SCHUSS MOUNTAIN

Marcelona, MI 49659 (616) 587-9162

AREA INFORMATION

BASE ELEVATION
740 feet
HOURS
9:00 a.m. - 4:30 p.m.
LIFTS
3 chairlifts, 1 T-bar, 1 tow, 5,000 capacity per hour
LONGEST RUN
4,800 feet
NURSERY
Ages 1 to 5, call Ski Area
SEASON
Late November to April, snowmaking
SNOW PHONE
Call Ski Area, or in Michigan . . . . . . (800) 632-7170
TRAILS
25% beginner, 40% intermediate, 35% advanced
TRAVEL
From Mancelona, 4 miles west, Rt. 85
VERTICAL DROP
400 feet

SHERIDAN VALLEY

Lewiston, MI 49756 (517) 785-4822

AREA INFORMATION

HOURS
Weekends, daily for Christmas holidays
LIFTS
2 pomas, 1 tow
SEASON
Mid-December to early April, snowmaking
SNOW PHONE
Call Ski Area
TRAILS
Beginner and intermediate
TRAVEL
Between Atlanta and Lewiston, M-33

SKI BRULE MOUNTAIN

Iron River, MI 49935 (906) 265-4957

AREA INFORMATION

BASE ELEVATION
1,430 feet
HOURS
9:30 a.m. - 4:30 p.m.
LIFTS
1 chairlift, 1 bar, 3 tows
LONGEST RUN
1 mile
NURSERY
Age 2 & up, call Ski Area
SEASON
Late November to early April, snowmaking
SNOW PHONE 265-4957
Outside Michigan . . . . (800) 338-7174
TRAILS
30% beginner, 40% intermediate, 30% advanced
TRAVEL
35 miles west of Iron Mountain, U.S. 2
VERTICAL DROP
410 feet

SKYLINE

Grayling, MI 49738 (517) 275-5445

AREA INFORMATION

BASE ELEVATION
1,300 feet
HOURS
10:00 a.m. - 5:00 p.m., 7:00 - 10:00 p.m.
LIFTS
1 chairlift, 10 tows, 9,000 capacity per hour
LONGEST RUN
2,000 feet
SEASON
Mid-December to early April
SNOW PHONE
Call Ski Area
TRAVEL
I-75 to exit 251, 4 miles to Ski Area
VERTICAL DROP
210 feet

SNOWSNAKE MOUNTAIN

Harrison, MI 48625 (517) 539-6583

AREA INFORMATION

HOURS
10:00 a.m. - 5:00 p.m., daily
6:00 - 10:00 p.m., Tues. - Sat.
1 T-bar, 5 tows
LONGEST RUN
1,200 feet
SEASON
Early December to mid-March, snowmaking
SNOW PHONE
Call Ski Area
TRAILS
15 slopes
TRAVEL
10 miles north of Clare, I-75, U.S. 27
VERTICAL DROP
200 feet

SUGAR LOAF MOUNTAIN

Rt. 1, Cedar, MI 49621 (616) 228-5461

AREA INFORMATION

HOURS
9:00 a.m. - 4:30 p.m.
LIFTS
5 chairlifts, 1 J-bar, 6,000 capacity per hour
LODGING
Convention facilities . . . . (800) 632-9802
LONGEST RUN
Over one mile
NURSERY
Day Care Center, call Ski Area
SEASON
Late November to early April, snowmaking
SNOW PHONE
Call Ski Area
TRAILS
80% beginner & intermediate, 20% advanced
TRAVEL
From Traverse City, 18 miles northwest, Rt. 72
Lighted 4,300 foot sod air strip, plowed in winter
VERTICAL DROP
600 feet

SWISS VALLEY

Jones, MI 49061 (616) 228-5461

AREA INFORMATION

HOURS
12:00 - 10:00 p.m., Mon. - Fri.
9:00 a.m. - 10:00 p.m., Saturdays
9:00 a.m. - 6:00 p.m., Sundays
LIFTS
1 chairlift, 2 bars, 10 tows, 2,400 capacity per hour
LONGEST RUN
1,800 feet
NURSERY
3 years & up, call Ski Area
SEASON
Mid-December to mid-March, snowmaking
SNOW PHONE
Call Ski Area
TRAILS
10 slopes
TRAVEL
10 miles from Three Rivers, M-60 W., Patterson Hill Rd.
VERTICAL DROP
225 feet

SYLVAN KNOB

Gaylord, MI 49735 (517) 732-4733

AREA INFORMATION

HOURS
9:30 a.m. - 4:30 p.m., closed Christmas day
LIFTS
1 chairlift, 4 pomas, 3 tows, 4,700 capacity per hour
LONGEST RUN
1,500 feet
SEASON
Middle of December to early April
SNOW PHONE
Call Ski Area
TRAILS
Beginner to advanced
TRAVEL
5 miles from Gaylord, M-44 West
VERTICAL DROP
225 feet

THUNDER MOUNTAIN

Kalamazoo, MI 49055 (616) 694-9449

AREA INFORMATION

HOURS
1:00 - 10:00 p.m., Mon. - Fri.
9:30 a.m. - 8:00 p.m., Saturdays
9:30 a.m. - 6:00 p.m., Sundays
LIFTS
2 chairlifts, 1 bar, 7 tows, 2,800 capacity per hour
LONGEST RUN
2,000 feet
NURSERY
Saturday & Sunday, call Ski Area
SEASON
Late November to early March, snowmaking
TRAILS
40% beginner, 40% intermediate, 20% advanced
TRAVEL
15 miles Kalamazoo, U.S. 131, D Ave., watch signs
VERTICAL DROP
230 feet

TIMBERLEE

Traverse City, MI 49684 (616) 946-2600

AREA INFORMATION

HOURS
12:00 p.m. - 10:00 p.m., weekdays
10:00 a.m. - 10:00 p.m., weekends
LIFTS
2 chairlifts, 1 poma, 2 tows, 3,800 capacity per hour
LONGEST RUN
4,100 feet
SEASON
Early December to mid-March, snowmaking
SNOW PHONE
Call Ski Area
TRAILS
25% beginner, 50% intermediate, 25% advanced
TRAVEL
6 miles from Traverse City, M-22 N., Cherry Bend Rd.
VERTICAL DROP
380 feet

TIMBER RIDGE

Boyne Falls, MI 49713 (616) 549-2441

AREA INFORMATION

HOURS
Weekends; Christmas to New Years, daily
LIFTS
2 chairlifts, 2 tows
LONGEST RUN
3,000 feet
SEASON
December to March, snowmaking

SNOW PHONE
Call Ski Area
TRAVEL
5 miles from Boyne Falls
VERTICAL DROP
410 feet

TRAVERSE CITY HOLIDAY

Traverse City, MI 49684 (616) 938-1360

AREA INFORMATION

HOURS
Day and night skiing
LIFTS
2 bars, 5 tows
SEASON
Mid-December to mid-March, snowmaking
SNOW PHONE
Call Ski Area
TRAILS
Beginner and intermediate
TRAVEL
3 miles from Traverse City, U.S. 31 North
VERTICAL DROP
210 feet

TYROLEAN

Gaylord, MI 49735 (517) 732-2743

AREA INFORMATION

HOURS
10:00 a.m. - 5:00 p.m., daily
7:00 - 10:00 p.m., Fri. & Sat.
LIFTS
1 chairlift, 1 bar, 2 tows, 2,800 capacity per hour
LONGEST RUN
½ mile
SEASON
Late November to late March
SNOW PHONE
Call Ski Area
TRAVEL
13 miles from Gaylord, Rt. 32 E., F-44, Sawyer Rd.
VERTICAL DROP
270 feet

WARD HILLS

Irons, MI 49644 (616) 266-5202

AREA INFORMATION

HOURS
Saturday, Sunday and holidays, daily
Wednesday and Saturday nights
LIFTS
6 tows
SEASON
December to March, snowmaking
SNOW PHONE
Call Ski Area
TRAILS
8 runs
TRAVEL
North of U.S. 10, 7 miles from Branch

WINTERSKOL

Lakeview, MI 48850 (517) 352-7920, 352-6898

AREA INFORMATION

HOURS
4:00 - 10:00 p.m., Mon. - Fri.
9:00 a.m. - 9:30 p.m., Saturdays
9:00 a.m. - 8:00 p.m., Sundays
12:00 p.m. - 10:00 p.m., holidays
LIFTS
1 poma, 6 tows
SEASON
December to March
SNOW PHONE
Call Ski Area
TRAILS
12 runs
TRAVEL
West of Lakeview, M-46

AFTON ALPS

Hastings, MN 55033 (612) 436-5245

AREA INFORMATION

HOURS
9:00 a.m. - 10:00 p.m., 5:00 - 10:00 p.m.
LIFTS
18 chairlifts, 2 tows, 20,000 capacity per hour
LONGEST RUN
3,000 feet
SEASON
Late November to late March, snowmaking
SNOW PHONE
Call Ski Area
TRAILS
20% beginner, 60% intermediate, 20% advanced
TRAVEL
Rt. 20, four miles south of Afton
Hastings, 12 miles; Twin Cities, 20
VERTICAL DROP
330 feet

BATTLE CREEK

St. Paul, MN 55109 (612) 777-1361

AREA INFORMATION

BASE ELEVATION
880 feet
HOURS
5:00 p.m. - 9:00 p.m., weekdays
9:00 a.m. - 9:00 p.m., Saturdays
12:00 p.m. - 9:00 p.m., Sundays
LIFTS
4 tows
LONGEST RUN
600 feet
SEASON
Mid-December to early February
SNOW PHONE
Call Ski Area
TRAILS
4 slopes, 1 for lessons
TRAVEL
I-94 E. from St. Paul to Ruth, Upper
Afton Rd. to Winthrop to Ski Area
VERTICAL DROP
115 feet

BUCK HILL

Burnsville, MN 55337 (612) 435-7187

AREA INFORMATION

BASE ELEVATION
900 feet
HOURS
10:00 a.m. - 10:00 p.m., weekdays
9:00 a.m. - 10:00 p.m., weekends
5:00 - 10:00 p.m., night skiing
LIFTS
4 chairs, 1 bar, 3 tows
LONGEST RUN
2,000 feet
NURSERY
Age 2 to 6, call Ski Area
SEASON
Mid-November to early April, snowmaking
SNOW PHONE
Call Ski Area
TRAILS
40% beginner, 45% intermediate, 15% advanced
TRAVEL
South of Minneapolis via Rt. 52 S. to Brunsville
VERTICAL DROP
320 feet

BUENA VISTA

Bemidji, MN 56601 (218) 243-2231

AREA INFORMATION

HOURS
12:00 - 9:00 p.m., Tuesday thru Friday
10:00 a.m. - 4:30 p.m., Saturday, Sunday
LIFTS
2 chairlifts, 6 tows, 4,500 capacity per hour
LONGEST RUN
1,800 feet
SNOW PHONE
Call Ski Area
TRAILS
Beginner to advanced
TRAVEL
12 miles north of Bemidji, County Rd. 15
VERTICAL DROP
220 feet

COFFEE MILL

Wabasha, MN 55981 (612) 565-4561

AREA INFORMATION

BASE ELEVATION
730 feet

HOURS
1:00 - 10:00 p.m., Wednesday - Friday
10:00 a.m. - 4:00 p.m., Saturday, Sunday
10:00 a.m. - 10:00 p.m., holiday weeks
LIFTS
2 chairlifts, 1 poma lift, 2,300 capacity per hour
LONGEST RUN
4,000 feet
SEASON
Late December to mid-March, snowmaking
SNOW PHONE
Call Ski Area
TRAILS
Beginner to advanced
TRAVEL
In Wabasha at junction of U.S. 61 & Rt. 60
VERTICAL DROP
500 feet

COMO PARK

St. Paul, MN 55101 (612) 489-1804

AREA INFORMATION

HOURS
12:30 p.m. - 10:00 p.m., Monday and Wednesday
4:00 p.m. - 10:00 p.m., Tuesday, Thursday and Friday
9:00 a.m. - 8:00 p.m., Sat., 11:00 a.m. - 7:00 p.m., Sun.
LIFTS
2 tows
SEASON
December through March, snowmaking
SNOW PHONE
Call Ski Area
TRAILS
Beginner area under the St. Paul Park Dept.

DETROIT MOUNTAIN

Detroit Lakes, MN 56501 (218) 847-4703

AREA INFORMATION

HOURS
9:30 a.m. - 4:30 p.m., Tues., Wed., holidays
9:30 a.m. - 10:00 p.m., Thursday - Saturday
LIFTS
1 chairlift, 2 bars, 6 tows, 4,500 capacity per hour
LONGEST RUN
2,400 feet
SEASON
December to March, snowmaking
SNOW PHONE
Call Ski Area
TRAILS
13 runs
TRAVEL
From Minneapolis, 200 miles, U.S. 10
VERTICAL DROP
230 feet

EAGLE MOUNTAIN

Grey Eagle, MN 56336 (612) 285-4567

AREA INFORMATION

HOURS
1:00 - 10:00 p.m., Wednesday - Friday
10:00 a.m. - 10:00 p.m., Saturdays
10:00 a.m. - 7:00 p.m., Sundays
LIFTS
1 poma, 5 tows
LONGEST RUN
2,000 feet
SEASON
Late November to late March, snowmaking
TRAVEL
I-94 to Rt. 238 to Upsula, then 5 miles
VERTICAL DROP
200 feet

GIANTS RIDGE

Biwabik, MN 55708 (218) 865-6315

AREA INFORMATION

BASE ELEVATION
1260 feet
HOURS
Weekends and holidays
LIFTS
1 T-bar, 1 poma, 8 tows
LONGEST RUN
3,700 feet
SEASON
December to March
SNOW PHONE
Call Ski Area
TRAVEL
Access route from Biwabik,
2 miles east and 4 miles north
VERTICAL DROP
200 feet

GLENHAVEN

Glenwood, MN 56334 (612) 634-9912

AREA INFORMATION

HOURS
10:00 a.m. - 9:00 p.m., Saturdays
1:00 p.m. - 5:00 p.m., Sundays
LIFTS
2 tows
LONGEST RUN
950 feet
SEASON
December to March
SNOW PHONE
Call Ski Area
TRAVEL
one-half mile south of Glenwood, Rt. 104
VERTICAL DROP
150 feet

GOLDEN GATE TO FUN CAMPGROUND

Sleepy Eye, MN 56085 (507) 794-6586

AREA INFORMATION

HOURS
1:00 - 5:00 p.m., weekends
LIFTS
5 tows
LONGEST RUN
1,300 feet
SEASON
December to March
TRAILS
50% beginner, 50% intermediate
TRAVEL
6 miles north of the junction of Rt. 4 & 14
VERTICAL DROP
130 feet

HIDDEN VALLEY

Ely, MN 55731 (218) 365-3097

AREA INFORMATION

HOURS
10:00 a.m. - 9:00 p.m., Wed. - Sun., holidays
LIFTS
1 bar, 2 tows, 450 capacity per hour
LONGEST RUN
1,800 feet
SEASON
Mid-December to mid-March
SNOW PHONE
Call Ski Area
TRAILS
5 runs
TRAVEL
Northeast Minnesota, 120 miles north of Duluth
VERTICAL DROP
160 feet

HOLE-IN-THE-MOUNTAIN

Lake Benton, MN 56149 (507) 368-9350

AREA INFORMATION

HOURS
10:00 a.m. - 5:00 p.m., Saturday
12:00 - 5:00 p.m., Sun., holidays
6:30 - 9:30 p.m., Tues., Thurs., Sat.
LIFTS
3 tows, 900 capacity per hour
LONGEST RUN
1,000 feet
SEASON
December to March
TRAVEL
Hole-In-The-Mtn. County Park, Rt. 14, 75
VERTICAL DROP
170 feet

HYLAND HILLS

Bloomington, MN 55437 (612) 835-4604

AREA INFORMATION

HOURS
10:00 a.m. - 10:00 p.m., Mon. - Sat.
10:00 a.m. - 5:00 p.m., Sundays
LIFTS
1 chairlift, 1 bar, 5 tows, 3,800 capacity per hour
No reservations, lift tickets limited to 2,500
LONGEST RUN
2,000 feet
SEASON
Late November to mid-March, snowmaking
TRAILS
60% beginner, 30% intermediate, 10% advanced
TRAVEL
I-494 to Bush Lake Road, south 2 miles
VERTICAL DROP
170 feet

LUTSEN MOUNTAINS

Box 86, Lutsen, MN 55612 (218) 663-7281

AREA INFORMATION

HOURS
9:00 a.m. - 4:30 p.m.
LIFTS
3 chairlifts, 2 bars, 1 tow, 5,800 capacity per hour
LONGEST RUN
1½ miles
NURSERY
At the slopes, call Ski Area
SEASON
Late November to mid-April, snowmaking
SNOW PHONE 436-5218
TRAVEL
90 miles from Duluth, U.S. 61 along Lake Superior
VERTICAL DROP
650 feet

MARTHALER

West St. Paul, MN 55118 (612) 445-9937

AREA INFORMATION

HOURS
Weekends and evenings
LIFTS
1 tow
LONGEST RUN
1,000 feet
SEASON
December to March
SNOW PHONE
Call Ski Area
TRAILS
2 runs
TRAVEL
Inside the city limits
VERTICAL DROP
300 feet

MT. FRONTENAC

Red Wing, MN 55066 (612) 388-5826

AREA INFORMATION

BASE ELEVATION
700 feet
HOURS
4:30 - 10:00 p.m., Tuesday - Saturday
9:00 a.m. - 10:00 p.m., Sun., holidays
LIFTS
1 chairlift, 2 bars, 6 tows, 1,200 capacity per hour
LONGEST RUN
1 mile
SEASON
Early December to March, snowmaking
TRAILS
10 slopes
TRAVEL
9 miles from Red Wing; Lake City, 6 miles
VERTICAL DROP
420 feet

MT. ITASCA

Coleraine, MN 55722 (218) 245 1463

AREA INFORMATION

HOURS
12:00 - 4:30 p.m., weekends
6:30 - 9:30 p.m., Wednesday
LIFTS
1 tow
LONGEST RUN
1,800 feet
SEASON
December to March
SNOW PHONE
Call Ski Area
TRAVEL
TRAVEL
Near Grand Rapids, U.S. 169
VERTICAL DROP
270 feet

MT. KATO

Mankato, MN 56001 (507) 625-3363

AREA INFORMATION

HOURS
9:00 a.m. - 10:00 p.m.
LIFTS
6 chairlifts, 2 tows, 8,500 capacity per hour
LONGEST RUN
Over 1 mile
SEASON
Late November to April, snowmaking
SNOW PHONE
Call Ski Area
TRAVEL
From Minneapolis/St. Paul, I-35 to U.S. 169
VERTICAL DROP
240 feet

MT. WIRTH

Minneapolis, MN 55422 (612) 522-4584

AREA INFORMATION

HOURS
6:00 - 10:00 p.m., Mon. - Thurs.
9:00 a.m. - 5:00 p.m., Sat., Sun.
LIFTS
3 tows
LONGEST RUN
300 feet
SEASON
Early December to early March, snowmaking
SNOW PHONE
Call Ski Area
TRAVEL
Outskirts of Minneapolis
VERTICAL DROP
200 feet

OLD SMOKEY

Fergus Falls, MN 56537 (218) 736-2251

AREA INFORMATION

HOURS
6:00 - 9:00 p.m., daily
LIFTS
2 tows
LONGEST RUN
600 feet
SEASON
Mid-December to mid-March
SNOW PHONE
Call Ski Area
TRAVEL
In Fergus Falls, Route 94
VERTICAL DROP
110 feet

POWDER RIDGE

Kimball, MN 55353 (612) 398-7200

AREA INFORMATION

HOURS
9:00 a.m. - 5:00 p.m., 5:00 - 10:00 p.m.
LIFTS
2 chairlifts, 2 bars, 3 tows, 11,000 capacity per hour
LONGEST RUN
2,600 feet
SEASON
Call Ski Area
TRAVEL
15 miles from St. Cloud, Rt. 15
VERTICAL DROP
310 feet

QUADNA

Hill City, MN 55748 (218) 697-2324

AREA INFORMATION

HOURS
9:30 a.m. - 4:30 p.m., daily
LIFTS
3 bars, 2 tows
LONGEST RUN
½ mile
SEASON
Late November to early April, snowmaking
SNOW PHONE
Call Ski Area
TRAVEL
90 miles from Duluth, Route 2
VERTICAL DROP
320 feet

ROCHESTER SKI HILL

Rochester, MN 55901 (507) 288-6767

AREA INFORMATION

HOURS
6:00 - 10:00 p.m., Tuesdays and Thursdays
10:00 a.m. - 10:00 p.m., weekends, holidays
LIFTS
1 poma, 1 tow
LONGEST RUN
800 feet
SEASON
December to March
SNOW PHONE
Call Ski Area
TRAVEL
Inside the city
VERTICAL DROP
140 feet

SKI GULL

Brainerd, MN 56401 (218) 963-4353

AREA INFORMATION

HOURS
4:30 - 9:30 p.m., Mon., Wed. and Thurs.
9:30 a.m. - 4:30 p.m., weekends, holidays

LIFTS
1 bar, 3 tows
LONGEST RUN
1,700 feet
SEASON
December to March
SNOW PHONE
Call Ski Area
TRAILS
12 runs
VERTICAL DROP
280 feet

SKI TONKA

Orono, MN 55960 (612) 472-2827

AREA INFORMATION

HOURS
4:00 p.m. - 10:00 p.m., Fridays
10:00 a.m. - 5:00 p.m., Sat., Sun., holidays
LIFTS
19 tows
LONGEST RUN
1,000 feet
SEASON
December to March, snowmaking
SNOW PHONE
Call Ski Area
TRAILS
14 open slopes
TRAVEL
From Minneapolis, Routes 7 & 19 to 84 junction
VERTICAL DROP
200 feet

SUGAR HILLS

Box 369, Grand Rapids, MN 55744 (218) 326-9461

AREA INFORMATION

HOURS
9:30 a.m. - 5:00 p.m., daily
5:00 - 10:00 p.m., Mon. - Sat.
LIFTS
2 chairlifts, 3 T-bars, 4 ropee tows
LONGEST RUN
3,000 feet
NURSERY
Under 6 years, call Ski Area
SEASON
Late December to mid-April, snowmaking
SNOW PHONE
Call Ski Area
TRAILS
2 beginner, 17 intermediate, 4 advanced
TRAVEL
175 miles north of Minneapolis, Rt. 169 to 17 W.
VERTICAL DROP
400 feet

TIMBERLANE

Red Lake Falls, MN 56750 (218) 732-4364

AREA INFORMATION

HOURS
12:00 - 5:00 p.m., weekends, holidays
5:00 p.m. - 9:00 p.m., Thursday nights
LIFTS
4 tows
LONGEST RUN
1,200 feet
SEASON
December to March
SNOW PHONE
Call Ski Area
TRAILS
7 runs
TRAVEL
I-94 to Rt. 32 from Grand Forks
VERTICAL DROP
110 feet

VAL CHATEL

Park Rapids, MN 56470 (218) 266-3306

AREA INFORMATION

HOURS
9:30 a.m. - 4:30 p.m., daily
7:00 - 10:00 p.m., Saturday
LIFTS
1 chairlift, 5 tows
LONGEST RUN
2,200 feet
SEASON
Late November to late March
SNOW PHONE
Call Ski Area
TRAVEL
16 miles from Park Rapids, Routes 34 E., 4 N.
VERTICAL DROP
270 feet

VIKING VALLEY

Ashby, MN 56309 (218) 747-2542

AREA INFORMATION

HOURS
10:00 a.m. - 10:00 p.m., Saturday
10:00 a.m. until dusk, Sunday
LIFTS
6 tows, 1,900 capacity per hour
LONGEST RUN
2,200 feet
SEASON
December to March, snowmaking
SNOW PHONE
Call Ski Area
TRAILS
7 runs
TRAVEL
On Rt. 126 between Battle and Ashby

WELCH VILLAGE

Welch, MN 55089 (612) 222-7079

AREA INFORMATION

BASE ELEVATION
700 feet
HOURS
9:00 a.m. - 4:00 p.m., daily
4:00 - 10:00 p.m., night skiing
LIFTS
5 chairlifts, 2 T-bars, 2 J-bars, 9,000 capacity per hour
LONGEST RUN
4,000 feet
SEASON
Mid-November to early April, snowmaking
SNOW PHONE
Call Ski Area
TRAILS
11 beginner, 15 intermediate, 4 advanced
TRAVEL
From Twin Cities, Rt. 61 S. past Miesville to Welch
VERTICAL DROP
350 feet

WILD MOUNTAIN

Taylor Falls, MN 55084 (612) 465-6365, 291-7980

AREA INFORMATION

BASE ELEVATION
810 feet
HOURS
10:00 a.m. - 10:00 p.m., weekdays
9:30 a.m. - 10:00 p.m., weekends
4:00 - 10:00 p.m., night skiing
LIFTS
3 chairlifts, 2 tows
LONGEST RUN
4,500 feet
SEASON
Mid-November to late March, snowmaking
SNOW PHONE
Call Ski Area
TRAILS
30% beginner, 40% intermediate, 30% advanced
TRAVEL
7 miles north of Taylors Falls, Routes 95, 8 & 16
VERTICAL DROP
300 feet

LODGING

THE BEST WESTERN DALLES HOUSE MOTEL
(dining room, coffee shop, cocktail lounge)
Rt. 8 & 35, St. Croix Falls, WI . . . . . (715) 483-3206
THE NEW PINES MOTEL (near restaurants)
Taylors Falls. 465-4422
THE SPRINGS INN (dining, entertainment Fri. night)
Near Ski Area . . . . (800) 328-5511
Minnesota Area . . . . (800) 462-5355
Twin City Area 331-5204

M I S S O U R I

MARRIOTT'S TAN-TAR-A

Osage Beach, MO 65065 (314) 348-3131

AREA INFORMATION

HOURS
9:30 a.m. - 4:30 p.m., 6:00 - 9:00 p.m.
LIFTS
1 bar, 1 tow, 850 capacity per hour
LONGEST RUN
1,200 feet
SEASON
Mid-December to early March, snowmaking
SNOW PHONE
Call Ski Area
TRAILS
Beginner and intermediate
TRAVEL
35 miles from Jefferson City via Rt. 54,
left on State Rd. KK to the Ski Area

MONTANA

BEEF TRAIL

Butte, MT 59701 (406) 792-2242

AREA INFORMATION

BASE ELEVATION
2,670 feet
HOURS
11:00 a.m. - 4:00 p.m., Saturday, Sunday
7:00 - 10:00 p.m., Tuesday - Thursday
LIFTS
1 T-bar, 1 tow, 500 capacity per hour
LONGEST RUN
3,600 feet
SEASON
Mid-December to mid-April, snowmaking
SNOW PHONE
Call Ski Area
TRAVEL
5 miles south of Butte
VERTICAL DROP
2,600 feet

BELMONT

Helena, MT 59601 (406) 442-8246

AREA INFORMATION

BASE ELEVATION
5,800 feet
HOURS
9:30 a.m. - 4:00 p.m., Thurs. - Sun.
Every day during Christmas vacation
LIFTS
1 T-bar, 1 poma, 2 tows
LONGEST RUN
1 mile
SEASON
Mid-December to mid-April
SNOW PHONE
Call Ski Area
TRAILS
Beginner to advanced
TRAVEL
25 miles northwest from Helena
VERTICAL DROP
1,500 feet

BRIDGER BOWL

Bozeman, MT 59715 (406) 586-2787, 586-2111

AREA INFORMATION

BASE ELEVATION
6,100 feet
HOURS
9:30 a.m. - 4:00 p.m.
LIFTS
5 chairlifts, 2 tows, 1 bar, 3,400 capacity per hour
LONGEST RUN
2½ miles
SEASON
Mid-December to early April, no snowmaking
SNOW PHONE 586-2389
TRAILS
25% beginner, 45% intermediate, 30% advanced
TRAVEL
I-90 to Bozeman, then 16 miles via Rt. 86 North
VERTICAL DROP
2,000 feet

DEEP CREEK

Wise River, MT 59762 (406) 839-2129

AREA INFORMATION

BASE ELEVATION
5,100 feet
HOURS
Thurs., Sat., Sun. & holidays
10:30 a.m. - 4:15 p.m.,
LIFTS
1 T-bar
SEASON
December to early April
SNOW PHONE
Call Ski Area
TRAILS
Beginner to advanced
TRAVEL
43 miles southwest from Butte
VERTICAL DROP
1,000 feet

DISCOVERY BASIN

Anaconda, MT 59711 (406) 563-2184

AREA INFORMATION

BASE ELEVATION
6,800 feet
HOURS
9:30 a.m. - 4:30 p.m., Wednesday thru Sunday
LIFTS
1 chairlift, 1 tow
LONGEST RUN
1¾ miles

DISCOVERY BASIN CONT.

NURSERY
At the slopes, call Ski Area
SEASON
December to April
SNOW PHONE
Call Ski Area
TRAILS
Mainly intermediate
TRAVEL
20 miles from Anaconda, Rt. 10A West
VERTICAL DROP
1,300 feet

LOST TRAIL

Darby, MT 59829 (406) 821-3495

AREA INFORMATION

BASE ELEVATION
7,050 feet
HOURS
10:00 a.m. - 4:00 p.m., Wed., Sat. & Sun.
LIFTS
1 chairlift, 2 tows, 700 capacity per hour
LONGEST RUN
1¼ miles
NURSERY
At the slopes, call Ski Area
SEASON
November to May
TRAILS
Beginner to advanced
TRAVEL
30 miles from Darby
VERTICAL DROP
650 feet

MARSHALL MOUNTAIN

Missoula, MT 59801 (406) 258-6619

AREA INFORMATION

BASE ELEVATION
4,000 feet
HOURS
1:00 - 4:30 p.m., weekdays
9:30 a.m. - 4:30 p.m., weekends
7:00 - 10:00 p.m., Mon. - Fri.
LIFTS
1 chairlift, 1 T-bar, 1 poma,
2 tows, 5,800 capacity per hour
LONGEST RUN
7,000 feet
NURSERY
At the slopes, call Ski Area
SEASON
Late November to late April, snowmaking
SNOW PHONE
Call Ski Area
TRAVEL
7 miles from Missoula, Rt. 200
VERTICAL DROP
1,500 feet

MAVERICK MOUNTAIN

Polaris, MT 59746 (406) 834-2412

AREA INFORMATION

LIFTS
1 chairlift, 1 pony lift, 1 rope tow
LONGEST RUN
2½ miles
SEASON
November to March
SNOW PHONE
Call Ski Area
TRAILS
25% beginner, 50% intermediate, 25% advanced
TRAVEL
38 miles southwest of Dillon, Rt. 278
VERTICAL DROP
1,650 feet

MONTANA SNOW BOWL

Missoula, MT 59801 (406) 549-9777

AREA INFORMATION

HOURS
Wednesday thru Sunday
LIFTS
1 chairlift, 1 T-bar, 1 poma, 1 rope tow
1,800 capacity per hour
LONGEST RUN
3½ miles
SEASON
Late November to early April
SNOW PHONE
Call Ski Area
TRAILS
4 intermediate, 14 advanced
TRAVEL
13 miles northwest of Missoula
VERTICAL DROP
2,600 feet

RED LODGE MOUNTAIN

Drawer R, Red Lodge, MT 59068 (406) 446-2288

AREA INFORMATION

BASE ELEVATION
7,400 feet
HOURS
9:30 a.m. - 4:00 p.m.
LIFTS
4 chairlifts, 1 tow, 4,500 capacity per hour
LONGEST RUN
2½ miles
SEASON
Late November to Mid-April, snowmaking
SNOW PHONE
Call Ski Area
TRAILS
15% beginner, 60% intermediate, 25% advanced
TRAVEL
60 miles south of Billings, U.S. 212, six miles from Red Lodge on West Fork Rd.
VERTICAL DROP
2,010 feet

LODGING

CENTRAL RESERVATIONS 446-2288

ALPINE VILLAGE MOTEL
Phone, TV 446-2213
BEST WESTERN LU PINE INN
Indoor pool, whirlpool, phone, TV 446-1321
CHATEAU ROUGE
Condo units, ski wax room 446-1601
EAGLES NEST MOTEL
Cable TV, kitchenettes. 446-2312
POLLARD MOTOR HOTEL (since 1893)
Phone, TV, ski lockers 446-1345
ROCK CREEK MINE GRIZZLY CONDO
To 3 bedrooms, TV, next to restaurant 446-1111
SKYVIEW MOTEL
1 & 2 bedrooms, TV, kitchenettes 446-1510
VALLI HI MOTOR LODGE (downtown)
Family room & suites. 446-1414
YODELER MOTEL
Subscription TV, kitchen, phone 446-1435

SHOWDOWN

Box 92, Neihart, MT 59465 (406) 236-5522

AREA INFORMATION

BASE ELEVATION
6,800 feet
HOURS
9:30 a.m. - 4:00 p.m., Wed. - Sun., holidays
LIFTS
2 chairlifts, 1 poma, 1 rope tow
3,200 capacity per hour
LONGEST RUN
2 miles
SEASON
Late November to mid-April
SNOW PHONE 727-8080
TRAILS
30% beginner, 60% intermediate, 10% expert
TRAVEL
60 miles south of Great Falls, U.S. 89
VERTICAL DROP
1,400 feet

TETON PASS

Choteau, MT 59422 (406) 466-2672

AREA INFORMATION

BASE ELEVATION
6,190 feet
HOURS
Wednesday, Saturday, Sunday, holidays
LIFTS
1 chairlift, 2 pomas, 1 tow, 1,200 capacity per hour
SEASON
December to March
SNOW PHONE
Call Ski Area
TRAVEL
33 miles from Choteau, Route 89
VERTICAL DROP
1,000 feet

WRAITH HILL

Anaconda, MT 59711 (406) 563-2357

AREA INFORMATION

BASE ELEVATION
6,300 feet
HOURS
10:00 a.m. - 4:30 p.m., weekends, holidays
LIFTS
1 T-bar, 1 tow, 1,300 capacity per hour
LONGEST RUN
1 mile
SEASON
Early January to April
SNOW PHONE
Call Ski Area
TRAVEL
15 miles west of Anaconda, Route 10A
VERTICAL DROP
500 feet

N E V A D A

LEE CANYON

Las Vegas, NV 89101 (702) 870-4778

AREA INFORMATION

BASE ELEVATION
8,500 feet
HOURS
9:00 a.m. - 4:00 p.m., daily
6:00 - 10:00 p.m., holidays
LIFTS
1 chairlift, 1 bar, 2 tows, 2,600 capacity per hour
LONGEST RUN
5,000 feet
SEASON
Late November to mid-April, snowmaking
SNOW PHONE
Call Ski Area
TRAVEL
45 miles from Las Vegas, U.S. 95, Rt. 52
VERTICAL DROP
1,030 feet

TANNENBAUM

Reno, NV 89501 (702) 849-9925

AREA INFORMATION

BASE ELEVATION
6,600 feet
HOURS
10:00 a.m. - 4:00 p.m., Tuesday thru Sunday
LIFTS
2 bars, 1 tow
LONGEST RUN
1,800 feet
SEASON
Late December to mid-April
SNOW PHONE
Call Ski Area
TRAILS
Beginner
TRAVEL
17 miles from Reno, Rt. 27
VERTICAL DROP
400 feet

NEW HAMPSHIRE

ALPINE RIDGE

Laconia, NH 03246 (603) 293-4304

AREA INFORMATION

HOURS
9:00 a.m. - 4:00 p.m., weekends, holidays
6:00 - 10:00 p.m., Wednesday thru Friday
LIFTS
1 chairlift, 1 T-bar, 1 tow
LONGEST RUN
1¼ mile
SEASON
Mid-December to April, snowmaking
SNOW PHONE
Call Ski Area
TRAVEL
Next to Gunstock Ski Area in Gilford, Rt. 11A
VERTICAL DROP
850 feet

BALSAM'S WILDERNESS

Dixville Notch, NH 03576 (603) 255-3400, (617) 227-8288

AREA INFORMATION

LIFTS
1 chairlift, 2 T-bars
NURSERY
At the slopes, call Ski Area
SEASON
December to March
SNOW PHONE
Call Ski Area
TRAILS
4 beginner, 3 intermediate, 5 advanced
TRAVEL
10 miles from Colebrook, Rt. 26 E.
VERTICAL DROP
1,000 feet

BIG BEAR

Brookline, NH 03033 (603) 673-9892

AREA INFORMATION

BASE ELEVATION
650 feet
HOURS
10:00 a.m. - 4:00 p.m., 7:00 - 10:00 p.m.
LIFTS
1 bar, 1 tow
LONGEST RUN
1,800 feet
SEASON
Late December to early March
SNOW PHONE
Call Ski Area
TRAVEL
10 miles from Boston, Route 3
VERTICAL DROP
600 feet

BOBCAT

Bennington, NH 03442 (603) 588-6330

AREA INFORMATION

BASE ELEVATION
1,350 feet
HOURS
9:00 a.m. - 4:30 p.m.
LIFTS
2 chairlifts, 2 bars, 3,000 capacity per hour
Lift tickets are limited to 2,000
LONGEST RUN
1 mile
NURSERY
At the slopes, call Ski Area
SEASON
Late November to April, snowmaking
SNOW PHONE
Call Ski Area
TRAILS
Beginner to advanced
TRAVEL
10 miles from Peterborough, Route 202
VERTICAL DROP
900 feet

BRICKYARD MOUNTAIN INN

Laconia, NH 03246 (800) 258-0343

AREA INFORMATION

BASE ELEVATION
580 feet
HOURS
9:00 a.m. - 4:00 p.m., 6:00 - 9:30 p.m.
LIFTS
1 chairlift, 1 tow, 1,200 capacity per hour
Lift tickets limited to 500
LONGEST RUN
3,000 feet
NURSERY
At the slopes, call Ski Area
SEASON
Late November to late March, snowmaking
SNOW PHONE
Call Ski Area
TRAVEL
I-93 to Routes 104 and 3
VERTICAL DROP
420 feet

CAMPTON MOUNTAIN

Campton, NH 03223 (603) 726-3082

AREA INFORMATION

BASE ELEVATION
1,600 feet
HOURS
9:00 a.m. - 4:00 p.m., weekends, holidays
6:30 p.m. - 10:00 p.m., night skiing
LIFTS
1 chairlift, 1,000 capacity per hour
LONGEST RUN
3,000 feet
SEASON
Late December to late March
SNOW PHONE
Call Ski Area
TRAILS
Beginner to advanced
TRAVEL
From Boston, I-93 N., exit 28
VERTICAL DROP
400 feet

CANNON MOUNTAIN

Franconia, NH 03580 (603) 823-5661

AREA INFORMATION

BASE ELEVATION
2,000 feet
HOURS
8:00 a.m. - 4:30 p.m.
LIFTS
1 tramway, 3 chairlifts, 2 T-bars,
1 beginner's tow, 5,500 capacity per hour
LONGEST RUN
2 1/3 miles
NURSERY
Babysitter available, call Ski Area
SEASON
Late November to mid-April, snowmaking
SNOW PHONE . . . . . . (603) 823-7771, (617) 338-6911
TRAILS
30% beginner, 45% intermediate, 25% advanced
TRAVEL
I-93, 190 miles from Providence
VERTICAL DROP
2,140 feet

LODGING

BEST WESTERN HILLWINDS INN
Route 18 823-7711
FRANCONIA INN (French restaurant)
Rt. 116, Easton Rd. 823-5542
GALE RIVER MOTEL
Main St. 823-5655
THE HORSE & HOUND INN (dining)
Fronconia 823-5501

CANNON CONT.

LOVETT'S INN (dining)
Franconia 823-7761
MITTERSILL ALPINE INN
Off Rt. 18 823-5511
NOTCHWAY MOTOR INN & RESTAURANT
U.S. Rt. 3, Box 474W, Franconia Notch 823-5525
RAYNOR'S MOTOR LODGE
Corner of Routes 18 & 142 823-5651
STONYBROOK MOTOR LODGE
Route 18. 823-8192
WESTWIND VACATION COTTAGES & MOTEL
Route 18. 823-5532

CROTCHED MOUNTAIN

Francestown, NH 03043 (603) 588-2836

AREA INFORMATION

BASE ELEVATION
1,200 feet
HOURS
9:00 a.m. - 4:00 p.m., daily
5:30 - 10:00 p.m., Saturday
LIFTS
3 chairs, 3 T-bars, 1 pony lift
LONGEST RUN
1 mile
NURSERY
No age limit, call Ski Area
SEASON
Late November to early April, snowmaking
SNOW PHONE
Call Ski Area
TRAILS
5 beginner, 17 intermediate, 3 advanced
TRAVEL
2½ miles from Francestown, Route 47
VERTICAL DROP
750 feet

EASTMOND POND

Grantham, NH 03753 (603) 863-4240

AREA INFORMATION

LIFTS
1 chairlift, 700 capacity per hour
HOURS
9:00 a.m. - 4:00 p.m., weekends, holidays
SEASON
Mid-December to March, no snowmaking
SNOW PHONE
Call Ski Area
TRAILS
3 open and tree-lined trails
TRAVEL
38 miles east of Concord, I-89 to exit 13
VERTICAL DROP
240 feet

HIGHLAND

Northfield, NH 03276 (603) 286-4055

AREA INFORMATION

HOURS
Daily, Wed. and Fri. nights
LIFTS
2 bars, 1 tow, 2,100 capacity per hour
NURSERY
Call Ski Area
SEASON
Mid-December to April
SNOW PHONE
Call Ski Area
TRAVEL
I-93 to Bean Hill Road
VERTICAL DROP
700 feet

THE INN AT EAST HILL FARM

Troy, NH 03465 (603) 242-6495

AREA INFORMATION

HOURS
10:00 a.m. - 12:00 p.m., 1:00 - 4:00 p.m.
January, weekends; February, daily
LIFTS
1 tow
LONGEST RUN
400 feet
NURSERY
At the slopes, call Ski Area
SEASON
Late December to late February
SNOW PHONE
Call Ski Area
TRAILS
Small open beginner slope
TRAVEL
From Boston, Routes 2, 140 and 12

KING PINE

East Madison, NH 03849 (603) 367-4648

AREA INFORMATION

BASE ELEVATION
500 feet

HOURS
9:00 a.m. - 4:00 p.m.
LIFTS
2 chairlifts, 1 bar, 1 tow
2,300 capacity per hour
LONGEST RUN
¾ mile
NURSERY
To Age 8, call Ski Area
SEASON
Late December to late March
SNOW PHONE
Call Ski Area
TRAVEL
9 miles from Conway, Route 153
VERTICAL DROP
350 feet

KING'S GRANT

Laconia, NH 03246 (603) 293-4431

AREA INFORMATION

BASE ELEVATION
700 feet
HOURS
Daily, 10:00 a.m. - 12:00 p.m.
2:00 - 5:00, 7:00 - 10:00 p.m.
LIFTS
2 tows, 500 capacity per hour
LONGEST RUN
1,500 feet
NURSERY
At the slopes, call Ski Area
SEASON
Late December to April
SNOW PHONE
Call Ski Area
TRAVEL
6 miles from Laconia, Routes 11 B & C North
VERTICAL DROP
100 feet

MC INTYRE

Manchester, NH 03104 (603) 669-7931

AREA INFORMATION

HOURS
9:30 a.m. - 4:30 p.m., daily
6:00 - 9:30 p.m., Tues. - Sat.
LIFTS
2 chairlifts, 1 tow, 1,000 capacity per hour
LONGEST RUN
1,000 feet
SEASON
Late December to mid-March, snowmaking
SNOW PHONE
Call Ski Area
TRAVEL
20 miles from Concord, I-935
VERTICAL DROP
160 feet

MONTEAU

Haverhill, MN 03765 (603) 787-2781

AREA INFORMATION

BASE ELEVATION
840 feet
HOURS
9:00 a.m. - 4:00 p.m., weekends, holidays
6:00 - 10:00 p.m., Wednesdays & Fridays
LIFTS
1 chairlift, 1 tow, 1,100 capacity per hour
SEASON
Mid-December to mid-March
SNOW PHONE
Call Ski Area
TRAILS
35% beginner, 40% intermediate, 35% advanced
TRAVEL
I-93 to Route 112 West
VERTICAL DROP
600 feet

MOOSE MOUNTAIN

Brookfield, NH 03872 (603) 522-3639

AREA INFORMATION

BASE ELEVATION
630 feet
HOURS
9:00 a.m. - 4:00 p.m., 7:00 - 10:00 p.m.
LIFTS
1 chairlift, 2 bars, 1 tow, 1,900 capacity per hour
LONGEST RUN
1 mile
NURSERY
Age 2 to 7, call Ski Area
SEASON
December to March, snowmaking
SNOW PHONE
Call Ski Area
TRAVEL
17½ miles from Rochester, Rt. 16
VERTICAL DROP
1,220 feet

MT. WHITTIER

West Ossipee, NH 03890 (603) 539-2268

AREA INFORMATION

BASE ELEVATION
400 feet
HOURS
9:00 a.m. - 4:00 p.m.
LIFTS
1 gondola, 1 chairlift, 1 bar,
1 tow, 5,800 capacity per hour
LONGEST RUN
1 mile
NURSERY
Arrangements for babysitter, call Ski Area
SEASON
December to early April
SNOW PHONE
Call Ski Area
TRAILS
50 acres, beginner to advanced
TRAVEL
At junction of Routes 25 & 16
VERTICAL DROP
1,700 feet

OAK HILL

Hanover, NH 03755 (603) 643-4129

AREA INFORMATION

HOURS
12:00 - 4:15 p.m., Tuesday through Friday
10:00 a.m. - 4:15 p.m., weekends, holidays
LIFTS
1 bar
SEASON
December to March
SNOW PHONE
Call Ski Area
TRAILS
50% beginner, 50% intermediate
TRAVEL
Route 10 North to Reservoir Rd.

OSSIPEE MOUNTAIN

Moultonboro, NH 03254 (603) 476-8491

AREA INFORMATION

BASE ELEVATION
1,130 feet
HOURS
Weekends, daily at Christmas & school vacations
LIFTS
1 bar, 1,200 capacity per hour
LONGEST RUN
½ mile
SEASON
Mid-December to mid-March
SNOW PHONE
Call Ski Area
TRAVEL
2 miles from Moultonboro, Routes 25, 109
VERTICAL DROP
370 feet

STORR'S HILL

Lebanon, NH 03766 (603) 448-2101

AREA INFORMATION

HOURS
1:30 - 4:00 p.m., Tuesday thru Friday
10:00 a.m. - 4:00 p.m., Sat., Sun., holidays
6:30 - 9:30 p.m., Tuesday thru Saturday
LIFTS
1 poma, 700 capacity per hour
SEASON
December to March
SNOW PHONE
Call Ski Area
TRAVEL
Route 4 to Spring Street in Lebanon

TEMPLE MOUNTAIN

Petersborough, NH 03458 (603) 924-6949

AREA INFORMATION

BASE ELEVATION
1,480 feet
HOURS
9:00 a.m. - 4:15 p.m., weekends, holidays
LIFTS
1 bar, 1 tow
SEASON
December to April
SNOW PHONE
Call Ski Area
TRAVEL
4 miles from Peterborough, Rt. 101 A, 101 W.
VERTICAL DROP
550 feet

TENNEY MOUNTAIN

Plymouth, NH 03264 (603) 536-1717

AREA INFORMATION

BASE ELEVATION
850 feet
HOURS
9:00 a.m. - 4:00 p.m.
LIFTS
2 chairlifts, 1 tow, 2,600 capacity per hour
Lift tickets are limited, call Ski Area
LONGEST RUN
1½ miles
SEASON
Mid-December to mid-April
SNOW PHONE
Call Ski Area
TRAVEL
I-93, exit 26, 6 miles from Plymouth
VERTICAL DROP
1,300 feet

VETERANS MEMORIAL

West Franklin, NH 03235 (603) 934-3539

AREA INFORMATION

HOURS
9:30 a.m. - 4:30 p.m., weekends, holidays
Night skiing on Thursdays
LIFTS
1 bar, 1 tow
SEASON
December to March
SNOW PHONE
Call Ski Area
TRAVEL
20 miles south of Concord, Route 3
VERTICAL DROP
760 feet

WATERVILLE VALLEY – SNOW'S MTN

Waterville Valley, NH 03223 (603) 236-8391

AREA INFORMATION

BASE ELEVATION
1,520 feet
HOURS
9:00 a.m. - 4:00 p.m., weekdays, holidays
LIFTS
1 chairlift, 900 capacity per hour
LONGEST RUN
4,000 feet
NURSERY
6 months to 12 years, call Ski Area
SEASON
Late December to late March
SNOW PHONE
Call Ski Area
TRAVEL
24 miles from Plymouth, I-93 N., Rt. 49 E.
VERTICAL DROP
580 feet

WILDERNESS

Dixville Notch, NH 03576 (603) 225-3400

AREA INFORMATION

BASE ELEVATION
1,700 feet
HOURS
9:00 a.m. - 4:00 p.m.
LIFTS
1 chairlift, 2 bars, 2,800 capacity per hour
LONGEST RUN
2 miles
SEASON
Early December to April
SNOW PHONE
Call Ski Area
TRAILS
10% beginner, 65% intermediate, 25% advanced
VERTICAL DROP
1,000 feet

WOODBOUND INN

Jaffrey, NH 03452 (603) 532-8341

AREA INFORMATION

BASE ELEVATION
720 feet
HOURS
9:00 a.m. - 4:30 p.m.
LIFTS
2 tows
SEASON
Late December to mid-March
SNOW PHONE
Call Ski Area
TRAVEL
65 miles from Boston, bus & limo service
VERTICAL DROP
600 feet

NEW JERSEY

ARROWHEAD

Marlboro, NJ 07746 (201) 946-4598

AREA INFORMATION

HOURS
3:00 - 10:00 p.m., weekdays
10:00 a.m. - 10:00 p.m., Wed., Sat.
10:00 a.m. - 6:00 p.m., Sundays
LIFTS
4 tows, 500 capacity per hour
LONGEST RUN
600 feet
SEASON
December to February, snowmaking
SNOW PHONE
Call Ski Area
TRAILS
Beginner and intermediate
TRAVEL
40 miles from New York City
N.J. Turnpike to Route 9 S.
VERTICAL DROP
100 feet

BELLE MOUNTAIN

Hopwell, NJ 08525 (609) 397-0043

AREA INFORMATION

HOURS
10:00 a.m. - 4:30 p.m.
Night skiing, weekends, holidays
LIFTS
1 chairlift, 3 tows, 1,500 capacity per hour
SEASON
December to March, snowmaking
SNOW PHONE
Call Ski Area
TRAVEL
Route 29 to Valley Road
VERTICAL DROP
190 feet

Mahwah, NJ 07430 (201) 327-7800

AREA INFORMATION

BASE ELEVATION
450 feet
HOURS
1:00 - 10:00 p.m., weekdays
10:00 - 5:00 p.m., weekends
3:00 - 10:00 p.m., weekends
LIFTS
2 chairlifts, 1 bar, 2,700 capacity per hour
LONGEST RUN
1,800 feet
SEASON
December to March, snowmaking
SNOW PHONE
Call Ski Area
TRAVEL
I-80 to Rt. 17 North
VERTICAL DROP
270 feet

CRAIGMEUR

Newfoundland, NJ 07435 (201) 697-4501

AREA INFORMATION

BASE ELEVATION
1,050 feet
HOURS
8:30 a.m. - 6:00 p.m., 6:00 - 10:30 p.m.
LIFTS
1 chairlift, 1 bar, 2 tows, 3,000 capacity per hour
LONGEST RUN
1,700 feet
SEASON
Mid-November to late March, snowmaking
SNOW PHONE
Call Ski Area
TRAVEL
I-80, Rt. 513 North
VERTICAL DROP
250 feet

GALLOPING HILL

Kenilworth, NJ 07073 (201) 352-8431

AREA INFORMATION

HOURS
10:00 a.m. - 6:00 p.m., 7:00 - 10:00 p.m.
LIFTS
1 tow, 200 capacity per hour
SEASON
Mid-December to early March, no snowmaking
SNOW PHONE
Call Ski Area
TRAIL
One 800 foot run
TRAVEL
I-287 to U.S. 22 E., Galloping Hill Golf Course
VERTICAL DROP
150 feet

HOLLY MOUNTAIN

Salem County, NJ 08069 (609) 935-4600

AREA INFORMATION

HOURS
10:00 a.m. - 4:00 p.m., weekdays
9:00 a.m. - 4:00 p.m., weekends
6:00 - 11:00 p.m., night skiing
LIFTS
1 chairlift, 1 tow, 1,500 capacity per hour
LONGEST RUN
1,500 feet
SEASON
December to March, snowmaking
SNOW PHONE 935-4550
TRAVEL
15 miles from Salem, Rt. 49,
Jericho and Hells Neck Roads
VERTICAL DROP
150 feet

PEAPACK

Brookside, NJ 07926 (201) 543-4589

AREA INFORMATION

HOURS
10:00 a.m. - 4:15 p.m., weekends, holidays
7:30 a.m. - 10:15 p.m., Monday - Thursday
LIFTS
1 tow, 700 capacity per hour
LONGEST RUN
1,200 feet
SEASON
Late December to mid-March
SNOW PHONE 234-1344
TRAVEL
2 miles north of junction of Routes 202 & 206
VERTICAL DROP
200 feet

SKI MOUNTAIN

Pine Hill, NJ 08021 (609) 783-8484

AREA INFORMATION

HOURS
9:00 a.m. - 5:00 p.m., 6:00 - 11:00 p.m.
LIFTS
1 chairlift, 1 bar, 3 tows
LONGEST RUN
2,000 feet
NURSERY
At the slopes, call Ski Area
SEASON
Late November to early March
SNOW PHONE
Call Ski Area
TRAVEL
9 miles from Philadelphia, Rt. 42 E., Rt. 534
VERTICAL DROP
230 feet

NEW MEXICO

RATON SKI BASIN

Raton 87740 (505) 445-3015

AREA INFORMATION

BASE ELEVATION
8,000 feet
HOURS
10:00 a.m. - 4:00 p.m.
LIFTS
1 chairlift, 1 tow, 1,200 capacity per hour
LONGEST RUN
2 miles
SEASON
December to April, snowmaking
SNOW PHONE
Call Ski Area
TRAVEL
I-25, 12 miles from Raton
VERTICAL DROP
820 feet

SIPAPU

Vadito, NM 87579 (505) 587-2240

AREA INFORMATION

BASE ELEVATION
8,200 feet
HOURS
9:30 a.m. - 4:00 p.m.
LIFTS
3 pomas, 1,800 capacity per hour
LONGEST RUN
1½ miles
SEASON
Mid-December to late March
SNOW PHONE
Call Ski Area
TRAVEL
25 miles from Taos, Rt. 3 S.
VERTICAL DROP
800 feet

VAL VERDE

Eagle Nest, NM 87718 (505) 377-2957

AREA INFORMATION

BASE ELEVATION
8,300 feet
HOURS
9:00 a.m. - 4:00 p.m.
LIFTS
1 bar, 1 tow, 500 capacity per hour
LONGEST RUN
½ mile
SEASON
Late November to mid-April
SNOW PHONE
Call Ski Area
TRAILS
65% beginner, 35% intermediate
TRAVEL
25 miles from Taos, U.S. 64 E.
VERTICAL DROP
350 feet

NEW YORK

ADIRONDACK

Porter Corners, NY 12859 (518) 893-9484

AREA INFORMATION

HOURS
Weekends, holidays, Saturday nights
LIFTS
3 bars, 1,100 capacity per hour
LONGEST RUN
2½ miles
SEASON
Mid-December to mid-April
SNOW PHONE
Call Ski Area
TRAVEL
Near Saratoga Springs
VERTICAL DROP
1,000 feet

BEARTOWN

West Chazy, NY 12992 (518) 563-2975

AREA INFORMATION

HOURS
Wednesday, Saturday, Sunday
Wednesday and Friday nights
LIFTS
2 bars, 2 tows
SEASON
December to March, snowmaking
SNOW PHONE
Call Ski Area
TRAILS
Beginner and intermediate
TRAVEL
Near Canadian border, Rt. 22
VERTICAL DROP
125 feet

BETHPAGE STATE PARK

Farmingdale, NY 11735 (516) 249-0701

AREA INFORMATION

HOURS
Open every day
LIFTS
1 tow
LONGEST RUN
400 feet
SEASON
Mid-December to mid-March, snowmaking
SNOW PHONE
Call Ski Area
TRAILS
One slope
TRAVEL
Long Island, 1 mile from Farmingdale
VERTICAL DROP
100 feet

BIG BIRCH

Patterson, NY 12563 (914) 878-3181

AREA INFORMATION

BASE ELEVATION
820 feet
HOURS
10:00 a.m. - 6:00 p.m., weekdays
9:00 a.m. - 6:00 p.m., weekends
6:00 - 10:00 p.m., Mon. thru Sat.
LIFTS
2 chairlifts, 1 bar, 2 tows, 1,000 capacity per hour
LONGEST RUN
2,400 feet
SEASON
Mid-December to mid-March, snowmaking
SNOW PHONE 878-6292
TRAILS
40% beginner, 30% intermediate, 40% advanced
TRAVEL
10 miles from Brewster, Route 22
VERTICAL DROP
450 feet

BIG VANILLA AT DAVOS

Woodridge, NY 12789 (914) 434-5321

AREA INFORMATION

HOURS
9:00 a.m. - 4:30 p.m., 4:30 - 10:00 p.m.
LIFTS
3 chairlifts, 4 T-bars, 2 rope tows
3,800 capacity per hour
LONGEST RUN
3,900 feet
NURSERY
Weekends, call Ski Area
SEASON
December to March, snowmaking
SNOW PHONE
Call Ski Area
TRAILS
7 beginner, 5 intermediate, 7 advanced
TRAVEL
92 miles from New York City
N.Y. Thruway and Route 17
VERTICAL DROP
500 feet

BLACKHEAD MOUNTAIN

Round Top, NY 12473 (518) 622-3157

AREA INFORMATION

HOURS
Saturday and Sunday
LIFTS
1 tow
SEASON
December to March
SNOW PHONE
Call Ski Area
TRAILS
Beginner
TRAVEL
N.Y. Thruway, south of U.S. 20
VERTICAL DROP
110 feet

BOBCAT AT CATSKILL SKI CENTER

Andes, NY 13731 (914) 676-3143

AREA INFORMATION

BASE ELEVATION
2,310 feet
HOURS
10:00 a.m. - 4:00 p.m., Mondays, Fridays
9:00 a.m. - 4:15 p.m., weekends, holidays
LIFTS
2 bars, 1,800 capacity per hour
LONGEST RUN
1¾ mile
SEASON
Mid-December to late March
SNOW PHONE
Call Ski Area
TRAVEL
Under 3 miles from Andes, Rt. 28
VERTICAL DROP
1,050 feet

BOVA SKI SLOPES

Salamanca, NY 14779 (916) 354-2535

AREA INFORMATION

BASE ELEVATION
1,500 feet
HOURS
9:00 a.m. - 5:00 p.m., weekends, holidays
LIFTS
2 tows, 600 capacity per hour
LONGEST RUN
1,000 feet
SEASON
Mid-December to mid-March
SNOW PHONE
Call Ski Area
TRAVEL
In Allegany State Park, U.S. 19
VERTICAL DROP
200 feet

BRANTLING SKI SLOPES

Sodus, NY 14551 (315) 331-2365

AREA INFORMATION

HOURS
Day and night skiing
LIFTS
2 bars, 3 tows, 2,700 capacity per hour
LONGEST RUN
1,400 feet
SEASON
Early December to early March, snowmaking
SNOW PHONE
Call Ski Area
TRAILS
6 slopes
TRAVEL
43 miles east of Rochester
VERTICAL DROP
240 feet

BRISTOL MOUNTAIN

Canandaigua, NY 14424 (716) 374-6331

AREA INFORMATION

BASE ELEVATION
1,000 feet
HOURS
9:00 a.m. - 10:30 p.m., Mon. - Sat.
9:00 a.m. - 8:00 p.m., Sundays
LIFTS
4 chairlifts, 2 tows, 6,500 capacity per hour
LONGEST RUN
1½ miles
NURSERY
At the slopes, call Ski Area
SEASON
Late November to Late March, snowmaking
SNOW PHONE 271-5000, 374-6421
TRAILS
3 beginner, 10 intermediate, 5 advanced
TRAVEL
13 miles from Canandaigua, Rt. 64 South
VERTICAL DROP
1,100 feet

CAMILLUS

Camillus, NY 13031 (315) 487-2778

AREA INFORMATION

BASE ELEVATION
720 feet
HOURS
7:00 - 10:00 p.m., Wed., Thurs., Fri.
9:00 a.m. - 4:30 p.m., weekends
LIFTS
1 bar, 2 tows, 500 capacity per hour
LONGEST RUN
400 feet
SEASON
January to mid-March
SNOW PHONE
Call Ski Area
TRAVEL
7 miles west of Syracuse, Rt. 15
VERTICAL DROP
125 feet

CATAMOUNT

Hillsdale, NY 12529 (518) 325-3200, (413) 528-1262

AREA INFORMATION

BASE ELEVATION
1,000 feet
HOURS
9:30 a.m. - 4:30 p.m., weekdays
8:00 a.m. - 4:30 p.m., weekends, holidays
4:00 p.m. - 10:00 p.m., Tues., Weds., Fri.
LIFTS
3 chairlifts, 2 T-bars, 1 J-bar, 5,400 capacity per hour
LONGEST RUN
2 miles
NURSERY
Call Ski Area
SEASON
Early December to early April, snowmaking
SNOW PHONE
Call Ski Area
TRAILS
40% beginner, 40% intermediate, 20% advanced
TRAVEL
2 hours from New York City
Taconic State Pkwy., Rt. 23 E.
VERTICAL DROP
1,000 feet

COCKAIGNE

Cherry Creek, NY 14723 (716) 287-3223

AREA INFORMATION

BASE ELEVATION
1,590 feet
HOURS
10:00 a.m. - 10:00 p.m., weekdays
8:30 a.m. - 10:00 p.m., weekends, holidays
LIFTS
2 chairlifts, 1 bar, 1,500 capacity per hour
LONGEST RUN
3,100 feet
SEASON
Mid-November to mid-April, snowmaking
SNOW PHONE 287-3545, (216) 221-5070
TRAILS
20% beginner, 50% intermediate, 30% advanced
TRAVEL
60 miles from Buffalo, I-90, Rt. 60 South
VERTICAL DROP
430 feet

CONCORD

Kiamesha Lake, NY 12751 (914) 794-4000

AREA INFORMATION

HOURS
8:30 a.m. - 4:00 p.m.
LIFTS
2 bars, 2 tows, 1,800 capacity per hour

LONGEST RUN
1,200 feet
NURSERY
For hotel guests' children, call Ski Area
SEASON
December until snow melts, snowmaking
SNOW PHONE
Call Ski Area
TRAILS
Beginner
TRAVEL
95 miles from New York City, Thruway, Rt. 17 N.
VERTICAL DROP
400 feet

DRY HILL

Watertown, NY 13601 (315) 782-9712

AREA INFORMATION

HOURS
Days, Tuesday through Sunday
Nights, Monday through Saturday
LIFTS
1 chairlift, 1 bar, 1,900 capacity per hour
SEASON
December to March, snowmaking
SNOW PHONE
Call Ski Area
TRAILS
Beginner to Advanced
TRAVEL
In Watertown, U.S. 11
VERTICAL DROP
300 feet

EAGLE MOUNTAIN

Pattersonville, NY 12137 (518) 887-2511

AREA INFORMATION

HOURS
Wednesday through Sunday
LIFTS
1 bar, 3 tows, 2,000 capacity per hour
LONGEST RUN
3,000 feet
SEASON
December to March
SNOW PHONE
Call Ski Area
TRAILS
30% beginner, 40% intermediate, 30% advanced
TRAVEL
8 miles from Schenectady, U.S. 20
VERTICAL DROP
400 feet

FAHNESTOCK

Carmel, NY 10512 (914) 225-3223

AREA INFORMATION

BASE ELEVATION
750 feet
HOURS
10:00 a.m. - 5:00 p.m., weekdays
9:00 a.m. - 5:00 p.m., weekends, holidays
4:00 - 10:30 p.m., Wednesdays, Fridays
LIFTS
2 bars, 2 tows, 2,300 capacity per hour
LONGEST RUN
1,500 feet
SEASON
Mid-December to early April, snowmaking
SNOW PHONE
Call Ski Area
TRAVEL
Taconic State Parkway from New York City
VERTICAL DROP
250 feet

FROST RIDGE

Le Roy, NY 14482 (716) 768-9730

AREA INFORMATION

BASE ELEVATION
640 feet
HOURS
1:00 - 10:00 p.m., Tuesday thru Friday
9:00 a.m. - 4:30 p.m., Sat., Sun., holidays
LIFTS
1 bar, 3 tows, 2,400 capacity per hour
LONGEST RUN
850 feet
SEASON
Mid-December to early April
SNOW PHONE
Call Ski Area
TRAVEL
20 miles from Rochester, 490 W., Rt. 19 E.
VERTICAL DROP
150 feet

FUN HAVEN

Lebanon, NY 13085 (315) 837-4812

AREA INFORMATION

HOURS
Saturday and Sunday

FUN HAVEN CONT.

LIFTS
1 tow
SEASON
December to March
SNOW PHONE
Call Ski Area
TRAILS
One beginner slope
TRAVEL
Route 12B, north of Norwich
VERTICAL DROP
250 feet

GROSSINGER SKI VALLEY

Grossinger, NY 12734 (914) 292-5000

AREA INFORMATION

HOURS
9:30 a.m. - 4:30 p.m.
LIFTS
1 bar, 1 tow, 600 capacity per hour
LONGEST RUN
1,600 feet
SEASON
Late November to mid-March, snowmaking
SNOW PHONE
Call Ski Area
TRAVEL
Route 17 from New York City
VERTICAL DROP
190 feet

GUNSET SKI BOWL

Richfield Springs, NY 13439 (315) 858-1140

AREA INFORMATION

BASE ELEVATION
1,340 feet
HOURS
Weekends, daily during Christmas week
LIFTS
2 bars, 1 tow, 1,500 capacity per hour
LONGEST RUN
3,000 feet
SEASON
Mid-December to Mid-April
SNOW PHONE
Call Ski Area
TRAVEL
68 miles from Albany, N.Y. Thruway
VERTICAL DROP
330 feet

HAPPY VALLEY SKI CENTER

Alfred, NY 14802 (607) 587-8825

AREA INFORMATION

BASE ELEVATION
1,950 feet
HOURS
7:30 - 10:00 p.m., Wednesday - Saturday
LIFTS
1 bar, 1 tow, 400 capacity per hour
LONGEST RUN
3,000 feet
SEASON
December to March
SNOW PHONE
Call Ski Area
TRAVEL
12 miles south of Hornell, Western N.Y.
VERTICAL DROP
350 feet

HI POINT

Huntington, NY 11743 (516) 271-6690

AREA INFORMATION

HOURS
Monday through Saturday nights
LIFTS
2 tows
SEASON
December to March, snowmaking
SNOW PHONE
Call Ski Area
TRAILS
Beginner and intermediate
TRAVEL
Long Island, on Dix Hills Road
VERTICAL DROP
115 feet

HICKORY SKI CENTER

Warrensburg, NY 12885 (518) 623-9866

AREA INFORMATION

BASE ELEVATION
700 feet
HOURS
9:00 a.m. - 4:00 p.m., weekends and holidays
LIFTS
1 T-bar, 2 pomas, 1 tow, 2,100 capacity per hour

LONGEST RUN
1¼ miles
SEASON
Late December to early April
SNOW PHONE
Call Ski Area
TRAVEL
I-87, Routes 9 and 418 W. to access road
VERTICAL DROP
1,200 feet

HIDDEN VALLEY

Lake Luzerne, NY 12846 (518) 696-2431

AREA INFORMATION

BASE ELEVATION
700 feet
HOURS
9:00 a.m. - 4:30 p.m., daily
7:00 - 10:00 p.m., Fri., Sat.
LIFTS
1 chairlift, 1,200 capacity per hour
LONGEST RUN
1,000 feet
SEASON
December to March, snowmaking
SNOW PHONE
Call Ski Area
TRAVEL
20 miles from Glenn Falls, I-87, exit 61 South
VERTICAL DROP
110 feet

HIGHMOUNT SKI CENTER

Highmount, NY 12441 (914) 254-5494

AREA INFORMATION

BASE ELEVATION
2,100 feet
HOURS
8:30 a.m. - 4:00 p.m., Friday, Saturday, Sunday
Daily during Christmas & Feb. school vacations
LIFTS
4 bars, 1 tow, 3,800 capacity per hour
LONGEST RUN
1½ miles
NURSERY
Ski School, ages 3 to 7, call Ski Area
SEASON
December to April, snowmaking
SNOW PHONE
Call Ski Area
TRAILS
Beginner to advanced
TRAVEL
125 miles from New York City; Thruway, Rt. 28 W.
VERTICAL DROP
1,050 feet

HOLIDAY MOUNTAIN

Monticello, NY 12701 (914) 796-3161

AREA INFORMATION

BASE ELEVATION
900 feet
HOURS
8:30 a.m. - 4:30 p.m., daily
4:30 - 10:00 p.m., Mon. - Sat.
LIFTS
2 chairlifts, 4 bars, 4 tows, 7,000 capacity per hour
LONGEST RUN
4,500 feet
SEASON
Early December to March, snowmaking
SNOW PHONE
Call Ski Area
TRAILS
30% beginner, 40% intermediate, 30% advanced
TRAVEL
4 miles from Monticello, Route 17
VERTICAL DROP
400 feet

HONEY HILL

Warsaw, NY 14569 (716) 786-5793

AREA INFORMATION

BASE ELEVATION
1,000 feet
HOURS
5:00 a.m. - 10:00 p.m., Tuesday - Friday
9:00 a.m. - 10:00 p.m., Saturday, Sunday
LIFTS
1 bar, 3 tows, 3,200 capacity per hour
LONGEST RUN
1,500 feet
SEASON
Early December to March, snowmaking
SNOW PHONE
Call Ski Area
TRAVEL
40 miles from Rochester, Routes 490 W. & 19
VERTICAL DROP
200 feet

INDIAN LAKE

Indian Lake, NY 12842 (518) 648-5112

AREA INFORMATION

HOURS
Weekends, holidays
LIFTS
1 bar
SEASON
December to March
SNOW PHONE
Call Ski Area
TRAILS
Beginner, some intermediate
TRAVEL
Near Rt. 30, south of junction of Rt. 28
VERTICAL DROP
210 feet

IRONWOOD RIDGE

Cazenovia, NY 13035 (315) 655-9551

AREA INFORMATION

BASE ELEVATION
750 feet
HOURS
12:00 - 10:00 p.m., Wednesday - Sunday
LIFTS
1 bar, 3 tows, 800 capacity per hour
Lift tickets limited, call Ski Area
LONGEST RUN
4,700 feet
SEASON
Mid-December to mid-March, snowmaking
SNOW PHONE
Call Ski Area
TRAVEL
Central New York, 10 miles from Syracuse
VERTICAL DROP
500 feet

JUNIPER HILLS

Harrisville, NY 13648 (315) 543-2492

AREA INFORMATION

HOURS
Saturday, Sunday and holidays
LIFTS
2 bars
SEASON
December to March, no snowmaking
SNOW PHONE
Call Ski Area
TRAILS
Beginner to advanced
TRAVEL
West of Harrisville, Route 3
VERTICAL DROP
200 feet

KISSING BRIDGE

Lake Luzerne 12846 (518) 696-2431

AREA INFORMATION

BASE ELEVATION
1,200 feet
HOURS
9:00 a.m. - 5:00 p.m., weekdays
8:00 a.m. - 5:00 p.m., weekends
Choice of 3:00 or 5:00 - 11:00 p.m.
LIFTS
3 chairlifts, 5 bars, 3 tows, 10,000 capacity per hour
NURSERY
Age one and up, call Ski Area
SEASON
Early December to mid-March, snowmaking
SNOW PHONE 592-4961
TRAILS
30% beginner, 50% intermediate, 20% advanced
TRAVEL
I-90, Rt. 400 S., Rt. 16 S.; airport in Buffalo, 35 miles
VERTICAL DROP
500 feet

LABRADOR

Truxton 13158 (607) 842-6221

AREA INFORMATION

HOURS
9:00 a.m. - 10:00 p.m., weekdays
8:00 a.m. - 4:30 p.m., weekends
4:30 - 10:00 p.m., Monday - Friday
LIFTS
2 chairlifts, 3 bars, 1,400 capacity per hour
LONGEST RUN
4,500 feet
NURSERY
Age 1½ and up, call Ski Area
SEASON
Early December to early April, snowmaking
SNOW PHONE
Call Ski Area
TRAILS
40% beginner, 30% intermediate, 30% advanced
TRAVEL
2 miles north of Truxton, Route 13
VERTICAL DROP
680 feet

MC CAULEY MOUNTAIN

Old Forge, NY 13420 (315) 369-3225

AREA INFORMATION

BASE ELEVATION
1,720 feet
HOURS
9:30 a.m. - 4:30 p.m.
LIFTS
1 chairlift, 4 bars, 1 tow, 4,300 capacity per hour
LONGEST RUN
¾ mile
SEASON
December to March
SNOW PHONE
Call Ski Area
TRAILS
9 slopes
TRAVEL
50 miles from Utica, Routes 12 and 28
VERTICAL DROP
480 feet

MOON VALLEY SKI CENTER

Malone, NY 12953 (518) 483-7320

AREA INFORMATION

HOURS
9:00 a.m. - 5:00 p.m., Sat., Sun.
7:00 p.m. - 10:00 p.m., Fridays
LIFTS
1 chairlift, 1 bar, 800 capacity per hour
LONGEST RUN
1 mile
SEASON
Mid-December to mid-April, no snowmaking
SNOW PHONE
Call Ski Area
TRAILS
10% beginner, 80% intermediate, 10% advanced
TRAVEL
Northwest of Lake Placid
VERTICAL DROP
600 feet

MT. CATHALIA

Ellenville, NY 12428 (914) 647-7171

AREA INFORMATION

BASE ELEVATION
1,200 feet
HOURS
9:00 a.m. - 4:30 p.m.
LIFTS
1 chairlift, 1 bar, 900 capacity per hour
LONGEST RUN
3,000 feet
SEASON
November to April, snowmaking
SNOW PHONE
Call Ski Area
TRAVEL
Southeastern New York, Rt. 52
VERTICAL DROP
520 feet

MT. OTSEGO

Cooperstown, NY 13326 (607) 547-9805

AREA INFORMATION

HOURS
Weekends, school holidays
LIFTS
1 T-bar, 3 tows, 1,900 capacity per hour
LONGEST RUN
¾ mile
SEASON
Mid-December to early April
SNOW PHONE
Call Ski Area
TRAILS
Beginner and intermediate
TRAVEL
20 miles from Oneonta, Rt. 28
VERTICAL DROP
300 feet

MT. PETER

Greenwood Lake, NY 10925 (914) 986-4992

AREA INFORMATION

BASE ELEVATION
600 feet
HOURS
9:00 a.m. - 11:00 p.m., weekdays
8:30 a.m. - 11:00 p.m., weekends
Night skiing begins at 5:00 p.m.
LIFTS
2 chairlifts, 2,300 capacity per hour
LONGEST RUN
½ mile
SEASON
Mid-December to mid-March, snowmaking
SNOW PHONE
Call Ski Area
TRAILS
50% beginner, 35% intermediate, 15% advanced
TRAVEL
50 miles from New York City, Routes 17 & 17A
VERTICAL DROP
400 feet

MT. PISGAH SKI CENTER

Saranac Lake, NY (518) 891-1990

AREA INFORMATION

HOURS
2:00 - 8:45 p.m., Tuesday - Saturday
10:00 a.m. - 5:00 p.m., Sundays
LIFTS
1 bar, 600 capacity per hour
LONGEST RUN
½ mile
SEASON
Mid-December to mid-March
SNOW PHONE
Call Ski Area
TRAVEL
Northwest of Lake Placid, Rt. 3
VERTICAL DROP
300 feet

MOUNT RAIMER

Petersburg, NY 12138 (518) 658-3399

AREA INFORMATION

BASE ELEVATION
1,000 feet
HOURS
9:00 a.m. - 10:30 p.m., Tuesday - Friday
8:30 a.m. till dark, Saturday and Sunday
LIFTS
1 chairlift, 1 bar, 1 tow, 1,200 capacity per hour
LONGEST RUN
3½ miles
SEASON
Early December to mid-April, snowmaking
SNOW PHONE
Call Ski Area
TRAVEL
Near Massachusetts border, Northway or Rt. 3
VERTICAL DROP
1,600 feet

MT. STORM

Stormville, NY 12582 (914) 226-4288

AREA INFORMATION

HOURS
12:00 - 5:00 p.m., weekdays
9:00 a.m. - 5:00 p.m., weekends
6:00 - 10:00 p.m., Wed., Fri., Sat.
LIFTS
1 bar, 1 tow
LONGEST RUN
1,800 feet
SEASON
Mid-December to mid-March
SNOW PHONE
Call Ski Area
TRAVEL
50 miles from New York City
I-68 N., I-84 W., Rt. 52 West
VERTICAL DROP
600 feet

MT. WHITNEY

Lake Placid, NY 12946 (518) 523-3361

AREA INFORMATION

BASE ELEVATION
2,000 feet
HOURS
9:00 a.m. - 4:15 p.m., daily
6:30 - 10:00 p.m., Wed., Fri., Sat.
LIFTS
2 bars, 800 capacity per hour
LONGEST RUN
¾ mile
SEASON
Mid-December to mid-March
SNOW PHONE
Call Ski Area
TRAILS
5 slopes
TRAVEL
3 miles from Lake Placid
VERTICAL DROP
400 feet

MYSTIC MOUNTAIN

New Woodstock, NY 13122 (315) 662-3322

AREA INFORMATION

HOURS
4:30 - 10:00 p.m., Monday
10:00 a.m. - 10:00 p.m., Tues. - Fri.
9:00 a.m. - 10:00 p.m., Saturday
9:00 a.m. - 4:30 p.m., Sunday
LIFTS
1 chairlift, 1 T-bar, 1 J-bar
LONGEST RUN
½ mile
NURSERY
At the slopes, call Ski Area
SEASON
Mid-December to early April, snowmaking
SNOW PHONE 662-7600

TRAILS
12 slopes
TRAVEL
At junction of Routes 13 and 80
VERTICAL DROP
590 feet

90 ACRES SKI CENTER

Fayetteville, NY 13066 (315) 637-9023

AREA INFORMATION

BASE ELEVATION
450 feet
HOURS
4:00 p.m. - 10:00 p.m., weekdays
10:00 a.m. - 4:30 p.m., weekends
LIFTS
1 bar, 1 tow, 1,700 capacity per hour
LONGEST RUN
1,500 feet
SEASON
Early December to mid-March, snowmaking
SNOW PHONE
Call Ski Area
TRAILS
Beginner
TRAVEL
8 miles from Syracuse
VERTICAL DROP
100 feet

NORTH CREEK

North Creek, NY 12853 (518) 998-2021

AREA INFORMATION

HOURS
Saturday and Sunday, days only
LIFTS
2 bars
SEASON
December to March
SNOW PHONE
Call Ski Area
TRAILS
Beginner and intermediate
TRAVEL
I-87 to Route 28
VERTICAL DROP
960 feet

OAK MOUNTAIN SKI CENTER

Speculator, NY 12164 (518) 548-6141

AREA INFORMATION

BASE ELEVATION
1,600 feet
HOURS
10:00 a.m. - 4:00 p.m., weekdays
9:00 a.m. - 4:00 p.m., weekends
LIFTS
3 bars, 1 tow, 2,800 capacity per hour
LONGEST RUN
1¼ miles
SEASON
Mid-December to mid-April
SNOW PHONE
Call Ski Area
TRAVEL
N.Y. Thruway, Route 30, from Albany
VERTICAL DROP
650 feet

ORANGE COUNTY

Montgomery, NY 12549 (914) 457-3000

AREA INFORMATION

BASE ELEVATION
400 feet
HOURS
1:00 till dark, Tuesday thru Friday
10:00 a.m. till dark, weekends, holidays
6:00 - 10:00 p.m., Friday and Saturday
LIFTS
1 bar, 1,200 capacity per hour
LONGEST RUN
1,800 feet
SEASON
Mid-December to mid-March, snowmaking
SNOW PHONE
Call Ski Area
TRAILS
Beginner and intermediate
TRAVEL
60 miles from New York City, Rt. 416
VERTICAL DROP
130 feet

OTIS MOUNTAIN SKI CENTER

Elizabethtown, NY 12932 (518) 873-6448

AREA INFORMATION

BASE ELEVATION
1,420 feet
HOURS
10:00 a.m. - 4:00 p.m., weekends
7:00 - 9:30 p.m., Wednesday
Daily during week of Christmas

OTIS CONT.

LIFTS
1 bar, 2 tows
SEASON
Mid-December to late March
SNOW PHONE
Call Ski Area
TRAVEL
40 miles from Plattsburg via Northway
VERTICAL DROP
370 feet

PALEFACE SKI CENTER

Jay, NY 12941 (518) 946-2272

AREA INFORMATION

BASE ELEVATION
1,120 feet
HOURS
8:30 a.m. - 5:00 p.m., daily
6:30 - 10:00 p.m., Friday
LIFTS
1 chairlift, 1 bar, 1,100 capacity per hour
LONGEST RUN
2,000 feet
NURSERY
Through age 11, call Ski Area
SEASON
Mid-December to mid-April, snowmaking
SNOW PHONE
Call Ski Area
TRAILS
15 trails
TRAVEL
15 miles from Lake Placid, Rt. 86 East
VERTICAL DROP
730 feet

PEEK 'N PEAK

Clymer, NY 14724 (716) 355-4141

AREA INFORMATION

BASE ELEVATION
1,400 feet
HOURS
9:30 a.m. - 5:00 p.m., daily
6:30 - 10:30 p.m., night skiing
LIFTS
3 chairlifts, 2 T-bars, 2 J-bars
7,000 capacity per hour
LONGEST RUN
4,100 feet
SEASON
Mid-November to early April, snowmaking
SNOW PHONE
Call Ski Area
TRAILS
25% beginner, 50% intermediate, 25% advanced
TRAVEL
From Jamestown, I-90, Routes 394 S. & 474 E.
From Erie, PA, 30 miles via Routes 8 & 474
VERTICAL DROP
400 feet

PINES

South Fallsberg, NY 12779 (914) 434-6000

AREA INFORMATION

BASE ELEVATION
1,600 feet
HOURS
9:00 a.m. - 4:30 p.m., 7:00 - 10:00 p.m.
LIFTS
1 chairlift, 2 tows, 600 capacity per hour
LONGEST RUN
2,000 feet
SEASON
Late November to early April, snowmaking
SNOW PHONE
Call Ski Area
TRAVEL
Northwest of Middletown, Route 17
VERTICAL DROP
270 feet

PLATTEKILL MOUNTAIN SKI CENTER

Roxbury, NY 12474 (607) 326-7574

AREA INFORMATION

BASE ELEVATION
2,350 feet
HOURS
9:00 a.m. - 4:00 p.m., Fri., Sat., Sun. and holidays
LIFTS
1 chairlift, 2 bars, 1 tow, 2,400 capacity per hour
LONGEST RUN
7,400 feet
NURSERY
Babysitter, call Ski Area
SEASON
December to April, snowmaking
SNOW PHONE
Call Ski Area
TRAVEL
80 miles from Albany, Route 305
VERTICAL DROP
1,000 feet

ROYAL MOUNTAIN

Johnstown, NY 12095 (518) 835-6445

AREA INFORMATION

HOURS
Saturday and Sunday
LIFTS
2 bars
SEASON
December to March, no snowmaking
SNOW PHONE
Call Ski Area
TRAILS
Beginner to advanced
TRAVEL
East of Utica, Route 10
VERTICAL DROP
550 feet

SCOTCH VALLEY

Stamford, NY 12167 (607) 652-7332

AREA INFORMATION

BASE ELEVATION
2,200 feet
HOURS
9:00 a.m. - 4:00 p.m.
LIFTS
3 chairlifts, 1 bar, 1 tow, 3,500 capacity per hour
LONGEST RUN
1 mile
SEASON
Late November to mid-April, snowmaking
SNOW PHONE
Call Ski Area
TRAILS
20% beginner, 60% intermediate, 20% advanced
TRAVEL
I-88, Oneonta exit to Route 23 East
VERTICAL DROP
700 feet

SHU MAKER MOUNTAIN

Little Falls, NY 13365 (315) 823-1111

AREA INFORMATION

HOURS
Days, Wednesday - Sunday; nights, Tuesday - Friday
LIFTS
2 chairlifts, 1 bar, 1 tow, 2,900 capacity per hour
SEASON
December to March, snowmaking
SNOW PHONE
Call Ski Area
TRAVEL
Little Falls, Route 167
VERTICAL DROP
750 feet

SILVER MINE SKI CENTER

Bear Mountain, NY 10911 (914) 786-3791

AREA INFORMATION

BASE ELEVATION
1,750 feet
HOURS
9:00 a.m. - 5:00 p.m., daily
5:00 - 10:30 p.m., Wed. - Fri.
LIFTS
2 bars, 3 tows
LONGEST RUN
1,400 feet
SEASON
Mid-December to early April, snowmaking
SNOW PHONE
Call Ski Area
TRAVEL
From New York City, Palisades Interstate Pkwy.
VERTICAL DROP
350 feet

SKI MAPLE RIDGE

Schenectady, NY 12301 (518) 377-5172

AREA INFORMATION

HOURS
Saturday and Sunday; Tuesday - Saturday nights
LIFTS
1 chairlift, 4 tows
SEASON
December to March, snowmaking
SNOW PHONE
Call Ski Area
TRAILS
Beginner to advanced
TRAVEL
159 West from Schenectady
VERTICAL DROP
225 feet

SKI MINNEWASKA

New Paltz, NY 12501 (914) 255-6000

AREA INFORMATION

BASE ELEVATION
870 feet
HOURS
9:00 a.m. - 5:00 p.m., weekends, holidays
First lift closing, 4:30 p.m.; last at 5:00 p.m.
LIFTS
1 chairlift, 2 bars, 1 tow, 3,300 capacity per hour
NURSERY
Call Ski Area
SEASON
Mid-December to mid-March, snowmaking
SNOW PHONE
Call Ski Area
TRAVEL
Southeastern New York, 10 miles from New Paltz
VERTICAL DROP
380 feet

SKI STONY POINT

Stony Point, NY 10986 (201) 786-2787

AREA INFORMATION

HOURS
10:00 a.m. - 5:00 p.m., weekdays
9:00 a.m. - 5:00 p.m., weekends
5:00 a.m. - 10:00 p.m., Wed. - Fri.
LIFTS
1 chairlift, 1 bar, 1 tow, 2,200 capacity per hour
LONGEST RUN
2,000 feet
SEASON
December to March, snowmaking
SNOW PHONE
Call Ski Area
TRAVEL
From Palisades Parkway, exit 14
VERTICAL DROP
250 feet

SKI WINDHAM

Windham, NY 12496 (518) 734-4300

AREA INFORMATION

BASE ELEVATION
1,500 feet
HOURS
9:00 a.m. - 4:30 p.m.
LIFTS
4 chairlifts, 1 poma, 4,700 capacity per hour
LONGEST RUN
2½ miles
NURSERY
At the slopes, call Ski Area
SEASON
Mid-December to mid-April, snowmaking
SNOW PHONE
Call Ski Area
TRAILS
20% beginner, 40% intermediate, 40% advanced
TRAVEL
From New York City, N.Y. Thruway, Rt. 23 W.
VERTICAL DROP
1,500 feet

SNOW RIDGE

Turin, NY 13473 (315) 348-8456

AREA INFORMATION

BASE ELEVATION
1,250 feet
HOURS
9:00 a.m. - 5:00 p.m., daily
5:00 - 9:30 p.m., night skiing
LIFTS
3 chairlifts, 3 bars, 2 tows, 6,800 capacity per hour
LONGEST RUN
Under one-half mile
NURSERY
At the slopes, call Ski Area
SEASON
First snow to April, no snowmaking
SNOW PHONE
Call Ski Area, in N.Y. call . . . . (800) 962-8419
TRAILS
20% beginner, 60% intermediate, 20% advanced
TRAVEL
Northern New York, I-81, Routes 12 and 26
VERTICAL DROP
500 feet

SONG MOUNTAIN

Tully, NY 13159 (315) 696-5711

AREA INFORMATION

BASE ELEVATION
1,200 feet
HOURS
10:00 a.m. - 4:30 p.m., weekdays
9:00 a.m. - 4:30 p.m., weekends
4:30 - 10:30 p.m., night skiing
LIFTS
1 chairlift, 4 bars, 4,900 capacity per hour

LONGEST RUN
1 mile
NURSERY
At the slopes, call Ski Area
SEASON
Mid-December to early April, snowmaking
SNOW PHONE
Call Ski Area
TRAVEL
30 miles from Syracuse, I-81
VERTICAL DROP
700 feet

STERLING FOREST

Tuxedo, NY 10987 (914) 351-2163

AREA INFORMATION

BASE ELEVATION
950 feet
HOURS
9:00 a.m. - 5:00 p.m., daily
5:00 - 9:00 p.m., Wed. - Sat.
5:00 - 10:00 p.m., Fridays
2:00 till closing, "Twilight"
LIFTS
4 chairlifts, 3,500 capacity per hour
LONGEST RUN
3,000 feet
SEASON
Mid-December to early March, snowmaking
SNOW PHONE
Call Ski Area
TRAILS
20% beginner, 70% intermediate, 10% advanced
TRAVEL
Near N.J. line, 40 miles from New York City, I-87
VERTICAL DROP
450 feet

SWAIN SKI CENTER

Swain, NY 14884 (607) 545-6511

AREA INFORMATION

BASE ELEVATION
1,400 feet
HOURS
10:00 a.m. - 10:00 p.m., Mon. - Fri.
9:00 a.m. - 10:00 p.m., Sat., holidays
9:00 a.m. - 5:00 p.m., Sundays
LIFTS
2 chairlifts, 2 bars, 5,800 capacity per hour
LONGEST RUN
Over 1 mile
SEASON
Late November to mid-April, snowmaking
SNOW PHONE
Call Ski Area
TRAILS
40% beginner, 45% intermediate, 15% advanced
TRAVEL
50 miles south of Rochester, U.S. 15, Rt. 70
VERTICAL DROP
600 feet

TOGGENBURG SKI CENTER

Fabius, NY 13063 (315) 683-5842

AREA INFORMATION

BASE ELEVATION
1,400 feet
HOURS
10:00 a.m. - 10:00 p.m., weekdays
8:30 a.m. - 4:30 p.m., weekends
4:30 - 10:00 p.m., night skiing
LIFTS
1 chairlift, 3 bars, 1 tow, 4,800 capacity per hour
LONGEST RUN
6,000 feet
NURSERY
At the slopes, call Ski Area
SEASON
December to April
SNOW PHONE 446-6666
TRAVEL
20 miles from Syracuse, Routes 81 S. & 80 E.
VERTICAL DROP
600 feet

TRAINER HILL

Colgate Univ., Hamilton, NY 13346 (315) 824-1000 X 613

AREA INFORMATION

BASE ELEVATION
1,200 feet
HOURS
1:00 p.m. - 6:30 p.m., weekdays
10:00 a.m. - 5:00 p.m., Saturdays
11:00 a.m. - 6:00 p.m., Sundays
LIFTS
1 bar, 800 capacity per hour
LONGEST RUN
2,500 feet
SEASON
Mid-December to mid-March, snowmaking
SNOW PHONE
Call office
TRAVEL
In Hamilton, 35 miles southwest of Utica
VERTICAL DROP
370 feet

VAL BIALAS SKI CENTER

Utica, NY 13501 (315) 798-3294

AREA INFORMATION

HOURS
10:00 a.m. - 10:00 p.m.
LIFTS
1 chairlifts, 1 bar, 1 tow
SEASON
December to March, snowmaking
SNOW PHONE
Call Ski Area
TRAILS
Beginner to advanced
TRAVEL
In Utica, Memorial Parkway
VERTICAL DROP
380 feet

WEST MOUNTAIN

Glens Falls, NY 12801 (518) 793-6606

AREA INFORMATION

BASE ELEVATION
450 feet
HOURS
8:30 a.m. - 6:00 p.m., Mon. - Sat.
8:30 a.m. - 4:30 p.m., Sundays
6:00 - 11:00 p.m., except Sundays
LIFTS
3 chairlifts, 1 J-bar, 2 rope tows
4,100 capacity per hour
LONGEST RUN
8,000 feet
SEASON
December to April, snowmaking
SNOW PHONE
Call Ski Area
TRAILS
20% beginner, 65% intermediate, 15% advanced
TRAVEL
5 miles from Glens Falls, I-87
VERTICAL DROP
1,000 feet

WILLARD MOUNTAIN

Greenwich, NY 12834 (518) 692-7337

AREA INFORMATION

BASE ELEVATION
950 feet
HOURS
3:30 - 10:00 p.m., weekdays
Night skiing begins at 6:30 p.m.
9:00 a.m. - 4:30 p.m., weekends
LIFTS
1 chairlift, 2 bars, 1 tow, 2,800 capacity per hour
LONGEST RUN
3,000 feet
NURSERY
Child care, all ages
SEASON
Mid-December to early April, snowmaking
SNOW PHONE
Call Ski Area
TRAVEL
20 miles from Troy, Route 40
VERTICAL DROP
460 feet

WILLIAMS LAKE

Rosendale, NY 12472 (914) 658-3101

AREA INFORMATION

HOURS
Open every day
LIFTS
1 tow
NURSERY
Babysitters, call Ski Area
SEASON
December to March, no snowmaking
SNOW PHONE
Call Ski Area
TRAILS
One beginner slope
TRAVEL
New York State Thruway and Route 8
VERTICAL DROP
100 feet

WING HOLLOW

Allegany, NY 14706 (716) 372-2288

AREA INFORMATION

HOURS
10:00 a.m. - 10:00 p.m., Mon. - Fri.
8:30 a.m. - 10:00 p.m., Saturdays
8:30 a.m. - 4:30 p.m., Sundays
LIFTS
1 chairlift, 2 bars, 750 capacity per hour
LONGEST RUN
2 miles

SEASON
Mid-November to mid-April, snowmaking
SNOW PHONE
Call Ski Area
TRAVEL
80 miles from Buffalo, Routes 219 S. & 17 E.
VERTICAL DROP
810 feet

WOODS VALLEY

Westernville, NY 13486 (315) 827-4721

AREA INFORMATION

HOURS
Tuesday - Sunday; Wednesday - Friday nights
LIFTS
2 chairlifts, 1 bar, 3,500 capacity per hour
SEASON
December to March, no snowmaking
SNOW PHONE
Call Ski Area
TRAILS
Beginner to advanced
TRAVEL
7 miles north of Rome, Route 46
VERTICAL DROP
500 feet

NORTH CAROLINA

APPALACHIAN SKI MOUNTAIN

Blowing Rock, NC 28605 (704) 295-7828

AREA INFORMATION

BASE ELEVATION
3,630 feet
HOURS
9:00 a.m. - 4:00 p.m., daily
6:00 - 10:00 p.m., except Mon. & Thurs.
LIFTS
2 chairlifts, 3 tows, 4,200 capacity per hour
LONGEST RUN
2,700 feet
SEASON
Late November to mid-March, snowmaking
SNOW PHONE
Call Ski Area
TRAILS
Beginner to advanced
TRAVEL
Rt. 16 & U.S. 321 from Charlotte, 90 miles
VERTICAL DROP
360 feet

HIGH MEADOWS

Roaring Gap, NC 28668 (919) 363-2221

AREA INFORMATION

BASE ELEVATION
3,420 feet
HOURS
9:00 a.m. - 4:00 p.m., weekends
6:00 - 10:00 p.m., Mon. thru Sat.
LIFTS
2 tows
LONGEST RUN
800 feet
SEASON
Early December to late March, snowmaking
SNOW PHONE
Call Ski Area
TRAILS
2 slopes
TRAVEL
70 miles from Winston-Salem, Rt. 21 N.
VERTICAL DROP
80 feet

HOUNDS EAR

Blowing Rock, NC 28605 (704) 963-4321

AREA INFORMATION

HOURS
9:00 a.m. - 5:30 p.m.
LIFTS
1 chairlift, 1 tow, 1,500 capacity per hour
LONGEST RUN
1,200 feet
SEASON
Mid-December to late February, snowmaking
SNOW PHONE
Call Ski Area
TRAILS
7 slopes
TRAVEL
5½ miles from Blowing Rock, Rt. 105
VERTICAL DROP
105 feet

MILL RIDGE

Boone, NC 28607 (704) 963-4500

AREA INFORMATION

HOURS
Open every day

MILL RIDGE CONT.

LIFTS
1 chairlift, 1 bar
SEASON
December to mid-March, snowmaking
SNOW PHONE
Call Ski Area
TRAILS
1 beginner, 2 intermediate and 2 advanced slopes
TRAVEL
From Boone, 9 miles west, Route 105
VERTICAL DROP
225 feet

SAPPHIRE VALLEY

Sapphire NC 28774 (704) 743-3441

AREA INFORMATION

HOURS
9:00 a.m. - 4:00 p.m., daily
7:00 - 10:00 p.m., Thurs. - Sat.
LIFTS
1 chairlift, 1 tow, 1,400 capacity per hour
LONGEST RUN
1,800 feet
SEASON
Mid-December to early March
SNOW PHONE
Call Ski Area
TRAILS
3 slopes
TRAVEL
4 miles from Cashiers, Route 64
VERTICAL DROP
320 feet

SEVEN DEVILS RESORT

Banner Elk, NC 28604 (704) 963-5665

AREA INFORMATION

BASE ELEVATION
4,215 feet
HOURS
8:30 a.m. - 4:30 p.m., daily
7:00 - 9:00 p.m., night skiing
LIFTS
2 chairlifts, 2 tows, 1,900 capacity per hour
LONGEST RUN
3,300 feet
SEASON
Early December to mid-March, snowmaking
SNOW PHONE
Call Ski Area
TRAILS
5 slopes
TRAVEL
8 miles from Boone, Rt. 105 South
VERTICAL DROP
600 feet

SKI BEECH

Banner Elk, NC 28604 (704) 387-4231

AREA INFORMATION

BASE ELEVATION
4,670 feet
HOURS
9:00 a.m. - 5:00 p.m., daily
7:00 - 10:00 p.m., Wed., Fri. & Sat.
LIFTS
5 chairlifts, 2 bars, 3 tows
10,000 capacity per hour
LONGEST RUN
1½ miles
NURSERY
At the slopes, call Ski Area
SEASON
Mid-November to March, snowmaking
SNOW PHONE
Call Ski Area
TRAILS
50% beginner, 30% intermediate, 20% advanced
TRAVEL
100 miles from Charlotte, I-85 E., Rt. 321 North
VERTICAL DROP
800 feet

SUGAR MOUNTAIN

Banner Elk, NC 28604 (704) 898-4521

AREA INFORMATION

BASE ELEVATION
4,100 feet
HOURS
9:00 a.m. - 4:30 p.m., daily
6:00 - 10:00 p.m., night skiing
LIFTS
3 chairlifts, 2 bars, 1 tow, 6,200 capacity per hour
LONGEST RUN
1½ miles
NURSERY
At the slopes, call Ski Area
SEASON
Mid-December to mid-March, snowmaking

SNOW PHONE 898-5256
TRAILS
35% beginner, 30% intermediate, 30% advanced
TRAVEL
3 miles from Banner Elk, Rt 105 S.
VERTICAL DROP
1,200 feet

WOLF LAUREL

Mars Hill, NC 28754 (704) 689-4111

AREA INFORMATION

BASE ELEVATION
4,000 feet
HOURS
10:00 a.m. - 4:30 p.m., weekdays
9:00 a.m. - 4:30 p.m., weekends
7:00 - 10:30 p.m., Wed., Fri., Sat.
LIFTS
1 chairlift, 2 tows, 950 capacity per hour
LONGEST RUN
3,500 feet
SEASON
December to mid-March, snowmaking
TRAILS
Beginner to advanced
TRAVEL
28 miles from Asheville, U.S. 23 N.
VERTICAL DROP
700 feet

NORTH DAKOTA

BOTTINEAU

Bottineau, ND 58318 (701) 263-4556

AREA INFORMATION

HOURS
9:00 a.m. - 10:00 p.m., Thurs., Sat.
9:00 a.m. - 5:00 p.m., Fri. & Sun.
5:30 p.m. - 10:00 p.m., Friday
LIFTS
2 bars, 3 tows, 2,000 capacity per hour
LONGEST RUN
1,200 feet
SEASON
December to March
SNOW PHONE . . . . (800) 437-2077
North Dakota . . . . (800) 472-2100
TRAILS
8 runs
TRAVEL
15 miles from Canada, Routes 14 and 5
VERTICAL DROP
200 feet

FT. RANSOM

Ft. Ransom, ND 58033 (701) 683-4834

AREA INFORMATION

HOURS
12:00 - 10:00 p.m., Wednesday
11:00 a.m. - 6:00 p.m., weekends
LIFTS
4 tows
LONGEST RUN
½ mile
SEASON
December to March
SNOW PHONE . . . . (800) 437-2077
North Dakota . . . . (800) 472-2100
TRAILS
6 slopes
TRAVEL
10 miles from Canada, Routes 5 and 30
VERTICAL DROP
300 feet

FROSTFIRE

Walhalla, ND 58282 (701) 549-3600

AREA INFORMATION

HOURS
1:00 p.m. - 9:00 p.m., Friday
10:00 a.m. - 5:00 p.m., Sat., Sun.
LIFTS
1 bar, 2 tows, 1,400 capacity per hour
SEASON
Late November to mid-March
SNOW PHONE
Call Ski Area
TRAVEL
6 miles from Walhalla, Route 6 W.
VERTICAL DROP
400 feet

ROLLA VIEW

Rolla View, ND 58364 (701) 477-5389

AREA INFORMATION

HOURS
1:00 - 5:00 p.m., weekends, holidays
7:00 - 9:30 p.m., Monday nights
LIFTS
3 tows
LONGEST RUN
1,200 feet
SEASON
December to March
SNOW PHONE . . . . (800) 437-2077
North Dakota . . . . (800) 472-2100
TRAILS
3 slopes
TRAVEL
Near Canada, U.S. 281
VERTICAL DROP
140 feet

SKYLINE SKIWAY

Devil's Lake, ND 58301 (701) 766-4479

AREA INFORMATION

BASE ELEVATION
1,430 feet
HOURS
12:00 - 5:00 p.m., Saturday
1:00 - 5:00 p.m., Sunday
6:00 - 10:00 p.m., Wednesday
LIFTS
2 tows, 900 capacity per hour
LONGEST RUN
¼ mile
SEASON
Mid-December to early March, no snowmaking
SNOW PHONE 662-5618
TRAVEL
U.S. 2 to Devils Lake, south on access route
VERTICAL DROP
310 feet

TRESTLE VALLEY

Minot, ND 58701 (701) 839-5321

AREA INFORMATION

BASE ELEVATION
1,310 feet
HOURS
12:00 - 9:00 p.m., Mon. - Thurs.
12:00 p.m. - 5:00 p.m., Saturday
1:00 p.m. - 5:00 p.m., Sunday
LIFTS
2 bars, 1 tow, 2,300 capacity per hour
LONGEST RUN
1,400 feet
SEASON
December to March, snowmaking
SNOW PHONE
Call Ski Area
TRAILS
10 trails
TRAVEL
From Minot, Rt. 2 W., 52, County Rd. 7
VERTICAL DROP
190 feet

VILLA VISTA

Grand Forks, ND 58201 (701) 594-4234

AREA INFORMATION

BASE ELEVATION
900 feet
HOURS
4:00 - 10:00 p.m., Thursday, Friday
10:00 a.m. - 10:00 p.m., weekends
LIFTS
4 tows, 3,600 capacity per hour
LONGEST RUN
900 feet
SEASON
December to March, no snowmaking
SNOW PHONE
Call Ski Area
TRAILS
4 slopes
TRAVEL
20 miles from Grand Forks, Route 2
VERTICAL DROP
100 feet

O H I O

ALPINE VALLEY

Alpine Valley, OH 44026 (216) 285-2211

AREA INFORMATION

HOURS
3:00 p.m. - 10:30 p.m., Mon. - Fri.
10:00 a.m. - 10:30 p.m., Tues. - Thurs.
9:00 a.m. - 11:00 p.m., Sat. & Sun.
LIFTS
2 chairlifts, 2 bars, 2 tows, 6,300 capacity per hour
LONGEST RUN
1,500 feet
SEASON
December to March, no snowmaking

SNOW PHONE 729-9775
TRAVEL
19 miles from Cleveland, Rt. 322 East
VERTICAL DROP
250 feet

BOSTON MILLS

Peninsula, OH 44264 (216) 657-2334

AREA INFORMATION

HOURS
10:00 a.m. - 11:00 p.m., Monday - Friday
8:30 a.m. - 11:00 p.m., Sat., Sun., holidays
Night skiing begins at 6:00 p.m. each night
LIFTS
5 chairlifts, 5 tows, 6,500 capacity per hour
LONGEST RUN
1,800 feet
SEASON
December to March, snowmaking
SNOW PHONE
Call Ski Area
TRAILS
50% beginner, 40% intermediate, 10% advanced
TRAVEL
Between Cleveland and Akron, Turnpike exit 11
to Route 21 S. and Route 303 E. to Peninsula
VERTICAL DROP
240 feet

BRANDYWINE

Northfield, OH 44067 (216) 467-8197

AREA INFORMATION

BASE ELEVATION
670 feet
HOURS
10:00 a.m. - 10:00 p.m., daily
8:30 a.m. - 11:00 p.m., Sat., Sun.
Night skiing begins at 6:00 p.m.
LIFTS
4 chairlifts, 2 bars, 10 tows
LONGEST RUN
1,700 feet
SEASON
Early December to mid-March, snowmaking
TRAILS
50% beginner, 40% intermediate, 10% advanced
This area has graduated slopes for beginners
TRAVEL
Southeast of Cleveland, I-271 to Rt. 8 N.
VERTICAL DROP
240 feet

CLEAR FORK

Butler, OH 44822 (419) 883-2000

AREA INFORMATION

HOURS
12:00 - 10:00 p.m., Monday
10:00 a.m. - 10:00 p.m., Tues. - Fri.
9:00 a.m. - 10:00 p.m., Sat., Sun.
Night skiing begins at 4:00 p.m.
LIFTS
3 chairlifts, 2 J-bars, 4 rope tows
LONGEST RUN
3,500 feet
SEASON
December to March, snowmaking
SNOW PHONE 522-2464
TRAILS
30% beginner, 40% intermediate, 30% advanced
TRAVEL
From I-71, take Route 97 to Butler
Airports: Mansfield and Columbus
VERTICAL DROP
325 feet

ECHO HILLS

Logan, OH 43138 (614) 384-8760

AREA INFORMATION

BASE ELEVATION
1,000 feet
HOURS
10:00 a.m. - 10:00 p.m.
LIFTS
1 T-bar, 2 tows, 2,300 capacity per hour
LONGEST RUN
2,600 feet
SEASON
Mid-December to late March, snowmaking

ECHO HILLS CONT.

SNOW PHONE
Call Ski Area
TRAILS
4 tree-lined slopes
TRAVEL
Southeast Ohio, Route 180
VERTICAL DROP
250 feet

MAD RIVER MOUNTAIN

Bellefontaine, OH 43311 (513) 599-1015

AREA INFORMATION

BASE ELEVATION
1,150 feet
HOURS
11:00 a.m. - 10:00 p.m., weekdays
9:30 a.m. - 10:00 p.m., weekends
Night skiing begins at 4:00 p.m.
LIFTS
3 chairlifts, 1 bar, 4 tows, 5,500 capacity per hour
LONGEST RUN
3,000 feet
SEASON
Early December to March, snowmaking
SNOW PHONE 599-4225
In Ohio. (800) 282-0250
TRAILS
15% beginner, 70% intermediate, 15% advanced
TRAVEL
From Columbus, U.S. 33, 6 miles from Bellefontaine
VERTICAL DROP
300 feet

SUGAR CREEK

Bellbrook, OH 45305 (513) 868-6211

AREA INFORMATION

HOURS
9:30 a.m. - 10:30 p.m.
LIFTS
2 chairlifts, 2 tows, 4,800 capacity per hour
LONGEST RUN
1,600 feet
SEASON
Mid-November to mid-March, snowmaking
SNOW PHONE
Call Ski Area
TRAILS
20% beginner, 60% intermediate, 20% advanced
TRAVEL
15 miles from Dayton, I-75, Route 725
VERTICAL DROP
200 feet

O R E G O N

ANTHONY LAKES

North Powder, OR 97867 (503) 963-8282

AREA INFORMATION

BASE ELEVATION
7,120 feet
HOURS
9:00 a.m. - 4:30 p.m.
LIFTS
1 chairlift, 1 bar, 1,800 capacity per hour
NURSERY
At the slopes, call Ski Area
SEASON
Mid-November to early May, snowmaking
SNOW PHONE
Call Ski Area
TRAILS
25% beginner, 50% intermediate, 25% advanced
TRAVEL
Northeastern Oregon, 23 mile access route
from U.S. 30 between La Grande and Baker
VERTICAL DROP
850 feet

COOPER SPUR

Hood River, OR 97031 (503) 386-3381

AREA INFORMATION

BASE ELEVATION
4,000 feet
HOURS
Weekends & holidays to 9:30 p.m., except Sundays
LIFTS
1 T-bar, 1 tow
SEASON
Mid-December to mid-April
SNOW PHONE
Call Ski Area
TRAVEL
North side of Mt. Hood, 86 miles from Portland
VERTICAL DROP
500 feet

HIGH WALLOWAS

Joseph, OR 97846 (503) 432-5331

AREA INFORMATION

BASE ELEVATION
4,300 feet
HOURS
Wednesday to Sunday, 9:00 a.m. - 4:00 p.m.
LIFTS
1 gondola, 1 chairlift
LONGEST RUN
3½ miles
SEASON
December to mid-June
SNOW PHONE
Call Ski Area
TRAVEL
Northeastern Oregon, I-80, Rt. 82 from Pendleton
VERTICAL DROP
3,700 feet

HOODOO

Sisters, OR 97759 Phone Hoodoo Toll Station No. 2

AREA INFORMATION

BASE ELEVATION
4,660 feet
HOURS
9:00 a.m. - 4:00 p.m., daily
4:00 - 9:00 p.m., Thurs. - Sat.
LIFTS
3 chairlifts, 2 rope tows, 4,800 capacity per hour
LONGEST RUN
1 mile
SEASON
Late November to mid-April, no snowmaking
SNOW PHONE 549-8255
TRAILS
30% beginner, 40% intermediate, 30% advanced
VERTICAL DROP
1,000 feet

MT. ASHLAND

Ashland, OR 97520 (503) 482-2897

AREA INFORMATION

BASE ELEVATION
6,000 feet
HOURS
9:00 a.m. - 4:00 p.m.
LIFTS
2 chairlifts, 2 bars, 1 tow, 3,300 capacity per hour
LONGEST RUN
1 mile
SEASON
December to April
SNOW PHONE
Call Ski Area
TRAILS
10% beginner, 25% intermediate, 65% advanced
TRAVEL
I-5 to Mt. Ashland exit, 8 mile access route
VERTICAL DROP
1,500 feet

MULTORPOR

Government Camp, OR 97028 (503) 272-3522

AREA INFORMATION

BASE ELEVATION
3,700 feet
HOURS
9:00 a.m. - 10:00 p.m., Wednesday - Sunday
1:00 - 10:00 p.m., Tuesday, closed Monday
LIFTS
4 chairlifts, 8 tows, 4,800 capacity per hour
LONGEST RUN
2½ miles
SEASON
Mid-November to mid-April, no snowmaking
SNOW PHONE 224-9221
TRAILS
20% beginner, 50% intermediate, 30% advanced
TRAVEL
53 miles from Portland, Route 26
VERTICAL DROP
1,500 feet

SPOUT SPRINGS

Weston, OR 97886 (503) 566-2015

AREA INFORMATION

BASE ELEVATION
4,950 feet
HOURS
9:00 a.m. - 4:00 p.m., Wed. - Sun.
4:00 - 10:00 p.m., night skiing
LIFTS
2 chairlifts, 2 bars, 1 tow, 4,600 capacity per hour
LONGEST RUN
4,000 feet

SPOUT SPRINGS CONT.

SEASON
Mid-November to mid-April
SNOW PHONE
Call Ski Area
TRAILS
30% beginner, 60% intermediate, 10% advanced
TRAVEL
40 miles from La Grande, Rt. 204
VERTICAL DROP
550 feet

SUMMIT

Government Camp, OR 97028 (503) 272-3351, 272-3255

AREA INFORMATION

BASE ELEVATION
4,000 feet
HOURS
8:00 a.m. - 4:30 p.m., weekends, holidays
LIFTS
1 bar, 4 tows, 900 capacity per hour
LONGEST RUN
¼ mile
SEASON
December to March
SNOW PHONE
Call Ski Area
TRAVEL
56 miles from Portland, Route 26
VERTICAL DROP
600 feet

TOMAHAWK SKI BOWL

Klamath Falls, OR 97601 (503) 884-9227

AREA INFORMATION

BASE ELEVATION
4,200 feet
HOURS
10:00 a.m. - 4:00 p.m., Sat., Sun.
12:00 - 4:00 p.m., Wednesdays
LIFTS
1 bars, 1 tow, 600 capacity per hour
LONGEST RUN
1½ miles
SEASON
Mid-December to late March
SNOW PHONE
Call Ski Area
TRAILS
5 slopes
TRAVEL
U.S. 97 to Klamath Falls, then 25 miles west
VERTICAL DROP
630 feet

WARNER CANYON

Lakeview, OR 97630 (503) 947-2932

AREA INFORMATION

BASE ELEVATION
5,750 feet
HOURS
10:00 a.m. - 4:00 p.m., Thurs., weekends, holidays
LIFTS
1 bar
LONGEST RUN
½ mile
SEASON
Early January to mid-April
SNOW PHONE
Call Ski Area
TRAVEL
Southern Central Oregon, Route 140
VERTICAL DROP
700 feet

WILLAMETTE

Sisters, OR 97759 (503) 433-2705

AREA INFORMATION

BASE ELEVATION
5,200 feet
HOURS
Days: Sundays, holidays
Nights: Wed., Fri. & Sat.
LIFTS
1 poma, 4 tows
SEASON
Late November to May
SNOW PHONE
Call Ski Area
TRAVEL
70 miles from Eugene, Rt. 58 East
VERTICAL DROP
1,500 feet

PENNSYLVANIA

BIG BOULDER

Lake Harmony, PA 18624 (717) 722-0101

AREA INFORMATION

BASE ELEVATION
1,720 feet
HOURS
9:00 a.m. - 4:15 p.m.
LIFTS
6 chairlifts, 1 J-bar, 7,200 capacity per hour
LONGEST RUN
2,900 feet
NURSERY
Babysitters, call Ski Area
SEASON
Early December to late March, snowmaking
SNOW PHONE
Call Ski Area
TRAILS
40% beginner, 40% intermediate, 20% advanced
TRAVEL
North-South Turnpike, I-80 East to
Routes 115, 903, Lake Harmony Rd.
VERTICAL DROP
470 feet

BLACK MOUNTAIN

Philipsburg, PA 16866 (814) 342-1101

AREA INFORMATION

HOURS
9:30 a.m. - 4:30 p.m.
LIFTS
2 bars, 1,300 capacity per hour
SEASON
Mid-December to mid-March
SNOW PHONE
Call Ski Area
TRAVEL
10 miles east of Philipsburg, U.S. 322, 220
VERTICAL DROP
250 feet

BOYCE PARK

Pittsburgh, PA 15239 (412) 325-1516

AREA INFORMATION

HOURS
10:00 a.m. - 4:30 p.m., Mon. - Fri.
9:30 a.m. - 4:30 p.m., Saturdays
9:30 a.m. - 5:00 p.m., Sundays
6:00 - 10:30 p.m., Mon. - Sat.
LIFTS
4 bars
LONGEST RUN
1,200 feet
SEASON
Mid-December to early March
SNOW PHONE
Call Ski Area
TRAVEL
Parkway East, I-376 to Plum exit
VERTICAL DROP
170 feet

BUCK HILL

Buck Hill Falls, PA 18323 (717) 595-7441

AREA INFORMATION

HOURS
Open every day
LIFTS
2 pomas
SEASON
December to March, snowmaking
SNOW PHONE
Call Ski Area
TRAILS
2 slopes
TRAVEL
I-80, 15 miles from Stroudsburg
VERTICAL DROP
320 feet

BUCKALOONS

Youngsville, PA 16371 (814) 563-9210

AREA INFORMATION

BASE ELEVATION
1,200 feet
HOURS
4:30 - 10:30 p.m., Tues. - Fri.
9:30 a.m. - 10:30 p.m., weekends
9:30 a.m. - 5:00 p.m., Sundays
LIFTS
1 chairlift, 2 bars, 1 tow, 2,800 capacity per hour

BUCKALOONS CONT.

LONGEST RUN
1 mile
SEASON
Mid-December to mid-March
SNOW PHONE
Call Ski Area
TRAVEL
10 miles from Warren, Rt. 6 West
VERTICAL DROP
570 feet

CHADDS PEAK

Chadds Ford, PA 19317 (215) 388-6476

AREA INFORMATION

HOURS
9:00 a.m. - 10:00 p.m., daily
Night skiing begins at 4:00 p.m.
LIFTS
1 bar, 3 tows, 4,800 capacity per hour
LONGEST RUN
1,000 feet
NURSERY
At the slopes, call Ski Area
SEASON
Mid-December to late March, snowmaking
SNOW PHONE
Call Ski Area
TRAILS
Beginner to advanced
TRAVEL
30 miles west of Philadelphia
VERTICAL DROP
280 feet

DENTON HILL STATE PARK

Coudersport, PA 16915 (814) 435-6372

AREA INFORMATION

BASE ELEVATION
1,800 feet
HOURS
9:00 a.m. - 4:30 p.m.
LIFTS
1 chairlift, 3 bars, 3,700 capacity per hour
LONGEST RUN
4,800 feet
SEASON
Early December to late March, snowmaking
SNOW PHONE
Call Ski Area
TRAILS
Beginner to advanced
TRAVEL
North-Central Pennsylvania, U.S. 6
VERTICAL DROP
570 feet

DOE MOUNTAIN

Macungie, PA 18062 (215) 682-7109

AREA INFORMATION

BASE ELEVATION
600 feet
HOURS
9:00 a.m. - 10:30 p.m., weekdays
9:00 a.m. - 10:00 p.m., Saturday
9:00 a.m. - 7:00 p.m., Sunday
Weekday nights from 5:30 p.m.
LIFTS
3 chairlifts, 1 bar, 1 tow, 3,800 capacity per hour
LONGEST RUN
4,000 feet
SEASON
Early December to March, snowmaking
SNOW PHONE 682-7107
TRAILS
Beginner to advanced
TRAVEL
28 miles northeast of Reading
VERTICAL DROP
500 feet

EAGLE ROCK

Hazleton, PA 18201 (717) 384-3231

AREA INFORMATION

BASE ELEVATION
1,220 feet
HOURS
9:00 a.m. - 4:00 p.m., 5:00 - 10:00 p.m.
LIFTS
3 chairlifts, 1 tows, 3,900 capacity per hour
LONGEST RUN
Over 1 mile
SEASON
Late November to late March, snowmaking
SNOW PHONE
Call Ski Area
TRAILS
Beginner to advanced
TRAVEL
I-81 to Route 924, 4 miles south of Hazleton
VERTICAL DROP
620 feet

ELK MOUNTAIN

Union Dale, PA 18470 (717) 679-2611

AREA INFORMATION

BASE ELEVATION
1,690 feet
HOURS
9:00 a.m. - 4:00 p.m., weekdays
8:30 a.m. - 4:30 p.m., weekends
5:00 - 10:00 p.m., night skiing
LIFTS
5 chairlifts, 5,200 capacity per hour
LONGEST RUN
1¾ miles
SEASON
Early December to mid-April, snowmaking
SNOW PHONE
Call Ski Area
TRAILS
30% beginner, 30% intermediate, 40% advanced
TRAVEL
I-81 to Lenoxville, access route signs posted
VERTICAL DROP
1,000 feet

FERNWOOD

Bushkill, PA 18324 (717) 588-6661

AREA INFORMATION

HOURS
9:00 a.m. - 4:30 p.m.
LIFTS
2 T-bars, 1 tow
SEASON
Early December to early April
SNOW PHONE,
Call Ski Area, out of state . . . . (800) 233-8103
TRAILS
Beginner to advanced
TRAVEL
I-80, U.S. 209 N., btwn. Philadelphia & New York City
VERTICAL DROP
300 feet

HAHN MOUNTAIN

Kempton, PA 19529 (215) 756-6351

AREA INFORMATION

BASE ELEVATION
400 feet
HOURS
10:00 a.m. - 5:00 p.m., 6:00 - 10:00 p.m., weekdays
9:00 a.m. - 5:00 p.m., 6:00 - 10:00 p.m., weekends
LIFTS
1 chairlift, 1 T-bar, 1 tow, 4,000 capacity per hour
LONGEST RUN
2,600 feet
SEASON
Mid-December to early March, snowmaking
SNOW PHONE
Call Ski Area
TRAVEL
25 miles from Allentown, Routes 22 and 143
VERTICAL DROP
500 feet

HANLEY'S HAPPY HILL

Eagles Mere, PA 17731 (717) 525-3461

AREA INFORMATION

HOURS
Weekends and holidays
LIFTS
2 tows, 1,000 capacity per hour
SEASON
Late December to March
SNOW PHONE
Call Ski Area
TRAVEL
36 miles from Williamsport, Route 42 N.
VERTICAL DROP
200 feet

HICKORY RIDGE

Honesdale, PA 18431 (717) 253-2000

AREA INFORMATION

HOURS
9:00 a.m. - 4:30 p.m., weekends, holidays
LIFTS
1 bar, 1 tow, 1,200 capacity per hour
LONGEST RUN
1 mile
SEASON
Late December to mid-March, snowmaking
TRAVEL
25 miles from Scranton, Routes 6 and 191
VERTICAL DROP
360 feet

HIDDEN VALLEY

Somerset, PA 15501 (814) 445-6014, 445-8575

AREA INFORMATION

BASE ELEVATION
2,550 feet
HOURS
9:30 a.m. - 4:30 p.m., daily
6:30 - 10:30 p.m., Mon. - Sat.
LIFTS
4 chairlifts, 2 pomas, 1 tow, 4,800 capacity per hour
LONGEST RUN
3,600 feet
NURSERY
9:30 a.m. - 4:00 p.m., call Ski Area
SEASON
Mid-December to mid-March, snowmaking
SNOW PHONE
Call Ski Area
TRAILS
25% beginner, 50% intermediate, 25% advanced
TRAVEL
13 miles from Somerset, Rt. 31 West
VERTICAL DROP
400 feet

JACK FROST

White Haven, PA 18661 (717) 443-8425

AREA INFORMATION

BASE ELEVATION
1,500 feet
HOURS
9:00 a.m. - 4:30 p.m.
LIFTS
6 chairlifts, 1 J-bar, 6,600 capacity per hour
LONGEST RUN
3,300 feet
NURSERY
At the slopes, call Ski Area
SEASON
Mid-November to late March, snowmaking
SNOW PHONE
Call Ski Area
TRAILS
25% beginner, 50% intermediate, 25% advanced
TRAVEL
Turnpike, Northeast Extension to Rt. 940 East
VERTICAL DROP
600 feet

LAUREL MOUNTAIN

Ligonier, PA 15658 (412) 238-6688

AREA INFORMATION

HOURS
9:30 a.m. - 4:30 p.m., except Tuesday
6:00 - 10:00 p.m., Thursday, Friday
LIFTS
1 chairlift, 2 pomas, 2 tows, 3,800 capacity per hour
LONGEST RUN
1¼ miles
SEASON
Late December to late March, snowmaking
SNOW PHONE 238-4460
TRAILS
3 beginner, 8 intermediate, 2 advanced
TRAVEL
Route 30 East from Ligonier, 8 miles
VERTICAL DROP
900 feet

LEMON DROP

Ebensburg, PA 15931 (814) 344-8749

AREA INFORMATION

BASE ELEVATION
1,880 feet
HOURS
10:00 a.m. - 5:00 p.m., 6:00 - 10:30 p.m.
LIFTS
2 bars
LONGEST RUN
2,300 feet
SEASON
December to March, snowmaking
SNOW PHONE
Call Ski Area
TRAILS
Beginner and intermediate
TRAVEL
20 miles northeast of Johnstown
VERTICAL DROP
300 feet

LITTLE GAP

Palmerton, PA 18071 (215) 826-7700, 826-3565

AREA INFORMATION

BASE ELEVATION
1,200 feet
HOURS
3:00 p.m. - 10:00 p.m., Monday thru Friday
8:00 a.m. - 10:00 p.m., weekends, holidays
LIFTS
1 chairlift, 1 bar, 1,800 capacity per hour

LONGEST RUN
1,700 feet
SEASON
Mid-December to mid-March, snowmaking
SNOW PHONE
Call Ski Area
TRAILS
35% beginner, 30% intermeidiate, 35% advanced
TRAVEL
I-80 to Palmerton, 5 miles east to Ski Area
VERTICAL DROP
300 feet

MASTHOPE

Lackawaxen, PA 18435 (717) 685-7101

AREA INFORMATION

BASE ELEVATION
700 feet
HOURS
9:30 a.m. - 4:30 p.m., weekdays
8:30 a.m. - 4:30 p.m., weekends
LIFTS
1 chairlift, 1 bar, 1,800 capacity per hour
LONGEST RUN
5,400 feet
SEASON
Late November to late March, snowmaking
SNOW PHONE
Call Ski Area
TRAILS
Beginner to advanced
TRAVEL
Northeastern Pennsylvania, Route 590
VERTICAL DROP
650 feet

MONT SAINT ONGE

Hughesville, PA 17737 (717) 584-2698

AREA INFORMATION

BASE ELEVATION
1,850 feet
HOURS
10:00 a.m. - 5:00 p.m., weekends
LIFTS
1 poma, 1 tow, 700 capacity per hour
LONGEST RUN
½ mile
SEASON
Mid-December to late March, no snowmaking
SNOW PHONE
Call Ski Area
TRAVEL
28 miles from Williamsport, Rt. 220 North
VERTICAL DROP
250 feet

MT. HEIDELBERG

Bernville, PA 19506 (215) 488-9533

AREA INFORMATION

BASE ELEVATION
300 feet
HOURS
10:00 a.m. - 5:00 p.m., Wed., Sat., Sun., holidays
6:30 p.m. - 10:30 p.m., night skiing every night
LIFTS
1 bar, 1 tow, 1,500 capacity per hour
LONGEST RUN
2,500 feet
SEASON
Mid-December to mid-March
SNOW PHONE
Call Ski Area
TRAILS
Beginner to advanced
TRAVEL
10 miles from Reading, Rt. 183 North
VERTICAL DROP
250 feet

MT. PLEASANT

Cambridge Springs, PA 16403 (814) 734-1641

AREA INFORMATION

BASE ELEVATION
1,200 feet
HOURS
5:00 - 10:00 p.m., Mon. - Fri.
9:30 a.m. - 10:00 p.m., Saturday
9:30 a.m. - 5:00 p.m., Sunday
LIFTS
3 bars, 2,200 capacity per hour
LONGEST RUN
3,100 feet
SEASON
Early December to late March, snowmaking
SNOW PHONE
Call Ski Area
TRAVEL
From Erie, U.S. 19, U.S. 6, Rt. 86
VERTICAL DROP
350 feet

MT. TONE

Lake Como, PA 18437 (717) 798-2707

AREA INFORMATION

HOURS
Days: Friday, Saturday and Sunday
Nights: Wednesday, Friday, Saturday
LIFTS
1 chairlift, 1 T-bar, 2 tows
SEASON
December to March
SNOW PHONE
Call Ski Area
TRAVEL
Northeastern Pennsylvania, Rt. 247
VERTICAL DROP
450 feet

NORTH MOUNTAIN

Muncy Valley, PA 17758 (717) 482-2541

AREA INFORMATION

BASE ELEVATION
1,100 feet
HOURS
10:00 a.m. - 4:00 p.m., weekends, holidays
LIFTS
1 J-bar, 1 poma, 1 tow
LONGEST RUN
1,200 feet
SEASON
Late December to early April, snowmaking
SNOW PHONE
Call Ski Area
TRAILS
Beginner
TRAVEL
Northern Pennsylvania, U.S. 220
Two miles from Muncy Valley
VERTICAL DROP
170 feet

OREGON HILL

Morris, PA 16938 (717) 353-7521

AREA INFORMATION

BASE ELEVATION
1,700 feet
HOURS
9:00 a.m. - 5:00 p.m., daily
Until 10:00 p.m., Mon. - Fri.
LIFTS
1 chairlift, 3 T-bars, 3,400 capacity per hour
LONGEST RUN
7,000 feet
SEASON
Mid-November to late March, snowmaking
SNOW PHONE
Call Ski Area
TRAVEL
36 miles from Williamsport, U.S. 220 to 287
VERTICAL DROP
350 feet

POCONO MANOR

Pocono Manor, PA 18349 (717) 839-7111

AREA INFORMATION

HOURS
Weekdays, some weekends
LIFTS
1 J-bar, 1 T-bar
NURSERY
Babysitters, call Ski Area
SEASON
December to March, snowmaking
TRAILS
4 slopes
TRAVEL
Northeastern Pennsylvania, Route 611
VERTICAL DROP
250 feet

RICHMOND HILL

Fort Loudon, PA 17224 (717) 369-2643

AREA INFORMATION

BASE ELEVATION
850 feet
HOURS
10:00 a.m. - 5:00 p.m., weekends
LIFTS
1 bar
SEASON
December to March
TRAILS
Small intermediate area
TRAVEL
Rt. 30 to Rt. 75, 4 miles north
VERTICAL DROP
120 feet

SAW CREEK

Bushkill, PA 18324 (717) 588-6611

AREA INFORMATION

HOURS
10:00 a.m. - 5:00 p.m.
LIFTS
1 chairlift, 1,100 capacity per hour
SEASON
Mid-December to late February, snowmaking
SNOW PHONE
Call Ski Area
TRAILS
7 slopes
TRAVEL
Central Pennsylvania, U.S. 522, north of Harrisburg
VERTICAL DROP
300 feet

SHAWNEE MOUNTAIN

Shawnee-on-Delaware, PA 18356 (717) 421-7231

AREA INFORMATION

BASE ELEVATION
650 feet
HOURS
9:00 a.m. - 4:30 p.m., weekdays
8:30 a.m. - 4:30 p.m., weekends
LIFTS
4 chairlifts, 4,500 capacity per hour
LONGEST RUN
1 mile
NURSERY
Babysitters, call Ski Area
SEASON
Late November to late March, snowmaking
SNOW PHONE
Call Ski Area
TRAILS
4 beginner, 5 intermediate, 3 advanced
TRAVEL
Eastern Pennsylvania; I-80 to Rt. 209 N.
Four miles north of East Stroudsburg
VERTICAL DROP
700 feet

SKI LIBERTY

Fairfield, PA 17320 (717) 642-8282

AREA INFORMATION

BASE ELEVATION
580 feet
HOURS
9:00 a.m. - 6:00 p.m., weekdays
8:00 a.m. - 6:00 p.m., weekends
6:00 - 10:00 p.m., night skiing
LIFTS
4 chairlifts, 1 J-bar, 3,500 capacity per hour
LONGEST RUN
4,300 feet
NURSERY
Age 1½ and up, call Ski Area
SEASON
Late November to mid-March, snowmaking
SNOW PHONE 642-8297
Outside state. . . . . (800) 233-7521
TRAILS
25% beginner, 50% intermediate, 25% advanced
TRAVEL
From Gettysburg, Routes 30E., 94 S. and 116 E.
VERTICAL DROP
600 feet

SKI ROUNDTOP

Lewisberry, PA 17339 (717) 432-9631

AREA INFORMATION

BASE ELEVATION
650 feet
HOURS
9:00 a.m. - 5:00 p.m., weekdays
8:00 a.m. - 5:00 p.m., weekends
6:00 - 10:00 p.m., night skiing
LIFTS
5 chairlifts, 2 J-bars, 7,000 capacity per hour
LONGEST RUN
4,100 feet
NURSERY
From age 1½, call Ski Area
SEASON
Mid-November to mid-March, snowmaking
SNOW PHONE . . . . (800) 382-1390
Outside state. . . . . (800) 233-1134
TRAILS
25% beginner, 45% intermediate, 30% advanced
TRAVEL
Near Harrisburg, Turnpike, I-81
or I-83 to Routes 382 N. & 177 S.
VERTICAL DROP
550 feet

SPLIT ROCK

Lake Harmony, PA 18624 (717) 722-9111

AREA INFORMATION

BASE ELEVATION
2,000 feet

SPLIT ROCK CONT.

HOURS
9:00 a.m. - 4:30 p.m., daily
6:00 - 10:00 p.m., Wed., Fri.
LIFTS
1 bar, 500 capacity per hour
LONGEST RUN
1,400 feet
SEASON
Late November to March, snowmaking
SNOW PHONE
Call Ski Area
TRAILS
2 slopes
TRAVEL
15 miles from Hazleton, I-80 to Rt. 940
VERTICAL DROP
150 miles

SPRING MOUNTAIN

Spring Mount, PA 19478 (215) 287-7900

AREA INFORMATION

BASE ELEVATION
50 feet
HOURS
10:00 a.m. - 5:00 p.m., daily
9:00 a.m. - 5:00 p.m., weekends
6:00 - 11:00 p.m., night skiing
LIFTS
3 chairlifts, 2 tows, 3,600 capacity per hour
LONGEST RUN
3,000 feet
SEASON
Mid-December to mid-March
SNOW PHONE
Call Ski Area
TRAVEL
30 miles from Philadelphia, Northeast
Extension of Turnpike, Routes 73 & 29
VERTICAL DROP
450 feet

SUGARBUSH MOUNTAIN

Latrobe, PA 15650 (412) 238-9655

AREA INFORMATION

BASE ELEVATION
1,800 feet
HOURS
12:00 - 5:00 p.m., Sat., Sun., holidays
6:30 p.m. - 10:30 p.m., Tues. thru Sun.
LIFTS
2 tows
LONGEST RUN
1,800 feet
SEASON
Early December to early April
SNOW PHONE
Call Ski Area
TRAILS
2 slopes
TRAVEL
Southwestern Pennsylvania, U.S. 30, Rt. 982
VERTICAL DROP
200 feet

TAMIMENT RESORT HOTEL

Tamiment, PA 18371 (717) 588-6652

AREA INFORMATION

BASE ELEVATION
1,840 feet
LIFTS
1 chairlift, 1,100 capacity per hour
LONGEST RUN
1,200 feet
SEASON
Late December to mid-March, snowmaking
SNOW PHONE
Call Ski Area
TRAILS
2 slopes
TRAVEL
Eastern Pennsylvania near state line, U.S. 209
VERTICAL DROP
120 feet

TIMBER HILL

Canadensis, PA 18325 (717) 595-7571

AREA INFORMATION

BASE ELEVATION
700 feet
HOURS
9:00 a.m. - 4:30 p.m.
LIFTS
3 bars
LONGEST RUN
5,000 feet
SEASON
Mid-December to mid-March, snowmaking
SNOW PHONE
Call Ski Area

TRAILS
2 slopes
TRAVEL
Northeastern Pennsylvania, Route 447
VERTICAL DROP
400 feet

VACATION VILLAGE

Zion Grove, PA 17985 (717) 384-3214

AREA INFORMATION

HOURS
8:30 a.m. - 4:30 p.m., weekends, holidays
LIFTS
1 chairlift, 1 tow, 700 capacity per hour
SEASON
January to March
SNOW PHONE
Call Ski Area
TRAILS
20% beginner, 60% intermediate, 20% advanced
TRAVEL
I-81 to Route 924 South
VERTICAL DROP
410 feet

RHODE ISLAND

PINE TOP

West Greenwich, RI 02818 Phone Unlisted

AREA INFORMATION

BASE ELEVATION
300 feet
HOURS
10:00 a.m. - 4:30 p.m., 5:00 - 10:00 p.m.
LIFTS
2 bars, 2 tows, 3,800 capacity per hour
LONGEST RUN
½ mile
SEASON
December to mid-March, snowmaking
SNOW PHONE
Call Ski Area
TRAILS
Beginner, 4 slopes
TRAVEL
20 miles from Providence, I-95 South
VERTICAL DROP
280 feet

SKI VALLEY

Cumberland, RI 02864 (401) 333-6406

AREA INFORMATION

BASE ELEVATION
200 feet
HOURS
9:00 a.m. - 10:00 p.m., , 7:00 - 10:00 p.m.
LIFTS
1 bar, 5 tows, 1,800 capacity per hour
LONGEST RUN
3,000 feet
SEASON
Early December to mid-March, snowmaking
SNOW PHONE
Call Ski Area
TRAILS
5 open slopes
TRAVEL
North of Providence, Route 122
VERTICAL DROP
270 feet

YAWGOO VALLEY

Exeter, RI 02882 (401) 295-5366, 294-3802

AREA INFORMATION

HOURS
10:00 a.m. - 10:00 p.m., Monday - Friday
9:00 a.m. - 10:00 p.m., weekends, holidays
LIFTS
1 chairlift, 3 rope tows, 2,100 capacity per hour
LONGEST RUN
1,800 feet
NURSERY
From age 1, call Ski Area
SEASON
December to March, snowmaking
SNOW PHONE
Call Ski Area
TRAILS
1 intermediate and 3 beginner slopes
TRAVEL
I-95 and Rt. 2, south of Providence
VERTICAL DROP
280 feet

SOUTH DAKOTA

DEER MOUNTAIN

Deadwood, SD 57732 (605) 584-3230

AREA INFORMATION

BASE ELEVATION
6,000 feet
HOURS
9:00 a.m. - 4:00 p.m., except Monday
6:30 - 9:30 p.m., Wednesday - Friday
Open holidays, closed Christmas day
LIFTS
1 chairlift, 2 pomas, 1 tow, 2,300 capacity per hour
LONGEST RUN
5,000 feet
SEASON
Late November to April
SNOW PHONE
Call Ski Area
TRAVEL
2 miles from Lead, Route 85
VERTICAL DROP
600 feet

GREAT BEAR SKI VALLEY

Sioux Falls, SD 57101 (605) 338-1351

AREA INFORMATION

HOURS
Thursday through Sunday and holidays
10:00 a.m. - 10:00 p.m., Sunday till six
LIFTS
4 tows, 1,100 capacity per hour
LONGEST RUN
1,500 feet
SEASON
Early December to mid-March, snowmaking
SNOW PHONE
Call Ski Area
TRAILS
3 open slopes
TRAVEL
I-299 to Sioux Falls, Rice Street exit
VERTICAL DROP
250 feet

INKPA-DU-TA

Big Stone City 57216 (612) 839-3315

AREA INFORMATION

HOURS
7:00 - 10:00 p.m., Tues. - Thurs.
1:00 - 5:00 p.m., weekends
LIFTS
3 tows
SEASON
Mid-December to mid-March
SNOW PHONE
Call Ski Area
TRAILS
1 beginner, 3 intermediate, 1 advanced
TRAVEL
I-29 and Route 77 N. to Big Stone City
VERTICAL DROP
150 feet

TERRY PEAK

Lead, SD 57754 (605) 584-2165

AREA INFORMATION

BASE ELEVATION
5,800 feet
HOURS
Open days and nights
LIFTS
3 chairlifts, 3 pomas
LONGEST RUN
8,000 feet
SEASON
Early December to early April, snowmaking
SNOW PHONE
Call Ski Area, outside state . . . . (800) 843-1930
TRAILS
25% beginner, 50% intermediate, 25% advanced
TRAVEL
Near Wyoming, I-90 to U.S. 85
VERTICAL DROP
1,270 feet

TENNESSEE

OBER GATLINBURG

Gatlinburg, TN 37738 (615) 436-5423

AREA INFORMATION

BASE ELEVATION
2,700 feet
HOURS
8:00 a.m. - 4:30 p.m., daily
6:00 - 10:00 p.m., Mon. - Sat.

LIFTS
1 tram, 3 chairlifts, 5 tows, 2,000 capacity per hour
LONGEST RUN
¾ mile
SEASON
December to mid-March, snowmaking
SNOW PHONE
Call Ski Area
TRAVEL
40 miles from Knoxville, I-40 E., Rt. 66, U.S. 441
VERTICAL DROP
800 feet

U T A H

BEAVER MOUNTAIN

Logan, UT 84321 (801) 753-0921, 563-5677

AREA INFORMATION

BASE ELEVATION
7,200 feet
HOURS
9:30 a.m. - 4:20 p.m., Tuesday thru Sunday
5:00 p.m. - 9:30 p.m., Tuesday thru Friday
Open holidays, except Christmas Day
LIFTS
3 chairlifts, 1 bar, 3,000 capacity per hour
LONGEST RUN
2¼ miles
SEASON
December to April, no snowmaking
SNOW PHONE 753-4822
TRAILS
25% beginner, 35% intermediate, 40% advanced
TRAVEL
27 miles from Logan, Rt. 89 East
VERTICAL DROP
1,630 feet

DEER VALLEY

Park City, UT 84060 (801) 649-1000, 649-4149

AREA INFORMATION

BASE ELEVATION
7,200 feet
HOURS
9:00 a.m. - 4:00 p.m.
LIFTS
5 chairlifts, 8,400 capacity per hour
Limited tickets, reservations. . . . . . . (800) 453-3833
LONGEST RUN
1.1 miles
NURSERY
At the slopes, call Ski Area
SEASON
Mid-December to late April
SNOW PHONE
Call Ski Area
TRAILS
20% beginner, 50% intermediate, 30% advanced
TRAVEL
35 miles from Salt Lake Int'l Airport, I-80, Rt. 224
VERTICAL DROP
2,200 feet

MT. HOLLY

Beaver, UT 84713 (801) 438-5030

AREA INFORMATION

BASE ELEVATION
9,200 feet
HOURS
9:30 a.m. - 4:30 p.m., weekends and holidays
LIFTS
1 chairlift, 1 T-bar, 1 tow, 2,900 capacity per hour
SEASON
Late November to early April
SNOW PHONE
Call Ski Area
TRAILS
Beginner to advanced
TRAVEL
60 miles from Cedar City, I-15 North
VERTICAL DROP
1,000 feet

NORDIC VALLEY

Eden, UT 84310 (801) 745-3771

AREA INFORMATION

HOURS
9:30 a.m. - 4:30 p.m., Tues. - Sun.
5:30 p.m. - 10:00 p.m., Mon. - Sat.
LIFTS
2 chairlifts, 1,800 capacity per hour
SEASON
Early December to early April
SNOW PHONE
Call Ski Area
TRAILS
Beginner to advanced
TRAVEL
I-15 North to 12th Street in Ogden
East to Ogden Canyon, signs posted
VERTICAL DROP
1,000 feet

PARLEY'S SUMMIT

Park City 84060 (801) 649-9840

AREA INFORMATION

HOURS
Open every day
LIFTS
2 chairlifts, 1,900 capacity per hour
SEASON
December to early May
SNOW PHONE
Call Ski Area
TRAILS
Beginner, open bowl
TRAVEL
I-80, 20 miles east of Salt Lake City
VERTICAL DROP
450 feet

POWDER MOUNTAIN

Eden 84310 (801) 745-3771

AREA INFORMATION

BASE ELEVATION
7,680 feet
HOURS
9:30 a.m. - 10:00 p.m., daily
9:30 a.m. - 4:30 p.m., Sunday
LIFTS
3 chairlifts, 1 tow, 4,500 capacity per hour
LONGEST RUN
3 miles
SEASON
Mid-November to May, no snowmaking
SNOW PHONE
Call Ski Area
TRAILS
15% beginner, 70% intermediate, 15% advanced
TRAVEL
55 miles from Salt Lake City via I-15 to
12th St. exit to Ogden Cyn., watch signs
VERTICAL DROP
1,300 feet

SNOWLAND

Fairview, UT 84629 (801) 427-3827

AREA INFORMATION

BASE ELEVATION
8,600 feet
HOURS
Weekends and holidays
LIFTS
1 tow, 300 capacity per hour
LONGEST RUN
3,500 feet
SEASON
December to April
SNOW PHONE
Call Ski Area
TRAILS
Beginner and intermediate
TRAVEL
Central Utah, U.S. 89, Route 31
VERTICAL DROP
200 feet

SOLITUDE

Salt Lake City, UT 84117 (801) 534-1400

AREA INFORMATION

BASE ELEVATION
8,000 feet
HOURS
9:30 a.m. - 4:30 p.m., daily
3:30 - 9:30 p.m., Wed. - Sat.
LIFTS
3 chairlifts, 1 tow, 4,000 capacity per hour
LONGEST RUN
2½ miles
SEASON
November to May, no snowmaking
SNOW PHONE
Call Ski Area
TRAILS
25% beginner, 30% intermediate, 45% advanced
TRAVEL
From Salt Lake City, 23 miles via I-215 to Wasatch Bl.,
left onto Rt. 152, Big Cottonwood Cyn. Rd., 12 miles
VERTICAL DROP
1,800 feet

SUNDANCE

Provo, UT 84601 (801) 225-4100, (800) 662-5901

AREA INFORMATION

BASE ELEVATION
6,100 feet
HOURS
9:00 a.m. - 4:00 p.m., daily
4:00 - 9:00 p.m., Mon. - Fri.
LIFTS
3 chairlifts, 3,500 capacity per hour

LONGEST RUN
2½ miles
SEASON
December to April, no snowmaking
SNOW PHONE
Call Ski Area
TRAILS
10% beginner, 50% intermediate, 40% advanced
TRAVEL
60 miles from Salt Lake Int'l Airport, I-15 South
Exit 189, east seven miles through Provo Canyon
VERTICAL DROP
1,740 feet

V E R M O N T

CARINTHIA

West Dover, VT 05356 (802) 464-5461

AREA INFORMATION

BASE ELEVATION
1,900 feet
HOURS
9:00 a.m. - 4:00 p.m., weekends, holiday weeks
LIFTS
1 chairlift, 1 bar, 1,200 capacity per hour
LONGEST RUN
4,000 feet
SEASON
December to April
SNOW PHONE
Call Ski Area
TRAILS
8 slopes
TRAVEL
I-91 N., Routes 9 W. and 100 N.
VERTICAL DROP
800 feet

COCHRAN

Richmond, VT 05477 (802) 434-2479

AREA INFORMATION

BASE ELEVATION
350 feet
HOURS
9:30 a.m. - 4:00 p.m., weekends, holiday weeks
2:30 - 5:00 p.m., Tuesday, Thursday, Friday
LIFTS
1 bar, 3 tows, 1,900 capacity per hour
LONGEST RUN
3,000 feet
SEASON
Mid-December to March
SNOW PHONE
Call Ski Area
TRAVEL
I-89, 25 miles from Montpelier
VERTICAL DROP
500 feet

DUTCH MOUNTAIN

Readsboro, VT 05350 (802) 423-5312

AREA INFORMATION

BASE ELEVATION
1,970 feet
HOURS
Weekends, holiday weeks
LIFTS
1 T-bar, 1 J-bar, 1,700 capacity per hour
SEASON
Late December to April
SNOW PHONE
Call Ski Area
TRAVEL
Southern Vermont near state line, Route 100
VERTICAL DROP
570 feet

HAYSTACK

Wilmington, VT 05363 (802) 464-5321

AREA INFORMATION

BASE ELEVATION
1,800 feet
HOURS
9:00 a.m. - 4:00 p.m.
LIFTS
3 chairlifts, 3 bars, 4,100 capacity per hour
LONGEST RUN
Over 2 miles
NURSERY
Ages 3 to 7, call Ski Area
SEASON
Early December to late March, snowmaking
SNOW PHONE 229-0531
TRAILS
25% beginner, 50% intermediate, 25% advanced
TRAVEL
In Southern Vermont between U.S. 7 and I-91
Routes 9 or 100 to Wilmington, 2 miles to Area
VERTICAL DROP
1,400 feet

HOGBACK MOUNTAIN

Marlboro, VT 05301 (802) 464-3942

AREA INFORMATION

HOURS
Open every day
LIFTS
4 bars
SEASON
December to April
SNOW PHONE
Call Ski Area
TOP ELEVATION
2,350 feet
TRAILS
Beginner to advanced
TRAVEL
Route 9, Southeastern Vermont

JAY PEAK

Jay Peak, VT 05859 (802) 988-2611

AREA INFORMATION

BASE ELEVATION
1,800 feet
HOURS
9:00 a.m. - 4:00 p.m.
LIFTS
1 tram, 2 chairlifts, 3 bars, 6,300 capacity per hour
LONGEST RUN
2½ miles
NURSERY
Babysitter for ages 2 to 7, call Ski Area
SEASON
Early November to early May, snowmaking
SNOW PHONE
Call Ski Area, Montreal. 866-1284
TRAILS
40% beginner, 35% intermediate, 25% advanced
TRAVEL
From Montreal, Autoroute No. 10 to the Eastman Exit, Routes No. 245 and 243; U.S., I-89 or I-91 to Rt. 105
VERTICAL DROP
2,100 feet

LIVING MEMORIAL PARK

Brattleboro, VT 05301 (802) 254-5868

AREA INFORMATION

HOURS
1:00 - 5:00 p.m., school vacations
7:00 - 10:00 p.m., Mon. - Sat.
10:00 a.m. - 5:00 p.m., Saturday
1:00 p.m. - 5:00 p.m., Sunday
LIFTS
1 bar, 900 capacity per hour
LONGEST RUN
1,200 feet
SEASON
December to mid-March
SNOW PHONE
Call Ski Area
TRAILS
Beginner, open slope
TRAVEL
1¼ miles from Brattleboro, Route 9 W.
VERTICAL DROP
200 feet

LYNDON OUTING CLUB

Lyndonville, VT 05851 (802) 626-8465, (800) 451-4205

AREA INFORMATION

HOURS
Tues., Wed., Fri. nights, weekends and holidays
LIFTS
1 bar, 2 tows
SEASON
December to April
SNOW PHONE
Call Ski Area
TRAILS
Beginner and intermediate
TRAVEL
Southern Vermont, north of Route 9

MAGIC MOUNTAIN

Londonderry, VT 05148 (802) 824-5566

AREA INFORMATION

BASE ELEVATION
1,400 feet
HOURS
9:00 a.m. - 4:00 p.m.
LIFTS
3 chairlifts, 1 bar, 1 tow, 3,500 capacity per hour
LONGEST RUN
2½ miles
NURSERY
Ages 3 to 6, call Ski Area
SEASON
Late November to early April, snowmaking
SNOW PHONE
Call Ski Area
TRAILS
25% beginner, 50% intermediate, 25% advanced
TRAVEL
Between I-91 and U.S. 7, on Route 11
VERTICAL DROP
1,600 feet

MAPLE VALLEY

West Dummerston, VT 05357 (802) 254-6083

AREA INFORMATION

HOURS
Open days, nights
LIFTS
2 chairlifts, 1 bar, 1 tow
SEASON
December to April, snowmaking
SNOW PHONE
Call Ski Area
TRAVEL
Southeastern Vermont, Route 30

MIDDLEBURY COLLEGE

Middlebury, VT 05753 (802) 388-4356

AREA INFORMATION

BASE ELEVATION
1,500 feet
HOURS
9:00 a.m. - 4:00 p.m.
LIFTS
1 chairlift, 3 bars
LONGEST RUN
2½ miles
SEASON
Mid-December to mid-April
SNOW PHONE
Call Ski Area
TRAILS
4 slopes
TRAVEL
Central Vermont, west of Hancock, Rt.125
VERTICAL DROP
1,100 feet

MT. ASCUTNEY

Brownsville, VT 05037 (802) 484-7711

AREA INFORMATION

BASE ELEVATION
800 feet
HOURS
9:00 a.m. - 4:00 p.m., daily
6:30 - 10:00 p.m., Fri., Sat.
LONGEST RUN
2½ miles
NURSERY
Ages 1 to 6, call Ski Area
SEASON
Mid-December to mid-April, snowmaking
SNOW PHONE
Call Ski Area
TRAILS
30% beginner, 40% intermediate, 30% advanced
VERTICAL DROP
1,480 feet

NORWICH UNIVERSITY

Northfield, VT 05663 (802) 485-9312

AREA INFORMATION

BASE ELEVATION
850 feet
HOURS
Open every day
LIFTS
1 chairlift, 2 bars
SNOW PHONE
Call Ski Area
TRAILS
3 open slopes
TRAVEL
Williamstown exit from I-89
VERTICAL DROP
900 feet

OKEMO MOUNTAIN

Ludlow, VT 05149 (802) 228-4041

AREA INFORMATION

BASE ELEVATION
1,200 feet
HOURS
9:00 a.m. - 4:30 p.m., weekdays
8:30 a.m. - 4:30 p.m., weekends, holidays
LONGEST RUN
4½ miles
NURSERY
Through age 6, call Ski Area
SEASON
Late November to mid-April, snowmaking
SNOW PHONE 228-5222
TRAILS
50% beginner, 30% intermediate, 20% advanced
TRAVEL
On Rt. 103 at Ludlow, between Rutland and Claremont; I-91 to Routes 131 E. or 103 N.
VERTICAL DROP
2,100 feet

PICO

Rutland, VT 05701 (802) 775-4345

AREA INFORMATION

BASE ELEVATION
2,000 feet
HOURS
8:30 a.m. - 4:30 p.m.
LIFTS
6 chairlifts, 3 bars, 9,000 capacity per hour
LONGEST RUN
2½ miles
NURSERY
Out of diapers to age five, call Ski Area
SEASON
Late November to early May, snowmaking
SNOW PHONE
Call Ski Area
TRAILS
20% beginner, 60% intermediate, 20% advanced
TRAVEL
Near New York line, between I-87 and I-91
Along U.S. Route 4, 9 miles from Rutland
VERTICAL DROP
1,900 feet

PROSPECT MOUNTAIN

Bennington, VT 05201 (802) 442-2575

AREA INFORMATION

BASE ELEVATION
2,250 feet
HOURS
Wednesday thru Sunday, holiday weeks
LIFTS
2 T-bars, 1 tow, 2,100 capacity per hour
SEASON
December to April
SNOW PHONE
Call Ski Area
TRAVEL
8 miles from Bennington, Rt. 9 East
VERTICAL DROP
670 feet

ROUND TOP

Plymouth VT 05056 (802) 672-5152

AREA INFORMATION

BASE ELEVATION
1,300 feet
HOURS
9:00 a.m. - 4:00 p.m., daily
6:00 - 10:00 p.m., Fri., Sat.
LIFTS
2 chairlifts, 1 bar, 1 tow, 2,900 capacity per hour
LONGEST RUN
1½ miles
NURSERY
For children out of diapers, call Ski Area
SEASON
Late December to April, snowmaking
SNOW PHONE
Call Ski Area
TRAILS
30% beginner, 35% intermediate, 35% advanced
TRAVEL
South of Killington, Route 100
VERTICAL DROP
1,300 feet

SMUGGLERS' NOTCH

Jeffersonville, VT 05464 (802) 644-8851

AREA INFORMATION

BASE ELEVATION
1,100 feet
HOURS
9:00 a.m. - 4:00 p.m.
LIFTS
4 chairlifts, 1 tow, 3,000 capacity per hour
LONGEST RUN
3½ miles
NURSERY
At the slopes, call Ski Area
SEASON
Late November to early May, snowmaking
SNOW PHONE
Call Ski Area, out of state . . . . (800) 451-3222
TRAILS
25% beginner, 40% intermediate, 35% advanced
TRAVEL
From Burlington, I-89 S., Routes 100 N. and 108 N.
Advance arrangement courtesy pick up at terminals
VERTICAL DROP
2,500 feet

SNOW VALLEY

Londonderry, VT 05148 (802) 297-1000

AREA INFORMATION

BASE ELEVATION
1,600 feet

HOURS
9:00 a.m. - 4:30 p.m., weekends and holidays
LIFTS
1 chairlift, 1 T-bar, 1 poma, 1 tow
1,400 capacity per hour
LONGEST RUN
1 mile
SEASON
December to early April
SNOW PHONE
Call Ski Area
TRAILS
10 slopes
TRAVEL
Southern Vermont, between Stratton & Bromley
VERTICAL DROP
900 feet

SONNENBURG

Barnard, VT 05031 (802) 234-9874

AREA INFORMATION

BASE ELEVATION
1,450 feet
HOURS
9:00 a.m. - 4:00 p.m., weekends
LIFTS
2 bars, 500 capacity per hour
LONGEST RUN
3,200 feet
SEASON
Mid-December to late March
SNOW PHONE
Call Ski Area
TRAVEL
East-Central Vermont, I-89, north of U.S. 4
VERTICAL DROP
2,600 feet

TIMBER RIDGE

Windham, VT 05359 (802) 824-6806

AREA INFORMATION

BASE ELEVATION
2,000 feet
HOURS
9:00 a.m. - 4:00 p.m., weekends, holiday weeks
LIFTS
1 chairlift, 1 bar, 2,200 capacity per hour
LONGEST RUN
1½ miles
SEASON
Mid-December to mid-April
SNOW PHONE
Call Ski Area
TRAVEL
Southeastern Vermont, west of Springfield, Rt. 11
VERTICAL DROP
800 feet

UNDERHILL SKI BOWL

Underhill Center, VT 05490 (802) 899-4677

AREA INFORMATION

BASE ELEVATION
1,650 feet
HOURS
10:00 a.m. - 4:30 p.m.
LIFTS
1 poma, 1 tow
LONGEST RUN
¼ mile
SEASON
Mid-December to early April
SNOW PHONE
Call Ski Area
TRAILS
Intermediate
TRAVEL
Northern Vermont, Rt. 100, Stevensville Rd.
VERTICAL DROP
150 feet

V I R G I N I A

BRYCE RESORT

Basye, VA 22810 (703) 856-2121

AREA INFORMATION

BASE ELEVATION
1,250 feet
HOURS
9:00 a.m. - 4:30 p.m., daily
7:00 - 10:00, Mon. - Sat.
LIFTS
2 chairlifts, 3 rope tows, 2,200 capacity per hour
LONGEST RUN
3,500 feet
NURSERY
At the slopes, call Ski Area
SEASON
Mid-December to mid-March, snowmaking

BRYCE CONT.

SNOW PHONE 856-2151
From Washington, D.C. . . . . (202) 554-8414
TRAILS
25% beginner, 50% intermediate, 25% advanced
TRAVEL
120 miles from Washington, D.C., I-66, I-81, to Route 263, 12 miles west of Mt. Jackson
VERTICAL DROP
500 feet

CASCADE MOUNTAIN

Fancy Gap, VA 24328 (703) 728-3161

AREA INFORMATION

BASE ELEVATION
2,740 feet
HOURS
9:00 a.m. - 4:30 p.m., weekends, holidays
LIFTS
1 chairlifts, 1 tow
LONGEST RUN
3,000 feet
SEASON
Mid-December to early March, snowmaking
SNOW PHONE
Call Ski Area
TRAVEL
Southwestern Virginia, U.S. 221, Route 52
VERTICAL DROP
250 feet

THE HOMESTEAD

Hot Springs, VA 24445 (703) 839-5079

AREA INFORMATION

BASE ELEVATION
2,500 feet
HOURS
9:00 a.m. - 5:00 p.m.
LIFTS
1 chairlift, 2 tows, 1 bar, 1,900 capacity per hour
LONGEST RUN
4,000 feet
SEASON
Mid-December to mid-March, snowmaking
SNOW PHONE 361-2100
TRAILS
15% beginner, 50% intermediate, 35% advanced
TRAVEL
West-Central Virginia, U.S. 11 and 60
VERTICAL DROP
600 feet

MASSANUTTEN

Harrisonburg, VA 22801 (703) 289-9441

AREA INFORMATION

BASE ELEVATION
1,720 feet
HOURS
9:00 a.m. - 4:30 p.m., daily
6:30 - 10:00 p.m., Mon. - Sat.
LIFTS
4 chairlifts, 1 bar, 5,000 capacity per hour
LONGEST RUN
Over 1 mile
NURSERY
At the slopes, call Ski Area
SEASON
Early December to mid-March, snowmaking
SNOW PHONE 289-5700
TRAILS
25% beginner, 50% intermediate, 25% advanced
TRAVEL
From Richmond, 130 miles, I-64 N., I-81 N., Rt. 33
VERTICAL DROP
800 feet

WINTERGREEN

Wintergreen, VA 22958 (804) 361-2200

AREA INFORMATION

BASE ELEVATION
2,920 feet
HOURS
9:00 a.m. - 4:30 p.m., daily
7:00 - 11:00 p.m., Tues. - Sun.
LIFTS
3 chairlifts, 4,600 capacity per hour
LONGEST RUN
2,800 feet
NURSERY
Day Care Center, Call Ski Area
SEASON
Early December to mid-March, snowmaking
SNOW PHONE 361-2100
TRAILS
15% beginner, 65% intermediate, 20% advanced
TRAVEL
Near Charlottesville, I-64
VERTICAL DROP
520 feet

WASHINGTON

ALPENTAL

Snoqualmie Pass, WA 98068 (206) 434-6112

AREA INFORMATION

BASE ELEVATION
3,200 feet
HOURS
9:30 a.m. - 10:30 p.m., Mon. - Thurs.
9:30 a.m. - 12:30 a.m., Fri., Sat.
9:30 a.m. - 8:30 p.m., Sunday
LIFTS
4 chairlifts, 1 bar, 4 tows, 4,300 capacity per hour
NURSERY
Age 3 & up, call Ski Area
SEASON
Late November to early May, no snowmaking
SNOW PHONE 623-3418
TRAILS
20% beginner, 40% intermediate, 40% advanced
TRAVEL
55 miles from Seattle, I-90 East
VERTICAL DROP
2,200 feet

BADGER MOUNTAIN

Waterville, WA 98858 (509) 745-4201

AREA INFORMATION

BASE ELEVATION
3,000 feet
HOURS
Weekends and holidays
LIFTS
5 tows, 1,600 capacity per hour
SEASON
December to March
SNOW PHONE
Call Ski Area
TRAILS
Beginner to advanced
TRAVEL
4 miles south of Waterville, U.S. 2, U.S. 97
VERTICAL DROP
1,500 feet

BLUEWOOD

Dayton, WA 99328 (509) 525-8410

AREA INFORMATION

BASE ELEVATION
4,450 feet
HOURS
9:00 a.m. - 4:00 p.m., see "Season"
LIFTS
1 chairlift, 1 tow, 2,200 capacity per hour
LONGEST RUN
2¼ miles
SEASON
Mid-November to early May
Mid-December to early April, daily
Balance of season, weekends only
SNOW PHONE
Call Ski Area
TRAVEL
S.E. Washington, northeast of Walla Walla, U.S. 12
VERTICAL DROP
1,200 feet

49 DEGREES NORTH

Chewelah, WA 99109 (509) 935-6649

AREA INFORMATION

BASE ELEVATION
3,930 feet
HOURS
9:00 a.m. - 4:00 p.m.
LIFTS
4 chairs, 4,200 capacity per hour
LONGEST RUN
About 3¼ miles
NURSERY
At the slopes, call Ski Area
SEASON
Early December to mid-April, no snowmaking
SNOW PHONE 838-4966, 924-5252
TRAILS
30% beginner, 30% intermediate, 40% advanced
TRAVEL
47 miles from Spokane, Rt. 395 to Chewelah,
Black Top Flowery Trail Road to Ski Area
VERTICAL DROP
1,840 feet

HURRICANE RIDGE

Port Angeles, WA 98362 (206) 452-9235

AREA INFORMATION

BASE ELEVATION
4,800 feet
HOURS
10:00 a.m. - 4:00 p.m., weekends, holidays
LIFTS
1 bar, 2 tows, 1,200 capacity per hour
LONGEST RUN
3,000 feet
SEASON
Mid-December to late April
SNOW PHONE
Call Ski Area
TRAVEL
Olympic Nat'l Park, 70 miles from Seattle, U.S. 101
VERTICAL DROP
420 feet

LOUP LOUP

Twisp, WA 98856 (509) 826-0537

AREA INFORMATION

BASE ELEVATION
4,040 feet
HOURS
Wednesdays, weekends, holidays
LIFTS
2 bars, 2 tows
SEASON
December to March
SNOW PHONE
Call Ski Area
TRAVEL
N. Central Washington, Rt. 20, east of Twisp
VERTICAL DROP
1,200 feet

MT. BAKER

Bellingham, WA 98225 (206) 734-6771

AREA INFORMATION

BASE ELEVATION
3,500 feet
HOURS
8:30 a.m. - 4:00 p.m., weekdays
8:00 a.m. - 4:00 p.m., weekends, holidays
Open Fridays beginning in January
LIFTS
6 chairlifts, 4 tows, 6,000 capacity per hour
LONGEST RUN
1¼ miles
SEASON
Late October to mid-May, no snowmaking
SNOW PHONE
Call Ski Area
TRAILS
15% beginner, 60% intermediate, 25% advanced
TRAVEL
110 miles from Vancouver, Provincial Hwy. 99, I-5
to Bellingham, then 55 miles via Rt. 542 to Area
VERTICAL DROP
1,500 feet

MT. SPOKANE

Spokane, WA 99208 (509) 484-3908

AREA INFORMATION

BASE ELEVATION
4,370 feet
HOURS
9:00 a.m. - 10:30 p.m., Wed. - Sun.
1:00 - 10:30 p.m., Monday, Tuesday
4:00 - 10:30 p.m., night skiing
LIFTS
5 chairlifts, 2 tows, 5,000 capacity per hour
LONGEST RUN
1½ miles
NURSERY
Weekends & holidays, call Ski Area
SEASON
Mid-December to mid-April, no snowmaking
SNOW PHONE 238-6223
TRAILS
20% beginner, 50% intermediate, 30% advanced
TRAVEL
Mt. Spokane State Park, U.S. 395, 2 & Rt. 206
VERTICAL DROP
1,500 feet

SITZMARK

Tonasket, WA 98855 (509) 485-3208

AREA INFORMATION

BASE ELEVATION
4,300 feet
LIFTS
2 bars, 1 tow, 900 capacity per hour
SEASON
December to March

SNOW PHONE
Call Ski Area
TRAILS
Intermediate
TRAVEL
Northern Washington, 20 miles east of Tonasket
VERTICAL DROP
630 feet

SKI ACRES

Snoqualmie Pass, WA 98068 (206) 434-6671

AREA INFORMATION

BASE ELEVATION
2,600 feet
HOURS
9:00 a.m. - 5:00 p.m., daily
5:00 - 11:00 p.m., 12:00, Fri. & Sat.
LIFTS
7 chairlifts, 7 tows, 8,000 capacity per hour
LONGEST RUN
1½ miles
NURSERY
Saturday and Sunday, call Ski Area
SEASON
Early November to early May, no snowmaking
SNOW PHONE 634-0200
TRAILS
25% beginner, 50% intermediate, 25% advanced
TRAVEL
47 miles from Seattle, I-90 East
VERTICAL DROP
900 feet

SNOQUALMIE SUMMIT

Snoqualmie Pass, WA 98068 (206) 434-6161

AREA INFORMATION

BASE ELEVATION
3,000 feet
HOURS
9:00 a.m. - 6:00 p.m., or 1:30 - 10:30 p.m.
5:00 p.m. - midnight, night skiing
LIFTS
8 chairlifts, 2 bars, 8 tows, 11,500 capacity per hour
SEASON
Mid-November to April, no snowmaking
SNOW PHONE 634-0200
TRAILS
20% beginner, 40% intermediate, 40% advanced
TRAVEL
From Seattle, 47 miles via I-90 East, exit 52
VERTICAL DROP
980 feet

SQUILCHUCK

Wenatchee, WA 98801 (206) 663-1303

AREA INFORMATION

BASE ELEVATION
3,300 feet
HOURS
Open days and nights
LIFTS
2 tows, 700 capacity per hour
SEASON
December to March
SNOW PHONE
Call Ski Area
TRAILS
Beginner and intermediate
TRAVEL
U.S. 2 to Wenatchee, then 9 miles south
VERTICAL DROP
200 feet

WHITE PASS VILLAGE

White Pass, WA 98937 Ask for Area 509, White Pass No. 1

AREA INFORMATION

BASE ELEVATION
4,500 feet
HOURS
8:45 a.m. - 5:00 p.m., daily
6:00 - 10:00 p.m., Thurs. - Sat.
LIFTS
3 chairlifts, 1 bar, 1 tow, 3,300 capacity per hour
LONGEST RUN
2 miles
SEASON
Late November to late May, no snowmaking
SNOW PHONE . . . . . . (206) 634-0200, (503) 222-9128
TRAILS
20% beginner, 60% intermediate, 20% advanced
TRAVEL
85 miles from Tacoma, Rt. 7 & U.S. 12
15 miles S.E. of Mt. Ranier Nat'l Park
VERTICAL DROP
1,500 feet

WEST VIRGINIA

ALPINE LAKE

Terra Alta, WV 26764 (304) 789-2481

AREA INFORMATION

BASE ELEVATION
2,550 feet
HOURS
6:00 - 10:00 p.m., Friday
10:00 - 10:00 p.m., Sat., Sun.
Every day the week of Christmas
LIFTS
2 bars, 1 tow, 500 capacity per hour
LONGEST RUN
5,000 feet
SEASON
Late November to March, snowmaking
SNOW PHONE
Call Ski Area
TRAILS
Beginner
TRAVEL
U.S. 219, south of Morgantown
VERTICAL DROP
450 feet

CHESTNUT RIDGE

Morgantown, WV 26505 (304) 292-4773

AREA INFORMATION

BASE ELEVATION
2,100 feet
HOURS
6:00 a.m. - 10:00 p.m., weekdays
1:00 p.m. - 10:00 p.m., weekends
LIFTS
1 tow
LONGEST RUN
1,200 feet
SEASON
December to February
SNOW PHONE
Call Ski Area
TRAVEL
15 miles from Morgantown, U.S. 48
VERTICAL DROP
170 feet

COONSKIN PARK

Charlestown, WV 25311 (304) 245-8000

AREA INFORMATION

BASE ELEVATION
720 feet
HOURS
12:00 - 10:00 p.m.
LIFTS
1 tow, 200 capacity per hour
LONGEST RUN
600 feet
SEASON
December to March
SNOW PHONE
Call Ski Area
TRAILS
One slope
VERTICAL DROP
120 feet

OGELBAY PARK

Wheeling, WV 26003 (304) 242-3000

AREA INFORMATION

HOURS
Weekdays, weekends, nights
LIFTS
2 bars, 1 tow
LONGEST RUN
1,600 feet
SEASON
December to early March, snowmaking
SNOW PHONE
Call Ski Area
TRAVEL
3 miles from Wheeling, Route 88
VERTICAL DROP
330 feet

WISCONSIN

ALPINE VALLEY

East Troy, WI 53120 (414) 642-7374

AREA INFORMATION

HOURS
10:00 a.m. - 11:00 p.m., weekdays
9:00 a.m. - 11:00 p.m., weekends

LIFTS
12 chairlifts, 5 rope tows
LONGEST RUN
3,000 feet
NURSERY
Advance arrangement, call Ski Area
SEASON
Early December to mid-March, snowmaking
SNOW PHONE
Call Ski Area, Chicago 263-5884
TRAILS
20% beginner, 60% intermediate, 20% advanced
TRAVEL
From Chicago, Routes 12 N., 15 E., G South, D West
VERTICAL DROP
280 feet

BIRCH PARK

Eight Flags, Houlton, WI (715) 549-6777

AREA INFORMATION

BASE ELEVATION
700 feet
HOURS
10:00 a.m. - 4:30 p.m., weekdays
9:30 a.m. - 4:30 p.m., weekends
4:30 - 10:00 p.m., night skiing
LIFTS
3 chairlifts, 7 tows, 10,000 capacity per hour
LONGEST RUN
1,800 feet
NURSERY
Wed. & Thurs., age 1½ to 6, call Ski Area
SEASON
Mid-November to late March, snowmaking
SNOW PHONE
Call Ski Area
TRAILS
30% beginner, 50% intermediate, 20% advanced
TRAVEL
Near Minnesota line; I-94 and Route 35
VERTICAL DROP
200 feet

BRUCE MOUND WINTER SPORTS

Neillsville, WI 54456 (715) 743-2490

AREA INFORMATION

HOURS
11:00 a.m. - 4:00 p.m., Fri. - Sun., holidays
LIFTS
2 bars, 2 tows
LONGEST RUN
2,400 feet
SEASON
Late December to March, snowmaking
SNOW PHONE
Call Ski Area
TRAVEL
12 miles S.W. of Neillsville, U.S. 10 E. & 12 S.
VERTICAL DROP
200 feet

BULL RUN

Boscobel, WI 53805 (608) 375-4789, 375-5869

AREA INFORMATION

HOURS
Saturdays, Sundays, Christmas
7:00 - 10:00 p.m., night skiing
LIFTS
2 tows
LONGEST RUN
3,800 feet
NURSERY
Advance arrangement, call Ski Area
SEASON
December to March
SNOW PHONE
Call Ski Area
TRAVEL
S.W. Wisconsin, U.S. 14 E. & 61 S. from Madison
VERTICAL DROP
230 feet

BULL VALLEY

Lake Geneva, WI 53147 (414) 248-6553

AREA INFORMATION

LIFTS
4 chairlifts, 1 T-bar, 2 rope tows
LONGEST RUN
3,600 feet
SEASON
December to March, snowmaking
SNOW PHONE
Call Ski Area
TRAILS
Intermediate
TRAVEL
2 miles from Lake Geneva, Route 36 & Krueger Rd.
VERTICAL DROP
230 feet

CALUMET

Hilbert, WI 54129 (414) 439-1008

AREA INFORMATION

HOURS
11:00 a.m. - 4:30 p.m., Friday to Sunday
LIFTS
1 bar, 5 tows, 800 capacity per hour
SEASON
Late December to mid-March
SNOW PHONE
Call Ski Area
TRAVEL
East-Central Wisconsin, Routes 10, 55
VERTICAL DROP
200 feet

CAMP 10

Rhinelander, WI 54501 (715) 362-6754

AREA INFORMATION

HOURS
9:00 a.m. - 4:00 p.m., Wed., Fri. to Sun., holidays
LIFTS
2 bars, 3 tows, 1,000 capacity per hour
LONGEST RUN
2,000 feet
SEASON
Mid-December to mid-March
SNOW PHONE
Call Ski Area
TRAVEL
Southeast of junction of U.S. 51 & 8
VERTICAL DROP
220 feet

CASCADE MOUNTAIN

Portage, WI 53901 (608) 742-5588

AREA INFORMATION

BASE ELEVATION
810 feet
HOURS
10:00 a.m. - 10:30 p.m., weekdays
Weekends, 9:00 a.m. - 10:30 p.m.
LIFTS
2 chairlifts, 2 bars, 3 tows, 5,400 capacity per hour
LONGEST RUN
5,300 feet
SEASON
December to April, snowmaking
SNOW PHONE
Call Ski Area
TRAVEL
35 miles from Madison, I-90, I-94
VERTICAL DROP
460 feet

CHRISTIE MOUNTAIN

Bruce, WI 54819 (715) 868-7800

AREA INFORMATION

BASE ELEVATION
1,300 feet
HOURS
10:30 a.m. - 4:30 p.m., Wed. thru Fri.
9:30 a.m. - 4:30 p.m., weekends, holidays
4:30 - 9:30 p.m., Friday, Saturday
LIFTS
1 chairlift, 1 bar, 1 tow, 2,800 capacity per hour
LONGEST RUN
¾ mile
SEASON
Late November to early April, snowmaking
SNOW PHONE
Call Ski Area
TRAVEL
North of U.S. 8, Northeast Wisconsin
VERTICAL DROP
350 feet

CHRISTMAS MOUNTAIN

Wisconsin Dells, WI 53965 (608) 254-2531

AREA INFORMATION

HOURS
5:00 - 10:00 p.m., Wed. - Fri.
9:00 - 10:00 p.m., weekends
LIFTS
2 chairlifts, 2 tows
LONGEST RUN
2,800 feet
SEASON
Mid-December to March, snowmaking
SNOW PHONE
Call Ski Area
TRAVEL
North of U.S. 8, Northwest Wisconsin
VERTICAL DROP
200 feet

CURRIE PARK

Milwaukee, WI 53233 (414) 453-7030

AREA INFORMATION

HOURS
6:00 - 10:00 p.m., Monday through Friday
1:00 - 5:00 & 6:00 - 10:00 p.m., Sat., Sun.
LIFTS
1 tow
SEASON
December to March, snowmaking
SNOW PHONE
Call Ski Area
TRAIL
One 820 foot run, city operated
TRAVEL
Wauwautosa, Rt. 100 & Capitol Drive
VERTICAL DROP
50 feet

DEEPWOOD

Wheeler, WI 54772 (715) 658-1394

AREA INFORMATION

HOURS
Monday, Saturday, Sunday, holidays
Night skiing by prior arrangement
LIFTS
2 bars, 8 tows
LONGEST RUN
3,200 feet
SEASON
December to March, snowmaking
SNOW PHONE
Call Ski Area
TRAILS
Beginner to advanced
TRAVEL
I-94 to Menomonie, then 15 miles north
VERTICAL DROP
300 feet

DRETZKA PARK

Milwaukee, WI 53233 (618) 278-4348

AREA INFORMATION

HOURS
6:00 - 10:00 p.m., Monday thru Friday
1:00 - 5:00 & 6:00 - 10:00 p.m., Sat., Sun.
LIFTS
4 tows
LONGEST RUN
1,000 feet
SEASON
December to March, snowmaking
SNOW PHONE 278-4343
TRAILS
2 runs, county operated
TRAVEL
In Milwaukee, 12020 W. Bradley Road

GATEWAY LODGE

Land O'Lakes, WI 54540 (715) 547-3321

AREA INFORMATION

HOURS
2 days each week, days & nights
9:00 a.m. - 9:00 p.m., weekends
LIFTS
3 tows
LONGEST RUN
2,000 feet
SEASON
December to March, no snowmaking
SNOW PHONE
Call Ski Area
TRAILS
11 runs
VERTICAL DROP
110 feet

GREENBUSH WINTER SPORTS

Cambellsport, WI 53010 (414) 626-2116

AREA INFORMATION

HOURS
10:00 a.m. - 4:00 p.m., Sat., Sun., holidays
LIFTS
1 tow
LONGEST RUN
700 feet
SEASON
December to March
SNOW PHONE
Call Ski Area
TRAILS
Beginner, 2 runs, operated by
Dept. of Natural Resources
TRAVEL
Eastern Wisconsin, south of Greenbush
VERTICAL DROP
100 feet

HARDSCRABBLE

Rice Lake, WI 54868 (715) 234-3412

AREA INFORMATION

HOURS
Wed., Fri. to Sun., Christmas holidays
LIFTS
2 bars, 5 tows, 2,800 capacity per hour
LONGEST RUN
4,000 feet
SEASON
November to March, snowmaking
SNOW PHONE
Call Ski Area
TRAILS
10 runs
TRAVEL
60 miles from Eau Claire, U.S. 53, N.W. Wisconsin
VERTICAL DROP
400 feet

HARRISON HILLS

Gleason, WI 54435 (715) 536-8588

AREA INFORMATION

HOURS
Sat., Sun., Christmas holidays
LIFTS
3 tows
LONGEST RUN
2,000 feet
SEASON
December to March
SNOW PHONE
Call Ski Area
TRAILS
5 runs
TRAVEL
Northwest Wisconsin, Route 17
VERTICAL DROP
200 feet

HILLY HAVEN

De Pere, WI 54115 (414) 336-6204

AREA INFORMATION

HOURS
10:00 a.m. - 4:00 p.m., weekends
7:00 - 10:00 p.m., Thursdays
LIFTS
5 tows, 1,800 capacity per hour
LONGEST RUN
500 feet
SEASON
Mid-December to mid-March
SNOW PHONE
Call Ski Area
TRAILS
One slope
TRAVEL
U.S. 141, 15 miles from Green Bay
VERTICAL DROP
100 feet

INTERLAKEN

Lake Geneva, WI 53147 (414) 248-9121

AREA INFORMATION

HOURS
10:00 a.m. - 10:00 p.m., Mon. - Fri.
9:00 a.m. - 10:00 p.m., Sat., Sun.
LIFTS
2 tows
LONGEST RUN
900 feet
SEASON
Mid-December to mid-March, snowmaking
SNOW PHONE
Call Ski Area
TRAILS
Beginner and intermediate
TRAVEL
50 miles from Milwaukee, near state line
VERTICAL DROP
80 feet

KETTLEBOWL

Antigo, WI 54409 (715) 623-3560

AREA INFORMATION

HOURS
12:00 - 4:00 p.m., Sat., Sun., holidays
LIFTS
5 tows
LONGEST RUN
2,000 feet
SEASON
December to March
SNOW PHONE
Call Ski Area
TRAILS
Beginner and intermediate
TRAVEL
Northeastern Wisconsin, Route 52
VERTICAL DROP
200 feet

KEYES PEAK

Florence, WI 54121 (715) 528-3228

AREA INFORMATION

HOURS
10:00 a.m. - 9:00 p.m., Thurs. - Sun. & Christmas
LIFTS
3 tows
LONGEST RUN
1,760 feet
SEASON
Mid-December to late March, no snowmaking
SNOW PHONE
Call Ski Area
TRAILS
4 slopes
TRAVEL
U.S. 2, 15 miles from Iron Mountain, MI
VERTICAL DROP
200 feet

LITTLE SWITZERLAND

Slinger, WI 53086 (414) 644-5020

AREA INFORMATION

HOURS
10:00 a.m. - 10:30 p.m., daily
LIFTS
5 chairlifts, 3 tows
LONGEST RUN
1,800 feet
SNOW PHONE
Call Ski Area
TRAVEL
From Milwaukee, U.S. 41 N.
VERTICAL DROP
200 feet

MONT DU LAC

Superior, WI 55808 (715) 636-9991

AREA INFORMATION

BASE ELEVATION
610 feet
HOURS
9:30 a.m. - 4:30 p.m., weekends, holidays
7:00 - 10:00 p.m., Tues., Weds., Thurs.
LIFTS
1 chairlift, 1 bar, 3 tow, 2,300 capacity per hour
LONGEST RUN
2,400 feet
SEASON
Early December to late March, snowmaking
SNOW PHONE
Call Ski Area
TRAILS
7 slopes
TRAVEL
Northwest Wisconsin, Rt. 23 from Duluth
VERTICAL DROP
300 feet

MT. FUJI

Lake Geneva, WI 53147 (414) 248-6553

AREA INFORMATION

HOURS
9:00 a.m. - 4:00 p.m., 5:30 - 10:00 p.m.
LIFTS
4 chairlifts, 1 bar, 2 tows
LONGEST RUN
½ mile
SNOW PHONE
Call Ski Area
TRAVEL
From Milwaukee, Rt. 15 S., U.S. 12,
VERTICAL DROP
230 feet

MT. LA CROSSE

La Crosse, WI 54601 (608) 788-0044

AREA INFORMATION

BASE ELEVATION
620 feet
HOURS
10:00 a.m. - 5:00 p.m., Monday
10:00 a.m. - 10:00 p.m., Tues. - Fri.
9:30 a.m. - 5:00 p.m., Sat., Sun.
LIFTS
2 chairlifts, 3 tows, 3,300 feet
LONGEST RUN
5,300 feet
NURSERY
Call Ski Area in advance
SEASON
Late November to mid-March, snowmaking
SNOW PHONE
Call Ski Area
TRAILS
20% beginner, 50% intermediate, 30% advanced
TRAVEL
Southwestern Wisconsin, 2 miles from La Crosse
VERTICAL DROP
510 feet

MT. LE BETT

Coleman, WI 54112 (414) 897-2290

AREA INFORMATION

HOURS
10:00 a.m. - 4:30 p.m., weekends
Womens' Day is every Thursday
LIFTS
3 tows
LONGEST RUN
1,500 feet
SEASON
December to March, snowmaking
SNOW PHONE
Call Ski Area
TRAILS
10 slopes
TRAVEL
Green Bay, 14 miles, U.S. 141 & County Trunk B
VERTICAL DROP
350 feet

NAVARINO HILLS

Shiocton, WI 54170 (715) 758-2211

AREA INFORMATION

HOURS
9:30 a.m. - 4:30 p.m., Saturday, Sunday
6:00 - 10:00 p.m., Tues. - Sat., holidays
LIFTS
1 chairlift, 5 tows, 1,100 capacity per hour
SEASON
Mid-December to mid-March, snowmaking
SNOW PHONE
Call Ski Area
TRAILS
10 runs
TRAVEL
U.S. 45, Rt. 156, northwest of Milwaukee
VERTICAL DROP
100 feet

NEST OF EAGLES

Spooner, WI 54801 (715) 635-8447

AREA INFORMATION

BASE ELEVATION
1,200 feet
HOURS
Wed., Sat., Sun., Christmas or by appointment
LIFTS
1 bar, 250 capacity per hour
LONGEST RUN
1,500 feet
SEASON
Late November to early April
SNOW PHONE
Call Ski Area
TRAILS
3 tree-lined runs
TRAVEL
From Spooner, U.S. 53 N., County A & E
VERTICAL DROP
160 feet

NORDIC MOUNTAIN

Wild Rose, WI 54984 (414) 787-3324

AREA INFORMATION

BASE ELEVATION
880 feet
HOURS
6:00 - 10:00 p.m., Tues., Weds., Fri.
1:00 p.m. - 10:00 p.m., Thursdays
10:00 a.m. - 10:00 p.m., Sat., Sun., holidays
LIFTS
1 chairlift, 2 bars, 4 tows, 3,800 capacity per hour
LONGEST RUN
3,500 feet
SEASON
Early December to mid-March, snowmaking
SNOW PHONE
Call Ski Area
TRAILS
15% beginner, 50% intermediate, 35% advanced
TRAVEL
Northwest of Sheboygan and Oshkosh, Rt. 152
VERTICAL DROP
240 feet

OLYMPIA

Oconomowoc, WI 53066 (414) 567-0311

AREA INFORMATION

HOURS
10:00 a.m. - 10:30 p.m., night skiing from 4:30 p.m.
LIFTS
2 chairlifts, 2 tows
LONGEST RUN
2,800 feet
NURSERY
Babysitters, call Ski Area

SEASON
Late November to mid-March, snowmaking
SNOW PHONE
Call Ski Area
TRAILS
11 slopes
TRAVEL
I-94, Rt. 67 from Milwaukee
VERTICAL DROP
190 feet

PARADISE VALLEY

Burlington, WI 53105 (414) 763-5121

AREA INFORMATION

HOURS
10:00 a.m. - 6:00 p.m., Sat., Sun., Christmas
6:00 p.m. - 10:30 p.m., Friday and Saturday
LIFTS
4 bars, 1 tow, 3,800 capacity per hour
LONGEST RUN
1,750 feet
SEASON
Early December to early March
TRAILS
2 slopes, beginner and intermediate
SNOW PHONE
Call Ski Area
TRAVEL
40 miles from Milwaukee, Routes 36 and 11
VERTICAL DROP
190 feet

PAUL BUNYAN SKI HILL

Lakewood, WI 54138 (715) 276-7143

AREA INFORMATION

HOURS
10:00 a.m. - 4:30 p.m., Fri., Sat., Sun., Christmas
LIFTS
1 bars, 4 tows
LONGEST RUN
800 feet
SEASON
Late December to March, snowmaking
SNOW PHONE
Call Ski Area
TRAVEL
Northeastern Wisconsin, 2 miles N. of Lakewood
VERTICAL DROP
120 feet

PORT MOUNTAIN

Bayfield, WI 54814 (715) 779-3227

AREA INFORMATION

BASE ELEVATION
960 feet
HOURS
9:30 a.m. - 4:30 p.m., Wed., Sat., Sun., holidays
6:30 p.m. - 10:00 p.m., Tuesday and Thursday
LIFTS
1 bar, 4 tows, 4,800 capacity per hour
LONGEST RUN
3,200 feet
SEASON
Early December to early April
SNOW PHONE
Call Ski Area
TRAVEL
Northern tip of Wisconsin, U.S. 2 to Rt. 13 N.
VERTICAL DROP
310 feet

POTAWATOMI PARK

Sturgeon Bay, WI 54235 (414) 743-5123, 743-9818

AREA INFORMATION

HOURS
12:00 - 5:00 p.m., Sat., Sun.
6:30 - 9:30 p.m., Wednesday
LIFTS
2 tows
LONGEST RUN
500 feet
SEASON
December to March, snowmaking
SNOW PHONE
Call Ski Area
TRAILS
2 runs
TRAVEL
On Peninsula, Routes 42 and 57
VERTICAL DROP
120 feet

POWERS BLUFF

Wisconsin Rapids, WI 54494 (715) 423-3000 X 190

AREA INFORMATION

HOURS
6:00 - 9:30 p.m., Wed., Thurs.
1:00 - 9:30 p.m., Saturdays
1:00 - 7:00 p.m., Sun. & holidays

POWERS BLUFF CONT.

LIFTS
1 tow
LONGEST RUN
1,400 feet
SEASON
December to March
SNOW PHONE
Call Ski Area
TRAILS
4 runs
TRAVEL
U.S. 51 to U.S. 10 East, Central Wisconsin
VERTICAL DROP
250 feet

RIB MOUNTAIN

Wausau, WI 54401 (715) 845-2846

AREA INFORMATION

BASE ELEVATION
1,240 feet
HOURS
9:30 a.m. - 4:30 p.m., daily
5:30 - 10:30 p.m., Mon. - Sat.
LIFTS
2 chairlifts, 2 T-bars, 4 tows, 5,800 capacity per hour
LONGEST RUN
3,830 feet
SEASON
Early December to mid-March
SNOW PHONE
Call Ski Area
TRAILS
3 beginner, 4 intermediate, 4 advanced
TRAVEL
Central Wisconsin, U.S. 10 to 51 N.
VERTICAL DROP
680 feet

SHELTERED VALLEY

Three Lakes, WI 54562 (715) 546-3535

AREA INFORMATION

HOURS
9:00 a.m. - 4:30 p.m.
LIFTS
1 bar, 3 tows
LONGEST RUN
2,000 feet
SEASON
December to March
SNOW PHONE
Call Ski Area
TRAILS
Beginner and intermediate
TRAVEL
N.E. Wisconsin, Rt. 32, north of U.S. 8
VERTICAL DROP
200 feet

SKI MAJESTIC

Lake Geneva, WI 53147 (414) 248-6128

AREA INFORMATION

HOURS
9:30 a.m. - 11:00 p.m.
LIFTS
3 chairlifts, 4 tows, 4,500 capacity per hour
LONGEST RUN
1,400 feet
SEASON
Early December to mid-March
SNOW PHONE
Call Ski Area
TRAILS
9 runs
TRAVEL
From Milwaukee, Rt. 15 S., U.S. 12
VERTICAL DROP
230 feet

SNOWBURST

De Pere, WI 54115 (414) 336-1122

AREA INFORMATION

HOURS
Days: Tuesday, Thursday thru Sunday
Night skiing: Tuesday thru Sunday
LIFTS
1 T-bar, 3 tows
LONGEST RUN
1,000 feet
SEASON
December to March
SNOW PHONE
Call Ski Area
TRAILS
Beginner, 6 runs
TRAVEL
Eastern Wisconsin, U.S. 141, Rt. 32

SNOWCREST

Somerset, WI 54025 (612) 439-2427

AREA INFORMATION

HOURS
9:00 a.m. - 4:30 p.m., daily
4:30 - 10:00 p.m., Sun. - Tues.
4:30 - 11:00 p.m., Weds. - Sat.
LIFTS
3 chairlifts, 7 tows, 9,000 capacity per hour
LONGEST RUN
¾ mile
NURSERY
Must be out of diapers, call Ski Area
SEASON
Mid-November to late March, snowmaking
SNOW PHONE
Call Ski Area
TRAILS
25% beginner, 50% intermediate, 25% advanced
TRAVEL
From Twin Cities, I-94 to Rt. 35 N.
12 miles from Hudson to Somerset
VERTICAL DROP
290 feet

STANDING ROCK

Stevens Point, WI 54481 (715) 824-3949

AREA INFORMATION

HOURS
10:00 a.m. - 4:30 p.m., Sat., Sun., Christmas
LIFTS
3 tows
LONGEST RUN
1,200 feet
SEASON
December to March
SNOW PHONE
Call Ski Area
TRAILS
5 runs
TRAVEL
Central Wisconsin, south of U.S. 10
VERTICAL DROP
100 feet

SYLVAN HILL

Wausau, WI 54401 (715) 842-0471

AREA INFORMATION

BASE ELEVATION
1,190 feet
HOURS
Saturdays, Sundays and holidays
9:00 a.m. - 4:30, 6:00 - 9:00 p.m.
LIFTS
4 tows
LONGEST RUN
1,800 feet
SEASON
Late December to early March, no snowmaking
SNOW PHONE
Call Ski Area
TRAILS
4 slopes
TRAVEL
In Wausau, U.S. 51, north of U.S. 10
VERTICAL DROP
110 feet

TIMBERLINE SKI HILL

Arena, WI 53503 (608) 753-2315

AREA INFORMATION

BASE ELEVATION
820 feet
HOURS
9:00 a.m. - 5:00 p.m., Wed. - Sun.
5:00 - 10:00 p.m., Wed. - Sat.
LIFTS
1 chairlifts, 1 bar, 1 tow, 1,900 capacity per hour
SEASON
Mid-December to March, snowmaking
SNOW PHONE
Call Ski Area
TRAILS
Beginner to advanced
TRAVEL
30 miles from Madison, U.S. 14 West
VERTICAL DROP
390 feet

TROLLHAUGEN

Dresser, WI 54009 (715) 755-2955

AREA INFORMATION

HOURS
10:00 a.m. - 10:00 p.m., Mon. - Fri.
9:00 a.m. - 10:00 p.m., Saturday
9:00 a.m. - 6:00 p.m., Sunday
Night skiing begins at 4:30 p.m.
LIFTS
3 chairlifts, 5 tows, 8,000 capacity per hour
LONGEST RUN
2,500 feet

TROLLHAUGEN CONT.

NURSERY
Weds. & Thurs., call Ski Area
SEASON
Mid-November to mid-March, snowmaking
SNOW PHONE
Call Ski Area
TRAILS
30% beginner, 40% intermediate, 30% advanced
TRAVEL
From Twin Cities, I-94 E., Rt. 35, County Rd. F
VERTICAL DROP
250 feet

TYROL SKI BASIN

Mt. Horeb, WI 53572 (608) 437-3076, 833-8827

AREA INFORMATION

BASE ELEVATION
850 feet
HOURS
9:30 a.m. - 5:00 p.m., Wed. - Sun.
6:00 - 10:30 p.m., night skiing
LIFTS
1 chairlift, 1 T-bar, 3 tows, 2,700 capacity per hour
LONGEST RUN
3,600 feet
SEASON
Late November to mid-March, snowmaking
SNOW PHONE
Call Ski Area
TRAILS
30% beginner, 35% intermediate, 35% advanced
TRAVEL
19 miles S.W. of Madison, U.S. 18
and 151, north on County Rd. JG
VERTICAL DROP
320 feet

WHITNALL PARK

Hales Corners, WI 53130 (414) 425-1132

AREA INFORMATION

HOURS
6:00 - 10:00 p.m., Monday through Friday
1:00 - 5:00, 6:00 - 10:00 p.m., weekends, holidays
LIFTS
1 tow
SEASON
December to March, no snowmaking
SNOW PHONE
Call Ski Area
TRAILS
One 1,100 foot run
TRAVEL
Outskirts of Milwaukee, County operated
VERTICAL DROP
60 feet

WILMOT MOUNTAIN

Wilmot, WI 53192 (414) 862-2301

AREA INFORMATION

HOURS
9:30 a.m. - 4:30 p.m., daily
4:30 - 11:00 p.m., night skiing
LIFTS
8 chairlifts, 6 rope tows, 18,000 capacity per hour
LONGEST RUN
2,500 feet
SEASON
Early December to late March, snowmaking
SNOW PHONE
Call Ski Area
TRAILS
12 beginner, 9 intermediate, 9 advanced
TRAVEL
S.E. corner of Wisconsin, ½ mile south of Wilmot
From Chicago, I-94, U.S. 12, Rt. 173 to Wilmot Rd.
VERTICAL DROP
230 feet

THE WINTERGREEN

Spring Green, WI 53588 (608) 588-2124

AREA INFORMATION

BASE ELEVATION
790 feet
HOURS
10:00 a.m. - 10:00 p.m., Tues. - Fri.
9:00 a.m. - 10:00 p.m., Saturday
9:00 a.m. - 5:00 p.m., Sunday
LIFTS
2 chairlifts, 1 bar, 2,200 capacity per hour
LONGEST RUN
4,100 feet
SEASON
Early December to mid-March, snowmaking
SNOW PHONE
Call Ski Area
TRAILS
9 slopes
TRAVEL
Southeastern Wisconsin, U.S. 14
VERTICAL DROP
400 feet

WINTER HAVEN

Delafield, WI 53018 (414) 646-8418

AREA INFORMATION

HOURS
4:00 - 10:30 p.m., weekdays
9:00 a.m. - 10:30 p.m., weekends
LIFTS
1 T-bar, 3 tows
LONGEST RUN
1,400 feet
SEASON
Early December to early March, snowmaking
SNOW PHONE
Call Ski Area
TRAILS
Beginner to advanced
TRAVEL
25 miles west of Milwaukee, I-94, Rt. 83
VERTICAL DROP
180 feet

WINTERSET

Crivitz, WI 54114 (715) 854-7935

AREA INFORMATION

HOURS
10:00 a.m. - 4:30 p.m., weekends, holidays
LIFTS
4 tows
LONGEST RUN
1,800 feet
SEASON
Late December to mid-March
SNOW PHONE
Call Ski Area
TRAILS
6 runs
TRAVEL
N.E. Wisconsin, U.S. 141, W. on County Rd. A
VERTICAL DROP
180 feet

W Y O M I N G

ANTELOPE BUTTE

Greybull, WY 82426 (307) 765-2806

AREA INFORMATION

BASE ELEVATION
7,900 feet
HOURS
10:00 a.m. - 4:00 p.m., Fri., Sun., holidays
LIFTS
2 bars
LONGEST RUN
4,300 feet
SEASON
Late November to mid-April
SNOW PHONE
Call Ski Area
TRAILS
3 slopes
TRAVEL
N. Central Wyoming, U.S. 14, 40 miles E. of Greybull
VERTICAL DROP
900 feet

EAGLE ROCK

Evanston, WY 82930 (307) 789-9903

AREA INFORMATION

HOURS
Weekends, holidays
LIFTS
2 tows, 1,100 capacity per hour
SEASON
Mid-November to mid-April
SNOW PHONE
Call Ski Area
TRAILS
Beginner and intermediate
TRAVEL
S.W. Wyoming, U.S. 189, I-80, old U.S. 30
VERTICAL DROP
680 feet

HOGADON

Casper Mountain, WY 82601 (307) 266-1600

AREA INFORMATION

BASE ELEVATION
8,000 feet
HOURS
9:00 a.m. - 4:30 p.m., weekends, holidays
LIFTS
2 bars, 1,400 capacity per hour
LONGEST RUN
2,200 feet
SEASON
December to April
SNOW PHONE
Call Ski Area
TRAILS
Beginner to advanced
TRAVEL
E. Central Wyoming, south of Casper, Rt. 251
VERTICAL DROP
650 feet

MEADOWLARK

Worland, WY 82401 (307) 366-2409

AREA INFORMATION

BASE ELEVATION
8,500 feet
HOURS
11:00 a.m. - 4:00 p.m., Weds., Fri., holidays
10:00 a.m. - 4:00 p.m., weekends
LIFTS
2 tows, 400 capacity per hour
LONGEST RUN
1 mile
SEASON
Late November to mid-April
SNOW PHONE
Call Ski Area
TRAILS
5 slopes
TRAVEL
U.S. 16, North-Central Wyoming
VERTICAL DROP
600 feet

MEDICINE BOW

Centennial, WY 82055 (307) 745-5750

AREA INFORMATION

BASE ELEVATION
9,000 feet
HOURS
9:30 a.m. - 4:00 p.m., Wed. - Sun., holidays
LIFTS
1 chairlift, 2 bars, 1 tow, 2,800 capacity per hour
SEASON
November to April
SNOW PHONE
Call Ski Area

TRAILS
30% beginner, 40% intermediate, 30% advanced
TRAVEL
Southern Wyoming, Medicine Bow Nat'l Forest
Route 130, west of Laramie and Centennial
VERTICAL DROP
600 feet

PINE CREEK

Pine Creek Cyn., WY 83114 (307) 279-3227, 279-3201

AREA INFORMATION

HOURS
Weekends, holidays, operated by town
LIFTS
1 chairlift, 1 tow
SEASON
Mid-November to March
SNOW PHONE
Call Ski Area
TRAILS
Beginner to advanced
TRAVEL
Rt. 232, 7 miles north of Cokeville
VERTICAL DROP
1,200 feet

SLEEPING GIANT

Cody, WY 82414 (307) 587-4044

AREA INFORMATION

BASE ELEVATION
6,700 feet
HOURS
10:00 a.m. - 4:00 p.m., Tues., Fri.,
Sat., Sun., holidays, closed Christmas
LIFTS
1 bar, 1 tow, 1,100 capacity per hour
SEASON
Mid-December to mid-April
SNOW PHONE
Call Ski Area
TRAVEL
E. of Yellowstone Nat'l Park, N.W. Wyoming
50 miles west of Cody, U.S. 14 A, 16 and 20
VERTICAL DROP
500 feet

SNOW KING MOUNTAIN

Jackson, WY 83001 (307) 733-2851

AREA INFORMATION

BASE ELEVATION
6,230 feet
HOURS
9:30 a.m. - 4:00 p.m.
LIFTS
2 chairlifts, 2 tows, 1,600 capacity per hour
LONGEST RUN
1 mile
NURSERY
At the slopes, call Ski Area
SEASON
Mid-December to mid-April, no snowmaking
SNOW PHONE
Call Ski Area
TRAILS
20% beginner, 30% intermediate, 50% advanced
TRAVEL
W. Wyoming, U.S. 187/189, south of Teton Park
VERTICAL DROP
1,570 feet

WHITE PINE

Pinedale, WY 82941 (307) 367-2913

AREA INFORMATION

BASE ELEVATION
8,500 feet
HOURS
Weekends, holidays
LIFTS
1 bar, 1 tow
SEASON
Mid-November to March
SNOW PHONE
Call Ski Area
TRAILS
Beginner to advanced
TRAVEL
W. Wyoming, U.S. 187/189
In Bridger National Park
VERTICAL DROP
1,000 feet

C A N A D A

A L B E R T A

CANYON SKI AREA

Red Deer, AL (403) 346-5588

AREA INFORMATION

BASE ELEVATION
750 feet
HOURS
1:00 - 5:00, 6:00 - 10:00 p.m., Monday through Friday
9:00 a.m. - 5:00, 6:00 - 10:00 p.m., Sat., Sun., holidays
LIFTS
1 chairlift, 2 bars, 2 tows, 4,700 capacity per hour
LONGEST RUN
2,700 feet
NURSERY
Age 2 & up, prior arrangement, call Ski Area
SEASON
November to March, snowmaking
SNOW PHONE
Call Ski Area
TRAILS
40% beginner, 40% intermediate, 20% advanced
TRAVEL
From Calgary, Hwy. 2 North
VERTICAL DROP
440 feet

CYPRESS

Elkwater, AL 50J 1C0 (403) 893-3961

AREA INFORMATION

HOURS
10:00 a.m. - 4:00 p.m., Wed., Sat., Sun.
LIFTS
1 bar, 900 capacity per hour
LONGEST RUN
2,500 feet
SEASON
November to March, no snowmaking
SNOW PHONE
Call Ski Area
TRAVEL
Southeast Alberta, Hwy. 48
VERTICAL DROP
530 feet

DAKOTA SKI HILL

Ponoka, AL T0C 2H0 (403) 783-2112

AREA INFORMATION

HOURS
1:00 - 6:30 p.m., Sundays
Night skiing, Friday nights
LIFTS
1 tow, 1,000 capacity per hour
SEASON
Late November to mid-March
SNOW PHONE
Call Ski Area
TRAILS
Mostly intermediate, some beginner and advanced
TRAVEL
S. of Edmonton, Hwy. 53 W. to Ponoka, then north
VERTICAL DROP
100 feet

DRAYTON VALLEY SKI CLUB

Drayton Valley, AL T0E 0M0 (403) 542-2837

AREA INFORMATION

HOURS
10:00 a.m. - 9:00 p.m., Saturday
11:00 a.m. - 9:00 p.m., Sunday
LIFTS
1 T-bar, 3 tows, 2,000 capacity per hour
LONGEST RUN
1,000 feet
SNOW PHONE
Call Ski Area
TRAVEL
West of Edmonton, 8 km from Drayton Valley
VERTICAL DROP
270 feet

EDMONTON SKI CLUB

Edmonton, AL (403) 469-4369

AREA INFORMATION

HOURS
10:00 a.m. - 10:00 p.m., weekdays
9:00 a.m. - 10:00 p.m., weekends

LIFTS
5 tows, 1,800 capacity per hour
LONGEST RUN
600 feet
SEASON
November to March, snowmaking
SNOW PHONE
Call Ski Area
TRAVEL
In Edmonton at 9613 96th Avenue
VERTICAL DROP
80 feet

GRAND PRAIRIE SKI CLUB

Grand Prairie, AL T8V (403) 532-6796

AREA INFORMATION

BASE ELEVATION
1,740 feet
HOURS
7:00 - 10:00 p.m., Monday - Friday
11:00 a.m. - 10:00 p.m., Saturday
10:00 a.m. - 6:00 p.m., Sunday
LIFTS
1 T-bar
LONGEST RUN
6,100 feet
SEASON
Mid-December to mid-March, snowmaking
SNOW PHONE
Call Ski Area
TRAILS
Beginner to advanced
TRAVEL
West-Central Alberta, Hwy. 2, Wapiti Road
VERTICAL DROP
460 feet

LAKE EDEN RESORT

Stony Plain, Edmonton, AL (403) 963-3411

AREA INFORMATION

HOURS
10:00 a.m. - 10:00 p.m., weekdays
9:00 a.m. - 6:00 p.m., weekends
LIFTS
1 chairlift, 2 T-bars, 5 tows
LONGEST RUN
800 feet
SEASON
Mid-November to March, snowmaking
SNOW PHONE
Call Ski Area
TRAILS
8 slopes
TRAVEL
Hwy. 16, west of Edmonton
VERTICAL DROP
160 feet

LONG LAKE

Newbrook, AL T0A 2P0 (403) 576-9905

AREA INFORMATION

HOURS
9:30 a.m. - 4:30 p.m.
LIFTS
1 bar, 1 tow, 1,000 capacity per hour
LONGEST RUN
½ mile
SEASON
December to April
SNOW PHONE
Call Ski Area
TRAILS
9 runs
TRAVEL
Northeast of Edmonton
VERTICAL DROP
200 feet

PASKAPOO

Calgary, AL (403) 288-4112

AREA INFORMATION

BASE ELEVATION
3,600 feet
HOURS
10:00 a.m. - 6:00 p.m., 5:00 - 10:00 p.m.
LIFTS
2 chairlifts, 2 bars, 2 tows
LONGEST RUN
3,500 feet
SEASON
Mid-November to late March, snowmaking
SNOW PHONE 286-2002
TRAILS
60% beginner, 40% intermediate
TRAVEL
W. Calgary, Trans Canada Hwy. & Bowford Rd., N.W.
VERTICAL DROP
400 feet

RABBIT HILL

Edmonton, AL (403) 955-2121

AREA INFORMATION

HOURS
10:00 a.m. - 10:00 p.m., Monday - Friday
10:00 a.m. - 6:00 p.m., Saturday, Sunday
LIFTS
1 chairlift, 2 bars, 3 tows, 3,400 capacity per hour
LONGEST RUN
2,900 feet
SEASON
Mid-November to mid-March, snowmaking
SNOW PHONE 955-2440
TRAILS
40% beginner, 40% intermediate, 20% advanced
TRAVEL
Southwest of Edmonton, Hwy. 2 South to
Ellerslie Corner, then access route, 12 miles
VERTICAL DROP
300 feet

SILVER SUMMIT

Edson, AL T0E 0P0 (403) 436-1728

AREA INFORMATION

BASE ELEVATION
3,780 feet
HOURS
9:00 a.m. - 4:30 p.m.
LIFTS
1 chairlift, 1 T-bar, 1 tow, 2,200 capacity per hour
LONGEST RUN
4,000 feet
SNOW PHONE
Call Ski Area
TRAILS
11 slopes
TRAVEL
N.W. of Edmonton, Hwy. 16, 30 miles from Edson
VERTICAL DROP
960 feet

SWAN RIDGE

Swan Hills, AL T0G 2C0 (403) 333-2127

AREA INFORMATION

HOURS
10:00 a.m. - 4:00 p.m., weekends
LIFTS
1 T-bar, 250 capacity per hour
LONGEST RUN
1,200 feet
SEASON
Late November to late April
SNOW PHONE
Call Ski Area
TRAILS
Beginner and intermediate
TRAVEL
Central Alberta, Hwy. 33
7 miles north of Swan Hills
VERTICAL DROP
550 feet

TAWATINAW VALLEY

Westlock (403) 698-2212

AREA INFORMATION

HOURS
10:00 a.m. - 4:30 p.m., Fri., Sat., Sun., holidays
LIFTS
2 T-bars, 1 tow, 2,000 capacity per hour
LONGEST RUN
1,900 feet
SEASON
Mid-December to late March
SNOW PHONE
Call Ski Area
TRAILS
18 runs
TRAVEL
55 miles north of Edmonton, Hwy. 2, sign posted
VERTICAL DROP
210 feet

BRITISH COLUMBIA

APEX ALPINE

P.O. Box 486, Pentincton, BC V2A 6K9 (604) 493-3200

AREA INFORMATION

BASE ELEVATION
5,450 feet

HOURS
9:30 a.m. - 4:00 p.m.
Night skiing, beginner run
LIFTS
3 chairlifts, 1 T-bar, 1 poma, 2 tows
3,600 capacity per hour
LONGEST RUN
1¼ miles
SEASON
Late December to mid-April
SNOW PHONE 493-3606
Alberta, Saskatchewan . . . . (403) 246-2736
TRAILS
15% beginner, 45% intermediate, 40% advanced
TRAVEL
S. British Columbia, 23 miles southwest
of Penticton via Green Mountain Road
VERTICAL DROP
2,000 feet

LODGING

CENTRAL RESERVATIONS. . . . . (604) 492-4181

KREEKSIDE MOTEL (near restaurants)
1706 Main St., V2A 5G8
MAJESTIC FLAG INN
152 Riverside Dr., V2A 5Y4
PENTICTON INN (dining, pub & night club)
333 Martin St., V2A 5K7
PENTICTON SANDMAN INN (dining, entertainment)
939 Burnaby Ave., V2A 1G7
PENTICTON SLUMBERLODGE (indoor pool)
274 Lakeshore Dr., V2A 1B8
PENTICTON TRAVELODGE (dining, indoor pool)
950 Westminster Ave., V2A 1L2
PLAZA MOTEL (heated indoor pool)
1485 Main St., V2A 5G4
RIVERSIDE MOTEL (near restaurants)
110 Riverside Dr., V2A 5Y4
THE "SHEILING" MOTEL
2509 S. Main St., V2A 5J4
THREE GABLES HOTEL (dining room)
353 Main St., V2A 5B7
WESTERN MOTEL (near restaurants)
38 Warren Ave., East, V2A 3L8

ARROWSMITH MOUNTAIN

Port Alberni, BC V9Y   Radio to Area (604) 723-7512

AREA INFORMATION

BASE ELEVATION
3,100 feet
HOURS
9:00 a.m. - 4:00 p.m.
LIFTS
1 chairlift, 2 bars, 2 tows, 1,200 capacity per hour
LONGEST RUN
1½ miles
SEASON
Early November to late April, no snowmaking
SNOW PHONE 687-5422
TRAILS
Beginner to advanced, helicopter skiing available
TRAVEL
20 miles from Port Alberni, Nanaimo Hwy.
to 12 mile logging access road, sign posted
VERTICAL DROP
1,300 feet

AZU

Dawson Creek, BC V1G   (604) 782-8531

AREA INFORMATION

BASE ELEVATION
3,000 feet
HOURS
9:00 a.m. - 4:00 p.m.
LIFTS
1 T-bar, 400 capacity per hour, helicopter skiing
LONGEST RUN
1½ miles
SEASON
November to late April
SNOW PHONE
Call Ski Area
TRAVEL
Near Alberta, 250 miles N.E. of Prince George
Jet service to Prince George and Dawson Creek

BIG BAM

Fort St. John, BC V1J   (604) 785-6977

AREA INFORMATION

HOURS
7:00 - 9:30 p.m., Tues. - Thurs., Sat.
11:00 a.m. - 5:00 p.m., Sat. & Sun.
LIFTS
1 T-bar, 1 tow
LONGEST RUN
2,700 feet
SEASON
December to March
SNOW PHONE
Call Ski Area

BIG BAM CONT.

TRAILS
6 slopes
TRAVEL
Jet service to Dawson Creek, 47 miles to Area
VERTICAL DROP
700 feet

BLACKCOMB MOUNTAIN

Whistler, BC V0N 1B0 (604) 932-3141

AREA INFORMATION

BASE ELEVATION
2,140 feet
HOURS
9:00 a.m. - 3:30 p.m., weekdays
8:00 a.m. - 3:30 p.m., weekends, holidays
LIFTS
5 chairlifts, interchangeable with Whistler Mtn.
Both mountains meet at Whistler Town Centre
LONGEST RUN
7 miles
NURSERY
Call Ski Area
SEASON
November to early May, no snowmaking
SNOW PHONE
Call Ski Area
TRAILS
350 acres of trails from steep chutes to novice runs
TRAVEL
80 miles north of Vancouver, Hwy. 99
VERTICAL DROP
4,000 feet

BLUE RIVER

Blue River, BC V0E 1J0

AREA INFORMATION

HOURS
11:00 a.m. - 9:00 p.m., Fri. - Sun. & Tues.
LIFTS
1 tow, 400 capacity per hour
LONGEST RUN
900 feet
SEASON
Late December to late March
TRAVEL
Eastern B.C., Hwy. 5, south of Blue River
VERTICAL DROP
300 feet

BOTANIE BUMP

Lytton, BC V0K 1Z0

AREA INFORMATION

HOURS
10:00 a.m. - 4:00 p.m., Sundays
LIFTS
1 tow, 450 capacity per hour
LONGEST RUN
1,200 feet
SEASON
Mid-December to mid-March
TRAILS
Mostly beginner
TRAVEL
Trans Canada Hwy. 1, 110 miles from
Kamloops, just inside Fraser Canyon
VERTICAL DROP
200 feet

CYPRESS PROVINCIAL PARK

Vancouver, BC (604) 929-2358

AREA INFORMATION

BASE ELEVATION
2,990 feet
HOURS
9:30 a.m. - 4:00 p.m., weekdays
9:00 a.m. - 4:00 p.m., weekends, holidays
LIFTS
2 chairlifts, 2 tows, 2,200 capacity per hour
SNOW PHONE
Call Ski Area
TRAVEL
16 km west of Vancouver, Lions Gate Bridge, Hwy. 99
VERTICAL DROP
1,170 feet

DAWSON

Dawson Creek, BC V1G (604) 782-4988

AREA INFORMATION

BASE ELEVATION
2,550 feet
HOURS
10:00 a.m. - 5:00 p.m., weekends, holidays
7:00 p.m. - 10:00 p.m., night skiing
Also Wednesday & Friday afternoons

LIFTS
1 T-bar, 550 capacity per hour
LONGEST RUN
3,500 feet
SEASON
Mid-December to mid-March, snowmaking
SNOW PHONE
Call Ski Area
TRAILS
4 slopes
TRAVEL
255 miles N.E. of Prince George, near Alberta
Jet service to Prince George and Dawson Creek
VERTICAL DROP
410 feet

FAIRMONT HOT SPRINGS

Fairmont Hot Springs, BC V0B 1L0 (604) 345-6311

AREA INFORMATION

BASE ELEVATION
4,200 feet
HOURS
9:00 a.m. - 10:00 p.m., night skiing from 6:00 p.m.
LIFTS
1 chairlift, 1 poma, 1 tow, 2,200 capacity per hour
LONGEST RUN
5,000 feet
SEASON
Mid-December to late March, snowmaking
SNOW PHONE
Call Ski Area
TRAILS
Beginner to advanced, more than 50% intermediate
TRAVEL
Southeastern edge of British Columbia, seventy
miles from Cranbrook, Hwy. 93 to Hwy. 95
VERTICAL DROP
1,000 feet

FERNIE SNOW VALLEY

Fernie, BC V0B 1M0 (604) 423-6041

AREA INFORMATION

BASE ELEVATION
3,500 feet
HOURS
9:00 a.m. - 4:00 p.m.
LIFTS
1 chairlift, 3 bars, 1 tow, 3,000 capacity per hour
NURSERY
Age 1 & up, call Ski Area
SEASON
Mid-November to late April, no snowmaking
SNOW PHONE 423-6464
TRAILS
25% beginner, 40% intermediate, 35% advanced
TRAVEL
Trans Canada Hwy. No. 3, S.E. British Columbia
VERTICAL DROP
2,100 feet

FORBIDDEN PLATEAU

Courtenay, BC V9N 5N4 (604) 334-4744

AREA INFORMATION

BASE ELEVATION
2,300 feet
HOURS
9:00 a.m. - 4:00 p.m.
LIFTS
1 chairlift, 3 bars, 2 tows, 4,700 capacity per hour
SEASON
Early December to late April, no snowmaking
SNOW PHONE
Call Ski Area
TRAILS
25% beginner, 65% intermediate, 10% advanced
TRAVEL
15 miles west of Courtenay, Island of Vancouver
VERTICAL DROP
1,150 feet

GRANDVIEW SKI ACRES

Kamloops, BC V2C 5M8 (604) 374-6070

AREA INFORMATION

HOURS
9:00 a.m. - 3:30 p.m., daily
7:00 - 10:00 p.m., Tues. - Sat.
LIFTS
1 chairlift, 1 bar, 1 tow, 2,000 capacity per hour
LONGEST RUN
1 mile
SEASON
December to March
SNOW PHONE
Call Ski Area
TRAVEL
From Kamloops to Ski Area, 7 miles,
Hwy. 1 to Hwy. 5 South to access road
VERTICAL DROP
580 feet

GREEN MOUNTAIN

Nanaimo, Vancouver Island, BC

AREA INFORMATION

BASE ELEVATION
3,800 feet
HOURS
9:00 a.m. - 4:00 p.m.
LIFTS
2 tows, 700 capacity per hour
LONGEST RUN
1½ miles
SEASON
Mid-December to April
TRAILS
600 acres
TRAVEL
Nanaimo Lakes Rd. W., paved and gravel roads, 2,000 foot climb, chains required
VERTICAL DROP
700 feet

GROUSE MOUNTAIN

North Vancouver, BC V7R 4N4 (604) 984-0661

AREA INFORMATION

BASE ELEVATION
2,900 feet
HOURS
9:00 a.m. - 10:30 p.m., weekdays
8:00 a.m. - 10:30 p.m., Saturday, holidays
8:00 a.m. - 10:00 p.m., Sunday
LIFTS
2 aerial tramways, 4 chairlifts, 2 T-bars, 3 rope tows, 1 handle tow, 10,500 per hour
LONGEST RUN
1 mile
NURSERY. 987-0210
SEASON
November to April, no snowmaking
SNOW PHONE 986-6262
TRAILS
30% beginner, 50% intermediate, 20% advanced
TRAVEL
20 minutes from downtown Vancouver, bus service on the half hour, B.C. Hydro from the mainland
VERTICAL DROP
1,200 feet

HARPER MOUNTAIN

Kamloops, BC (604) 573-5115

AREA INFORMATION

BASE ELEVATION
4,000 feet
HOURS
9:30 a.m. - 4:00 p.m.
7:00 - 10:00 p.m., Tues. - Fri.
LIFTS
1 chairlift, 2 bars, 1 tow, 3,400 capacity per hour
SEASON
Early December to early April, no snowmaking
SNOW PHONE
Call Ski Area
TRAILS
25% beginner, 50% intermediate, 25% advanced
TRAVEL
15 miles from Kamloops, Yellowhead Hwy. North for 2 miles to access road, signs posted
VERTICAL DROP
1,400 feet

HEMLOCK VALLEY

Harrison Mills, BC V0M 1L0 (604) 685-2205, 525-3732

AREA INFORMATION

BASE ELEVATION
3,300 feet
HOURS
9:00 a.m. - 4:00 p.m., daily
4:00 - 10:00 p.m., Fri., Sat.
LIFTS
3 chairlifts, 3 tows, 4,100 capacity per hour
LONGEST RUN
Over 1 mile
SEASON
December to May, no snowmaking
SNOW PHONE 253-5121, 859-6211
TRAILS
30% beginner, 35% intermediate, 35% advanced
TRAVEL
76 miles from Vancouver, Route 7 East
Bus service is available from Vancouver
VERTICAL DROP
1,200 feet

HUDSON BAY MOUNTAIN

Smithers, BC V0J 2N0 (604) 847-2058

AREA INFORMATION

BASE ELEVATION
4,500 feet
HOURS
9:30 a.m. - 4:00 p.m.
LIFTS
2 bars, 1 tow, 1,600 capacity per hour
LONGEST RUN
1½ miles
SEASON
Mid-November to late April
SNOW PHONE
Call Ski Area
TRAILS
25 miles of runs, 8 miles tree-lined
TRAVEL
West-Central British Columbia, 12 miles south of Smithers, Yellowhead Highway
VERTICAL DROP
1,000 feet

KITIMAT ALPINE SKI CLUB

Kitimat, BC V8C 1B4 (504) 632-2892

AREA INFORMATION

BASE ELEVATION
500 feet
HOURS
7:00 - 9:00 p.m., weekdays
1:00 - 4:00 p.m., weekends
LIFTS
1 tow
LONGEST RUN
900 feet
SEASON
December to March, no snowmaking
SNOW PHONE
Call Ski Area
TRAILS
Beginner area
TRAVEL
W. Central British Columbia, 2 miles N. of Kitimat
VERTICAL DROP
250 feet

KITSUMKALUM MOUNTAIN

Terrace, BC V8G (604) 638-1616

AREA INFORMATION

BASE ELEVATION
1,000 feet
HOURS
10:00 a.m. - 4:00 p.m., Mon. - Sun.
Wednesday & Thursday, night skiing
LIFTS
1 chairlift, 1 bar, 2 tows, 1,800 capacity per hour
LONGEST RUN
4 miles
SEASON
Late November to April
SNOW PHONE
Call Ski Area
TRAILS
2 tree-lined slopes
TRAVEL
W. Central British Columbia, air service from Vancouver to Terrace, 7 miles to Ski Area
VERTICAL DROP
1,400 feet

LAST MOUNTAIN

Westbank, BC V0H 2A0 (604) 768-5189

AREA INFORMATION

HOURS
Open every day and Tuesday thru Saturday nights
LIFTS
1 chairlift, 2 bars, 2,800 capacity per hour
LONGEST RUN
6,000 feet
SEASON
December to April
SNOW PHONE
Call Ski Area
TRAVEL
Near United States border, eight miles from Hwy. 97, 30 miles S. of Penticton
VERTICAL DROP
600 feet

LE JEUNE LODGE

Kamloops, BC (604) 374-2165

AREA INFORMATION

BASE ELEVATION
4,300 feet
HOURS
9:00 - 3:30 p.m.
LIFTS
1 bar, 2 tows, 1,400 capacity per hour
LONGEST RUN
4,500 feet
SEASON
Early December to late March
SNOW PHONE
Call Ski Area
TRAILS
Intermediate, some beginner and advanced
TRAVEL
5 miles west of Kamloops
VERTICAL DROP
800 feet

LITTLE MAC SKI HILL

Mackenzie, BC V0J 2C0 (604) 997-3221

AREA INFORMATION

HOURS
1:00 - 4:00, 7:00 - 9:30 p.m., Sat. & Sun.
LIFTS
2 tows, 450 capacity per hour
SEASON
November to late March
SNOW PHONE
Call Ski Area
TRAILS
2 slopes, beginner
TRAVEL
North of Dawson Creek, 112 miles north of Prince George, jet service to both cities

MORNING MOUNTAIN

Nelson (604) 352-9969

AREA INFORMATION

BASE ELEVATION
1,600 feet
HOURS
9:30 a.m. - 3:30 p.m., Sat. - Mon.
6:30 - 9:30 p.m., Tues. - Thurs.
LIFTS
1 bar, 900 capacity per hour
LONGEST RUN
2,300 feet
SEASON
Early December to late March
SNOW PHONE
Call Ski Area
TRAILS
6 runs
TRAVEL
Highway 3A, 5 miles west of Nelson
VERTICAL DROP
400 feet

MOUNT BALDY

Osoyoos, BC V0H 1V0 (604) 495-6534

AREA INFORMATION

BASE ELEVATION
5,600 feet
HOURS
9:30 a.m. - 4:00 p.m.
LIFTS
2 bars, 1 tow, 1,800 capacity per hour
SEASON
Late November to mid-April
SNOW PHONE
Call Ski Area
TRAILS
Beginner to advanced
TRAVEL
Near United States border, Highway 3 to Rock Canyon Bridge, 11 mile access road
VERTICAL DROP
7,000 feet

MT. MC KENZIE

Revelstoke, BC V0E 2S0 (604) 837-3641, 837-4883

AREA INFORMATION

BASE ELEVATION
1,050 feet
HOURS
10:00 a.m. - 4:00 p.m., Sat. - Mon. & Weds.
7:30 - 10:00 p.m., Tues., Weds., Fri.
LIFTS
1 chairlift, 1 bar, 1 tow, 1,200 capacity per hour
LONGEST RUN
5 miles
SEASON
Mid-December to late March, no snowmaking

SNOW PHONE
Call Ski Area
TRAILS
5 slopes
TRAVEL
Trans Canada Hwy. 1 to Revelstoke
south on 5 mile access road to Area
VERTICAL DROP
2,600 feet

MOUNT SEYMOUR PROVINCIAL PARK

Vancouver, BC (604) 929-5212

AREA INFORMATION

HOURS
9:00 a.m. - 4:00 p.m., Mon. - Sat.
4:00 p.m. - 10:00 p.m., Saturday
4:00 p.m. - 8:00 p.m., Sunday
LIFTS
2 chairlifts, 4 tows, 2,500 capacity per hour
LONGEST RUN
1,030 feet
SEASON
Early December to early April
SNOW PHONE
Call Ski Area
TRAVEL
From Vancouver, 15 km, Second Narrows
Bridge, Keith Road, Mt. Seymour Parkway
VERTICAL DROP
125 feet

MT. WASHINGTON

Campbell River, BC V9W (604) 287-8912

AREA INFORMATION

BASE ELEVATION
3,500 feet
LIFTS
2 chairlifts, 1 tow, 2,400 capacity per hour
LONGEST RUN
3 miles
SEASON
November to May
SNOW PHONE
Call Ski Area
TRAVEL
Vancouver Island, 128 miles northwest of Victoria
VERTICAL DROP
1,700 feet

PANORAMA

P.O. Box 458, Invermere V0A 1K0 (604) 342-3211

AREA INFORMATION

BASE ELEVATION
3,700 feet
HOURS
9:30 a.m. - 4:00 p.m.
LIFTS
3 chairlifts, 1 T-bar, 1 platter pull, 1 rope tow
5,900 capacity per hour
LODGING. . . . . (403) 266-9829
LONGEST RUN
2½ miles
SEASON
Early December to mid-April, no snowmaking
SNOW PHONE 342-3223, (403) 246-2736
TRAILS
5 beginner, 5 intermediate, 11 advanced
TRAVEL
12 miles southwest of Invermere on Toby Creek Road
Trans Canada Hwy. No. 1 to Radium, Hwy. No. 93/95
VERTICAL DROP
3,200 feet

RAINBOW LAKE SKI CLUB

Prince Rupert, BC V8J (604) 624-6263, 624-2236

AREA INFORMATION

HOURS
10:00 a.m. - 5:00 p.m., Sat., Sun., holidays
7:00 p.m. - 10:30 p.m., Saturday nights
LIFTS
1 bar, 2 tows, 1,600 capacity per hour
LONGEST RUN
2,700 feet
SEASON
December to April
SNOW PHONE
Call Ski Area
TRAVEL
Near Southern Alaska, take ferry,
train, plane, bus to access gondola
VERTICAL DROP
550 feet

RED MOUNTAIN

Rossland, BC V0G 1Y0 (604) 362-7384

AREA INFORMATION

BASE ELEVATION
3,800 feet
HOURS
8:30 a.m. - 3:30 p.m., 3:30 - 9:00 p.m., Mon. - Fri.
8:30 a.m. - Noon, Saturday; Noon - 3:30 p.m., Sunday
LIFTS
3 chairlifts, 1 T-bar, 1 tow, 4,000 capacity per hour
LONGEST RUN
4½ miles
NURSERY
To grade school age, Base Lodge
SEASON
Mid-November to late April, no snowmaking
SNOW PHONE 362-5500
TRAILS
20% beginner, 40% intermediate, 40% advanced
TRAVEL
2 miles from Rossland on Hwy. 3 B
Between Vancouver and Calgary
VERTICAL DROP
2,700 feet

SALMO

Salmo, BC V0G 1Z0 (604) 357-2232

AREA INFORMATION

HOURS
9:30 a.m. - 4:00 p.m., Saturday, Sunday
6:00 - 10:00 p.m., Monday - Thursday
LIFTS
1 T-bar, 2 tows, 1,400 capacity per hour
LONGEST RUN
4,200 feet
SEASON
December to March
SNOW PHONE
Call Ski Area
TRAILS
Beginner to advanced
TRAVEL
Near U.S. border, 2 miles south of Salmo
VERTICAL DROP
1,100 feet

SILVER STAR

Box 1720, Vernon, BC V1T 8C3 (604) 545-3618

AREA INFORMATION

BASE ELEVATION
4,680 feet
HOURS
9:00 a.m. - 3:30 p.m., extended holidays & Spring
LIFTS
3 chairlifts, 3 T-bars, 1 poma, 7,500 capacity per hour
LONGEST RUN
10,000 feet
NURSERY
Age 2 & up, must be toilet trained, call Ski Area
SEASON
Mid-November to mid-April
SNOW PHONE 542-0224
TRAILS
35% beginner, 50% intermediate, 15% advanced
TRAVEL
Trans Canada Hwy. 1 to Hwy. 17 South, thirteen
miles on Silver Star Road; airport is near Vernon
VERTICAL DROP
1,600 feet

SKI LOOS

McBride, BC V0J 2E0

AREA INFORMATION

HOURS
9:00 a.m. - 4:30 p.m., weekends, holidays
LIFTS
1 bar, 300 capacity per hour
SEASON
Late December to late March
TRAVEL
35 miles west from McBride to Crescent Spur
and Loos Roads, signs posted from this point
VERTICAL DROP
260 feet

SNOWPATCH SKI AREA

Princeton, BC V0X 1W0 (604) 295-7248, 295-3353

AREA INFORMATION

BASE ELEVATION
3,700 feet
HOURS
10:00 a.m. - 4:00 p.m., weekends, holidays
Every day during Christmas holidays
January & February, Wednesday thru Sunday
LIFTS
1 bar, 3 tows, 500 capacity per hour

LONGEST RUN
½ mile
SEASON
Mid-December to late March
SNOW PHONE
Call Ski Area
TRAVEL
180 miles east of Vancouver, 5 miles north of Princeton
VERTICAL DROP
500 feet

TABOR MOUNTAIN

Prince George, BC V2N 2J6 (604) 963-7542

AREA INFORMATION

HOURS
9:00 a.m. - 4:00 p.m., Mon. - Sun.
6:00 - 10:30 p.m., Mon. - Fri.
LIFTS
1 T-bar, 2 tows, 1,200 capacity per hour
LONGEST RUN
2 miles
SEASON
December to March
SNOW PHONE
Call Ski Area
TRAVEL
From Prince George, 8 miles on Hwy. 16 East
VERTICAL DROP
800 feet

TILLICUM VALLEY

Vernon, BC V1T 8C3 (604) 542-1109

AREA INFORMATION

BASE ELEVATION
2,500 feet
HOURS
10:00 a.m. - 5:00 p.m., 5:00 - 10:00 p.m.
LIFTS
1 chairlift, 1 T-bar, 1 tow, 2,600 capacity per hour
LONGEST RUN
6,000 feet
SNOW PHONE
Call Ski Area
TRAILS
Beginner to advanced
TRAVEL
From Vernon, 5 miles east, Silver Star Road
VERTICAL DROP
700 feet

TIMBERLAND

Williams Lake, BC V2G

AREA INFORMATION

HOURS
9:30 a.m. - 3:30 p.m., 7:00 - 9:30 p.m.
LIFTS
1 bar, 1 tow, 500 capacity per hour
SEASON
December to late March
TRAILS
11 runs, open bowl
TRAVEL
10 miles south of Williams Lake
VERTICAL DROP
800 feet

WHISTLER MOUNTAIN

Box 181, Whistler, BC V0N 1B0 (604) 681-1014

AREA INFORMATION

BASE ELEVATION
2,140 feet
HOURS
9:00 a.m. - 3:30 p.m., Monday - Friday
8:00 a.m. - 3:30 p.m., weekends, holidays
LIFTS
1 gondola, 10 chairlifts, 2 T-bars, over 10,000 per hour
Interchangeable lifts with Blackcomb Ski Area
Both mountains meet at the Whistler Town Centre
LODGING. 932-4222
LONGEST RUN
7 miles
NURSERY
Must be toilet trained, call Ski Area
SEASON
November to early May, no snowmaking
SNOW PHONE
Call Ski Area
TRAILS
35% beginner, 45% intermediate, 20% advanced
TRAVEL
80 miles north of Vancouver via Rt. 99. By air to Vancouver, then train, bus or rental car to Area
VERTICAL DROP
4,280 feet

WHITEWATER

Box 60, Nelson, BC V1L 5P7 (604) 352-7669

AREA INFORMATION

BASE ELEVATION
5,400 feet
HOURS
9:00 a.m. - 3:30 p.m.
LIFTS
2 chairlifts, 1 T-bar, 3,000 capacity per hour
LONGEST RUN
1.2 miles
NURSERY
Call Ski Area
SEASON
Mid-November to late April, no snowmaking
SNOW PHONE 352-7669
TRAILS
20% beginner, 30% intermediate, 50% advanced
TRAVEL
12 miles south of Nelson; Cranbrook, 150 miles
Spokane, 120 miles; 3,000 ft. airstrip at Castlegar
VERTICAL DROP
1,300 feet

M A N I T O B A

FALCON SKI SLOPES

Whiteshell Pk., Falcon Lake, MT R0E 0N0 (204) 347-2201

AREA INFORMATION

HOURS
10:00 a.m. - 4:30 p.m., weekends, holidays
LIFTS
4 tows, 1,800 capacity per hour
LONGEST RUN
1,120 feet
SEASON
December to March
SNOW PHONE
Call Ski Area
TRAILS
4 slopes
TRAVEL
95 miles east of Winnipeg, Trans Canada Hwy.
VERTICAL DROP
140 feet

FLIN FLON SKI CLUB

Flin Flon, MT R8A (204) 687-3446

AREA INFORMATION

BASE ELEVATION
1,000 feet
HOURS
11:00 a.m. - 5:00 p.m., weekends
LIFTS
2 tows, 850 capacity per hour
LONGEST RUN
1,000 feet
SEASON
Mid-December to early April
SNOW PHONE
Call Ski Area
TRAILS
2 slopes
TRAVEL
Central Manitoba, near Saskatchewan
VERTICAL DROP
200 feet

HOLIDAY MOUNTAIN

La Riviere, MT R0G 1A0 (204) 242-2172

AREA INFORMATION

BASE ELEVATION
1,250 feet
HOURS
9:00 a.m. - 4:30 p.m., daily
7:00 - 10:30 p.m., Weds., Fri., Sat.
LIFTS
3 bars, 2 tows, 3,800 capacity per hour
LONGEST RUN
2,000 feet
SEASON
Mid-November to mid-March, snowmaking
SNOW PHONE
Call Ski Area
TRAILS
9 slopes
TRAVEL
100 miles S.W. of Winnipeg, P.T.H. No. 3
VERTICAL DROP
300 feet

MT. AGASSIZ

McCreary, MT R0J 1B0 (204) 835-2246, 956-2676

AREA INFORMATION

BASE ELEVATION
2,300 feet
HOURS
9:00 a.m. - 5:00 p.m.

LIFTS
1 chairlift, 2 T-bars, 2 tows, 3,100 capacity per hour
LONGEST RUN
4,600 feet
SEASON
Early December to early April, snowmaking
SNOW PHONE 835-2302
TRAILS
1 beginner, 5 intermediate, 2 advanced
TRAVEL
150 miles N.W. of Winnipeg, P.T.H. No. 1, 4, & 5
VERTICAL DROP
500 feet

MT. GLENORKEY

Brandon, MT

AREA INFORMATION

HOURS
9:30 a.m. - 4:30 p.m., weekends, holidays
LIFTS
1 bar, 2 tows, 1,200 capacity per hour
SEASON
December to March
TRAILS
Beginner and intermediate
TRAVEL
Southwest Manitoba, 10 miles west of Brandon

STONY MOUNTAIN WINTER PARK

Winnipeg, MT (204) 344-5977, 338-9503

AREA INFORMATION

HOURS
7:00 - 10:00 p.m., Tues. - Thurs.
10:00 a.m. - 4:00 p.m., Sat., Sun.
Friday nights, groups by reservation
LIFTS
2 tows, 750 capacity per hour
LONGEST RUN
400 feet
SEASON
Early December to late March, snowmaking
SNOW PHONE
Call Ski Area
TRAILS
Beginner and intermediate
TRAVEL
15 miles from Winnipeg, Hwy. 7, Stony Mtn. exit
VERTICAL DROP
125 feet

WINNIPEG SKI CLUB

Winnipeg, MT (204) 284-2852

AREA INFORMATION

HOURS
Days, Saturday and Sunday
Nights, Monday thru Thursday
LIFTS
1 tow, 300 capacity per hour
LONGEST RUN
200 feet
SEASON
December to April
SNOW PHONE
Call Ski Area
TRAILS
4 runs, beginner and intermediate
TRAVEL
In Winnipeg, Togo and Osborne Streets
VERTICAL DROP
100 feet

NEW BRUNSWICK

CRABBE MOUNTAIN WINTER PARK

Millville, NB E0H 1M0 (506) 463-2686

AREA INFORMATION

BASE ELEVATION
470 feet
HOURS
1:00 - 4:30 p.m., Weds., Thurs.
9:30 a.m. - 4:30 p.m., Fri. - Sun.
LIFTS
2 T-bar, 1 tow, 1,800 capacity per hour
LONGEST RUN
1½ miles
SEASON
Late December to late March
SNOW PHONE
Call Ski Area
TRAILS
Beginner to advanced
TRAVEL
35 miles north of Fredericton, Route 104
VERTICAL DROP
850 feet

ROCKWOOD PARK SKI HILLS

Saint John, NB (508) 658-2844

AREA INFORMATION

HOURS
9:00 a.m. - 12:30, 1:00 - 4:30 p.m., Saturday
1:00 - 4:30 p.m., 8:00 - 10:30 p.m., Sunday
7:00 - 10:00 p.m., Monday through Friday
LIFTS
1 bar, 1 tow, 1,300 capacity per hour
LONGEST RUN
1,350 feet
SEASON
Mid-December to mid-March
SNOW PHONE
Call Ski Area
TRAVEL
In Saint John, Southern New Brunswick
VERTICAL DROP
150 feet

SILVERWOOD WINTER PARK

Fredericton, NB E3B 5C3 (506) 454-3151

AREA INFORMATION

BASE ELEVATION
60 feet
HOURS
1:00 - 10:00 p.m., Monday - Friday
9:00 a.m. - 10:00 p.m., Saturday, Sunday
LIFTS
1 bar, 1 tow, 1,600 capacity per hour
LONGEST RUN
2,600 feet
SEASON
December to March
SNOW PHONE
Call Ski Area
TRAILS
3 trails
TRAVEL
5 miles west of Fredericton Centre
Trans Canada Highway No. 2
VERTICAL DROP
300 feet

SUGARLOAF PROVINCIAL PARK

Campbellton, NB E3N (506) 753-6258

AREA INFORMATION

BASE ELEVATION
150 feet
HOURS
1:00 - 4:30 p.m., 7:00 - 10:00 p.m., Thursday
10:00 a.m. - 4:30, 7:00 - 10:00 p.m., Fri. - Sun.
7:00 p.m. - 10:00 p.m., Wednesday nights
LIFTS
1 chairlift, 3 bars, 3,100 capacity per hour
SEASON
Mid-December to early April
SNOW PHONE
Call Ski Area
TRAILS
Beginner to advanced
TRAVEL
2 miles from Campbellton, N. New Brunswick
VERTICAL DROP
500 feet

NEWFOUNDLAND

CHURCHILL FALLS

Churchill Falls, NF A0R 1A0 (709) 924-3311

AREA INFORMATION

LIFTS
1 bar, 1 tow, 1,300 capacity per hour
LONGEST RUN
1,450 feet
SEASON
December to March, no snowmaking
SNOW PHONE
Call Ski Area
TRAILS
4 slopes
TRAVEL
About 100 miles from Labrador City
VERTICAL DROP
690 feet

SMOKEY MOUNTAIN

P.O. Box 9, Labrador City, NF A2V (709) 944-3505

AREA INFORMATION

LIFTS
1 chairlift, 3 pomas, 3,600 capacity per hour
LONGEST RUN
5,000 feet
SEASON
December to March
SNOW PHONE
Call Ski Area

TRAILS
1 beginner, 4 intermediate, 3 advanced
TRAVEL
Near Labrador City
VERTICAL DROP
1,000 feet

NOVA SCOTIA

BEN EOIN RECREATION CENTRE

Sydney, NS (902) 828-2222

AREA INFORMATION

BASE ELEVATION
30 feet
HOURS
10:00 a.m. - 4:30 p.m., Saturday, Sunday
10:00 a.m. - 10:00 p.m., Monday - Friday
LIFTS
1 bar, 1 tow, 1,100 capacity per hour
LONGEST RUN
2,700 feet
SEASON
December to March
SNOW PHONE 539-9999
TRAVEL
Northern Nova Scotia
VERTICAL DROP
470 feet

KELTIC'S CAPE SMOKEY

Ingonish Beach, NS 1L0 (902) 285-2778

AREA INFORMATION

BASE ELEVATION
100 feet
HOURS
8:30 a.m. - 4:30 p.m.
LIFTS
1 chairlift, 1 tow, 700 capacity per hour
LONGEST RUN
1¼ miles
SEASON
Mid-December to mid-April
SNOW PHONE
Call Ski Area
TRAILS
Beginner to intermediate
TRAVEL
From Sydney, 80 miles, Route 105 West
35 miles from interception of Cabot Trail
VERTICAL DROP
1,000 feet

KEPPOCH MOUNTAIN

Antigonish, NS B2G (902) 863-1764

AREA INFORMATION

BASE ELEVATION
400 feet
HOURS
Tuesday through Sunday, days
LIFTS
1 bar, 900 capacity per hour
LONGEST RUN
4,000 feet
SEASON
Late December to April, snowmaking
SNOW PHONE
Call Ski Area
TRAILS
Beginner to advanced
TRAVEL
7 miles from Antigonish
VERTICAL DROP
460 feet

MARTOCK II SKI AREA

Windsor, NS B0N 2T0 (902) 798-4728

AREA INFORMATION

BASE ELEVATION
95 feet
HOURS
1:00 - 10:00 p.m., weekdays
9:00 a.m. - 10:00 p.m., weekends
LIFTS
2 bars, 2,200 capacity per hour
LONGEST RUN
1½ miles
SEASON
Mid-December to early April, snowmaking
SNOW PHONE 798-5421
TRAILS
3 mile total
TRAVEL
45 miles from Halifax, Routes No. 1 and 14
VERTICAL DROP
600 feet

SKI WENTWORTH

Wentworth, NS B0M 1Z0 (902) 548-2089

AREA INFORMATION

BASE ELEVATION
400 feet

SKI WENTWORTH CONT.

HOURS
9:30 a.m. - 4:30 p.m., Tuesday thru Sunday
LIFTS
2 bars, 1 tow, 1,400 capacity per hour
LONGEST RUN
1¾ miles
SEASON
Mid-December to late March, snowmaking
SNOW PHONE
Call Ski Area
TRAILS
Beginner, intermediate, some advanced
TRAVEL
From Halifax, 90 miles, Trans Canada Hwy. 104
VERTICAL DROP
700 feet

O N T A R I O

ABERFOYLE COUNTRY CLUB

Puslinch, ON N0B 2J0 (519) 822-5764

AREA INFORMATION

HOURS
6:00 - 10:00 p.m., Tuesday thru Friday
9:00 a.m. - 4:30 p.m., Sat., Sun., holidays
LIFTS
1 bar, 1 tow, 1,200 capacity per hour
LONGEST RUN
2,500 feet
SNOW PHONE
Call Ski Area
SEASON
Mid-December to mid-March, snowmaking
TRAVEL
South of Ottawa, 2 miles east of Puslinch
VERTICAL DROP
180 feet

ADANAC SKI CENTRE

Sudbury, ON (705) 566-9911

AREA INFORMATION

BASE ELEVATION
840 feet
HOURS
10:00 a.m. - 4:00 p.m., Friday thru Sunday
7:00 - 10:00 p.m., Wednesday thru Friday
LIFTS
1 bar, 1 tow, 1,700 capacity per hour
LONGEST RUN
1,500 feet
SEASON
Mid-December to late March, snowmaking
SNOW PHONE
Call Ski Area
TRAILS
Beginner and intermediate
TRAVEL
In Sudbury, Beatrice Crescent
VERTICAL DROP
200 feet

ALBION HILLS

Palgrave, ON L0N 1P0 (416) 661-6600

AREA INFORMATION

BASE ELEVATION
850 feet
HOURS
9:30 a.m. - 4:30 p.m., weekends
LIFTS
3 tows, 1,200 capacity per hour
LONGEST RUN
700 feet
SEASON
Early December to mid-March
SNOW PHONE
Call Ski Area
TRAILS
2 beginner slopes
TRAVEL
About 4 miles from Bolton, Hwy. 50 North
VERTICAL DROP
120 feet

ALICE HILL PARK

Pembroke, ON K8A (613) 732-2776

AREA INFORMATION

BASE ELEVATION
300 feet
HOURS
10:00 a.m. - 5:00 p.m., Sat., Sun., holidays
8:00 - 11:00 p.m., Wednesday and Friday
LIFTS
1 bar, 1 tow, 950 capacity per hour
LONGEST RUN
4,000 feet
SEASON
Early December to late March

SNOW PHONE
Call Ski Area
TRAILS
2 slopes
TRAVEL
14 miles from Pembroke
VERTICAL DROP
210 feet

ATIKOKAN SKI CLUB

Atikokan, ON P0T 1C0 (807) 597-4475

AREA INFORMATION

BASE ELEVATION
1,230 feet
HOURS
11:00 a.m. - 4:30 p.m., Saturday and Sunday
LIFTS
1 bar, 2 tows, 1,000 capacity per hour
LONGEST RUN
2,000 feet
SEASON
Late November to late March
SNOW PHONE
Call Ski Area
TRAVEL
132 miles from Thunder Bay to Ski Area,
Highways 17, 11 and 11 B to Route 622
VERTICAL DROP
240 feet

BATAWA SKI CLUB

Batawa, ON K0K 1E0 (613) 398-6568

AREA INFORMATION

HOURS
Weekends, Tuesday and Thursday nights
LIFTS
2 bars, 2 tows, 1,700 capacity per hour
LONGEST RUN
1,800 feet
SEASON
December to March
SNOW PHONE
Call Ski Area
TRAVEL
From Trenton, 5 miles north to Ski Area
VERTICAL DROP
180 feet

BEAVER VALLEY

Markdale, ON N0C 1H0 (519) 986-2520

AREA INFORMATION

BASE ELEVATION
840 feet
HOURS
9:00 a.m. - 4:00 p.m., Fri., Sat., Sun., holidays
6:00 p.m. - 10:00 p.m., Saturday, night skiing
LIFTS
2 chairlifts, 2 T-bars, 1 J-bar, 1 tow
4,100 capacity per hour
LONGEST RUN
Almost 1 mile
NURSERY
At the slopes, call Ski Area
SEASON
December to early April, snowmaking
SNOW PHONE
Call Ski Area
TRAILS
20% beginner, 50% intermediate, 30% advanced
TRAVEL
From Toronto, Hwy. No. 10 N., 4 E., County No. 13 N.
VERTICAL DROP
500 feet

BETHANY SKI CLUB

Peterborough, ON (705) 277-2311

AREA INFORMATION

HOURS
9:00 a.m. - 4:00 p.m., daily
4:00 - 10:00 p.m., Mon. - Fri.
LIFTS
1 chairlift, 2 T-bars, 2,800 capacity per hour
LONGEST RUN
2,500 feet
SEASON
Mid-December to mid-April, snowmaking
SNOW PHONE
Call Ski Area
TRAILS
14 slopes
TRAVEL
From Bethany, Hwy. No. 35, 7A, north 2 miles
VERTICAL DROP
360 feet

BLUE MOUNTAIN

Collingwood, ON L9Y 3Z2 (705) 445-0231

AREA INFORMATION

BASE ELEVATION
720 feet
HOURS
9:00 a.m. - 4:30 p.m., daily
4:30 - 10:00 p.m., Weds., Thurs., Sat.
4:30 - 11:00 p.m., Friday nights
LIFTS
12 chairlifts, 4 poma lifts, 1 T-bar, 5 tows
Over 15,000 capacity per hour
LONGEST RUN
1½ miles
NURSERY
Age 2 & up, toilet trained,
SEASON
Early December to mid-April, snowmaking
SNOW PHONE
Call Ski Area, or. . . . . (416) 967-7152
TRAILS
25% beginner, 55% intermediate, 20% advanced
TRAVEL
From Toronto, 90 miles via Routes 400 N., 26 W.; from Collingwood to Area, 7 miles; bus service from Toronto
VERTICAL DROP
820 feet

BROCKVILLE "Y" SKI CENTRE

YMCA/YWCA, Brockville, ON K6V (613) 342-7961

AREA INFORMATION

HOURS
12:00 - 5:00 p.m., Saturday
1:00 - 4:00 p.m., Sunday
Tuesday & Thursday nights
LIFTS
1 bar, 500 capacity per hour
LONGEST RUN
600 feet
SEASON
Late December to late March
SNOW PHONE
Call Ski Area
TRAILS
One open slope
TRAVEL
Area is beyond Athens, Highways 29 N. & 42 W.
VERTICAL DROP
200 feet

BUTTERMILK

Goulais Bay, ON (705) 649-2061

AREA INFORMATION

BASE ELEVATION
720 feet
HOURS
10:30 a.m. - 4:30 p.m., 7:30 - 11:00 p.m.
LIFTS
1 bar, 750 capacity per hour
SEASON
Mid-November to late March
SNOW PHONE
Call Ski Area
TRAILS
2 slopes
TRAVEL
18 miles from Sault Ste. Marie, Hwy. 17 N., 8 miles north of Heyden Ski Hill, Restaurant, and Motel
VERTICAL DROP
180 feet

CALABOGIE PEAKS

Box 6136, Sta. J, Ottawa, ON K2A 1T2 (613) 752-2720

AREA INFORMATION

BASE ELEVATION
500 feet
HOURS
9:30 a.m. - 4:30 p.m.
LIFTS
1 chairlift, 3 T-bars, 1 handle tow
5,100 capacity per hour
LONGEST RUN
8,800 feet
NURSERY
Toilet trained, call Ski Area
SEASON
Early December to mid-April, snowmaking
SNOW PHONE
Call Ski Area
TRAILS
3 beginner, 6 intermediate, 3 advanced
TRAVEL
Hwy. 508 West, three miles from Calabogie
Hwy. 17 to 508 W., 60 miles from Ottawa
VERTICAL DROP
750 feet

CAMBORNE VILLAGE SKI CLUB

Cobourg, ON K9A (416) 342-5323

AREA INFORMATION

HOURS
Tuesday, Wednesday, and weekends
10:00 a.m. - 4:30, 7:00 - 10:00 p.m.
LIFTS
1 bars, 2 tows, 1,600 capacity per hour
LONGEST RUN
1,300 feet
SEASON
Early December to mid-March
SNOW PHONE
Call Ski Area
TRAVEL
From Toronto to Coburg, Hwy. 401 E., 70 miles
From Coburg to Ski Area, County Road 18 North
VERTICAL DROP
180 feet

CANDIAC SKIWAYS

Dacre, ON K0J 1N0 (613) 432-5305

AREA INFORMATION

HOURS
9:30 a.m. - 4:00 p.m., Wednesday, weekends, holidays
LIFTS
3 bars, 1,800 capacity per hour
LONGEST RUN
Almost 2 miles
SEASON
December to April
SNOW PHONE
Call Ski Area
TRAILS
7 trails
TRAVEL
Route 17 and Hwy. 132 West, 70 miles
from Ottawa, 3 miles south of Dacre
VERTICAL DROP
600 feet

CANDY MOUNTAIN

Thunder Bay, ON P7C 4Z2 (807) 939-6033

AREA INFORMATION

BASE ELEVATION
810 feet
HOURS
9:30 a.m. - 4:15 p.m., Tues. - Sun., holidays
LIFTS
1 chairlift, 1 T-bar, 1 tow, 2,300 capacity per hour
LONGEST RUN
1 mile
SEASON
Early December to early April, snowmaking
SNOW PHONE
Call Ski Area
TRAILS
9 trails
TRAVEL
Hwy. 30 to Hwy. 17 or 61 West
16 miles west of Thunder Bay
VERTICAL DROP
730 feet

CARLINGTON PARK

Raven Ave., Ottawa, ON (613) 729-8202

AREA INFORMATION

HOURS
4:00 - 10:00 p.m., weekdays
9:00 a.m. - 5:00 p.m., weekends
LIFTS
1 bar, 1,100 capacity per hour
SEASON
Late November to late March, snowmaking
SNOW PHONE
Call Ski Area
TRAILS
Beginner slope, 700 feet
TRAVEL
In Ottawa, lodging nearby
VERTICAL DROP
70 feet

CASWELL RESORT

Sundridge, ON P0A 1Z0 (705) 384-5371

AREA INFORMATION

HOURS
Weekends
LIFTS
1 bar, 1 tow, 1,200 capacity per hour
LONGEST RUN
1,800 feet
SEASON
December to March, snowmaking
SNOW PHONE
Call Ski Area
TRAVEL
Hwy. No. 11
VERTICAL DROP
170 feet

CEDAR MOUNTAIN

Peterborough, ON (705) 745-5251

AREA INFORMATION

HOURS
10:00 a.m. - 4:30 p.m., 6:00 - 10:00 p.m.
LIFTS
2 bars, 1 tow, 700 capacity per hour
LONGEST RUN
2,000 feet
SEASON
Mid-December to late March, snowmaking
SNOW PHONE
Call Ski Area
TRAILS
11 slopes
TRAVEL
1 mile east of Peterborough
VERTICAL DROP
230 feet

CENTENNIAL PARK SKI HILL

Toronto, ON (416) 621-3702

AREA INFORMATION

HOURS
12:00 - 6:00 p.m., Monday - Friday
9:00 a.m. - 5:00 p.m., Saturday, Sunday
7:00 p.m. - 10:00 p.m., every night
LIFTS
2 bars, 1,800 capacity per hour
LONGEST RUN
700 feet
SEASON
December to March, snowmaking
SNOW PHONE
Call Ski Area
TRAVEL
Renforth Drive in Toronto
VERTICAL DROP
130 feet

CHICOPEE SKI CLUB

Kitchener, ON (519) 724-5844

AREA INFORMATION

HOURS
10:00 a.m. - 10:00 p.m., Mon. - Fri.
9:00 a.m. - 10:00 p.m., Saturday
9:00 a.m. - 5:00 p.m., Sunday
LIFTS
2 chairlifts, 4 bars, 8,100 capacity per hour
LONGEST RUN
2,000 feet
SEASON
December to March
SNOW PHONE 742-8307
TRAVEL
Morrison Road in Kitchener
VERTICAL DROP
190 feet

COCHENOUR SKI AREA

City Rd., Bolton, ON L0P 1A0 (416) 857-3120

AREA INFORMATION

HOURS
Wednesday night, Saturday, Sunday
LIFTS
1 tow, 150 capacity per hour
SEASON
Mid-December to late March
SNOW PHONE
Call Ski Area
TRAVEL
Northwestern Ontario, Hwy. 105 to Cochenour
VERTICAL DROP
200 feet

DEVIL'S ELBOW

Bethany (705) 277-2012

AREA INFORMATION

HOURS
10:00 a.m. - 4:30 p.m., weekdays
9:00 a.m. - 4:30 p.m., weekends
LIFTS
3 chairlifts, 3 T-bars, 7,500 capacity per hour
LONGEST RUN
¾ mile
SEASON
Early December to early April
SNOW PHONE
Call Ski Area
TRAVEL
From Toronto, Routes 401 E., 35 N., 71 W.
Area is three miles north of Bethany Village
VERTICAL DROP
350 feet

EDELWEISS

City Road, Bolton (416) 857-3120

AREA INFORMATION

HOURS
Days, Tuesday through Sunday
Nights, Monday through Saturday
LIFTS
2 cables, 3 bars, 3,700 capacity per hour
LONGEST RUN
2,000 feet
SEASON
December to March, snowmaking
SNOW PHONE
Call Ski Area
TRAVEL
West of Bolton
VERTICAL DROP
150 feet

FONTHILL SKI CENTRE

St. Catharine's, ON (416) 934-2682

AREA INFORMATION

HOURS
10:00 a.m. - 4:30 p.m., Sat., Sun., holidays
7:00 - 10:00 p.m., Wednesday and Thursday
LIFTS
1 bar, 3 tows, 2,200 capacity per hour
LONGEST RUN
800 feet
SEASON
Mid-December to early March
SNOW PHONE 934-8400
TRAILS
4 runs
TRAVEL
Town of Fonthill, Hwy. No. 20 to Lookout Point
VERTICAL DROP
120 feet

GEORGIAN PEAKS

Thornbury, ON N0H 2P0 (519) 599-3737

AREA INFORMATION

BASE ELEVATION
600 feet
HOURS
8:30 a.m. - 4:30 p.m.
LIFTS
4 chairlifts, 1 bar, 2 tows, 5,000 capacity per hour
SEASON
Early December to early April
SNOW PHONE
Call Ski Area
TRAILS
Beginner to advanced
TRAVEL
From Toronto, Rt. 400 through Barrie, Rt. 26 through Collingwood, then 8 miles to Thornbury to Ski Area
VERTICAL DROP
820 feet

GLEN EDEN

Milton, ON L9T (416) 878-4131

AREA INFORMATION

BASE ELEVATION
800 feet
HOURS
1:00 - 5:00 p.m., Tues. - Thurs.
10:00 a.m. - 5:00 p.m., Friday
9:30 a.m. - 4:30 p.m., Sat., Sun.
6:30 - 10:00 p.m., Mon. - Sat.
LIFTS
1 chairlift, 3 T-bars, 3 tows, 4,500 capacity per hour
LONGEST RUN
2,000 feet
SEASON
Early December to early April, snowmaking
SNOW PHONE
Call Ski Area
TRAILS
Beginner and intermediate
TRAVEL
From Toronto, Highways No. 401 and 25 to 4 mile access route, signs posted from Hwy. 25 to Area
VERTICAL DROP
240 feet

HAPPY VALLEY

Walkerton, ON N0G 2V0 (519) 881-1590

AREA INFORMATION

HOURS
9:30 a.m. - 4:30 p.m., 7:00 - 10:00 p.m., Wed. - Sun.
LIFTS
1 bar, 1 tow, 650 capacity per hour
LONGEST RUN
1,800 feet
SEASON
Mid-December to mid-April
SNOW PHONE
Call Ski Area

TRAILS
7 slopes
TRAVEL
Southwestern Ontario, 1 mile from Walkerton
VERTICAL DROP
170 feet

HEYDEN SKI HILL

Sault Ste. Marie, ON (705) 777-2082

AREA INFORMATION

HOURS
10:00 a.m. - 4:00 p.m., Wednesday - Sunday
7:00 p.m. - 10:30 p.m., Tuesday - Sunday
LIFTS
1 bar, 800 capacity per hour
LONGEST RUN
2,000 feet
SEASON
Mid-December to early April
SNOW PHONE
Call Ski Area
TRAILS
4 runs
TRAVEL
Hwy. 17 N., 10 miles from Sault Ste. Marie
Eight miles south of Buttermilk Ski Resort
VERTICAL DROP
200 feet

HIDDEN VALLEY HIGHLANDS

Huntsville, ON P0A 1K0 (705) 789-5942, (416) 364-2011

AREA INFORMATION

BASE ELEVATION
940 feet
HOURS
9:30 a.m. - 4:30 p.m., weekdays
9:00 a.m. - 4:30 p.m., weekends
LIFTS
2 chairlifts, 1 T-bar, 1 tow, 3,400 capacity per hour
NURSERY
At the Holiday Inn 789-2301
SEASON
Mid-December to early April, snowmaking
SNOW PHONE
Call Ski Area
TRAILS
30% beginner, 50% intermediate, 20% advanced
TRAVEL
From Toronto, Highways No. 400 N., 11 and 60; six miles from Huntsville to Area
VERTICAL DROP
320 feet

HONEY POT

Duffering St., Maple ON L0J 1E0

AREA INFORMATION

BASE ELEVATION
20 feet
HOURS
1:00 - 5:00, 7:00 - 10:30 p.m., Tues. - Fri.
9:00 a.m. - 5:00 p.m., Saturday and Sunday
LIFTS
3 bars, 3 tows, 1,500 capacity per hour
LONGEST RUN
300 feet
SEASON
December to March, snowmaking
TRAILS
Beginner and some intermediate
TRAVEL
In Maple, Southern Ontario
VERTICAL DROP
100 feet

HORSESHOE VALLEY

Horsehoe Valley, ON (705) 835-2014, (416) 364-9509

AREA INFORMATION

HOURS
9:00 a.m. - 4:30 p.m.
LIFTS
3 chairlifts, 3 T-bars, 7,500 capacity per hour
LONGEST RUN
¾ mile
NURSERY
Weekends, other times by appointment
SEASON
Late November to mid-April, snowmaking
SNOW PHONE
Call Ski Area
TRAILS
30% beginner, 50% intermediate, 20% advanced
TRAVEL
70 miles from Toronto via Route 400 to
Horshoe Valley Rd., 15 miles past Barrie
VERTICAL DROP
400 feet

JIGSAW

Madoc, ON K0K 2K0

AREA INFORMATION

HOURS
Saturday and Sunday
LIFTS
2 tows, 300 capacity per hour
LONGEST RUN
1,200 feet
SEASON
Mid-December to late March
TRAILS
5 slopes
TRAVEL
Hwy. 62 N. Through Bannockburn to access road
VERTICAL DROP
200 feet

KAMISKOTIA

Timmins, ON (705) 264-8114, 264-9057

AREA INFORMATION

BASE ELEVATION
1,000 feet
HOURS
10:00 a.m. - 4:30 p.m., Sat., Sun.
7:00 - 10:30 p.m., Tues., Weds., Sat.
Also open on Wednesday afternoons
LIFTS
3 T-bars, 2,600 capacity per hour
LONGEST RUN
3,000 feet
SEASON
Early December to mid-April
SNOW PHONE
Call Ski Area
TRAILS
14 trails
TRAVEL
Highways 101 W. and 576 N., 12 miles from Timmins
VERTICAL DROP
350 feet

KING'S FOREST WINTER PARK

Hamilton, ON (416) 547-9042

AREA INFORMATION

HOURS
6:30 - 10:00 p.m., Mon. - Thurs.
1:00 - 5:00 p.m., Tues., Thurs.
10:00 a.m. - 5:00 p.m., Sat., Sun.
LIFTS
2 T-bars, 1 poma, 2,600 capacity per hour
LONGEST RUN
3,000 feet
SEASON
Late December to March, snowmaking
SNOW PHONE
Call Ski Area
TRAILS
2 open slopes
TRAVEL
In Hamilton, Cochrane Road S. and Greenhill Ave.
VERTICAL DROP
240 feet

KINGSTON SKI HILLS

Kingston, ON (613) 542-7166

AREA INFORMATION

HOURS
9:30 a.m. - 4:30 p.m., weekends, holidays
7:30 - 10:00 p.m., Tuesday - Thursday
LIFTS
1 bar, 4 tows, 2,400 capacity per hour
LONGEST RUN
800 feet
SEASON
Mid-December to late March
SNOW PHONE
Call Ski Area
TRAILS
5 open slopes
TRAVEL
Southeastern Ontario, 3 miles northeast of Sydenham
VERTICAL DROP
120 feet

KIWISSA

Old Wilpay, Manitouwadge, ON P0T 2C0 (807) 826-3870

AREA INFORMATION

BASE ELEVATION
1,120 feet
HOURS
10:30 a.m. - 4:30 p.m., Saturday
12:00 - 4:30 p.m., Sunday
Weds. night, Christmas holidays
LIFTS
1 T-bar, 1 tow, 750 capacity per hour
LONGEST RUN
2,600 feet
SEASON
Mid-December to March

KIWASSA CONT.

SNOW PHONE
Call Ski Area
TRAILS
1 slope with 5 runs
TRAVEL
250 miles northeast of Thunder Bay
VERTICAL DROP
330 feet

LARDER SKI CLUB

Larder Lake, ON P0K 1L0 (705) 643-2523

AREA INFORMATION

HOURS
Fri. night, Sat., Sun., Christmas/Easter weeks
1:00 p.m. - 5:00 p.m., 7:00 p.m. - 10:00 p.m.
LIFTS
1 tow, 200 capacity per hour
LONGEST RUN
850 feet
SEASON
December to April
SNOW PHONE
Call Ski Area
TRAILS
4 slopes
TRAVEL
Near S.W. Quebec, just south of Larder Lake
VERTICAL DROP
170 feet

LOCH LOMOND

R.R. 4, Thunder Bay, ON P7C 4Z2 (807) 577-5787

AREA INFORMATION

BASE ELEVATION
700 feet
HOURS
9:30 a.m. - 5:00 p.m., 7:30 - 10:00 p.m.
LIFTS
3 chairlifts, 1 T-bar, 4,600 capacity per hour
LONGEST RUN
1¼ miles
SEASON
Late November to mid-April, snowmaking
SNOW PHONE 577-5787
TRAILS
15 beginner, 3 intermediate, 8 advanced
TRAVEL
Near the Ontario/Minnesota border and Lake Superior
8 miles from Thunder Bay, Hwy. 17 to Hwy. 61 South
U.S. Rt. 61 along Lake Superior to Ontario Hwy. 61
VERTICAL DROP
800 feet

LORETTO SKI RESORT

Mississauga, ON (416) 277-8230

AREA INFORMATION

HOURS
9:00 a.m. - 4:30 p.m., Tues., Weds., weekends, holidays
LIFTS
2 bars, 1 tow, 2,400 capacity per hour
LONGEST RUN
1,500 feet
SEASON
Early December to late March, snowmaking
SNOW PHONE
Call Ski Area
TRAILS
5 runs
TRAVEL
Hwy. No. 50 from Toronto
VERTICAL DROP
180 feet

MANSFIELD SKIWAYS

Mansfield, ON L0N 1M0 (705) 435-5302

AREA INFORMATION

BASE ELEVATION
970 feet
HOURS
9:00 a.m. - 5:00 p.m.
LIFTS
5 bars, 1 tow, 5,200 capacity per hour
LONGEST RUN
2,600 feet
SEASON
Mid-December to early April, snowmaking
SNOW PHONE
Call Ski Area
TRAILS
30% beginner, 60% intermediate, 10% advanced
TRAVEL
30 miles from Barrie, Hwy. No. 89 and 400
VERTICAL DROP
400 feet

MEDONTE MOUNTAIN

Barrie, ON L4M 4Y8 (705) 835-2001

AREA INFORMATION

HOURS
Tuesday thru Sunday
LIFTS
4 bars, 2 tows, 5,400 capacity per hour
LONGEST RUN
4,000 feet
SEASON
December to April, snowmaking
SNOW PHONE
Call Ski Area
TRAILS
Beginner to advanced
TRAVEL
15 miles from Barrie, Hwy. 400 North
Turn right onto Horseshoe Valley Road
VERTICAL DROP
400 feet

MINTO GLEN SPORTS CENTRE

Harriston, ON N0G 1Z0 (519) 338-2007

AREA INFORMATION

HOURS
10:30 a.m. - 5:00 p.m., weekends
7:30 - 10:00 p.m., Saturday
LIFTS
1 tow
LONGEST RUN
1,000 feet
SEASON
December to March
SNOW PHONE 338-2722
TRAILS
25% beginner, 75% intermediate
TRAVEL
Hwy. 89 to County Road 2, 6½ miles N. of Harriston
VERTICAL DROP
180 feet

MOONSTONE

Coldwater, ON L0K 1E0 (705) 835-2018

AREA INFORMATION

HOURS
9:00 a.m. - 4:30 p.m.
LIFTS
3 chairlifts, 2 poma lifts, 1 T-bar, 1 tow
6,300 capacity per hour
LONGEST RUN
5,000 feet
NURSERY
Age 4 and up, call Ski Area
SEASON
Mid-December to late March, snowmaking
SNOW PHONE 368-6900
TRAILS
25% beginner, 50% intermediate, 25% advanced
TRAVEL
Hwy. 400 from Toronto, 60 miles
VERTICAL DROP
450 feet

MOUNTAIN VIEW SKI AREA

Midland, ON L4R (705) 526-8149

AREA INFORMATION

BASE ELEVATION
150 feet
HOURS
9:00 a.m. - 4:30 p.m., weekends, holidays
LIFTS
2 bars, 1 tow, 1,400 capacity per hour
LONGEST RUN
1,300 feet
SEASON
Late December to mid-March
SNOW PHONE
Call Ski Area
TRAILS
Beginner to advanced, 7 open slopes
TRAVEL
90 miles from Toronto, Highways 400 and 27
VERTICAL DROP
150 feet

MT. ANTOINE

Mattawa, ON P0H 1V0 (705) 472-7440, 744-2159

AREA INFORMATION

BASE ELEVATION
520 feet
HOURS
9:30 a.m. - 4:00 p.m., Monday - Friday
9:00 a.m. - 4:00 p.m., Saturday, Sunday
LIFTS
1 chairlift, 1,100 capacity per hour
Interchangeable ticket, North Bay-Laurentian

MT. ANTOINE CONT.

LONGEST RUN
10,000 feet
SEASON
Mid-December to early April
SNOW PHONE
Call Ski Area
TRAILS
Beginner to advanced
TRAVEL
40 miles from North Bay
VERTICAL DROP
640 feet

MT. BALDY

Box 2124, Thunder Bay, ON P7B 5E7 (807) 683-8441

AREA INFORMATION

HOURS
12:00 - 5:00 p.m., weekdays
9:00 a.m. - 5:00 , weekends
7:00 - 10:00 p.m., Weds., Fri.
LIFTS
1 chairlift, 1 T-bar, 1 J-bar, 1 rope tow
3,800 capacity per hour
LONGEST RUN
7,000 feet
SEASON
Late November to early April, snowmaking
SNOW PHONE
Call Ski Area
TRAILS
25% beginner, 50% intermediate, 25% advanced
TRAVEL
7 miles east of Thunder Bay, Hwy. 17-11, 527 N.
VERTICAL DROP
700 feet

MT. CHINGUACOUSY

Brampton, ON (416) 791-6510

AREA INFORMATION

HOURS
Weekends and holidays
6:00 - 10:00 p.m., nights
LIFTS
1 bar, 1 tow, 850 capacity per hour
LONGEST RUN
750 feet
SEASON
December to March, snowmaking
SNOW PHONE
Call Ski Area
TRAVEL
Southeastern Ontario, Hwy. No. 7 to Bramalea Rd. N.
VERTICAL DROP
130 feet

MOUNT DUFOUR

Elliot Lake, ON (705) 848-6655

AREA INFORMATION

HOURS
10:00 a.m. - 4:00 p.m., weekends
LIFTS
1 bar, 600 capacity per hour
SEASON
Late December to March
SNOW PHONE
Call Ski Area
TRAILS
3 slopes, beginner to advanced
TRAVEL
North of Spanish, east of Elliot Lake
VERTICAL DROP
310 feet

MT. EVERGREEN SKI CLUB

Kenora, ON P9N (807) 548-5100

AREA INFORMATION

BASE ELEVATION
1,000 feet
HOURS
1:00 - 4:00 p.m., Wednesday
7:00 - 10:00 p.m., Weds., Fri.
9:30 a.m. - 4:30 p.m., Sat., Sun.
Daily during Christmas week
LIFTS
2 bars, 1 tow, 1,400 capacity per hour
LONGEST RUN
2,100 feet
NURSERY
At the slopes, call Ski Area
SEASON
Early December to mid-March, snowmaking
SNOW PHONE
Call Ski Area
TRAILS
Mostly intermediate
TRAVEL
130 miles from Winnipeg, Hwy. No. 17 to 604
VERTICAL DROP
250 feet

MOUNT MC KAY

R.R. 4, Thunder Bay, ON P7C 4Z2 (807) 623-6822

AREA INFORMATION

HOURS
Open days, every day; night skiing, Tuesday - Friday
LIFTS
3 chairlifts, 1 bar, 1 tow, 3,900 capacity per hour
LONGEST RUN
Over 1 mile
SNOW PHONE
Call Ski Area
TRAVEL
Highways 17 and 61, U.S. 61 connects with Hwy. 61
VERTICAL DROP
620 feet

MOUNT NORWAY

Thunder Bay, ON P7C 4Z2 (807) 577-8813

AREA INFORMATION

HOURS
10:00 a.m. - 4:30 p.m., Mon., Weds. - Fri.
10:00 a.m. - 5:00 p.m., weekends
7:00 p.m. - 10:00 p.m., night skiing
LIFTS
1 chairlift, 1 T-bar, 1,700 capacity per hour
LONGEST RUN
1½ miles
SEASON
Late November to April, snowmaking
SNOW PHONE
Call Ski Area
TRAVEL
Nine miles from Thunder Bay
Hwy. 61, Little Norway Road
VERTICAL DROP
750 feet

MOUNT PAKENHAM

Pakenham, ON K0A 2X0 (613) 624-5290

AREA INFORMATION

BASE ELEVATION
450 feet
HOURS
9:00 a.m. - 5:00 p.m., Weds. - Sun.
6:30 - 10:30 p.m., night skiing
LIFTS
1 chairlift, 1 T-bar, 1 tow, 2,200 capacity per hour
LONGEST RUN
3,000 feet
SEASON
December to early April, snowmaking
SNOW PHONE
Call Ski Area
TRAILS
50% beginner, 25% intermediate, 25% advanced
TRAVEL
Ottawa, 30 miles, Hwy. No. 17, 2 miles from Pakenham
VERTICAL DROP
270 feet

NEW HOCKEY HILLS

Orangeville, ON L9W (519) 941-7802

AREA INFORMATION

BASE ELEVATION
230 feet
HOURS
10:00 a.m. - 10:30 p.m.
LIFTS
1 chairlift, 1 T-bar, 1 poma, 1 tow
2,400 capacity per hour
LONGEST RUN
2,400 feet
SEASON
Mid-December to late March, snowmaking
SNOW PHONE
Call Ski Area
TRAILS
13 runs
TRAVEL
33 miles north of Toronto; Orangeville, 7 miles
VERTICAL DROP
110 feet

NIPISSING RIDGE

Callander, ON P0H 1H0 (705) 472-2827

AREA INFORMATION

BASE ELEVATION
720 feet
HOURS
9:30 a.m. - 4:30 p.m., Fri. - Sun., holidays
LIFTS
2 bars, 1 tow, 1,400 capacity per hour
LONGEST RUN
4,500 feet
SEASON
Early December to mid-April, snowmaking
SNOW PHONE
Call Ski Area
TRAILS
Area tree-lined, variety of terrain
TRAVEL
Highways 11 and 534 West, 20 miles from North Bay
VERTICAL DROP
400 feet

NORDIC HILLS

Sudbury, ON (705) 522-6663, 675-8487

AREA INFORMATION

HOURS
Wednesday and weekend days
Wednesday and Thursday nights
LIFTS
2 bars, 2 tows, 2,200 capacity per hour
LONGEST RUN
2,400 feet
SEASON
December to March
SNOW PHONE
Call Ski Area
TRAVEL
2 miles southwest of Sudbury
VERTICAL DROP
250 feet

NORTHBAY LAURENTIAN

North Bay, ON (705) 472-7440

AREA INFORMATION

BASE ELEVATION
310 feet
HOURS
1:00 - 4:00 p.m., Monday thru Wednesday
7:00 - 10:00 p.m., Tuesday thru Friday
9:00 a.m. - 4:00 p.m., weekends, holidays
LIFTS
3 T-bars, 2,500 capacity per hour
LONGEST RUN
1,800 capacity per hour
SEASON
Mid-December to March
SNOW PHONE
Call Ski Area
TRAILS
2 open slopes
TRAVEL
In North Bay, northwest of Ottawa
VERTICAL DROP
310 feet

NORTH YORK SKI CENTRE

Bathurst St., Downsview, ON M3N 1S4 (416) 638-5315

AREA INFORMATION

HOURS
10:00 a.m. - 5:00, 6:30 - 10:30 p.m., Tues. - Sun.
LIFTS
2 bars, 1 tow, 2,200 capacity per hour
LONGEST RUN
1,000 feet
SEASON
Early December to late March, snowmaking
SNOW PHONE
Call Ski Area
TRAILS
3 slopes
TRAVEL
In Downsview, southwest of Ottawa
VERTICAL DROP
130 feet

ONAPING

Onaping, ON P0M 2R0 (705) 966-3939

AREA INFORMATION

BASE ELEVATION
1,100 feet
HOURS
10:00 a.m. - 4:30 p.m., weekends, holiday weeks
1:00 p.m. - 4:30 p.m., Wednesday afternoons
LIFTS
3 bars, 2,900 capacity per hour
LONGEST RUN
2,400 feet
SEASON
Mid-December to mid-April
SNOW PHONE
Call Ski Area
TRAILS
Beginner to advanced
TRAVEL
28 miles from Sudbury, Hwy. 144 N. to Hwy. 544
VERTICAL DROP
320 feet

OSHAWA KIRBY

Oshawa, ON (416) 983-5983

AREA INFORMATION

BASE ELEVATION
870 feet
HOURS
9:30 a.m. - 4:30, 5:30 - 10:00 p.m., Weds., Thurs.
9:30 a.m. - 4:30 p.m., Saturday and Sunday
LIFTS
5 bars, 3 tows, 5,800 capacity per hour
SEASON
Mid-December to mid-April, snowmaking

SNOW PHONE
Call Ski Area
TRAILS
10 tree-lined slopes, 3 open slopes, 1 bowl
TRAVEL
30 miles from Oshawa, Routes 401, 115, 35 North to Area access road
VERTICAL DROP
300 feet

OTTAWA YM/YWCA

South March, ON (613) 832-1234

AREA INFORMATION

HOURS
9:00 a.m. - 4:00 p.m., weekends
LIFTS
1 bar, 500 capacity per hour
LONGEST RUN
1,000 feet
SEASON
January to mid-March
SNOW PHONE
Call Ski Area
TRAVEL
9 miles from Queensway at Kanata
VERTICAL DROP
100 feet

PINE TOP

Thunder Bay, ON (807) 683-8061

AREA INFORMATION

BASE ELEVATION
1,100 feet
HOURS
1:00 - 5:00 p.m., Wednesday, Thursday, Friday
10:00 a.m. - 5:00 p.m., Saturday and Sunday
LIFTS
1 bar, 750 capacity per hour
LONGEST RUN
3,000 feet
SEASON
Mid-December to early April
SNOW PHONE
Call Ski Area
TRAILS
4 slopes
TRAVEL
6 miles from Thunder Bay, Hwy. 17-11 E., 527 N.
VERTICAL DROP
500 feet

REMI LAKE WINTER RECREATION AREA

Moonbeam, ON P0L 1V0 (705) 367-2442

AREA INFORMATION

HOURS
Days, Wednesdays and weekends
Nights, Tuesdays and Fridays
LIFTS
2 tows, 800 capacity per hour
LONGEST RUN
620 feet
SEASON
December to March
SNOW PHONE
Call Ski Area
TRAVEL
two miles west of Moonbeam, east of northern border of Ontario & Quebec
VERTICAL DROP
140 feet

ROUGE VALLEY SKI CENTRE

Toronto, ON (416) 284-0249, 859-0292

AREA INFORMATION

HOURS
1:00 - 5:00 p.m., weekdays
10:00 a.m. - 5:00 p.m., weekends
6:00 - 10:00 p.m., Wed. - Fri.
LIFTS
1 T-bar, 2 tows, 2,200 capacity per hour
LONGEST RUN
800 feet
SEASON
Early December to March, snowmaking
SNOW PHONE
Call Ski Area
TRAILS
4 slopes, beginner and intermediate, some advanced
TRAVEL
From Toronto, five miles via Highway 401 East to Meadowvale Rd. North, east on Shepherd and Twyn River Drive to Ski Area
VERTICAL DROP
130 feet

THE SAULT SKI CLUB

Sault Ste. Marie, ON

AREA INFORMATION

HOURS
7:00 - 10:00 p.m., Tuesday, Thursday
10:00 a.m. - 4:00 p.m., Saturday, Sunday
LIFTS
1 bar, 350 capacity per hour
LONGEST RUN
1,300 feet
SEASON
Late December to late March
TRAILS
Bowl and 1 advanced tree-lined run
TRAVEL
Northeastern outskirts of Sault Ste. Marie
VERTICAL DROP
160 feet

SEARCHMONT VALLEY

Searchmont, ON P0S 1J0 (705) 253-4179

AREA INFORMATION

BASE ELEVATION
900 feet
HOURS
10:00 a.m. - 4:30 p.m., weekdays
9:00 a.m. - 4:30 p.m., weekends
LIFTS
1 chairlift, 1 J-bar, 1 poma, 2,200 capacity per hour
LONGEST RUN
6,000 feet
SEASON
Mid-December to early April, no snowmaking
SNOW PHONE
Call Ski Area
TRAVEL
From Sault Ste. Marie, Trans Canada Highway West
14 miles; Hwy. 556 North from Heyden, 16 miles
VERTICAL DROP
700 feet

SKEE-HI

Thamesford, ON N0M 2M0 (519) 461-1720

AREA INFORMATION

HOURS
1:00 - 5:00 p.m., weekdays
10:00 a.m. - 5:00 p.m., weekends
7:00 - 10:00 p.m., weekend nights
LIFTS
2 bars, 4 tows
LONGEST RUN
1,500 feet
SEASON
Mid-December to mid-March
SNOW PHONE
Call Ski Area
TRAILS
Intermediate
TRAVEL
East of Toronto, 15 miles north of London
VERTICAL DROP
150 feet

SKI DAGMAR

Ashburn, ON L0B 1A0 (416) 649-2002

AREA INFORMATION

HOURS
9:00 a.m. - 4:30 p.m., daily
6:00 - 10:00 p.m., Tues. - Fri.
LIFTS
1 chairlift, 3 bars, 2 tows, 6,100 capacity per hour
LONGEST RUN
2,000 feet
SEASON
Early December to late March, snowmaking
SNOW PHONE
Call Ski Area
TRAILS
15 tree-lined slopes
TRAVEL
Northeast of Toronto, Hwy. 401 E. to Brock Road, Pickering, north 10 miles to Claremont, 5 miles east
VERTICAL DROP
200 feet

SNOW VALLEY

Barrie, ON (705) 728-9541

AREA INFORMATION

HOURS
10:00 a.m. - 4:30 p.m., Wednesday - Sunday
7:30 - 11:00 p.m., Wednesday - Saturday
LIFTS
1 chairlift, 3 T-bars, 1 tow, 5,100 capacity per hour
LONGEST RUN
3,200 feet
SEASON
December to March, snowmaking
SNOW PHONE
Call Ski Area

TRAILS
11 slopes, beginner to advanced
TRAVEL
From Barrie, 5 miles northwest via Hwy. 26/27
VERTICAL DROP
320 feet

SUNDANCE

Box 1234, Thunder Bay P7C 4X9 (807) 577-8813

AREA INFORMATION

LIFTS
1 chairlift, 1 T-bar, 1 grip tow
LONGEST RUN
1½ miles
NURSERY
At the slopes, call Ski Area
SEASON
December to March
SNOW PHONE
Call Ski Area
TRAILS
3 beginner, 8 intermediate, 4 advanced
TRAVEL
Thunder Bay, 1 mile, Hwy. 61 to Little Norway Rd.
VERTICAL DROP
750 feet

TALISMAN

Kimberley, ON N0C 1G0 (519) 599-2520

AREA INFORMATION

HOURS
9:00 a.m. - 4:30 p.m., daily
7:00 - 10:00 p.m., night skiing
LIFTS
3 chairs, 1 T-bar, 1 tow, 4,100 capacity per hour
LONGEST RUN
¾ mile
SEASON
December to April
SNOW PHONE
Call Ski Area
TRAVEL
From Toronto to Flesherton, ninety miles via Hwy. 10 N., 10 miles from Flesherton to Area
VERTICAL DROP
600 feet

TALLY-HO WINTER PARK

Huntsville, ON P0A 1K0 (705) 635-2720

AREA INFORMATION

BASE ELEVATION
990 feet
HOURS
10:00 a.m. - 4:30 p.m., weekdays
9:00 a.m. - 4:30 p.m., weekends
LIFTS
2 bars, 1 tow, 2,300 capacity per hour
LONGEST RUN
1,800 feet
SEASON
December to late March
SNOW PHONE
Call Ski Area
TRAILS
50% beginner, 50% intermediate
TRAVEL
150 miles north of Toronto; Huntsville, 9 miles
VERTICAL DROP
200 feet

THORNE SKI RESORT

Thorne, ON P0H 2J0 (819) 627-3529

AREA INFORMATION

BASE ELEVATION
420 feet
HOURS
1:00 - 5:00 p.m., Fri., Sat., Sun.
7:00 - 10:00 p.m., Friday nights
LIFTS
1 tow, 850 capacity per hour
LONGEST RUN
5,000 feet
SEASON
Mid-December to mid-April
SNOW PHONE
Call Ski Area
TRAILS
6 slopes
TRAVEL
From North Bay, 35 miles via Hwy. 63 East
VERTICAL DROP
670 feet

THUNDER BAY CENTENNIAL PARK

Thunder Bay, ON P7B 5E7 (807) 683-6511

HOURS
Nights and weekends
LIFTS
1 tow, 400 capacity per hour
LONGEST RUN
600 feet
SEASON
December to March
SNOW PHONE
Call Ski Area
TRAVEL
Hwy. 17-11 or U.S. 61 to Trans Canada Hwy. 61
VERTICAL DROP
100 feet

TRI-TOWN SKI VILLAGE

New Liskeard, ON P0J 1P0 (705) 647-4056

AREA INFORMATION

HOURS
Days: Wed., Sat., Sun., holidays; night skiing, Wed.
LIFTS
2 bars, 650 capacity per hour
LONGEST RUN
2,600 feet
SEASON
Mid-December to early April
SNOW PHONE
Call Ski Area
TRAILS
7 slopes, beginner and intermediate, some advanced
TRAVEL
Near Quebec border, 8 miles S.E. of New Liskeard
VERTICAL DROP
320 feet

UPLANDS SKI CENTRE

Thornhill, ON (416) 889-9405

AREA INFORMATION

HOURS
1:00 - 5:00, 7:00 - 10:30 p.m., Tuesday - Friday
9:00 a.m. - 5:00 p.m., Saturday, Sunday, holidays
LIFTS
2 T-bars, 1 tow, 2,100 capacity per hour
LONGEST RUN
1,200 feet
SEASON
Mid-December to March, snowmaking
SNOW PHONE
Call Ski Area
TRAILS
5 slopes, beginner to advanced
TRAVEL
In Thornhill, Younge St., 3 miles north of Toronto
VERTICAL DROP
110 feet

VALLEY SCHUSS SKI CLUB

Orangeville (519) 941-3487

AREA INFORMATION

HOURS
9:00 a.m. - 4:45 p.m., Fri., Sat., Sun.
LIFTS
2 tows, 3 bars, 2,500 capacity per hour
Limited to 150 non-members
LONGEST RUN
1½ miles
NURSERY
Call Ski Area
SEASON
Mid-December to early April, snowmaking
SNOW PHONE
Call Ski Area
TRAILS
15 slopes,
TRAVEL
37 miles north of Toronto, Airport and Hockley Roads
VERTICAL DROP
350 feet

WINDSOR VALLEY

Kirkland Lake (705) 567-7065

AREA INFORMATION

HOURS
10:00 a.m. - 4:30 p.m., Sat., Sun.
Night skiing by prior arrangement
LIFTS
1 tow
LONGEST RUN
1,300 feet
SEASON
Early December to late April
SNOW PHONE
Call Ski Area
TRAILS
4 slopes; 1 open, 3 tree-lined

TRAVEL
8 miles east of Kirkland Lake
175 miles north of North Bay
VERTICAL DROP
120 feet

WOODSTOCK SKI CLUB

Woodstock, ON N4S (519) 462-2625

AREA INFORMATION

BASE ELEVATION
800 feet
HOURS
7:30 - 10:30 p.m., weekdays
10:00 a.m. - 4:30 p.m., weekends
LIFTS
1 bar, 3 tows, 2,100 capacity per hour
LONGEST RUN
1,600 feet
SEASON
Mid-December to mid-March, snowmaking
SNOW PHONE
Call Ski Area
TRAILS
Beginner and intermediate
TRAVEL
Eight miles from Woodstock via Highway 59 for 5 miles, then west 2 miles to access road
VERTICAL DROP
110 feet

PRINCE EDWARD ISLAND

BROOKVALE PROVINCIAL PARK

Charlottetown, PE (902) 892-7411

AREA INFORMATION

BASE ELEVATION
120 feet
HOURS
1:00 - 5:00 p.m., weekdays
9:30 a.m. - 5:00 p.m., weekends
6:00 - 9:00 p.m., Wed. and Fri.
LIFTS
1 T-bar, 3 tows, 1,600 capacity per hour
LONGEST RUN
1,400 feet
SEASON
Mid-December to late March
SNOW PHONE
Call Ski Area
TRAILS
6 tree-lined slopes
TRAVEL
From Charlottetown, 15 miles west, Hwy. 13
VERTICAL DROP
180 feet

ALTA

Val-David, QU J0T 2N0 (819) 322-3206

AREA INFORMATION

BASE ELEVATION
1,100 feet
HOURS
8:30 a.m. - 4:00 p.m., weekends, holidays
9:00 a.m. - 4:00 p.m., Mon., Wed., Fri.
LIFTS
1 chairlift, 1 poma, 1,800 capacity per hour
LONGEST RUN
1½ miles
NURSERY
At the slopes, call Ski Area
SEASON
Late November to late April, no snowmaking
SNOW PHONE
Call Ski Area
TRAILS
25% beginner, 25% intermediate, 50% advanced
TRAVEL
2 miles from Ste. Agathe, exit 86
from Autoroute 15 to Route 117
VERTICAL DROP
770 feet

BELLE NEIGE

Val-Morin, QU J0T 2R0 (819) 322-3011

AREA INFORMATION

BASE ELEVATION
500 feet
HOURS
9:00 a.m. - 4:00 p.m.
LIFTS
4 T-bars, 1,800 capacity per hour
LONGEST RUN
¾ mile
SEASON
Late December to early April, snowmaking
SNOWPHONE
Call Ski Area
TRAILS
10 slopes
TRAVEL
48 miles from Montreal, exit 76
from the Laurentian Autoroute
VERTICAL DROP
500 feet

BELLEVUE SKI CENTER

Morin-Heights, QU J0R 1H0 (514) 226-2003

AREA INFORMATION

BASE ELEVATION
800 feet
HOURS
9:00 a.m. - 4:30 p.m., weekends, holidays
LIFTS
2 T-bars, 1,600 capacity per hour
LONGEST RUN
1,500 feet
SEASON
December to Early April, no snowmaking
SNOW PHONE
Call Ski Area
TRAILS
3 open slopes, mostly intermediate
TRAVEL
Laurentian Autoroute 15 N.W. to exit 60
40 miles from Montreal, then east 5 miles
VERTICAL DROP
300 feet

BROMONT

Bromont, QU J0E 1L0 (514) 534-2200

AREA INFORMATION

BASE ELEVATION
550 feet
HOURS
9:00 a.m. - 4:00 p.m., daily
6:30 - 10:00 p.m., night skiing
LIFTS
3 chairlifts, 1 T-bar, 1 tow, 5,000 capacity per hour
LONGEST RUN
2½ miles
SEASON
Early December to late April, snowmaking
SNOW PHONE
Call Ski Area
TRAILS
35% beginner, 50% intermediate, 15% advanced
TRAVEL
From Montreal, Autoroute 10 E., exit 78. From
Vermont, I-91 N., Quebec 55 N., Autoroute 10 W.
VERTICAL DROP
600 feet

CAMP FORTUNE

Old Chelsea, QU J0X 2N0 (819) 827-1717

AREA INFORMATION

BASE ELEVATION
600 feet
HOURS
9:00 a.m. - 5:00 p.m., weekdays
8:45 a.m. - 5:00 p.m., Sat., Sun.
6:30 - 10:30 p.m., Mon. - Sat.
LIFTS
2 chairlifts, 4 T-bars, 1 poma, 8,200 capacity per hour
NURSERY
Ages two to six, 9:00 a.m. - 4:30 p.m.
SEASON
Early December to mid-April, snowmaking
SNOW PHONE
Call Ski Area
TRAILS
15 slopes
TRAVEL
In Gatineau Park, Autoroute A5 from Ottawa
VERTICAL DROP
600 feet

CHALET SUISSE

La Sarre, QU J9Z (819) 333-6727

AREA INFORMATION

HOURS
12:00 - 4:00 p.m., Saturday, Sunday
7:00 - 9:00 p.m., Tuesday, Thursday
LIFTS
1 tow, 600 capacity per hour
LONGEST RUN
800 feet
SEASON
Mid-November to early April, no snowmaking
SNOW PHONE
Call Ski Area
TRAILS
2 slopes
TRAVEL
North of North Bay, Ontario, N.W. of Lake Abitibi
From Noranda, Quebec, Hwy. 101 N. to 111 West
VERTICAL DROP
120 feet

EDELWEISS VALLEY

Wakefield, QU J0X 3G0 (819) 459-2859

AREA INFORMATION

BASE ELEVATION
570 feet
HOURS
9:00 a.m. - 11:00 p.m., weekdays
8:00 a.m. - 11:00 p.m., weekends
LIFTS
2 chairlifts, 3 T-bars, 1 poma, 5,800 capacity per hour
LONGEST RUN
5,000 feet
SEASON
Mid-November to mid-April, snowmaking
SNOW PHONE
Call Ski Area
TRAILS
9 beginner, 3 intermediate, 3 advanced
TRAVEL
18 miles north of Ottawa, Hwy. 11
VERTICAL DROP
650 feet

GRAY ROCKS

Box 1,000, St-Jovite, QU J0T 2H0 (819) 425-2771

AREA INFORMATION

BASE ELEVATION
730 feet
HOURS
8:30 a.m. - 4:30 p.m., daily until mid-April
Afterwards, weekends only
LIFTS
3 chairlifts, 2 T-bars, 5,200 capacity per hour
LONGEST RUN
1 mile
SEASON
Mid-November to mid-May, snowmaking
SNOW PHONE
Call Ski Area
TRAILS
30% beginner, 30% intermediate, 40% advanced
TRAVEL
From Montreal 75 miles northwest via Autoroute 15
and Rt. 117 to St.-Jovite, 327 N. for 3 miles to Area
VERTICAL DROP
610 feet

LAC L'ARGILE

Notre-Dame-de-la-Salette, QU J0X 2L0 (819) 766-2341

AREA INFORMATION

HOURS
9:00 a.m. - 5:00 p.m.
LIFTS
1 bar, 750 capacity per hour
LONGEST RUN
2,000 feet
SEASON
Mid-December to late March, snowmaking
SNOW PHONE
Call Ski Area
TRAILS
3 open slopes
TRAVEL
44 miles from Ottawa, Hwy. 148 E., 309 N.
VERTICAL DROP
600 feet

LA TUQUE

La Tuque, QU G9X (819) 523-2204, 523-4422

AREA INFORMATION

HOURS
1:00 - 4:00 p.m., Monday thru Friday
9:00 a.m. - 4:00 p.m., Saturday, Sunday
7:00 - 10:00 p.m., Monday thru Saturday
LIFTS
1 chairlift, 1 bar, 1,700 capacity per hour
LONGEST RUN
Almost 1 mile
SEASON
November to April, no snowmaking
SNOW PHONE
Call Ski Area
TRAILS
11 slopes
TRAVEL
75 miles north of Shawinigan, Hwy. 155
VERTICAL DROP
430 feet

L'AVALANCHE

St-Adolphe-D'Howard, QU J0T 2B0 (819) 327-2411

AREA INFORMATION

BASE ELEVATION
1,550 feet
HOURS
9:00 a.m. - 4:30 p.m., no snowmaking
LIFTS
2 bars, 1,800 capacity per hour
LONGEST RUN
3,200 feet
SEASON
November to April, no snowmaking
SNOW PHONE
Call Ski Area
TRAVEL
A short distance from Montreal and St.-Jerome
VERTICAL DROP
400 feet

LE CHANTECLER

Ste-Adele, QU J0R 1L0 (514) 229-2717

AREA INFORMATION

HOURS
9:00 a.m. - 4:30 p.m.
LIFTS
2 chairlifts, 5 T-bars, 2 pomas, 8,400 capacity per hour
LONGEST RUN
3,000 feet
NURSERY
At the slopes, call Ski Area
SEASON
Mid-November to mid-April, snowmaking
SNOW PHONE
Call Ski Area
TRAILS
13 slopes
TRAVEL
41 miles N.W. of Montreal, Autoroute 15, exit 67
VERTICAL DROP
650 feet

LE RELAIS

Lac Beauport (418) 849-3073

AREA INFORMATION

BASE ELEVATION
700 feet
HOURS
Open daily and five nights a week
8:00 a.m. - 5:00, 6:30 - 10:00 p.m.
LIFTS
1 chairlift, 2 T-bars, 2 pomas, 3,800 capacity per hour
LONGEST RUN
4,700 feet
NURSERY
At the slopes, call Ski Area

SEASON
Late November to mid-April, snowmaking
SNOW PHONE
Call Ski Area
TRAILS
7 tree-lined slopes
TRAVEL
North of City of Quebec, Hwy. 73 to Lac Beauport
VERTICAL DROP
650 feet

MONT ADSTOCK

Thetford Mines, QU G6G (418) 487-2242

AREA INFORMATION

HOURS
1:00 - 4:00, 7:00 - 9:00 p.m., Tuesday - Friday
10:00 a.m. - 4:00 p.m., Saturday and Sunday
LIFTS
1 chairlift, 3 bars, 3,600 capacity per hour
LONGEST RUN
5,300 feet
SEASON
Mid-November to early April
SNOW PHONE
Call Ski Area
TRAILS
8 slopes
TRAVEL
From City of Quebec, south via Hwy. 73, 173 and 112
VERTICAL DROP
720 feet

MONT ALOUETTE

Ste. Adele (514) 229-2717

AREA INFORMATION

HOURS
8:30 a.m. - 4:30 p.m.
LIFTS
4 bars, 3,700 capacity per hour
LONGEST RUN
4,800 feet
SEASON
November to April
SNOW PHONE
Call Ski Area
TRAILS
Beginner to advanced
TRAVEL
44 miles northwest from Montreal, exit 67
of Autoroute 15, 3 miles from Ste. Adele
VERTICAL DROP
500 feet

MONT APIC

St-Pierre Baptiste, QU G0P 1K0 (819) 362-2109

AREA INFORMATION

HOURS
9:30 a.m. - 4:00 p.m., Saturday, Sunday
LIFTS
1 bar, 850 capacity per hour
LONGEST RUN
4,900 capacity per hour
SEASON
November to April, no snowmaking
SNOW PHONE
Call Ski Area
TRAILS
6 slopes
TRAVEL
South of Quebec, Highways 73, 173, 271
VERTICAL DROP
300 feet

MONT AVILA

Piedmont, QU J0R 1K0 (514) 861-6578

AREA INFORMATION

HOURS
9:00 a.m. - 4:30, 6:30 - 10:30 p.m.
LIFTS
1 chairlift, 3 bars, 1 tow, 4,600 capacity per hour
LONGEST RUN
4,900 feet
NURSERY
At the slopes, call Ski Area
SEASON
November to April, snowmaking
SNOW PHONE
Call Ski Area
TRAILS
8 slopes
TRAVEL
Northwest of Montreal via Autoroute 15
38 miles to exit, turn west to Piedmont
VERTICAL DROP
600 feet

MONT BELLEVUE

Ste-Anne-des-Monts, QU G0E 2G0 (418) 763-5511

AREA INFORMATION

BASE ELEVATION
200 feet

MONT BELLEVUE CONT.

HOURS
Tuesday and Friday thru Sunday
LIFTS
1 T-bar, 900 capacity per hour
LONGEST RUN
2,500 feet
SEASON
December to April
SNOW PHONE
Call Ski Area
TRAILS
50% beginner, 50% intermediate, advanced
TRAVEL
Eastern Quebec, Routes 132 and 299
VERTICAL DROP
350 feet

MONT BELU

Port Alfred, QU G7B (418) 544-5044

AREA INFORMATION

BASE ELEVATION
80 feet
HOURS
10:00 a.m. - 4:00, 7:30 - 10:00 p.m.
LIFTS
1-T bar, 800 capacity per hour
LONGEST RUN
1 mile
SEASON
Mid-December to late March
SNOW PHONE
Call Ski Area
TRAILS
5 tree-lined slopes
TRAVEL
Northeast of Quebec, Routes 138 and 170
VERTICAL DROP
550 feet

MONT BLANC

St-Faustin, QU J0T 2G0 (819) 688-2444

AREA INFORMATION

HOURS
9:00 a.m. - 4:00 p.m.
LIFTS
1 chairlift, 2 bars, 2,200 capacity per hour
LONGEST RUN
5,400 feet
NURSERY
At the slopes, call Ski Area
SEASON
December to April, snowmaking
SNOW PHONE
Call Ski Area
TRAILS
9 runs
TRAVEL
60 miles northwest of Montreal, Autoroute 15, 117
VERTICAL DROP
600 feet

MONT CARMEL

Mont-Carmel, QU G0L 1W0 (819) 374-4534

AREA INFORMATION

HOURS
9:00 a.m. - 4:00, 7:00 - 10:30 p.m.
LIFTS
3 bars, 1,100 capacity per hour
LONGEST RUN
3,150 feet
SEASON
Mid-November to mid-April, snowmaking
SNOW PHONE
Call Ski Area
TRAILS
Beginner and intermediate
TRAVEL
14 miles from Trois-Rivieres
VERTICAL DROP
490 feet

MONT CASCADES

Cantley, QU J0X 1L0 (819) 827-0136

AREA INFORMATION

HOURS
9:00 a.m. - 10:30 p.m.
LIFTS
2 chairlifts, 2 T-bars, 4,200 capacity per hour
SEASON
December to April, snowmaking
SNOW PHONE
Call Ski Area
TRAILS
9 slopes
TRAVEL
From Ottawa, Hwy. 5, Alonzo Wright Bridge, 307 N.
VERTICAL DROP
500 feet

MONT CHRISTIE

Christieville, QU (514) 226-2412

AREA INFORMATION

HOURS
December-January, weekends, holidays
February to mid-April, Wed. thru Sun.
9:00 a.m. - 4:30 p.m., no night skiing
LIFTS
3 bars, 3,000 capacity per hour
LONGEST RUN
4,000 feet
SEASON
December to mid-April
SNOW PHONE
Call Ski Area
TRAILS
12 slopes, mostly intermediate
TRAVEL
42 miles from Montreal, Autoroute 15, exit 60
VERTICAL DROP
560 feet

MONT COMI (PARC)

St-Donat, QU (418) 739-4066

AREA INFORMATION

BASE ELEVATION
880 feet
LIFTS
1 chairlift, 1 T-bar, 1 poma, 2,700 capacity per hour
LONGEST RUN
6,000 feet
SEASON
Mid-November to late April, no snowmaking
SNOW PHONE
Call Ski Area
TRAILS
13 tree-lined slopes
TRAVEL
74 miles from Montreal via Laurentian Autoroute 15
to Hwy. 329, 22 miles north of Ste.-Agathe-des-Monts
VERTICAL DROP
990 feet

MT. CITADELLE SKI CLUB

St-Honore, QU G0M 1V0 (418) 497-3792

AREA INFORMATION

BASE
300 feet
HOURS
Tuesday - Thursday, Saturday and Sunday
9:00 a.m. - 4:00 p.m., 7:00 - 10:00 p.m.
LIFTS
1 bar, 750 capacity per hour
LONGEST RUN
3,000 feet
SEASON
December to mid-April
SNOW PHONE
Call Ski Area
TRAILS
Beginner to advanced, 6 runs
TRAVEL
131 miles north of City of Quebec via
Hwy. 175 to Chicoutimi, 8 miles north
VERTICAL DROP
700 feet

MONT ELAN

East Angus, QU J0B 1R0 (819) 832-9011

AREA INFORMATION

BASE ELEVATION
930 feet
HOURS
9:30 a.m. - 4:00 p.m., weekends
7:00 - 10:00 p.m., night skiing
LIFTS
2 bars, 1,500 capacity per hour
LONGEST RUN
2,600 feet
SEASON
Mid-December to early April
SNOW PHONE
Call Ski Area
TRAILS
3 beginner, 1 intermediate, 2 advanced
TRAVEL
15 miles N.E. of Sherbrooke, S.E. of Quebec
VERTICAL DROP
320 feet

MONT FAUSTIN

St-Jovite, QU J0T 2H0 (819) 425-2461

AREA INFORMATION

BASE ELEVATION
800 feet
HOURS
9:00 a.m. - 4:30 p.m.
LIFTS
3 bars, 2,800 capacity per hour
LONGEST RUN
1½ miles
SEASON
Mid-December to mid-April
SNOW PHONE
Call Ski Area
TRAILS
Beginner to advanced
TRAVEL
70 miles from Montreal, Autoroute 15 to Hwy. 117 N., 5 miles from St. Jovite
VERTICAL DROP
700 feet

MONT FORTIN

Jonquiere, QU G7X (418) 542-5711

AREA INFORMATION

HOURS
1:00 - 4:00 p.m., Monday - Friday
10:00 a.m. - 4:00 p.m., Sat. - Sun.
7:30 - 10:30 p.m., night skiing
LIFTS
1 chairlift, 2 bars, 2,700 capacity per hour
LONGEST RUN
3,280 feet
SEASON
December to April, snowmaking
SNOW PHONE
Call Ski Area
TRAILS
7 slopes
TRAVEL
140 miles from Quebec, Hwy. 175 N., 170 West, ten miles from Chicoutimi
VERTICAL DROP
160 feet

MONT-GABRIEL

Mont Gabriel, QU J0R 1R0 (514) 229-3547

AREA INFORMATION

BASE ELEVATION
570 feet
HOURS
9:00 a.m. - 4:30 p.m., 6:30 - 10:30 p.m.
LIFTS
2 chairlifts, 9 T-bars, 4,800 capacity per hour
LONGEST RUN
5,000 feet
NURSERY
Weekends, call Ski Area
SEASON
Mid-November to mid-April, snowmaking
SNOW PHONE
Call Ski Area
TRAILS
15% beginner, 45% intermediate, 40% advanced
TRAVEL
40 miles from Montreal, Autoroute 15 N., exit 64
VERTICAL DROP
750 feet

MONT GRAND FONDS

La Malbaie, QU G0T 1J0 (418) 665-2334

AREA INFORMATION

BASE ELEVATION
50 feet
HOURS
10:00 a.m. - 4:00 p.m., weekdays
9:00 a.m. - 4:00 p.m., weekends
LIFTS
1 chairlift, 1 T-bar, 1,100 capacity per hour
LONGEST RUN
7,500 feet
SEASON
November to April
SNOW PHONE
Call Ski Area
TRAILS
8 runs
TRAVEL
100 miles north of Quebec, Hwy. 138
VERTICAL DROP
1,200 feet

MONT HABITANT

St-Sauveur-des-Monts, QU J0R 1R0 (514) 227-2637

AREA INFORMATION

BASE ELEVATION
700 feet
HOURS
8:30 a.m. - 4:30 p.m., 6:30 - 10:30 p.m.
LIFTS
1 chairlift, 4 T-bars, 1 tow, 4,800 capacity per hour

NURSERY
Call Ski Area for information
SEASON
Late November to mid-April, snowmaking
SNOW PHONE 861-2283
TRAILS
30% beginner, 40% intermediate, 30% advanced
TRAVEL
37 miles from Montreal, Autoroute 15 N., exit 38
VERTICAL DROP
Call Ski Area

MONT JACOB

Jonquiere, QU G7X (418) 542-5711

AREA INFORMATION

HOURS
10:00 a.m. - 4:00, 7:00 - 10:00 p.m., Sat., Sun.
LIFTS
1 bar, 950 capacity per hour
LONGEST RUN
1,640 feet
SEASON
December to April
SNOW PHONE
Call Ski Area
TRAILS
3 slopes
TRAVEL
141 miles from Quebec, Hwy. 175 N. to 170 W.
VERTICAL DROP
130 feet

MONT LA RESERVE

St-Donat, QU (819) 424-2377

AREA INFORMATION

HOURS
8:00 a.m. - 4:30 p.m.
LIFTS
1 T-bar, 1 poma, 1,800 capacity per hour
LONGEST RUN
1 mile
SEASON
Early December to late April
SNOW PHONE
Call Ski Area
TRAILS
8 slopes
TRAVEL
74 miles northwest of Montreal
Autoroute 15, Hwy. 329 North
VERTICAL DROP
1,150 feet

MONT MARS

Port Alfred, QU G7B (418) 544-5115

AREA INFORMATION

BASE ELEVATION
30 feet
HOURS
10:00 a.m. - 4:30 p.m., 7:30 - 10:00 p.m.
LIFTS
2 T-bars, 1,200 capacity per hour
LONGEST RUN
1½ miles
SEASON
December to March
SNOW PHONE
Call Ski Area
TRAILS
5 slopes, beginner to advanced
TRAVEL
146 miles from Quebec, Hwy. 175 North
and Hwy. 170 West to Area access route
VERTICAL DROP
570 feet

MONT MILLER

Murdochville, QU GOE 1WO (418) 784-2908

AREA INFORMATION

HOURS
10:00 a.m. - 4:00 p.m., Thursday - Sunday
LIFTS
1 chairlift, 1 bar, 900 capacity per hour
LONGEST RUN
6,000 feet
SEASON
December to April
SNOW PHONE
Call Ski Area
TRAILS
6 slopes
TRAVEL
Eastern Quebec, 50 miles N.E. from Gaspe
Twenty miles south of Ruisseau-des-Olives
VERTICAL DROP
760 feet

MONT ORGNAL

Lac-Etchemin, QU GOR 1SO (418) 625-1551

AREA INFORMATION

HOURS
9:00 a.m. - 4:30 p.m.

MONT ORGNAL CONT.

LIFTS
1 chairlift, 1 bar, 1,800 capacity per hour
LONGEST RUN
6,500 feet
NURSERY
At the slopes, call Ski Area
SEASON
Mid-November to early April
SNOW PHONE
Call Ski Area
TRAILS
6 slopes
TRAVEL
51 miles southeast of Quebec, Autoroute 73
to Autoroute 20 East, Highway 277 South
VERTICAL DROP
850 feet

MONT PLANTE

Val-David, QU J0T 2N0

AREA INFORMATION

HOURS
8:30 a.m. - 4:00 p.m., daily
7:00 - 10:00 p.m., Saturday
LIFTS
2 bars, 1,800 capacity per hour
LONGEST RUN
1 mile
SEASON
December to April
TRAILS
11 slopes
TRAVEL
40 miles northwest of Montreal
Autoroute 10 N., Hwy. 117 N.
VERTICAL DROP
450 feet

MONT SAINTE-ANNE

Box 200, Beaupre, QU G0A 1E0 (418) 827-4561

AREA INFORMATION

BASE ELEVATION
570 feet
HOURS
8:30 a.m. - 4:30 p.m., varies with amount of daylight
LIFTS
1 gondola, 4 chairlifts, 4 T-bars, 4 J-bars,
1 tow, 9,000 capacity per hour
LONGEST RUN
3 miles
NURSERY
One year and up, call Ski Area
SEASON
Late November to early May, snowmaking
SNOW PHONE 827-4579
Other areas. . . . . . . (416) 482-1796, (514) 861-6670
TRAILS
25% beginner, 40% intermediate, 35% advanced
TRAVEL
N.E. of Quebec, twenty miles via Hwy. 138; Montreal
to Quebec, 180 miles via Trans-Canada Highway 20
VERTICAL DROP
2,000 feet

MONT ST. CASTIN DES NEIGES

Lac-Beauport, QU G0A 2C0 (418) 849-4461

AREA INFORMATION

HOURS
10:00 a.m. - 4:30 p.m., daily
7:00 - 10:00 p.m., Mon. - Sat.
LIFTS
2 chairlifts, 4 bars, 1 tow, 6,400 capacity per hour
LONGEST RUN
2,700 feet
SEASON
Mid-November to mid-March, snowmaking
SNOW PHONE
Call Ski Area
TRAILS
6 slopes
TRAVEL
Under 1 hour from Quebec, Hwy. 40, 73 N.
VERTICAL DROP
550 feet

MONT SAINT-SAUVEUR

St-Sauveur-des-Monts, QU J0R 1R0 (514) 866-7190

AREA INFORMATION

HOURS
8:30 a.m. - 4:30 p.m., daily
6:30 - 10:30 p.m., night skiing
LIFTS
3 chairlifts, 5 T-bars, 8,000 capacity per hour
LONGEST RUN
.8 mile
NURSERY
Call Ski Area

SEASON
Late November to early March, snowmaking
SNOW PHONE
Call Ski Area
TRAVEL
35 miles northwest of Montreal, Autoroute 15
VERTICAL DROP
700 feet

MONT SAUVAGE

Val-Morin, QU J0T 2R0 (819) 322-2337

AREA INFORMATION

BASE ELEVATION
600 feet
HOURS
9:00 a.m. - 4:00 p.m.
LIFTS
3 bars, 3,200 capacity per hour
LONGEST RUN
1 mile
SEASON
Mid-December to mid-April
SNOW PHONE
Call Ski Area
TRAILS
9 slopes
TRAVEL
From Montreal, Autoroute 15 N., exit 72, 5 miles
VERTICAL DROP
600 feet

MONT VIDEO

Abitibi, QU (819) 734-2193

AREA INFORMATION

BASE ELEVATION
1,200 feet
HOURS
Wednesday, Friday through Sunday
10:00 a.m. - 5:00, 7:00 - 10:00 p.m.
LIFTS
1 chairlift, 1,000 capacity per hour
LONGEST RUN
4,000 feet
SEASON
Early December to mid-April
SNOW PHONE
Call Ski Area
TRAILS
5 slopes
TRAVEL
Northwest of Ottawa, Highways 105, 117 N. to Val d'Or, thirty miles north
VERTICAL DROP
350 feet

OWL'S HEAD

Box 35, Mansonville, QU J0E 1X0 (514) 292-5592

AREA INFORMATION

BASE ELEVATION
680 feet
HOURS
9:00 a.m. - 4:00 p.m.
LIFTS
5 chairlifts, 1 T-bar, 5,500 capacity per hour
LONGEST RUN
2¼ miles
SEASON
Early December to late April, no snowmaking
SNOW PHONE
Call Ski Area
TRAILS
25% beginner, 50% intermediate, 25% advanced
TRAVEL
From Montreal, Autoroute 10, Hwy. 245, 243 S.
Near the U.S. border, N.W. of Newport, Vermont
VERTICAL DROP
1,700 feet

SAGUENAY LAC ST. JEAN

Alma, QU G8B (418) 662-2901

AREA INFORMATION

HOURS
1:00 - 4:00 p.m., daily
7:00 - 10:00 p.m., weekdays
LIFTS
1 bar, 750 capacity per hour
LONGEST RUN
1,200 feet
SEASON
Mid-December to mid-April, snowmaking
SNOW PHONE
Call Ski Area
TRAILS
3 tree-lined slopes
TRAVEL
210 miles from Quebec, Hwy. 175 and 169 North
VERTICAL DROP
170 feet

SKI MONTCALM

Rawdon, QU J0K 1S0 (514) 834-3139

AREA INFORMATION

BASE ELEVATION
1,000 feet
HOURS
9:00 a.m. - 4:00 p.m., Sat., Sun.
1:00 p.m. - 5:00 p.m., Friday
LIFTS
2 chairlifts, 5 bars, 6,400 capacity per hour
LONGEST RUN
3,000 feet
SEASON
Late November to March, no snowmaking
SNOW PHONE
Call Ski Area
TRAILS
12 slopes
TRAVEL
40 miles north of Montreal, Highways 25, 125 & 337
VERTICAL DROP
400 feet

ST. EDGAR

New Richmond, QU G0C 2B0 (418) 392-4684

AREA INFORMATION

BASE ELEVATION
200 feet
HOURS
9:00 a.m. - 4:00 p.m., weekends
1:00 - 4:00 p.m., Wednesdays
LIFTS
2 bars, 1,500 capacity per hour
LONGEST RUN
3,400 feet
SEASON
December to April
SNOW PHONE
Call Ski Area
TRAILS
6 tree-lined slopes
TRAVEL
North of New Brunswick, Hwy. 132
VERTICAL DROP
300 feet

SAINTE FOY

Ste-Foy, QU (418) 657-4298

AREA INFORMATION

HOURS
1:00 - 4:30, 7:00 - 10:00 p.m., weekdays
9:00 a.m. - 4:30 p.m., weekends
LIFTS
1 bar, 1 tow, 1,200 capacity per hour
LONGEST RUN
1,350 feet
SEASON
December to April, snowmaking
SNOW PHONE
Call Ski Area
TRAILS
2 slopes
TRAVEL
Edge of Quebec City, Hwy. 73 or 540 to Sainte-Foy
VERTICAL DROP
290 feet

ST. GEORGES

St-Georges, QU (418) 228-8151

AREA INFORMATION

HOURS
1:00 - 4:00 p.m., Tuesday - Friday
7:00 - 10:00 p.m., Tuesday - Saturday
9:30 a.m. - 4:00 p.m., Saturday, Sunday
LIFTS
2 bars, 1,800 capacity per hour
LONGEST RUN
2,300 feet
SEASON
December to April
SNOW PHONE
Call Ski Area
TRAILS
6 slopes
TRAVEL
65 miles from Quebec City, Hwy. 73 and 173 South
VERTICAL DROP
260 feet

ST. GERARD

St-Mathieu, Lac Bellemare, QU G0X 1N0 (819) 539-5451

AREA INFORMATION

HOURS
1:00 - 4:30, 7:00 - 10:00 p.m., weekdays
9:00 a.m. - 4:30, 7:00 - 10:00 p.m., weekends
LIFTS
6 bars, 6,900 capacity per hour

LONGEST RUN
3,900 feet
NURSERY
Weekends, call Ski Area
SEASON
November to April
SNOW PHONE
Call Ski Area
TRAILS
50% beginner, 50% intermediate and advanced
TRAVEL
31 miles from Trois-Rivieres, Hwy. 55N., exit at Shawinigan, then 6 miles to Area
VERTICAL DROP
400 feet

ST. RAYMOND

St-Raymond, QU G0A 4G0 (418) 337-2866

AREA INFORMATION

BASE ELEVATION
500 feet
HOURS
Tuesday thru Friday, 3 hours
Saturday, Sunday, 7 hours
LIFTS
1 bar, 1,100 capacity per hour
LONGEST RUN
2,000 feet
SEASON
Mid-December to mid-April
SNOW PHONE
Call Ski Area
TRAILS
6 slopes, 1 tree-lined
TRAVEL
In St.-Raymond, 25 miles N.W. of Quebec City, Highway 367
VERTICAL DROP
350 feet

STONEHAM

1420 Ave. du Hibou
Stoneham, QU G0A 4P0 (418) 848-2411

AREA INFORMATION

LIFTS
2 chairlifts, 2 T-bars, 1 poma
LONGEST RUN
10,500 feet
NURSERY
At the slopes, call Ski Area
SEASON
December to April
SNOW PHONE
Call Ski Area
TRAILS
30% beginner, 30% intermediate, 40% advanced
TRAVEL
17 miles north of Quebec, Hwy. 54
VERTICAL DROP
1,250 feet

SUN VALLEY

Ste-Adele, QU J0R 1L0 (514) 229-3511, 861-4801

AREA INFORMATION

BASE ELEVATION
1,800 feet
HOURS
8:30 a.m. - 4:00 p.m.
LIFTS
1 chairlift, 4 T-bars, 5,600 capacity per hour
LONGEST RUN
1 mile
SEASON
Mid-November to March
SNOW PHONE
Call Ski Area
TRAILS
10 runs
TRAVEL
28 miles N.W. of Montreal via Laurentian Autoroute 15, exit 42, 4 miles on 117 N.
VERTICAL DROP
500 feet

UNIVERSITE DE MONTREAL

Montreal, QU (514) 343-6150

AREA INFORMATION

BASE ELEVATION
440 feet
HOURS
Monday thru Friday to 10:00 p.m.
9:00 a.m. - 5:00 p.m., weekends
LIFTS
1 bar, 850 capacity per hour
LONGEST RUN
950 feet
SEASON
Mid-December to early April
SNOW PHONE
Call office
TRAILS
Beginner
TRAVEL
In Montreal
VERTICAL DROP
170 feet

VAL D'IRENE

Matapedia Valley, QU G0J 1V0 (418) 629-3040

AREA INFORMATION

BASE ELEVATION
1,400 feet
HOURS
9:00 a.m. - 4:00 p.m., Friday thru Monday
LIFTS
1 chairlift, 1 T-bar, 1 poma, 2,400 capacity per hour
LONGEST RUN
2 miles
SEASON
Early December to early May, no snowmaking
SNOW PHONE
Call Ski Area
TRAILS
20% beginner, 45% intermediate, 35% advanced
TRAVEL
Hwy. 132 from New Brunswick or Mont-Joli
Hwy. 195 from Matane, 10 miles from Amqui
VERTICAL DROP
900 feet

VALLEE BLEUE SKI CENTRE

Val-David, QU J0T 2N0 (819) 322-3427

AREA INFORMATION

BASE ELEVATION
1,100 feet
HOURS
9:00 a.m. - 4:00 p.m.
LIFTS
4 bars, 4,300 capacity per hour
LONGEST RUN
3,000 feet
SNOW PHONE
Call Ski Area
TRAILS
10 runs
TRAVEL
40 miles northwest of Montreal
Autoroute 10 N., Hwy. 117 N.
VERTICAL DROP
360 feet

VALLEE DU PARK

Blvd. Vallee du Park, Grand'Mere, QU G9T (819) 538-1639

AREA INFORMATION

BASE ELEVATION
500 feet
HOURS
9:00 a.m. - 4:30 p.m., daily
7:00 - 10:00 p.m., Mon. - Sat.
LIFTS
1 chairlift, 3 T-bar, 4,600 capacity per hour
LONGEST RUN
4,800 feet
SEASON
Late November to mid-April, snowmaking
SNOW PHONE
Call Ski Area
TRAILS
14 slopes
TRAVEL
28 miles north of Trois-Rivieres, Hwy. 55 N.
VERTICAL DROP
550 feet

YVAN COUTU/AUBERGE

Ste-Marguerite, QU (514) 228-2511

AREA INFORMATION

HOURS
9:00 a.m. - 4:00 p.m.

LIFTS
1 chairlift, 4 T-bars, 2 pomas, 5,900 capacity per hour
LONGEST RUN
1,800 feet
SEASON
December to March, no snowmaking
SNOW PHONE
Call Ski Area
TRAILS
15 slopes
TRAVEL
Hwy. 117, north of Montreal
VERTICAL DROP
370 feet

SASKATCHEWAN

BLACKSTRAP RECREATION SITE

Saskatoon, SA (306) 492-2276

AREA INFORMATION

HOURS
1:00 - 5:00 p.m., Wednesday, Friday
10:00 a.m. - 4:30 pm., Saturday, Sunday
LIFTS
1 bar, 2 tows, 1,700 capacity per hour
LONGEST RUN
1,200 feet
SEASON
Mid-December to late March, snowmaking
SNOW PHONE 373-5930
TRAILS
12 runs
TRAVEL
35 miles from Saskatoon, Hwy. 11 South
VERTICAL
DROP
290 feet

CYPRESS HILLS

Maple Creek, SA S0N 1N0 (306) 667-2981

AREA INFORMATION

BASE ELEVATION
3,620 feet
HOURS
10:00 a.m. - 4:30 p.m., weekends, Mondays
Christmas holidays and some Wednesdays
LIFTS
1 bar, 1 tow, 750 capacity per hour
SEASON
Mid-December to early March
SNOW PHONE
Call Ski Area
TRAVEL
S.W. Saskatchewan, 18 miles from Maple Creek
Hwy. 21 South to Cypress Hills Provincial Park
VERTICAL DROP
360 feet

LITTLE RED RIVER PARK

Prince Albert, SA S6V (306) 764-5464

AREA INFORMATION

LIFTS
3 tows
SEASON
December to March
SNOW PHONE
Call Ski Area
TRAILS
5 slopes, beginner and intermediate
TRAVEL
4 miles from Prince Albert

MINATINAS

Domremy, SA S0K 1G0 (306) 423-5728

AREA INFORMATION

HOURS
10:00 a.m. - 5:00 p.m.
LIFTS
1 bar, 1 tow, 650 capacity per hour
LONGEST RUN
3,000 feet
SEASON
Late December to early March
SNOW PHONE
Call Ski Area
TRAILS
12 runs
TRAVEL
28 miles south of Prince Albert
Highway 2, south of Domremy
VERTICAL DROP
230 feet

SNOASIS

Regina, SA

AREA INFORMATION

HOURS
1:00 - 10:00 p.m., Monday - Friday
10:00 a.m. - 10:00 p.m., Sat., holidays
10:00 a.m. - 6:00 p.m., Sunday
LIFTS
2 chairlifts, 1 tow, 2,600 capacity per hour
LONGEST RUN
2,000 feet
SEASON
December to March, snowmaking
TRAVEL
19 miles north of Regina, Hwy. 6, signs posted
VERTICAL DROP
250 feet

TABLE MOUNTAIN

North Battleford, SA S9A (306) 446-2455

AREA INFORMATION

HOURS
1:00 - 9:30 p.m., Wednesday
1:00 - 5:00 p.m., school groups, Friday
7:00 - 9:30 p.m., open to public, Friday
10:00 a.m. - 5:00 p.m., Sat., Sun., holidays
LIFTS
2 bars, 2 tows, 2,600 capacity per hour
LONGEST RUN
3,370 feet
SEASON
December to March, snowmaking
SNOW PHONE
Call Ski Area
TRAVEL
Twenty miles west of Battleford,
Hwy. 40, Table Mtn. Regional Park
VERTICAL DROP
390 feet

TWIN TOWERS

Stanraer, SA (306) 337-4502 X 9091

AREA INFORMATION

HOURS
1:00 - 4:00 p.m., Wednesday
6:00 - 9:30 p.m., Friday
1:00 - 9:30 p.m., Saturday
1:00 - 5:30 p.m., Sunday
LIFTS
3 tows, 1,050 capacity per hour
LONGEST RUN
2,500 feet
SEASON
December to March
TRAVEL
From Saskatoon, 73 miles via Hwy. 7 S., 30 miles northwest on Hwy. 31, two miles east of Stanraer
VERTICAL DROP
320 feet

WHITE TRACK

Moose Jaw, SA S6H (306) 692-8114

BASE ELEVATION
600 feet
HOURS
2:00 - 4:30, 5:30 - 10:00 p.m., Wednesday, Friday
10:00 a.m. - 4:30 p.m., Sat., Sun. and Christmas
LIFTS
1 bar, 2 tows, 350 capacity per hour
LONGEST RUN
2,600 feet
SEASON
Mid-December to mid-March, snowmaking
TRAILS
4 slopes, 1 bowl
TRAVEL
20 miles N.E. of Moose Jaw, Hwy. 2 N., 301 E.
VERTICAL DROP
300 feet

CROSS-COUNTRY

UNITED STATES

ALASKA

ALYESKA RESORT

Box 249, Girdwood, AK 99587 (907) 783-2222

AREA INFORMATION

TOURING
Situated within 10 square miles of Alpine meadows
Two to ten mile tours through Glacier Creek's bed

TRAILS
At the resort, 2½, 3 & 5 km loops, some maintenance

TRAVEL
40 miles southeast of Anchorage

FAIRBANKS

BIRCH HILL NORDIC SKI CENTER

Chamber of Commerce, Fairbanks, AK 97701

AREA INFORMATION

TRAILS
7½ km machine-groomed trails, warm up - waxing hut
Most trails in city groomed, 1 - 20 km, warm up huts

UNIVERSITY OF ALASKA

Phys. Ed. Dept., Fairbanks, AK 99701 (907) 479-7208

AREA INFORMATION

RENTAL
Beaver Sports Shop, Fairbanks 479-2494
TRAILS
30 km of trails, 20 km marked, 12 km machine-groomed
Trails start on campus, open to the public at no charge
TRAVEL
N.W. Fairbanks, northeast of College, Alaska

NORDIC SKI CLUB OF FAIRBANKS

Box 80111, Fairbanks, AK 99708 (907) 479-6742

AREA INFORMATION

EVENTS
Citizen and USSA races
SEASON
Fairbanks area has six month season
TOURING
Organized tours, lessons

NORDIC SKI CLUB OF ANCHORAGE

Box 3301, Anchorage, AK 99501 (907) 344-1740

AREA INFORMATION

EVENTS
Races conducted by Club
LODGING
Cabins in Chugach Nat'l Forest, 50 miles east
TOURING
Club lessons, clinics, day and overnight tours
TRAILS
50 km of groomed trails maintained by Club.
Some of the trails are lighted for night skiing.

A R I Z O N A

APACHE NATIONAL FOREST/GREER

Chamber of Commerce
Box 254, Greer AZ 85927 (602) 735-7583

AREA INFORMATION

ELEVATION
From 8,300 feet
LODGING
In Greer, lodges and housekeeping cabins
RENTALS/LESSONS
Circle B Market, Box 121 . . . . (602) 735-7540
TRAILS
Through Little Colorado River Valley, all levels
30 km marked, maintained; 2.4 to 11.2 km loops
The trail network begins two miles from Greer.
TRAVEL
East-Central Arizona, I-40 to U.S. 666 S. to Rt. 260 W.

MORMON LAKE

Ski Touring Ctr., Mormon Lake, AZ 86038 (602) 354-2240

AREA INFORMATION

ELEVATION
7,200 feet
TOURING
At lake basin, beginner to advanced
TRAILS
80 km marked
TRAVEL
30 miles southeast of Flagstaff

SACRED MOUNTAIN SKI TOURS

406 S. Beaver St., Flagstaff, AZ 86001 (602) 774-7809

AREA INFORMATION

ELEVATION
Coconino National Forest, 7,000 to 12,500 feet
RENTALS
Complete rentals
TOURING
Back country, mountaineering, downhill Nordic instruction, clinics, moonlight tours, races, guided group tours
TRAILS
6 to 15 km trails, for ski school and races

C A L I F O R N I A

BEAR VALLEY

Touring Ctr., Box 5, Bear Valley, CA 95223 (209) 753-2844

AREA INFORMATION

EVENTS
NASTAR races every weekend
TOURING
Off-track and prepared-track skiing, ski school
Guided day tours and overnight snowcamping

TRAILS
25 km marked, 15 to 25 km maintained weekly
TRAVEL
East of Stockton, south of Lake Tahoe, Rt. 4

BIG CHIEF GUIDES

Box 2427, Truckee, CA 95734 (916) 587-4723

AREA INFORMATION

LODGING
Touring Center dorm, cabins
RESTAURANT
Big Chief Lodge
TOURING
Guide services and snow survival instruction
TRAILS
Pole Creek area, 30 km marked and maintained
TRAVEL
On Rt. 89, north of Tahoe City, south of I-80

CHILDS MEADOWS NORDIC

Rt. 36, Mill Creek, CA 96061 (916) 595-4411

AREA INFORMATION

ELEVATION
5,000 feet
EVENTS
NASTAR races twice each month
LODGING
Motel and cabins
RESTAURANTS
At Center
TOURING
Beginner instruction; all day tours, reservations
TRAILS
30 km marked and maintained after snowfall
50 miles of logging and Forest Service roads
National Park Service marked, unmarked trails
TRAVEL
I-5 to Red Bluff, Rt. 36 E., Lassen National Forest, near Lassen Volcanic National Park

EBBETTS PASS

Tamarack Lodge
Box 56, Bear Valley, CA 95223 (209) 753-2594

AREA INFORMATION

LODGING
Dorms, private rooms, meals
TOURING
Guided tours through the Stanislaus National Forest
TRAILS
10 km marked, lessons and tours through Ski School
TRAVEL
Route 4, two miles south of Bear Valley
South of Lake Tahoe, east of Stockton

KIRKWOOD SKI TOURING CENTER

Box 77, Kirkwood, CA 95646 (209) 258-8864

AREA INFORMATION

ELEVATION
7,800 feet
EVENTS
Last weekend of March, Echo Summit to Kirkwood Race
Rt. 50 to Rt. 88, 12 miles across top of the Sierra Range
LODGING
Kirkwood Ski Area, Silver Lake Resort & S. Lake Tahoe
TOURING
Beginner and intermediate lessons; for wilderness camping, contact Nordic Ski Patrol at the Center.
TRAILS
30 km marked, 15 km maintained
TRAVEL
U.S. 50 from Sacramento to Route 88 south of Lake Tahoe, 30 miles from Grover Hot Springs, Markleeville

LASSEN NATIONAL PARK

Lassen Ski Touring, Mineral, CA 96063 (916) 595-3376

AREA INFORMATION

TOURING
One mile daily trip on packed-track to Sulphur Works
TRAILS
Marked trails and backcountry skiing
TRAVEL
I-5 to Red Bluff, then 52 miles via Routes 36 E., 89 N.

MAMMOTH

Box 102, Mammoth Lake, CA 93546 (714) 934-6955

AREA INFORMATION

EVENTS
NASTAR and citizens' races, 42 km Mammoth Marathon
LODGING
Mammoth vicinity
SKI SHOPS
In town and at Center
TOURING
Center staffed by F.W.S.A. certified instructors.
Guided day, moonlight and hot springs tours
Wilderness and winter camping courses & trips

TRAILS
55 km marked, 25 km maintained twice each week
TRAVEL
East of Modesto, northeast of Los Angeles, U.S. 395
Touring Center is on Twin Lakes, on the eastern side of the Sierra Range, 2 miles from Mammoth Lakes.

MONTECITO-SEQUOIA LODGE

Sequoia National Park, CA 93262 (209) 565-3389

AREA INFORMATION

ELEVATION
7,350 feet
EVENTS
NASTAR races weekly
LODGING
Sequoia Lodge, meals, trail usage
RENTALS
Complete rentals at Center
TOURING
Half-day lessons, wilderness survival clinics
Snow camping and moonlight tours
TRAILS
80 km marked
TRAVEL
From Fresno, Rt. 168, General's Hwy. to access road
Center between Sequoia and Kings Canyon Nat'l Parks

NORTHSTAR NORDIC

Box 129, Truckee, CA 95734 (916) 562-0396

AREA INFORMATION

ELEVATION
6,000 to 7,200 feet
EVENTS
NASTAR races, Thursday and Saturday Noon
LODGING
At Center, deli, jacuzzi, sauna, exercise room
Shuttle service within the touring center
RESTAURANT
Big Springs Day Lodge, meals and snacks
Located 1.5 km inside the trail network
SKI SHOP
Complete Nordic equipment
TOURING
Lessons, guided day, picnic and moonlight tours
Overnight tours, lodging at a mountain cabin
TRAILS
50 km marked, 20 km maintained
Network is secluded, 2,500 acres
TRAVEL
7½ miles from Central Truckee exit, off I-80

ROYAL GORGE

Box 178, Soda Springs, CA 95728 (916) 426-3871

AREA INFORMATION

EVENTS
3 race Royal Gorge Cup series, 45 km CA Vasa Marathon, weekly NASTAR races, Telemark Turn contests
LODGING
Wilderness Lodge provides divided loft sleeping, Continental Cuisine, sauna and hot tub, and is reached on skis; other lodging in Soda Springs
TOURING
Lessons, seminars, including wilderness instruction
One week helicopter touring in Canadian Rockies
Touring in Yellowstone National Park, Argentina, Norway, in the French Alps and other countries
TRAILS
218 km marked and machine-groomed, warming huts
TRAVEL
Donner Pass Rd., Soda Springs exit from I-80

SEQUOIA SKI TOURING

Sequoia National Park, CA 93262 (209) 565-3308

AREA INFORMATION

ELEVATION
7,250 to 9,000 + feet
LODGING
Walking distance from Center
TOURING
In Giant Forest, largest Giant Sequoia tree forest
Lessons, advanced winter courses, glacier tours
Downhill touring, 4 miles by skis to downhill area
TRAILS
50 km marked
TRAVEL
Rt. 198 N.E. from Visalia or Rt. 180 S.E. from Fresno
Center is located in Giant Forest, Sequoia National Park.

SIERRA SKI TOURING

Box C-9, Mammoth Lakes, CA 93546 (714) 934-4495

AREA INFORMATION

TOURING
Sierra backcountry, base huts 8 km in to lighten packs

Overnight trips to either Mammoth Lake or June Lake
Wilderness six day tours, see "Trails", Center provides food, cooking gear, tents, avalanche beacons, first aid

TRAILS
Yellowstone, White Mountains, Trans-Sierra-Yosemite, Trans-Sierra-California Haute Rt., Bighorn Plateau Loop

TRAVEL
East of Modesto, U.S. 395, East-Central California

SQUAW VALLEY

Box 2499, Olympic Valley, CA 95730 (916) 583-2499

AREA INFORMATION

EVENTS
Monthly citizens' races, junior race program

LODGING
Squaw Valley Inn and Lodge

SKI SHOP
At Center, sales and rentals

TOURING
Center is staffed by Far West certified instructors.
Daily classes including instruction for blind skiers
Alpine Meadows, backcountry, moonlight touring

TRAILS
20 km marked, 5 km maintained

TRAVEL
The Nordic Center is near the Blyth Ice Arena, within Squaw Valley, north of Tahoe City, I-80 to Rt. 89 S.

SUGAR HOUSE WEST

Meyers, CA 95708 (916) 577-6811

AREA INFORMATION

SKI SHOP
At Center, sale and rental

SNOW CONDITIONS
Tahoe radio station KRLT-FM

TOURING
All level instruction on prepared tracks
Guided tours to the high Sierra

TRAILS
4 km marked and maintained

TRAVEL
U.S. 50, near S. Lake Tahoe

TAHOE NORDIC

Box 1632, Tahoe City, CA 95730 (916) 583-9858

AREA INFORMATION

EVENTS
30 km Great Race to Truckee

NEWSLETTER
Monthly, lists events

TOURING
Tahoe City and Carmelian Bay, full-moon guided tours
Untracked snow to Mt. Pluto, Painted Rock, Mt. Wilson

TRAILS
55 km marked, 25 km machine-groomed each snowfall

TRAVEL
2 miles from Tahoe City, Route 28 East

YOSEMITE

Mountaineering School/Park & Curry Co. (209) 372-4611
Yosemite National Park, CA 95389 372-4611

AREA INFORMATION

EVENTS
Annual Nordic Holiday race, early March

LODGING
Ahwannee Hotel, Curry Village, Yosemite Lodge

TOURING
Lessons and survival technique courses
Day, snowcamping and overnight tours
Popular 3 mile trail to view, Dewey Point

TRAILS
150 km marked

TRAVEL
North of Fresno, Route 41

COLORADO

AMERICAN WILDERNESS ALLIANCE

4260 E. Evans, Denver, CO 80222 (303) 758-5018

AREA INFORMATION

TOURING
2 to 7 day wilderness tours in Colorado and Montana
Guides experienced in wilderness touring, snowshoeing and camping help in developing skills, new techniques.

ASHCROFT SKI TOURING

Box 1572, Aspen 81611 (303) 925-1971

AREA INFORMATION

EVENTS
Annual citizens' race in January
LODGING
2 miles north at Ruby Park, morning-evening shuttle
RESTAURANT
Pine Creek Cookhouse, Hungarian-Swiss food, wine
Reachable by skis in one hour; reservations required.
SNOW CONDITIONS
Local radio stations
TOURING
Warming-waxing-hot drink huts, 3, 4 and 6 km
Guided day, overnight and backcountry touring
TRAILS
30 km marked, machine-groomed daily
TRAVEL
I-70, Rt. 82 W. to Castle Creek/Maroon Creek exit, left fork from exit to Touring Center, twelve miles

BEAR POLE RANCH

Star Rt. 1, Steamboat Springs, CO 80477 (303) 879-0567

AREA INFORMATION

TOURING
Guided day, moonlight and hot springs tours
TRAILS
30 km marked
TRAVEL
Next to Routt National Forest
Steamboat Springs, 10 minutes

BERTHOUD PASS TOURING CENTER

Box 520, Idaho Springs, CO 80452 (303) 572-8014

AREA INFORMATION

ELEVATION
11,000 feet at base
EVENTS
High Ridge Rally, Berthoud Pass to Mary-Jane
Telemark slalom and powder-8 competitions
Parallel-on-pins giant slalom
LODGING
Berthoud Pass Lodge, top of the pass
SEASON
Early November to June
TOURING
Beginner instruction on 6 km flat track in forest
Downhill instruction on pin bindings
Avalanche-backcountry hazards seminars
TRAILS
30 km marked
TRAVEL
60 miles from Denver, I-70 West

BRECKENRIDGE

Box 1058, Breckenridge, CO 80424 (303) 453-2368

AREA INFORMATION

EVENTS
Annual Telemark Festival: freestyle on touring skis, dual Telemark slalom races, dances and parades
SKI SHOPS
Advance Ski Shop & Rental, 401 S. Main . . . 453-6868
Nordica Specialty Store, 540 S. Main. 453-9513
Trygve Sports, 100 S. Main 453-2717
TOURING
Personalized lessons, mountaineering
Adequate advanced skiing terrain
Day, moonlight and overnight tours
TRAILS
25 km marked, 20 km maintained mainly by tracksetter
TRAVEL
70 miles from Denver, I-70 W. to Rt. 9 S., 9 miles

C LAZY U RANCH

Box 378, Rt. 125, Granby, CO 80446 (303) 887-3344

AREA INFORMATION

SEASON
Late December to early April

TOURING
3,000 acres privately owned
Equipment and instruction, guided touring
TRAILS
10 km marked and groomed
TRAVEL
Northwest of Denver, I-70 to U.S. 40 N. to Rt. 125
WINTER ACTIVITIES
Ice skating, sledding, tubing, sleigh rides, and downhill skiing nearby; indoor racquet court, sauna, whirlpool

COPPER MOUNTAIN

Box 1, Copper Mountain, CO 80443 (303) 668-2220

AREA INFORMATION

EVENTS
Rocky Mountain Ski Association Touring Series Finale, Copper Derby Citizens' race, downhill and level with touring skis, the Kamikazi Kup, touring skis downhill
LODGING
Condominiums at Ski Area
RESTAURANTS
At Ski Area
TOURING
Beginner and intermediate instruction
Moonlight and overnight tours
TRAILS
30 km marked, 20 km maintained
6 km beginner track, 80 km of touring routes
TRAVEL
75 miles from Denver, I-70 W., exit 195
Center located west of downhill area

CRESTED BUTTE

Box 528, Crested Butte, CO 81224 (303) 349-6611

AREA INFORMATION

LODGING
At Ski Area
TOURING
Instruction in Telemark turns, winter camping, survival
Backcountry in Gunnison National Forest
Guided day and overnight tours
TRAILS
10 km marked and maintained
TRAVEL
U.S. 50 to Gunnison, then Rt. 135 N., 16 miles

CUCHARA VALLEY

West Peak, Box 459, La Veta, CO 81055 (303) 742-3661

AREA INFORMATION

LODGING
La Veta Lodge, dining
TOURING
Beginner to advanced, San Isabel National Forest
Instruction; day, photography and moonlight tours
TRAILS
40 km marked, 75 km total
TRAVEL
60 miles S.W. of Pueblo, I-25 to Rt. 160, then 5 miles
WINTER ACTIVITIES
Mountaineering, snowshoeing

DEVIL'S THUMB

Box 98, Fraser, CO 80442 (303) 726-8298, (800) 525-3051

AREA INFORMATION

EVENTS
Altitude International Ski Race, December
TOURING
780 acres of private land, view of Continental Divide
Instruction, children's and handicapped programs
TRAILS
60 km marked, maintained daily; 2 Telemark Hills
TRAVEL
I-70 W., U.S. 40 past Fraser, right on County Rd. 83

GLEN EDEN RANCH

Box 867, Clark, CO 80428 (303) 879-3906

AREA INFORMATION

EVENTS/RECREATION
Glen Eden Classic race, wine and cheese parties, ice skating, hot tub and pool
LODGING
Cabins at Center
RESTAURANT
Main Lodge, wines, western music, dancing weekends
TOURING
Elk River Valley, Routt National Forest
Moonlight and other tours by reservation
TRAILS
20 km marked, machine-groomed daily
TRAVEL
U.S. 40 north of Steamboat Springs, Elk River Road

KEYSTONE

Box 38, Keystone, CO 80435 (303) 468-2316

AREA INFORMATION

EVENTS
Annual Keystone Caper Race, 3rd weekend in Feb.
TOURING
Beginner lessons, other level instruction by reservation
Day, picnic and moonlight tours, reservations also
TRAILS
20 km marked
TRAVEL
I-70 W. from Denver, 73 miles

LAKE ELDORA

Box 430, Nederland, CO 80466 (303) 447-8011

AREA INFORMATION

LODGING
In Nederland, 5 miles from Center
RESTAURANT
Eldora Ski Lodge, nearby
TOURING
Instruction at the Center
TRAILS
30 km marked, 20 km maintained
patrolled, some one-way trails
TRAVEL
21 miles from Boulder, Rt. 119 S., 1 mile past
Nederland, then west on access road to Eldora

NOKAHU MOUNTAIN GUIDES

Granby, CO 80446 (303) 887-3777

AREA INFORMATION

LODGING
Condominiums nearby
TOURING
Backcountry, hot springs, Continental Divide tours
Lessons, winter camping, ski equipment rental
TRAILS
55 km marked system from the Beaver Ski Chalet
TRAVEL
Near Granby, Junction of U.S. 34 and 40

PEACEFUL VALLEY

Touring, Peaceful Valley Lodge
Star Route, Lyons, CO 80540 (303) 747-2582

AREA INFORMATION

SKI SHOP
Nordic equipment, accessories and clothing
LODGING
At Center, dining, covered pool, sauna, whirlpool
TOURING
6 acre instruction-practice area
Guided tours into forest
TRAILS
75 km marked, 800,000 acres of national forest
TRAVEL
60 miles N.W. of Denver, Rt. 72

ROCKY MOUNTAIN EXPEDITIONS

Box 1, Buena Vista, CO 81211 (303) 395-8466

AREA INFORMATION

TOURING
Center in ghost town, St. Elmo
Private lessons, beginner to advanced
Telemark and mountaineering instruction
TRAILS
75 km marked
TRAVEL
U.S. 24, south of Leadville

ST. PAUL SKI LODGE

Box 463, Silverton, CO 81433 (303) 387-5494

AREA INFORMATION

LODGING
Dormitory style
SKI SHOP
Nordic equipment, accessories
TOURING
Instruction, guided tours, mostly untracked
TRAILS
10 km marked
TRAVEL
1 mile from Rt. 550 by skis to Lodge
12 miles from Silverton to the Center

SCANDINAVIAN LODGE

Box 5040, Steamboat Springs, CO 80499 (303) 879-0517

AREA INFORMATION

LODGING
Scandinavian food, pool, sauna, gym
TOURING
All-level instruction, complete program
Backcountry tours, annual clinics
TRAILS
3 km marked and maintained
TRAVEL
165 miles N.W. of Denver, I-70, U.S. 40 North

SNOWMASS

Snowmass Country Club
Snowmass Village, CO 81615 (303) 923-4012

AREA INFORMATION

EVENTS
Weekly cross-country NASTAR races
LODGING
In Snowmass Village 923-2000
RESTAURANT
Courts & Course, at the Center
TOURING
Children's programs, ladies days, guided tours
All-level instruction, handicapped program
TRAILS
10 km marked, 25 km total
Shelter 8 km in, unheated
TRAVEL
10 miles N.W. of Aspen, Rt. 82 N. to access road

SNOW MOUNTAIN RANCH YMCA

Box 558, Granby, CO 80446 (303) 887-2152

AREA INFORMATION

EVENTS/RECREATION
Ice skating, roller skating, snowshoeing
LODGING
At Center
TOURING
Night lessons, moonlight tours
TRAILS
60 km marked, over 2,500 acres
Unheated winter campsites
TRAVEL
U.S. 40, south of Granby, near Winter Park

STEAMBOAT SPRINGS

Box 771178, Steamboat Springs, CO 80477 (303) 879-6111

AREA INFORMATION

ELEVATION
6,900 feet at Center
EVENTS
Winterstart Classified and Citizens' Races, December
Winter Carnival and variety of races, February
Cross-Country Citizens' Obstacle Race, April
LODGING
At Ski Area or in town
SKI SHOP
Rental and repair, at Center
TOURING
All-level group lessons or private instruction
Guided wilderness tours, scheduled or personalized
TRAILS
20 km marked, maintained
TRAVEL
157 miles from Denver via I-70, exit 205 to Rt. 9 N. to Kremmling, U.S. 40 West to Steamboat Springs

TELLURIDE SKI TOURING

Box 307, Telluride, CO 81435 (303) 728-3856

AREA INFORMATION

ELEVATION
8,730 feet at Center
TOURING
San Juan Mountains, guides advised for backcountry
Lessons and guided day, starlight, and group tours
Telemark clinics, call Center for reservation
TRAILS
10 km marked
TRAVEL
South of Montrose, U.S. 550, Rt. 62 W., Rt. 145 S.

TOUR IDLEWILD

Box 3, Winter Park, CO 80482 (303) 726-5564

AREA INFORMATION

LODGING
Idlewild Lodge, dining, outdoor heated pool
SKI SHOP
Complete cross-country equipment
TOURING
Advanced touring via ski lifts
Day, photography and overnight touring

TOUR IDLEWILD CONT.

TRAILS
45 km marked, machine-groomed
TRAVEL
70 miles west of Denver, I-70, exit 232, U.S. 40 to ½ mile access road, 2 miles from Winter Park

VAIL

Ski Touring, Box 811, Vail, CO 81657 (303) 476-5601

AREA INFORMATION

ELEVATION
8,200 feet at the Center
EVENTS
Citizens' races
TOURING
Instruction on golf course, guides advised beyond
Mountain and night headlamp guided tours
LODGING
In Vail
TRAILS
Not marked nor maintained except for occasional grooming of a 16 km trail from top of mountain
TRAVEL
100 miles west of Denver, I-70 West

VISTA VERDE

Vista Verde Guest Ranch
Box 465, Steamboat Springs, CO 80477 (303) 879-3858

AREA INFORMATION

EVENTS/RECREATION
Sleigh rides, ice fishing on Steamboat Lake
TOURING
600 acres in Routt National Forest
Wilderness touring, guided tours
TRAILS
22 km marked, maintained
TRAVEL
25 miles from Steamboat Springs, U.S. 40, exit 129

CONNECTICUT

BLACKBERRY RIVER

Touring Ctr., Rt. 44, Norfolk, CT 06058 (203) 542-5614

AREA INFORMATION

LODGING
Blackberry River Inn, meals, live entertainment
SKI SHOP
At Center, sale and rental
TOURING
Instruction, group night tours
TRAILS
32 km marked, maintained
TRAVEL
Northwest Connecticut, U.S. 44

GREAT WORLD TOURING CENTER

250 Farms Village Road
West Simsbury, CT 06092 (203) 658-4461

AREA INFORMATION

EVENTS
NASTAR races weekly
TOURING
EPSTI certified instructors
Nordic Ski Patrol
TRAILS
20 km marked, maintained
TRAVEL
U.S. 202 to Rt. 309 W., N.W. of Hartford

PINE MOUNTAIN

Great World, 250 Farms Village Road
Box 250, West Simsbury, CT 06092 (203) 658-4461

AREA INFORMATION

EVENTS
NASTAR citizens' races
TOURING
EPSTI certified instructors
Nordic Ski Patrol
TRAILS
32 km marked, maintained, trail reports. . . . 658-4471
TRAVEL
U.S. 202 to Rt. 309 W., N.W. of Hartford

POWDER RIDGE

Middlefield, CT 06455 (203) 349-3454

AREA INFORMATION

LODGING
Base Lodge Inn or in Meriden, five miles
TOURING
250 acres of field touring, 30 miles of state hiking trails
Climb to trail system or use chairlifts from Base Area
Instruction , guided day tours, lighted night skiing

TRAILS
10 km marked, maintained daily
TRAVEL
20 miles from Hartford, I-91 S., E. Main Street for 2 miles, Rt. 147 East to Powder Hill Road

RIVERRUNNING EXPEDITIONS

Main Street, Falls Village, CT 06031 (203) 824-5579

AREA INFORMATION

EVENTS
Citizens' races
SKI SHOP
Equipment, accessories and clothing
TOURING
Warming shelters at start and 3 km into trail network
EPSTI certified instructors, group and moonlight tours
TRAILS
24 km marked, 16 km maintained
TRAVEL
N.E. Connecticut, U.S. 7 to Route 126 West

WHITE MEMORIAL FOUNDATION

Rt. 202, Litchfield, CT 06759 (203) 567-0857

AREA INFORMATION

SKI SHOP
The Wilderness Shop 567-5905
TOURING
4,000 acre preserve, 35 miles tree-lined and lakeshore
Trails free, charge for map at Conservation Center
Equipment and accessories at ski shop in Litchfield
TRAILS
57 km marked
TRAVEL
U.S. 202 S. from Torrington, 2½ miles S.W. of Litchfield

WOODBURY SKI & RACQUET

Rt. 47, Woodbury, CT 06798 (203) 263-2203

AREA INFORMATION

LODGING
Inn on Lake Waramaug, Lake Preston 868-2168
Mayflower Inn, Washington 868-0515
SKI SHOP
At Ski Area
TOURING
Steep Rock Park and Flanders Nature Center
Trails free, some unheated shelters at ends of trails
Beginner lessons and advanced instruction tours
TRAILS
30 km marked, 60 km total
TRAVEL
4 miles from Woodbury, Rt. 47 North

I D A H O

BUSTERBACK RANCH

Star Route, Ketchum, ID 83340 (208) 774-2217

AREA INFORMATION

LODGING
At the ranch, meals
TOURING
2,500 acres of ranch land and Sawtooth Nat'l Rec. Area
Guided tours, Salmon River Valley and two mountains
TRAILS
40 km marked, maintained
TRAVEL
From Ketchum and Sun Valley,
40 miles, Rt. 75 N. to access road

GALENA LODGE

Star Route, Ketchum, ID 83340 (208) 726-4010

AREA INFORMATION

EVENTS/RECREATION
Siberian husky sled rides by reservation
LODGING
Cabins at trail start
RESTAURANT
Galena Lodge, breakfast, lunch, box lunches
Evening meals for 15 or more, 48 hr. reservation
SKI SHOP
Equipment, accessories
TOURING
Sawtooth National Recreation Area
Day, moonlight and overnight tours
All-level instruction, Telemark turns
TRAILS
50 km machine-groomed, 100 km total
TRAVEL
24 miles from Ketchum and Sun Valley, Rt. 75 N.

SUN VALLEY

Box 272, Sun Valley, ID 83353 (208) 622-4111

AREA INFORMATION

LODGING
At Ski Area

SUN VALLEY CONT.

RESTAURANT
    Trail Creek Cabin, lighted trail at night
SKI SHOP
    At the Center, rentals
TOURING
    Morning and afternoon lessons
    Day, helicopter and moonlight tours
TRAILS
    30 km maintained, over 160 km total
    Sun Valley Ski Touring Guide at Center
TRAVEL
    80 miles north of Twin Falls, Route 75

TIMBER RIDGE RANCH

Box 34, Harrison, ID 83833   (208) 689-3421, 689-3315

AREA INFORMATION

LODGING
    Dormitory cabins, rooms, ranch-style meals
TOURING
    Between Blue Lane and Coeur d'Alene National Forest
TRAILS
    24 km groomed, marked by level of difficulty
    Unmarked trails in mountains, powder
TRAVEL
    29 miles south of Coeur d'Alene, Rt. 97

I L L I N O I S

THE GALENA TERRITORY

Box 777, Galena, IL 61036   (815) 777-2444

AREA INFORMATION

LODGING
    At the Inn, register at the ski shop
RESTAURANT
    At the Inn, cocktails
TOURING
    Tree-lined area, hills and lakes
TRAILS
    50 km marked
TRAVEL
    Northwestern Illinois, U.S. 20

MORAINE HILLS STATE PARK

914 S. River Rd., McHenry, IL 60050   (815) 385-1624

AREA INFORMATION

TOURING
    Open and wooded terrain
    Clinics, rentals at Park Bldg.
TRAILS
    17 km marked, 3 loops
TRAVEL
    Northeastern Illinois, Route 120

I N D I A N A

DUNES STATE PARK

M.R. Box 322, Chesterton, IN 46304   (219) 926-1215

AREA INFORMATION

TOURING
    Skiing permitted on over 300 acres in the park
    Skis, shoes and pole rentals handled by state
TRAILS
    5 km in state park and 15 km bicycle trail,
    Mineral Springs Rd. to Country Line Rd.
TRAVEL
    30 miles east of Gary, U.S. 12, near Lake Michigan

I O W A

YELLOW RIVER STATION

R.F.D., Monona, IA 52159   (319) 539-2425

AREA INFORMATION

TOURING
    280 acres, wooded hills, meadows
    Beginner instruction, rentals and sales
TRAILS
    15 km marked and maintained
TRAVEL
    Northeast Iowa, U.S. 18/52

M A I N E

AKERS SKI

Andover, ME 04216 (207) 392-4582

AREA INFORMATION

TOURING
Waxing-warming shelter at start; shelter at 3 km
Lessons pre-arranged, off-track skiing near network
TRAILS
25 km marked, 10 km maintained after snowfall
Mini trail, 1 km loop for beginners near warehouse
TRAVEL
Western Maine, U.S. 2 to Rt. 5 North

THE BIRCHES

Ski Center, Rockwood, ME 04478 (207) 534-7305

AREA INFORMATION

LODGING
Cabins at the Center
RENTALS
Skiing equipment and snowshoes
TOURING
Moosehead lakeshore, logging roads, snowmobile system
Instruction, guided tours, six day touring trip
TRAILS
20 km marked, 14 km maintained
320 km snowmobile system, groomed
TRAVEL
In Rockwood, near Squaw Valley and Quebec border

CARRABASSETT VALLEY

Box 518, Carrabassett Valley, ME 04947 (207) 237-2205

AREA INFORMATION

SKI SHOP
Sale, rental, repair
TOURING
Beginner to advanced trails, level to steep climbs
Flagstaff Lake and Appalachian wilderness touring
Warming room and cafeteria in lodge at Center
TRAILS
80 km marked, 50 km maintained
TRAVEL
I-95 to Waterville, U.S. 201/201 A to Rt. 16 N.
Center is one mile south of Sugarloaf Mountain.

DEER FARM

Touring Center, Kingsfield, ME 04947 (207) 265-2241

AREA INFORMATION

SKI SHOP
At the Center, rental, sale
LODGING
Farmhouse and log cabins, meals
TOURING
Lunch, moonlight and other guided tours
TRAILS
57 km marked, 48 km maintained
TRAVEL
I-95 to Waterville, U.S. 202/202 A, Rt. 16 North
Center is 17 miles south of Sugarloaf Mountain.

LITTLE LYFORD POND CAMPS

Box 688, Brownville, ME 04414

AREA INFORMATION

LODGING
Guest cabins, meals at dining lodge nearby
TOURING
Logging roads, forest touring with map and compass
Guided day tours, instruction, limited rentals
TRAILS
69 km marked, not groomed
TRAVEL
U.S. 95, Routes 16 and 11 North to Brownville
Center is six miles from roads, access by skis or by
Folsoms Air Service, Greenville, (207) 695-2821.

LOST VALLEY

Box 260, Auburn, ME 04210 (207) 784-1561

AREA INFORMATION

LODGING
Nearby, dining and lounge at the Center
TRAILS
6.5 km, groomed unmarked trails
TRAVEL
Center is in N.W. Maine, 8 miles from the
junction of Routes 16 and 17 at Rangeley.

SADDLEBACK

Box 490, Rangeley, ME 04970 (207) 864-3380

AREA INFORMATION

LODGING
At the Area and nearby
RESTAURANT
Base Lodge, Alpine Area
TOURING
Men's Day, Wednesday; Women's Day, Thursday
Lessons and rentals are provided at the Center.
TRAILS
40 km marked, not groomed
TRAVEL
Turnpike, Rt. 4 to Saddleback Rd.
Seven miles southeast of Rangeley

SQUAW MOUNTAIN

Box D, Greenville, ME 04441 (207) 695-2272

AREA INFORMATION

LODGING
At Ski Area, restaurant, cocktail lounge, dancing
TOURING
Open land with scattered frozen lakes and ponds
Golf course and surrounding wooded area, 3 miles
Alpine, guided wilderness and group touring
TRAILS
80 km marked
TRAVEL
Route 6/15, six miles from Greenville
Near southern tip of Moosehead Lake

MARYLAND

SWALLAW FALLS STATE PARK

Superintendent, Oakland, MD 21550 (301) 334-9180

AREA INFORMATION

LODGING
In vicinity and at nearby Wisp Ski Area 387-4911
TOURING
Winter camping permitted
TRAILS
16 km marked; 8.2 km marked and groomed at New Germany State Park, Grantsville, 895-5453; 6.7 km maintained at Herrington Manor State Park, Garrett State Forest, N.W. of Oakland, 5 miles, 334-9180.
TRAVEL
Western tip of Maryland, U.S. 219, north of Oakland

MASSACHUSETTS

BUTTERNUT

Rt. 23, Great Barrington, MA 01230 (413) 528-0610

AREA INFORMATION

LODGING
Nearby, cafeteria and nursery at Alpine Area
TOURING
Snowmaking in instruction area
State Forest touring beyond trails
TRAILS
7 km maintained; 10 km wilderness trail
45 km system in Beartown State Forest
TRAVEL
S.W. Massachusetts, U.S. 7 to Rt. 23, two miles east

CUMMINGTON FARM

South Road, Cummington, MA 01026 (413) 634-2111

AREA INFORMATION

ELEVATION
1,200 feet
LODGING
At the farm and nearby
RESTAURANT
Cummington Farm Restaurant
SEASON
Area has a long season.
TOURING
PSIA instruction, clinics and races
Guided full-moon and other guided tours
TRAILS
45 km marked, maintained, 2½ km lighted loop
TRAVEL
23 miles northwest of Northampton, Route 9

EGREMONT COUNTRY CLUB

Rt. 23, Great Barrington, MA 01230 (413) 528-4222

AREA INFORMATION

TOURING
Trail system on golf courses and surrounding area
Instruction, maximum of six in group lessons
TRAILS
10 km marked, maintained
TRAVEL
S.W. Massachusetts, U.S. 7, Route 23 East

FLYING CLOUD INN

Box 143, New Marlboro, MA 01230 (413) 229-2113

AREA INFORMATION

LODGING
Included are meals, equipment, trail use, ice skating, snowshoeing, no instruction.
TOURING
Trail system for guests, maximum of 20
TRAILS
10 km marked
TRAVEL
S.W. Massachusetts, U.S. 7 to Routes 23, 57 East, 10 miles from Great Barrington

JUG END RESORT

South Egremont, MA 01258 (413) 528-0434

AREA INFORMATION

LODGING
Base lodge of Alpine Area, dining, nightlife
RECREATION
Ice skating and indoor swimming
TOURING
Trail system is on golf course and logging roads.
TRAILS
16 km marked, 5 km maintained
TRAVEL
U.S. 7 to Route 23, southwest of Great Barrington

MT. TOM

Ski Area, Holyoke, MA 01040 (413) 536-0146

AREA INFORMATION

LODGING
In Springfield and Holyoke
RESTAURANTS
Mt. Tom Lodge, Tom's Tavern
TRAILS
10 km, ungroomed, no trail fee
TRAVEL
10 miles north of Holyoke, I-91, exit 17 to Rt. 5 N. to access road

NORTHFIELD MOUNTAIN

Ski Touring Center
RR 1, Box 377, Northfield, MA 01360 (413) 659-3713

AREA INFORMATION

TOURING
2,000 acres of wooded area, Nordic Ski Patrol
Part of National Recreational Trail System
Food at trail start and 2 km, weekends, holidays
TRAILS
40 km marked, maintained
TRAVEL
Near Vermont, I-91 to Rt. 10 east; access road continues on where Routes 10 and 63 meet.

OTIS RIDGE

Route 23, Otis, MA 01253 (413) 269-4444

AREA INFORMATION

LODGING
The Grouse House, Alpine Area
RESTAURANT
½ mile from Center at Base Lodge
SKI SHOP
Base Area, equipment, accessories, clothing
TOURING
Beyond trails are unplowed roads in Otis State Forest.
2 unheated shelters in trail system at 4 km and 10 km
TRAILS
5 km marked, maintained
TRAVEL
S.W. Massachusetts, I-90 to Rt. 23

RED FOX

Ski Center, New Marlboro, MA 01230 (413) 229-7790

AREA INFORMATION

LODGING
Daffers, Sandisfield 258-4453
SKI SHOP
Rental and instruction
TOURING
1,800 acres connect with Sandisfield State Forest
TRAILS
25 km marked, maintained
TRAVEL
S.W. Massachusetts, Rt. 57 to New Marlboro, southeast to South Sandisfield Rd. to Center

RIVERRUN NORTH

Route 7, Sheffield, MA 01257 (413) 528-1100

AREA INFORMATION

TOURING
Warming shelter at trail start, hot drinks, food
TRAILS
5 km marked, double-tracked after adequate snow
TRAVEL
S.E. Massachusetts, U.S. 7

WILDER SKI TRACK

Springfield, MA 01119 (413) 783-4411

AREA INFORMATION

EVENTS
Citizens' races
SKI SHOP
Complete touring equipment, rental
TOURING
Golf course, wooded park area, moonlight tours
Instruction, Bill Koch Ski League junior program
TRAILS
10 km marked and maintained
TRAVEL
Veterans Golf Course, South Branch Parkway

MICHIGAN

BINTZ APPLE MOUNTAIN

4535 N. River Rd., Freeland, MI 48623 (517) 781-2550

AREA INFORMATION

LODGING
In Bay City, Saginaw and Midland
SKI SHOP
At Ski Area
TOURING
Apple orchards and fields
TRAILS
8 km marked
TRAVEL
Route 47, south of Midland

BOYNE HIGHLANDS

Harbor Springs, MI 49740 (616) 526-2171

AREA INFORMATION

NURSERY
Alpine Area nearby
TOURING
Lessons, rentals
TRAILS
24 km, marked, 20 km maintained
TRAVEL
N.W. tip of peninsula, U.S. 31 to Rt. 119 North

BOYNE MOUNTAIN

Boyne Falls, MI 49713 (616) 549-2441

AREA INFORMATION

NURSERY
Alpine Area nearby
TOURING
Lessons, rentals
TRAILS
16 km marked, maintained
TRAVEL
I-75, Routes 32 W. and U.S. 131 N.

CROSS-COUNTRY SKI HEADQUARTERS

Higgins Lake, MI 48653 (517) 821-5868

AREA INFORMATION

LODGING
Roscommon, Houghton Lake, Higgins Lake
TOURING
Beginner instruction, equipment rental
TRAILS
14 km marked, maintained
TRAVEL
I-75, Center is 3 miles north of
South Higgins Lake State Park.

GREENWOOD CAMPGROUND

636 W. Greenwood Rd., Alger, MI 48610 (517) 345-2778

AREA INFORMATION

LODGING
Camping, motels several miles away

SKI SHOP
Equipment sale and rental
TOURING
Beginner, instruction given
TRAILS
3, 5 and 10 km loops, marked and maintained
Warming room at Center, unheated shelter, 5 km
TRAVEL
I-75, east side of Higgins Lake

HANSON RECREATION AREA

Box 361, Grayling, MI 49738 (517) 348-9266

AREA INFORMATION

EVENTS
Citizens, races and treasure hunt in February
Fleischmann's Margarine cross-country race
TRAILS
10, 15 and 30 km, maintained by use
Food and warming shelter at trail start
TRAVEL
I-75, south of Harwick Pines State Park

HILTON SHANTY CREEK

Box 355, Bellaire, MI 49615 (616) 533-8621

AREA INFORMATION

LODGING
At Alpine Area, dining, cocktails, cafeteria, pool
TOURING
Instruction, rentals for adults and children
TRAILS
28 km marked, double-tracked, 13 trails
TRAVEL
U.S. 131 to Rt. 88 N., 2 miles south of Bellaire; from Eastport at Grand Traverse Bay, 17 miles southeast

HINCHMAN ACRES RESORT

Box 146, Mio, MI 48647 (517) 826-3991

AREA INFORMATION

LODGING
Cottages with kitchens, 2 chalets
TOURING
Huron National Forest, novice and intermediate
TRAILS
26 km marked and maintained, 1.7 to 10 km loops
TRAVEL
I-75, Grayling exit to Rt. 72 East, 31 miles

KEN-MAR

Box 679, Gaylord, MI 49735 (517) 732-4950

AREA INFORMATION

EVENTS
Annual Ken-Mar Classic
TOURING
140 acres of forest, orchards and marsh
Some trails can be skied side by side
Instruction, clinics and equipment rental
TRAILS
18.5 km marked and maintained, warming hut at start
3 km lighted loop, 7:30 - 10:00 p.m., Wed., Fri. & Sat.
TRAVEL
Junction of I-75, Rt. 32, 4 miles south of Gaylord

LAKE DOSTER

135 Golf View Dr., Plainwell, MI 49080 (616) 685-5304

AREA INFORMATION

SEASON
Center opens in December, Tuesday thru Sunday
TOURING
Over 2,200 acres surrounding trail system
TRAILS
18 km marked, maintained
TRAVEL
S.W. Michigan, near junction of U.S. 131, Rt. 81

LOST LAKE RESORT

Paradise, MI 49768 (906) 492-3464

AREA INFORMATION

LODGING
Housekeeping cottages, no lessons or equipment
TOURING
Extended touring in state park, 3 miles from Center
TRAILS
45 km
TRAVEL
Northern Michigan I-75 to Routes 28 W., 123 N.

PORCUPINE MOUNTAINS

Dept. of Natural Resources
Ontonagon, MI 49953 (906) 885-5798

AREA INFORMATION

LODGING
In Ontonagon and Silver City
SEASON
December to April
RESTAURANT
Alpine Area, 9:00 a.m. - 4:00 p.m.
SKI SHOP
Alpine Area, rentals, sale, repair
TOURING
View of Lake Superior from part of trail system
TRAILS
32 km maintained
TRAVEL
Northwest Michigan, U.S. 45, Routes 64, 107 W.

RANCH RUDOLF

Box 587, Traverse City, MI 49684 (616) 946-5410

AREA INFORMATION

EVENTS
NASTAR races Sundays
LODGING
At the ranch
SKI SHOP
Equipment sale and rental
TOURING
Next to Fife Lake State Forest, 123,000 acres
Lessons, CSIA certification courses, group tours
TRAILS
24 km marked, maintained; connections with 4-loop Muncie Lake Trail Network, loops into State Forest, logging roads and hiking trails
TRAVEL
I-75 or U.S. 131 to Route 72 West

SCHUSS MOUNTAIN

Mancelona, MI 49659 (616) 587-9162

AREA INFORMATION

LODGING
Dining, cocktail lounges, night club, pool
NURSERY
Day care
TOURING
1,400 acres extend beyond trail network
Instruction and tours, equipment rental
TRAILS
19 km marked and maintained
TRAVEL
U.S. 131 to Route 88 West, N.E. of Traverse City

SHAROCO FARM

Savage & Baldhill Rds., Jones, MI 49061 (616) 476-2464

AREA INFORMATION

SKI SHOP
Equipment rental and sale
TOURING
Woods and open fields, private and group lessons
TRAILS
25.5 km, snack bar, warming shelter at start
TRAVEL
Southwest Michigan, near Jones

SKY VALLEY RANCH

Rt. 1, Box 11, Kalkaska, MI 49646 (616) 258-5982

AREA INFORMATION

LODGING
15 rooms, meals
TOURING
500 acres, woods and hills; equipment rentals
TRAILS
30 km, arranged by level of ability
TRAVEL
N.W. Peninsula, junction of U.S. 131, Rt. 72

SUGAR LOAF

Rt. 1, Cedar, MI 49621 (616) 228-5461

AREA INFORMATION

LODGING
Dining room, cafeteria, cocktail lounges
NURSERY
At Ski Area
RECREATION
Indoor tennis, heated outdoor pool, downhill skiing
SKI SHOP
Complete touring equipment
TOURING
2,000 acres of wooded hills; instruction, guided tours
TRAILS
21 km marked, groomed; coded by degree of difficulty
TRAVEL
18 miles northwest of Traverse City, Rt. 72 West, for 5½ miles, then north past Cedar City to Area

SUICIDE BOWL

Chamber of Commerce
202 E. Division St., Ishpeming, MI 49849 (906) 486-4841

AREA INFORMATION

EVENTS
Int'l ski jumping, Ishpeming Invitational and Paul Bietila Memorial in February; 10, 50 and 70 meter hills, cross-country citizens' races, sponsored by Ispeming Ski Club
LODGING
Ishpeming area
SKI SHOPS
Bietila Sports Shop, Ishpeming 486-8671
Champion Nordic Ski Shop, Ishpeming 339-2294
TRAILS
2.5, 5 and 7.5 km, approved by the Int'l Ski Federation
The 2.5 km trail is lighted until 10:00 p.m. every night.
TRAVEL
U.S. 41, between Lake Superior and Wisconsin

SYLVANIA OUTFITTERS

West U.S. 2, Watersmeet, MI 49969 (906) 358-4766

AREA INFORMATION

LODGING
Watersmeet area
TOURING
21,000 acres in Ottawa National Forest
Winter camping, register at ski shop, U.S. 2
TRAILS
32 km marked, maintained, mostly for advanced skiers.
1, 3 and 5 km easier loops from Information Center
TRAVEL
Junction of U.S. 2 and 45, 8 miles from Wisconsin

TAHQUAMENON FALLS STATE PARK

Paradise, MI 29768 (906) 492-3415, 293-5131

AREA INFORMATION

TOURING
Over 16,000 acres; northern route, experienced only
TRAILS
21 km marked, shared by snowshoers
TRAVEL
Northern Michigan, I-75 to Routes 28 West, 123 North
Except for the access routes, area is closed to vehicles.

WOODS & WATERS

Route 1, White Cloud, MI 49349 (616) 689-6701

AREA INFORMATION

LODGING
280 Campsites, 8 motels, indoor swimming pool with sauna
TOURING
Instructor, Rolling hills, ice skating, snowmobiling
TRAILS
280 acres, marked and maintained
TRAVEL
50 mi. No. of Grand Rapids on M-37

MINNESOTA

EAGLE MOUNTAIN

Box 98, Grey Eagle, MN 56336 (612) 285-4567

AREA INFORMATION

LODGING
At the area, breakfast
TOURING
Adjacent 1,500 acre wildlife preserve, winter camping
TRAILS
10 km marked and maintained, 3 unheated shelters
TRAVEL
50 miles northwest of St. Cloud, I-94 to Rt. 28 North

HENNEPIN COUNTY PARKS

BAKER PARK RESERVE

Maple Plain, MN 55359 (612) 473-4693

AREA INFORMATION

TOURING
Lessons and rentals; snack bar at trail start
TRAILS
15.5 km, unheated shelter at 8 km
TRAVEL
20 miles west of Minneapolis via U.S. 12

CARVER PARK RESERVE

Rt. 1, Box 690, Excelsior, MN 55331 (612) 472-4911

AREA INFORMATION

SNOW PHONE 473-4693
TOURING
Lessons and rentals
TRAILS
29 km, Lowry Nature Center at 9 km, heated
TRAVEL
Southwestern outskirts of Minneapolis, Route 7

CLEARY LAKE REGIONAL PARK

Rt. 1, Box 61, Prior Lake, MN 55372 (612) 447-2171

AREA INFORMATION

TOURING
Lessons and rentals, night skiing
TRAILS
14.5 km, three loops, 2.5 to 7 km
TRAVEL
Southern outskirts of Minneapolis, I-35

ELM CREEK PARK RESERVE

Route 3, Osseo, MN 55369 (612) 425-2324

AREA INFORMATION

TOURING
Lessons and rentals
TRAILS
22 km machine-groomed, connection with trails at Whitney Eastman Nature Center
TRAVEL
Northwest of Minneapolis, U.S. 52/169

HYLAND LAKE PARK RESERVE

Bloomington, MN 55438 (612) 941-1344

AREA INFORMATION

TOURING
Rentals, some guided tours
TRAILS
11 km maintained, Richardson Nature Ctr. at 3.5 km
TRAVEL
8737 East Bush Lake Road in Bloomington

THE HOME PLACE

Squaw Point Rd., Cass Lake, MN 56633 (218) 335-8802

AREA INFORMATION

TOURING
1 million acres, Chippewa National Forest
Instruction, rentals, winterized cabins
TRAILS
25 km, marked and maintained
TRAVEL
32 miles southeast of Bemidji, U.S. 2

LUTSEN

Box 86, Lutsen, MN 55612 (218) 663-7212

AREA INFORMATION

LODGING
Alpine Area, cafeteria, cocktail lounge

TOURING
Superior National Forest; lessons and rentals
TRAILS
40 km groomed, 6 loops
TRAVEL
90 miles from Duluth, U.S. 61 North

MINNEAPOLIS

Park and Recreation Board
250 S. 4th St., Minneapolis, MN 55415 (612) 348-2121

COLUMBIA SKI TOURING CENTER

33rd Street, Minneapolis, MN (612) 789-2627

AREA INFORMATION

HOURS
Wednesday, Saturday and Sunday
TOURING
Lessons and rentals
TRAVEL
33rd St. and Central N.E.

HIAWATHA SKI TOURING CENTER

46th Street, Minneapolis, MN (612) 724-7715

AREA INFORMATION

HOURS
Tuesday thru Thursday, Saturday, Sunday
TOURING
Lessons and rentals
TRAILS
Lighted for night skiing
TRAVEL
46th Street and Longfellow Avenue

WIRTH PAR 3 SKI TOURING CENTER

Plymouth Ave., Minneapolis, MN (612) 522-2818

AREA INFORMATION

HOURS
Wednesday, Saturday and Sunday
TOURING
Lessons and rentals; blind skier program
TRAVEL
Plymouth Ave. and Theodore Wirth Pkwy.

NATIONAL FOREST LODGE

Isabella, MN 55607 (218) 293-4411

AREA INFORMATION

LODGING
Cabins with bunkbeds, family-style meals
TOURING
140 acres, Superior Nat'l Forest, S. Lake Gegoka
Logging roads and other trails supplement network.
TRAILS
60 km, no snowmobiles
TRAVEL
N.E. Minnesota, 17 miles north of U.S. 61 on Rt. 1

QUADNA MOUNTAIN

Hill City, MN 55748 (218) 697-2303

AREA INFORMATION

LODGING
Lodge, motel and townhouses at Area
RECREATION
Indoor tennis, pool, sauna, lounges
TOURING
Heavily wooded, level to steep terrain
TRAVEL
Nineteen miles south of Grand Rapids
near U.S. 2 and Route 200 junction

RADISSON INN/GRAND PORTAGE

Grand Portage, MN 55605 (218) 475-2401

AREA INFORMATION

LODGING
At the Area
TOURING
The Historic native American Grand Portage Trail
Guides, trail system map and rentals at the Center
Facility owned and run by the Chippewa Indians.
TRAILS
80 km marked, 50 km maintained
TRAVEL
Northeastern tip of Minnesota, near Ontario, U.S. 61

REMOTE LAKE SOLITUDE AREA

Sandy Lake Ranger Station
McGregor, MN 55760 (218) 426-3407

AREA INFORMATION

LODGING
McGregor Activities and Trail Assoc., McGregor 55760
Kare Phree Pines Resort, Big Sandy Lake . . . 426-3333
TOURING
Savanna State Forest, Savanna Portage State Park
Intermediate level skiing; no rentals, no instruction
TRAILS
25 km marked, groomed after heavy snowfall
Unheated shelter at 8 km, no motor vehicles in park
TRAVEL
62 miles west of Duluth, Routes 210 and 65 North

SPIRIT MOUNTAIN

9500 Spirit Mtn. Pl., Duluth, MN 55810 (218) 628-2891

AREA INFORMATION

EVENTS
Citizens' races
LODGING
At Ski Area, food services, nursery
TOURING
200 acres, instruction, rentals
TRAILS
12 km marked and groomed, double track
TRAVEL
I-35 to Boundary Ave. exit, signs posted

SUGAR HILLS

Box 369, Grand Rapids, MN 55744 (218) 326-3473

AREA INFORMATION

ELEVATION
1,300 to 1,750 feet
LODGING
At Ski Area, dining room, cafeteria, cocktail lounge
TOURING
Guided tours, rental, lessons, Telemark instruction
TRAILS
80 km, 100,000 acres
TRAVEL
U.S. 169, ten miles south of Grand Rapids

VAL CHATEL

Park Rapids, MN 56470 (218) 266-3306

AREA INFORMATION

LODGING
At Ski Area, dining; entertainment, Thurs. - Sun.
TOURING
Connection to Paul Bunyan State Forest
Instruction and equipment rental
TRAILS
12 km marked and maintained
TRAVEL
U.S. 71 to Route 4 south of the town of Lake George
Ski Area is 22 miles north of Park Rapids, Rt. 4 North

M O N T A N A

BIG SKY

Lone Mountain Ranch
Box 145, Big Sky, MT 59716 (406) 995-4644

AREA INFORMATION

LODGING
Family-style dining, saloon, entertainment
TOURING
Instruction, Telemark skiing, guided tours to
Yellowstone Nat'l Park and the Spanish Peaks
Ski to buffet-on-the-snow lunch, Sundays.
TRAILS
96 km total, 56 km machine-set
TRAVEL
43 miles south of Bozeman, U.S. 191

CRYSTAL LAKES RESORT

Fortine, MT 59918 (406) 882-4455

AREA INFORMATION

LODGING
At the lodge
TOURING
Kootenai Nat'l Forest, Ten Lakes Scenic Area
Some trails loop through winter game range.
Instruction, rentals, maps, mountaineering gear
TRAILS
Groomed trail system
TRAVEL
55 miles from Kalispell, U.S. 93 N.

NORTHERN NORDIC

Box 895, Whitefish, MT 59937 (406) 862-4082

AREA INFORMATION

EVENTS
Citizens' and other races
LODGING
Big Mountain Ski Area or Whitefish
SKI SHOP
Equipment sale and rental
TOURING
Lessons, guided day tours, backpacking
TRAILS
10 km marked and maintained
TRAVEL
15 miles from Whitefish, U.S. 93 North to access road; 70 miles from Elko, B.C.

WOODY CREEK

Box 1044, Cooke City, MT 59020 (406) 838-2305

AREA INFORMATION

LODGING
Watuck Lodge, dining, heated pool, entertainment
TOURING
Northeastern edge of Yellowstone Nat'l Park
Lessons, rentals, guided day and overnight tours
TRAILS
Tracked by use, meadows and mountains
TRAVEL
U.S. 212, 80 miles S.W. of Billings, near Wyoming line

YELLOWSTONE NORDIC

Box 488, West Yellowstone, MT 59758 (406) 646-7319

AREA INFORMATION

LODGING
West Yellowstone
TOURING
Guided tours through Yellowstone National Park, Gallatin National Forest, Lone Mtn. Guest Ranch
TRAILS
300 km marked, 15 km maintained
TRAVEL
90 miles south of Bozeman, U.S. 191, 287

YELLOWSTONE RENDEZVOUS

Box 429, West Yellowstone, MT 59758 (406) 646-7712

AREA INFORMATION

LODGING
West Yellowstone
TOURING
Guided tours through Yellowstone and National Forests
TRAILS
50 km marked, 25 km maintained
U.S. Cross-Country Ski Team training area
TRAVEL
90 miles south of Bozeman, U.S. 191, 287

N E B R A S K A

PONCA STATE PARK

Ponca, NB 68770 (402) 755-2284

AREA INFORMATION

LODGING
South Sioux City
TOURING
830 acres along the Missouri River
TRAILS
14 km
TRAVEL
N.E. Nebraska, 21 miles from South Sioux City

INDIAN CAVE STATE PARK

Barada, NB 68437 (402) 883-2575

AREA INFORMATION

LODGING
Falls City
TOURING
3,000 acres of forest
TRAILS
26 km, 9 Adirondack shelters
TRAVEL
S.E. Nebraska, 19 miles from Falls City
U.S. 159 E., turn north on access road

FORT ROBINSON STATE PARK

Fort Robinson 69339 (308) 665-2660

AREA INFORMATION

LODGING
Crawford
TOURING
31,000 acres of park and federal land
TRAILS
45 km total, 22 km maintained
TRAVEL
N.W. Nebraska, 27 miles from Chadron, U.S. 20

CHADRON STATE PARK

Chadron 69337 (308) 432-2036

AREA INFORMATION

LODGING
In Chadron or at group facility in park
TOURING
840 acres of pine forest
TRAILS
12 km total, 5 km groomed
TRAVEL
11 miles south of Chadron, U.S. 385

N E V A D A

INCLINE NORDIC

Box 488, Carnelian Bay, CA 95711 (702) 831-2700

AREA INFORMATION

LODGING
Incline Village or North Lake Tahoe
TOURING
Geared to beginners, equipment rental
Instruction and weekly guided tours
TRAILS
3.2 km marked and maintained
TRAVEL
Rt. 28, N. Lake Tahoe, 6 miles from CA line

NEW HAMPSHIRE

BALSAMS

Dixville Notch, NH 03576 (603) 255-3400

AREA INFORMATION

ELEVATION
From 1,870 feet
LODGING
Resort Hotel
SKI SHOP
Retail shop, equipment, accessories and clothing
TOURING
15,000 acres, guided tours by appointment
TRAILS
40 km marked, 25 km maintained
TRAVEL
Northern New Hampshire, 41 miles
from Berlin, Rt. 16 N. to Rt. 26 W.

BRETTON WOODS

Bretton Woods, NH 03575 (603) 278-5000

AREA INFORMATION

EVENTS
Citizens' races
LODGING
At Ski Resort, cafeteria, nursery
SKI SHOPS
At the Center, rental, sale and repair
TOURING
10,000 acres and into White Mtn. Nat'l Forest
Instruction, guided tours, overnight camping
Cafe at touring center and tavern on the trails
TRAILS
100 km marked, 66 km maintained
Racing trails included in this system
TRAVEL
23 miles from Littleton, U.S. 302 East

CANNON MOUNTAIN

Franconia, NH 03580 (603) 823-5563

AREA INFORMATION

ELEVATION
2,000 feet

SNOW PHONE 823-7771
TOURING
Franconia Notch State Park, instruction, rental, repair
TRAILS
9 km, not maintained, system combines
Old U.S. 3 and abandoned logging roads
TRAVEL
8 miles from Franconia, I-93 to U.S. 3 South

CHARMINGFARE

South Road, Candia, NH 03034 (603) 483-2307

AREA INFORMATION

EVENTS
Citizens' races
TOURING
Instruction, clinics and ski shop
TRAILS
16 km marked and maintained
Warming shelter at 5 km
TRAVEL
28 miles N.E. of Manchester, Routes 28, 101 B

DEXTER'S INN

Box S, Sunapee, NH 03782 (603) 763-5571

AREA INFORMATION

LODGING
17 rooms, some with bunks
TOURING
450 acres include town's recreation area
Instruction, rental, beginner to expert
TRAILS
19 km marked and maintained
TRAVEL
46 miles from Concord, I-89 N., Rt. 11 W.

EASTMAN TOURING CENTER

Box 53, Grantham, NH 03753 (603) 863-4500

AREA INFORMATION

LODGING
Grantham
TOURING
Harvey's Ski Cap Lounge at tralhead, food & cocktails
Instruction, guided tours and trail system patrol
TRAILS
30 km marked, 20 km maintained
TRAVEL
10 miles from Newport, Rt. 10 N.; I-89, exit 13

FRANCONIA INN

Rt. 116, Franconia, NH 03580 (603) 823-5542

AREA INFORMATION

LODGING
At the Inn, dining
TOURING
System connects with area inns and restaurants.
Guided tours; safeguard, check in and out at Inn
TRAILS
80 km marked, 60 km maintained daily
One trail has a vertical rise of 1,200 feet.
TRAVEL
N.W. New Hampshire, I-93 S. from Littleton, 10 miles

GRAY LEDGES FARM

Grantham, NH 03753 (603) 863-1002

AREA INFORMATION

LODGING
At the farm, motel, bunkhouses, restaurant
TOURING
Woods, orchards, pastureland, logging roads
Instruction, rentals and guided tours
TRAILS
40 km marked, 80 km maintained
TRAVEL
Rt. 10 N. from Newport, 10 miles; I-89, exit 13

GUNSTOCK

Box 336, Laconia, NH 03246 (603) 293-4341

AREA INFORMATION

LODGING
Franklin, Tilton and Laconia
TOURING
Instruction, rentals, sales, repairs, trail maps
TRAILS
15 km marked and maintained , warming hut
TRAVEL
I-93, 20 miles northeast of Franklin

THE INN AT EAST HILL FARM

Troy, NH 03465 (603) 242-6495

AREA INFORMATION

LODGING
At the Inn, meals, indoor pool
RECREATION
Skating, tobogganing, downhill skiing
TOURING
300 acres
TRAILS
11 km groomed
TRAVEL
S.W. part of state, 8 miles from Keene, Rt. 12 S.

JACKSON SKI TOURING FOUNDATION

Box 216, Main St., Jackson, NH 03846 (603) 383-9355

AREA INFORMATION

ELEVATION
700 to 4,000 feet
EVENTS
Citizens' races
LODGING
Inns at Jackson
NURSERY
Babysitting services, call Foundation
RECREATION
Ice skating, indoor swimming and tennis, camping
SEASON
December to April
SNOW PHONE 383-9356
TOURING
Guided tours, instruction, rentals, repairs, junior racing program, workshops, wax and equipment clinics:
Eastern Mountain Sports. 356-5433
The Jack Frost Shop 383-4391
TRAILS
140 km total, 60 km machine-set; system connects with inns, the trails at the base of Mt. Washington and Alpine Areas at Tyrol, Black Mountain and Wildcat Mountain.
TRAVEL
E. Central NH, 8 miles north of Conway, Rt. 16/16 A

LOCH LYME LODGE

Lyme, NH 03768 (603) 795-2141

AREA INFORMATION

LODGING
200 year old farmhouse, meals
RECREATION
Ice fishing, snowshoeing, downhill skiing, 4 miles
TOURING
Over 100 acres including 40 acre lake
Lessons, tours, rentals by reservation
TRAVEL
I-91, exit 14, 13 miles north of I-89 junction

LOON MOUNTAIN

Lincoln, NH 03251 (603) 785-8111

AREA INFORMATION

LODGING
Inn at Loon Mountain, cafeterias, dining room
NURSERY
Alpine Area
TOURING
Logging roads in the White Mountain Preserve
Extended touring into White National Forest
Instruction, guided tours, rentals, waxing clinics
TRAILS
20 km groomed, beginner and intermediate
TRAVEL
I-93, exit 32, 2 miles east

MOOSE MOUNTAIN LODGE

Etna, NH 03750 (603) 643-3529

AREA INFORMATION

ELEVATION
700 to 2,400 feet; the Lodge is at 1,500 feet.
LODGING
At the Lodge, reservations; call for road conditions.
TOURING
For lodge guests; guided tours, instruction, rentals
TRAILS
40 km marked
TRAVEL
I-91 to Hanover, exit 13, 7 miles east

NORSK TOURING CENTER

Rt. 11, New London, NH 03257 (603) 526-6040

AREA INFORMATION

EVENTS
Citizens' races
TOURING
200 acres of wooded and open land
Instruction, ski shop, moonlight tours

TRAILS
30 km marked, 25 km maintained
One-third of trails are for beginners.
TRAVEL
I-89, exit 11 to Rt. 11 E., Lake Sunapee Country Club

POLE & PEDAL TOURING CENTER

Box 327, Henniker, NH 03242 (603) 428-3242

AREA INFORMATION

EVENTS
NASTAR races on 5 km lighted track
TOURING
Proctor Hill, 400 ft. vertical rise
Guided day and overnight tours
TRAILS
20 km marked and maintained, 30 km logging roads
TRAVEL
I-89, exit 5 to U.S. 202 W., 9 miles

SARGENT CAMP

R.F.D. 2, Peterborough, NH 03458 (603) 525-9338

AREA INFORMATION

ELEVATION
950 to 1,100 feet
LODGING
At the camp, meals
TOURING
Lessons, rentals, tours
TRAILS
35 km marked, 15 km maintained
TRAVEL
Southern New Hampshire, near the
junction of U.S. 202 and Route 101

SUMMERS SKI TOURING

Box F, Rt. 101, Dublin, NH 03444 (603) 563-8556

AREA INFORMATION

LODGING
Countryside Lodging 924-3715
The Guest House 563-8561
Knight Homestead 924-3746
TOURING
Instruction and guided tours, advance arrangement
Winter camping is by permit, obtain at Ski Shop.
TRAILS
25 km, 10 km maintained
TRAVEL
Southwestern part of state, ½ mile west of Rt. 137

SUNSET HILL HOUSE

Sugar Hill, NH 03505 (603) 823-5522

AREA INFORMATION

LODGING
At the Lodge, dining; see also "Franconia Inn"
TOURING
Guided tours, night touring
TRAILS
50 km marked, 20 km maintained
Connect with inns in Franconia.
TRAVEL
N.W. part of state, I-93, exit 38, two miles

TEMPLE MOUNTAIN

Rt. 101, Peterborough, NH 03458 (603) 924-6949

AREA INFORMATION

EVENTS
Annual Souhegan Lions Citizens' Race, January
LODGING
In Peterborough
TOURING
Instruction, guided tours, rentals, winter camping
TRAILS
50 km marked, 20 km maintained
Includes Wapack Trail, 36 km at 2,000 feet
TRAVEL
32 miles S.W. of Manchester, Rt. 101

WATERVILLE VALLEY

Box 10, Waterville Valley, NH 03223 (603) 236-8311

AREA INFORMATION

EVENTS
Citizens' races are in February and March; Annual
Fleischmann's Margarine 50 km Marathon, March.
LODGING
Walking distance or free shuttle to Area
RESTAURANTS
At the Center
TOURING
Lessons, guided day and moonlight tours, rental, repair
Eastern Training Center for U.S. Nordic Olympic Team
TRAILS
55 km marked, maintained daily and patrolled
TRAVEL
18 miles from Plymouth, I-93, exit 28, Rt. 49 N.

WATERVILLE VALLEY GATEWAY

Campton, NH 03223 (603) 726-3724

AREA INFORMATION

EVENTS
  NASTAR races
LODGING
  At the Resort, restaurant, cafeteria, nursery
RECREATION
  Sleigh rides, tobogganing, ice skating
TOURING
  Connects with White Mountain National Forest
  Instruction, including freestyle and racing clinics
TRAILS
  34 km marked and maintained
TRAVEL
  I-93, exit 28, Rt. 49 to Upper Mad River Road

WHITE MOUNTAIN COUNTRY CLUB

Ashland, NH 03217 (603) 536-2214

AREA INFORMATION

EVENTS
  Citizens' races, children's competition
LODGING
  In Plymouth, 3 miles
TOURING
  Golf course, woods and meadows
TRAILS
  20 km marked, maintained daily
TRAVEL
  I-93, exit 24, 2 miles

WINDBLOWN

Turnpike Road, New Ipswich, NH 03701 (603) 878-2869

AREA INFORMATION

TOURING
  Rentals, reservations advised, warming hut at 1½ km
TRAILS
  32 km marked, 16 km maintained
TRAVEL
  Southern part of state, Rt. 124, west of U.S. 202

WOLFBORO

The Nordic Skier, Wolfboro, NH 03894 (603) 569-3151

AREA INFORMATION

LODGING
  Wolfboro area
SEASON
  December to April
TOURING
  Lessons, tours, rentals, sales, trail maps
  Network connects with old logging trails
TRAILS
  32 km marked and maintained
TRAVEL
  I-93 to Rt. 11 E., 25 miles past Laconia
  Rt. 109 N. ten miles, 19 N. Main Street

NEW JERSEY

CRAIGMEUR

Newfoundland, NJ 07435 (201) 697-4501

AREA INFORMATION

TOURING
  Instruction, rentals; check in with ski patrol
TRAILS
  3 km marked and maintained; part of
  trails has snowmaking and night skiing.
TRAVEL
  I-80, then 13 miles via Rt. 23 N. and access road

FAIRVIEW LAKE

R.D. 5, Box 210, Newton, NH 07860 (201) 383-9282

AREA INFORMATION

LODGING
  At this YMCA Camp, meals
TOURING
  Ski School, winter survival courses
  Day and overnight tours, rentals
TRAILS
  30 km marked, 15 km maintained
TRAVEL
  17 miles north of I-80 on U.S. 202

VERNON VALLEY/GREAT GORGE

Rt. 94, Vernon, NJ 07462 (201) 827-2000

AREA INFORMATION

LODGING
At Area, Playboy Club or motels
TOURING
Acres of wooded land at Area
Ski school, equipment rental
TRAILS
3 km marked and maintained
TRAVEL
Rt. 94, 6 miles from NY line and Rt. 23

NEW MEXICO

ANGEL FIRE

Drawer B, Angel Fire, NM 87710 (505) 377-2301

AREA INFORMATION

LODGING
Condos at Area
RESTAURANT
At Center
TOURING
Instruction, guided tours, rental and repair
TRAILS
65 km maintained; 5 and 10 km racing tracks
TRAVEL
32 miles S.E. of Taos, U.S. 64 E., Rt. 38 S.

NEW YORK

ADIRONDAK LOJ

Box 867, Lake Placid, NY 12946 (518) 523-3441

AREA INFORMATION

LODGING
At the lodge, meals
TOURING
Instruction, guided tours, rental and repair
TRAILS
320 km
TRAVEL
I-87 to Rt. 73, 8 miles south of Lake Placid

ALPINE RECREATION

298 Ellicott Rd., West Falls, NY 14170 (716) 662-1400

AREA INFORMATION

EVENTS
Cross-country races
LODGING
Orchard Park
TOURING
Lessons, rentals, sales
TRAILS
20 km marked, 15 km maintained frequently
TRAVEL
19 miles south of Buffalo, U.S. 219 to Rt. 240

APPLE BARN

Hanson's Trail North, Latham, NY 12110 (518) 785-0340

AREA INFORMATION

LODGING
Schenectady
TOURING
200 acre apple orchard area; instruction,
cross-country rentals, store and restaurant
TRAILS
11 km marked and maintained
TRAVEL
S.E. of Schenectady, 11 miles via Rt. 7
895 New Loudon Rd., which is U.S. 9

BELLEAYRE

Highmount, NY 12441 (914) 254-5603

AREA INFORMATION

TOURING
Instruction, rentals; hiking trails in the Catskills
TRAILS
Longest loop is 12 km using part of Alpine slopes
TRAVEL
40 miles west of I-87, Kingston exit 19 via Rt. 28

BERESFORD FARMS

R.D. 1, Delanson, NY 12053 (518) 895-2345

AREA INFORMATION

ELEVATION
950 to 1,200 feet

TOURING
800 acres, equipment rental
TRAILS
25 km marked, maintained daily; 3.2 km lighted
TRAVEL
3½ miles from Duanesburg; from U.S. 20 take Rt. 7 W., turn north on Chadwick Rd.

BIG TUPPER

Box 820, Tupper Lake, NY 12986 (518) 359-3651

AREA INFORMATION

LODGING
Tupper Lake
TOURING
Instruction and rentals
TRAILS
22 km marked and maintained
TRAVEL
N. NY, Rt. 30 S., 3 miles from Tupper Lake

CASCADE SKI TOURING CENTER

Box 190, Lake Placid, NY 12946 (518) 523-3374

AREA INFORMATION

TOURING
200 acres; instruction, equipment rental and sales; restaurant and bar at trailhead
TRAILS
10 km marked, groomed; system connects with Mt. Van Hoevenberg trail network
TRAVEL
Northern NY, I-87 to Rt. 73 West, 30 miles

COUNTRY HILLS FARMS

North Road, Tully, NY 13159 (315) 696-8774

AREA INFORMATION

LODGING
Lodge at Center
TOURING
Connects with Meeker Hill Game Preserve
Instruction, equipment rental and sales
TRAILS
40 km marked, 15 km groomed daily
TRAVEL
20 miles south of Syracuse, I-81, exit 14

ERIE BRIDGE INN

R.D. 2, Camden, NY 13316 (315) 245-1555

AREA INFORMATION

LODGING
At the Inn
TOURING
Mad River State Park, 2,000 acres
TRAILS
35 km, night skiing
TRAVEL
22 miles east of I-81, exit 33

GARNET HILL LODGE

North River, NY 12856 (518) 251-2821

AREA INFORMATION

TOURING
Instruction, guided tours, equipment rental
TRAILS
30 km marked, groomed daily; system connects with the bordering state forest's trails, 80 km.
TRAVEL
45 miles from Glens Falls, I-87 N., U.S. 9 N., Rt. 28 W.

GLENS FALLS

Recreation Dept., Glens Falls, NY 12801 (518) 793-5676

AREA INFORMATION

EVENTS
Races Wednesday night
TOURING
In Crandall Park; instruction, guided tours, rentals
TRAILS
10 km groomed frequently; 7 km track lighted
TRAVEL
E. Central NY, I-87, exit 18

GORE MOUNTAIN

Ski Center, North Creek, NY 12853 (518) 251-2411

AREA INFORMATION

LODGING
In North Creek
TOURING
Instruction and rentals

TRAILS
17 km marked, maintained daily
TRAVEL
18 miles west of I-87, exit 25, Routes 8 & 28

INDIAN LAKE

Geaudreau's Ski Touring Center
Box 408, Indian Lake Village, NY 12842 (518) 648-5500

AREA INFORMATION

LODGING
Cabins at resort
TOURING
Adirondack Mountains; instruction, tours, rentals
TRAILS
230 km marked
TRAVEL
38 miles N.W. of I-87, exit 23, Routes 8 & 28

INLET

Ski Touring Center, Inlet, NY 13360 (315) 357-3453

AREA INFORMATION

EVENTS
Annual Adirondack Marathon Citizens' Race, March
TOURING
Instruction, guided tours, rentals
TRAILS
75 km marked, 30 km maintaned daily
System connects with trails on state land
TRAVEL
51 miles from Utica, Routes 12 and 28 North

LAKE MINNEWASKA

Ski Area, Lake Minnewaska, NY 12561 (914) 255-6000

AREA INFORMATION

ELEVATION
1,800 to over 2,000 feet
TOURING
Shawangunk Mountains
TRAILS
244 km marked, 24 km maintained
TRAVEL
S. NY, I-87, New Paltz exit 18, west 12 miles

LAKE PLACID RESORT HOTEL

Lake Placid, NY 12946 (518) 523-3361

AREA INFORMATION

TOURING
1980 Winter Olympics Area
Instruction, guided tours, rentals
TRAILS
19 km marked, 2 shelters, 1 heated
TRAVEL
N. NY, I-87, 34 miles west via Rt. 9N
and Rt. 86; 30 miles west via Rt. 73

MOHONK MOUNTAIN HOUSE

Lake Mohonk, New Paltz, NY 12561 (914) 255-1000

AREA INFORMATION

LODGING
258 rooms, some cottages
TOURING
7,500 acres, equipment rental
TRAILS
86 km marked and maintained
TRAVEL
S. NY, I-87, New Paltz exit 18, west 6 miles

MT. VAN HOEVENBERG

State Dept. of Conservation
50 Wolf Road, Albany, NY 12233 (518) 457-2500

AREA INFORMATION

SKI SHOPS
At Centers and communities nearby
TOURING
2,260,000 acres in Adirondack Park
TRAILS
48 km maintained, also used for racing; system
connects with 1,600 km of backcountry trails
TRAVEL
I-87, exit 30, N.W. 21 miles; exit 34, S.W. 33 miles

90 ACRES SKI CENTER

Route 5, Fayetteville, NY 13066 (315) 637-9023

AREA INFORMATION

TOURING
Instruction, guided tours, rentals and sales
TRAILS
15 km marked and maintained
Lighted trails, warming shelter
TRAVEL
12 miles southeast of Syracuse, Rt. 5

THE NORDIC WAY

8536 Center Rd., Holland, NY 14080 (716) 941-6675

AREA INFORMATION

ELEVATION
1,700 feet
EVENTS
David Noll Memorial Relay, December
American Lung Association Race, February
LODGING
South Wales
RESTAURANT
At the Center, cocktails
TOURING
Instruction, tours, rentals and sales
TRAILS
13 km marked and maintained; warming hut
TRAVEL
35 miles from Buffalo, Routes 400 E. and 16 S.

OMI SKI TOURING CENTER

West Ghent, NY 12075 (518) 828-7007

AREA INFORMATION

TOURING
Instruction, rentals, restaurant and bar
TRAILS
15 km marked and maintained
TRAVEL
10 miles northeast of Hudson, Rt. 66

PALEFACE

Rt. 86, Box 163, Jay, NY 12941 (518) 946-2272

AREA INFORMATION

LODGING
At the Lodge
TOURING
Lessons, rentals, novice and intermediate
Check in and out as a safeguard
TRAILS
40 km maintained
TRAVEL
I-87, exit 34, southwest 16 miles, Rt. 9N

PECHLER'S TRAILS

Shilling Road, Palmyra, NY 14522 (315) 597-4210

AREA INFORMATION

TOURING
400 acres; instruction, tours and rentals
TRAILS
20 km marked, 10 km maintained
TRAVEL
I-90, exit 43, north 7 miles, Rt. 21
Palmyra is southeast of Rochester.

PODUNK

Podunk Rd., Trumansburg, NY 14886 (607) 387-6716

AREA INFORMATION

EVENTS
Citizens' races, Winter Carnival in February
TOURING
Extends into state and federal land
Rentals and sales, guided tours
TRAILS
10 km marked
TRAVEL
10 miles northwest of Ithaca, Rt. 96

SARATOGA MTN.

Saratoga Springs, NY 12866 (518) 584-2008

AREA INFORMATION

LODGING
Gideon Putnam Hotel in Saratoga Park
RACES
NASTAR races, weekends; Saratoga Cup Race, January
Washington's Birthday Race, St. Patrick's Day carnival
TOURING
2,000 acres in Saratoga Park; instruction, clinics, tours
TRAILS
20 km marked and maintained
TRAVEL
South of Saratoga Springs, I-87, exit 13, east 2 miles

SKANEATELES SKI ROSSIGNOL

Rt. 20, Skaneateles, NY 13152 (315) 685-7558

AREA INFORMATION

RESTAURANTS
Within 1 mile of the center; also an inn
TOURING
Two high elevation forest preserves, no steep grades
TRAILS
7 km marked and maintained often
TRAVEL
16 mi. from I-81 at U.S. 20, Lafayette exit
Area operates out of the Sailboat Shop.

SNOW RIDGE

Turin, NY 13473 (315) 348-8456

AREA INFORMATION

LODGING
Numerous in Turin
RESTAURANTS
At the Alpine Area and in Turin
TRAILS
60 km, marked and maintained
TRAVEL
Exit 33, 40 mi. from Utica or
off I-90, 60 mi.

SOJOURN FARM

RD1, Cayuga, NY 13034 (315) 252-1092

AREA INFORMATION

EVENTS
Moonlight tours, citizen races, children's league races on Saturdays, winterfest
LODGE
Full service at area, with shops, repair and rental facilities
RESTAURANTS
With bar and lounge, at the lodge
TOURING
550 acres, 5 drumlins
TRAILS
40 km marked and maintained; 7 km night-skiing
TRAVEL
RD1, 4 mi. N. of Cayuga Lake

STAR LAKE

State University College at Potsdam
SUC Potsdam, NY 13676 (315) 268-3735

AREA INFORMATION

EVENTS
Moonlight skiing, clinics
LODGING
Housing for 90 people
RESTAURANTS
Meals provided with housing
TOURING
Overnight and guided tours and rentals
TRAILS
100 km not maintained, 10 km marked
TRAVEL
From Star Lake Campus, off Hwy. 56, through upper Oswegatchie areas

SWAIN

Swain Ski School, Swain, NY 14884 (607) 545-6511

AREA INFORMATION

LODGING
in town of Hornell
TOURING
Guided tour, Alpine facilities
TRAILS
45km marked, 5 km maintained
TRAVEL
50 mi. S. of Rochester off Hwy. 390

WARD POUND RIDGE

Cross River, NY 10518 (914) 763-3993

AREA INFORMATION

TOURING
Nordic instruction, guided tours
TRAILS
15 km marked, 3 km loop, 32 km unmarked
TRAVEL
Exit 6, Saw Mill River Pkwy. or I684 to Rt. 35

WHITE BIRCHES

Windham, NY 12496 (518) 734-3266

AREA INFORMATION

LODGING
Lodge with rental shop, snack bar, camping
TOURING
400 acres, scenic trails
TRAILS
25.5 km marked, 25.5 km maintained
Machine packed
TRAVEL
Thruway Exit 21, W. on Rt. 23, past junction of Rts. 23 and 296

WILLIAMS LAKE HOTEL

Rosendale, NY 12472 (212) 427-1211

AREA INFORMATION

LODGING
At the hotel
TOURING
Guided tours available
TRAILS
15 km marked and maintained
TRAVEL
N.Y. Thruway I-87, 90 miles from NYC, eight miles off Exit 18

WILLS RUN

Hoffman Rd., Schroon Lake, NY 12870 (518) 532-7936

AREA INFORMATION

LODGING
In Schroon Lake
RESTAURANTS
In Schroon Lake
TOURING
Guided tours, moonlight skiing, ski shop, seminars
TRAILS
32 km. marked, 6 km. maintained, in wilderness area
TRAVEL
I-87 to Exit 27, two hrs. from Albany

NORTH CAROLINA

NANTAHALA OUTDOOR CENTER

Star Rt. Box 68, Bryson Cty., NC 28713 (704) 488-2176

AREA INFORMATION

LODGING
By weekend, week or month
TOURING
Guided tour
TRAILS
Numerous in area along Blue Ridge Pkwy.
TRAVEL
Hwy. 19 from Bryson City

NORTH DAKOTA

STATE PARK

GRAND FORKS

Villa Vista Area, Grand Forks, ND 58201 (701) 594-4234

AREA INFORMATION

LODGING
In Grand Forks
RECREATION
Ice skating, snowmobiling, tubing, tobogganing
TOURING
At Alpine Area
TRAVEL
22 miles west of Grand Forks, Route 2

STATE PARK

MINOT

Trestle Valley Ski Area, Minot, ND 58701 (701) 839-5321

AREA INFORMATION

RECREATION
Ice fishing, indoor tennis, curling
SEASON
December to March
TOURING
Instruction, rental and repair
TRAILS
16 km
TRAVEL
11 miles from Minot, off U.S. 52 N.

LAKE METIGOSHE STATE PARK

c/o Parks and Recreation Dept.
Box 139, Mandan, ND 58554 (701) 663-9571

AREA INFORMATION

LODGING
For groups in Park by reservation, and in Bottineau
SNOW PHONE . . . . (800) 437-2077
In North Dakota . . . . (800) 472-2100
TRAILS
Small network, rangers on duty
TRAVEL
N. Central part of state, Rt. 5 W. from Bottineau, 1½ miles to access road, then north two miles

TURTLE RIVER STATE PARK

c/o Parks and Recreation Dept.
Box 139, Mandan, ND 58554 (701) 663-9571

AREA INFORMATION

LODGING
Grand Forks
TRAILS
Small network, rangers on duty
TRAVEL
Near Villa Vista Ski Area, 21 miles from Grand Forks via Route 2 West

O H I O

TOWNER'S WOODS

County Park Dept., Ravenna, OH 44266 (216) 678-8851

AREA INFORMATION

EVENTS
Annual Towner's Woods Citizens' Race, January
TOURING
175 acres, lessons, night tours
TRAILS
10 km marked and maintained
TRAVEL
15 miles from Akron, I-77 S., Routes 619 & 43

O R E G O N

MT. BACHELOR

Box 828, Bend, OR 97701 (503) 382-2442

AREA INFORMATION

EVENTS
NASTAR and Citizens' races every 2 weeks
TOURING
Deschutes Nat'l Forest, Three Sisters Wilderness Area; instruction, tours, equipment rental, sales
Overnight camping is permitted in parking area.
TRAILS
22 km marked and double-tracked; trail system patrolled daily; Nat'l Patrol, weekends in forest
TRAVEL
U.S. 20 or 97 to Bend, then 22 miles east

ODELL LAKE LODGE

Box 72, Crescent Lake, OR 97425 (503) 433-2540

AREA INFORMATION

LODGING
Cabins, small hotel; dormitory, need sleeping bag
TOURING
Extends into Diamond Peak Wilderness Area
Instruction and equipment rental
TRAILS
50 km marked, 20 km maintained
TRAVEL
70 miles S.E. of Springfield, I-5 & Rt. 58

SUN RIVER

Nordic Center, Sunriver, OR 97701 (503) 593-1221

AREA INFORMATION

LODGING
At the Resort, restaurants, lounge, dancing
TOURING
In the Deschutes National Forest
Instruction, equipment rental, sales
Unplowed fire roads, 200 km
TRAILS
30 km marked, 10 km maintained
TRAVEL
U.S. 20 or 97 to Bend, then 8 miles west on Mt. Bachelor access road, turn south, 9 miles

TELEMARK CROSS-COUNTRY

3735 N.E. Shaver St., Portland, OR 97212 (503) 281-9030

AREA INFORMATION

SNOW PHONE 272-3427
TOURING
At Mt. Hood, lessons, guided tours
Equipment rentals, overnight camping
TRAILS
100 km marked
TRAVEL
50 miles from Portland, U.S. 26 to access road
Bus transportation, weekends by reservation

TIMBERLINE LODGE

Government Camp, OR 97028 (503) 272-3311

AREA INFORMATION

ELEVATION
From 4,000 feet
LODGING
At the Area, restaurant
TOURING
Lessons, telemark skiing, rentals and repairs
TRAILS
110 km marked
TRAVEL
68 miles from Portland, U.S. 26 to access road

PENNSYLVANIA

APPLE VALLEY

R.D. 1, Zionsville, PA 18092 (215) 697-9360

AREA INFORMATION

LODGING
Near Area
TOURING
Woods and fields, view from High Point
Lessons, rentals, equipment rental, sales
TRAILS
8 km marked, heated lodge at trailhead
TRAVEL
Off Hwy. 9, 12 miles south of Allentown

BLUE KNOB

Box 344, Claysburg, PA 16625 (814) 239-5106

AREA INFORMATION

TOURING
Flat to steep inclines; guided tours, rentals
TRAILS
20 km marked, warming hut, enclosed picnic area
TRAVEL
17 miles south of Altoona, U.S. 220

CRYSTAL LAKE CAMPS

R.D. 1, Hughesville, PA 17737 (717) 584-2698

AREA INFORMATION

LODGING
At Center by reservation
TOURING
Instruction, guided tours, rentals
TRAILS
24 km marked and maintained
Adirondack shelter at 3.2 km
TRAVEL
29 miles west of Williamsport via U.S. 220
Seven miles north of Tivoli on access road

HIDDEN VALLEY

R.D. 4, Somerset, PA 15501 (814) 455-6014

AREA INFORMATION

EVENTS
Citizens' races
LODGING
At the Area, meals
TOURING
Laurel Highlands, Moonlight tours, waxing clinics
TRAILS
50 km marked, 30 km maintained daily
TRAVEL
S.W. part of state, I-70/76 Turnpike to Somerset

INN AT STARLIGHT LAKE

Starlight, PA 18461 (717) 798-2519

AREA INFORMATION

LODGING
At the Inn, meals
TOURING
Woods near Delaware River, lakes
Instruction, guided tours, rentals
TRAILS
29 km marked, 24 km maintained
TRAVEL
N.E. PA, Rt. 370, 5 miles south of Hancock, NY

POCONO CROSS-COUNTRY

Pocono 500 Ski Lodge, Reeders, PA 18352 (717) 629-4443

AREA INFORMATION

LODGING
At the Lodge
TOURING
Pocono Mountains, 400 acres, woods and fields
Private and group instruction, equipment rental
TRAILS
10 km marked and maintained daily
TRAVEL
11 miles west of Stroudsburg, I-80, 115 S.

TANGLWOOD

Lake Wallenpaupack, Tafton, PA 18464 (717) 226-9500

AREA INFORMATION

EVENTS
Citizens' races
LODGING
At Alpine Area
NURSERY
Babysitting
TOURING
Instruction, day and moonlight tours
TRAILS
15 km marked and maintained
TRAVEL
36 miles from Scranton, I-81 N.E. to I-380 W.
I-84, exit 7, north to access road near Tafton

TIADAGHTON STATE FOREST

Pennsylvania Bureau of Forestry
South Williamsport, PA 17701 (717) 326-3576

AREA INFORMATION

ELEVATION
Around 2,000 feet
TOURING
On a plateau, old railroad beds and logging roads
TRAILS
60 km marked
TRAVEL
29 miles north of Williamsport, Route 14

WILDERNESS LODGE

R.D. 2, Wattsburg, PA 16442 (814) 739-2946

AREA INFORMATION

EVENTS
Citizens' races
LODGING
At the lodge, meals
TOURING
Tours, ski shop
TRAILS
40 km marked and maintained
TRAVEL
18 miles south of Erie, Routes 8 & 89

SOUTH DAKOTA

DEER MOUNTAIN

Box 622, Deadwood, SD 57732 (605) 584-3230

AREA INFORMATION

TOURING
Black Hills, instruction, rentals
TRAILS
20 km marked, 10 km maintained; system connects with other trails in the Black Hills
TRAVEL
55 miles from Rapid City, I-90 North to Sturgis exit, U.S. 14 A to Deadwood

TERRY PEAK

136 Sherman St., Deadwood, SD 57732 (605) 578-1501

AREA INFORMATION

LODGING
Near Ski Area
TOURING
Black Hills, instruction, rentals and repair
TRAILS
4.8 km marked and maintained; system connects with other Black Hills trails
TRAILS
53 miles from Rapid City, I-90 North to Sturgis exit, U.S. 14 A to Deadwood

U T A H

BRIAN HEAD

Box 30, Brian Head, UT 84719 (801) 586-8825

AREA INFORMATION

LODGING
At the Area, restaurants
TOURING
Dixie National Forest, instruction, rentals, sales
Day and overnight tours, Guides for extended trips
TRAILS
15 km marked, 10 km packed
TRAVEL
S.W. Utah, I-15, exit 70, east of Summit

BRIGHTON SKI TOURING CENTER

Brighton, UT 84121 (801) 649-9156

AREA INFORMATION

LODGING
At the Area, dining room, state liquor store
TOURING
Tours of Wasatch Mountains, powder bowls
Instruction, all ages; downhill cross-country
Racing and Telemark clinics, rentals
TRAILS
50 km marked, 20 km maintained
TRAVEL
35 miles from Salt Lake City, I-80 E.
Eight miles southwest of Park City

BRYCE CANYON NATIONAL PARK

Bryce Canyon, UT 84717 (801) 834-5233

AREA INFORMATION

TOURING
56 square miles, no facilities or rentals
TRAILS
102 km marked, not maintained
Register with Nat'l Park Service
TRAVEL
S.W. Utah, U.S. 89 to Rt. 12; Panguitch, 24 miles

CEDAR BREAKS NATIONAL MONUMENT

Box 749, Cedar City, UT 84720 (801) 586-9451

AREA INFORMATION

LODGING
At Brian Head Ski Area
TOURING
On 8 km park road closed to motor vehicles
Instruction and rentals at the Brian Head Area
TRAVEL
Southwest Utah, I-15 to the Cedar City exit,
Routes 14 & 143, 4 miles from Brian Head

SNOWBIRD

Ski Resort, Snowbird, UT 84070 (801) 742-2222

AREA INFORMATION

LODGING
At the Resort, restaurants, lounges
TOURING
Red Pine, White Pine and Cottonwood Canyons
Nordic skiing on Alpine slopes, use of chairlifts
Instruction, guided tours, rentals, sales
TRAILS
Marked trail system joining with Brighton & Park City
TRAVEL
26 miles S.E. of Salt Lake City, I-80, I-215 S.
to Route 210, one mile from Alta

SNOW BASIN

Ogden, UT 84404 (801) 392-3911

AREA INFORMATION

LODGING
In Ogden
TOURING
Limited, Cross-country lessons
TRAILS
12 km marked
TRAVEL
Northern Utah, I-15 to 12th St. exit in Ogden, continue to Ogden Canyon, signs posted

WHITE PINE

Box 417, Park City, UT 84060 (801) 649-8701

AREA INFORMATION

EVENTS
Weekly citizens' races
TOURING
Lessons, include instruction in Nordic downhill, Telemark, racing, winter survival, avalanche safety. Day tours in the Wasatch Mountains, extended touring in the Uinta Mountains
TRAILS
5 km marked and maintained daily
TRAVEL
27 miles from Salt Lake City, I-80 East

V E R M O N T

BLUEBERRY HILL

Goshen, VT 05733 (802) 247-6735

AREA INFORMATION

LODGING
At the Inn, meals
TOURING
Green Mountains, Power Co. & Nat'l Forest land
Instruction, guided tours, equipment rental, sales
TRAILS
60 km maintained daily; 2 shelters on trails
TRAVEL
W. Central VT, U.S. 7 to Rt. 73, 5 miles

BOLTON VALLEY

Bolton, VT 05477 (802) 434-2131

AREA INFORMATION

LODGING
Full service lodging at the resort, Shops, food stores, motels nearby
RESTAURANTS
With entertainment, full meals, numerous nearby, and at resort
TOURING
Full service touring area
TRAILS
45 km marked and groomed, access to Stowe via trail
TRAVEL
Rt. 93 to Exit 10 from Boston, Rt. 89 W. to ski area

BURKE MOUNTAIN

East Burke, VT 05832 (802) 626-3305

AREA INFORMATION

ELEVATION
1,200 feet
EVENTS
Citizen's races, carnival
LODGINGS
At the mountain and in nearby towns
RESTAURANTS
Lodge has cafeteria, lounge. Numerous restaurants nearby in East Burke and Lyndonville
TOURING
Lear to Ski available
TRAILS
52km marked and maintained, Through varying countryside
TRAVEL
7 miles off I-91, Exit 24 to Rt. 114

BURKLYN SKI TOURING CENTER

East Burke, VT 05832 (800)451-4163, (802) 626-9332

AREA INFORMATION

EVENTS
Burklyn Stampede, USSA Nordic qualifier, Burklyn Cup Series

BURKLYN CONT.

RESTAURANTS
Tavern at area
TOURING
Guided moonlight tours, instruction
TRAILS
50 km marked and maintained, all levels of ability
TRAVEL
N.E. Vermont, access via Hwy. 21 to 114

CHURCHILL HOUSE

RFD 3, Brandon, VT 05733 (802) 247-3300

AREA INFORMATION

EVENTS
League races, American Ski Marathon, Triathlon
LODGING
At Churchill House Inn
RESTAURANTS
At the Inn, to go lunches also
TOURING
Lessons, guided tours, night skiing
TRAILS
40 km marked, 20 km maintained
TRAVEL
Exit 4 off I-89 West

CORTINA INN

Killington, VT 05751 (802) 773-3331

AREA INFORMATION

LODGING
At the Inn; also rentals
RESTAURANTS
At the inn, with lounge
TOURING
Instruction, guided tours
TRAILS
40 km marked, 25 km maintained
TRAVEL
Rt. 4, 7 miles E. of Rutland

CRAFTSBURY CENTER

Box 56, Craftsbury Common, VT 05827 (802) 586-2514

AREA INFORMATION

LODGING
Dorms, cottage, apts, sauna
RESTAURANTS
Family meals at area
TOURING
Racing clinics, coaching
TRAILS
30 km marked, 30 km maintained, 140 acres
TRAVEL
8 miles N. of Rt. 14 from Hardwick

EDSON HILL

RR 1, Eson Hill Rd., Stowe, VT 05672 (802) 253-7371

AREA INFORMATION

LODGING
At Edson Hill Manor and in nearby Stowe
RESTAURANTS
Lunches at the manor
TOURING
Ski instruction, equipment rentals, ski shop
TRAILS
60 km marked, 30 km maintained, through various countryside, 400 acres
TRAVEL
From Burlington, Hwy. 89 E. to Rt. 100 N.

GREEN MOUNTAIN TOURING

Randolph, VT 05060 (802) 728-5575

AREA INFORMATION

LODGING
At the area, with sauna
RESTAURANT
Meals at the lodge
TOURING
Guided tours, night skiing
TRAILS
35 km marked and maintained
TRAVEL
I-89, 2 mi. from Exit 4

GREEN TRAILS

Brookfield, VT 05036 (802) 276-2012

AREA INFORMATION

EVENTS
Tobogganing, sledding
LODGING
Apartments at area
RESTAURANTS
At the area
TOURING
Looping system over lakes and various terrain
TRAILS
25 km marked
TRAVEL
Exit 4, 7 miles from I-89, South of Montpelier

HAZEN'S NOTCH

Montgomery Center, VT 05471 (802) 326-5708

AREA INFORMATION

EVENTS
Cross country race, Pig Roast in late March
LODGING
Day lodge with rentals, also in Montgomery Center
TOURING
Instruction, guided tours, night tours
TRAILS
32 km marked and maintained
TRAVEL
Access via Rt. 58, Rt. 242, Northermonst VT

HIGHLAND LODGE

Greensboro, VT 05841 (802) 533-2647

AREA INFORMATION

LODGING
At the lodge, plus cottages
RESTAURANT
Food at the lodge
TOURING
Guided tours, rentals
TRAILS
45km marked 35 km maintained
TRAVEL
Eight miles off Rt. 15

MOUNTAIN MEADOWS

100 Thundering Brook Rd.
Killington, VT 05751 (802) 775-7077, 775-1010

AREA INFORMATION

EVENTS
Citizen's races
LODGING
At tthe lodge, also repairs and rentals
TOURING
Guided tours, moonlight racing
TRAILS
40 km marked, 25 km maintained
TRAVEL
East of Rutland, central Vermont, near junction of U.S. 4 and U.S. 100

MOUNTAIN TOP

Chittenden, VT 05737 (802) 483-2311

AREA INFORMATION

ELEVATION
2,200 feet
LODGING
At Killington or in Rutland
RESTAURANT
At the Mountain Top Inn
TOURING
Night skiing, group tours through variable terrain
TRAILS
91 km marked, 25 km maintained, racing camp
TRAVEL
7 miles away is Rt. 7 and 4

MT. ASCUTNEY

Rt. 44, Brownsville, VT 05037 (802) 484-7711

AREA INFORMATION

LODGING
Nearby, within six miles
TOURING
Connecting trails
TRAILS
8 km marked
TRAVEL
Exit 8 off I-91

MT. MANSFIELD

Stowe, VT 05672 (802) 253-7311

AREA INFORMATION

EVENTS
NASTAR racing
LODGING
Numerous in nearby Stowe
RESTAURANTS
Numerous in nearby Stowe,
Meals and drinks at the center
TOURING
Full service area, rentals, instruction,
class lessons
TRAILS
50 km marked, 25 km maintained
TRAVEL
7.5 miles W. of Stowe via Hwy. 108

NORDIC INN

Rt. 11, Landgrove, VT 05148 (802) 824-6444

AREA INFORMATION

LODGING
At Bromley, Stratton area, nearby
Also at the Inn, Rt. 11
RESTAURANTS
At Bromley, Stratton area, nearby
TOURING
Instruction, rentals, EPSTI instruction
TRAILS
30 km marked and maintained
TRAVEL
14 mi. from Manchester, Rt. 11

OKEMO

RFD 1, Ludlow, VT 05149 (802) 228-4041

AREA INFORMATION

LODGING
Available one mile from the area, in Ludlow
RESTAURANTS
In Ludlow
TOURING
Guided tours
TRAILS
10 km marked and maintained
TRAVEL
Rt. 103, Ludlow

OLE'S CROSS-COUNTRY CENTER

Warren, VT 05674 (802) 496-3430

AREA INFORMATION

LODGING
In Sugarbush
RESTAURANTS
One at the area
TOURING
Lessons; area caters to beginners
TRAILS
35 km marked, 25 km maintained
TRAVEL
At Sugarbush airport, Mad River Valley

ON THE ROCKS

Wilmington, VT 05363 (802) 464-8364

AREA INFORMATION

LODGE
At the area, equipment rentals
RESTAURANT
At the lodge, patio dining
TOURING
Group tour, mountain climbing, night skiing
TRAILS
55 km marked, 30 km maintained
TRAVEL
Green Mountains, Off Hwy. 9, S'W' Vermont

GRE Green Mountain, Off Hwy. 9, S.W. Vermont

RABBIT HILL

Lower Waterford, VT 05848 (802) 748-5168

AREA INFORMATION

LODGING
Inn at area
RESTAURANTS
At the Inn
TOURING
EPSTI instruction, rentals
TRAILS
20 km marked, 5 km maintained
TRAVEL
Rt. 18, outside St. Johnsbury

SNOW VALLEY

Londonderry, VT 05148 (201) 622-2800

AREA INFORMATION

LODGING
Base lodge, and in Bromley, Stratton
RESTAURANTS
In nearby Bromley, Stratton
TOURING
Instruction, rentals, Alpine facilities
TRAILS
20 km marked and maintained
TRAVEL
Winhall, 1 mile fr. Rt. 30

STRATTON

Stratton Mtn., VT 05155 (802) 297-2200

AREA INFORMATION

EVENTS
NASTAR racing yearly
LODGING
Full service resort, Bromley is 10 miles away
RESTAURANTS
At most lodgings and nearby
TOURING
Rentals, nightime skiing, certified instruction
TRAILS
32 km marked, 8 km maintained
TRAVEL
I-91 to Rt. 30

SUNSHINE

Rt. 242, Jay, VT 05859 (802) 988-4459

AREA INFORMATION

LODGING
In the Jay area
RESTAURANTS
In the Jay area
TOURING
Trails through variable terrain,
clinics, citizens' races
TRAILS
65 km marked, 25 km maintained
TRAVEL
Off Rt. 242, off I-91

THE HERMITAGE

Coldbrook Rd., Wilmington VT 05363 (802) 464-3759

AREA INFORMATION

LODGING
Fuest rooms at the Inn
Guest rooms at the Inn
RESTAURANT
At the Inn
TOURING
Group tours, guided
TRAILS
32 km marked, mostly maintained
TRAVEL
Exit 9 off Hwy. I-91

TOPNOTCH

Mountain Rd., Stowe, VT 05672 (802) 253-8585

AREA INFORMATION

LODGING
In Stowe, full service
RESTAURANTS
Warm drinks & snacks at warming hut,
Full service restaurants in Stowe
TOURING
Full service, guided tours, ski shop
TRAILS
65 km marked, 45 km maintained
TRAVEL
Exit 10, I-89

TRAPP FAMILY LODGE

Stowe, VT 05672 (802) 253-8511

LODGING
At the lodge and full service in Stowe
RESTAURANTS
At the lodge and in Stowe
TOURING
Instruction, beginner and super advanced skiing,
ski shop, rentals
TRAILS
100 km marked, 50 km maintained
TRAVEL
2 miles from Stowe, Exit 10 off I-89

VIKING SKI TOURING CENTRE

Little Pond Rd., Londonderry, VT 05148 (802) 824-3933

AREA INFORMATION

LODGING
Contact Manchester C. of C. (, Manchester, VT 05255
RESTAURANTS
Breakfast and lunch, wine and beer
TOURING
All levels of skiing, ski shop, night skiing and night races
TRAILS
35 km marked, 25 km maintained
TRAVEL
Green Mountain National Forest, outside of Manchester, via Hwy. 7

WILD WINGS

Peru, VT 05152 (802) 824-6793

AREA INFORMATION

LODGING
Numerous nearby
RESTAURANTS
Numerous nearby
TOURING
certified instruction, rental equipment, for all levels of skiers
TRAILS
14 km marked, 11 km maintained
TRAVEL
Exit 6 off I-91

WOODSTOCK

Woodstock, VT 05091 (802) 457-1100

AREA INFORMATION

LODGING
At Suicide Six, and at Woodstock Inn
RESTAURANTS
Full service at Suicide Six
TOURING
instruction, rental equipment, tours
TRAILS
70 km marked, 40 km maintained
TRAVEL
Rt. 106, S. of Woodstock Inn, or I-89 to Rt. 4 to Rt. 12 N. to Suicide Six

V I R G I N I A

MT. ROGERS RECREATION AREA

Appalachian Outfitters
Rt. 3, Box 7A, Salem, VA 24153 (703) 389-1056

TOURING
One marked trail, 20 miles of uncharter skiing in Jefferson National Forest.
TRAVEL
South of I-81

W A S H I N G T O N

ADVENTURE CHALET

P.O. Box 312, Leavenworth, WA 98826 (509) 548-7330

AREA INFORMATION

LODGING
At the lodge, in cabins
RESTAURANT
At the chalet
TOURING
Instruction, rentals
TRAILS
55 km marked, 12 km maintained
TRAVEL
Off Hwy. 2, Leavenworth

BATNUNI LAKE RESORT

1628 Ninth Ave., Seattle, WA 98101 (206) 622-6074

AREA INFORMATION

LODGING
Cabins at area
RESTAURANT
Meals served family style
TOURING
85 km unmarked trails for experienced skiers
TRAVEL
In Cariboo District, contact the resort office for instructions

THE CROSS-COUNTRY CENTER

Snoqualmie Pass, WA 98068 (206) 434-6503

AREA INFORMATION

TOURING
Training clinics, instructions for visually handicapped
TRAILS
25 km marked

TRAVEL
Snoqualmie Pass, Off Hwy. 2 at the Cascade Range

DUCK CREEK SKI TOURING

Box 356, Cedar City, UT 84720 (801) 648-2495

AREA INFORMATION

RESTAURANT
At the Meadowview Lodge
TOURING
Day and overnight
TRAILS
Unmarked
TRAVEL
Hwy. 14 to 30 mi. E. of Cedar City

MOUNT RANIER

Star Route, Ashwood, WA 98304 (206) 569-2343

AREA INFORMATION

LODGING
Campgrounds
RESTAURANTS
At Longmire Campground
TOURING
5 km marked, instruction, rentals
TRAVEL
State Hwy. 706 btwn. State Hwy. 7 & Hwy. 12

MOUNTAINHOLM

The Ski Rack
2126 Westlake Ave., Seattle, WA 98121 (206) 623-5595

AREA INFORMATION

LODGING
In Easton, nearest town
RESTAURANTS
At the lodge
TOURING
Night skiing, instruction, rentals
TRAILS
15 marked
TRAVEL
I-90 Exit 70

SUN MOUNTAIN LODGE

P.O. Box 1000, Winthrop, WA 98862 (509) 996-2211

AREA INFORMATION

LODGING
At lodge, call ahead
RESTAURANTS
At the lodge
TOURING
Certified instruction, group and private
TRAILS
75 km marked, 35 km maintained
TRAVEL
98 miles N. of Winatchee, near U.S. Hwy. 97

WEST VIRGINIA

MONONGAHELA NATIONAL FOREST

SPRUCE KNOB

U.S. Forest Service District Ranger
Petersburg, WV 26847 (304) 257-4488

AREA INFORMATION

ELEVATION
4,863 feet
TOURING
From Laneville Wildlife Cabin, straight up

SOUTHWEST NATIONAL FOREST AREA

U.S. Forest Service District Ranger
Box 110, Richwood, WV 26261 (304) 846-6558

AREA INFORMATION

LODGING
In city of Richwood
TOURING
Restricted Traffic
TRAILS
35 km unmarked roads
TRAVEL
At U.S. Hwy. 33 and State Hwy. 18

SNOWSHOE

Slatyfork, WV 26291 (304) 799-6630

AREA INFORMATION

LODGING
2 cabins at area, lodge on mountain top
RESTAURANTS
Dining room, cafeteria at lodge
TOURING
Charlift down
TRAILS
31 km marked, 31 km maintained
TRAVEL
White Sulphur Springs exit off I-64,
65 miles East

TRANSMONTANE

Box 325, Davis, WV 26260 (304) 259-5117

AREA INFORMATION

LODGING
At area
TOURING
Multiple day excursions
TRAILS
Through Monongahela National Forest,
High altitudes
TRAVEL
E. Panhandle, Monongahela Forest

W I S C O N S I N

ANVIL LAKE TRAILS

Chamber of Commerce
Eagle River, Wisconsin 54521 (715) 479-4026

AREA INFORMATION

LODGING
Eagle River
TOURING
Instruction
TRAILS
45 km, all levels, 1 very difficult expert trail
Heated cabin and warming shelter
TRAVEL
N. Wisconsin, 9 miles east of Eagle River, Rt. 70

BLACKHAWK RIDGE

Box 92, Sauk City, WI 53583 (608) 643-3775

AREA INFORMATION

LODGING
Cabins at Center
TOURING
650 acres of forest land and meadows
Instruction, rentals, snack bar
TRAILS
60 km marked, 25 km maintained
5 km lighted, warming shelter
TRAVEL
28 miles N.W. of Madison, U.S. 12

BLACK RIVER STATE FOREST

Rt. 4, Box 5, Black River Falls, WI 54615 (715) 284-5301

AREA INFORMATION

TOURING
Camping permitted along trail system
TRAILS
22 km marked and groomed; shelter at 4 km
Picnic facilities, restrooms
TRAVEL
60 miles S.E. of Eau Claire, I-94, Millston exit 128

CHANTICLEER INN

Rt. 3, Eagle River, WI 54521 (715) 479-4486

AREA INFORMATION

LODGING
At the Inn
TOURING
Nicolet National Forest, Eagle Chain of lakes
Instruction, rentals and sales
TRAILS
7 km marked and maintained
TRAVEL
N.E. Wisconsin, 3 miles from junction of
U.S. 45 and Route 17

CONSOLIDATED TRAILS

Box 50, Wisconsin Rapids, WI 54494 (715) 422-3956

AREA INFORMATION

TOURING
3 sections of land owned by Consolidated Papers, Inc.
TRAILS
Biron, 60 acres of forest land, mapped
Manitowish Waters, mapped
Monico, 8 km, beginner to intermediate
TRAVEL
Biron, 5 miles N.E. of Wisconsin Rapids
Manitowish Waters, N.E. WI, U.S. 51
Monico, N.E. WI at U.S. 8 & 45

COPPER FALLS STATE PARK

County Chamber of Commerce
111 W. Front St., Ashland, WI 54806 (715) 682-2500

AREA INFORMATION

TOURING
Bad River Gorge, no ski patrol
TRAILS
Marked hiking trails
TRAVEL
N. WI, 3 miles north of Mellen, Rt. 169

EAGLE RIVER NORDIC

Box 936, Eagle River, WI 54521 (715) 479-7285

AREA INFORMATION

EVENTS
Citizens' races
LODGING
Northernaire Lodge, meals
SEASON
Late November to March
TOURING
Instruction, guided tours, rentals
TRAILS
70 km marked, 50 km maintained
TRAVEL
15 miles from Eagle River, Rt. 70 East

EGG HARBOR LODGE

Box 57, Egg Harbor, WI 54209 (414) 868-3115

AREA INFORMATION

LODGING
At the Lodge, meals
TOURING
Overlooks Green Bay, instruction, rentals, sales
TRAILS
Novice trail connects with 10 km trail
at Egg Harbor; marked and groomed.
TRAVEL
60 miles N.W. of Green Bay, Routes 57 & 42 N.

FOX HILLS INN

Box 129, Mishicot, WI 54228 (414) 755-2376

AREA INFORMATION

LODGING
At the Inn, dining room
TOURING
Fox Hills and Point Beach State Forest
TRAILS
15 km marked and maintained
TRAVEL
E. WI, 8 miles N.W. of Two Rivers, Rt. 147

GERBICK LAKE TRAIL

Birkensee Resort, Tomahawk, WI 55487 (715) 453-5103

AREA INFORMATION

LODGING
Cottages, meals
TOURING
Connects with Otter Run Trail, rentals
TRAILS
40 km maintained
TRAVEL
U.S. 51 north of Merrill to Tomahawk,
turn east onto access route, 7 miles

GREENBUSH AREA

Dept. of Natural Resources
Box 426, Campbellsport, WI 53010 (414) 626-2116

AREA INFORMATION

LODGING
In Plymouth
TOURING
Kettle Moraine State Forest, unheated shelters, restrooms, no rentals or lessons
TRAILS
18 km and 40 km hiking trail marked
TRAVEL
21 miles north of West Bend, U.S. 45 to Dundee turnoff, 5 miles past Dundee

HOOFBEAT RIDGE

Rt. 2, Mazomanie, WI 53560 (608) 767-3667

AREA INFORMATION

LODGING
The Hoofroof, 40 with sleeping bags, warm clothing; cabin for six at 12 km
TOURING
Instruction and rentals, lounge
TRAILS
32 km marked and maintained
TRAVEL
26 miles N.E. of Madison, U.S. 14

MT. HARDSCRABBLE

Rice Lake, WI 54868 (715) 234-3412

AREA INFORMATION

LODGING
Rice Lake, 5 miles
TOURING
Lessons, rentals, cafeteria
TRAILS
16 km
TRAVEL
68 miles from Eau Claire, U.S. 53 North to County Rd. C East

MT. LA CROSSE

La Crosse, WI 54601 (608) 788-0044

AREA INFORMATION

LODGING
La Crosse
TOURING
Instruction, rentals, sales
TRAILS
10 km marked and maintained
TRAVEL
6 miles south of La Crosse, U.S. 14 at Rt. 35

NEWMAN SPRINGS TRAIL

Chequamegon National Forest
Box 280, Park Falls, WI 54552 (715) 762-2461

AREA INFORMATION

TRAILS
2.5, 4 and 5.5 km, well-marked and mapped
TRAVEL
Route 13 & 182, 12 miles east of Park Falls

NEWPORT STATE PARK

Ellison Bay, WI 54210 (414) 854-2500

AREA INFORMATION

LODGING
Ellison Bay
TOURING
2,000 acres, 12 km lakeshore, 13 campsites
TRAILS
32 km
TRAVEL
84 miles N.W. of Green Bay, Routes 57 & 42

OLYMPIA RESORT

Oconomowoc, WI 53066 (414) 567-0311

AREA INFORMATION

LODGING
Hotel and condos
RECREATION
Swimming and tennis
TOURING
400 acres, instruction, rentals
TRAILS
12 km
TRAVEL
26 miles from Milwaukee, I-94 & Rt. 16 West

OLYMPIA SPORT VILLAGE

Box 3, Upson, WI 54565 (715) 561-4427

AREA INFORMATION

LODGING
Heated cabins
TOURING
Wilderness touring in the Penokee Range
TRAILS
45 km, marked and maintained
TRAVEL
N. WI, U.S. 2 or 51 to Rt. 77 to Upson, 5 miles south on access road

OMNIBUS

Fish Creek, WI 54212 (414) 868-3013

AREA INFORMATION

LODGING
Races weekends
LODGING
Fish Creek
TOURING
Lessons, including instruction for certification
TRAILS
35 km marked and maintained
TRAVEL
61 miles from Green Bay, Routes 57 & 42

OTTER RUN TRAILS

Lincoln County Resources Agency
Merrill, WI 54452 (715) 536-7151

AREA INFORMATION

LODGING
Merrill and Tomahawk
TOURING
Rentals, camping
TRAILS
25.5 km
TRAVEL
From Merrill, U.S. 51 N. to Tomahawk, east on County Rd. D, Town Hall and Grundy Roads

PENINSULA STATE PARK

Fish Creek, WI 54212 (414) 868-3258

AREA INFORMATION

LODGING
Fish Creek
TOURING
3,700 acres of wooded area and beach, camping
TRAILS
Marked and maintained, warming hut
TRAVEL
64 miles from Green Bay, Routes 57 & 42

PIKE LAKE STATE PARK

Expedition Supply, Hartford, WI 53027 (414) 673-7313

AREA INFORMATION

TOURING
Equipment, trail map at Expedition Supply
TRAILS
8 km marked, mapped
TRAVEL
29 miles from Milwaukee, U.S. 41 N., Rt. 60 W.

PORT MOUNTAIN

P.O. Box 99, Bayfield, WI 54814 (715) 779-3227

AREA INFORMATION

LODGING
Condominiums at area
TOURING
Area has adjacent lifts
TRAILS
24 km marked and maintained
TRAVEL
N. on Hwy. 2 between Ashalnd and Bayfield

TELEMARK

Telemark Lodge, Cable, WI 54821 (715) 798-3811

AREA INFORMATION

EVENTS
NASTAR races, Gitchi Gami Games
LODGING
Lodge at area with pool, saunas, jacuzzi,
More lodging in Cable, Hayward and Lake Owen

RESTAURANTS
Full service at the lodge, other restaurants in Cable and Hayward
TOURING
All skill levels, ski school
TRAILS
93 km marked and maintained
TRAVEL
Northern Wisconsin, U.S. Hwy. 63 to Cable, E. 3 miles on County Rd. M

THE FARM

Box 191, Brantwood, WI 54513 (715) 564-2558

AREA INFORMATION

LODGING
Farmhouse and cottages, meals
RECREATION
Sleigh rides on weekends
TOURING
800 acres connect with Chequamegon National Forest; instruction and guided tours
TRAILS
21 km marked
TRAVEL
37 miles N.W. of Merrill, U.S. 51 to Rt. 86 W.

TIMBERLAKE LODGE

Rt. 2, Turtle Lake, WI 54889 (715) 986-2484

AREA INFORMATION

LODGE
At area, overlooking Sugarbush Lake, group accomodations
RESTAURANTS
Kitchen facilities; in nearby Twin Cities
TOURING
Through various terrain and by the river, rentals, lessons
TRAILS
30 km marked and maintained
TRAVEL
70 miles from Twin Cities, I-35 North, U.S. Hwy. 8 West

TREES FOR TOMORROW

P.O. Box 609, Eagle River, WI 54521 (715) 479-6456

AREA INFORMATION

LODGING
In Eagle River, full service
RESTAURANTS
At Eagle River, meals
TOURING
Environmental center, lessons, guides, night programs
TRAILS
25 km marked and maintained
TRAVEL
Northern Wisconsin near junction of U.S. 45 and Rt. 70

UNDERDOWN WILDERNESS AREA

Lincoln County Resource Agency 1106 E. 7th St.
Merrill, WI 54452 (715) 536-7151

AREA INFORMATION

LODGING
In Merrill on Hwy. 51
RESTAURANTS
In Merrill
TOURING
in Lincoln County, for all levels of skiers
TRAILS
33 km marked
TRAVEL
From U.S. Hwy. 51, btwn. Tomahawk and Merrill, east onto Copper Lake Rd., 3 miles

WHITECAP

Montreal, WI 54550 (715) 561-2227

AREA INFORMATION

EVENTS
NASTAR races, citizenz' races, other events
LODGINGS
In Ironwood, MI, Mercer, At Whitecap Lodge, in Herley

RESTAURANTS
At the towns listed above, in Manitowish Waters
TOURING
Full service area adjoining
TRAILS
32 km marked and maintained
TRAVEL
8 miles W. of Ironwood, MI on Rt. 77 to Montreal, Airplane access at Iron - Gogebic Airport, Republic Airlines

WILDCAT MOUNTAIN

Box 98, Ontario, WI 54651 (608) 387-4775

AREA INFORMATION

LODGING
Camping, numerous lodgings nearby
RESTAURANTS
Near the area
TOURING
For experience skiers, beginners
TRAILS
11 km marked
TRAVEL
37 mi. East of La Crosse, Rt. 33

THE WINTERGREEN

Box 467, Spring Green, WI 53588 (608) 588-9047

AREA INFORMATION

LODGING
Available nearby
TOURING
Not for experts, through the woods
TRAILS
27 km marked, 20 maintained
TRAVEL
43 miles N.W. of Madison, U.S. 14

WOLF RIVER LODGE

White Lake, WI 54491 (715) 882-2182

AREA INFORMATION

LODGINGS
Call ahead for reservations
RESTAURANTS
At the center
TOURING
On road trails
TRAILS
60 km marked and maintained
TRAVEL
White Lake, WI, at Rts. 55 & 64

WOODSIDE RANCH RESORT

235 E. State St., Mauston, WI 53948 (608) 847-4275

AREA INFORMATION

EVENTS
Working tanch with animals, sleigh rides
LODGINGS
Main lodge, cabins
RESTAURANTS
Food available
TOURING
Equipment rentals
TRAILS
20 km marked, 10 km maintained
TRAVEL
41 mi. N.W. of Portage, I-94, exit 69

W Y O M I N G

CACHE CREEK

Bridger-Teton National Forest
Box 1689, Jackson, WY 83001 (307) 733-2664

AREA INFORMATION

LODGING
In Jackson
TOURING
Wilderness, some difficult skiing
TRAILS
Not marked or maintained
TRAVEL
Western Wyoming, U.S. Hwy. 187, outside of Jackson

FLAGG RANCH VILLAGE

Box 187, Moran, WY 83013 (307) 733-4818

AREA INFORMATION

LODGING
In Jackson
TOURING
Complete resort
TRAVEL
Southeastern end of Yellowstone, 55 miles north Jackson, U.S. 89

GRAND TARGHEE RESORT

Alta, WY, via Drigs, ID 83422 (307) 353-2304
Out of state phone (800) 443-8146

AREA INFORMATION

LODGING
Full service area, lodging at the resort, near the lifts
RESTAURANTS
Two at base area
TOURING
Instruction, rentals, full service
TRAILS
Open terrain, 4 km groomed
TRAVEL
Rt. 33 to Driggs, head 7 miles east, just inside the border

GRAND TETON NATIONAL PARK

P.O. Drawer 170, Moose, WY 83012 (307) 733-2880

AREA INFORMATION

LODGING
See "FLAGG RANCH VILLAGE"
TOURING
Open area
TRAILS
Not marked or maintained
TRAVEL
14 mi. north of Jackson, U.S. 187 to Moose Visitor Center

SNOW KING

Box 427, Jackson Hole, WY 83001 (307) 733-2453

AREA INFORMATION

EVENTS
In Jackson Hole
LODGING
In Jackson
TOURING
This Touring Center is at Jackson Hole. Refer to "Jackson Hole" in the Alpine Skiing section of this book
TRAVEL
Hwy. 75 from town of Jackson

TOGWOTEE MOUNTAIN

P.O. Box 91, Moran WY 83013 (307) 543-2847

AREA INFORMATION

LODGING
At the lodge
RESTAURANTS
At lodge, plus coffee shop
TOURING
For any level of skill, over varied terrain
TRAILS
Unlimited, marked and maintained at lodge
TRAVEL
1 hr. east of Jackson

C A N A D A

A L B E R T A

BANFF NATIONAL PARK

Box 1258, BANFF, AL TOL 0C0 (403) 762-4421

AREA INFORMATION

LODGING
Full service resort, see "SUNSHINE VILLAGE" in the Alpine Skiing section of this book
RESTAURANTS
Numerous
TOURING
Rentals, ski shop, lower elevations for winter, upper elevations for early spring, late winter skiing
TRAILS
450 km marked, 20 km maintained
TRAVEL
70 miles east of Calgary, Trans Canada Hwy. 1

CANADIAN MOUNTAIN HOLIDAYS

P.O. Box 1660, Banff, AL %0L 0C0 (403) 762-4531

AREA INFORMATION

LODGING
Heated cabins
TOURING
Excursions for experience skiers
TRAILS
500 km marked, 20 km maintained
TRAVEL
Call or write for Rockies expeditions

JASPER NATIONAL PARK

Box 1300, Jasper, AL T0E 1E0 (403) 853-4401

AREA INFORMATION

LODGING
Lodge at Maligne Lake, lodgin in Jasper
RESTAURANTS
In Jasper
TOURING
Full range of services at Marmot Basin
TRAILS
50 km marked, 30 km maintained
TRAVEL
Hwy. 33, 175 miles northwest of Banff

MALIGNE LAKE

Box 280, Jasper, Alberta R0E 1E0 (403) 852-3370

AREA INFORMATION

LODGING
In Jasper
RESTAURANTS
Cafeteria
TOURING
Rentals, ski shop
TRAILS
28 km marked and maintained
TRAVEL
Outside of Jasper off Hwy. 16, SE from town

MARMOT BASIN

Box 1300, Jasper, AL T0E 1E0 (403) 853-3816

AREA INFORMATION
See "MARMOT BASIN" in the Canadian Alpine Skiing Section of this book.

TOURING
Rentals, instructions, tours by reservation
TRAILS
25 km marked and maintained
TRAVEL
Hwy. 93 north of Calgary and Lake Louise, rail service

SUNSHINE VILLAGE

Box 1150, Banff, Al, TOL0C0 (403) 762-3383

AREA INFORMATION

LODGING
Full service area, listed in the Alpine Skiing section of this book.
RESTAURANTS
At ski area
TOURING
Open touring, full service
TRAILS
16 km marked and maintained
TRAVEL
Trans-Canada Hwy. 1, Sunshine Exit

BRITISH COLUMBIA

BOWRON LAKE PARK

District Super., Barkersville, BC V0K 1B0 (604) 994-3209

AREA INFORMATION

LODGING
Unheated shelters, campground at lake
TOURING
Wilderness skiing for experts
TRAILS
115 km, not marked or maintained
TRAVEL
Rt. 92, Exit 26

CHILANKO LODGE

Kleena Kleene, BC (206) 822-9241

AREA INFORMATION

LODGING
At the lodge
RESTAURANT
Food at the lodge
TOURING
Overnighters to cabins
TRAILS
Wilderness area
TRAVEL
Near Mt. Waddington, Northern BC

CIRCLE H NORDIC TOURING CENTER

555 Richard St., Vancouver, BC V6B 2Z5 (604) 687-7885

AREA INFORMATION

LODGING
Cabins, lodge
TOURING
Instruction, ski shop, long season
TRAILS
90 km groomed, 50 km maintained
TRAVEL
400 km north of Vancouver,
35 km west of Clinton, south Caribou,
call ahead

CROOKED RIVER PROVINCIAL PARK

Superintendent, Provicial Park Branch Box 245
Prince George, BC V2N 2J6 (604) 562-8288

AREA INFORMATION

LODGING
In Prince George
RESTAURANTS
Picnic tables; meals in Prince George
TOURING
Toboggan run, unsupervised touring
TRAILS
26 km marked and maintained
TRAVEL
Hwy. 97 N., 72 km N. of Prince George

CYPRESS PARK

Provincial Parks Branch
1600 Indian River Dr. N. Vancouver, BC V7G 1L3
(604) 923-3911

AREA INFORMATION

LODGING
Heated shelter along touring area
TOURING
All degrees of experience
TRAILS
30 km marked, 18 km maintained
TRAVEL
Trans Canada Hwy. 1, 13 km from W. Vancouver

FAIRMONT HOT SPRINGS

BC V0B 1L0 9604) 345-6311

AREA INFORMATION

LODGING
Lodge at ski center
RESTAURANTS
Dining facilities at lodge
TOURING
Instruction, ski shop, swimming pool, various activities
TRAILS
50 km marked, 30 km maintained
TRAVEL
Rt. 93-95, 100 miles south of Banff

FORBIDDEN PLATEAU LODGE

Box 3271, Courtenay, BC V9N 5N4 (ask for Plateau Lodge

AREA INFORMATION

RESTAURANTS
Coffee shop open weekends, to-go lunch
TOURING
Rentals
TRAILS
25 km marked
TRAVEL
Island Hwy., 13 miles from Courtenay

MANNING PARK

BC V0X 1R0 (604) 840-8836

AREA INFORMATION

LODGING
Camping
TOURING
Full service at Gibson Pass, instruction
TRAILS
100 km marked, 35 km maintained
TRAVEL
Rt. 3, btwn. Hope and Princeton

MT. ASSINIBOINE

Provincial Parks Branch
P.O. Box 118, Wasa, BC CV0B 0C0

AREA INFORMATION

TOURING
Not accessible by car, call ahead for helicopter
Alpine shelters available
TRAILS
Open touring, for experienced skiers
TRAVEL
From Sunshine Ski Area to Magog Lake, by trail

MT. REVELSTOKE

Glacier National Park
Box 350, Revelstoke, BC V0E 2S0 (604) 837-5155

AREA INFORMATION

LODGING
In Revelstoke
TOURING
Unheated shelters along route
TRAILS
36 km marked
TRAVEL
Trans Canada Hwy. 1, Mt. Revelstoke exit

MT. SEYMOUR

Provincial Parks Branch
1600 Indian River Dr., N. Vancouver BC V7G 1L3
(604) 929-2358

AREA INFORMATION

TOURING
Loops for beginners
TRAILS
4 km marked and maintained
TRAVEL
3 km from Vancouver

108 RESORT RANCH

RR1, 100 Mi. House, BC V0K 2E0 (604) 791-5211

AREA INFORMATION

LODGING
At the ranch
RESTAURANTS
At the center
TOURING
Rentals, ice skating
TRAILS
65 km marked and maintained
TRAVEL
Rail service from Vancouver

PRINCE GEORGE

Chamber of Commerce, Prince George BC (604) 563-5493

AREA INFORMATION

LODGING
In town
RESTAURANTS
In town
TOURING
Racing and touring
TRAILS
68 km marked and maintained
TRAVEL
Northern provice, 550 mi. from Vancouver

PTARMIGAN TOURS

290 Wallinger, Kimberly, BC (604) 427-2221

AREA INFORMATION

LODGING
Heated cabins
RESTAURANT
Meals
TOURING
Small groups through Purcell Range
TRAILS
Open touring
TRAVEL
Contact Ptarmigan Tours

RED COACH INN

P.O. Box 760, 100 Mi. House, BC V0K 2E0 (604) 395-2266

AREA INFORMATION

LODGING
Cabins
RESTAURANT
Dining room and lounge
TOURING
Wilderness trail, many services
TRAILS
35 km marked and maintained
TRAVEL
Fraser Plateau, 100 Mile House

TEN MILE LAKE PARK

District Mgr., Ministry of Lands, Parks and Housing
Barkerville, BC V0K 1B0 (604) 994-3209

AREA INFORMATION

TOURING
Snowshoeing, ice-fishing, various activities
TRAILS
10 km marked and maintained
TRAVEL
Hwy. 97, 8 mi. north of Quesnel

WHISTLER

Whistler Heli Ski
Box 258, Whistler, BC V0N 1B0 (604) 932-5331

AREA INFORMATION

LODGING
Full service, all types
RESTAURANTS
Numerous
TOURING
Helicopter tours, all types of skiing
TRAILS
Unlimited, a few maintained
TRAVEL
From Whistler, transportation available

MANITOBA

BIRD'S HILL

AREA INFORMATION

LODGING
Shelters
TOURING
Many areas nearby
TRAILS
50 km not maintained, facilities along route
TRAVEL
15 N.E. of Winnipeg

PROVINCIAL PARKS

Canadian Ski Association, Manitoba Division
1301 Ellice Ave., Winnipeg, Manitoba (204) 786-5641

AREA INFORMATION

TOURING
Limited facilities
TRAILS
Unlimited
TRAVEL
Contact the Ski Association for directions and instructions

RIDING MOUNTAIN

Wasagaming, Manitoba R0J 2H0 (204) 848-2811

AREA INFORMATION

LODGING
Shelter, and rooms in Wasagaming, Onanocle, Mc Creary
TOURING
Tours
TRAILS
240 km in various states of maintenance
TRAVEL
Rt. 10, 60 mi. from Brandon

SPRUCE WOODS

Canadian Ski Association
1301 Ellice Ave, Winnipeg, Manitoba (204) 786-5641

AREA INFORMATION

LODGING
Shelters
TRAILS
75 km marked and maintained
TRAVEL
Trans Canada Hwy. 1, 100 miles west of Winnipeg

WINNIPEG

Canadian Ski Association

See "Manitoba Provincial Parks

AREA INFORMATION

LODGING
In the city
RESTAURANTS
In the city
TOURING
Through various terrain
TRAILS
Unlimited, marked and maintained
TRAVEL
Contact Ski Assoc. for areas to ski

NEW BRUNSWICK

FREDERICTON

Wostawea Ski Club
RR4, New Brunswick E3B 5C3 (506) 887-5000

AREA INFORMATION

LODGING
In Fredericton
RESTAURANTS
In Fredericton, at trails
TOURING
Instruction, tours
TRAILS
60 km marked and maintained
TRAVEL
Trans Canada Hwy. 1 to Fredericton

FUNDY NATIONAL PARK

Box 12345, New Brunswick E3B 5C3 (506) 887-2000

AREA INFORMATION

TOURING
Rolling terrain with a shelter
TRAILS
34 km marked
TRAVEL
Rt. 114, near Alma

KOUCHIBOUGUAC NATIONAL PARK

Kent Co., New Brunswick E0A 2A0 (506) 876-2320

AREA INFORMATION

TOURING
Through various terrain
TRAILS
30 km marked, 25 km maintained
TRAVEL
Rt. 11, 30 miles S. of Chatham

MT. FARLAGNE

31 Canada Rd.
Edmundston, New Brunswick (506) 735-6617

AREA INFORMATION

LODGING
Nearby, beds
TOURING
Alpine and Nordic area
TRAILS
15 km marked and maintained
TRAVEL
Trans Canada Hwy. 1, near Maine border, between Fredericton and Edmundston

PROVINCIAL PARKS

MACTAQUAC

Tourism New Brunswick (506) 363-3011

AREA INFORMATION

RESTAURANT
Canteen and bar
TOURING
Various outdoor activities
TRAILS
30 km marked and maintained
TRAVEL
Rt. 105, 29 km W. of Fredericton

SUGARLOAF

Tourism New Brunswick
Fredericton, New Brunswick E3B 5C3

P.O. Box 12345
(506) 753-3381

AREA INFORMATION

RESTAURANT
Chalet with lunch
TOURING
Rentals
TRAILS
15 km marked and maintained
TRAVEL
Rt. 270, 2 mi. from Campbellton

POLEY MOUNTAIN

General Delivery
Sussex, New Brunswick

(506) 433-2201

AREA INFORMATION

LODGING
Chalet
RESTAURANT
Cafeteria
TOURING
Through various territory
TRAILS
Winding marked trails
TRAVEL
Rts. 1 & 2, 6 miles from Sussex

SILVERWOOD WINTER PARK

Wostawea Ski Club
New Brunswick E3B 4R7

RR4, Fredericton
(506) 472-1819

AREA INFORMATION

TOURING
Near Fredericton, various terrain
TRAILS
26 km not maintained
TRAVEL
Trans Canada Hwy., 5 mi. from Fredericton

NEWFOUNDLAND

GROS MORNE NATIONAL PARK

Box 130
Newfoundland

Rocky Harbour
A0K 4N0

AREA INFORMATION

LODGING
Camping, at Con Head, Woody Point
TOURING
1,900 square km
TRAILS
Some marked and maintained
TRAVEL
Write for info., Gros Morne Mountain

NOVA SCOTIA

CANADIAN HOSTELLING ASSOCIATION

P.O. Box 3010 South, Halifax, NS B3J 3G6

AREA INFORMATION

LODGING
At the Outpost
RESTAURANT
Reserve meals
TOURING
Logging roads, forests
TRAILS
70 km some marked and maintained
TRAVEL
Trans Canada Hwy., Wentworth Hostel, between Amherst and Truro

OLD ORCHARD INN

P.O. Box 1090, Wolfville, NS

(902) 542-5751

AREA INFORMATION

LODGING
Inn
RESTAURANT
Food and bar, dancing
TOURING
Tracksetter, rentals, ski shop
TRAILS
25 km marked
TRAVEL
Rt. 101, Exit 11, 60 mi. from Halifax

ONTARIO

ALBION HILLS

Metro Region Conservation — 5 Shoreham Dr.
Downsview, ONT M3N 1S4 — (416) 661-6600

AREA INFORMATION

LODGING
In Toronto
RESTAURANTS
Chalet with food
TOURING
Skiing in various terrain, instruction
TRAILS
987 acres
TRAVEL
Hwy. 50 8 km N. of Bolton, 35 minutes from Toronto

ALGOMA KINNIWABI

Algoma Central Railway — P.O. Box 7000
Sault Ste. Mario, ONT — P6A 5P6

AREA INFORMATION

RESTAURANT
Sault Finnish Lodge for meals
TOURING
Wilderness area
TRAILS
24 km marked and maintained, large open area
TRAVEL
Train, Algoma Railway, into area, area is E. of Lake Superior, N. of Sault Ste. Marie

BEAR TRAIL INN RESORT

Whitney, ONT K-J 2M0 — (705) 637-2662

AREA INFORMATION

LODGING
At the resort
RESTAURANT
At the resort
TOURING
Rentals, guides, wilderness tours
TRAILS
45 km marked, 20 km maintained
TRAVEL
Rt. 60, off the route by ½ mi., Whitney Centre 200 mi. from Toronto

BLUE MOUNTAIN

RR3, Colingwood, ONT L9Y 3Z2 — (705) 445-0231

AREA INFORMATION

LODGING
Numerous, over 30 lodgings
RESTAURANTS
Full service area, bars
TOURING
Also Alpine area, all levels of skiing, rentals, instruction
TRAILS
18 km marked and maintained
TRAVEL
Hwy. 26, 5 mi. W. of Collingwood

BURCE'S MILL

Metro Region Conservation — 5 Shoreham Drive
Downsview, ONT M3N 1S4 — (416) 661-6600

AREA INFORMATION

LODGING
In nearby Toronto
TOURING
instruction, many facilities
TRAILS
8 km marked and maintained
TRAVEL
Woodbine Ave., N. from Hwy. 404, E. on Gormley-Stouffville sideroad

CANDY MOUNTAIN

RR6, Thunder Bay, ONT — (807) 939-6033

AREA INFORMATION

LODGING
In Thunder Bay
RESTAURANTS
In Thunder Bay
TOURING
Alpine area also, rentals, instruction
TRAILS
8 km marked and maintained
TRAVEL
Area is outside Thunder Bay, 15 mi. from town

GUINDON PARK

Cornwall
360 Pitt St.

P.O. Box 877
Cornwall, ONT K6H 5T9

AREA INFORMATION

LODGING
In towns nearby
RESTAURANTS
Nearby in the towns
TOURING
Rentals, ski shop
TRAILS
16 km marked and maintained
TRAVEL
Hwy. 2, 2 miles west of Cornwall

HIDDEN VALLEY HIGHLANDS

Group Box 74, RR 2
Ontario P0A 1K0

Huntsville
(705) 789-5942

AREA INFORMATION

EVENTS
Muskoka Loppet
LODGING
Inn at premises
RESTAURANT
At the Inn
TOURING
Alpine skiing also
TRAILS
7 km marked 6 km maintained
TRAVEL
By Huntsville, overlooking Peninsula Lake

HOMESTEAD

AREA INFORMATION

RESTAURANT
Steaks, bar, dancing
TOURING
Instruction, tours
TRAILS
40 km marked, 30 km maintained
TRAVEL
Rt. 6, near Durham

HOOK 'N HORN

Box 280, Nestor Falls ONT P0X 1K0 (807) 484-5364

AREA INFORMATION

LODGING
Log cabin, also in Nestor Falls
TOURING
Ski shop, tours
TRAILS
45 km marked
TRAVEL
Fly in air service from Nestor Falls

HORSESHOE VALLEY

RR 1, Barrie, ONT L4M 4Y8 (705) 835-2014

AREA INFORMATION

LODGING
Numerous, in Barrie and Orillia
RESTAURANTS
Numerous in the two towns
TOURING
Full service skiing, ski shop
TRAILS
63 km marked and maintained
TRAVEL
14 mi. from Barrie, 72 mi. N.E. of Toronto

MOLSON'S PARK

1 Big Bay Rd., Barrie, ONT L4N 4T2 (416) 361-1407

AREA INFORMATION

LODGING
In Barrie
RESTAURANTS
In town
TOURING
Open skiing, 700 acres
TRAILS
20 km marked
TRAVEL
In Barrie, Ontario

MOUNTAIN VIEW

RR2, Midland, ONT L4R 4K4 (705) 526-8149

AREA INFORMATION

LODGING
In Midland
RESTAURANTS
In Midland
TOURING
Instruction ski shop, shelter
TRAILS
8 km marked, maintained
TRAVEL
Off Rt. 22, 90 mi. N. of Toronto, train from Barrie

NAKKERTOK

Box 4476, Station E, Ottawa, ONT K1S 5B4

AREA INFORMATION

LODGING
In Ottawa
RESTAURANTS
In Ottawa
TOURING
Day and Night, day for members
TRAILS
60 km marked and maintained
TRAVEL
20 minutes from Ottawa

NANGOR

Westmeath, ONT K0J 2L0 (613) 587-4455

AREA INFORMATION

LODGING
At the area
TOURING
400 acres, rentals, instruction
TRAILS
36 km marked and maintained
TRAVEL
25 miles from Pembroke

NORDIC INN

Box 155, Dorset, ONT P0A 1E0 (705) 766-2343

AREA INFORMATION

LODGING
At the Inn
TOURING
Some night skiing
TRAILS
19 km marked and maintained
TRAVEL
Near Dorset, 25 mi. from Huntsville

SENECA KING

Seneca College King Campus
Dufferin St. N., RR3, King City
Ontario L0G 1K0 (416) 883-1701

AREA INFORMATION

LODGING
In Toronto, nearby, sometimes in King City
RESTAURANTS
In Toronto
TOURING
Instruction, night racing, many programs
TRAILS
13 km marked and maintained
TRAVEL
On the campus in King City, N. of Toronto

SHANTY BAY

Ontario L0L 2L0 (705) 726-1911

AREA INFORMATION

LODGING
In Barrie
TOURING
Ski shop at area, instruction, rentals
TRAILS
25 km marked and maintained
TRAVEL
Rt. 11, 7 mi. N. of Barrie

SKI HAVEN

RR1, Gilford, ONT L0L 1R0 (705) 456-2026

AREA INFORMATION

LODGING
At the club
RESTAURANTS
Dining at the club
TOURING
800 acres, cooking, shelters on trail
TRAILS
20 km marked and maintained
TRAVEL
Rt. 400, 15 miles from Barrie

SOO FINNISH SKI CLUB

Landslide Rd., Sault Ste. Marie, Ontario

AREA INFORMATION

LODGING
Nearby
RESTAURANT
At the lodge
TOURING
Many events at area, double tracked
TRAILS
40 km marked and maintained
TRAVEL
Outside Sault Ste. Marie, call for info.

STOKELY CREEK LODGE

AREA INFORMATION

LODGING
Camping, lodge
RESTAURANTS
At the lodge
TOURING
Many facilities, wilderness terrain
TRAILS
50 km marked and maintained
TRAVEL
20 mi. N. of Sault Ste. Marie, Algoma Kinniwabi

TALISMAN

Kimberley, ONT N0C 1G0 (519) 599-2520

AREA INFORMATION

LODGING
Full service area
RESTAURANT
At the area resort, lounge
TOURING
Also Alpine area, ski shop, full svcs.
TRAILS
25 km marked and maintained

PRINCE EDWARD ISLAND

PEI NATIONAL PARK

Visitor Services Officer PEI National Park
Box 487, Charlottetown, PEI (802) 672-2211

AREA INFORMATION

LODGING
In Charlottetown
TOURING
No facilities in area
TRAILS
11 km marked
TRAVEL
Call, must be arranged in advance

QUEBEC

ALPINE INN

Ste. Marguerite Station, Quebec (514) 229-3516

AREA INFORMATION

LODGING
Main lodge, chalets
RESTAURANT
At the lodge
TOURING
Rentals, instruction, activities
TRAILS
10 km marked and maintained
TRAVEL
45 miles from Montreal via Rts. 155, 117

AUBERGE NORMANDE

Box 723, Lake Beauport, QU J0E 2C0 (514) 534-2670

AREA INFORMATION

LODGING
At the resort
RESTAURANT
At the resort
TOURING
Sauna, night skiing
TRAILS
200 km marked and maintained
TRAVEL
12 miles N. of Quebec via 175

BROMONT SKI CENTER

C.P. 29, Bromont, QU J0E 1L0 (514) 534-2670

AREA INFORMATION

LODGING
At Mt. Brome
RESTAURANT
Also bar
TOURING
Also Alpine area, full service
TRAILS
25 km marked and maintained
TRAVEL
Call ahead for directions

CAMP FORTUNE

Old Chelsea, QU J0X 2N0 (819) 423-6341

AREA INFORMATION

LODGING
In nearby Ottawa
RESTAURANTS
In Ottawa
TOURING
Also Alpine area, ski club, Gatineau Park
TRAILS
160 km marked and maintained
TRAVEL
10 miles from Ottawa

CHATEAU MONTEBELLO

Montebello, QU J0V 1L0 (819) 423-6341

AREA INFORMATION

LODGING
At the hotel
RESTAURANT
At the hotel
TOURING
Canadian Ski Marathon, rentals, saunas, sporting activities
TRAILS
Numerous cross-country opportunities
TRAVEL
80 miles W. of Montreal, Hwy. 17

FORILLON NATIONAL PARK

Box 1220, Gaspe, QU G0C 1R0 (418) 368-5505

AREA INFORMATION

LODGING
Cap des Rosiers, close by
TOURING
Open area, no facilities
TRAILS
50 km marked, 40 km maintained
TRAVEL
Rt. 132, Gaspe, to Park

GRAY ROCKS INN

St. Jovite, Mt. Tremblant Box 1000
St. Jovite, QU J0T 2H0 (819) 425-2771

AREA INFORMATION

LODGING
At the inn
RESTAURANT
Food at the inn
TOURING
Also Alpine skiing, ski club, rentals, Instruction, shop
TRAILS
19 km marked
TRAVEL
Rt. 327 btwn. Mt. Tremblant & St. Jovite

LAURENTIDES PARK

150 Boule St. Cyrille St. East
Box 8888, QU G1K 7W3 (418) 848-2422

AREA INFORMATION

LODGING
Cottages by reservation
RESTAURANT
At reception center
TOURING
Relay stations, ski shop, rentals, Guided tours
TRAILS
49 km marked
TRAVEL
Camp Mercier, 38 mi. from Quebec, buses from Quebec

LE CHANTECLER RESORT

Ste. Adele, QU J0R 1L0 (514) 229-3555

AREA INFORMATION

LODGING
At the resort
RESTAURANT
At the resort, dancing
TOURING
Rentals, shop, Maple Leaf Trail access
TRAILS
16 km marked, 4 km maintained
TRAVEL
Ste. Adele Village, 40 mi. from Montreal

L'ESTEREL

Ministrere du Tourisme de la Chasse et de la Peche
Administration Region-Sud 2265 de la Province
Longueil, QU J4G 1G3 (514) 873-2843

AREA INFORMATION

LODGING
In Montreal
RESTAURANT
Cafeteria
TOURING
Skating, open daily
TRAILS
25 km marked and maintained
TRAVEL
Rt. 30, Exit 121, W. of Montreal

MONT ADSTOCK

C.P. 38 Ville d'Esterel
Ct. Prevost, QU J0T 1E0 (514) 228-2571

AREA INFORMATION

LODGING
At the hotel
RESTAURANT
Entertainment, activities
TOURING
Many indoor and outdoor activities, instruction, tours, sauna, pool
TRAILS
50 km marked and maintained
TRAVEL
Exit 69 off Rt. 15 N.

MONT ORFORD PARK

C.P. 261, Thetford Mines, QU (418) 487-2242

AREA INFORMATION

LODGING
In Thedford Mines
TOURING
No accomodations at the area
TRAILS
19 km marked and maintained
TRAVEL
100 mi. S. of Quebec

MONT ST. BRUNO PARK

Box 248, Magog QU J1X 3W8 *819) 843-6548
Lodging (819) 843-4200

AREA INFORMATION

LODGING
In Magog, see MT. ORFORD, in the Alpine skiing section of this book
RESTAURANTS
Full service at Mt. Orford
TOURING
Rentals, many services
TRAILS
35 km marked
TRAVEL
67 mi. from Montreal via Rt. 10 to Eastman to Ski Area

MONT STE. ANNE PARK

Box 400, Beaupre, QU G0A 1E0 (418) 827-4561

AREA INFORMATION

LODGING
In Beaupre
RESTAURANT
At the area
TOURING
Also Alpine area, rentals
TRAILS
140 km marked and maintained
TRAVEL
Rt. 138, Exit 360

MONT TREMBLANT LODGE

Quebec J0T 1Z0 (819) 425-2711

AREA INFORMATION

LODGING
Full service ski area, see MT. TREMBLANT in the Alpine Skiing section of this book
RESTAURANTS
Full service, entertainment
TOURING
Rentals, instruction
TRAILS
4 km marked and maintained
TRAVEL
From Montreal, 80 mi. via Rt. 15 & Hwy. 117

PROVINCIAL PARKS

Quebec Dept. of Tourism
150 est. bd. St. Cyrille
Place de la Capitale
Quebec G1R 4Y3

AREA INFORMATION

RESTAURANTS
Dining rooms
TOURING
Many facilities, relax stations
TRAILS
Numerous, 470 km in varying states of grooming
TRAVEL
Call for Info, booklets available to various areas

SCAN SPORT

Box 151, Morin Hts., QU (514) 226-2344

AREA INFORMATION

LODGING
In Morin Heights
RESTAURANTS
At various inns
TOURING
Night skiing, tours
TRAILS
110 km marked, a few maintained
TRAVEL
Morin Heeights, via Hwy. 117 & 15

VILLA BELLEVUE

AREA INFORMATION

LODGING
At the hotel, other hotels nearby
RESTAURANTS
Numerous in nearby inns, St. Jovite, Mt. Tremblant
TOURING
Touring, instruction, many activities
TRAILS
95 km marked 30 km maintained
TRAVEL
Hwy. 117, N. of Montreal

SASKATCHEWAN

DEPT. OF TOURISM

1825 Lorne St.
Saskatchewan S4P 3V7
Regina
(306) 565-2304

AREA INFORMATION

LODGING
In nearby towns
RESTAURANTS
Limited, in towns
TOURING
40 areas with various activities, Saskatchewan Ski Club activities, 50 km run, some instruction and rentals through ski clubs
TRAILS
Unlimited
TRAVEL
For travel to various areas, contact the Dept. of Tourism or Saskatchewan Ski Assoc., 26 Porteous Crescent, Saskatoon, Saskatchewan S7J 2S8

AUTO RENTALS

AJAX
- 200 Stuart St. 542-4196
- 161 Orleans, E. Boston (24 hrs.) 569-3550

AMERICAN INTERNATIONAL RENT-A-CAR
- Government Center. 523-5441
- Prudential Center 267-6661
- 164 Orleans St., E. Boston (24 hrs.) 569-5525
- Toll Free . . . . (800) 527-6346

AVIS
- 60 Park Sq. 267-8500
- 70 High St.. 482-6876
- Logan Airport, E. Boston (24 hrs.) 569-3300
- Toll free . . . . (800) 331-1212

BUDGET RENT A CAR
- 19 Huntington Ave.. 266-3537
- 62 Elliot St. 426-2600
- Logan Airport, E. Boston (24 hrs.) 569-4000

DOLLAR RENT-A-CAR
- 39 Dalton St. 523-5098
- Logan Airport, E. Boston (24 hrs.) 569-5300

ECONO-CAR
- Downtown. 542-9800
- Logan Airport, E. Boston (24 hrs.) 569-5770
- Toll free . . . . (800) 228-1000

HERTZ
- Park Square 482-9100
- 13 Holyoke, Cambridge 547-0336
- Logan Airport, E. Boston 569-5930
- Toll free . . . . (800) 654-3131

NATIONAL CAR RENTAL
- 183 Dartmouth 426-6830
- Logan Airport, E. Boston 569-6700
- Toll free . . . . (800) 328-4567

PURITAN
- Downtown. 523-5441
- Prudential Center 267-6661
- Logan Airport, E. Boston 569-5524

TRAV L CAR
- 200 Milk St. 482-9010
- 226 Stuart St. 482-8015
- 285 McClellan Hwy., Airport 567-1950

Toll free
- In Boston . . . . (800) 732-3423
- Out-of-town . . . . (800) 225-3539

HOSPITALS

BOSTON CITY HOSPITAL
- 818 Harrison Ave.. 424-5000

BOSTON UNIVERSITY MEDICAL CENTER
- 75 E. Newton 247-5000

MASSACHUSETTS GENERAL HOSPITAL
- Fruit St. 726-2000

MT. AUBURN HOSPITAL
- 330 Mt. Auburn (Cambridge) 492-3500

TUFTS - NEW ENGLAND MEDICAL CENTER
- Harrison Ave. 956-5000
- Emergency - Adult 956-5566

UNIVERSITY HOSPITAL INC.
- 75 E. Newton 247-5000

LOGAN INT'L. AIRPORT

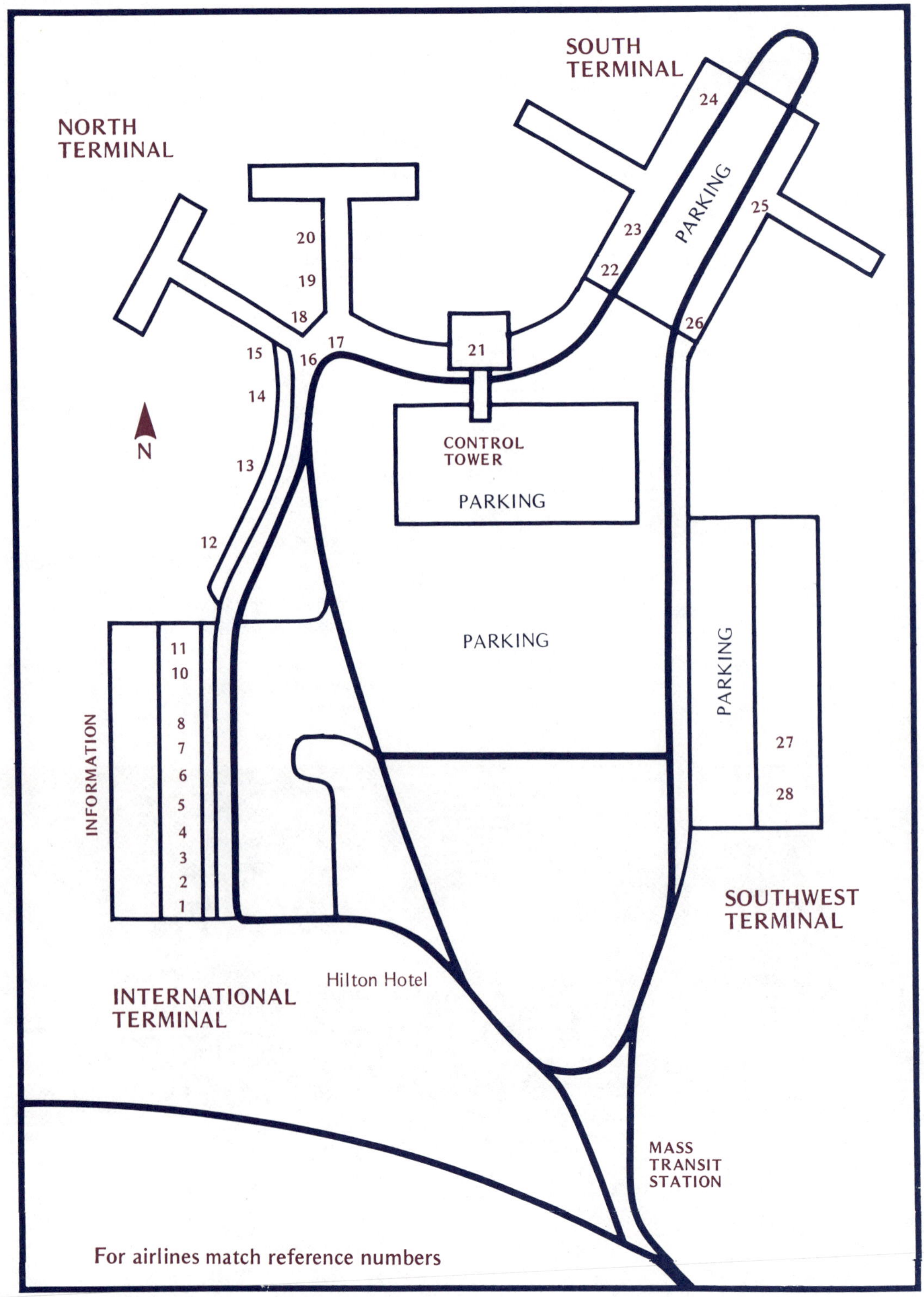

LOGAN INT'L. AIRPORT

2	AER LINGUS	(800) 631-7917
13	AIR CANADA	482-4300
14	AIR NEW ENGLAND	569-5510
25	AIR US	(800) 525-1849
7	ALLEGHENY	482-3160
8	ALITALIA	542-9060
23	AMERICAN	542-6700
15	BAR HARBOR	542-0791
11	BRANIFF	423-2100
1	BRITISH	426-4105
9	CAPITOL	262-2500
12	COMMUTER-PRINCETON	(800) 847-1462
22	COMMAND	423-5750
22	COSMOPOLITAN	(516) 420-0800
17	DELTA	567-4100
20	DOWNEAST	569-3126
28	EASTERN	262-3700
26	EMPIRE	(800) 862-5665
22	GREEN MOUNTAIN	
22	HYANNIS	775-5543
10	LUFTHANSA	(800) 645-3860
26	MERRIMACK	(800) 342-8898
5	NORTHWEST INT.	267-4885
24	NORTHWEST ORIENT	(800) 221-2300
21	PIEDMONT	523-1100
22	PILGRIM	569-1414
26	PRECISION	(800) 451-4221
27	PROVINCETOWN-BOSTON	567-6090
18	REPUBLIC	482-4332
3	SWISSAIR	(800) 221-6600
6	TRANSAMERICA	
4	TWA INTERNATIONAL	(800) 322-4883
16	TWA	742-8800
19	UNITED	482-7900
28	WINNIPESAUKEE	482-4232

TRANSPORTATION

MASSPORT INTERTERMINAL SHUTTLE stops every 6 to 12 minutes, depending on the time of day, at all terminals, the Airport Hilton Hotel, and the MBTA Airport subway station with connections to downtown and greater Boston. The fare is $.25, exact change. Children under 6 ride free. Daily from 5:30 a.m. to 1 a.m.

SHARE-A-CAB – Shared taxis are available for a reduced flat fee to 138 suburban Boston towns and are available at all terminals.

LIMO & BUS services are available at all terminals, along with car rentals.

PARKING – Parking is available for both long and short terms adjacent to all terminals. Metered parking is also available. The rate is .75 per hour, $6.00 a day. Meters are .75 p/hr.

SERVICES

INFORMATION BOOTH – Foreign language aides are available for general help and information. Open 12-6 winter, 12-8 summer.

CUSTOMER SERVICE PHONES – Yellow phones are located on the lower level curbside at each terminal taxicab stand for any questions concerning Airport ground transportation services, 24 hours a day.

EMERGENCY & POLICE – Located at the Administration Bldg., Medical Station hours are Mon. thru Fri. 8 a.m. to 8 p.m., 8 a.m. to 2 p.m. Sundays. State Police: Phone 567-2233.

TRAVELERS AID – Open from 12:30 to 7 weekdays, to 6 weekends, in the International Terminal.

FOREIGN CURRENCY EXCHANGE – 12 to 9:30 p.m. Mon. thru Sat, 1 to 6 p.m. Sunday. Call 569-5999.

OTHER SERVICES – Duty free shops are at the North, South and Int'l. Terminals. A chapel is on the lower level, and a lounge with a view of Boston is on the 17th floor of the tower. Detailed information displays are located throughout the airport.

AUTO RENTALS

AGENCY RENT-A-CAR
6825 E. Tennesse Ave. 821-8188
AIRCAR AUTO RENTALS
850 Bannock 534-1771
AMERICAN INTERNATIONAL RENT A CAR
1919 Broadway 629-6153
Airport Office, 6800 Smith Rd.. 399-5020
THE ARRANGERS INC.
Stapleton International Airport 398-3666
AVIS RENT A CAR SYSTEM INC.
7500 E. 32nd Ave. 398-5340
BUDGET RENT A CAR OF COLORADO
7400 E. 32nd Ave. 320-1676
COMPACTS ONLY RENT A CAR SYSTEM
3970 Monaco Pkwy. 388-0940
CONTINENTAL RENT A CAR
Denver Airport, 8906 E. Colfax Ave.. 399-6600
DOLLAR RENT A CAR SYSTEMS
7450 E. 29th Ave. 398-2323
E-Z WAY RENTALS INC.
5190 Morrison Rd. 935-2498
THE HERTZ CORPORATION
7600 E. 32nd Ave. 398-3693
18 E. 16th 861-2128
HOLIDAY RENT A CAR
1229 Lincoln St. 831-8828
MOTOR HOME RENTALS OF DENVER/ROCKIES
345½-355 Sheridan Bl., Lakewood 23306718
Toll Free . . . . (800) 525-8327

EMERGENCY

AURORA COMMUNITY HOSPITAL
1501 S. Potomac 751-5353
COLORADO
HIGHWAY PATROL. 757-9475, 757-9422
DENVER
EMERGENCY HELP. 911
DENVER GENERAL HOSPITAL
W. 8th Ave. & Cherokee 893-6000
LUTHERAN MEDICAL CENTER
E. 17th Ave. & Milwaukee
Medical Center 388-6288
Family Care Center 321-8859
Pharmacy 388-2435
PORTER MEMORIAL HOSPITAL
2525 S. Dowing 778-1955
RALEIGH HILLS HOSPITAL
1920 High 388-2491
SWEDISH MEDICAL CENTER
501 E. Hamden Ave. 789-6789
UNIVERSITY OF COLORADO MEDICAL CENTER
4200 E. 9th. Ave. 399-1211

WINTER RESORTS

A-BASIN SKI AREA
Dillon. . . . . .468-2608, (from Denver) 892-0577
ARAPAHOE BASIN - KEYSTONE RESORT
0163 Summit County Rd. 8, Dillon 468-2316
ARAPAHOE EAST SKI AREA
Exit 58, I-70, 1164 S. Grape Vine Rd.
Lookout Mountain 526-0833
ARAPAHOE SKI AREA
A-Basin Ski Area, Dillon 468-2608, 892-0577
ASPEN HIGHLANDS SKI AREA
1600 Maroon Creek Rd., Aspen. 925-5300
ASPEN SKIING CORP.
406 S. Mill Aspen 925-1220
BRECKENRIDGE SKI AREA
1599 Summit County Rd. 3 453-2368
BRECKENRIDGE TRAILS END CONDOMINIUMS
6850 Evans Ave. 757-7836
CANADAS OF VAIL LTD.
108 S. Frontage Rd. West, Vail 534-4830
COLORADO CONVENTION & RESERVATIONS INC.
1665 Grant 861-2418
COLORADO COUNTRY INC.
Shuttle Service to Ski Resorts
1648 S. Ironton 752-3879
COPPER MOUNTAIN
Frisco. . . . .(info., Denver no.) 623-4641
COPPER MOUNTAIN RESORT
178 Ten Mile Circle, Copper Mtn.. 668-6477
CRESTED BUTTE SKI AREA
Mt. Crested Butte 349-6611
FOOTHILLS LODGE
0063 W. Hwy. 149, S. Fork 873-5969
FROSTY BASIN SKI AREA
440 4 Granby 887-9950
GASTHOF GRAMSHAMMER
231 E. Gore Creek Dr., Vail 476-5626
HI-COUNTRY HAUS CONDOMINIUM RESORT
Hideaway Park . . . . (Denver No.) 825-0705
HIGH COUNTRY INN
Winter Park . . . . (Denver No.) 573-1082
KEYSTONE RESORT - ARAPAHOE BASIN (Dillon)
0163 Summit County Rd. 8 . . . . .534-7712, 468-2316
LAKE ELDORA CORPORATION
West of Nederland . . . . (Boulder No.) 447-8011
LION SQUARE LODGE & CONFERENCE CENTER
655 W. Lionshead Pl., Vail. . . . (Denver No.) 534-5987
LODGE AT VAIL
174 E. Gore Creek Dr., Vail 623-7300, 476-5011
LOVELAND BASIN SKI AREA
Loveland Pass, Georgetown 571-5580, 569-2288
MANOR VAIL LODGE
Vail 571-5629
MEADOW RIDGE LODGE CONDOMINIUMS
Winter Park Ranch . . . . (Denver No.) 892-1602
MOUNTAIN MEN JEEP SIGHTSEEING TOURS
Cross-Country Ski Tours from Denver
11100 E. Dartmouth Ave. 750-0090

MOUNTAIN STATES SKI ASSOCIATION
1670 York 399-5066

PARK MEADOWS AT ASPEN (Condo units)
21873 W. Hwy. 82, Aspen 925-3767

PONDEROSA GUEST RANCH
9010 County Rd. 240, Salida 539-2730

R M A TRAVEL & TOURS INC.
1660 S. Albion 759-4600

RAMADA INN 220 Tanglewood Lane
Silverthorne . . . . (Denver no.) 629-1359

SCI MANAGEMENT COMPANY INC. (Condos)
120 S. Main, Breckenridge 571-5620, 453-2288

SILVERHEELS LODGE
81 Buffalo Dr., Dillon 468-2926

SITZMARK SKI LODGE & GUEST RANCH
Hideaway Park 726-5453

SKI COUNTRY ENTERPRISES INC. (Mt. Werner)
Steamboat Springs . . . . (Denver no.) 623-1976

SKI IDLEWILD
Hideaway Park . . . . (Denver no.) 572-9523

SKI TIP RANCH (Dillon)
0764 Summit County Rd. 5 . . . . .468-9928, 468-2004

SNOWMASS RESORT ASSOCIATION
45 Village Sq., Snowmass Village 923-2000

STEAMBOAT CENTRAL RESERVATION
1201 Lincoln Ave., Steamboat Springs. 879-0740

STEAMBOAT VILLAGE RESORT (Steamboat Springs)
2200 Village Inn Court. 879-2220

STORM MEADOWS CONDOMINIUMS
Mt. Werner, Steamboat Springs 623-1976

STORMWATCH CONDOS
Mt. Werner, Steamboat Springs 879-4187

TAMARRON
40292 US Hwy. 550 N., Durango. 247-8801

TELLURIDE SKI AREA LODGE
666 W. Colorado Ave., Telluride 728-3831

TOP OF THE VILLAGE CONDOMINIUMS
855 Carriage Way, Aspen. 923-3673

TUMBLING RIVER RANCH
Grant 838-5981

VAIL ASSOCIATES INC.
150 S. Washington, Denver 733-3668

VAIL RESORT ASSOCIATION
Vail . . . . (Denver no.) 623-6624

WINTER PARK MEADOWS LODGE CO.
Fraser (North of Winter Park) 726-5942

WINTER PARK RESERVATIONS INC.
Hideaway Park 726-5733

WINTER PARK SKI AREA
Winter Park . . . . (Denver no.) 892-0961
Ski Lessons, Mary Jane, Winter Park 726-5762
Ski Rentals. . . . . (Denver no.) 573-9397
Ski & Snow Report . . . . (Denver no.) 892-1453

STAPLETON INT'L. AIRPORT

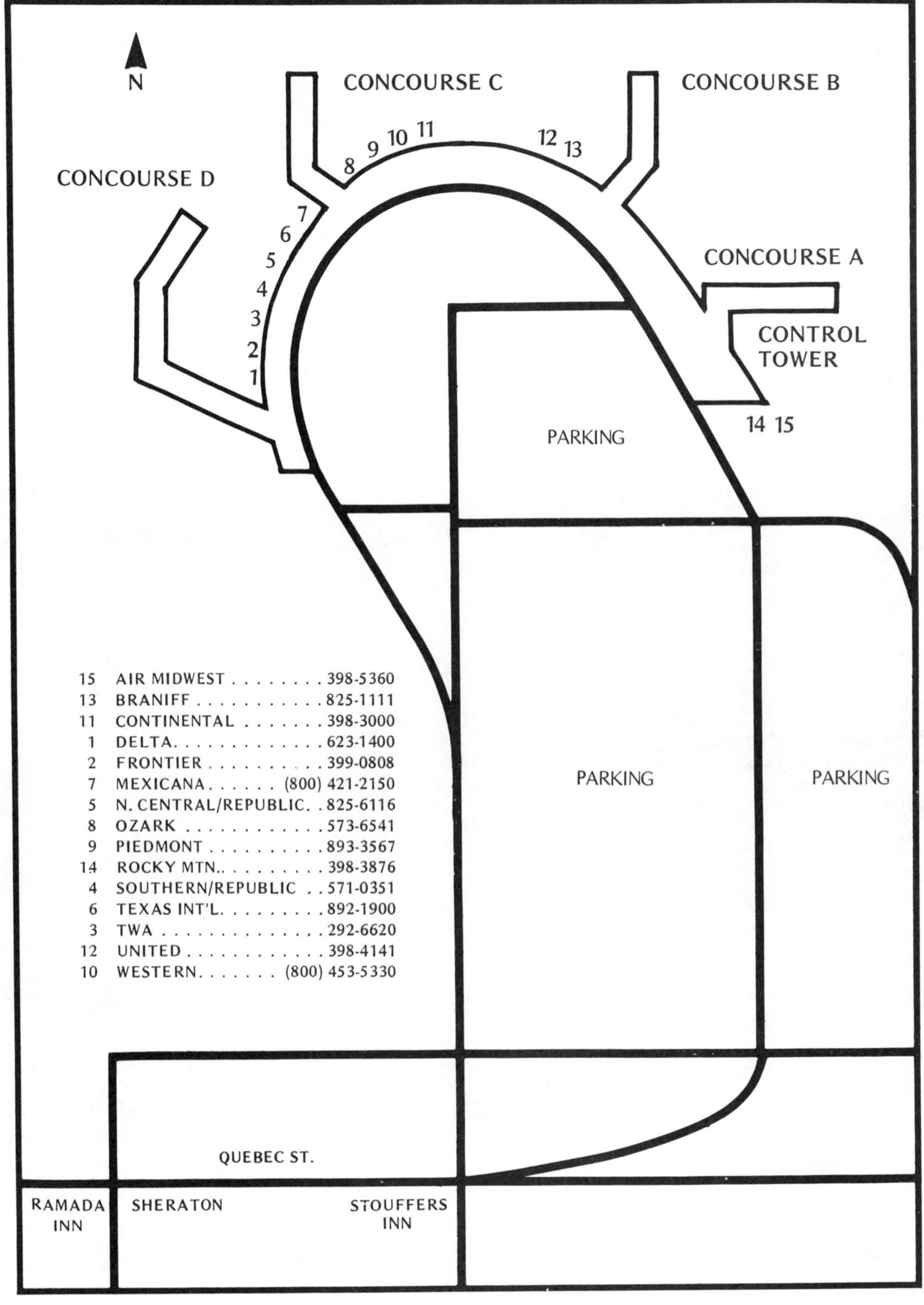

STAPLETON INT'L. AIRPORT

TRANSPORTATION

CAR RENTAL AGENCIES – Avis Rent A Car, 398-5340; Budget Rent A Car, 320-1674; Hertz Rent A Car, 398-3990; National Rent A Car, 388-1677; Dollar Rent A Car, 399-1568.

BUS LINES – During the week, buses run from 7:05 to 12:20. On Saturdays, Sundays and Holidays, service is available from 8:10 to 12:20. The rate from the Airport to Denver is $.75 on the express bus. The Airport to Boulder rate is $1.25. Passengers 65 years and older may ride during off-peak hours free. Handicapped passengers may ride for reduced fare with RTD identification. Information service is available for patrons with hearing and speech impairments at 778-6000.

FREIGHT COMPANIES–Federal Express, call 377-8946. The Flying Tiger Line is located in the Old Control Tower Building.

OTHER TRANPORTATION – Airport Limo Service, 893-6464; American Auto Tours, Inc., 429-7106; Continental Trailways, 573-7005; Greyhound, 623-1075. Mellow Yellow Taxi Company, 925-2282; Ritz Cab Company, 534-2702; San Juan Tours, Inc., 398-5399; Vail Guides, 476-5387; Yellow Cab, 893-6464; Zone Cab, 623-7171.

PARKING – Close-In: $4.50 per day. Outlying: $2.50 per day. Remote: $2.50 per day (includes shuttle bus service). Short Term: 50 cents per half hour, no maximum.

HOTELS – Located from East to West on Quebec Street are the following hotels: Stouffers Inn, Sheraton Inn, Ramada Inn, Holiday Inn, Rodeway Inn.

SERVICES

MEDICAL EMERGENCY – The Airport Clinic is located at 3600 Circle Way. Phone 398-5310.

SECURITY – The Airport Security Office is located on the ground level of the terminal. Call 398-3855.

Stapleton International Airport is divided into three levels. The ticket level is on the second floor.

FIRST FLOOR – Baggage Reclaim, Bank, Car Rental, Ground Transportation, Postal Service, Security Office, Travelers Aid.

SECOND FLOOR, TICKET LEVEL – See other side for airlines. The following services are located on this level: Candy shop, Travelers Aid, Barber Shop, Game Room, Ice Cream Stand, Afro Shop, Spanish Shop, Oriental Shop. There are two restaurants at opposite ends of the floor, as weel as two Western Shops. Newsstands, Insurance Booths and Phones are located throughout the airport.

THIRD FLOOR – Mexicana, United, Continental and Western Offices, Military Lounge, Nursery, Observation Deck, Chapel, Aviation Historical Society.

FLYING CLUBS – Aero Training of the Rockies, Flightcraft, Inc., Star Airways, Inc.

GOVERNMENT AGENCIES – Federal Aviation Administration, call 837-3646. U.S. Customs are located at Concourse C and the Air Cargo Building.

WEATHER – National Weather Service Forecast Office, call 399-2541 or 837-3611.

TRAINS

AMTRAK
- Metroliner 736-3967
- Penn & Grand Central Terminals 736-4545
- Package Express 239-6388
  - Penn Station 239-6328
  - Grand Central 239-6388
  - Nights, Holidays, Weekends 239-6912
- Lost & Found
  - Penn Station 239-6193
  - Grand Central 239-6388

AUTO TRAIN
- Toll Free . . . . . (800) 424-1111

BRITRAIL TRAVEL
- 270 Madison Ave.. 725-7711

CANADIAN NATIONAL RAILROAD
- 630 Fifth Ave.. 581-3977

CONRAIL
- Grand Central Terminal 532-4900
- Penn Station 736-6000
- Tickets by Mail 340-3000
- Lost and Found
  - Grand Central 340-2572
  - Penn Station 239-6193
- Stationmaster 340-2553

FRENCH NATIONAL RAILROAD
- 615 Fifth Ave.. 582-2110

GERMAN FEDERAL RAILROAD
- 630 Fifth Ave.. 977-9300

ITALIAN STATE RAILROAD
- 500 Fifth Ave.. 354-9830

METROLINER
- Information & Reservations 736-3967

ROCK ISLAND LINE
- 500 Fifth Ave.. 279-9790

TOUREX OF AMERICA
- 29 Broadway 480-0240

JOHN F. KENNEDY INT'L. AIRPORT

TRANSPORTATION

BETWEEN AIRLINE TERMINALS – The Port Authority provides an airline connection bus service operating between all terminal buildings. Buses run 24 hours a day. Fare is $.50. Phone 656-5510.

BETWEEN CENTRAL TERMINAL AREA & LONG TERM LOTS – The Port Authority provides a free bus service between the Central Terminal Areas and Lots 8 & 9. Buses run 24 hrs. a day. Phone 656-5510.

NEW YORK CITY – Carey Transportation, Inc. provides express coach service to and from the East Side Airlines Terminal at 37th St. & First Ave. Fare is $4.00. Carey furnishes free shuttle bus service between the Eastside Airlines Terminal, midtown hotels, and the Port Authority Bus Terminal, weekdays only The fare, including the trip to the airport, is $7.00. For info call 632-0500. New York Airways provides helicopter flights to and from the World Trade Center in Manhattan. Flights operate weekdays only. Fares are $17.36 to $23.15. Reduced rates are available for some flights. Transit type bus service is furnished by the Green Bus Lines (Q-10 Bus) to subway stations at Leffers Blvd and Kew Gardens-Union Turnpike. For information call 995-4700.

LIMOS – Salem Transportation operates a fleet of 11 limos every day except Saturday. Reservations must be made in advance. The service desk is in the Main Lobby and courtesy phones are available at all other terminals.

PASSENGER SERVICES

MEDICAL SERVICES – 24 hr. service is available at the Medical Clinic, Bldg. 198 at 150th St. Phone 656-5344.

POLICE – Call 656-4333 or 656-4668.

NURSERY – A nursery is located on the second floor of the International Arrivals Bldg. Other facilities are located in the British Airways, TWA and National Terminals.

DENTAL OFFICE – A dental office is located in Suite 2311 in the East Wing of the International Arrivals Bldg. Phone 656-5426.

JFK GENERAL AIRPORT INFORMATION – A centrally located counter staffed by multi-lingual personnel is provided in the main lobby of the International Arrivals Bldg. Phone 656-4520.

TRAVELERS AID – The office is in the International Arrivals Bldg. Phone 656-4870.

POSTAL SERBICES – A Post Office is located in an annex to the Air Mail Facility Bldg. 179, at S. Cargo and 150th St. Phone 995-3732.

LOST AND FOUND – Report baggage to your airline. As a final step, call 656-4120.

ANIMAL SHELTER – A 24 hr. ASPCA shelter is in Bldg. 189 on N. Service Court. Phone 656-6042.

CENTRAL TERMINAL AREA – Lots 1 thru 5: Up to 1 hr, $1.00, $6.00 maximum for the day.

PARKING LOT 6, PAN AM ROOFTOP – Lot 6 is for short term parking. Maximum rate is $13.00 for the first 24 hours.

LONG TERM LOTS – The Reduced Rate for lots 8 & 9 is $3.00 for the first 24 hours, $1.50 for each further 12 hour period. Phone 656-5699.

JOHN F. KENNEDY INT'L. AIRPORT

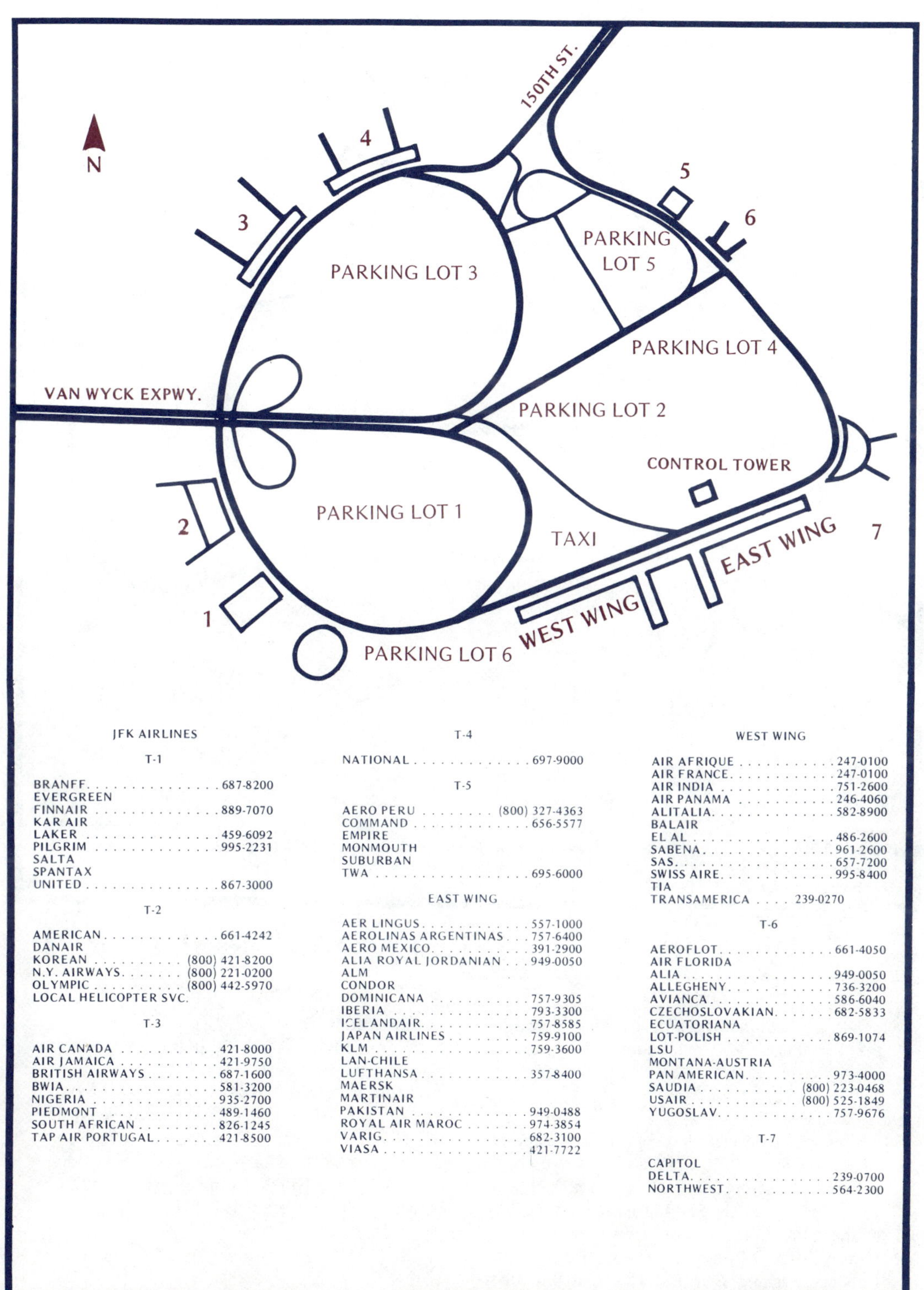

JFK AIRLINES

T-1

BRANFF	687-8200
EVERGREEN	
FINNAIR	889-7070
KAR AIR	
LAKER	459-6092
PILGRIM	995-2231
SALTA	
SPANTAX	
UNITED	867-3000

T-2

AMERICAN	661-4242
DANAIR	
KOREAN	(800) 421-8200
N.Y. AIRWAYS	(800) 221-0200
OLYMPIC	(800) 442-5970
LOCAL HELICOPTER SVC.	

T-3

AIR CANADA	421-8000
AIR JAMAICA	421-9750
BRITISH AIRWAYS	687-1600
BWIA	581-3200
NIGERIA	935-2700
PIEDMONT	489-1460
SOUTH AFRICAN	826-1245
TAP AIR PORTUGAL	421-8500

T-4

NATIONAL	697-9000

T-5

AERO PERU	(800) 327-4363
COMMAND	656-5577
EMPIRE	
MONMOUTH	
SUBURBAN	
TWA	695-6000

EAST WING

AER LINGUS	557-1000
AEROLINAS ARGENTINAS	757-6400
AERO MEXICO	391-2900
ALIA ROYAL JORDANIAN	949-0050
ALM	
CONDOR	
DOMINICANA	757-9305
IBERIA	793-3300
ICELANDAIR	757-8585
JAPAN AIRLINES	759-9100
KLM	759-3600
LAN-CHILE	
LUFTHANSA	357-8400
MAERSK	
MARTINAIR	
PAKISTAN	949-0488
ROYAL AIR MAROC	974-3854
VARIG	682-3100
VIASA	421-7722

WEST WING

AIR AFRIQUE	247-0100
AIR FRANCE	247-0100
AIR INDIA	751-2600
AIR PANAMA	246-4060
ALITALIA	582-8900
BALAIR	
EL AL	486-2600
SABENA	961-2600
SAS	657-7200
SWISS AIRE	995-8400
TIA	
TRANSAMERICA	239-0270

T-6

AEROFLOT	661-4050
AIR FLORIDA	
ALIA	949-0050
ALLEGHENY	736-3200
AVIANCA	586-6040
CZECHOSLOVAKIAN	682-5833
ECUATORIANA	
LOT-POLISH	869-1074
LSU	
MONTANA-AUSTRIA	
PAN AMERICAN	973-4000
SAUDIA	(800) 223-0468
USAIR	(800) 525-1849
YUGOSLAV	757-9676

T-7

CAPITOL	
DELTA	239-0700
NORTHWEST	564-2300

LA GUARDIA INT'L. AIRPORT

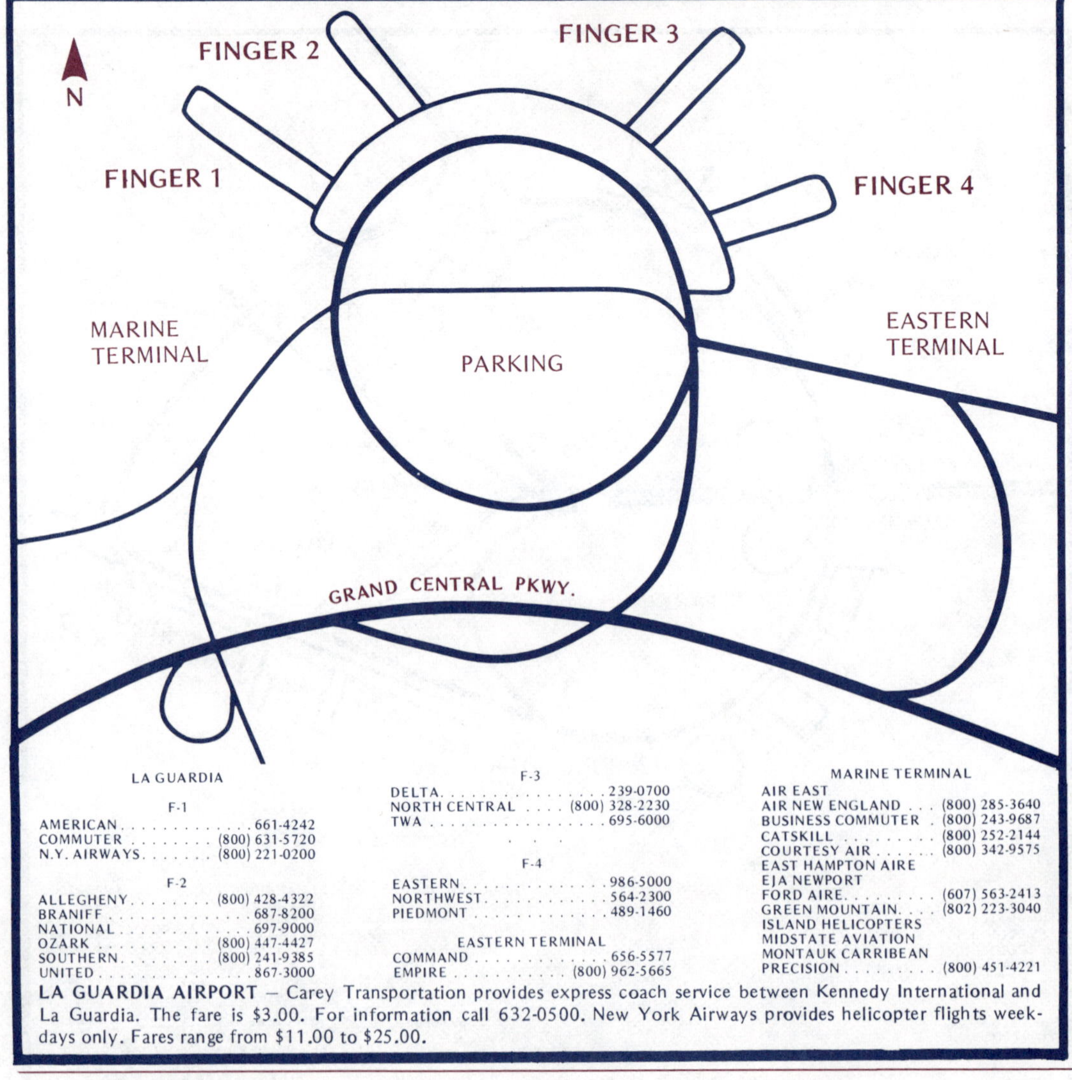

LA GUARDIA

F-1

AMERICAN 661-4242
COMMUTER . . . . (800) 631-5720
N.Y. AIRWAYS. . . . . . . (800) 221-0200

F-2

ALLEGHENY. . . . . (800) 428-4322
BRANIFF 687-8200
NATIONAL 697-9000
OZARK . . . . (800) 447-4427
SOUTHERN. . . . . (800) 241-9385
UNITED 867-3000

F-3

DELTA. 239-0700
NORTH CENTRAL . . . . (800) 328-2230
TWA 695-6000

F-4

EASTERN. 986-5000
NORTHWEST. 564-2300
PIEDMONT 489-1460

EASTERN TERMINAL

COMMAND 656-5577
EMPIRE . . . . (800) 962-5665

MARINE TERMINAL

AIR EAST
AIR NEW ENGLAND . . . (800) 285-3640
BUSINESS COMMUTER . (800) 243-9687
CATSKILL . . . . (800) 252-2144
COURTESY AIR . . . . . . (800) 342-9575
EAST HAMPTON AIRE
EJA NEWPORT
FORD AIRE. . . . . (607) 563-2413
GREEN MOUNTAIN. . . . (802) 223-3040
ISLAND HELICOPTERS
MIDSTATE AVIATION
MONTAUK CARRIBEAN
PRECISION . . . . (800) 451-4221

LA GUARDIA AIRPORT – Carey Transportation provides express coach service between Kennedy International and La Guardia. The fare is $3.00. For information call 632-0500. New York Airways provides helicopter flights weekdays only. Fares range from $11.00 to $25.00.

NEWARK INT'L. AIRPORT

PARKING

North Terminal–Parking Lot 1 is opposite the terminal. $3.00 maximum for 24 hours, hourly rates are posted. For information call 961-2012.

Central Terminal Parking–Hourly Parking is in Lots A & B is intended for pickup and delivery of passengers. $1.00 per hour, $16.00 for 24 hours. Daily Parking is in Lots A,B & C and is intended for overnight parking up to two nights. $7.00 for 24 hours. Long Term Reduced Parking is in Lot D and is intended for three or more days. $3.00 per 24 hrs.

TRANSPORTATION

Free connecting bus service is available between Terminals A & B, at the arrivals level at ten minute intervals from 7 a.m. to 11 p.m. At night, the bus goes to Long Term Parking Lot D. Free bus service is provided between the North Terminal & Terminals A & B every 30 minutes from 6 a.m. to 8 p.m. Stops are in front of the North Terminal and on the departure levels of Terminals A & B.

NEWARK INT'L. AIRPORT

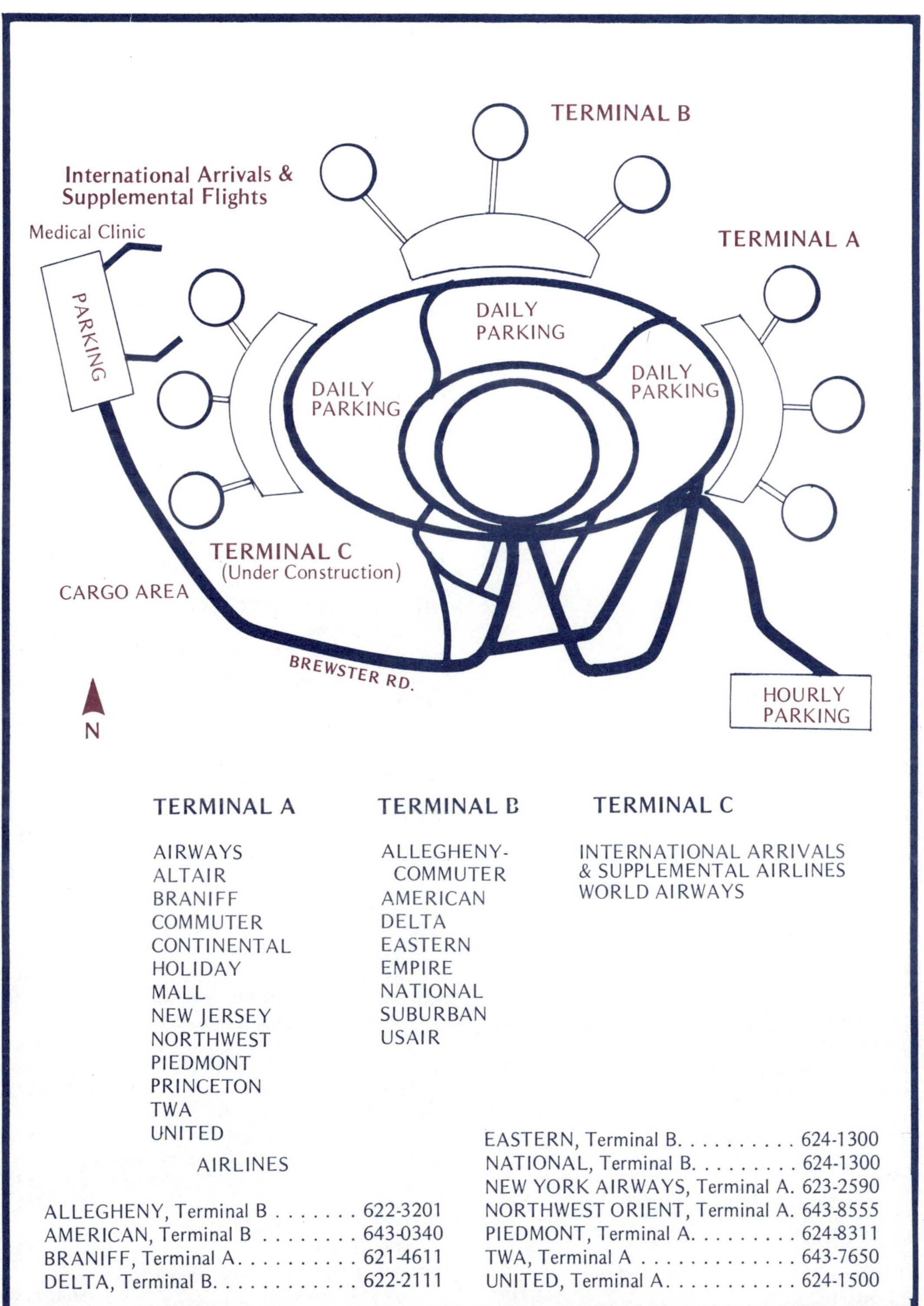

TERMINAL A	TERMINAL B	TERMINAL C
AIRWAYS	ALLEGHENY-COMMUTER	INTERNATIONAL ARRIVALS & SUPPLEMENTAL AIRLINES
ALTAIR	AMERICAN	WORLD AIRWAYS
BRANIFF	DELTA	
COMMUTER	EASTERN	
CONTINENTAL	EMPIRE	
HOLIDAY	NATIONAL	
MALL	SUBURBAN	
NEW JERSEY	USAIR	
NORTHWEST		
PIEDMONT		
PRINCETON		
TWA		
UNITED		

AIRLINES

ALLEGHENY, Terminal B 622-3201
AMERICAN, Terminal B 643-0340
BRANIFF, Terminal A. 621-4611
DELTA, Terminal B. 622-2111
EASTERN, Terminal B. 624-1300
NATIONAL, Terminal B. 624-1300
NEW YORK AIRWAYS, Terminal A. 623-2590
NORTHWEST ORIENT, Terminal A. 643-8555
PIEDMONT, Terminal A. 624-8311
TWA, Terminal A 643-7650
UNITED, Terminal A. 624-1500

SALT LAKE CITY

AUTO RENTALS

AMERICAN INTERNATIONAL
1355 W. North Temple. . . . 322-2488, (800) 527-0202
AVIS
611 South West Temple 539-2177
BUDGET
Salt Lake Int'l. Airport. 363-1500
DOLLAR
Salt Lake Int'l. Airport. 521-2590
HERTZ
Salt Lake Int'l. Airport. . . . 328-2088, (800) 654-3131
HOLIDAY
1935 West North Temple 322-1311
NATIONAL
468 South Main St.. . . . . . . 328-3221, (800) 328-4567
Salt Lake Int'l. Airport. 539-0200
THRIFTY
1255 W. North Temple. . . . 328-2545, (800) 331-4200

BUS LINES

GREYHOUND BUS LINES
160 West South Temple 355-4684
LEWIS BROTHERS STAGES
549 West 5th South. 359-8677
TRAILWAYS BUS SYSTEM
77 West South Temple 328-8122
UTAH TRANSIT AUTHORITY
616 West 200 South 531-8600

HEALTH CLUBS

CAM II FITNESS CENTER
3335 South 900 East. 467-2727
NAUTILUS PLUS
3474 South State 262-4315
SALT LAKE ATHLETIC CLUB
255 East 2nd South. 328-8633
SPA FITNESS CENTERS
1033 East 2100 South 484-8786
4700 Highland Dr., Holladay 278-2846

HOTELS

AVENUES RESIDENTIAL CENTER (kitchen)
107 F Street. 363-8137
BEST WESTERN SANDMAN INN (restaurant, shuttle)
380 West 7200 South, Midvale 561-2256
Continental U.S. . . . . (800) 432-7045
BEST WESTERN WORLD MOTOR HOTEL
(restaurant, liquor store)
1900 South State 487-7801
COUNTRY CLUB MOTOR INN
2665 Parleys Way 486-1034
DOWNTOWN TRAVELODGE (car rentals, ski bus stop)
524 South West Temple . . . 531-7100, (800) 255-3050
FLYING J MOTEL (adjacent 24 hr. restaurant)
715 West North Temple 363-0062
FRIENDSHIP INN - SKYLINE MOTEL
2475 E. 1700 S.. 582-5350
HILTON HOTEL (5 restaurants, lounges, car rentals)
150 W. Fifth South 532-3344, (800) 528-0313
HILTON INN (full-service)
Airport, 5151 Wiley Post Way. 539-1515
City Center, 154 W. 6th South 521-2930
Toll free . . . . (800) 528-0313
HOLIDAY INN & HOLIDOME
(restaurant, indoor putting green & pool)
230 West 600 South 532-7000
HOTEL UTAH (restaurant, near tennis/spa - privileges)
Main St. @ South Temple 531-1000
INTERNATIONAL INN (dining, liquor store)
206 South West Temple 521-9500
LA QUINTA MOTOR INN (adjacent 24 hr. restaurant)
530 Catalpa Rd., Midvale. . . 566-3291, (800) 531-5900
LITTLE AMERICA (dining, shopping arcade)
500 S. Main 363-6781, (800) 453-9450
QUALITY INN (liquor store, adjacent 24 hr. restaurant)
4465 Century Dr.. 268-2533
Toll free . . . . (800) 228-5151
RAMADA INN (liquor store, car rental)
999 S. Main St. 531-7200
RINN'S ROYAL EXECUTIVE INN
(24 hr. coffee shop, airport courtesy car)
300 West North Temple 521-3450
RODEWAY INN - AIRPORT (restaurant)
2080 West North Temple 355-0088
Toll free . . . . (800) 228-2000
RODEWAY INN - SOUTH (restaurant)
280 West 7200 South, Midvale 566-4141
Toll free reservations . . . . (800) 228-2000
SALT LAKE MARRIOTT HOTEL (restaurant, liquor store)
75 South West Temple 531-0800, (800) 228-9290
SALT LAKE TRAVELODGE (near restaurants)
144 West North Temple . . . 533-8200, (800) 255-3050
SALT PALACE TRAVELODGE (restaurant)
215 West North Temple . . . 532-1000, (800) 255-3050
Canada . . . . (800) 261-3330
TEMPLE SQUARE HOTEL (restaurant)
75 West South Temple 355-2961
TRI-ARC HOTEL (restaurant, liquor store)
161 West 6th South. 521-7373, (800) 453-9466

LIMOUSINES

LEWIS BROTHERS STAGES LIMO SERVICE
549 W. Fifth South 359-8677

RESTAURANTS

BALSAM EMBERS (Continental)
2350 Foothill Dr.. 466-4496
BILL & NADA'S (American, open 24 hrs.)
479 S. 6th East 359-6984
CASA DEL SOL (Mexican, live entertainment)
Trolley Square. 531-8228
CATTLE BARON (steak)
2110 Emigration Canyon 582-8991
CHINA VILLAGE (Chinese)
7334 S. Main 355-5507
FINN'S (American, Continental)
2675 Parley's Way 466-4682
HEATHER (live entertainment)
2832 E. 6200 South 272-4468
HIBACHI (Japanese)
238 E. South Temple. 364-5456
HOTEL UTAH RESTAURANT (American)
S. Temple & Main Sts. 531-1000
TAYLOR'S CAFE (soul food)
244 W. South Temple 532-9272
LA CAILLE AT QUAIL RUN (French, Basque)
9565 S. Wasatch Bl.. 942-1751
LA FLEUR DE LIS (French)
338 S. State 359-5753
LAMB'S GRILL (American)
169 S. Main 364-7166
LE PARISIEN (French)
417 S. 3rd East 364-5223
RISTORANTE DELLA FONTANA (Italian)
336 S. 400 East 328-4243
ROYAL PALACE (Continental, American)
249 S. 4th East 359-5000
THE TOWNE HALL, Salt Lake Hilton
151 W. 5th South 532-3344

STORES & SHOPS

MAURICE ANDERSON MEN'S SHOP (clothing, shoes)
25 E. South Temple 359-8781
CLAIR OPTICAL CO. (prescription ski goggles)
319 S. Main 364-6616
THE HIGHLANDER (ski sales, rental)
3333 Highland Dr. 487-3508
HOLUBAR (ski sales, rental, touring advice)
4385 S. State 261-3071
JERRY'S SPORTS CENTER (ski sales, rental)
838 East 9400 South. 571-8812
LIFT HOUSE SKI SHOP
3698 East 7000 South 943-1056
MOUNTAINEER SPORTS
201 South 1300 East. 582-2338
Trolley Sq., 6th South 7th East. 363-6003
MURDOCK NUTRITION CENTER
260 S. Main 355-6665
NORDSTROM (dept. store)
50 S. Main 322-4200
STEVENS-BROWN SPORTS CO. (ski shop)
1176 East 2100 South 486-5447
STEVENSONS (women's clothing)
50 S. Main 322-4448
SUNSET SPORTS CENTER (ski sales, service, rental)
3500 South State 973-4224
50 S. Main 322-4460
UTAH WOOLEN MILLS
59 W. South Temple 364-1851
WEINSTOCKS (dept. store)
50 S. Main 524-2666
WOLFE'S SPORTMAN'S HEADQUARTERS (ski shop)
250 South State. 521-0550
6151 Highland Dr. 272-8661
ZCMI (dept. store)
15 S. Main 321-6666

TAXICABS

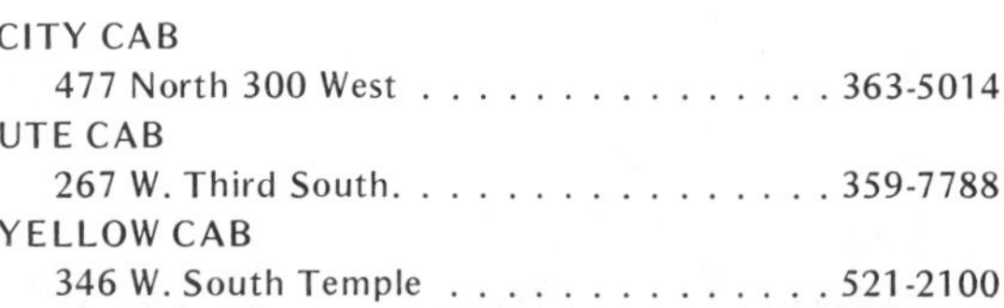
CITY CAB
477 North 300 West 363-5014
UTE CAB
267 W. Third South. 359-7788
YELLOW CAB
346 W. South Temple 521-2100

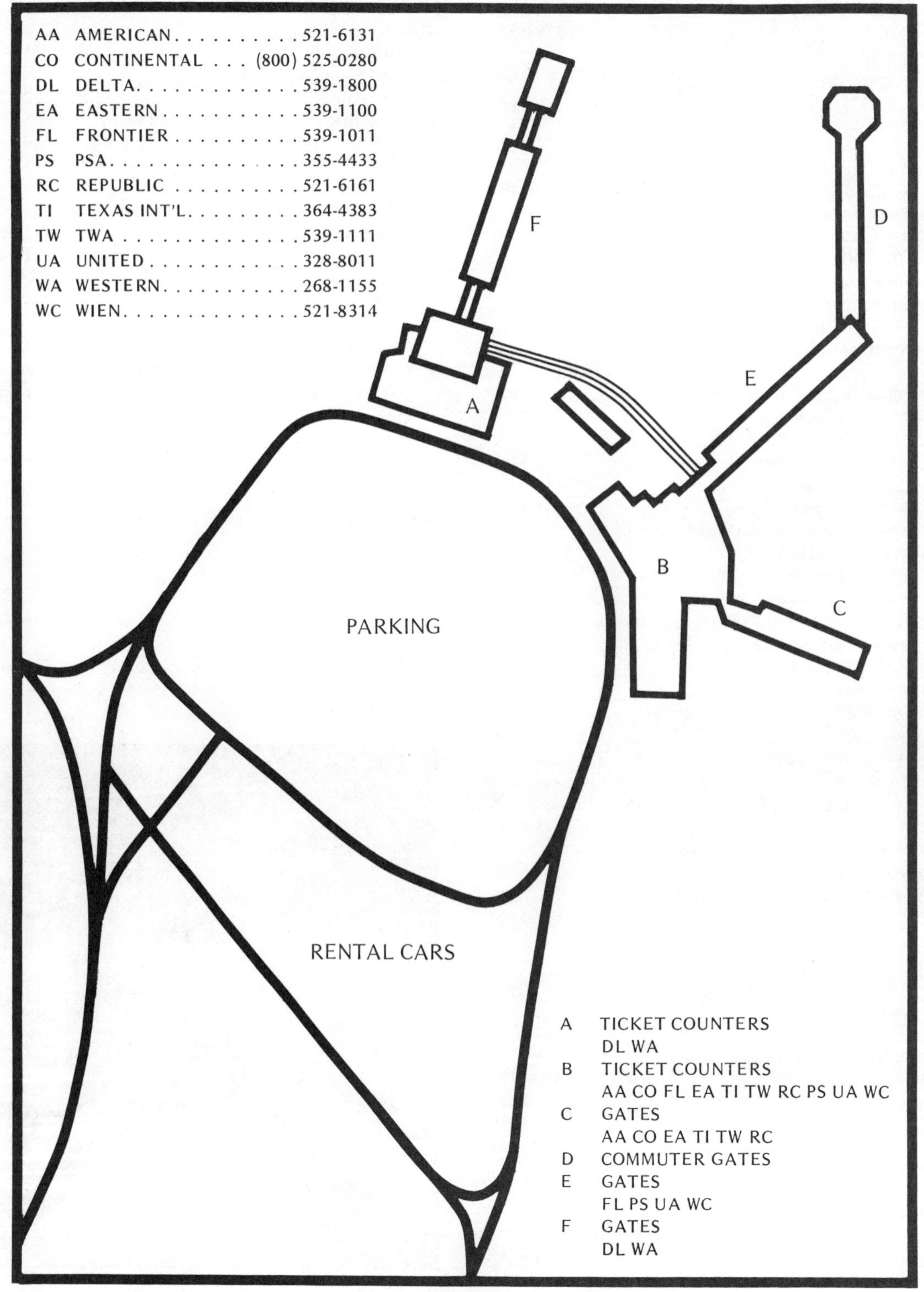
AA AMERICAN 521-6131
CO CONTINENTAL . . . (800) 525-0280
DL DELTA. 539-1800
EA EASTERN 539-1100
FL FRONTIER 539-1011
PS PSA. 355-4433
RC REPUBLIC 521-6161
TI TEXAS INT'L. 364-4383
TW TWA 539-1111
UA UNITED 328-8011
WA WESTERN. 268-1155
WC WIEN. 521-8314
F
D
E
A
B
C
PARKING
RENTAL CARS
A TICKET COUNTERS
DL WA
B TICKET COUNTERS
AA CO FL EA TI TW RC PS UA WC
C GATES
AA CO EA TI TW RC
D COMMUTER GATES
E GATES
FL PS UA WC
F GATES
DL WA

I N D E X

(A) – ADDENDUM
(XC) – CROSS COUNTRY
ALL OTHER AREAS ARE ALPINE

Billy Kidd grew up in Stowe, Vermont, and raced interationally for nine years on the United States Ski Team. In 1964 he won the Silver Medal in the Slalom at the Innsbruck, Austria, Olympics. In Val Gardena, Italy, at the 1970 World Championships, he captured the title and the first United States Gold Medal, going on to win the 1970 World Professional Ski Racing Championship in Verbier, Switzerland.

Currently, Billy devotes his time to the demands of the ski business. He is Director of Skiing at the Steamboat Springs Ski Area in Colorado and is a design consultant for Hart Skiis and Salomon Boots & Bindings. Billy has his own line of gloves, goggles, skis and Stetson hats.

Billy Kidd Racing Camps are the latest edition to his business activities. He is also head ski coach for the Special Olympics.

After a lifetime of total involvement in the sports world, Kidd still skis daily at Steamboat and seizes the opportunity to travel the world and keep abreast of what's happening in the ski industry. He's in it for the enjoyment and excitement—two things which are as much a part of skiing as the name Billy Kidd.